# LEGENDS, TRADITIONS AND HISTORY
# IN MEDIEVAL ENGLAND

# LEGENDS, TRADITIONS AND HISTORY IN MEDIEVAL ENGLAND

## ANTONIA GRANSDEN

THE HAMBLEDON PRESS

LONDON AND RIO GRANDE

Published by The Hambledon Press 1992

102 Gloucester Avenue, London NW1 8HX (U.K.)
P.O. Box 162, Rio Grande, Ohio 45672 (U.S.A.)

ISBN 1 85285 016 7

© Antonia Gransden 1992

A description of this book is available from the
British Library and from the Library of Congress

Printed on acid-free paper and
bound in Great Britain at the
University Press, Cambridge

# Contents

# Acknowledgements

The articles reprinted here appeared first in the following places and are reprinted by kind permission of the original publishers.

1. *Journal of Ecclesiastical History*, 32 (1981), 397-425.

2. *Journal of Ecclesiastical History*, 40 (1989), 159-207.

3. *English Historical Review*, c (1985), 1-24.

4. *Medieval Art and Architecture at Worcester Cathedral British Archaeological Association, Conference Transactions for the year 1975*, I (1978), 1-14.

5. *England in the Twelfth-Century, Proceedings of the 1988 Harlaxton Symposium*, edited by Daniel Williams (Woodbridge, 1990), pp. 55-81.

6. *Journal of Ecclesiastical History*, 27 (1976), 337-58.

7. *Speculum*, xlvii (1972), 29-51.

8. *Journal of Medieval History*, xvi (1990), 129-50, *ibid.*, xvii (1991), 217-43.

9. *Bulletin of the Institute of Historical Research*, xxxvi (1963), 77-82.

10. *Mediaeval Studies*, xxxvi (1974), 472-92.

11. *English Historical Review*, lxxxvii (1972), 333-44.

12. *English Historical Review*, lxxii (1957), 270-8.

13. *English Historical Review*, xcv (1980), 358-63.

14. *Antiquaries Journal*, lx (1980), 75-97.

# Preface

The value to the historian of narrative sources as quarries of facts has always been recognized. However, there is a growing consciousness that, unless these sources are properly understood, they can neither be correctly interpreted nor their historical worth assessed. Used uncritically, it can be argued, they provide less reliable factual information than charters, public records and other kinds of official documents. This is true, but an unwary historian can also be led astray by, for example, forged charters and political bias in public records. In any case, narrative sources have more to offer than just solid facts, as historians increasingly appreciate. They provide clues to what the author and, by implication, some of his contemporaries, thought about events and personalities in their times. They also give some idea about how the author saw the past. For instance, they raise the puzzling question of the extent to which the author understood the difference between true history and legend.

My interest in the narrative sources of English history was first aroused by Professor V.H. Galbraith, who was an excellent example of a scholar who successfully used narrative, particularly chronicle, evidence in conjunction with that of the public records. The enthusiasm, knowledge and perception with which he treated the chronicles of Richard II's reign in his seminars at Oxford made him an inspiring and invigorating teacher. I have also been especially indebted to two other eminent medievalists, Sir Goronwy Edwards and Dom David Knowles. Sir Goronwy, my supervisor for a London Ph.D., combined erudition with good sense and good humour – and a sense of humour – an invaluable combination in a supervisor. Later, Dom David's belief that my plan to write a history of historical writing in medieval England was feasible, and that such a book should be very useful, gave me confidence and encouragement, but without his sustained interest and help I might not have persisted. Both he and Sir Goronwy read chapters of the first volume of my *Historical Writing in England* in draft and always had valuable comments and suggestions to make.

The articles reprinted in the present book have been written in the last thirty-five years. They have been chosen because they all concern the study in medieval England of the past, medieval attitudes to history and medieval modes of historiographic expression. Most of them discuss in detail topics briefly alluded to in one or other of the two volumes of my *Historical Writing*. But Chapter 1, on Bede's reputation in medieval England, Chapter 5, on prologues to twelfth-century historical works, and nearly all Chapter 8, on the writing of chronicles, are independent of *Historical Writing*. Chapter 14, on fifteenth-century antiquarianism, deals thematically and more systematically with material which is scattered, though more detailed, in *Historical Writing*, ii. It has not been practicable to revise the articles thoroughly nor to bring them completely up to date. However, many corrections have been made, and to some extent bibiliographical references have been up-dated and new evidence taken into account. Wherever possible revisions are incorporated in the pre-existing text; if there was not enough room they have been put in a note at the end of the article; in three instances it has been necessary to put a revisory note at the end of the volume (see pp. 329-35, Additional Notes to Chapters 6, 8 and 10).

Debts to scholars who have helped me revise articles are acknowledged in the footnotes where appropriate. But here I must especially thank Dr Martin Brett for checking through Chapter 4, and Professor John Greatrex for telling me about, and sending me copies of, entries in the precentors' accounts of Worcester cathedral which throw light on the composing of a chronicle (cf. Article 8 and pp. 330-32). I am also deeply indebted to Mr Martin Sheppard of the Hambledon Press for his patient and sympathetic handling of the book, and to my daughter, Deborah Shields, for kindly and efficiently helping me with the index.

Antonia Gransden
Cambridge
January 1992

# List of Illustrations

To Jonathan

1

# Bede's Reputation as an Historian in Medieval England[1]

The *Hand-List of Bede Manuscripts* by M. L. W. Laistner and H. H. King is not definitive, since it is based partly on the evidence of catalogues and other printed material and not on the manuscripts themselves. However, it provides a useful rough guide. It lists approximately 160 surviving manuscripts of the *Historia Ecclesiastica*. Laistner constructed a table showing the percentage of the total number copied in each century:[2]

### BEDE MANUSCRIPTS

| Century copied | Percentage | Century copied | Percentage |
|---|---|---|---|
| eighth & eighth/ninth | 3·4 | thirteenth | 10·0 |
| ninth | 7·0 | fourteenth | 17·0 |
| tenth | 5·0 | fifteenth | 12·0 |
| eleventh | 9·0 | sixteenth | 1·2 |
| twelfth | 31·0 | doubtful | 4·4 |

Laistner estimated that at least 70 per cent of the extant manuscripts of the *Historia Ecclesiastica* were copied in England.[3] The pattern of survival can be seen, therefore, as throwing some light on the relative popularity of the *Historia Ecclesiastica* in one century and another. The most remarkable feature is the large percentage of manuscripts written in the twelfth century. It is also noteworthy that the *Historia Ecclesiastica* maintained its popularity in the late Middle Ages; in fact, a fairly high percentage of the copies were made in the fourteenth century.

[1] This article is based on a paper delivered at the British Library in September 1980, in a series of lectures on the Benedictines in Britain.

[2] M. L. W. Laistner, with the collaboration of H. H. King, *A Hand-List of Bede Manuscripts*, Ithaca, New York 1943, 7. The edition of the *Historia Ecclesiastica* cited below is *Venerabilis Baedae Historiam Ecclesiasticam . . .*, ed. C. Plummer, Oxford 1896, 2 vols.

[3] Laistner, op. cit., 8.

Evidence suggesting why the *Historia Ecclesiastica* was more popular in some centuries than in others can be sought in contemporary sources. The opinions the chroniclers express about Bede, and the use they make of the *Historia Ecclesiastica*, are particularly valuable, but references in other types of sources, for example, official documents, can also be revealing.

In such a study some account must be taken of Bede's minor historical works, the two universal histories in *De Temporibus*[4] and *De Temporum Ratione*,[5] the prose Life of St Cuthbert[6] and the metrical one,[7] and the Lives of the Abbots of Wearmouth.[8] Nor can Bede's reputation as an historian be wholly dissociated from his reputation as a saint and Father of the Church. The Anglo-Norman eulogies cited below make it plain that Bede's historical works were considered merely as one element in his total achievement. Moreover, his venerability and learning in the scriptures added weight to his authority on historical matters.[9]

The chronicles and other sources show that the *Historia Ecclesiastica* was used in the Middle Ages for various reasons. For instance, it could provide spiritual inspiration for a religious revival, since it was the main source of information about the Northumbrian renaissance, the golden age of the Anglo-Saxon Church, of which Bede was the principal luminary. Religious leaders often wanted their movement to emulate the achievements of that period and, therefore, consulted the *Historia Ecclesiastica* to discover details. Indeed, the *Historia Ecclesiastica* seems on occasion to have provided them with an initial incentive.

The chroniclers themselves used Bede's historical works for information, in order to establish the continuous sequence of English history. Occasionally, when a chronicler found Bede's narrative conflicted with someone else's account of the same period, he might prefer Bede's authority as being of greater weight. Some chroniclers had a tendentious purpose. The Northumbrian period provided the English Church with a glorious past. Therefore, a chronicler might extol Bede himself and use his works to paint a flattering picture of the Anglo-Saxon Church in the

---

[4] Printed in M.G.H., *Auctorum Antiquissimorum*, XIII, *Chronica Minorum saec. iv–vii*, iii, ed. T. Mommsen, Berlin 1898, 247–317.

[5] Printed in ibid., iii. 247–327.

[6] Printed in *Two Lives of St Cuthbert*, ed., with an English translation, B. Colgrave, Cambridge 1940.

[7] Printed as 'Bedas metrische Vita Sancti Cuthberti', ed. W. Jaager, *Palaestra*, cxcviii. Leipzig 1935.

[8] Printed in Plummer, *Venerabilis Baedae*, i. 364–87.

[9] Professor Laistner constructed a table which demonstrates the percentage of the surviving manuscripts of Bede's biblical commentaries belonging to each century, similar to his table for the *Historia Ecclesiastica*; Laistner, *Hand-List*, 4. The pattern resembles that for the *Historia Ecclesiastica*, in so far as there is a high percentage belonging to the twelfth century. However, as most of the extant manuscripts of the commentaries are of continental provenance, his table does not indicate their popularity in England as accurately as does that for the *Historia Ecclesiastica*.

seventh century. Above all, Bede's *Historia Ecclesiastica* was an authority. Ancient origins, whether of the English Church as a whole or of individual monasteries, attested by Bede had especial prestige. But the *Historia Ecclesiastica* did more than increase fame; it could also be appealed to in specific disputes as a storehouse of precedents. It could be cited by 'official' chroniclers presenting the case of a party to a dispute and by those actually involved in the proceedings.

The evidence supplied by the chroniclers and others concerning Bede's reputation as an historian in medieval England will be treated chronologically. This arrangement makes possible correlation with Laistner's table. However, it is not practicable to divide the material century by century, as Laistner did the manuscripts. This is because evidence is scarce or totally lacking in some periods, though plentiful in others. Moreover, when abundant, it tends to have distinctive characteristics which link it with one or more of the motives for interest in Bede outlined above. In the divisions and subdivisions adopted below, such characteristics have been taken into account.

## I. *The Anglo-Saxon Period*

Bede's influence as an historian was established soon after his death. He played a vital role in the genesis of annalistic historiography among the Anglo-Saxons. The chronological epitome which he had appended to the *Historia Ecclesiastica* became the stock from which contemporary annals grew. He himself had probably added annals from 731 to 734, the so-called Appendix, and shortly afterwards a continuation from 735 to 766 was written in Northumbria.[10] Another series of Northumbrian annals, incorporating the Appendix and continuing until 802, was added to the epitome in the late eighth and early ninth centuries.[11]

The importance of the *Historia Ecclesiastica* was recognised in King Alfred's reign. It was translated into the vernacular,[12] possibly at the king's instigation as part of his programme to raise the standard of education and Christian observance.[13] Moreover, Alfred needed to

[10] The epitome is printed in Plummer, *Venerabilis Baedae*, i. 352–6, and the continuations to 734 and 766 in ibid., i. 361–3. Cf. ibid., ii. 345 note.

[11] See *Chronica Magistri Rogeri de Houedene*, ed. W. Stubbs (Rolls Series (hereafter cited as R.S.), 1868/71, 4 vols), xxviii–xxx, and P. H. Blair, 'Some observations on the *Historia Regum* attributed to Symeon of Durham', *Celt and Saxon*, ed. N. K. Chadwick, Cambridge 1963, 86–99.

[12] Printed as *The Old English Version of Bede's Ecclesiastical History of the English People*, ed. T. Miller (Early English Text Society (hereafter cited as E.E.T.S.), o.s., xcv–xcvi, cx–cxi, 1890, 1898, 2 pts). Six manuscripts of the Old English Bede survive, all of the ninth and tenth centuries; Laistner, *Hand-List*, 111–12.

[13] Professor Whitelock, after a careful examination of the Old English Bede, concluded: 'That the work was undertaken at Alfred's instigation remains a probability'; D. Whitelock, 'The Old English Bede', *Proceedings of the British Academy*, xlviii (1962), 77.

improve the prestige of his dynasty and the morale of his subjects; an obvious expedient was to make accessible the history of the early achievements of the English people—as narrated by Bede. As mentioned above, Bede can be regarded as the father of the early Northumbrian annals. These annals were, of course, in Latin, but Bede can claim almost equal importance in the inception of vernacular annals in the south of England. The form of the Anglo-Saxon Chronicle, which King Alfred himself may have commissioned,[14] was partly determined by the epitome of the *Historia Ecclesiastica*, and both the epitome and the main text supplied some of the information.[15] In addition, at about the same time Bede made an important contribution to the hagiographical tradition, which had been fairly quiescent since the eighth century. The Old English martyrology was probably written under King Alfred. Much of its material was borrowed from the *Historia Ecclesiastica*; and some derived from Bede's Lives of St Cuthbert, and from the Lives of the Abbots.[16]

Bede's *Historia Ecclesiastica* and Lives of St Cuthbert were influential during the monastic revival in the last half of the tenth century. But their influence was on the actual course of the movement rather than on historical literature. The *Historia Ecclesiastica* provided the reformers, SS Dunstan, Ethelwold and Oswald, with a spiritual tradition native to England. Apparently they saw themselves to some extent as successors to the seventh-century religious leaders. The council at Winchester, summoned by King Edgar to draw up the *Regularis Concordia*, which imposed

[14] Plummer believed that King Alfred commissioned the Anglo-Saxon Chronicle; see *Two of the Saxon Chronicles Parallel*, ed. C. Plummer and J. Earle, Oxford 1892–9, 2 vols, II. civ–cv). A case can be made for regarding it as an official history; see A. Gransden, *Historical Writing in England c. 550–c. 1300*, London 1974, pp. 34–5. However, Professor Whitelock takes a cautious view; *The Anglo-Saxon Chronicle*, ed. D. Whitelock, with D. C. Douglas and S. I. Tucker, London 1961, xxii–xxiii.

[15] See Plummer and Earle, op. cit., II. xli and n. 2, lxviii–lxix, cxiii and n. 1. It is noteworthy that in the southern versions of the Anglo-Saxon Chronicle (Ā, B and C) nearly all the annals derived from the *Historia Ecclesiastica* are from the epitome, while in the northern version, that lying behind D and E, most such annals are from the main text. (The northern version also used the Northumbrian annals; see ibid., II. lxviii–lxxi.) The complex relationship of the Anglo-Saxon Chronicle to Bede is fully discussed by J. Bately, 'Bede and the Anglo-Saxon Chronicle', *Saints, Scholars and Heroes*, ed. M. H. King and W. M. Stevens, Hill Monastic MS Library, Minnesota 1979, 233–44.

[16] For the use of Bede in the Old English martyrology see *An Old English Martyrology*, ed. G. Herzfield (E.E.T.S., o.s., cxvi, 1900), xxxiii/xxxiv, xxxvi/xlii *passim*, and C. E. Fell, 'Edward King and Martyr and the Anglo-Saxon hagiographical tradition', *Ethelred the Unready: Papers from the Millenary Conference*, ed. D. Hill (British Archaeological Reports, British series, lix, 1978), 2, 3. For the date of the Old English Martyrology, and its probable association with King Alfred's reforms, see C. Sisam, 'An early fragment of the Old English Martyrology', *The Review of English Studies*, N.S., iv (1953), 217. It is probably based on a lost ninth-century Latin original; ibid., 212–13, Herzfeld, op. cit., xxxii, xxxvi, and F. Liebermann, 'Zum Old English Martyrology', *Archiv für das Studium der neueren Sprachen*, cv (1900), 86 et seq.

some unity on the monasteries, had a precedent in the synod of Whitby summoned by King Oswy to heal the division in the English Church and fully described by Bede. The *Regularis Concordia*, indeed, has an allusion to the *Historia Ecclesiastica*.[17]

Two of the monasteries founded by St Ethelwold during the revival, Peterborough and Ely, were in fact re-foundations, for there were monasteries on those sites in the seventh century, as Bede records (*Historia Ecclesiastica*, iv. 6, 19). And St Oswald apparently tried to re-found yet another 'Bedan' monastery, Ripon.[18] Both St Ethelwold and St Oswald venerated the early saints, whose acts Bede described. St Ethelwold included a solemn blessing for the feast of St Æthelthryth of Ely, and a full page miniature of her, in his Benedictional. (St Cuthbert figures in the miniature of the Confessors.)[19] And St Oswald searched Northumbria for relics of the ancient saints.[20]

In so far as Bede's *Historia Ecclesiastica* and Lives of St Cuthbert had a literary influence during the revival, it was on hagiography. St Ethelwold's pupil, Ælfric, used the *Historia Ecclesiastica* to provide the acts of SS Alban, Æthelthryth and Oswald for his *Lives of Saints*.[21] And possibly it was owing partly to the example of Bede's Lives of St Cuthbert that biographies were produced of the three tenth-century religious leaders, SS Dunstan, Ethelwold and Oswald.[22] Indeed, the Life of St Oswald contains evidence of Bede's influence. The author compares a miracle performed by St Oswald, the rescue of monks in a sinking boat, with one of St Cuthbert's—which is described in Bede's metrical Life.[23] And he has an allusion to the *Historia Ecclesiastica*; he comments that Foldbriht, abbot of Pershore, ignored the advice given by Bede in the *Historia Ecclesiastica* (iii. 25), that it is better to speak well than ill of those whom you do not know, and proceeds to relate, perhaps with Drythelm in mind (*Historia*

---

[17] *Regularis Concordia*, ed., with an English translation, T. Symons, Nelson's Medieval Texts 1953, 2 and n. 2. Cf. pp. xlv n. 1, 3 and n.c.

[18] *The Historians of the Church of York*, ed. J. Raine (R.S., 1879–94, 3 vols), i. 462.

[19] See *The Benedictional of Saint Æthelwold*, ed., in facsimile, G. F. Warner and H. A. Wilson (Roxburghe Club), Oxford 1910, xv–xvi, 37, and fos 1, 90v.

[20] Raine, op cit., i. 462.

[21] *Aelfric's Lives of Saints*, ed. W. W. Skeat (E.E.T.S., o.s., lxxvi, lxxxii, xciv, cxiv, 1881–1900, 2 vols), i. 414–41 (nos XIX, XX); ii. 124–43 (no. XXVI); cf. ibid., ii. xlviii. For Ælfric's use of Bede for his Lives see J. H. Ott, *Über die Quellen der Heiligenleben in Aelfrics Lives of Saints*, 1 (Inaugural-Dissertation), Halle 1892, 44–7 (for SS Alban and Æthelthryth), Ruth Waterhouse, 'Ælfric's use of discourse in some saints' lives', *Anglo-Saxon England*, v (1976), 83/91 and nn. *passim*, and Fell, 'Edward King and Martyr', 2, 3.

[22] The earliest Lives of SS Dunstan, Ethelwold and Oswald are printed respectively in: *Memorials of St Dunstan*, ed. W. Stubbs (R.S., 1874), 3–52; *Chronicon Monasterii de Abingdon*, ed. J. Stevenson (R.S., 1858, 2 vols), ii. 255–66; and Raine, op. cit., i. 399–475.

[23] Raine, op cit., i. 448. Cf. Bede's metrical life chap. ix (ed. Jaager, 'Bedas metrische Vita', 77–8).

*Ecclesiastica*, v. 12), how Foldbriht died and came alive again, having had a vision of the afterworld.[24]

However, Bede's influence as an historian on the tenth-century monastic revival was limited. Scholars were at least as interested in his computistical works as in his historical ones. Byrhtferth based his *Manual*[25] and Ælfric his *De Temporibus Anni*[26] on the *De Temporum Ratione*, the *De Temporibus* and the *De Natura Rerum*. Nor did the revival rely exclusively, or even mainly, for inspiration on the tradition of the seventh-century Anglo-Saxon Church. No serious attempt was made to revive monasticism in the North, and the English characteristics of the revival are less conspicuous than its continental ones; its strongest influences came from abroad.

Meanwhile, it seems that Bede's cult as a saint developed throughout the Anglo-Saxon period. His relics at Jarrow were reputed to work miracles at least by the late eighth century.[27] Then, in the mid-eleventh century, Alfred (or Alured), son of Westou, sacrist of Durham, thought it worth his while to steal Bede's relics from Jarrow and re-bury them in Durham cathedral, next to St Cuthbert.[28] Bede's reputation is also witnessed by the fact that one of the first acts of Wulfstan as bishop of Worcester, in 1062, was to dedicate a church to him: 'It is most fitting', wrote Wulfstan's biographer, Coleman (sometime between 1095 and 1113), 'that his first dedication should have been to him who is first in fame as a man of letters among the English people.'[29]

---

[24] Raine, op. cit., i. 439–41. Foldbriht was abbot of Pershore *c*. 970–88; M. D. Knowles, C. N. L. Brooke and V. C. M. London, *The Heads of Religious Houses, England and Wales 940–1216*, Cambridge 1972, 58. For later examples of visions resembling Drythelm's experienced by inhabitants of the north of England, see p. 8 n. 36 below.

[25] Printed as *Byrhtferth's Manual*, ed. S. J. Crawford (E.E.T.S, o.s., clxxvii, 1929; only one volume, comprising text with footnotes, published). For the use of Bede in the *Manual* see Crawford's footnotes and H. Henel, 'Byrhtferth's *Preface*: the Epilogue of his *Manual?*', *Speculum*, xviii (1943), 290. Byrhtferth has a eulogy on Bede, especially praising his contribution to computistics, in his 'epilogue', which was written to accompany a copy of Bede's computistical works, or perhaps as an epilogue to the *Manual*: see the printed text in G. F. Forsey, 'Byrhtferth's Preface', *Speculum*, iii (1928), 516–19; cf. Henel, op cit., 288–302, and M. Lapidge, 'The hermeneutic style in tenth-century Anglo-Latin literature', *Anglo-Saxon England*, iv (1975), 90 and n. 3.

[26] Printed as *Aelfric's De Temporibus Anni*, ed. H. Henel (E.E.T.S., o.s., ccxiii, 1942). For Ælfric's use of Bede therein see ibid., liii–lvi.

[27] Alcuin, *De Pontificibus et Sanctis Ecclesiae Eboracensis Carmen* in Raine, *Historians of . . . York*, i. 388.

[28] *Symeonis Monachi Opera Omnia*, ed. T. Arnold (R.S., 1882, 1885, 2 vols), i. 88–9. Cf. H. S. Offler, 'The date of Durham (*Carmen de Situ Dunelmi*)', *Jnl English and Germanic Philology*, lxi (1962), 592–3.

[29] *The Vita Wulfstani of William of Malmesbury*, ed. R. R. Darlington (Camden Society, 3rd ser., xl, 1928), 20.

## II. *c. 1066–c. 1136*

Perhaps at no time in medieval England were Bede's historical works more intensively studied than in the Anglo-Norman period. There were two main reasons for this.

### 1. *Bede as the inspiration for the monasticisation of the North in the late eleventh century*

Aldwin, a monk of Winchcombe, was moved by the *Historia Ecclesiastica* and the Lives of the Abbots of Wearmouth to try to revive religious life in the region formerly ancient Northumbria. A near contemporary, the chronicler Symeon of Durham, recorded that Aldwin 'learnt from the *Historia Anglorum* [i.e. the *Historia Ecclesiastica*] that the province of Northumbria was once crowded with communities of monks and packed with multitudes of saints'.[30] Accordingly, in 1073 or 1074, Aldwin went to Evesham, where he was joined by two monks, Elfwy and Reinfrid, and with them travelled north. The group went to Walcher, the bishop of Durham (1071–80).

Walcher, Symeon recorded, 'gave them the monastery of the blessed Paul, the apostle, formerly built by Abbot Benedict [Biscop] at Jarrow, the walls of which still stood, but roofless and hardly preserving any sign of its ancient dignity'.[31] The missionaries thatched the church and began to celebrate the divine office. Later, after they had failed to restore Whitby and Melrose,[32] Walcher gave them Wearmouth. The monastery, Symeon wrote, 'was formerly famous and noble, as Bede, who lived there from infancy, testifies; but at this time it was hardly possible to appreciate its antiquity because of its ruined condition'.[33] The missionaries built themselves a shack and began to lead the religious life there.

Walcher, who wanted to become a monk himself, planned to found a monastic community in the see of St Cuthbert at Durham.[34] However, his scheme was ended by his murder. It was revived by his successor, William of St Carilef, who finally instituted a monastic community in Durham cathedral in 1083. William acted under the direct influence of Bede's *Historia Ecclesiastica* and prose Life of St Cuthbert. (His copy of the latter still survives in Durham cathedral library.)[35] Symeon recorded that William, grieved at the desolate state of the see of St Cuthbert and the neglect of the saint's body, took advice how to amend the situation:

> He asked the wise old men of the bishopric how things were originally managed at St Cuthbert's: they replied that the see was on the island of

---

[30] *Symeonis Monachi Opera Omnia*, i. 108.

[31] Ibid., i. 109.

[32] Ibid., i. 111.

[33] Ibid., i. 112.

[34] Ibid., i. 113.

[35] MS B 11.35 in the chapter library at Durham; R. A. B. Mynors, *Durham Cathedral Manuscripts to the End of the Twelfth Century*, Oxford 1939, 41.

Lindisfarne and that monks served [St Cuthbert], both when he was alive and when he was dead, with due veneration; their assertion accords with the evidence in the Life [of St Cuthbert] and with the *Historia Ecclesiastica Gentis Anglorum*.[36]

The evidence cited shows that Bede's historical works made a positive contribution to the revival of monasticism in the North. It could even be claimed that they provided the initial incentive. The instigator of the movement, Aldwin, was an Englishman, and so were his two companions from Evesham, Elfwy and Reinfrid. They were continuing the tradition of the Anglo-Saxon Church, not only its missionary spirit but also the study of Bede.

However, it is possible that Aldwin and his companions had another motive besides missionary zeal and the inspiration of Bede. Perhaps they intended to augment the reputation of the Anglo-Saxon Church, in order to help protect its traditions against the new Norman rulers. Walcher and William of St Carilef, although Normans, may have co-operated with the English missionaries partly to strengthen their own positions. Possibly they hoped to placate the hostile English in their diocese by showing an appreciation of the Anglo-Saxon achievement.[37] Moreover, by increasing the prestige of Durham cathedral they may have hoped to be able to resist their enemies more effectively.[38] Therefore, the appeal to Bede may have been one by-product of the threat to the tradition of the English Church posed by the new regime and of the political instability in the North after the Norman Conquest.

2. *The use of Bede by chroniclers and controversialists in the Anglo-Norman period*
    The Norman Conquest put in jeopardy the traditions of the whole Church in England as well as of each monastery. The threat impelled monks to write chronicles and saints' Lives in order to establish continuity with the past. Monks wrote chronicles covering the period from the earliest times to their own day in order to demonstrate that English church history was long and unbroken. In addition, they wrote local histories

---

[36] *Symeonis Monachi Opera Omnia*, i. 120. An instance of the strength of the Bedan tradition in the Durham area is provided by Symeon who relates that a local man, Eadulf, died and came alive again, having had a vision of the afterworld; Symeon explicitly compares Eadulf's experience with Drythelm's; ibid., i. 114–15. A similar vision was experienced by a boy, Orm, who also lived in north-east England; an account was written in 1126 or soon after, and sent by Sigar, the parish priest of Newbald, in the East Riding of Yorkshire, to Symeon at Durham. See H. Farmer, 'The Vision of Orm', *Analecta Bollandiana*, lxxv (1957), 72–82. For a pre-Conquest example of a man having a vision like Drythelm's see p. 402 and n. 24 above.

[37] Walcher's attempt to placate the English in the political sphere was, ironically, one factor leading to his murder; see D. C. Douglas, *William the Conqueror*, London 1964, 240–1.

[38] William of St Carilef could not rely on the support even of the king. For his quarrel with William Rufus, 1087–8, see A. L. Poole, *From Domesday Book to Magna Carta*, Oxford 1951, 100–4.

and hagiographies to prove the antiquity of their own monasteries. They hoped in this way to increase the prestige of the English Church and of the particular monasteries, so that they could the better withstand the innovations of their new ecclesiastical masters and the onslaughts of the new secular ones.

In order to increase the prestige of the Church and of the monasteries, it was necessary to prove not only the continuity, but also the glory of their past history. Here writers faced a problem, since it was part of Norman propaganda to denigrate the eleventh-century Anglo-Saxon Church; one justification of the Conquest was that William I and Lanfranc had instigated a movement of ecclesiastical and monastic reform. A solution was that writers should turn to Bede, since he provided an account of a golden age of the Anglo-Saxon Church in the remote past.

At no period did the chroniclers pay greater tribute to Bede than under William Rufus and Henry I. Chroniclers of general history, and some of the local historians, expressed admiration for both the sanctity of his life and the profundity of his learning. Some did so in passing, but others devoted a page or more to Bede's life (based on the *Historia Ecclesiastica*, v. 24, and Cuthbert's letter to Cuthwin) and achievements. Orderic Vitalis[39] and Henry of Huntingdon,[40] who wrote about Bede at some length, commented especially on his saintliness and fame as a Father of the Church. Florence of Worcester concentrated mainly on his historiography. He recorded Bede's death, noting that he 'lucidly narrated the deeds of his people (his life and his History ended at one and the same time)';[41] he noted Bede's knowledge of chronology, a subject in which he himself was interested.[42]

The longest, most eloquent and most comprehensive, encomium of Bede by a chronicler of general history is William of Malmesbury's in the *Gesta Regum*.[43] Much of it is about Bede's saintly qualities and pre-eminence in biblical scholarship. Of Bede's fame in general, William wrote:

> He is a man easier to admire than adequately to extol. He was born in a remote corner of the earth. (Indeed, Britain is called another world by some because, being cut off by the sea, many cosmographers overlooked it.) And the place of his birth and education was in its remotest region, near

---

[39] *The Ecclesiastical History of Orderic Vitalis*, ed., with an English translation, M. Chibnall Oxford Medieval Texts 1969–81), iii. 66, 68.

[40] *Henrici Archidiaconi Huntendunensis Historia Anglorum*, ed. T. Arnold (R.S., 1879), 115–16.

[41] *Florentii Wigorniensis Monachi Chronicon ex Chronicis*, ed. B. Thorpe (English Historical Society, 1848–9, 2 vols), i. 53.

[42] ibid., i. 50. For other references to Bede see ibid., i. 44, 45, 46. For Florence's interest in chronology, see Gransden, *Historical Writing*, 144 and n. 56, 145 and n. 63, 146.

[43] *Willelmi Malmesbiriensis Monachi de Gestis Regum Anglorum* . . ., ed. W. Stubbs (R.S., 1887–9, 2 vols), i. 58–67.

Scotland. Nevertheless, the bright light of his learning illuminated the whole world.[44]

William commented twice on Bede's unique position in the historio-graphical tradition of the Anglo-Saxons, briefly at the beginning of the prologue to the *Gesta Regum*[45] and at some length in the encomium. In the latter he wrote:

> with [Bede] was buried almost all record of events until our own day; for there was no Englishman to rival his learning or imitate his virtues, none to emulate his glory and take up the thread of his teaching, now cut short. A few loved Jesus equally, but, although not ill-educated in letters, they spent their lives in graceless silence; others, after the merest taste of learning, preferred sloth and idleness. And thus, lazier men succeeded the lazy, and soon the love of scholarship grew cold throughout this island.[46]

Chroniclers could express their admiration of Bede in other ways than by eulogy. In some cases they explicitly stated that they wrote in order to continue Bede's work, and occasionally they imitated his method. Florence of Worcester wrote:

> We in truth, inspired by God, . . . have thought it fitting to leave a record of events from the death of Bede onwards, for our faithful successors.[47]

Similarly, William of Malmesbury wrote the *Gesta Regum* as a continuation of the *Historia Ecclesiastica*. Having deplored in the prologue the paucity of chroniclers after Bede's death, and the absence of any competent ones until his own day, he wrote: 'moved by love of my country and by the persuasion of others, I have decided to bridge the gap of interrupted time'.[48] And Henry of Huntingdon stated in the prologue to his chronicle that, on the advice of Alexander, bishop of Lincoln, he had 'continued the *Ecclesiastical History* of the venerable Bede to the best of his ability'.[49]

Appreciation by imitation is particularly apparent in William of Malmesbury's chronicles. He began the *Gesta Regum* by listing his authorities in the prologue, in the same way as Bede had done in the *Historia Ecclesiastica*.[50] Moreover, the section on each bishopric in the *Gesta Pontificum*[51] starts with a geographical description of the see, reminiscent of the description of Britain with which the *Historia Ecclesiastica* opens. Similarly, Henry of Huntingdon began his history with the

[44] Ibid., i. 59.
[45] Ibid., i. 1–2.
[46] Ibid., i. 66–7.
[47] *Chronicon ex Chronicis*, i. 53.
[48] *Gesta Regum*, i. 2.
[49] *Historia Anglorum*, 3.
[50] *Gesta Regum*, i. 1–2.
[51] *Willelmi Malmesbiriensis Monachi de Gestis Pontificum Anglorum ...*, ed. N. E. S. A. Hamilton (R.S., 1870).

geography of Britain (partly based on Bede's).[52] And Orderic (who made a copy of the *Historia Ecclesiastica* with his own hand)[53] may well have chosen the title of his work in imitation of Bede, and probably also borrowed from him (*Historia Ecclesiastica*, v. 24) the idea of appending an autobiography.[54]

Thus Bede's life and learning inspired the Anglo-Norman historians to eulogy, and his achievements as an historian in particular inspired them to continue his work and even to imitate his method. However, it cannot be claimed that the influence of the *Historia Ecclesiastica* on historical method in the Anglo-Norman period was profound; the chroniclers were subject to numerous other influences. Probably it had more effect on the content of the chronicles than on their form. As a quarry of information for early Anglo-Saxon history the *Historia Ecclesiastica* had no rivals; it was extensively used by Florence of Worcester, William of Malmesbury, Orderic Vitalis and Henry of Huntingdon. In general their use of the *Historia Ecclesiastica* was uncritical. Chroniclers extracted information, or copied passages verbatim from the *Historia Ecclesiastica* without comment, sometimes putting them alongside material from other, usually less reliable, sources. (For example, Henry of Huntingdon interposed an account based on Nennius of the Britons' Trojan origins.)[55] However, William of Malmesbury was on occasion scholarly in his approach to the *Historia Ecclesiastica*. In the *Gesta Regum* he pointed out a discrepancy between the estimated length of Ethelbert's reign as recorded in the *Historia Ecclesiastica*, of fifty-six years (ii. 5), and that given in the Anglo-Saxon Chronicle (s.a. 565), of fifty-three years; the matter, he wrote, must be left to the reader's judgement.[56] In the *Gesta Pontificum* he commented that Bede's account of St Wilfrid's life is incomplete; therefore, he will use the Life by Eddius Stephanus.[57] He also expressed doubt whether, as Bede recorded (*Historia Ecclesiastica*, iii. 6), St Oswald's arms were preserved at Bamburgh[58] and wondered at Bede's silence on the foundation of Evesham by St Ecgwin.[59]

Those local historians who, in the Anglo-Norman period, turned to Bede had a more limited purpose than the chroniclers of general events; they used him merely to prove the antiquity of their houses. The historian of Ely Abbey described Bede as the 'venerable' and 'most eloquent' doctor, and as 'a most truthful historian'.[60] His main authority

[52] *Historia Anglorum*, 5–7.
[53] Rouen MS 1343. See *Bede's Ecclesiastical History of the English People*, ed., with an English translation, B. Colgrave and R. A. B. Mynors (Oxford Medieval Texts, 1969), p. lxi.
[54] *The Ecclesiastical History of Orderic Vitalis*, ed. Chibnall, vi. 550–6. See ibid., vi. 556 n. 1.
[55] *Historia Anglorum*, 13.
[56] *Gesta Regum*, i. 13. Cf. *Historia Ecclesiastica*, ed. Plummer, ii. 85 note.
[57] *Gesta Pontificum*, 210; cf. ibid., 238–9.
[58] Ibid., 293; cf. *Historia Ecclesiastica*, ed. Plummer, ii. 141, 158, notes.
[59] *Gesta Pontificum*, 296.
[60] *Liber Eliensis*, ed. E. O. Blake (Camden Society, 3rd ser., xcii, 1962), 2, 13.

both for the abbey's foundation and for the life of its patron saint, Æthelthryth, was the *Historia Ecclesiastica*.[61] In addition, he used the universal chronicle in the *De Temporibus*, to provide St Æthelthryth's life with a comparative chronology.[62]

Symeon of Durham praised Bede at greater length than did the Ely writer. He included one eulogy in his history of the see of St Cuthbert (which covered the period from 635 to 1096)[63] and another in his letter about the early archbishops of York which he addressed to 'Hugh, dean of York'.[64] Bede, as the biographer of St Cuthbert, had especial importance to Symeon. And Bede himself was, in a sense, a patron saint of Durham; as has been seen, his relics had been removed to the cathedral in the mid-eleventh century, where they had become the centre of a cult.[65] Symeon wrote of Bede in almost intimate terms, referring to him as 'our Bede'.[66] He described Bede's 'study' at Jarrow in a way which suggests that he himself had visited it. It was 'a stone cottage; there Bede would sit, free from all disturbance, to meditate, read, dictate and write'.[67] He also recorded that the porticus 'on the north side of the church of St Paul at Jarrow was dedicated to Bede, to preserve his memory for the faithful'.[68]

Symeon's two eulogies of Bede resemble William of Malmesbury's, but they are shorter and alone mention Bede's knowledge of Greek.[69] Like William, Symeon seems to have been most impressed by the biblical commentaries,[70] and, again like William, he commented on the fact that Bede's genius flowered in such a distant place:

> It seems unbelievable to many that in a remote corner of the world, a man, who never crossed the sea to acquire knowledge and never frequented the schools of philosophers, should shine with such erudition, and that his books should be famed throughout the world.[71]

Moreover, Symeon wrote, Bede could describe far away lands which he had never visited:

> In his books he vividly describes the location, the nature, and the merits of many and diverse countries and regions, as if he himself had been there,

---

[61] See ibid., pp. xxviii, liii, 2–50 *passim*.

[62] Ibid., 50–1.

[63] *Libellus de exordio atque procursu istius, hoc est Dunelmensis Ecclesiae*, printed as *Historia Dunelmensis Ecclesiae* in *Symeonis Monachi Opera Omnia*, i. 3–135.

[64] Printed in ibid., i. 222–8. One Hugh was dean from 1090–*c*. 1109, and another from *c*. 1130–*c*. 1132; see J. Le Neve, *Fasti Ecclesiae Anglicanae*, Oxford 1854, 3 vols, iii. 120.

[65] See p. 402 above.

[66] See his letter to Hugh; *Symeonis Monachi Opera Omnia*, i. 227.

[67] Ibid., i. 43.

[68] Ibid., i. 42–3.

[69] Ibid., i. 29, 30, 228.

[70] Ibid., i. 29.

[71] The letter to Hugh; ibid., i. 227–8. See also the *Libellus*; ibid., i. 37. Cf. pp. 406–7 above.

although he had been reared from childhood in one monastery, where he spent his whole life until the day he died.[72]

But Symeon, unlike William, was not surprised that Bede surmounted the geographical isolation of his home; it seemed perfectly explicable in view of the excellent library at Wearmouth/Jarrow and the high standard of learning during the Northumbrian renaissance.[73] Moreover, he cited a passage from Bede's commentary on the Song of Songs, where Bede explained that he had had to rely on written authorities for his information about foreign lands, because he 'was born and nurtured far away in an island set in the midst of the sea'.[74]

Symeon's main sources for the early history of the see of St Cuthbert were the *Historia Ecclesiastica* and Bede's lives of St Cuthbert.[75] With their help he wrote a detailed account of the see's beginnings at Lindisfarne. His primary object was to augment in a general way the prestige of the see in its present site at Durham. However, in one instance Symeon defended the monastery on a particular issue, as if in response to a specific criticism, and appealed to Bede's authority to support his argument. He claimed that the appointment of the prior Turgot as archdeacon, with responsibility for spiritual matters throughout the bishopric, and the stipulation that subsequent priors should hold the same office were justified by precedent; the Life of St Cuthbert showed that Boisil, when he was 'praepositus' of the monastery (of Lindisfarne), had often gone on expeditions preaching to the people, following the example of St Cuthbert himself. Since 'praepositus' was merely the early name for 'prior', the precedent established by Boisil made it incumbent on those who succeeded him in the priorate to perform similar functions.[76]

The use of Bede's authority to support contending parties was not uncommon during the reigns of William Rufus and Henry I, when the definition of jurisdictions caused frequent disputes between rivals, each claiming privileges at the expense of the other. Towards the mid-twelfth century a history of the archbishops of York was composed, covering the period from the early seventh century to the death of Thurstan (1140).[77] The author was a partisan of the Church of York, and his object was to prove the independence of the metropolitan see of York from subjection

---

[72] Ibid., i. 41.

[73] See the letter to Hugh; ibid., i. 227–8.

[74] Ibid., i. 228. *Expositio in Cantica Canticorum*, Lib. 1 (the *Complete Works of the Venerable Bede*, ed. J. A. Giles, London 1843–4, 12 vols, ix. 200). A copy (now lost) of Bede's commentary on the Song of Songs was among the books given by William of St Carilef to the cathedral; see C. H. Turner, 'The earliest list of Durham MSS.', *J.T.S.*, xix (1918), 130, no. 40.

[75] Passages are cited verbatim from the prose Life. For a direct reference to the verse Life see *Symeonis Monachi Opera Omnia*, i. 38 and n. a.

[76] Ibid., i. 129. Cf. *Historia Ecclesiastica*, iv. 27; ed. Plummer, i. 269.

[77] Printed in *Historians of . . . York*, ed. Raine, ii. 312–87.

to the archbishop of Canterbury.[78] To achieve his end the York writer relied for the early period on Bede. He stated at the outset:

> Whoever reads the History of the English [i.e. the *Historia Ecclesiastica*] . . . will understand clearly that the exaction of profession [of obedience to the archbishop of Canterbury], is not only contrary to reason, but also undoubtedly contrary to the original institution of the church.[79]

In order to defend the claims of York the chronicler sought to glorify the achievements of the province in general. He praised its famous men, including a section on Bede's life and works based mainly on extracts from Symeon.[80] He called Bede the 'illustrious' and 'incomparable' doctor, whose 'immortal genius gave him and the whole of Britain everlasting fame', and whose 'writings were the admiration of Europe'.[81] But the York chronicler's tendentious purpose necessitated more specific arguments. He cited Gregory's instructions to St Augustine from the *Historia Ecclesiastica* in order to prove that the pope originally instituted two equal metropolitan sees, London and York. Then, still relying on Bede, he demonstrated how the see of Canterbury gained importance instead of that of London and explained why there was no archbishop of York in St Augustine's time.[82]

Disputants might cite Bede in the course of proceedings, either verbally or in documents. Lanfranc cited the authority of the *Historia Ecclesiastica* in the council he held at Winchester in April 1072 to try to settle the question of the primacy. He used the *Historia Ecclesiastica* to prove that from the time of St Augustine until Bede's death, a period of nearly a hundred and forty years, his predecessors had ruled York and 'the whole of Britain and Ireland', ordaining bishops and holding councils, to which they had summoned the archbishops of York; St Augustine had not consecrated an archbishop of York because there was none in his day.[83] Lanfranc's case was based on early history rather than on law. The evidence of Bede, although inconclusive, did provide, in the words of one historian, 'a satisfactory foundation for Lanfranc's claim to the historical precedence of Canterbury'.[84]

When the controversy was revived by Ralph d'Éscures, archbishop of Canterbury (1114–22), the Canterbury party again appealed to early history, as recorded in the *Historia Ecclesiastica*. Archbisop Ralph, writing in 1119 to Calixtus II, in order to complain that Archbishop Thurstan

[78] See ibid., ii, pp. xxi–xxii.

[79] Ibid., ii. 313.

[80] Ibid., ii. 332–5.

[81] Ibid., ii. 327–8, 331, 334.

[82] Ibid., ii. 313–16.

[83] See Lanfranc's letter to Alexander II; *The Letters of Lanfranc Archbishop of Canterbury*, ed., with an English translation, H. Clover and M. Gibson (Oxford Medieval Texts, 1979), 50–1. Cf. R. W. Southern, 'The Canterbury forgeries', *E.H.R.*, lxxiii (1958), 195.

[84] A. J. Macdonald, 'Eadmer and the Canterbury privileges', *J.T.S.*, xxxii (1931), 41.

had refused the oath of obedience, set forth Bede's evidence in detail.[85] He admitted that Pope Gregory established two equal metropolitans, but pointed out that the sees in question were London and York, not Canterbury and York. He proceeded to cite the *Historia Ecclesiastica* to supply historical precedents for the superiority which Canterbury now claimed: he asserted that the bishops of Northumbria were suffragans of Canterbury (*Historia Ecclesiastica*, i. 29). He also demonstrated that St Benedict exercised authority over the British bishops (*Historia Ecclesiastica*, i. 27; ii. 2), that Laurence succeeded to St Augustine's power (*Historia Ecclesiastica*, ii. 4), and that Archbishop Theodore had authority over all England and was active in the province of York.

Archbishop Ralph specifically stated that Canterbury, not York, had primacy over Scotland. He based this claim on the precedent of St Augustine's authority over the British bishops, arguing that the term 'British' included 'Scottish'.[86] Eadmer became involved in this dispute when in 1120 Alexander I of Scotland appointed him to the bishopric of St Andrews. Accepting Canterbury's right without question, Eadmer demanded to do obedience to Canterbury not York. Alexander refused, and within six months opposition had forced him to resign.[87] In the course of the dispute Eadmer wrote to Nicholas, prior of Worcester, for information to strengthen his case. In his reply Nicholas cited Bede to prove that York had no right to primacy over Scotland. He pointed out that it was Aidan who preached in Northumbria after Paulinus's expulsion, and that his four successors were all consecrated, and one even deposed, by the Scots.[88]

As is well known, the Anglo-Norman ecclesiastics and monks used forgery, besides legitimate weapons, in their disputes. Here again the importance of Bede as an historical source is manifest; he provided the forgers with essential information. Unlike the controversialists considered above, who cited Bede's authority openly, the forgers used the *Historia Ecclesiastica* covertly. They did not appeal to it to provide specific precedents relevant to the points at issue. (Indeed, had they been able to do so, they might not have considered forgery necessary.) Rather they borrowed phrases from the *Historia Ecclesiastica*, apparently with the intention of making the style of their spurious documents appropriate to the time when they were supposed to have been written. They also used Bede to provide a convincing historical background.

The monks of Christ Church and of St Augustine's, Canterbury,

---

[85] The letter is printed in *Historians of . . . York*, ed. Raine, ii. 228–51 (see esp. 228–39). See Southern, op. cit., 208–9.

[86] Raine, op. cit., ii. 235–6.

[87] *Eadmeri Historia Novorum in Anglia*, ed. M. Rule (R.S., 1884), 279–88. See R. W. Southern, *Saint Anselm and his Biographer*, Cambridge 1963, 236.

[88] Nicholas's letter is printed in *Councils and Ecclesiastical Documents relating to Great Britain and Ireland*, ed. A. W. Haddan and W. Stubbs, Oxford 1869–78, reprinted 1964, 3 vols, ii. 202–4.

resorted to forgery at much the same time, early in the 1070s. The Christ Church monks wanted to prove the antiquity of their community in order to show that it existed already in the seventh century.[89] For this purpose they forged, in about 1072, a bull of Boniface IV, which Lanfranc sent on their behalf as evidence to Alexander II.[90] It purported to have been granted at the request of King Ethelbert and stipulated that Archbishop Laurence might establish monks at Christ Church, who were to live according to the Rule of St Bendict. The *Historia Ecclesiastica* supplied the form of the date of the bull and the historical background.

The object of the monks of St Augustine's when they turned to forgery was to provide evidence to protect their privileges, notably of exemption from archiepiscopal control, against Lanfranc's encroachments. They produced a series of forged papal bulls and royal charters, granting St Augustine's various rights. Eleven of these documents still survive. Most of them purport to be of the seventh century; the *Historia Ecclesiastica* again supplied the historical background. It also provided occasional phrases.[91]

It can be seen, therefore, that the Anglo-Normans used Bede's reputation and his historical works in various ways. They used them as proof of the English Church's tradition: by eulogising Bede himself they added glory to the Northumbrian renaissance; by plundering his works they were able to describe in detail the achievements of the early Anglo-Saxon Church. Moreover, the historian of any monastery in existence in the seventh century used Bede's authority to increase its house's prestige by demonstrating its antiquity. In this way Bede made a vital contribution to salvaging the tradition of the English Church from the cataclysm of the Norman Conquest. In addition, the Anglo-Norman controversialists appealed to Bede for precedents in disputes over ecclesiastical jurisdiction and monastic privilege. And if they had to resort to forgery, Bede supplied them with background information and a stylistic model.

[89] According to Eadmer (*Historia Novorum*, 18–19), Walkelin, bishop of Winchester, planned to replace the monks by secular canons not only in his own cathedral but also in Christ Church, Canterbury. Professor Knowles, however, doubted the reliability of Eadmer's information on this point; see M. D. Knowles, *The Monastic Order in England*, 2nd edn, Cambridge 1963, 130 and n. 2.

[90] For the spurious bull of Boniface IV, see W. Levison, *England and the Continent in the Eighth Century*, Oxford 1946, 202–4, and C. N. L. Brooke, 'The Canterbury forgeries and their author', *Downside Review*, lxviii (1950), 465–7.

[91] See Levison, op. cit., 181 et seq. Professor Brooke argued that all the Canterbury forgeries were the work of one man, Guerno; Brooke, op. cit., 462–76, and the continuation of the same article, *Downside Review*, lxix (1951) 210–31, *passim*. This is unlikely, since the forgeries produced at Christ Church in relation to the primacy dispute, which do not concern us here, were probably produced 1121–2. However, it is quite possible that Guerno was responsible for the earliest Christ Church forgery, the bull of Boniface IV, as well as for the St Augustine's forgeries; see Southern, op. cit., 193–4 and n. 1.

## III. *c. 1136–c. 1200*

Once the monasteries had been restored to comparative security and the readjustments entailed by the Norman Conquest made, historians no longer had the incentives provided by insecurity and controversy for the study of Bede. The influence of Bede declined. However, two factors assured that it retained some importance during the rest of the twelfth century. These factors will be considered separately.

1. *Bede as an inspiration for the Cistercian settlement in the North in the last half of the twelfth century*

When the Cistercians settled in the North they found their ideals in harmony with the tradition of ancient Northumbria. Therefore, they adopted it in order to enrich their spiritual life, becoming, as it were, the spiritual heirs to the Northumbrian saints. Moreover, it is likely that it was not only in spiritual matters that the Northumbrian tradition was congenial to them. Northumbria had straddled what was in their day the border βetween England and Scotland, including part of southern Scotland. And so it provided some precedent for the spread of the Cistercian order into Scotland.

The centre of Bedan influence was Rievaulx. When Maurice, abbot from 1145 to 1147, moved there from St Cuthbert's, Durham, in 1132, he was already known as 'a second Bede'. His works, which have not survived, included one on the monastic life and one on the translation of St Cuthbert in 1104 (which Maurice himself may have witnessed).[92] The most famous north-country Cistercian, Ailred of Rievaulx (abbot of Rievaulx 1147–67), came of a family already well-established in the ecclesiastical life of Anglo-Saxon England, belonging to an area which had been part of ancient Northumbria.[93] Ailred's father, Eilaf, was hereditary priest of Hexham (he was ousted in 1113 to make room for a community of secular canons, when Thomas, archbishop of York, restored Wilfred's foundation); Eilaf's patron saint was St Cuthbert, and he became a monk of Durham in 1138 shortly before his death. And Ailred's great-grandfather was Alured, son of Westou, sacrist of Durham, the man responsible for the theft of Bede's relics from Jarrow.

It is not, therefore, surprising that Ailred was imbued with the Northumbrian tradition. His loyalty to the Anglo-Saxon past was reinforced by his education in the court of King David of Scotland. Ailred retained an affection and admiration for the Scottish royal family, which

---

[92] For Maurice and his works see F. M. Powicke, 'Maurice of Rievaulx', *E.H.R.*, xxxvi (1921), 17–29.

[93] For Ailred and his family see *The Life of Ailred of Rievaulx by Walter Daniel*, ed. F. M. Powicke Nelson's Medieval Texts 1950, pp. xxxiii–li *passim*. For his family tree see J. Raine, *Hexham Priory* (Surtees Society, xliv, xlvi, 1863–4, 2 vols), i. li–lii.

descended from the Anglo-Saxon one.[94] Like his father, he particularly venerated St Cuthbert,[95] whose austerities his own resembled, and he inspired and helped Reginald of Durham to write a book about him.[96] He probably attended the translation of the Hexham saints in 1155; he certainly wrote a tract for the occasion, the *De sanctis ecclesiae Hagustald-ensis*. Ailred's principal source for this tract was Bede's *Historia Ecclesiastica*, and in his account of Acca he refers to Bede's commentaries on the gospels of Luke and Mark (because Bede had composed them at Acca's suggestion).[97]

Bede's Lives of St Cuthbert and the *Historia Ecclesiastica* were, therefore, of value to the north-country Cistercians as authorities on St Cuthbert and the other saints of the Northumbrian period. It could be argued, therefore, that Bede contributed as an historian to the success of the Cistercians in the North. However, undoubtedly, he was mainly of importance as a saint and Father of the Church; his influence was primarily spiritual, not historiographical. The Cistercians' use of the *Historia Ecclesiastica* was limited. As a result of the regulations of their order, which virtually prohibited all literary activity unless of a religious nature,[98] the twelfth-century Cistercians in England produced no general chronicles. Thus they had no need of the *Historia Ecclesiastica* as a quarry of information for early Anglo-Saxon history as a whole. Nor, since their houses were of recent foundation, could they use it to increase the prestige of any of their monasteries in particular.

2. *The use of Bede by critics of Geoffrey of Monmouth*

The first writer who challenged, by implication, Bede's ascendancy as the primary authority for the early history of Britain was Geoffrey of Monmouth, whose *Historia Regum Britanniae* was published in 1136. However, it should be borne in mind that Geoffrey's work conflicted with the *Historia Ecclesiastica* only to a limited extent. Bede had written little, because he knew little, about the Anglo-Saxons' predecessors, the ancient Britons. Geoffrey began the *Historia* by observing that, except for Gildas and Bede, the chroniclers had totally ignored the British period, not even mentioning King Arthur and his many successors.[99] And Henry of Huntingdon explained, in his letter answering a query from 'Warin the Briton', that he had started his history with Julius Caesar because he had no information for the previous centuries.[100] It was this gap which

[94] Powicke, op. cit., pp. xxxix–xlii.

[95] Ibid., pp. xxxvii–xxxviii.

[96] See *Reginaldi Monachi Dunelmensis Libellus de Admirandis Beati Cuthberti Virtutibus*. ed. J. Raine (Surtees Society, i, 1835), viii, 4, 7, 32.

[97] Raine, *Hexham Priory*, i. 33.

[98] Consuetudines, c. lviii; P. Guignard, *Les Monuments primitifs de la Règle Cistercienne*, Dijon 1878, 266. Cf. Knowles, *The Monastic Order in England*, 643–4 and n. 6.

[99] *The Historia Regum Britanniae of Geoffrey of Monmouth*, ed. A. Griscom, London 1929, 219.

[100] *Historia Anglorum*, xx–xxi.

Geoffrey undertook to fill. But he wrote at fanciful length, not only about the Britons in the period before Caesar but also about them in the time of the Anglo-Saxon invasions and later, until King Arthur's final defeat. The narrative in the *Historia Ecclesiastica* conflicted with that in the *Historia Regum Britanniae* only to the extent that Bede was almost silent about the people whose exploits Geoffrey fully described. In addition, on some points Bede's statements were irreconcilable with Geoffrey's.

The *Historia Regum Britanniae* soon became a 'best-seller', and its fictional narrative gained general acceptance as sober history. Significantly, it was in the North, where Bede's reputation was most flourishing, that the few voices of dissent were raised. The first may have been that of Ailred himself, whose *Speculum Charitatis*, written between 1142 and 1143, contains what appears to be an oblique reference to Geoffrey's work; Ailred lamented that novices 'weep more readily over fictitious tales about someone (I know not whom) called Arthur', than over pious books, and dismissed the stories as 'fables and lies'.[101] The historicity of the *Historia Regum Britanniae* was explicitly, if rather hesitantly, called in question by Alfred (or Alured) of Beverley, treasurer and sacrist of Beverley Minster, in his *Annales sive Historia de Gestis Regum Britanniae*.[102] He probably composed the *Annales* in 1143: he explained that he wrote during a period of enforced idleness, when many people were under sentence of excommunication; this was probably a result of the legatine council held by Henry of Blois, bishop of Winchester, in 1143.[103] He turned to the study of history because everyone was talking of the new 'History of the Britons', and he was ashamed never to have read it.[104]

Alfred copied extracts from standard histories and chronicles and arranged them in chronological order. He stated the source of each extract, and mentioned which other authorities agreed with it and in some cases cited an alternative account. One of his principal sources for the early part was the *Historia Regum Britanniae*; he put copious extracts side by side with those from Bede's *Historia Ecclesiastica*, and from other reputable works. He made no systematic attempt to evaluate the relative reliability of his sources. However, comparison of one with another raised questions in his mind. He wondered, for example, whether the Ambrosius Aurelianus in Bede (*Historia Ecclesiastica*, i. 16) was the same man as the Ambrosius Aurelianus mentioned by Geoffrey.[105] More important, collation of sources combined with his common sense made him have doubts about some passages in the *Historia Regum Britanniae*. He noticed the anomaly that Trogus Pompeius, Suetonius and Orosius

---

[101] *Speculum Charitatis*, lib. ii. c. 17: P.L. cxcv, col. 565.

[102] *Aluredi Beverlacensis Annales sive Historia de Gestis Regum Britanniae*, ed. T. Hearne, Oxford 1716.

[103] Ibid., 1–2. Cf. J. S. P. Tatlock, *The Legendary History of Britain*, Berkeley, Cal. 1950, 210–11.

[104] *Aluredi Beverlacensis Annales*, 2.

[105] Ibid., 56. See *Historia Regum Britanniae*, 330, 360, 362, 365–6, etc.

did not mention the British kings whose deeds Geoffrey extolled, 'neither do Gildas Sapiens nor Bede—all are equally silent'.[106] And he admitted that he was uneasy about the historicity of King Arthur himself; 'neither the Roman nor the English historians record anything about the illustrious King Arthur, although he did such remarkable deeds with such skill and valour, not only in Britain against pagans, but also in Gaul against the Romans'.[107]

Alfred was faced, therefore, with a dilemma: on the one hand was his respect for authority (he stated that he would not presume to question Geoffrey's veracity);[108] and on the other was his doubt about the reliability of the *Historia Regum Britanniae*. His solution was to compromise. He decided, as he explained in the prologue, to borrow from the *Historia Regum Britanniae* 'only those passages which are not beyond belief'.[109] The fact that he nevertheless made fairly free use of it was the result not only of his respect for authority, but also, as he mentioned in the prologue, of his desire to please his readers;[110] like many other people, he recognised Geoffrey as a good read.

A generation later the *Historia Regum Britanniae* found a more intelligent and uncompromising critic than Alfred of Beverley. At the end of the twelfth century William of Newburgh, a canon of the Augustinian priory of Newburgh in the North Riding of Yorkshire, wrote his *Historia Rerum Anglicarum*[111] at the request of Ernald, abbot of Rievaulx.[112] (Ernald was inhibited by the regulations of his order from asking one of his own monks to undertake the task.) Since William's chronicle began at the Norman Conquest, the narrative itself had no need of the *Historia Regum Britanniae*. However, the prologue started with a survey of the sources for early British and Anglo-Saxon history and a resumé of the English settlements before it briefly described the purpose and scope of the actual chronicle (which continued to 1198). It is in the survey of sources that William demolished the credibility of the *Historia Regum Britanniae*. Indeed, this section and the short account of the English settlements seem to be distinct from the last part of the prologue, which constituted the true preface to the chronicle. The possibility must be considered that the prologue up to the 'true preface' was once a tract on its own.[113]

The question arises why anyone, presumably in this case William, should have written such a tract, which was subsequently incorporated

[106] *Aluredi Beverlaćensis Annales*, 24.

[107] Ibid., 76.

[108] Ibid., 76.

[109] Ibid., 2.

[110] Ibid., 2–3.

[111] Printed in *Chronicles of the Reigns of Stephen, Henry II, and Richard I*, ed. R. Howlett (R.S., 1884–9, 4 vols), i. 3–408; ii. 411–500.

[112] Ibid., i. 3–4.

[113] The suggested tract, as it survives in the prologue, might well have ended at 'ab omnibus respuatur' (ibid., i. 18, line 18), at which point William changes theme and starts leading up to his own chronicle.

in the prologue to the chronicle, to discredit Geoffrey of Monmouth. The reasons would probably have been political. The Celtic peoples could use the *Historia Regum Britanniae* as a weapon against the Angevin dynasty. It provided them with valiant predecessors, the greatest of whom was King Arthur. Arthur served as a focus of loyalty, becoming, as it were, their spiritual leader. Nor, indeed, was it certain that Arthur was dead; in his description of the wounded king's last refuge on the Isle of Avalon (Bk. xi. 2), Geoffrey left the possibility open that he would return once more and lead his people to victory. King Arthur became, therefore, the British 'hope'; and added zest to the rebellions of the Welsh and Bretons against the Angevin kings.[114]

William himself recorded the Welsh rising of 1157, commenting that the Welsh were descendants of the ancient Britons.[115] But he dwelt at greater length on Breton disaffection. He recorded the posthumous birth of a son in 1186 to Henry II's son Geoffrey, by a daughter of the duke of Brittany. And he recorded that the Bretons had the child solemnly acclaimed and baptised Arthur—although King Henry had expressly ordered that he should be named Henry after him. 'Thus', wrote William, 'the Bretons, who are said long to have awaited the return of the fabulous Arthur, are now nurturing a real one, according to certain prophets learned in the great and famous Arthurian legend.'[116] And almost at the end of the chronicle William noticed the Breton rebellion of 1196. The Bretons, 'who were rearing the boy Arthur under the mighty omen of his name', roused the French king to war against Richard I. The occasion, William explained, was Richard's request that the Bretons give him guardianship of his nephew, the young Arthur; by virtue of this concession Brittany would be bound to Richard against all enemies. But the Bretons, 'moved by suspicion rather than by prudence', refused and rallied to defend the child.[117]

It is noteworthy that William's passages on dissidence among the Welsh and Bretons do not show an undue preoccupation with the subject. This fact seems to corroborate the view that the attack on the *Historia Regum Britanniae* in the prologue was once a tract on its own. It is not improbable that William would have been commissioned to write such a tract. A remark in the prologue that Gildas's *De Excidio Britanniae* had come into his hands 'several years previously' proves that he had been studying history for a while,[118] and his reputation as an historian was sufficiently established for Ernald to ask him to write the chronicle.

---

[114] See R. F. Treharne, *The Glastonbury Legends*, London 1967, 105–6, and J. S. P. Tatlock 'Geoffrey and King Arthur in "Normannicus Draco"', *Modern Philology*, xxxi (1933–4), 122 and n. 7, 123.

[115] *Chrons. Stephen, Henry II and Richard I*, ed. Howlett, i. 106–7.

[116] Ibid., i. 235.

[117] Ibid., ii. 463–4.

[118] Ibid., i. 11.

However, it seems unlikely that Ernald would have commissioned a political tract; it is more probable that someone connected with the royal court, even Henry II or Richard I himself, would have done so.

Royal interest in anti-Arthurian propaganda was by no means unprecedented. Sometime between 1167 and 1169 the *Draco Normannicus* was composed in support of Henry II's suppression of the Breton rebellion.[119] Its author, Etienne of Rouen, may well have written specifically to please the king.[120] It relates the history of Normandy, drawing heavily on the *Historia Regum Britanniae*. But in it King Arthur is represented as a fay, and thus the Breton's hope of his return was reduced to an absurdity.[121] Again, when in 1191 the monks of Glastonbury exhumed the (supposed) bodies of King Arthur and Queen Guinevere, they may have acted at an earlier suggestion of Henry II. The purpose of this archaeological forgery was probably not only to increase the abbey's tourist trade; it may also have been intended to demonstrate, once and for all, for the instruction of the rebellious Welsh, that King Arthur was actually dead.[122]

It is likely, therefore that William's attack on Geoffrey in the prologue was a piece of political propaganda. He launched an eloquent tirade against the prophecies of Merlin and the Arthurian legends. Why, if the former was a greater prophet than Isaiah, and if the latter's victories were more glorious than Alexander's, had the ancient historians heard of neither?[123] Indeed, everything that 'that man' and others say concerning King Arthur is fictional; Geoffrey concocted his stories 'either because of his love of unbridled lying, or in order to please the Britons'.[124] In William's opinion, Gildas, despite his unpolished and illiterate style (the reason, William believed, why copies of Gildas's work were rare), was an author of integrity; 'for the sake of truth he did not spare his own people, but deplored their sins and shortcomings, showing them to be neither brave in war nor trustworthy in peace'.[125] William twice repeated that the Britons of his own day were so stupid as to believe that Arthur would return; they could not bear to think of him as dead, preferring the tale that he had retreated wounded to Avalon.[126]

Like the ecclesiastical and monastic controversialists, William took his stand particularly on the authority of Bede. He compared Bede's account of early Anglo-Saxon history with Geoffrey's and noticed a discrepancy; according to Geoffrey's chronology, King Arthur would have been a contemporary of King Ethelbert and would have been reigning when St

---

[119] See Tatlock, 'Geoffrey and King Arthur', 1–2, 124.

[120] Ibid., 124–5.

[121] Ibid., 3, 113–23.

[122] Cf. Treharne, op. cit. 105-6 and below p. 170.

[123] *Chrons. Stephen, Henry II and Richard I*, ed. Howlett, i. 17.

[124] Ibid., i. 14.

[125] Ibid., i. 11.

[126] Ibid., i. 14, 18.

Augustine came to England.[127] William stated that for this early period he would follow Bede's narrative, 'because the venerable Bede based it on historical truth and, therefore, it can be accepted as established beyond doubt'.[128] 'Everyone', William declared, 'should reject without hesitation both the fable teller [i.e. Geoffrey] and his fables', and instead 'put complete trust in Bede, whose wisdom and sincerity can never be doubted.'[129] Bede should be accepted as the authority even for the ancient Britons: 'he narrated the famous deeds of our people accurately and concisely; he began right at the beginning, including the Britons, who are recognised as the first inhabitants of our island, in order to provide a fitting introduction to what especially interested him.'[130]

Thus William drew the conclusion that all that can be known about the ancient Britons was what Bede and Gildas (whose work Bede used) recorded. Hence, since neither even mention the heroes, whose deeds Geoffrey so colourfully described, they were probably fictional—a supposition made the more likely by the fact that on Gildas's account the ancient Britons were cowardly and treacherous. The corollary of this conclusion was that the contemporary Britons had no glorious ancestors, and, since King Arthur had never lived, their belief that he would return was baseless.

## IV. *c. 1200–c. 1500*

Bede's reputation as an historian from the thirteenth to the fifteenth century was less than it had been in the late eleventh and twelfth centuries, but it was not negligible. He and his historical works retained widespread respect among the writers of general histories. Both Matthew Paris and Ranulf Higden gave eulogies on Bede and detailed accounts of his life. But these lack the immediacy of their Anglo-Norman prototypes, partly because they were mainly derived from the latter.[131] The *Historia Ecclesiastica* remained an important source for early Anglo-Saxon history. It was most often used purely for information, but on occasion it served as an authority in disputes. Thus, Gerald of Wales, in his attempt to obtain the bishopric at St David's, appealed to it to prove that the Church of Wales was independent of Canterbury. (He was elected bishop in 1198,

---

[127] Ibid., i. 15.
[128] Ibid., i. 14.
[129] Ibid., i. 18.
[130] Ibid., i. 11.
[131] Matthew Paris borrowed his account of Bede mainly from William of Malmesbury, but in addition he used Henry of Huntingdon; *Matthaei Parisiensis, Monachi Sancti Albani, Chronica Majora*, ed. H. R. Luard (R.S., 1872–83, 7 vols), i. 333–6. Higden also took his account mainly from William of Malmesbury; *Polychronicon Ranulphi Higden Monachi Cestrensis*, ed. C. Babington and J. R. Lumby (R.S., 1865–8, 9 vols), vi. 218–26.

but Archbishop Hubert Walter quashed the election; the consequent dispute lasted until 1203.)[132]

However, in this period the *Historia Ecclesiastica* was often cited alongside other, less respectable works, notably the *Historia Regum Britanniae*.[133] Indeed, an author, having quoted Bede by name, might proceed to an unacknowledged borrowing from Geoffrey and so give the impression that Bede is its authority too. An early example of this method is supplied by Ralph Diceto, writing in the late twelfth century. He recorded (*s.a.* A.D. 178), citing the *Historia Ecclesiastica*, Bk. I, chap. 4, that Pope Eleutherius wrote to the British King Lucius to convert him to Christianity. He continued, here using Geoffrey but without acknowledgement, that Eleutherius then sent Fagan and Duvian who baptised Lucius.[134] The fifteenth-century authors Thomas Rudborne, monk of St Swithun's, Winchester, and John Rous, the antiquary, provided similar examples.[135]

Exceptions to this uncritical use of sources are rare. The *Historia Regum Britanniae* was accepted almost without question. Scholars neglected William of Newburgh's devastating criticism until the early sixteenth century, when the humanist Polydore Vergil adopted it as the basis of his own strictures on the *Historia Regum Britanniae*.[136] Apparently, only three writers, Ranulf Higden,[137] Thomas Rudborne[138] and John Whethamsted (abbot of St Albans 1420–40, 1452–65),[139] cast doubt on its historicity, and then only on some of its statements. Nor does it seem that the first two were independent critics; Higden, who was sceptical about the Arthurian legends mainly because of the silence of Gildas and Bede, may have been influenced by Alfred of Beverley,[140] one of his sources, while

---

[132] For appeals to the *Historia Ecclesiastica* in Gerald's letter (1199) to Innocent III, in his *De Invectionibus* (1205), and in his *De Jure et Statu Menevensis Ecclesiae* (c. 1218), see *Giraldi Cambrensis Opera*, ed. J. S. Brewer *et alii* (R.S., 1861–91, 8 vols), iii. 169–76 *passim*, 44–51, 111, respectively.

[133] The *Historia Ecclesiastica* and the *Historia Regum Britanniae* are cited side by side by, for example, Matthew Paris, Higden and Gerald of Wales.

[134] See *Radulfi de Diceto Decani Lundoniensis Opera Historica*, ed. W. Stubbs (R.S., 1876, 2 vols), i. 66.

[135] Thomas Rudborne, *Historia Major . . . Ecclesiae Wintoniensis*, in H. Wharton, *Anglia Sacra*, London 1691, 2 vols, i. 180; John Rous, *Historia Regum Angliae*, ed. Thomas Hearne, Oxford 1716, 48.

[136] See *Historia Anglica*, Basle 1546, 15–19 (for a reference to William of Newburgh's criticisms see ibid., 17, line 3). For the passage in the sixteenth-century English translation see *Polydore Vergil's English History*, ed. Henry Ellis (Camden Society, original ser., xxxvi, 1846, xxix, 1844, 2 vols), i. 26–33.

[137] *Polychronicon*, v. 332–8.

[138] Wharton, *Anglia Sacra*, i. 188.

[139] Whethamsted in his *Granarium*, Pt. I, an encyclopaedia of historians and historical personages, disputes the Brutus legend; B.L. MS Nero C VI, fos. 33–33v. (His scepticism is noticed in L. Keeler, 'The *Historia Regum Britanniae* and four medieval chroniclers', *Speculum*, xxi (1946), 36.) However, he appears to accept the legend of Belinus and that of Brennus; ibid., fos. 28, 30v–32.

[140] See *Polychronicon*, i. 24.

Rudborne in his turn may have owed his doubts on the same subject to Higden.[141]

The comparative decline of Bede's influence as an historian is perhaps reflected by the printed editions of the *Historia Ecclesiastica*. The first edition was issued abroad, in a volume also including Eusebius's *Historia Ecclesiastica*, by Heinrich Eggestein of Strasburg, sometime between 1475 and 1482.[142] No other edition appeared before the end of the fifteenth century. (The first edition to be issued in England was that of 1643.)[143] The absence of an early edition printed in England probably has little significance, since it was normal for Latin texts to be printed abroad. Possibly more relevant to our argument is the fact that no English translation was available which might have formed the basis of a printed edition. William Caxton issued, in 1480 and 1482 respectively, English versions of the *Historia Regum Britanniae* and of the *Polychronicon*, but the first translation of the *Historia Ecclesiastica* to be printed was that by Thomas Stapleton, the Catholic polemicist; he published it in 1565 to provide proof that the Church of England was of papal origin.[144]

Bede's historiographical influence no doubt declined after the end of the twelfth century partly on account of contemporary circumstances. None of the factors which had encouraged writers of general history to study Bede's historical works in the early period existed in the later one: there was no monastic revival or new monastic order; there was no cataclysmic event comparable with the Norman Conquest to threaten the tradition of the Church of England; and there were no important controversies necessitating appeal to his authority. Nevertheless, in the late fourteenth and fifteenth centuries opinion in some quarters turned against monasticism; it was attacked by the Lollards, by other 'dispossessioners' and by the secular canons. The monks wrote in self-defence. It was a matter of consolidating their position and guarding against general aspersions rather than of defending themselves in specific disputes. They composed tracts justifying monasticism on historical grounds, by demonstrating its long tradition.[145] Since the monastic movement originated before Bede's time and abroad, the *Historia Ecclesiastica* was not very useful to such authors. However, the case with a

---

[141] Rudborne questioned the Arthurian legends because historic persons mentioned in them, notably the Emperors Lucius and Leo, did not rule at the time of King Arthur. He demonstrated these chronological flaws in the legends with some care, but Higden had already noticed them briefly. (For references see nn. 138, 137 above, respectively.)

[142] See *Catalogue of Books Printed in the Fifteenth Century now in the British Museum* (Trustees of the British Museum, lithographic reprint, 1912–67, 9 pts), i. 71.

[143] For a survey of the printed editions, see *Bede's Ecclesiastical History of the English People,* ed. Colgrave and Mynors, pp. lxx–lxxii.

[144] See M. McKisack, *Medieval History in the Tudor Age*, Oxford 1971, 39, and F. J. Levy, *Tudor Historical Thought*, Huntingdon Library, California 1967, 110–12.

[145] W. A. Pantin, 'Some medieval English treatises on the origins of monasticism', *Medieval Studies presented to Rose Graham*, ed. V. Ruffer and A. J. Taylor, Oxford 1950, 189–215.

local historian might be different; if his monastery was founded in the Northumbrian period, Bede's evidence could; as always, be invaluable in augmenting its prestige. For this reason the *Historia Ecclesiastica* was studied as carefully as ever before at St Augustine's, Canterbury, and at St Cuthbert's, Durham.

Thomas Elmham, monk of St Augustine's, Canterbury, wrote the *Speculum Augustinianum* shortly before 1414.[146] He conceived this history of St Augustine's on such a massive scale that he completed it only as far as the year 803. He intended the work to be a definitive record of the abbey's past glory and of its privileges, and to silence any detractors. He was particularly at pains to demonstrate its independence of archiepiscopal authority. (In fact the pope had finally confirmed its exemption in 1397, thus ending the struggle with the archbishops which had driven the monks to forgery in the late eleventh century and to the employment sporadically thereafter of harassing tactics.)[147]

Bede's *Historia Ecclesiastica* was Elmham's principal literary authority for the abbey's foundation and early history. He praised Bede as an historian in fulsome terms (though he borrowed most of his words from William of Malmesbury),[148] and he specifically appealed to his authority to defend St Augustine's against any allegation contrary to its interests. He objected to Higden's assertion that Archbishop Theodore appointed Benedict Biscop abbot of St Augustine's. If Biscop had been abbot, and if, as certain 'detractors' alleged, he was Theodore's chaplain, St Augustine's would have been under the archbishop's control. Elmham asserted that there is no evidence in the *Historia Ecclesiastica* either that Biscop was abbot of St Augustine's, or that he was Theodore's chaplain.[149] Similarly, Elmham

---

[146] Printed as *Historia Monasterii S. Augustini Cantuariensis, by Thomas of Elmham*, ed. C. Hardwick (R.S., 1858). For the original title, *Speculum Augustinianum*, see F. Taylor, 'A note on Rolls Series 8', *Bulletin of the John Rylands Library*, xx (1936), 379–82. The *Speculum* must have been written before 1414 because in that year Elmham joined the Cluniac order, becoming prior of Lenton, near Nottingham; see J. S. Roskell and F. Taylor, 'The authorship and purpose of the *Gesta Henrici Quinti*: 1', *Bull. of the John Rylands Library*, liii (1970–1), 436.

[147] For St Augustine's claim to exemption from archiepiscopal control see M. D. Knowles, 'Essays in monastic history. iv. The growth of exemption', *Downside Review*, l (1932), 401–15. For the dispute in the late eleventh century see pp. 411–12 and n. 91 above. The course of the struggle is described in the earlier chronicles of St Augustine's, the lost one by Thomas Sprott, which apparently ended in 1228, and William Thorne's to 1397, both of which Elmham used; see Hardwick, op. cit., 77. Thorne's chronicle is printed in Roger Twysden, *Historiae Anglicanae Scriptores X*, London 1652, 2 vols, i. cols 1757–2202; for a discussion of the chronicles of St Augustine's see *William Thorne's Chronicle of Saint Augustine's Abbey*, translated by A. H. Davis, with a preface by A. Hamilton Thompson, Oxford 1934, xx–xxvi.

[148] Hardwick, op. cit., 309.

[149] Ibid., 185–6, 202–5. Cf. *Historia Ecclesiastica*, iv. 1 (ed. Plummer, i. 204) and *Polychronicon*, vi. 78. Plummer (*Historia Ecclesiastica*, ed. Plummer, ii. 204) points out that Bede's *Historia Abbatum* §§3.4 (ibid. i. 366–7) has evidence that Biscop was once abbot of St Augustine's (for two years), despite Elmham's assertion to the contrary.

cites Bede to prove that Theodore in his capacity as papal legate, not as archbishop, appointed Hadrian to the abbacy; Hadrian, therefore, did not become his subordinate, but remained his friend and colleague.[150] Elmham also cites Bede in order to defend Theodore against those who accused him of treating Wilfrid harshly.[151] His concern for Theodore's reputation may well have been partly the result of his burial at St Augustine's (Wilfrid lay in Canterbury cathedral). Elmham's interest in the identity of Cadwaller (he compares the evidence of Bede, William of Malmesbury and Geoffrey of Monmouth) may have owed something to the (supposed) burial of Cadwaller's brother, Mul, at St Augustine's.[152]

Elmham's counterpart at Durham was John Wessington, prior from 1416 to 1446.[153] The situation at St Cuthbert's was not unlike that at St Augustine's: serious conflict between the cathedral priory and its diocesan was over by the fifteenth century; indeed, it had ended in the first third of the fourteenth century.[154] However, the monks were anxious to increase their prestige in general and to arm themselves against any new encroachment by the bishop. They too turned to past glory for present help. Bede's *Historia Ecclesiastica* and Lives of St Cuthbert were especially useful because they supplied a picture of St Cuthbert's see in its early days at Lindisfarne, when the bishop never interfered with the monastery.[155] The popularity at Durham of Bede's prose Life of St Cuthbert is witnessed by the fact that the monks had a new copy made just before the Dissolution.[156]

Wessington wrote a history of St Cuthbert's which he intended to be definitive.[157] His aims were similar to Elmham's; to increase his house's prestige by dwelling on its past achievements and to confirm its rights by putting them on record. He started with the see's origin in 635, but, like Elmham, he never finished his work; it ends in 1362. He included a long and eulogistic account of Bede's life and work: he borrowed most of it from Symeon of Durham, but added a passage from the 'Legenda Sanctorum';[158] this addition recounts two 'miracles' purporting to

---

[150] Hardwick, op. cit., 202–4.

[151] Ibid., 279.

[152] Ibid., 268–70. Cf. *Historia Ecclesiastica*, ed. Plummer, ii. 228, 265.

[153] For Wessington's career see R. B. Dobson, *Durham Priory 1400–1450*, Cambridge 1973, 89–113.

[154] Dobson, op. cit., 204–5, 222–4, and R. L. Storey, *Thomas Langley and the Bishopric of Durham, 1406–1437*, London 1961, 199–200.

[155] See Dobson, op. cit., 203.

[156] See (with further references) Dobson, op. cit., 32 and n. 1, 350 n. 4, 360.

[157] Wessington's history, the *Libellus de exordio et statu ecclesie cathedralis quondam Lindesfarnensis, post Conchestrensis, demum Dunelmensis, ac de gestis pontificum eiusdem*, is unprinted. Three manuscripts, all from Durham, are known to survive; one is cited in the next footnote. See H. H. E. Craster, 'The Red Book of Durham', *E.H.R.*, xl (1925), 504–14. *passim*. For the place of the *Libellus* in the historiography of Durham see H. S. Offler, *Medieval Historians of Durham*, Durham 1958, 17.

[158] B.L. MS Cotton Claudius D IV, fo. 14. The reference is presumably to John of

explain why Bede was called 'venerable' instead of 'saint' everywhere except at Durham. Wessington also relied mainly on Symeon for the early history of St Cuthbert's; as has been seen, Symeon himself had based his narrative mainly on the *Historia Ecclesiastica* and on the Lives of St Cuthbert, but Wessington amplified it with further additions from Bede.[159]

The same motives which caused Wessington to compose the history of St Cuthbert's, made him write numerous tracts on the see's antiquities and rights,[160] and for them he used Bede when appropriate. One, for example, comprised copies of the descriptive captions which he himself wrote beneath the 'images' (i.e. the statues or pictures) of saints at the altar of SS Jerome and Benedict; Bede was his authority for the Northumbrian ones.[161] And when Wessington collected evidences of the prior's rights to place before Thomas Langley, bishop of Durham, and his council in 1426, his 'declaration' began: 'the prior should have all the rights, offices and honours of an abbot, according to the dignity of the church of Lindisfarne, as set forth in Bede's *De Gestis Anglorum*, Bk. IV, chapter 25, and in the prose Life of St Cuthbert, chapter 16'; Wessington

---

Tynemouth's *Sanctilogium*, compiled between 1327 and 1347, for which see V. H. Galbraith, 'The *Historia Aurea* of John, vicar of Tynemouth, and the sources of the St. Albans Chronicle (1327–1377)', *Essays in History presented to Reginald Lane Poole*, ed. H. W. C. Davis, Oxford 1927, 385. The passage cited by Wessington is almost identical with that in the *Nova Legenda Anglie*, ed. Carl Horstman, Oxford 1901, 2 vols, i. 111, and in the *Historia Aurea*. The latter is a mid-fourteenth century version of the *Sanctilogium* in which the saints' Lives are arranged chronologically (see Galbraith, op. cit., 382–5); a late fourteenth-century copy from Durham priory is now Lambeth Palace MSS 10, 11 and 12. It is possible that Wessington in fact copied the passage in question from the *Historia Aurea* from which he derived his copy of Pope Sergius's letter (Claudius D IV, fo. 14), and not directly from the *Sanctilogium*. This is suggested by the fact that both he and the Durham copy of the *Historia Aurea* (Lambeth Palace MS 12, fo. 50) have the marginal note in the hand of the scribe, 'Legenda Sanctorum in fine'. However, it is unlikely that he was using the copy now in Lambeth Palace; his version of the passage on why Bede was called 'venerable' has, besides a few slight variants from that in the Lambeth MS, a different beginning. Wessington begins: 'Licet enim Beda in sanctorum cathalogo computetur et a Dunelmensibus sanctus Beda nominetur, non tamen a pluribus aliis "sanctus" sed "venerabilis" appellatur'; Claudius D IV, fo. 14v. The *Historia Aurea* (and the *Nova Legenda Anglie*) begins: 'Licet enim Beda in sanctorum cathalogo computetur, tamen ab ecclesia non "sanctus", sed "venerabilis" appellatur'; Lambeth Palace MS 12, fo. 50. Wessington's account of Bede is *in toto* much fuller than that in the *Historia Aurea*.

[159] Craster, 'The Red Book of Durham', 516–17.

[160] A contemporary of Wessington, who listed his tracts, comments that Wessington 'compiled them not without labour and study for the perpetual preservation and defence of the rights, liberties and possessions of the church of Durham against the malice and machinations of would-be molesters'; *Historiae Dunelmensis Scriptores Tres, Gaufridus de Coldingham, Robertus de Graystanes, et Willielmus de Chambre*, ed. J. Raine (Surtees Society, ix, 1839), cclxviii–cclxix. Cf. Dobson, *Durham Priory*, 379 and n. 2, and Craster, 'The Red Book', 515 and n. 2. For Wessington's tracts in general see Dobson, op. cit., 382–4.

[161] The text is printed in *Rites of Durham*, ed. J. T. Fowler (Surtees Society, cvii, 1903), 124–36.

proceeded with the extracts from Bede as quoted, and then gave copies of ten charters relevant to the issue.[162]

The cult of Bede flourished at Durham alongside that of St Cuthbert until the end ˙of the Middle Ages. In 1370 his relics were moved from the grave next to St Cuthbert's and re-interred in the Galilee chapel.[163] Bishop Robert Neville (1438–57) had a new shrine built for him, decorated with gold and silver,[164] and wanted to be buried in front of his altar (a wish which was not fulfilled).[165] And St Bede, almost equally with St Cuthbert, became an object of pilgrimage.[166]

This survey provides some explanation for the high percentage of twelfth-century copies of the *Historia Ecclesiastica* in Laistner's table of the surviving manuscripts. At the outset the twelfth century inherited a vigorous tradition of Bedan studies from the Anglo-Saxon period, a tradition which was adopted with enthusiasm by the missionaries to the North in the late eleventh century. In the twelfth century itself the exceptional religious and political circumstances account for the blossoming of Bede's reputation. This survey does not, however, explain the relatively high percentage of fourteenth- and fifteenth-century manuscripts. Perhaps one of the explanations which Laistner offers for the rather similar survival pattern of manuscripts of Bede's biblical commentaries is applicable here too; simply that old copies needed replacing.[167]

---

[162] *Historia Dunelmensis Scriptores Tres*, cclxx. The 'declaration', dated 17 June 1426, is now 1. 7. Pontificalia, no. 2, in the muniments of the dean and chapter of Durham. It is listed in R. B. Dobson, *The Priory of Durham in the Time of John Wessington Prior 1416–1446* (unpublished Oxford D.Phil. thesis, 1962), 583, no. 22.

[163] *Rites of Durham*, 46.

[164] Ibid., 45, 233.

[165] Ibid., 225.

[166] In his account of his visit to Durham on his return from the court of James I of Scotland, Aeneas Sylvius Piccolomini (later Pius II) apparently mentioned only Bede's tomb, not that of St Cuthbert: 'Exinde Dunelmiam venit, ubi sepulchrum venerabilis Bedae presbyteri sancti viri hodie visitur, quod accolae regionis devota religione colunt'; *Pii Secundi Max. Commentarii Rerum Memorabilium, quae temporibus suis contigerunt,* Frankfurt 1614, 5. This passage is mistranslated as 'Next he came to Durham, where today men go to see the tomb of the holy abbot, the Venerable Bede, which is piously revered by the inhabitants of the region', in *The Commentaries of Pius II*, translated by F. A. Gragg, ed. L. C. Gabel (Smith College Studies in History, xxii, nos 1–2, 1936–7), 20, The erroneous rendering of 'venerabilis Bedae presbyteri sancti viri' as 'the holy abbot, the venerable Bede', perhaps explains the assertion by a recent scholar that Aeneas Sylvius confused Bede's shrine with that of St Cuthbert's; Dobson, *Durham Priory*, 105.

[167] Laistner, *Hand List*, 7.

## ADDITIONAL NOTE

*Page* 7. For a more detailed treatment of Bede's influence on Anglo-Norman monasticism see now R. H. C. Davis, 'Bede after Bede', in *Studies in Medieval History presented to R. Allen Brown*, ed. C. Harper-Bill, C. J. Holdsworth and J. L. Nelson (Woodbridge, 1989), 103–16.

## 2

# Traditionalism and Continuity during the Last Century of Anglo-Saxon Monasticism

Those writing at the time, and subsequent historians, have tended to exaggerate the importance of the tenth-century monastic revival and of the reform movement which followed the Norman Conquest. During each period contemporary writers glorified the achievements of the reformation, of which they themselves were products, and belittled or even denigrated the religious life of the preceding era. This was partly because the hallmark of both reformations was the strict enforcement of the Rule of Benedict; the ideal of strict Benedictinism appealed to those writing during the reformations, since they themselves were strict Benedictines, and it has appealed to some historians in our own day. One result has been a tendency to emphasise the influence of continental models so much that it overshadows the importance of the Anglo-Saxon tradition. David Knowles makes continental influence on the tenth-century revival the theme of chapter 1 of his *The Monastic Order in England*. The fact that he starts his survey with a section which treats the preceding period, from the Northumbrian renaissance onwards, as

*BJRL* = *Bulletin of the John Rylands Library*; CCM = Corpus Consuetudinum Monasticarum; *Proceedings* = *Proceedings of the Battle Conference on Anglo-Norman Studies*; *A-SE* = *Anglo-Saxon England*; *Rev.Bén.* = *Revue Bénédictine*; EETS = Early English Text Society; *PCAS* = *Proceedings of the Cambridge Antiquarian Society*

I am deeply indebted to Dr Simon Keynes and Dr Michael Lapidge for reading this article in typescript; they pointed out some errors and made a number of valuable comments and suggestions and provided me with useful bibliographical information. After writing my article I heard the paper by Patrick Wormald, 'Æthelwold and his continental counterparts: contact, comparison, contrast', at the Anglo-American Conference of Historians, now publ. in *Æthelwold of Winchester: studies in his career and influence*, ed. Barbara Yorke, Woodbridge 1988, 13–42. Mr Wormald kindly allowed me to read the typescript of his article and read mine. He made some useful comments, in the light of which I have revised my article slightly. In general, Mr Wormald's article puts the case for continental influence on St Ethelwold, but concludes with a tribute to the contribution to the monastic revival of the Anglo-Saxon tradition (pp. 39–41), making a few of the same points which I had made.

introductory matter, would itself have hampered appreciation of the revival's full significance. Knowles, indeed, makes some sweeping statements about the revival: the daughter houses of St Oswald's foundation at Westbury-on-Trym were 'pure reproduction[s] of Fleury'; the *Life of St Oswald*, written at Ramsey *c.* 1000, 'is in tone and style wholly a product of the school of Fleury'. He tends to treat the post-Conquest period in a similar manner: thus Eadmer was 'wholly of the school of Lanfranc and Anselm'.[1] Eric John lays even greater emphasis than Knowles on continental influence. For example, speculating on the origin of the monastic ideals of Ælfheah, bishop of Winchester (who was himself a secular clerk), John suggests that they reached him from abroad, by way of Athelstan's court, since the king was in touch with Henry the Fowler of Germany.[2]

However, historians have not uniformly under-rated the native tradition.[3] Thomas Symons, in his discussion of the *Regularis concordia* issued by the reformers at Winchester *c.* 972, adopted a cautious and judicious approach to the problem of the origins, whether continental or indigenous, of the monastic and liturgical observances it contains.[4] Richard Southern has done ample justice to the English contribution to the post-Conquest reformation, particularly with regard to the cult of saints.[5] Moreover, historians increasingly recognise the achievements of the native tradition in the Viking Age and in the eleventh century prior to the Norman Conquest. Francis Wormald pointed out that 'from the reign of King Alfred onwards there was a steady stylistic development in the production of illuminated books in southern England'; this style was in the Anglo-Saxon tradition, although it was influenced by Carolingian models, and '[prepared] the way...for the much more

[1] D. Knowles, *The Monastic Order in England*, 2nd edn, Cambridge 1963, 42, 65, 79.

[2] Eric John, 'The king and the monks in the tenth-century reformation', *BJRL* xlii (1959), 63 n. 3. Another exponent of continental influence is D. A. Bullough, 'The continental background of the reform', in *Tenth-century Studies*, ed. David Parsons, London–Chichester 1975, 20–36.

[3] Knowles, op. cit. 37–9 (cf. p. 83), 45 (monks' prayers for the king and queen) (but cf. Wormald, op. cit. 33), 45–6 (monks' importance in national life and the institution of monastic cathedrals).

[4] Thomas Symons, 'Sources of the *Regularis concordia*', *Downside Review* xl (1941), 14–36, 143–70, 264–89 passim; see esp. pp. 32–3, 143–4, 168–70. However, much of what he says there has been superseded by the newly discovered customary of Fleury. See Lin Donnat, 'Recherches sur l'influence de Fleury au Xe siècle', in *Etudes ligériennes d'histoire et d'archéologie médiévales*, ed. René Louis, Auxerre 1975, 165–74; and *Consuetudinum Saeculi X/XI/XII Monumenta: Introductiones*, ed. Kassius Hallinger, CCM vii/1. 331–93.

[5] R. W. Southern, 'Aspects of the European tradition of historical writing: 4. The sense of the past', *Transactions of the Royal Historical Society* xxiii (1973), 251–2; and idem, *St Anselm and his Biographer*, Cambridge 1963, 246 ff. Cf. e.g. A. Gransden, *Historical Writing in England*, [i], *c. 550 to c. 1307*, London 1974, ch. vii passim; idem, 'Cultural transition at Worcester in the Anglo-Norman period', *British Archaeological Association Conference Transactions*, I: *Medieval Art and Architecture at Worcester Cathedral* (1978), 1–14; idem, 'Baldwin, abbot of Bury St Edmunds, 1065–1097', *Proceedings* iv (1981), 65–76, 187–95.

spectacular changes' of the monastic revival in the second half of the century.[6] J. Armitage Robinson demonstrated that the cult of saints and relics, an important feature of the Anglo-Saxon tradition (but one neglected by Knowles), flourished before the tenth-century revival – under King Athelstan and, of course, earlier.[7] Most recently Simon Keynes has discussed Athelstan's enthusiasm for relics which, he suggests, was the result of King Alfred's influence.[8] Knowles argued that, once the tenth-century revival was over, Anglo-Saxon monasticism recovered its distinctive form, and he pinpointed a few of its peculiarities.[9] And Keynes and other modern scholars have brought to light much new evidence of remarkable cultural activity in many fields both before and after the tenth-century revival, while John Blair has demonstrated the survival of numerous clerical communities, ranging from the more or less monastic to 'loosely ordered groups of priests', and serving 'superior' churches – 'minsters'.[10]

It is not the intention of this article to minimise the importance of continental influence on the monastic reformations (although it must be remembered that at no time has England been immune to influences from abroad). However, it seems time to try to assemble the evidence for the continuity of the Anglo-Saxon monastic tradition, which had been founded in seventh-century Northumbria, and survived through the tenth-century monastic revival and into the Anglo-Norman period without interruption. Furthermore, because of this continuity and the vigour of the tradition in the tenth and eleventh centuries at times other than those of monastic reformation, we ought to re-evaluate the reformers' achievements; they should now be seen as rather less momentous than they have been in the past.

Since the survival of the Anglo-Saxon tradition was a result of an essential feature of the Anglo-Saxon mentality, something should first be said about that subject in general. The Anglo-Saxons shared the backward-looking tendency so prevalent in the Middle Ages. This characteristic combined with intense pride in the achievements of the Anglo-Saxon people to produce a strong interest in their past. 'Nationalistic' traditionalism is very apparent at least as early as King Alfred's reign. It seems that Alfred and his circle wanted to recreate the

---

[6] Francis Wormald, 'The "Winchester School" before St Æthelwold', in *England before the Conquest: studies in primary sources presented to Dorothy Whitelock*, ed. Peter Clemoes and Kathleen Hughes, Cambridge 1971, 305–13.

[7] J. A. Robinson, *The Times of St Dunstan*, Oxford 1923, 51–5, 71–80, 101–2.

[8] Simon Keynes, 'King Athelstan's books', in *Learning and Literature in Anglo-Saxon England*, ed. Michael Lapidge and Helmut Gneuss, Cambridge 1985, 143–4.

[9] Knowles, *Monastic Order*, 80–1 and n. 4 (property owning by monks), 83 and n. 1.

[10] See e.g. Simon Keynes's introduction to *The Golden Age of Anglo-Saxon Art*, ed. Janet Backhouse, D. H. Turner and Leslie Webster, London 1984, 12–13; David N. Dumville's introduction to *The Historia Brittonum, 3, The 'Vatican' Recension*, ed. idem, Cambridge 1985, 18–23; John Blair, 'Secular minster churches in Domesday Book', in *Domesday Book, a Reassessment*, ed. Peter Sawyer, London 1985, 104–42 passim.

Golden Age of Northumbria.[11] The late ninth-century Old English translation of Bede's *Ecclesiastical History* can be seen as one outcome of this desire. Possibly Alfred's rule itself was to some extent influenced by the *Ecclesiastical History*. Alfred, like the Northumbrian kings, saw the value of the Church as a support for kingship. A more particular instance of possible influence is provided by Asser in his *Life of King Alfred* (C. cii). He asserts that Alfred, having divided his annual revenues in half, further divided the second half, which was to be devoted to the service of God, into four parts. The first part was to go to the poor and 'anyone who came to him'; the second to his two monastic foundations; the third to his school; and the fourth to monasteries throughout England and in Ireland and Brittany.[12] This quadripartite division is reminiscent of the first of Gregory the Great's *Responsiones* to St Augustine, which Asser could have read in the *Ecclesiastical History* (although he might have used an independent text).[13] Gregory states that, by custom, the pope instructs all newly consecrated bishops to divide their revenues into four parts. One was for the bishop and his household, to enable them to offer hospitality, the second for the clergy, the third for the poor and the fourth for the repair of churches. Alfred held Gregory's *Pastoral Care* in high regard and included it among the works which he translated for the benefit of priests. In his estimate of the *Pastoral Care*, and also in his recognition of the value of translations to the Church, Alfred was foreshadowed by Bede. Bede's letter to Bishop Ecgbert advises him to be guided by the *Pastoral Care* and advocates that the Creed and Lord's Prayer should be taught in the vernacular to those who knew no Latin.[14]

The monks of the later Anglo-Saxon period were backward-looking in their attitude to the Church in England; tradition and its preservation were a mental preoccupation. Like King Alfred they saw seventh-century Northumbria as laying the foundations of that tradition; this past gave healthy roots to the monasticism of their own day. It also provided the monks with examples of monastic observance and organisation which they could follow and advice which they should take; in addition, it

---

[11] See *Alfred the Great: Asser's Life of King Alfred and other contemporary sources*, ed. and trans. Simon Keynes and Michael Lapidge, Harmondsworth 1983, 25, 33.

[12] *Asser's Life of King Alfred*, ed. W. H. Stevenson, Oxford 1904, repr. 1959, 88–9.

[13] *Historia Ecclesiastica*, i. 27(1), *Venerabilis Baedae Opera Historica*, 2 vols, ed. Charles Plummer, Oxford 1896, i. 48. For the existence of independent texts of Gregory's answers see Paul Meyvaert, 'Bede's text of the *Libellus Responsionum* of Gregory the Great to Augustine of Canterbury', in Clemoes and Hughes, *England before the Conquest*, 23–8 (and nn. for further references).

[14] Bede enjoins Ecgbert to meditate on the epistles of St Paul to Timothy and Titus 'et verbis sanctissimi papae Gregorii, quibus de uita simul et uitiis rectorum siue in libro Regulae Pastoralis, seu in omeliis euangelii', and to impress the Creed and Lord's Prayer on the memories of his flock. 'Et quidem omnes, qui Latinam linguam lectionis usu didicerunt, etiam haec optime didicisse certissimum est; sed idiotas, hoc est, eos qui propriae tantum linguae notitiam habent, haec ipsa sua lingua discere, ac sedulo decantare facito': Letter to Egbert, §§3, 5, i. 406, 408–9.

supplied precedents and thus justification for their own methods and proceedings. (The reformers were undeterred by, or perhaps unaware of, the fact that Northumbrian monasticism, except at Wearmouth and Jarrow, did not in fact conform in many respects to their own Benedictine ideals.)

In order to use past history in the ways described, it was necessary to know about it. However, here inquirers were faced with almost insuperable difficulties. Material relevant to the state of monasticism in the Viking Age and, though to a lesser degree, in the eleventh century before the Conquest was very scarce. Neither, of course, did the monks have any aids to research to help them collect and evaluate what material there was. But, since reliance on tradition was such an essential part of their mentality, they had somehow to fill the vast gaps in their knowledge in order to reconstruct the past. One method of supplementing their defective information was to use literary *topoi*. The monks might use, for example, Bede's *Ecclesiastical History* and his two Lives of St Cuthbert (one in prose and one in verse). Later, in the post-Conquest period, works written during and shortly after the tenth-century revival could be used; Ælfric's and Wulfstan's Lives of St Ethelwold proved particularly serviceable. Such works provided literary models: a writer might discover what happened in one instance and apply it to another; thus he might use verifiable evidence concerning the foundation of one monastery as a *topos* for the foundation of another about which he had no specific material.

A conclusion reached by means of a *topos* is speculative. It is not *necessarily* false; on the contrary, because the Anglo-Saxons were so traditionalist, they must often have been tempted to imitate their forebears' acts. Nevertheless, since circumstances vary in different times and places, no conclusion obviously or possibly reached by means of a *topos* must be trusted unless supported by verifiable evidence. The historian may, of course, find it hard to decide whether or not a writer was using a literary model. Perhaps the substance of a later work has points in common with an earlier one, but other evidence makes its use as the exemplar problematical. For instance, the gist of some passages in the tenth-century reformers' writings is so very like parts of Bede's letter to Bishop Ecgbert that it is hard to believe that the reformers did not use it. However, there are no distinct verbal echoes, nor is it certain that Bede's letter to Ecgbert was readily available at the time of the revival. (It survives, as far as is known, only in three manuscripts, of the early tenth, early twelfth and fifteenth centuries.)[15] Even if the parallels do not

---

[15] M. L. W. Laistner, *A Hand-list of Bede Manuscripts*, Ithaca 1943, 120. Symons suggests that the authors of the *Regularis concordia*, when they prescribed daily communion, had in mind the passage in Bede's Letter to Ecgbert deploring the neglect of the eucharist in Northumbria and enjoining that people be taught the spiritual benefits of daily communion, Thomas Symons, 'Sources', 157–8; and idem (ed. and trans.), *Regularis concordia*, London 1953, 2 n.a. Patrick Wormald accepts that the reformers borrowed from the Letter to Ecgbert.

actually prove direct borrowing, they certainly do prove that, on the topics which concerned them, the tenth-century reformers felt and thought very like Bede.

The traditionalism of the Anglo-Saxon monks and the continuity of monastic history will be discussed in two parts: the tenth-century revival; and the period *c.* 1000–*c.* 1100.

## I. The Tenth-century Revival

From the reign of Edgar until that of William the Conqueror monasticism in England depended on royal patronage and protection. In fact King Edgar played as important a part in the tenth-century revival as did SS Dunstan, Ethelwold and Oswald. He must have believed in the revival's spiritual value. As a child he had spent some time in St Ethelwold's monastery at Abingdon,[16] and St Ethelwold translated the Rule of Benedict for him and his queen, Ælfthryth.[17] His alliance with the monks (typified by the fact that the royal palace at Winchester was situated immediately opposite St Ethelwold's cathedral)[18] won him the benefit of their prayers; the *Regularis concordia* stipulates that the monks should pray daily for the king and queen.[19] It also procured fitting burial places for royalty, since the monastic churches were the finest in the land. And the alliance gave him political advantages. The monks accorded an almost theocratic position to the king (the *Regularis concordia* even compares him with the Good Shepherd);[20] and the daily prayers for the king and queen were constant reminders of their allegiance. The king also gained more mundane benefits: since the monasteries had a virtual monopoly of literate education, they were the recruiting ground for the episcopate; and the king chose his ministers from the abbots and bishops.

Edgar, therefore, had both religious and political reasons for espousing the cause of the reformers. However, he was also probably influenced by the examples of earlier rulers. When he summoned the synod at Winchester *c.*972 in order to impose unity of observance on the monasteries, he may well have been following the example of Louis the Pious who had summoned a synod at Aachen for a similar purpose in 816.

---

[16] See St Ethelwold's account of the establishment of the monasteries, in *Councils and Synods*, I: *AD 871–1204*, ed. Dorothy Whitelock, Martin Brett and C. N. L. Brooke, 2 pts, Oxford 1981, i. 142–54; Eric John, *Orbis Britanniae and Other Studies*, Leicester 1966, 158–60.

[17] Printed in *Die Angelsächsischen Prosabearbeitungen der Benediktinerregel*, ed. Arnold Schröer, 2nd edn revised with suppl. by H. Gneuss, Darmstadt 1964. Cf. Mechthild Gretsch, *Die Regula Sancti Benedicti in England und ihre Altenglische Übersetzung*, Munich 1973; and idem, 'Aethelwold's translation of the Regula Sancti Benedicti and its Latin exemplar', *A-SE* iii (1974), 125–51.

[18] Martin Biddle, '*Felix urbs Winthonia*: Winchester in the age of monastic reform', in Parsons, *Tenth-century Studies*, 138.

[19] *Regularis concordia*, in *Consuetudinum Saeculi X/XI/XII Monumenta non-Cluniacensia*, ed. Kassius Hallinger, CCM vii 3. 74, 83.    [20] Ibid. 70.

It is certain that the reformers were influenced by the *Capitula* and *Regula canonicorum* issued by the synod of Aachen, since they borrowed from them for the *Regularis concordia*.[21] Nevertheless, Anglo-Saxon history could provide an example of a king who had patronised the monks and summoned a reforming synod. Oswy, king of Northumbria (654–70), had done so. The purpose of the synod of Whitby (664) was to heal the rift in the Northumbrian Church between the Roman and Celtic parties. Edgar and SS Dunstan, Ethelwold and Oswald would have learned about Oswy from Bede's *Ecclesiastical History* (iii. 24 25), with which they were undoubtedly well acquainted (the prologue to the *Regularis concordia* draws on it in a number of places, and a long passage in St Ethelwold's treatise on King Edgar's establishment of the Monasteries also derives from it).[22] It is likely that the reformers turned to the *Ecclesiastical History* for precedents and advice. The prologue to the *Regularis concordia* states that they summoned monks from Fleury and Ghent to the synod because they recalled 'the letters in which our holy patron Gregory instructed the blessed Augustine that, for the advancement of the rude English church, he should establish therein the seemly customs of the Gallic churches as well as of Rome'. The author probably read the text of Gregory's *Responsiones* in the *Ecclesiastical History* (although he, like Asser, might have used an independent text).[23]

Bede's letter to Bishop Ecgbert contains the model of a king, Ceolwulf, king of Northumbria (729–60/5), who, like Oswy, was a patron of monks. Bede tells Ecgbert to seek his help in the reform of his province and to summon a reforming synod.[24] Bede's description of Ceolwulf would have fitted Edgar, or at least the reformer's image of him (which probably represented the type of king he aspired to be). It reads:

qui et pro insita sibi dilectione religionis, quicquid ad regulam pietatis pertinet, firma protinus intentione adiuuare curabit, et maxime illa, quae tu, quum sis propinquus illius amantissimus, bona caeperis, ipse, ut perficiantur, opitulari curabit.[25]

Similarly, as Sally Vaughn has recently pointed out, a letter of Gregory the Great to King Ethelberht cited by Bede (*HE* i. 32) describes the attributes of a good Christian king. It tells Ethelberht to promote the Christian faith among his people and to follow the guidance of Bishop Augustine. Vaughn argues that this *exemplum* conditioned Eadmer's view of William the Conqueror and of his relationship with Lanfranc and Anselm.[26] Equally it could have influenced the tenth-century reformers' view of King Edgar.

Bede's advice to Bishop Ecgbert on the creation of monastic sees and the

---

[21] Ibid. 71 lines 7–11 and note. Cf. Symons, 'Sources', 165 70.
[22] *Councils and Synods*, ii. 143 and n. 1.      [23] *Reg. con.*, 71 2.
[24] Letter to Ecgbert, §9, i. 412.      [25] Ibid.
[26] Sally Vaughn, 'Eadmer's *Historia novorum*: a reinterpretation', *Proceedings* x (1987), pp. 263–4.

appointment of bishops resembles the regulations on these matters in the *Regularis concordia*. Bede reminds Ecgbert that Pope Gregory had stipulated that there should be twelve bishops in the province of York. Therefore, the reforming synod, in order to increase the existing number of bishops, should find monasteries suitable to serve as sees. Lest the abbot or community of a monastery chosen to be a see should oppose, the monks were to be allowed to choose one of their number to be bishop, and he was to rule both the monastery and the diocese; if there were no one suitable in the monastery, some suitable person in the diocese should be found. The passage reads:

Quapropter commodum duxerim, habito maiori concilio et consensu, pontificali simul et regali edicto prospiciatur locus aliquis monasteriorum, ubi sedes fiat episcopalis. Et ne forte abbas vel monachi huic decreto contraire ac resistere temptauerint, detur illis licentia, ut de suis ipsi eligant eum, qui episcopus ordinetur, et adiacentium locorum, quotquot ad eandem diocesim pertineant, una cum ipso monasterio curam gerat episcopalem; aut, si forte in ipso monasterio, qui episcopi ordinari debeat, inueniri nequeat, in ipsorum tamen iuxta statuta canonum pendeat examine, qui de sua diocesi ordinetur antistes.[27]

A passage in the *Regularis concordia* recalls this advice. It decrees that the monks of a cathedral monastery should elect the bishop, in the same way as monks of an ordinary monastery elect their abbot, from among their number, if there is a monk worthy of the office, and no one should oppose. But if, 'owing to their ignorance or sinfulness', there is no one suitable, a monk should be chosen from another monastery. Whoever is chosen should live with the monks and set an example of strict adherence to the Rule. The passage reads:

Praefato equidem synodali conciliabulo hoc attendendum magnopere cuncti decreuerunt...Episcoporum quoque electio uti abbatum, ubicumque in sede episcopali monachi regulares conuersantur, si Domini largiente gratia tanti profectus inibi monachus reperiri potuerit, eodem modo agatur; nec alio quolibet modo dum eiusdem sunt conuersationis a quoquam praesumatur. Si autem, imperitia impediente uel peccatis promerentibus, talis qui tanti gradus honore dignus sit in eadem congregatione reperiri non potuerit, ex *alio noto monachorum monasterio* [*Regula Benedicti, cap.* lxi. 31 ff.], concordi regis et fratrum quibus dedicari debet consilio eligatur.[28]

Knowles saw this passage in the *Regularis concordia* as a supreme example of St Dunstan's statesmanship. It put the characteristically English institution of the monastic cathedral on a firm basis, at a time when, on the continent, reformers were trying to emancipate monasteries from episcopal control. Knowles pointed out that the idea that bishops should live in ordered communities originated in Gregory's *Responsiones*,[29] but he does not mention the parallel in Bede's letter to Ecgbert.

[27] Letter to Ecgbert, §10, i. 413.    [28] *Reg. con.*, 74–5.
[29] Knowles, *Monastic Order*, 45–6. *HE*, i. 27; i. 48–9.

Characteristic of the writings of the tenth-century revival is the invective against the clerical communities which preceded the new Benedictine monasteries. The *Regularis concordia* states that Edgar rejected 'the abominations of the negligent clerks' ('eiectisque negligentium clericorum spurcitiis').[30] Edgar's foundation charter to the New Minster, Winchester, describes in disparaging terms the clerks whom he expelled from that church.[31] The earliest biography of St Oswald (*c.* 1000), which is attributed to Byrhtferth, thus depicts the character of the religious before the revival:

In diebus illis non monastici viri, nec ipsius sanctae institutionis regulae erant in regione Anglorum, sed erant religiosi et dignissimi clerici qui tamen thesauros suos, quos avidis acquirebant cordibus, non ad ecclesiae honorem, sed suis dare solebant uxoribus.[32]

Ælfric and Wulfstan, the early biographers of St Ethelwold, cast similar aspersions on the clerks who served the Old Minster, Winchester, before its reform. They, too, refer to the clerks' wives. Ælfric writes:

Erant autem tunc in ueteri monasterio, ubi cathedra episcopalis habetur, male morigerati clerici, elatione et insolentia ac luxuria preuenti, adeo ut nonnulli eorum dedignarentur missas suo ordine celebrare, repudiantes uxores quas inclite duxerant et alias accipientes, gulae et ebrietati iugiter dediti.[33]

Possibly Bede influenced the terms of this invective. The passage in the *Regularis concordia* and that in Edgar's charter to the New Minster which

[30] *Reg. con.*, 70. Knowles accepts the truth of such aspersions on the clerks, op. cit. 41 n. 3, and so, with some reservation, does Hallinger, *Reg. Con.*, 381–2.

[31] Walter de Gray Birch, *Cartularium Saxonicum*, 3 vols, London [1883]–1893, repr. 1963, iii. 456 no. 1190; P. H. Sawyer, *Anglo-Saxon Charters*, London 1968, 240 no. 745. Cf. other passages in the same charter: 'vitiosorum cuneos canonicorum, e diversis nostri regiminis coenobiis Christi vicarius eliminavi', 'rebelliones omnipotentis voluntati obviantes possessionem domini usurpare non sustinens clericos lascivientes repuli': Birch, op. cit. iii. 459. John cites this charter and quotes passages from two other Winchester charters (Birch, op. cit. nos 1147, 1159; Sawyer, op. cit. 258–9 nos 817, 818) which contain virulent abuse of the clerks, Eric John, 'The church of Winchester and the tenth-century reformation', *BJRL* xlvii (1964–5), 420–1. I have not included these among my examples since the charters in question are of dubious authenticity and may be post-Conquest, at least in their present form; see F. E. Harmer, *Anglo-Saxon Writs*, Manchester 1952, 374 and nn. 1, 2. If so, their invective could reflect Norman propaganda rather than tenth-century opinion.

[32] *Vita Oswaldi archiepiscopi Eboracensis*, in *The Historians of the Church of York and its Archbishops*, ed. James Raine, Jr, 3 vols (Rolls Series, 1879–94), i. 411.

[33] Ælfric's *Vita S. Æthelwoldi*, in *Three Lives of English Saints*, ed. Michael Winterbottom, Toronto 1972, 22–3. Knowles, *Monastic Order*, 41 n. 3, takes this passage seriously. A slightly longer version occurs in Wulfstan's *Vita gloriosi et beati patris Athelwoldi*, in *Three Lives*, 44. It should be noted that Ælfric's and Wulfstan's Lives are closely related; either Ælfric abbreviated Wulfstan's *Vita*, which is the fuller of the two, or Wulfstan expanded Ælfric's. Recent scholars conclude that Wulfstan's is the original. See Barbara York, 'Introduction', in idem, *Bishop .Ethelwold*, 1–2; Michael Lapidge, 'Æthelwold as scholar and teacher', in ibid. 89 n. 1. A new edition, with trans., of Wulfstan's *Vita*, by Michael Winterbottom and Michael Lapidge is forthcoming (Oxford).

refer to the clerks' 'abominations' seem to echo the *Ecclesiastical History*, ii.
4: Bede relates that Pope Boniface obtained the Pantheon from the
Emperor Phocas and, 'when all the abominations had been eliminated'
('eliminata omnia spurcitia'), converted it into a church.[34] Moreover,
there are parallels between the reformers' abuse and Bede's letter to
Ecgbert. Bede had dwelt on the luxurious lives and licentiousness of the
monks of his day and also inveighed against the immorality of young
noblemen.[35] In two particulars the resemblance between his invective and
that of the reformers is striking. The accusation of the latter that the clerks
were married, including the allegation in the *Life of St Oswald* that the
clerks squandered 'treasure' on their wives, recalls part of Bede's tirade
where he claims that the secular owners of monasteries divided their time
between monastic concerns and their wives and children and gave land to
their wives for the foundation of convents:

> Idem ipsi uiri modo coniugis ac liberorum procreandorum curam gerunt, modo
> exsurgentes de cubilibus, quid intra septa monasteriorum geri debeat, sedula
> intentione pertractant. Quin etiam suis coniugibus simili impudentia constru-
> endis, ut ipsi aiunt, monasteriis loca conquirunt, quae pari stultitia, cum sint
> laicae, famularum se Christi permittunt esse rectrices.[36]

The other parallel is Bede's attribution of the decline of monasticism to
secularisation resulting from the power of the lay nobility. Noblemen
obtained lands from the king in order to found monasteries; they then
lived in them like lords, ruling a motley crowd of men unworthy of the
monastic vocation:

> At alii grauiore adhuc flagitio, cum sint ipsi laici, et nullo uitae regularis uel usu
> exerciti, uel amore praediti, data regibus pecunia, emunt sibi sub praetextu
> construendorum monasteriorum territoria in quibus suae liberius uacent libidini,
> et haec insuper in ius sibi haereditarium regalibus edictis faciunt asscribi, ipsas
> quoque litteras priuilegiorum suorum quasi veraciter Deo dignas, pontificum,
> abbatum, et potestatum seculi obtinent subscriptione confirmari. Sicque
> usurpatis sibi agellulis siue uicis, liberi exinde a diuino simul et humano seruitio,
> suis tantum inibi desideriis, laici monachis imperantes, deseruiunt; immo non
> monachos ibi congregant, sed quoscunque ob culpam inobaedientiae ueris
> expulsos monasteriis alicubi forte oberrantes inuenerint, aut evocare monasteriis
> ipsi ualuerint; vel certe quos ipsi de suis a satellitibus ad suscipiendam tonsuram
> promissa sibi obaedientia monachica inuitare quiuerint.[37]

The prohibition in the *Regularis concordia* on monasteries to acknowledge
secular overlordship, with a particular reference to the ruin this had
caused in the past, is reminiscent of this passage:

> Saecularium uero prioratum, ne ad magni ruinam detrimenti uti olim acciderat
> miserabiliter deueniret, magna animaduersione atque anathemate suscipi
> coenobiis sacris sapienter prohibentes...[38]

---

[34] *Op. Hist.*, i. 88.                 [35] Bede's letter to Ecgbert, §§ 10–12, i. 413–16.
[36] Ibid. § 12, i. 416.                [37] Ibid. § 12, i. 415–16.
[38] *Reg. con.*, 7.

St Ethelwold, in his treatise on King Edgar's Establishment of the Monasteries, admonishes abbesses not to give 'God's estate to their kinsmen nor to great secular persons, neither for money nor flattery'. He also enjoins the king and secular lords not to seize the opportunity 'to rob God, who owns those possessions', if any abbess 'be convicted of a crime against church or state'.[39] On the evidence of these passages Eric John concludes that lay power alone accounted for lax observance in religious communities from the early eighth to the mid-tenth century.[40] He dismisses the Viking incursions as a factor. This conclusion, however, disregards the possible use in the *Regularis concordia* and Ethelwold's treatise of a *topos* derived from Bede. It also ignores the evidence of Asser and of Fulco in his letter to King Alfred, who both suggest the Vikings as another explanation. (Alfred, in the prologue to the *Pastoral Care*, treats the Vikings as instruments of divine punishment for the decline of monastic standards.)[41] Nor was the power of the nobility always inimical to monasticism: to cite just one example, during the revival itself Ramsey Abbey owed its site to a nobleman, Æthelwine, ealdorman of East Anglia. As its patron, he kept close contact with the monks, and he and one of his brothers were buried in the conventual church. During the reaction against the new monasteries which immediately followed the death of King Edgar, Æthelwine and his brothers and Byrhtnoth, ealdorman of Essex, fought in defence of the East Anglian houses. Nevertheless, the attacks were led by another thegn, Ælfhere, ealdorman of Mercia, and, while Æthelwine was regarded by the monks of his own monastery of Ramsey as 'amicus Dei', to those of Ely he was a bitter enemy (a usurper of their estates – in Ramsey's interest).[42]

In order to justify their take-over of the religious system and to strengthen their position, the reformers resorted to propaganda. Perhaps sometimes they objected to a clerical community because it did not conform to the new continental standards of observance. But in many cases they had worldly reasons for wanting to discredit the clerks; if a clerical community owned a church and property which a reformer needed for his monks, it had to be dispossessed. The property of the clerical communities was partly built up from the inheritance of individual

---

[39] *Councils and Synods*, 153–4.     [40] John, 'The king and the monks', 61.

[41] For the evidence of Asser and Fulco see Keynes and Lapidge, *Alfred the Great*, 103, 182–3. For Alfred's prologue to the *Pastoral Care* see ibid. 125.

[42] For Æthelwine's relations with Ramsey see *Vita Oswaldi*, 427–9, 447, 468, 475. For his defence of the East Anglian monasteries see D. J. V. Fisher, 'The anti-monastic reaction in the reign of Edward the Martyr', *Cambridge Historical Journal* x (1952), 254, 258, 265–6, 267; cf. Wormald, 'Æthelwold', 36. For his bad relations with Ely see Fisher, op. cit. 266–7. For lay lords as protectors of monasteries on the Continent in the late ninth and in the tenth century see H. E. J. Cowdrey, *The Cluniacs and the Gregorian Reform*, Oxford 1970, 11–12. For a careful assessment of Ælfhere's probable motives (which were apparently mainly political) for attacking the new monasteries see Ann Williams, 'Princeps Merciorum gentis: the family, career and connections of Ælfhere, ealdorman of Mercia, 956–83', *A-SE* x (1982), 159–61, 166–70.

clerks and from endowments given by their families. The clerks' relatives tended to be people of consequence in the neighbourhood and, apparently, to feel responsible for the communities with which they had a family connection. The clerks and their supporters were, therefore, powers to be reckoned with.[43] King Edgar had to resort to force to eject the clerks from the Old and New Minsters in Winchester and from Chertsey and Milton.[44] The reformers feared that such dispossessed clerks would try to recover their property, and the king in particular faced the danger of a hostile combination of them and their supporters. At least some people objected, in any case, to influence from abroad. The Anglo-Saxon Chronicle, in a eulogy of Edgar under 959, admits that he had one grave fault: 'he loved evil foreign customs and was excessively determined to introduce heathen manners into this land, and he encouraged foreigners and harmful people to come to this country'.[45] That the reformers' fears were not groundless is proved by the violence of the reaction against the new monasteries led by Ælfhere, ealdorman of Mercia, and his followers. Apparently they despoiled a number of Mercian monasteries and, in a few cases, dispersed the monks.[46]

The conclusion that the reformers' abuse of the clerks was part of their propaganda is supported by the fact that it only occurs in writings of monastic origin (of Worcester, Ramsey and Winchester provenance). There is no trace of it in the *Life of St Dunstan* by the anonymous author, whose name began with 'B', who was probably a secular clerk, not a monk.[47] Nor, in view of the achievements of the Anglo-Saxon Church in the tenth century before the monastic revival, is it likely that the clerks were as bad as the reformers painted them.

Scholars from the tenth century until recently, while tending to exaggerate the impact of the tenth-century monastic revival, have in general paid too little attention to the fate of the old clerical communities which were replaced by Benedictine ones. In fact the reformers made no clean sweep. The abruptness of the transition from clerical to monastic community at Winchester, Milton and Chertsey was exceptional. In most cases the change was gradual. The reformers, indeed, had grown up in the old tradition. St Dunstan was consecrated to the priesthood by a clerk, his

[43] For the clerks and their family connections see Fisher, op. cit. 255–64 passim; and D. J. Sheerin, 'The dedication of the Old Minster, Winchester, in 980', *Rev. Bén.* lxxxviii (1978), 265, 269–70.

[44] *The Anglo-Saxon Chronicle*, ed. Dorothy Whitelock with D. C. Douglas and S. I. Tucker, London 1961, 76.

[45] Ibid. 75.

[46] See Fisher, 'Anti-monastic reaction', 254–70; Williams, op. cit. 167–70; Blair, 'Secular minster churches', 119. According to later tradition the monks of Evesham were expelled and the clerks reinstated – but not for long. See *Chronicon Abbatiae de Evesham*, ed. W. D. Macray (Rolls Series, 1863), 78.

[47] I owe this comment about B's Life of St Dunstan to Dr Simon Keynes. The Life is printed in *Memorials of St Dunstan*, ed. William Stubbs (Rolls Series, 1874), pp. 3–52.

kinsman, Ælfheah, bishop of Winchester.[48] St Oswald was sent to Fleury to study monasticism by another clerk, his uncle, Oda, archbishop of Canterbury (942–58), himself a notable reformer. Before going to Fleury St Oswald had ruled some clerical community at Winchester; we only have the word of his first biographer, who, being a monk of Ramsey, would have been a biased witness on the matter, that he found the clerks' mode of living repulsively luxurious. His biographer writes that St Oswald, having habitually worn silk and feasted sumptuously every day, became discontented:

Cum his [clericis] mansitabat pius adolescens, velut Loth in Sodomis, quorum superfluas nenias cernens vir providus, coepit frequenter sollicitis cogitationibus, pulsari, et beatae mentis indagine praemeditari, quia carnis delicta magis augent quam debent, qui de alienis rebus vivunt et injuste agere non desistunt...![49]

The reformers must have recognised the merits of the old order and realised that its destruction, or any indiscriminate damage to it, would sap the vitality of their own movement. Their desire to minimise any break with the past is well illustrated by the fact that two of the foundations, Ely and Peterborough, were in fact refoundations of monasteries mentioned by Bede. Similarly, St Oswald attempted to re-establish a monastery at Ripon. His biographer vividly demonstrates his revivalist intention:

Oswaldus vero impiger miles Christi sua ovilia perlustrans pervenit gaudens ad moenia monasterii quod dictum est Ripun, quod tunc dirutum erat, quondam vero a reverentissimo viro Wilfridi celebriter constructum.[50]

When the reformers wanted to dispossess a community of clerks, sometimes, at least, they acted with moderation and tact. Even at the Old Minster, Winchester, whence King Edgar 'drove the clerks' to make room for St Ethelwold's monks, there was some continuity of personnel; the king, according to St Ethelwold's biographers, Ælfric and Wulfstan, gave the clerks the choice of conforming to the Benedictine Rule or of leaving. Three, Eadsige, Wulfsige and Wulfstan, did in fact eventually conform:

Misit quoque rex quendam ministrorum suorum famosissimum, Uulstanum vocabulo, cum episcopo, qui regia auctoritate mandauit clericis ocissime dare locum monachis aut monachicum suscipere habitum. At illi execrantes monachicam uitam ilico exierunt de aecclesia; sed tamen postmodum tres ex illis

---

[48] *Memorials of St Dunstan*, 13–14. William of Malmesbury in his *Life of St Dunstan* alleges that Ælfheah had been a monk of Glastonbury, ibid. 260. However, the earliest Life, that by 'B', makes no mention of this, and in any case even if William's statement were true (and it could have been a product of his desire to stress the antiquity of the monastery at Glastonbury), it would only signify that Ælfheah was a member of the 'clerical' community before Dunstan's reform. [49] *Vita Oswaldi*, 411.
[50] Ibid. 462. Cf. below p. 179.

conversi sunt ad regularem conuersationem, scilicet Eadsinus, Uulfsinus, Uuilstanus.[51]

Two post-Conquest authorities, 'Florence of Worcester' (*c.* 1100) and the Ramsey chronicler (*temp.* Henry II), give similar accounts of St Oswald's procedure at Worcester, asserting that he gave the clerks in the cathedral the choice of conforming to the Rule of Benedict or of leaving.[52] However, the Ramsey chronicler was probably here borrowing from 'Florence', and 'Florence' in turn was probably using as a *topos* Ælfric's or Wulfstan's account of St Ethelwold's treatment of the clerks of the Old Minster. Rather more convincing, because it has no obvious model in Ælfric or Wulfstan, is the Ramsey chronicler's statement that St Oswald sent one of the clerks from Worcester to Ramsey for training and then brought him back to rule the new monastic community in the cathedral:

unus [clericorum] Winsinus nomine, qui caeteris et dignitate generis et opum copia insignior habebatur, saeculo renuncians et habitu monastico amictus, Rameseiam missus est, regularis ordinis disciplina instruendus et instituendus, ac deinceps inde revocatus Wigorniae prioratum est promotus.[53]

Moreover, St Oswald treated even those clerks who remained obdurate leniently. He left them in possession of the old cathedral, which in any case was too small, and built a new one for his monks.[54]

[51] Ælfric's *Vita S. Æthelwoldi*, 23. For the similar passages in Wulfstan see ibid. 45. For Eadsig see *Ælfric's Lives of Saints*, 2 vols, ed. W. W. Skeat (EETS, orig. ser. lxxvi, lxxxii, xciv, cxiv, 1881–1900), i. 442–7. Knowles, *Monastic Order*, 41, notes that these three clerks became monks of St Ethelwold's new monastery; however, he then continues with this sweeping statement: 'The expulsion of the clerks from the New Minster was effected in the next year, and followed by similar action in other places throughout the country.' Knowles comments that 'the measure, if its causes and consequences are studied in contemporary documents, needs no elaborate defence' and cites contemporary 'evidence' of the clerks' misdemeanours: ibid. 41 n. 3.

[52] *Florentii Wigorniensis monachi Chronicon ex Chronicis*, 2 vols, ed. Benjamin Thorpe (English Historical Society, 1848–9), New York 1964, i. 141 (s.a. 969); *Chronicon Abbatiae Rameseiensis*, ed. W. D. Macray (Rolls Series, 1886), 41.

[53] Ibid. 41–2. 'Florence of Worcester' states that Wynsige was a monk of Ramsey (which is not, however, incompatible with the Ramsey chronicler's narrative), *Chron. ex Chronicis*, i. 141.

[54] See J. Armitage Robinson, *St Oswald and the Church of Worcester*, London 1919, passim, esp. at pp. 3–6, 20–1, 36–7. On the other hand John argues that the conversion at Worcester was more like that at Winchester rather than being peaceful, 'St Oswald and the Church of Worcester', in idem, *Orbis Britanniae and Other Studies*, Leicester 1966, 234–48. His case is based on the so-called *Altitonantis* charter purportedly of King Edgar to Worcester (Birch, *Cart. Sax.*, iii. 377–81 no. 1135), the authenticity of which he defends in his *Land Tenure in Early England*, Leicester 1960, 80–139. However, John's views have not persuaded Professor R. R. Darlington, *The Cartulary of Worcester Cathedral Priory* (Pipe Roll Society lxxvi (NS, xxxviii), 1962–3), pp. xiii–xxiv, esp. p. xviii n. 6, or Professor P. H. Sawyer, 'Charters of the reform movement: the Worcester archive', in Parsons, *Tenth-century Studies*, 84–93. They both decide in favour of Robinson's conclusions. It may also be noted that the chronicle evidence cited by John is unreliable in this context.

Nicholas Brooks has pointed out that, despite the tenth-century monastic revival, 'monastic cathedrals remained very much the exception in England'. St Dunstan, indeed, never replaced the clerks of Christ Church, Canterbury, by monks at all. The community's transformation took place probably in the early eleventh century, when it was brought about gradually. (The story that the clerks were dramatically expelled from the cathedral, which occurs in the forged 'foundation charter' of the second quarter of the eleventh century, is fictitious and was probably formulated under the influence of Edgar's procedure at Winchester). St Dunstan would have seen no reason to displace the clerks; by all accounts they fulfilled their duties in the cathedral well.[55]

In the north of England the community attached to the see of St Cuthbert remained clerical even longer – considerably longer – than that at Canterbury. It served St Cuthbert's shrine and the cathedral first at Chester-le-Street and then at Durham. Its prosperity is apparent in the *Historia de Sancto Cuthberto*, a history of the see written in the first instance in 946 but continued subsequently. The *Historia* records a visit to the shrine by King Athelstan in 934 on his way to campaign in Scotland. His gifts to the saint included extensive estates, rich treasures and precious books.[56] One of the books was probably the splendidly illuminated volume containing Bede's two Lives of St Cuthbert and a liturgical office for the saint which still survives.[57] The *Historia* asserts that Athelstan enjoined his brother, Edmund, that, if he himself were killed on the expedition, he should bear his body to St Cuthbert's and there commend his soul to God. In fact Athelstan survived, but Edmund, when king, visited St Cuthbert's for the sake of prayer, also on the way to Scotland. He placed two gold armlets (*armillas aureas*) and two Greek *pallia* on the body and confirmed 'peace and law' (*pacem vero et legem*) to all St Cuthbert's lands.[58] Clearly at the start of the monastic revival the see of St Cuthbert was flourishing, untouched by the reformers. In 995 the clerks moved St Cuthbert's body to Durham for greater security. There their community survived, serving the shrine and cathedral until after the Norman Conquest, when, in 1083, it was finally replaced by a Benedictine monastery.

At the same time the fortunes of the clerical community serving St Edmund's shrine at Beadericesworth (the later Bury St Edmunds) rose. Although the cult of St Edmund, king and martyr, had flourished in East

---

[55] See Nicholas Brooks, *The Early History of the Church of Canterbury: Christ Church from 597–1066*, Leicester 1984, 255–7.

[56] *Historia de Sancto Cuthberto*, in *Symeonis Monachi Opera Omnia*, 2 vols, ed. Thomas Arnold (Rolls Series, 1882–5), i. 211–12. For the *Historia* see Edmund Craster, 'The patrimony of St Cuthbert', *EHR* lxix (1954), 177–8. John Blair gives many examples of secular minsters which flourished in the tenth and eleventh centuries, 'Secular minster churches', 120–3.

[57] The book is now Corpus Christi College, Cambridge, MS 183. See Keynes, 'King Athelstan's books', 180–5.     [58] *Historia de S. Cuthberto*, 212.

Anglia for a generation after the saint's 'martyrdom' by the Vikings in 869,[59] it had subsequently lapsed. After the Norman Conquest the Bury monks contended that King Edmund (939–46) had granted to the clerks, who preceded them as guardians of St Edmund's shrine, jurisdictional privileges over Beadericesworth and the adjacent land. Although the charter, on which this claim rested, is of doubtful authenticity,[60] it is not unlikely that King Edmund would have held St Edmund, his namesake, in especial veneration and was a benefactor of the community at Beadericesworth. Certainly some of his relatives were its benefactors. His father-in-law, Ælfgar, bequeathed to his daughter Æthelflaed, Edmund's second wife, an estate at Cockfield (Suffolk) with reversion to St Edmund's some time between 946 and 951. Æthelflaed did not directly bequeath the estate to St Edmund's but, together with an estate at Chelsworth (Suffolk), bequeathed it to her sister, Ælflaed, and brother-in-law, Brihtnoth, again with reversion to St Edmund's. Ælflaed duly bequeathed Cockfield and Chelsworth and also Nedging (Suffolk) to St Edmund's in *c.*1000.[61] The fourteenth-century Benefactors' Lists state that King Edwy, King Edmund's son (955–9), gave Beccles (Suffolk) 'but without a charter'.[62]

Besides royal and royally connected benefactors, St Edmund's had one, or more probably two, episcopal patrons in the tenth century. Theodred, bishop of London (*c.* 909 × 926–951 × 953), who was on good terms with King Edmund, bequeathed estates at Nowton, Horningsheath, Ickworth and Whepstead (all in Suffolk) 'for the good of my soul'.[63] The later Benefactors' Lists state that Ælfric, bishop of East Anglia, gave estates at Soham, Bradfield, Brockford and Southwold (all in Suffolk), at Runcton (Norfolk) and at 'Thorpe'. One Benefactors' List identifies this Bishop Ælfric with Ælfric I (? × 970–970 × ?).[64] In addition, in about 961,

[59] See C. E. Blunt, 'The St. Edmund memorial coinage', *Proceedings of the Suffolk Institute of Archaeology* xxxi (1970), 234–55.

[60] For King Edmund's purported charter see Sawyer, *Anglo-Saxon Charters*, 191–2 no. 507; and C. R. Hart, *The Early Charters of Eastern England*, Leicester 1966, 54–8 no. 74. Hart believes that at least the part of the charter delineating the boundaries of St Edmund's jurisdictional area is pre-Conquest.

[61] For Ælfgar's, Æthelflaed's and Ælflaed's wills see Sawyer, op. cit. 414–16 passim, 418 nos 1483, 1486, 1494; Dorothy Whitelock, *Anglo-Saxon Wills*, Cambridge 1930, 7–9, 35–43 nos ii, xiv, xv, 103–8, 137–46. Æthelflaed had acquired Chelsworth from King Edgar, Sawyer, op cit. 231 no. 703.

[62] See the Benefactors' List, written in the last half of the thirteenth century, in Cambridge University Library MS Ff. 2. 33. fo. 50v; *The Pinchbeck Register*, 2 vols, ed. Francis Hervey, Brighton 1925, ii. 284. Domesday Book, ii. 369b, shows that St Edmund's had held there before 1066 and still did so in 1086.

[63] For Bishop Theodred's will see Whitelock, *Anglo-Saxon Wills*, 2–5 no. i, 99–103. Abbo mentions Theodred's generosity to St Edmund, *Passio S. Eadmundi*, in *Three Lives*, 83.

[64] St Edmund's certainly had landholdings at Bradfield, Brockford, Soham, Southwold and Runcton before the Norman Conquest, *Domesday Book*, ii. 362, 361b, 368b, 371b, 309 respectively. All these places except Southwold contributed a month's, or part of a month's, food-rent to the abbey, A. J. Robertson, *Anglo-Saxon Charters*, Cambridge 1956,

St Edmund's received a grant of land at Palgrave (Suffolk) from Wulfstan, a thegn, and between 961 and 995 the bequest of 'Northo' from another thegn, Ætheric.[65] By this time the reputation of St Edmund was well established in eastern England, sufficiently so to prompt the monks of Ramsey to commission Abbo of Fleury during his stay with them, *c.* 986–8, to write an account of his 'martyrdom' and early cult, the *Passio Sancti Eadmundi.*[66] There is no doubt that no attempt was made during the monastic revival to reform St Edmund's clerical community, which survived well into the eleventh century.

The community at Beadericesworth differed, it would appear, in an important respect from the one at Christ Church, Canterbury, and from that of St Cuthbert's: it was not attached to an episcopal see. However, there is a little evidence suggesting the possibility that Beadericesworth was a see for a time in the tenth century. In the eighth century East Anglia was divided into two dioceses. Bede records that the northern see was at Elmham and the southern one at Dunwich.[67] At some periods in the tenth and eleventh centuries the latter was at Hoxne;[68] its cathedral was dedicated to St Ethelbert, who, like St Edmund, was a martyred king of East Anglia. The evidence that Beadericesworth was ever a see is post-Conquest. It is to be found in literature produced during the quarrel between the monks of Bury St Edmunds and Herbert Losinga, bishop of East Anglia (1090 × 1091–1119), over the latter's attempt to move his see to Bury. In the course of the dispute Losinga's party produced a tract, a copy of which still survives, which supports the bishop's case partly by supplying an historical precedent; the tract 'proves' that Beadericesworth

94–200 passim. The abbot's claim to Southwold was disputed after the Conquest, see Hermann, *De miraculis Sancti Eadmundi,* in *Memorials of St Edmund's Abbey,* 3 vols, ed. Thomas Arnold (Rolls Series, 1890–6), i. 79. St Edmund's had landholdings before the Conquest at a number of places called 'Thorpe', 'Torp' or 'Torpa' in Domesday Book, namely Ixworth Thorpe and Thorpe Morieux (both within St Edmund's Liberty), and Abbot's Thorpe, Morningthorpe and Thorpland in Norfolk, *Domesday Book,* ii. 367 and 367b, 333, 369, 210b, 212, 209 respectively (see also ibid. ii. 360b). A 'Thorpa', together with Palgrave (Suffolk) provided a month's food-rent, Robertson, op. cit. 194, 200. Robertson identifies this as Westhorpe because it was the nearest 'Thorpe' to Palgrave, ibid. 443, and cf. *Domesday Book,* ii. 370b, 371 (Westtorp). However, not all the landholdings which combined to provide a month's food-rent were close together, and both Ixworth Thorpe and Thorpe Morieux, unlike Westhorp, were within St Edmund's Liberty. Hart identifies Bishop Ælfric as Ælfric III, 1039 × 1043, commenting that the Benefactors' Lists call him 'the good', Hart, *Early Charters,* 248 no. 248. However, the Pinchbeck Register, having noticed the gift by Ælfric *cognomento bonus* of the above-mentioned landholdings, writes: 'Fuerunt enim tres venerabiles episcopi elmanenses uno nomine alfrici dicti unus bonus alter niger et tercius paruus ob differencia uocati'; clearly Ælfric 'the good' was Ælfric I, *Pinchbeck Register,* ii. 287.

[65] For Wulfstan's grant see Sawyer, op. cit. 355 no. 1213. For Aetheric's bequest see ibid. 420 no. 1501; Whitelock, *Wills,* 42 no. 16/1, 146–8.

[66] Printed in *Three Lives,* 67–88.

[67] *HE,* ii. 15; iv. 5: i. 116–17, 217. Cf. ii. 108, 214–15.

[68] See Bishop Theodred's will, Whitelock, op. cit. 2, 102; and *Domesday Book,* ii. 379.

had once been an East Anglian see.[69] It asserts that: Felix, a colleague (mentioned by Bede) of St Augustine, founded a cathedral dedicated to the Virgin Mary at Beadericesworth; King Cnut made Ælfric, monk and prior of Ely, bishop of Beadericesworth, stipulating that he should replace the clerical community by a monastic one; after Cnut's death Harold transformed the cathedral priory into an abbey. This narrative is at variance with the account of the origins of the abbey propagated by the monks of Bury St Edmunds at the end of the eleventh century: they claimed that the abbey was founded by Cnut in 1020 on the advice of Bishop Ælfwine, monk of Ely, to replace the clerical community serving St Edmund's shrine.

V. H. Galbraith, who edited the Losinga tract, while concluding that it was 'an unconvincing perversion of the facts, so far as these are known',[70] admits that it may contain a grain of truth. He concedes that, if the writer 'had limited his claim to the period from *c.* 850 to *c.* 960, it would have been hard to disprove him, so great is our ignorance concerning the East Anglian see at that time'. Losinga had been abbot of Ramsey before becoming bishop of Thetford. The monks of Ramsey had had some part in the rise of Beadericesworth to importance as a cult centre and religious community – by asking Abbo to write the *Passio*. Therefore, some tradition about the early history of Beadericesworth could have survived at Ramsey. That the Losinga tract used Ramsey material is suggested by its reference to St Felix, whose body was translated to Ramsey in the eleventh century,[71] and by the dedication to St Mary; Ramsey Abbey was dedicated to St Mary (jointly with St Benedict) and so was St Oswald's Cathedral at Worcester.[72]

The tract differs from the Bury account not only in substance but also in one possibly significant detail: it calls the first bishop of Beadericesworth, Ælfric, 'monk and prior of Ely'; as has been seen, the Bury tradition calls the bishop who advised Cnut to found the monastery Ælfwine, describing him simply as 'monk of Ely'. Ælfwine was bishop ? × 1019–23 and Ælfric II 1023 × 1038–1038. Galbraith tacitly assumes that the author confused Ælfric II with Ælfwine. But perhaps the Losinga tract preserves here a piece of true information, that a bishop called Ælfric had had his see at Beadericesworth. This could have been the bishop in St Oswald's time, Ælfric I, bishop of East Anglia ? × 970–970 × ? who, as mentioned above, appears to have been a substantial benefactor of St Edmund's.

The choice of Beadericesworth as a see in the mid-tenth century would not be surprising. It was a more important place, a *villa regia* according to

---

[69] The tract is printed by V. H. Galbraith, 'The East Anglian see and the Abbey of Bury St Edmunds', *EHR* xl (1925), 226–8.

[70] Ibid. 222.

[71] *Chron. Ram.*, 127–8.

[72] Cf. Armitage Robinson, *St Oswald*, 3–6.

Abbo,[73] than Hoxne, and presumably St Edmund's cult under royal and episcopal patronage was more thriving than St Ethelberht's. It is known that Archbishop Oda, a zealous reformer, was concerned about the lack of ecclesiastical organisation in East Anglia, which had resulted from the Viking incursions of the ninth century. There is evidence suggesting that he revived the see of North Elmham,[74] and he may well also have turned his attention to East Anglia's southern see. Just possibly St Edmund attracted his attention for family reasons. His father was said to have been a soldier in the host of Ivarr, the Viking leader who, having conquered the north of England, attacked East Anglia and was, according to legend, responsible for St Edmund's 'martyrdom'.[75] Oda might have fostered St Edmund's cult in expiation for his father's complicity in rather the same way as Cnut was to promote the cult of St Ælfheah in order to expiate his murder by the Danes in 1012.

It is not inconceivable that Oda planned to raise St Edmund's to a status like that of St Cuthbert's. His north-country connections lend weight to this possibility. In this context it must be noted that comparison of the St Edmund legend in Abbo with the St Cuthbert legend in the earlier *Historia de Sancto Cuthberto* shows a relationship between the two. It is more likely that the St Cuthbert legend influenced the St Edmund one than *vice versa*, and Abbo himself might well have been responsible for the borrowing. If so, perhaps he first learned of the St Cuthbert legend from Oda, whom he mentions as one of his patrons.[76] However, since Oda died in 958 Abbo's contact with him must have been about thirty years before his visit to Ramsey. This perhaps makes it more likely that he would have owed any information about St Cuthbert to St Oswald. The St Edmund legend resembles the St Cuthbert one in its emphasis on the uncorruption of St Edmund's body. Indeed, it explicitly compares St Edmund's uncorruption with St Cuthbert's. More specifically, Abbo tells two stories which seem to derive from a story in the *Historia*. One is about Leofstan, the proud thegn, who insisted on gazing at St Edmund's body and consequently went mad and died. The other relates that thieves were

[73] *Passio S. Eadmundi*, 82. The description *villa regia* could, however, be a late eleventh-century interpolation in the *Passio*; see Gransden, 'Baldwin', 72.

[74] See Brooks, *Early History*, 223–4 and nn. 52, 53. For the scale of the possibly tenth-century rebuilding of the cathedral at North Elmham see S. E. Rigold, 'The Anglian cathedral of North Elmham, Norfolk. Analysis and excavation by the Ancient Monuments Branch of the Ministry of Public Buildings and Works', *Medieval Archaeology* vi–vii (1962–3), 68, 104–8; and idem, in Peter Wade-Martins, *Excavations in North Elmham Park 1967–1972*, 2 vols (consecutively paginated), Norfolk 1980, i. 6–8, 137–48; ii. I am indebted to Professor Brooks for these references.

[75] *Passio S. Eadmundi*, 73. For Oda's parentage see *Vita S. Oswaldi*, 404.

[76] Abbo's acrostic poem addressed to St Dunstan includes these lines: 'Solus Odo pius cenSor qui jure sacerdoS/ Te pater ante fuiT, sat nos amplexus amaviT': *Memorials of St Dunstan*, 410. Cf. Armitage Robinson, *St Oswald*, 45. For St Oswald's probable interest in St Cuthbert see below p. 50.

paralysed in the act of robbing St Edmund's shrine.[77] These passages are reminiscent of the story in the *Historia* of the proud Viking, Onalafball, who entered St Cuthbert's church, defied the saint, became paralysed and died.[78]

Oda's reforming activities had the full support of King Edmund. As has been seen, both he and his predecessor, King Athelstan, were benefactors of St Cuthbert's, and it is likely that he was also a patron of St Edmund's. Royal interest in these shrine churches was probably not only the result of piety. Two thriving Christian communities, one in the north, the other in East Anglia, headed by loyal bishops and in control of the surrounding areas, would have spread royal power. Robin Fleming has mentioned that, after the reconquest of the Danelaw, the monarchy by endowing monasteries created 'a network of... loyal ecclesiastical officials, and efficient administrative districts'.[79] St Cuthbert's and St Edmund's clerical communities served the same purpose. Moreover, they were Christian strongholds, where prayers could be said for the king's success in battle, and centres for the quick mobilisation of troops. Thus they served as outposts against invasion by heathens from Scandinavia, a constant threat at this time, exactly in those regions where the king most needed them. St Edmund was a particularly appropriate patron saint, since he had died defending the East Anglians against these very enemies. Fleming has demonstrated that, during the Viking Age, the monarchy had accumulated lands lost by the monasteries to create its own defensive blocs against the Danes.[80] It seems that now the monarchy was endowing at least St Cuthbert's and St Edmund's for the same defensive purpose.

It is clear, therefore, that the clerical communities at Chester-le-Street and Beadericesworth were flourishing at the beginning of the monastic revival and continued to do so throughout its course. There is no evidence that the reformers objected to them. St Oswald's veneration of the Northumbrian saints presumably included St Cuthbert. (His biographer at one point, apparently using Bede's prose Life of St Cuthbert as a source, compares a miracle worked by St Oswald with one of St Cuthbert's.) Perhaps he regarded St Edmund as the re-embodiment, so to speak, of his own namesake, St Oswald, king of Northumbria (634–42), another Anglo-Saxon king 'martyred' by heathens about whom he would have read in Bede. It was the monks of his foundation at Ramsey who commissioned Abbo to write the *Passio Sancti Eadmundi*, and St Dunstan himself, according to Abbo, provided information about St Edmund.[81] And although St Cuthbert's prospered in an area which was little affected

---

[77] *Passio S. Eadmundi*, 68. I have suggested elsewhere that possibly the *Passio*'s explicit comparison of St Edmund with St Cuthbert is a late eleventh-century interpolation, Gransden, 'Baldwin', 73–4.

[78] *Passio S. Eadmundi*, 85, 83. *Hist. de S. Cuthberto*, 209.

[79] Robin Fleming, 'Monastic lands and England's defence in the Viking Age', *EHR* c (1985), 265.              [80] Ibid. 247–65 passim.

[81] *Passio S. Eadmundi*, 67.

by the monastic revival, St Edmund's flourished in eastern England where there was no lack of reforming activity.

The shrine churches of St Cuthbert and St Edmund exemplify a marked characteristic of Anglo-Saxon religious life, the cult of saints. But that tradition was rooted in the Anglo-Saxon past, dating back to the period of the conversion to Christianity. Bede proves its existence in the seventh and eighth centuries. Although subsequently, until the mid-tenth century, evidence is scarce, it is known that King Alfred venerated saints: he apparently visited a saint's shrine in Cornwall to be cured of an infirmity.[82] The tenth-century reformers showed a lively interest in the cult of Anglo-Saxon saints. Perhaps their enthusiasm was fanned by Pope Gregory's letter to Mellitus, bishop of London, preserved in Bede's *Ecclesiastical History*;[83] Gregory recommended the use of relics as a means of encouraging popular worship. Bede himself informed the reformers about the seventh-century Anglo-Saxon saints. (It was under his influence that St Oswald excavated the bones of Northumbrian saints.)[84] But the reformers were also influenced by the continental example. Fleury claimed to have the body of St Benedict, and it was a monk of Fleury, Abbo, who wrote St Edmund's *Passio*.

The reformers recognised that relics gave prestige to individual churches. St Oswald used the relics of the Northumbrian saints for his attempted refoundation to Ripon. Having built a suitable church, he placed the bone of St Wilfrid, Ripon's original founder, together with those of the other saints, in a shrine. 'Ædificauit nouae Hierosolymae portas, construxit ipsius coenobii noua fundamenta, quae ad perfectionem perfecit et cum simplicitate cordis Deo obtulit.'[85]

Of all the reformers, St Ethelwold did the most to exploit the cult of saints in his monasteries. Ely had, as it were, inherited the body of St Ætheldreda; St Ethelwold included her feast, with full-page portrait, in his benedictional.[86] He was also active in acquiring relics for those of his foundations which had none. A contemporary writes that St Ethelwold gained King Edgar's permission 'to move those bodies of saints which lay in desolate, neglected places, where formerly noble churches had stood, to the new monasteries so that they could be venerated by the faithful as was fitting'.[87] He lavished relics on Thorney; 'every corner of

[82] *Asser's Life, cap.* lxxiv. 55. Cf. Keynes and Lapidge, *Alfred the Great*, 254–5. For the cult of relics in Anglo-Saxon England see Max Förster, *Zur Geschichte des Reliquienkultus in Altengland*, Munich 1943. Cf. D. W. Rollason, 'Lists of saints' resting-places in Anglo-Saxon England', *A-SE* vii (1978), 61–93 passim esp. at p. 81.

[83] *HE*, i. 30: i. 64–6.     [84] *Vita S. Oswaldi*, 462.     [85] Ibid. Cf. above p. 43.

[86] *The Benedictional of St. Æthelwold*, facsimile ed. by G. F. Warner and H. A. Wilson, Oxford 1910, 37.

[87] *Liber vitae: Register and Martyrology of New Minster and Hyde Abbey, Winchester*, ed. Walter de Gray Birch, London 1892, 286. Cf. Sheerin, 'Dedication of the Old Minster', 266 n. 4; and Alan Thacker, 'Æthelwold and Abingdon', in Yorke, *Bishop Æthelwold*, 59–63.

the church was crammed with them'.[88] Of particular interest is St Ethelwold's promotion of the cult of St Swithun, bishop of Winchester (852 × 3–862 × 5), in the Old Minster.[89] St Swithun, it was said, began to make known the presence of his body in the Old Minster in 968. Meanwhile, St Ethelwold was rebuilding the cathedral on a grand scale. On 15 July 971 he had St Swithun's body translated to a suitable shrine, and on 20 October 980 he solemnly dedicated the new cathedral, in the presence of King Ethelred and a vast concourse of people, including St Dunstan. The occasion and St Swithun's miracles were described by an eyewitness, the monk Lantfred, in the *Translatio et miracula Sancti Swithuni*.[90] It is not clear whether St Ethelwold in the first instance rebuilt the cathedral in order to provide a shrine church for St Swithun or whether he promoted the cult in order to increase his cathedral's prestige and help finance the rebuilding. However, the latter motives seem more likely; if they were his reasons, his choice of St Swithun could indicate an additional motive. Possibly he, in connivance with King Ethelred, intended to placate the clerks of the old dispensation, to whose class St Swithun had belonged.[91] The magnificent ceremony of the dedication can be seen as symbolising the healing of the breach between the clerical party and the monastic one, a breach which had been expressed by open hostility during the anti-monastic reaction following King Edgar's death.

It can be said that, although the tenth-century monastic revival was inspired by influences from abroad, it marked no break with the Anglo-Saxon tradition. That tradition had survived into the tenth century in an attenuated form, in the clerical communities. Benedictine monasteries replaced a few of the old communities, but the reformers, who had themselves grown up in the native tradition, did not treat the clerks as harshly as might at first appear. They preferred co-operation to confrontation; some clerks joined the new monasteries, and at least three clerical communities survived intact and prospered. The reformers turned for guidance mainly to the past, especially to the tradition's fountain-head, the Northumbrian renaissance, as revealed by Bede. Thus guided they were able to keep their movement in line with the indigenous tradition of Anglo-Saxon monasticism, at the same time supplementing it with what they learned from abroad.

[88] *Willelmi Malmesbiriensis monachi de gestis pontificum Anglorum libri quinque*, ed. N. E. S. A. Hamilton (Rolls Series, 1870), 327.

[89] Sheerin, op. cit. 264–70. Forthcoming is Michael Lapidge's important book, *The Cult of St Swithun* (Winchester Studies IV. 2), Oxford 1990.

[90] Ed. E. P. Sauvage in *Analecta Bollandiana* iv (1885), 367–410.

[91] Sheerin, op. cit. 269.

## II. *c.* 1000–*c.* 1100

St Ethelwold died in 984, St Dunstan in 988 and St Oswald in 992. The monks had already lost the patronage of a strong king with the death of Edgar in 975. Political instability had ensued, and law and order were soon further threatened by the resumption of Viking onslaughts. The extent of the injury which the Vikings inflicted on the monasteries is hard to assess, but it was greatest in East Anglia. Reputedly, they destroyed St Neots; the saint's body was moved to Crowland.[92] (They also seem to have disrupted the clerical community at Beadericesworth; according to tradition the body of St Edmund was taken temporarily for safety to London.)[93] Among those killed at *Assandun* (1016) were Wulfsige, abbot of Ramsey,[94] and a company of monks from Ely, who had gone there with their relics to pray for an English victory.[95] Nevertheless, there was no breach in the Anglo-Saxon religious tradition. The monks endeavoured, with a large measure of success, to preserve and continue the work of the reformers. They were as conscious as the reformers themselves had been of the inheritance from the Anglo-Saxon past – the recent, the more remote and the very remote past – and as anxious to be guided by it. Bede remained the predominant authority.

The cult of saints flourished in the late tenth and early eleventh centuries, as monastic liturgical calendars testify.[96] Eadnoth, abbot of Ramsey (993–1006), inherited St Oswald's love of relics. Inspired by a vision, it was said, he discovered the (supposed) body of St Ivo at Slepe and brought it to Ramsey.[97] As previously, cults were used to promote the prosperity of existing monasteries and to help establish new foundations. Eadnoth, continuing in a modest way St Oswald's policy of expansion, founded a small monastery at Slepe, the site of St Ivo's invention.[98] Perhaps he was also responsible for the translation of St Neot, whose shrine became the heart of another little monastery. This is suggested by the facts that the translation to Eynesbury apparently took place in Eadnoth's day and that St Neots, as the house was henceforth called, was endowed by Ramsey's lay patron, Æthelwine the ealdorman.[99] Mean-

---

[92] *Gesta pontificum*, 321; *Liber Eliensis*, ed. E. O. Blake (Camden Society, 3rd series xcii, 1962), 102. Cf. Cyril Hart, 'The East Anglian chronicle', *Journal of Medieval History* vii (1981), 279; and most recently, *The Anglo-Saxon Chronicles, a Collaborative Edition*, ed. David Dumville and Simon Keynes, xvii = *The Annals of St Neots with Vita prima Sancti Neoti*, ed. David Dumville and Michael Lapidge, Cambridge–Woodbridge, 1984, p. lxxxix.

[93] Hermann, *De miraculis S. Eadmundi*, i. 40–6.

[94] *Chron. Ram.* 118; *Lib. Eli.*, 148.          [95] Ibid. 148.

[96] See C. E. Fell, 'Edward king and martyr and the Anglo-Saxon hagiographic tradition', in *Ethelred the Unready: papers from the millenary conference*, ed. David Hill (British Archaeological Reports, British series lix, 1978), 1 ff.

[97] *Chron. Ram.*, 114–15; *Lib. Eli.*, 141.          [98] *Chron. Ram.* 115; *Lib. Eli.*, 141.

[99] Ibid. 103–4; cf. *Chron. Ram.*, 96. It was apparently in Eadnoth's day that the cult of St Neot first developed in the monastery at Eynesbury; see Marjorie Chibnall, 'History

while, Eadnoth's family endowed both Slepe and the nunnery which Eadnoth had founded at Chatteris, making his sister abbess.[100]

Moreover, at this time the claims to sanctity of SS Dunstan, Ethelwold and Oswald received literary recognition. St Dunstan's *Life* was written by the anonymous 'B'.[101] Two of St Ethelwold's pupils, Ælfric, monk of Cerne, previously a monk of the Old Minster, Winchester, perhaps the best known scholar of his day, and Wulfstan, reputedly precentor of the Old Minster, wrote biographies of him.[102] At Ramsey an anonymous author, who has been identified as the scholar, Byrhtferth, wrote a *Life of St Oswald*.[103] These Lives were intended to do more than depict their subjects as saints; they are not just hagiographies but have many features of 'straight' biography. They record the saints' achievements as reformers against the background of the tenth-century revival. They show particular interest in the saints' foundations and clearly intend the saints to shed reflected glory on them. The biographers were especially concerned in this respect with their own monasteries; for example, St Oswald's biographer, a monk of Ramsey, was at pains to include much information about that house.[104] In varying degrees the Lives were intended to foster cults. Ælfric and Wulfstan wrote partly to promote the cult of St Ethelwold in the Old Minster; therefore, they described the posthumous miracles which took place at St Ethelwold's shrine in the cathedral.[105] Already, during the tenth-century revival itself, hagiographies had been produced to support specific cults: the monk Lantfred had contributed to St Ethelwold's promotion of the cult of St Swithun in the Old Minster, with his *Translatio et miracula Sancti Swithuni*; and Abbo of Fleury, while staying at Ramsey, *c.* 986–8, had composed the *Passio Sancti Eadmundi* to promote St Edmund's cult at Beadericesworth. Even earlier, in the reign of Edred (946–55), a member of the clerical community at Ely, which preceded St Ethelwold's monastic foundation there, had written on the miracles of St Etheldreda.[106]

These early eleventh-century biographers were reviving a well-

of the priory at St Neots', *PCAS* lix (1966), 69; and *Annals of St Neots with Vita prima*, pp. lxxxvii–xcii. It should be noted that Christopher Hohler rejects the view that St Neot was translated from Cornwall; he argues that the Cornish St Neot and the Huntingdonshire one were two separate people; see Gransden, *Historical Writing*, 49 n. 52.

[100] See Hart, 'East Anglian chronicle', 277–9; and idem, 'Eadnoth, first abbot of Ramsey and the foundation of Chatteris and St Ives', *PCAS* lvi–lvii (1964), 61–7.

[101] Printed, and its authorship discussed, in *Memorials of Saint Dunstan*, pp. x–xxvi, 3–52. Cf. Brooks, *Early History*, 245–6.

[102] Ælfric's *Vita* and Wulfstan's *Vita gloriosi* are printed in *Three Lives*, 17–29 and 33–63. They are not independent authorities; see ibid. 2.

[103] Printed in Raine, *Historians of the Church of York*, i. 399–475. The case for Byrhtferth's authorship, based mainly on philological evidence, has been made most recently by Michael Lapidge, 'The hermeneutic style in tenth-century Anglo-Latin literature', *A-SE* iv (1975), 90–4; see 91 nn. 2–3 for references to the works of previous scholars who have discussed the problem of the authorship of the *Vita S. Oswaldi*.

[104] See e.g. *Vita S. Oswaldi*, 429–34, 447, 468, 475.

[105] *Three Lives*, 28, 62–3.            [106] *Lib. Eli.*, p. xxxii.

established, Anglo-Saxon, biographical tradition (It should, however, be remembered that, abroad, the tenth-century continental reformers were also the subjects of rather similar biographies.)[107] The practice of writing the biography of a saint or other churchman shortly after his death began during the Northumbrian renaissance. The biographers of SS Ethelwold and Oswald knew their respective saints well ('B' may have been an exception in this respect), like the biographers of the Northumbrian period. Although the Lives of saints produced during the Northumbrian period can be classed as 'hagiographies', they contain much non-hagiographic material. The Lives of St Cuthbert by an anonymous monk of Lindisfarne and by Bede[108] have much reliable information about St Cuthbert. Similarly, the anonymous *Life of Abbot Ceolfrid*,[109] Bede's *Lives of the Abbots of Wearmouth/Jarrow*[110] and the *Life of Wilfrid*, by Eddius Stephanus (or 'Stephanus' as it now seems we should call him),[111] are all free of the miraculous element. Moreover, the Lives of St Cuthbert, the *Life of Abbot Ceolfrid* and the *Life of Wilfrid* have information respectively about the monasteries of Lindisfarne, Wearmouth/Jarrow and Wilfrid's foundations at Hexham and Ripon, while Bede's *Lives of the Abbots of Wearmouth/Jarrow* is virtually a history of those twin houses. Nevertheless, one purpose of some of the Northumbrian saints' Lives was to foster cults. Thus the Lives of St Cuthbert were written partly to promote his cult at Lindisfarne. An even better example is the *Life* of Pope Gregory the Great composed at Whitby early in the eighth century;[112] its principal intention was to promote St Gregory's cult at Whitby, which claimed to have a relic of him. It is clear, therefore, that the Northumbrian renaissance provided would-be biographers of the tenth-century reformers with a usefully varied biographical tradition. It is likely that the reformers consciously revived that tradition. The influence of Bede on Ælfric is well known; for instance, Ælfric drew heavily on the *Ecclesiastical History* for his *Lives of Saints*.[113] Similarly, Byrhtferth was a Bedan scholar. He compiled a miscellany which strongly shows the influence of Bede. From this he derived most of the material which he used for his *Enchiridion*, which is

[107] The continental Lives are fully described by Patrick Wormald in 'Æthelwold', passim.
[108] *Two Lives of St Cuthbert: A Life by an Anonymous Monk of Lindisfarne and Bede's Prose Life*, ed. and trans. Bertram Colgrave, Cambridge 1940, repr. 1985; 'Bedas metrische *Vita Sancti Cuthbert*', ed. Werner Jaager, *Palaestra* cxcviii (1935).
[109] In *Op. Hist.*, i. 388–404.    [110] Ibid. i. 364–87.
[111] *The Life of Bishop Wilfrid by Eddius Stephanus*, ed. and trans. Bertram Colgrave, Cambridge 1927, repr. 1985. Cf. David Kirby, 'Bede, Eddius Stephanus and the Life of St Wilfred', *EHR* xcviii (1983), 101–14.
[112] *The Earliest Life of Gregory the Great by an Anonymous Monk of Whitby*, ed. and trans. Bertram Colgrave, Lawrence, Kan. 1968.
[113] See J. H. Ott, *Über die Quellen der Heiligenleben in Ælfrics Lives of Saints*, i. inaugural dissertation, Halle 1892, 44–7; and Ruth Waterhouse, 'Ælfric's use of discourse in some saints' lives', *A-SE* v (1976), 83–91. For Ælfric's use of Bede's *De temporum ratione, De temporibus* and *De natura rerum* for his *De temporibus anni* see *Ælfric's De temporibus anni*, ed. Heinrich Henel (EETS, orig. ser. ccxiii, 1942), pp. liii–lvi.

virtually a commentary on Bede's books on time.[114] The *Life of Oswald* has what appears to be a borrowing from Bede's prose Life of St Cuthbert.[115]

The Anglo-Saxon religious tradition continued in the late tenth and early eleventh centuries despite the facts that, after the death of Edgar, the monks lacked a strong royal patron and then suffered to an indeterminate degree from Viking incursions. After the accession in 1016 of Cnut the monks once again had a staunch royal supporter and one who imposed peace on the country. Even before he became king, Cnut had connections among the monks: Æthelwine, abbot of Abingdon (1016–30), was his friend, and Ælfweard, first a monk of Ramsey and then abbot of Evesham, his relative.[116] The chronicles of Ramsey, Abingdon and Ely have passages eloquent in his praise.[117] (Although these three chronicles were compiled after the Conquest, in Henry II's reign, they contain much pre-Conquest material.)[118] The Ramsey chronicler appreciated that Cnut's merit lay, not only in his respect for the Church and his patronage of the monks, but also in his success in the secular sphere – in establishing the rule of just laws throughout his empire; in the same way his personal virtue combined piety and love of peace with martial skill. The chronicler writes:

Interea Cnuto rex Christianissimus, nulli praecedecessorum suorum regum comparatione virtutum vel bellica exercitatione inferior, coepit sanctam ecclesiam enixissime venerari et religiosorum causis virorum patrocinari, eleemosynis profluere, justas leges vel novas condere vel antiquitus conditas observare. Quumque non solum Angliae sed et Daciae simul et Norguegiae principaretur, erat tamen humilitate cernuus, usus venerei parcus, alloquio dulcis, ad bona suadibilis, ad misericordiam proclivis, amatorum pacis amator fidissimus, in eos autem qui vel latrocinio vel depraedatione jura regni violassent ultor severissimus.[119]

Cnut, indeed, had political motives as well as religious ones for patronising the monks. No doubt he was pious and approved of monks, but there were practical reasons for winning their favour. Since he was by

[114] Byrhtferth's miscellany survives only in a late eleventh-century copy, St John's College, Oxford, MS 17. It contains many of Bede's works. See P. S. Baker, 'Byrhtferth's *Enchiridion* and the computus in Oxford, St John's College 17', *A-SE* x (1982), 123–42. I am grateful to Dr Lapidge for calling my attention to this manuscript. The *Enchiridion* is printed in *Byrhtferth's Manual*, ed. J. S. Crawford (EETS clxxvii, 1929). For the use of Bede in the *Manual* see Crawford's footnotes and Heinrich Henel, 'Byrhtferth's *Preface*: the Epilogue of his *Manual*', *Speculum* xviii (1943), 290. For the influence of Bede on Byrhtferth in general see Michael Lapidge, 'Byrhtferth of Ramsey and the early sections of the *Historia regum* attributed to Symeon of Durham', *A-SE* x (1982), esp. at pp. 120–1.

[115] *Vita S. Oswaldi*, 448. Raine suggests, probably wrongly, that Bede's metrical *Life of St Cuthbert* was the source, ibid. 448 n. 1.

[116] *Chronicon Monasterii de Abingdon*, 2 vols, ed. Joseph Stevenson (Rolls Series, 1858), i. 433. *Chron. Eve.*, 83.

[117] *Chron. Ram.*, 125–6 (extract cited below); *Chron. Ab.*, i. 433; *Lib. Eli.*, 152–4. Henry of Huntingdon also eulogises Cnut, *Henrici Archidiaconi Huntendunensis Historia Anglorum*, ed. Thomas Arnold (Rolls Series, 1879), 188–9.

[118] See Gransden, *Historical Writing*, 273–5.          [119] *Chron. Ram.*, 125–6.

origins a Viking warlord and had seized the throne by force, he needed support; the monks were invaluable allies. Possibly Cnut saw himself, and wished to be seen, as a second King Edgar. One version of Cnut's laws states in the preliminary matter that his councillors were determined to 'zealously observe Edgar's laws'.[120] In fact, although his codes draw partly on the laws of Edgar, they are more indebted to those of Ethelred. This disparity between claim and actuality suggests that Cnut wanted to be identified with the successful Edgar, not with the unfortunate Ethelred.

Cnut was a generous benefactor of the monasteries. He gave lands, for example, to the Old Minster, Winchester,[121] Bury St Edmunds[122] and Sherborne.[123] Sometimes he helped monasteries, for instance Abingdon and Ramsey, to acquire lands. And he made gifts of relics and other treasures, for example to Abingdon,[124] Evesham,[125] the New Minster, Winchester,[126] and to Christ Church, Canterbury.[127] According to post-Conquest tradition Cnut founded two monasteries, St Benet of Holme and Bury St Edmunds. However, the evidence for his foundation of these houses is by no means beyond dispute.[128] The evidence that he founded a nunnery at Ramsey is more convincing. It occurs in the Ramsey chronicle; the relevant passage reads:

... Ramesensem ecclesiam, circumquaque suavem spirantem jam bonae opinionis odorem, plurimum diligens, in ipsa insula quandam aliam ecclesiam juxta primam, eiusdem formae sed quantitatis paulo dissimilis, datis de fisco regio sumptibus, in honorem Sanctae Trinitatis construi fecit. In qua quum coetum monialium aggregare decrevisset, ut, sicut in altero monasterio collegium virorum, sic in hoc quoque chorus feminarum sedulum Deo obsequium exhiberet...[129]

---

[120] The so-called D version of 1018. See A. G. Kennedy, 'Cnut's law code of 1018', *A-SE* xi (1983), 62, 64, 72 (I owe this reference to Dr Simon Keynes). Whitelock argues that this version of Cnut's laws and also Cnut I and II were the work of Wulfstan I, bishop of Worcester 1002–16 and archbishop of York 1002–23; Dorothy Whitelock, 'Wulfstan and the laws of Cnut', *EHR* lxiii (1948), 433–52. Her conclusion is strongly supported with additional evidence by Kennedy, op. cit. 57–66. Whitelock, op. cit. 442–3, also contends that Wulfstan regarded Edgar's reign as a Golden Age. Since Wulfstan wrote the codes for Cnut and was the king's friend, it can be assumed that Cnut agreed with his views.

[121] Sawyer, *Anglo-Saxon Charters*, 292 no. 972.

[122] Ibid. 293–4 no. 980. Only part of this charter is apparently authentic; see Harmer, *Anglo-Saxon Writs*, 433–4.     [123] Sawyer, op. cit. 292 no. 975.

[124] *Chron. Ab.*, i. 433–4.     [125] *Chron. Eve.*, 83.

[126] A picture, executed c. 1020, of Cnut and Emma placing a large gold cross on the altar of New Minster, Winchester, is BL MS Stowe 944, fo. 6; reproduced, e.g. Frank Barlow, *Edward the Confessor*, London 1970, repr. 1979, plate facing p. 40. For a vivid (probably idealised) description of Cnut's demonstration of piety and his generosity when he visited St Bertin's and St Omer's, at St Omer in Flanders, see *Encomium Emmae reginae*, ed. Alistair Campbell (Camden Society, 3rd series lxxii, 1949), 36. His gift to the altar of each monastery was so large that it had to be brought not 'shut up in a bag' but 'wrapped in the folds of a cloak'.

[127] Harmer, op. cit. 168 and n. 1.

[128] See A. Gransden, 'The legends and traditions concerning the origins of the Abbey of Bury St. Edmunds', below pp. 90-104 passim.     [129] *Chron. Ram.*, 126.

Despite the Ramsey chronicle's late date (*temp.* Henry II), there seems no good reason for doubting its accuracy on this point. In this instance the chronicler had no obvious motive for fabrication. On the contrary, since his subsequent narrative shows that he was strongly opposed to any i'.ea of a nunnery next to a monastery, he might surely have been tempted to suppress such a piece of information. He follows the notice of the foundation with the statement that Cnut never fulfilled his plan; this was 'by divine providence', since 'it was not unknown how useful, or rather damaging, the close proximity of the sexes can be'. He observes that the crypt, which had lain underneath the high altar of the 'great church', could still be seen in his own day in the monks' cemetery.[130] We only have the chronicler's word for it that Cnut never brought his scheme to completion. Perhaps the chronicler was indulging in wishful thinking, unhampered by certain knowledge. By his time the climate of opinion tended to be hostile to 'double monasteries' – those comprising two houses, one for each sex – òf the Anglo-Saxon type. It is not impossible that a nunnery did exist for a while beside the monastery at Ramsey and that it subsequently languished to extinction from lack of support, leaving no trace except this notice in the Ramsey chronicle.[131]

Although Edward the Confessor is credited with no new monastic foundation, he restored and lavishly endowed Westminster Abbey,[132] besides being a generous benefactor of other houses.[133] In their patronage of the monks both Cnut and Edward the Confessor were supported by their queens, Emma and Edith, who were worthy successors of Edgar's queen, Ælfthryth, as patronesses of the religious. The *Regularis concordia* had made the queen responsible for the nuns;[134] Edith built a new church for those at Wilton.[135] Emma did not patronise the nuns in particular (unless her influence was responsible for Cnut's foundation of the nunnery at Ramsey), but she was generous to the monks. Goscelin, in his *Life of St Wulsin*, which he wrote towards the end of the eleventh century, relates

---

[130] 'Ex providentia tamen Dei, quam quid utilitatis aut damni ex vicinitate sexuum amborum provenire posset non latebat, propositum non implevit. Porro crypta, quae subtus majus ipsius ecclesiae altare fabricata fuerat, ejusdem aedificii testis et index, in coemiterio nostro hodieque indemnis perdurat': *Chron. Ram.*, 126.

[131] Dr Sally Thompson, whose book on post-Conquest nuns and nunneries is to be published by Oxford University Press, informs me that a number of post-Conquest nunneries disappeared leaving hardly any evidence of their previous existence, and that there must have been others which left no trace at all. Moreover, in the twelfth century it was not unusual for a monastery to act as protector to a group of nuns within its precincts (for example Christine of Markyate and her followers were sheltered by Geoffrey, abbot of St Albans). Later the tendency was for a nunnery under monastic protection to be founded at a distance from the monastery (an example is the nunnery of Sopewell, which was dependent on St Albans).

[132] *The Life of King Edward who Rests at Westminster*, ed. and trans. Frank Barlow, London 1962, 44–6.

[133] E.g. Bury St Edmunds, see Harmer, *Anglo-Saxon Writs*, 148–9, and Abingdon. See below p. 187 and n. 137.

[134] *Reg. con.* vii. 70.

[135] *Life of King Edward*, 46–9.

that Emma, during a visit with Cnut to Sherborne Abbey, was so shocked at the state of the roof of the church that she paid for its repair.[136] Queen Edith was also a benefactress of the monks. The Abingdon chronicler records her distress, when she visited Abingdon with Edward, to find that the monks, because of their poverty, could give the children of the cloisters nothing better to eat than bread. Therefore she persuaded Edward to grant jointly with her the vill of Lewknor  as an endowment to supply the boys with proper meals.[137]

Nevertheless, the position of the monks in religious life and in politics changed in the course of the eleventh century. No spiritual leaders of calibre comparable with that of Dunstan, Ethelwold and Oswald appeared. There were very few new foundations of importance. The most notable was Bury St Edmunds; some time fairly early in the century the clerical community serving St Edmund's shrine at Beadericesworth was replaced by a Benedictine one.[138] The tradition of the foundation of monasteries by the lay nobility just survived until the middle of the century. In about 1002 Wulfric Spott founded Burton, and in 1045 Leofric, earl of Mercia, and his wife Godgifu founded Coventry abbey.[139] Meanwhile, the monks' influence on the central government was on the wane. They lost their virtual monopoly of the episcopal bench.[140] One reason for this was that Edward the Confessor, who had spent the first thirty years or so of his life in Normandy and France, tended to give bishoprics to foreign clerics. Some of these men were trained in the Lotharingian school, whose reforms included the establishing of disciplined clerical communities in episcopal sees. Such were Edward's priests, Hermann, Leofric and Giso, to whom Edward gave Ramsbury (1045), Crediton (1046) and Wells (1060) respectively. However, the main reason why the monks lost their monopoly was the development of royal government. The king needed a permanent staff, and it was more convenient to use the secular priests of his own chapel rather than monks who belonged to their individual monasteries. Since the king had to reward the chaplains for their services, he gave some of them bishoprics. This development was already apparent in Cnut's reign.

The erosion of the monks' importance at the centre of national power encouraged the growth of localism, a trend not countered by any contrary force. The Rule of Benedict did not legislate for a unified order but for virtually autonomous monasteries; it provided no links between houses. It

---

[136] C. H. Taylor, 'The Life of St. Wulfsin of Sherborne by Goscelin', *Rev. Bén.* lxix (1959), 81 (*cap.* xiii). Emma also bequeathed a manor, Kirby Cane, to the Abbey of Bury St Edmunds, Harmer, *Anglo-Saxon Writs*, 148–9, 159 nos 16, 17.

[137] *Chron. Ab.* i. 460–1; ii. 283. See *Victoria County History, Oxfordshire*, 11 vols, 1939–83 (in progress), viii. 100.

[138] This is the argument I put forward, in preference to the traditional ascription of the foundation of the Benedictine monastery to Cnut, in the article cited above, n. 128.

[139] Frank Barlow, *The English Church 1000–1066*, 2nd edn, London 1979, 316.

[140] See R. R. Darlington, 'Ecclesiastical reform in the late Old English period', *EHR* li (1936), 395–6.

is true that, in England during the tenth-century revival, monasteries
founded by one or other of the spiritual leaders had been in close touch
with each other. But when the founders were dead, their 'families' of
houses tended to drift apart. Although Cnut and Edward the Confessor
were patrons of the monasteries, neither attempted to impose uniformity
on them by holding a synod comparable to Edgar's synod of Winchester.

Centrifugal tendencies had appeared early in the revival itself;
otherwise, the *Regularis concordia*, which was a product of a desire to impose
greater uniformity, would not have been necessary. Localism is a marked
feature of the *Life of St Oswald (c.* 1000); it is evident in the *Life*'s concern
for, and extensive information about, the early history of Ramsey
Abbey.[141] The cult of saints encouraged local attachments; a monastery's
patron saint became, as it were, its *persona*, and its relics in general added
to its individual reputation. The popularity of cults suffered no abatement
in the course of the eleventh century. Cnut himself was an enthusiast.[142]
(As has been seen, Ramsey under Abbot Eadnoth played an important
part in the dissemination of particular cults.) Nor did Eadnoth's
endeavours slacken after he became bishop of Dorchester (1007 × 9–1016);
his burial of the body of St Ælphege in London marked the start of the
cult of that saint.[143] Another Ramsey monk, Ælfweard, on becoming
abbot of Evesham (*c.* 1014–44), purchased relics of St Odulf for his new
home.[144] In this way the prestige of individual monasteries grew.

A monastery's prestige attracted gifts partly in the form of landed
property; and an increase in monastic estates led in its turn to an increase
in prestige. Indeed, during the period between the tenth-century revival
and the Norman Conquest endowment of the Anglo-Saxon foundations
was more lavish than at any other time in the history of medieval
England. In regard to monasteries in the east Midlands in general, and to
Thorney and Crowland in particular, a recent scholar has written:

The ultimate wealth and standing of any house was largely determined by its
date of foundation. Crowland and Thorney, like neighbouring Ramsey, Ely and
Peterborough, were among the richest because they were established early and
enjoyed the fruits of Anglo-Saxon patronage. It was in the pre-Conquest period
that they achieved their enduring control over land in the east midlands. Never
again was so much property to pass into the hands of the Church.[145]

The growth of monastic estates was not only owing to the patronage of
Anglo-Saxon kings, ecclesiastics, nobles and thegns. It was also indebted
to the ability of a number of outstanding abbots. For example, Æthelwig,
abbot of Evesham (1058–77), was spectacularly successful in increasing

[141] *Vita S. Oswaldi*, 429–34, 447, 463–8, 475.
[142] For Cnut's gifts of relics to monasteries see above p. 185 and nn. 125, 127. Cf. *Chron. Ab.* i. 433, and *Chron. Ram.*, 127.     [143] *Chron. Ram.*, 115.
[144] *Chron. Eve.*, 83.
[145] Sandra Raban, *The Estates of Thorney and Crowland*, Cambridge 1977, 88. Cf. below n. 147.

Evesham's landed property.[146] The result of the combination of the generosity of benefactors and the business acumen of abbots was that the holdings of at least a number of pre-Conquest foundations reached their greatest extent, despite fluctuations caused by Viking invasions, the rapacity of neighbours and political instability.[147] Moreover, to this period belongs the earliest evidence of the elaborate system of estate management which was to become common after the Conquest. The first surviving list of food-farms was drawn up for the Ely estates by Leofsige, abbot of Ely from 1029 to 1035. The system of food-farms was in fact well established and quite widespread before the Conquest; it certainly existed at Westminster, Abingdon, Bury St Edmunds, Peterborough and Ramsey, as well as at Ely.[148] At the same time the separation of the bishop's property from that of the monks was taking place in some cathedral monasteries. The similar division of property between abbot and convent was also probably evolving in the greater abbeys.[149]

The power of individual houses was increased by the grant of papal and royal privileges. It is impossible to be certain about the exact nature of these early privileges because the evidence tends to be scanty and its meaning obscure, and some of it is of dubious authenticity.[150] Already

[146] *Chron. Eve.*, 88–90, 94–6. For Æthelwig's career after the Norman Conquest see below p. 193.

[147] For the growth of the holdings of Thorney and Crowland in the late Anglo-Saxon period see Raban, op. cit. 6–29. Of Ramsey Professor Raftis writes, 'The long list of properties pertaining to Ramsey Abbey enumerated in [Domesday Book] is a fitting epitaph to the first century of growth... This Domesday map marked the end of an era of geographical expansion. It was the substantially complete ground plan upon which may be traced movements in agrarian history for the next four and one half centuries so that the list of properties compiled by Cromwell's inquisitors tallies markedly with that of his eleventh-century predecessor': J. A. Raftis, *The Estates of Ramsey Abbey*, Toronto 1957, 21. Dr Smith wrote of Christ Church, Canterbury, 'It is quite clear that the cathedral priory was primarily indebted to Saxon kings, nobles and thegns, for its vast endowment': R. A. L. Smith, *Canterbury Cathedral Priory*, Cambridge 1943, 9. The lands of Ely suffered considerable fluctuation during the period from the tenth-century monastic revival until the Conquest. They reached their greatest extent in the first decades of the eleventh century; see Edward Miller, *The Abbey and Bishopric of Ely*, Cambridge 1951, 16–25. For the formation of the Peterborough estates 966–1066 see Edmund King, *Peterborough Abbey 1086–1310*, Cambridge 1973, 6–11.

[148] See Miller, op. cit. 38; Raftis, op. cit. 34–5 and n. 42; Reginald Lennard, *Rural England 1086–1135*, Oxford 1959, 130–1 and n. 1, 132–3; and (with further references) Margaret Howell, 'Abbatial vacancies and the divided *mensa* in medieval England', this JOURNAL xxxiii (1982), 174 and n. 5.     [149] Ibid. 175–6 and nn.

[150] For the question of monastic exemption and protection in England and on the Continent, from the sixth to tenth centuries, see with further references, Wormald, 'Æthelwold', 21–2 and nn. 33–4, 23–4 and nn. 42–3, 34 and nn. 88, 89; and, for the early period, H. H. Anton, *Studien zu den Klosterprivilegien der Päpste im Frühen Mittelalter*, Berlin–New York 1975. I am indebted to Dr Rosamund McKitterick and Mr Wormald for help on this subject. Knowles's conclusions have, in fact, been more or less corroborated by later research. He believed that, in practice, a number of English monasteries before 1066 were free from subjection to the diocesan, though their *de facto* 'exemption' was rarely put to the test, M. D. Knowles, 'Essays in monastic history IV – the growth of exemption',

during the Northumbrian renaissance popes had granted privileges which gave virtual exemption from episcopal and royal authority. Benedict Biscop had obtained a privilege from Pope Agatho for Wearmouth/Jarrow ('pro tuitione sui monasterii'), stipulating that it should be free from outside interference ('ab omni prorsus extrinseca irruptione tutum perpetuo reddit ac liberum'). Pope Sergius confirmed this privilege at the request of Biscop's successor, Abbot Ceolfrid.[151] During the tenth-century revival the purpose of the privileges seems to have been to protect monasteries from oppression by the diocesan bishop (but probably not to prevent just episcopal supervision) and to give various degrees of freedom from temporal burdens. John xv apparently granted a privilege to Glastonbury, giving the monks the right to elect their own abbot and hold the Isle free from any outside interference.[152] Ramsey also claimed to have obtained a privilege from Pope John.[153] Moreover, during the revival, and in the eleventh century, kings alienated regalian rights to some of the greater abbeys. King Edgar granted extensive rights of jurisdiction to Worcester Cathedral and Ely.[154] Later such grants became more specific. Cnut gave royal rights of jurisdiction to Christ Church, Canterbury,[155] and probably to the Old Minster, Winchester.[156] Edward the Confessor was particularly generous to Bury St Edmunds, granting it the jurisdictional area of the eight-and-a-half hundreds, exemption from taxation and also the right to mint coins.[157]

Although there was great variation between monasteries, many flourished in the half century or so before the Norman Conquest, growing in prestige, wealth and power. The historian of Peterborough, then known as the 'Golden City', could write of Abbot Leofric (1052–autumn 1066): 'He did much for the benefit of the monastery of Peterborough,

*Downside Review* xxxi (1932), 211, 213, 225–6, 396, 401, 420–1. He concludes that 'it has become quite clear that the origins of exemption must be sought long before the Conquest, and that the changes within our period are precisions rather than developments': ibid. 423.

[151] Bede's *Lives of the Abbots*, vi, xv, in *Op. Hist.* i. 369, 380. Noticed by: Wilhelm Schwarz, 'Jurisdictio und Condicio. Eine Untersuchung zu Privilegia libertatis der Klöster', *Zeitschrift der Savigny-Stiftung für Rechtsgeschichte. Kanonistische Abteilung xlv* lxxvi (1959), 69–70; Heinrich Appelt, 'Die Anfänge des päpstlichen Schutzes', *Mitteilungen des Instituts für Österreichische Geschichtsforschung* lxii (1954), 106–7; Anton, op. cit. 62, 65.
[152] *The Early History of Glastonbury...William of Malmesbury's De antiquitate Glastonie ecclesie*, ed. and trans. John Scott, Woodbridge 1981, 129, 204. Noticed by Willy Szaivert, 'Die Entstehung und Entwicklung der Klosterexemtion', *Mitteilungen des Instituts für Österreichische Geschichtsforschung* lix (1951), 295.     [153] *Chron. Ram.*, 48.
[154] Unfortunately, certainty about the nature of the liberty of Oswaldslaw is impossible because our knowledge is dependent on charters of dubious authenticity, e.g. the *Altitonantis* charter, John, *Land Tenure*, 8off. and above n. 54. For Ely see Miller, *Ely*, 25–35.
[155] Sawyer, *Anglo-Saxon Charters*, 295 no. 985. Cf. Harmer, *Anglo-Saxon Writs*, 79, 168–71, 181–2 no. 26; and most recently and especially Brooks, *Early History*, 288–90.
[156] Sawyer, op. cit. 292 no. 976. Cf. Harmer, op. cit. 382, 397–8 no. 109.
[157] Ibid. 145–8 passim, 151, 156–65 passim. Cf. Gransden, 'Legends and traditions', below p. 92.

with gold and silver vestments and land, more indeed than any before or after him.'[158] Corporate pride served as a spur to the development of localism; monks were intent upon the interests, whether spiritual or temporal, of their own houses. Undoubtedly, this inward-looking mentality had some bad results. It could lead to corporate selfishness; one consequence of this could be unseemly quarrels between monasteries over land, relics and the like.[159] Nevertheless, the evils of localism can easily be exaggerated. Despite the existence in some monasteries of distinctive customs (for example, one which came perilously near to property owning by individual monks),[160] there is no evidence that, in general, the Rule of Benedict was flouted. Æthelwig, abbot of Evesham (1058–77), held maundies and was a generous alms-giver in accordance with the Rule.[161] There is even evidence that, at least at Christ Church, Canterbury, the *Regularis concordia* was not forgotten.[162] (As will be seen, the post-Conquest strictures on the Christ Church monks were ill-founded.) Moreover, on occasion monks resisted royal control. In 1052 those of Christ Church attempted, but failed, to elect one of their number to be head of their house – which meant, of course that he would also be archbishop.[163] In the same year the monks of Abingdon successfully insisted on their right to elect their abbot.[164]

Within the monasteries monks continued and developed the Anglo-Saxon cultural tradition, which had been revived during the tenth-century revival. Scholars now recognise the monks' achievements in many fields in the century prior to the Conquest. Evesham was especially famous for goldsmiths' work and sculpture under Abbot Mannig (1044–58).[165] The art of book illustration continued to thrive in a number of centres; the tenth-century technique of line-drawing survived, though its representational style was modified by Viking influence and by the infiltration of Romanesque art from France.[166] Vernacular literature, a tradition rooted in eighth-century Northumbria and promoted by King Alfred, also flourished.[167] The Anglo-Saxon Chronicle, which is disappointingly brief for the tenth century, has many detailed annals for the eleventh century in excellent prose, some of impressive power.[168]

---

[158] Whitelock, *Anglo-Saxon Chronicle*, 142 (s.a. 1066). Cf. Darlington, 'Ecclesiastical reform', 402.    [159] See e.g. *Chron. Ram.*, 118–19, 127–8, 166; *Lib. Eli.*, 135–6.

[160] See *Chron. Ab.*, i. 477. Cf. Knowles, *Monastic Order*, 80–1 and n. 4.

[161] *Chron. Eve.*, 90–3. Cf. *Sancti Benedicti Regula monachorum, cap.* liii.

[162] The only two surviving complete texts of the *Regularis concordia*, one of them probably post-Conquest, are from Christ Church; see Symons's edn, pp. liii–lix. For continued interest in it at Christ Church after the Conquest, see Southern, *St Anselm*, 245–8 passim.    [163] *Life of King Edward*, 18–19.

[164] *Chron. Ab.*, i. 463–4.    [165] *Chron. Eve.*, 86–7. Cf. Barlow, *English Church*, 336.

[166] Francis Wormald, *English Drawings of the Tenth and Eleventh Centuries*, London 1952, 49–53.

[167] See Peter Clemoes, 'Late Old English literature', in Parsons, *Tenth-century Studies*, 103–14, 230–3 nn.

[168] See Cecily Clark, 'The narrative mode of the Anglo-Saxon Chronicle before the Conquest', in Clemoes and Hughes, *England before the Conquest*, 230–3.

Particularly remarkable is a chronicle from 983 to 1044 composed retrospectively in the early 1040s at Abingdon; a copy soon went to St Augustine's, Canterbury, where it was incorporated into the Anglo-Saxon Chronicle. Its unusual feature is its strong political bias (in favour of the house of Godwin), which is in marked contrast to the non-committal tone of most annalistic writing.[169]

Pride in the possession of relics, themselves a source of prestige, was expressed in, and fostered by, the writing of hagiographies. The revival in the late tenth and early eleventh centuries of the Northumbrian tradition of sacred biography was sustained later in the eleventh century. A monk of Ramsey, probably Byrhtferth, supplied Evesham with a *Life* of its patron saint, Ecgwin.[170] (Contact between Ramsey and Evesham must have been encouraged by the succession *c.* 1014 of Ælfweard, a Ramsey monk, to the abbacy of Evesham.) It was probably later, in the mid-eleventh century, that a *Life of St Neot* was written for St Neot's.[171]

Hagiography, however, formed only part of the Anglo-Saxon tradition of sacred biography; a man did not need to be a saint to merit biographical attention. Although there is no evidence that complete biographies of churchmen other than saints were composed in the late Anglo-Saxon period, it is likely that biographical material highlighting particular activities of some such men was produced. It apparently concerned the abbots and benefactors of the specific monasteries where the authors wrote. An author's intention would have been partly to commemorate the individuals concerned but also, by recording in chronological sequence their associations with, and contributions to, the welfare of the monastery for which he wrote, to compose a virtual 'house history'. The prototype of 'house histories' structured round abbatial biographies was of course Bede's *Lives of the Abbots of Wearmouth/Jarrow*. Hitherto, scholars have neglected the possible existence of this type of literature in the late Anglo-Saxon period. The evidence for it is in the pre-Conquest sections of some post-Conquest chronicles. Just occasionally a chronicle refers to what seems to have been an early narrative source of this kind which is otherwise unknown. But the identification of a passage borrowed from a pre-Conquest abbatial history is nearly always suggested by another type of evidence: a passage may stand out from the adjoining narrative because of its precise and vivid detail and the sense of

---

[169] See David Dumville, 'Some aspects of annalistic writing at Canterbury in the eleventh and early twelfth centuries', *Peritia* ii (1983), 26–31, 38; Simon Keynes, 'The declining reputation of King Æthelred the Unready', in Hill, *Ethelred the Unready*, 227–53.

[170] See Lapidge, 'Hermeneutic style', 90–4; and idem, 'Byrhtferth and the *Vita S. Ecgwini*', *Mediæval Studies* xli (1979), 331–53. For the possibility that Byrhtferth also wrote for Ramsey Passions of SS Ethelred and Ethelbert, whose relics Æthelwine the ealdorman gave to the abbey, *Chron. Ram.*, 55, see idem, 'Byrhtferth of Ramsey', 119–20.

[171] See *Annals of St Neots with Vita prima*, pp. xciv–xcvi. Cf. Hart, 'East Anglian chronicle', 277–9; and idem, 'Eadnoth, first abbot of Ramsey and the foundation of Chatteris and St Ives', *PCAS* lvi–lvii (1964), 61–7.

immediacy it conveys. Such a passage could, of course, derive from some lost work written shortly after, and not before, the Conquest, based on oral information and the author's own observation. However, the impression that some post-Conquest chronicles did use pre-Conquest abbatial histories is deepened by comparison with other post-Conquest writings. For instance, Hermann's *De miraculis Sancti Eadmundi*, written by a monk of Bury St Edmunds *c.* 1100, shows the haziest knowledge of the abbots who preceded Baldwin (1065–98); this suggests that Bury had no pre-Conquest biographies of its abbots.[172] Even if we accept that a few monasteries did produce abbatial histories in the late Anglo-Saxon period, any such text can only be reconstructed very tentatively, since it could have been revised and interpolated at any time before the post-Conquest chronicler borrowed from it.

The chronicle of Abingdon, compiled in Henry II's reign and covering the period from the abbey's foundation to 1154, has considerable detail about the abbots from Siward (1030–44) to Ordric (1052–January 1066).[173] For instance, it has a graphic account of how the disreputable Abbot Spearhafoc (*c.* 1047–51), a goldsmith, packed the gold and jewels, which Edward the Confessor had given him to make a crown, into 'various receptacles' and absconded, never to be seen again.[174] The Abingdon chronicler certainly used the evidence of charters, many of which he copied in full.[175] He may also have drawn on the oral traditions of his house. But the fact that he was writing a century after the period in question, when memories were no longer fresh, combined with the precise detail and vivid touches in some of his narrative, strongly suggest that, in addition, he used some now lost abbatial history, possibly a pre-Conquest one.

At Evesham a Life of Abbot Æthelwig was written shortly after his death (1077). This Life no longer survives as an independent work, but it was incorporated in the early thirteenth-century chronicle of Evesham which is still extant.[176] The latter also contains well-informed accounts of Æthelwig's predecessors, Ælfweard (*c.* 1014–44) and Mannig (1044–58).[177] The section on Mannig is particularly colourful and detailed. The biographer of Æthelwig testified to the truth of his narrative about Æthelwig and 'the others' ('tam de illo [i.e. Æthelwig] quam de aliis'). His authorities were, he states, ancient charters, oral information and his own observation ('Partim namque in antiquis cartis huius loci reperimus, partim a fidelissimis viris audivimus, partim nos ipsi oculis nostris perspeximus').[178] However, the words 'de aliis' are imprecise and need not refer to 'the other [abbots]'; they could mean 'other things' or 'other people' mentioned in the Æthelwig narrative. Therefore, the

---

[172] Cf. Gransden, 'Baldwin', 65.     [173] *Chron. Ab.* i. 443–5, 451–2, 461–4.
[174] See e.g. ibid. i. 434–42, 446–50, 452–7.     [175] Ibid. i. 462–3.
[176] *Chron. Eve.*, 87–96. Cf. for this Life R. R. Darlington, 'Aethelwig, abbot of Evesham', *EHR* xlvii (1938), 1–22, 177–98.     [177] *Chron. Eve.*, 81–7.
[178] *Chron. Eve.*, 94.

possibility remains that the chronicler used some pre-Conquest abbatial history for Ælfweard and Mannig.

The Ramsey chronicle, compiled in Henry II's reign, has a much fuller pre-Conquest section than either the Abingdon chronicle or the Evesham one. This section includes much biographical material, which is interspersed with other types of entry (notably copies of charters). The description of the abbey's foundation and its early years centres on the joint roles of St Oswald and Earl Æthelwine.[179] The chronicle then has entries, some substantial, about the abbots from Eadnoth (993–1006) to Athelstan (1020–43).[180] Most remarkable are a number of passages, some quite long and amounting in all to about twenty-five printed pages, about Ætheric, bishop of Dorchester (1016–34), who had been educated at Ramsey and was buried there. The great detail of these passages and their lively tone suggest that the chronicler copied them from some now lost Life of Ætheric. Whether this is so or not, they are now an integral part of the Ramsey chronicle (they overlap with the passages concerning individual abbots of Ramsey, which will be discussed below).

The first passage about Ætheric relates how he, when a scholar of Ramsey, climbed with three fellow pupils among the great bells of the church and set them ringing discordantly, so that one cracked.[181] The abbot forgave the boys, despite the monks' anger with them, partly out of kindness, but also because he believed that the boys, all of noble birth, would amply recompense the abbey later in life. The next passage[182] begins with a notice of Ætheric's succession to the bishopric of Dorchester. It then relates how he visited Ramsey to hear the complaints of Abbot Wythman (1016–20), a German by birth, against his insubordinate monks who were exasperated by the severity of his rule. Ætheric, perhaps moved by loyalty to previous companions, decided in the monks' favour and reprimanded Wythman for his unreasonable behaviour. Also relating to Ætheric is the passage, quoted above, recording Cnut's foundation of a nunnery at Ramsey; Cnut took this action at Ætheric's urging ('cuius hortatu').[183] The same is true of the notice that the body of St Felix was translated from Soham to Ramsey; this was done with Cnut's support, again at Ætheric's instance ('Cnutone rege precibus Ætherici episcopi favente').[184] The chronicle also notes the death of Ætheric and his burial at Ramsey, referring to him in eulogistic terms.[185]

Before this final entry about Ætheric are five long passages which form a highly distinctive part of the chronicle. They describe in vivid detail how Ætheric acquired estates for Ramsey.[186] He purchased or otherwise obtained them, not necessarily by scrupulous means, but always with Cnut's help, from local Scandinavian landowners. An example is the story

---

[179] *Chron. Ram.*, 29–45, 85–108.     [180] Ibid. 109–10, 112–19, 121–5, 127–8, 155.
[181] Ibid. 112–14.     [182] Ibid. 120–6.
[183] Ibid. 126.     [184] Ibid. 127–8.
[185] Ibid. 147.
[186] Ibid. 128–44. This section of the Ramsey chronicle is not cited in Raftis, *Estates*.

of his acquisition of Ellington (Hunts). He was accompanying Cnut as he travelled through his kingdom, but on this occasion there was not room for him to stay in the same vill with the king. He, therefore, together with four royal clerks, lodged with a Dane, who gave them generous hospitality. The Dane himself became very drunk and entered into a wager with Ætheric; he undertook to sell him his vill if Ætheric could raise the (nominal) purchase money of fifty marks by morning. As soon as his host fell asleep in drunken torpor, Ætheric sent one of the clerks riding post haste to Cnut. The clerk, who interrupted Cnut at a game of chess, obtained a loan from the king which enabled Ætheric to buy the estate.[187] Another story, which tells how Ætheric acquired Therfield (Herts) for Ramsey, reveals that Ætheric employed a local agent to purchase land as opportunity arose.[188] Besides illustrating how monastic landholdings were built up, these stories throw light on relations between the Anglo-Saxons and Scandinavian settlers. Ætheric acquired two vills, Therfield and Shillington (Beds), because the Danish landowners fled through fear of the English.[189]

The Ramsey chronicle attributes Ætheric's generosity to Ramsey to his wish to recompense the abbey for cracking the bell.[190] In addition, the chronicle has information about the careers and achievements of the three other bell-crackers: Athelstan, who became abbot of Ramsey;[191] Eadnoth, who, after being a monk of Ramsey, succeeded Ætheric as bishop of Dorchester;[192] and Oswald, St Oswald's nephew, who became a monk of Ramsey and a noted writer and poet.[193] Bishop Ædnoth was, like Ætheric, a generous benefactor of his old home,[194] and Oswald, together with Abbot Wythman, persuaded Edward the Confessor to give lands and rights, which are specified in the chronicle, to Ramsey.[195]

The question arises as to the possible nature of the early biographical sources of the pre-Conquest section of the Ramsey chronicle. (The chronicler's use of charter evidence and of oral information is well known, although the extent to which he used the latter is impossible to determine.)[196] Information from some of these literary sources may have reached him indirectly through an intermediate source or sources. One intermediate source can be tentatively identified. An appreciable portion of the pre-Conquest section is in flowery Latin, characterised by the use of unusual words and verbose sentences, biblical quotations and direct speech. If passages in this prose style are isolated, they can be roughly

---

[187] *Chron. Ram.*, 135-40.  [188] Ibid. 142.

[189] Ibid. 140, 143.

[190] Ibid. 128-9, 146. Similarly, the chronicle attributes the gifts of another of the bell-crackers, Bishop Eadnoth, to penitence for his part in the incident.

[191] Ibid. 124, 127, 155.  [192] Ibid. 148, 159.

[193] Ibid. 159-60. For Oswald see Lapidge, 'Hermeneutic style', 94-5.

[194] *Chron. Ram.*, 159.  [195] Ibid. 159-60.

[196] In my emphasis below on the likelihood that the Ramsey chronicle used pre-Conquest written narrative sources, I revise the view expressed in my *Historical Writing*, 275, that it leaned heavily on oral evidence.

divided into two groups. The first mainly concerns the close co-operation of St Oswald and Earl Æthelwine in the foundation and early years of Ramsey. The second group includes the description of the bell-cracking incident and the culprits' later careers. Both groups have some thematic unity. The theme of the first group is the close friendship and co-operation of St Oswald and Æthelwine, who are jointly credited with Ramsey's foundation and successful early years; their partnership is given visual expression by the image of the twin towers of the abbey church.[197] The theme of the second group is provided by the bell-cracking incident itself, which forms the starting point for the accounts of the benefits done to the abbey by the four boys later in life. The ornate prose of the passages is reminiscent of the literary style of the forged charter, purportedly of King Edgar, granting privileges to the abbey. A copy of the charter occurs in the chronicle, introduced and followed by passages in the same style.[198]

It seems likely, therefore, that some of the chronicle's pre-Conquest sources suffered embellishment at about the time when the Edgar charter was concocted (perhaps even by the forger himself). Pierre Chaplais attributes the forgery to the Westminster monk, Osbert of Clare, who died *c.* 1170.[199] If Osbert did forge the Edgar charter, the dates of his period of literary activity make him a possible candidate also for the authorship of some of the flowery passages in the chronicle; the latter has an account of the rule of Abbot Walter (1135–60) which is partly in flowery prose.[200] However, it would be extremely rash to argue that all instances of this style in the chronicle must be post-Conquest, rasher still to attribute them, even tentatively, to one author. Ornate Latin was characteristic of prose-writing at Ramsey (and in many other monasteries) in the late Anglo-Saxon period and was fairly widespread after the Conquest and throughout the Middle Ages.

Most of the chronicle's flowery passages concerning St Oswald and Æthelwine were elaborations of information found in the first *Life of St Oswald*.[201] Other early written sources probably lie behind much of the rest of the narrative in the pre-Conquest section, both flowery and that in simple prose. The wealth of apparently contemporary detail leads to this conclusion. The latter is, moreover, supported by explicit references. Thus, the chronicler admits that he does not know why Abbot Ælfweard

---

[197] The towers of the late tenth-century church at Ramsey were obviously impressive; they are described in *Chron. Ram.*, 41. The main tower of the first stone church cracked and had to be rebuilt, ibid. 85–8. The image of St Oswald and Earl Æthelwine as the two towers originated in the early *Life of St Oswald*, i. 469; it states that a monk had a vision of the fall of the two towers, presaging the deaths of St Oswald and Earl Æthelwine. This idea is elaborated in *Chron. Ram.*, 102–3 passim.

[198] Ibid. 68–70 and n. 2 For the charter itself see ibid. 181–9; and Sawyer, *Anglo-Saxon Charters*, 254–5 no. 798.

[199] Pierre Chaplais, 'The original charters of Herbert and Gervase abbots of Westminster (1121–1157)', in *A Medieval Miscellany for Doris Mary Stenton* (Pipe Roll Society lxxvi, NS xxxvi, 1960), 92.

[200] *Chron. Ram.*, 325–36.          [201] See ibid. p. xxiv.

was afflicted with illness (he suffered from leprosy), because 'the chronicles are silent' ('Cuius valetudinis causam quamlibet chronica taceant').[202] The nature of this reference suggests that 'the chronicles' were domestic histories of the abbey. Again, to substantiate his statement that St Oswald acted as abbot of Ramsey during his lifetime, the chronicler appeals to a document containing monastic professions made in St Oswald's presence ('schedae quaedam in ecclesia nostra hodieque reperiuntur professiones virorum temporis illius in presentia ejus celebratas continentes').[203] Whether this document included any biographical details about the monks is impossible to say. However, another of the chronicler's references is perhaps more relevant to the investigation of his sources. For his account of Athelstan the 'Half-King', father of Ramsey's lay patron, Æthelwine, and his family, he cites the authority of a certain ancient document containing the names of kings and other benefactors of the abbey, noting their gifts:

Fidejubent sermonis nostri veritatem quaedam in archivis ecclesiae nostrae repertae vetustissimae scedulae, eorundem regum nomina et quibusdam personis factas ab eisdem terrarum donationes continentes; quae donationes etiam ab ipsis personis postmodum ecclesiae nostrae in perpetuam eleemosynam cum earundem scedularum munimento sunt collatae, in quarum singulis vir ille inter alios nobiles earundem donationum testis invenitur ascriptus.[204]

Since Athelstan was not (so far as is known) himself a benefactor of Ramsey, he must have been included in the document because he was Æthelwine's father. A very rough parallel would be the inclusion of a Life of Oda, St Oswald's uncle, in the *Life of St Oswald*.[205] His inclusion suggests that the document was quite a substantial work. Possibly the passages in the chronicle about Ætheric, including the narratives describing his acquisition of landholdings for Ramsey, were copied from it. If, indeed, it did contain this amount of detail, it would be comparable to the *Libellus quorundam insignium operum beati Æthelwoldi episcopi* composed to record St Ethelwold's acquisition of property for his monastery at Ely.[206] (A similar, but much shorter and more concise work was written to record St Ethelwold's gifts to another of his foundations, Peterborough.)[207] A distinctive feature of the *Libellus* is its use of charters containing lively narratives of how (purportedly, at least) St Ethelwold acquired the land.[208] The narratives in the Ramsey chronicle describing

[202] *Chron. Ram.*, 157.                [203] Ibid. 41–2.

[204] Ibid. 12–13. Cf. with references to the Ramsey chronicle, including this passage, Cyril Hart, 'Athelstan "Half King" and his family', *A-SE* ii (1973), 115–44.

[205] *Vita S. Oswaldi*, 401–10. Cf. Armitage Robinson, 'St Oswald', 38–42.

[206] The *Libellus quorundam insignium operum beati Æthelwoldi episcopi*, which was the source for much of book ii of the *Liber Eliensis*, was a translation of an OE work composed in the late tenth century, *Lib. Eli.*, pp. ix–x, li. (A new edn, with trans. and discussion, is being prepared by Simon Keynes and Alan Kennedy.) For two documents from Rochester, which contain graphic narrative similar to that found in the documents copied in the Ely *Libellus*, see Robertson, *Anglo-Saxon Charters*, 84–7, 122–5.

[207] Printed ibid. 72–5. Cf. ibid. 75–83.                [208] *Lib. Eli.*, pp. ix–x.

Ætheric's land acquisition could derive ultimately from similar charters. Some such charter could also underlie the account in the Abingdon chronicle of how Abingdon obtained Lewknor (Oxon) from Queen Edith and Edward the Confessor.[209]

It has been argued above that there is a distinct possibility that at least some of the biographical material in the pre-Conquest sections of the chronicles of Abingdon, Evesham and Ramsey was written before the Conquest. If so, it indicates considerable historiographical activity on a local level. But even if some, or all, of this material is post-Conquest, the information it contains is of value. The written record, as such, is no more reliable than near-contemporary, oral testimony, while personal observation carries more weight than either. The details preserved in these chronicles show that there were many admirable abbots and generous benefactors of the monks in the eleventh century prior to 1066. They give a generally favourable picture, which is what the other evidence leads one to expect.

The Norman Conquest could have resulted in irreparable damage to the monasteries. Not only did their estates suffer depredation and usurpation, but their cultural and intellectual inheritance was threatened with extinction. Although, of the thirty-five or so pre-Conquest abbots, only about half a dozen fled or were deposed, when, one by one in the course of nature, the others died, the Anglo-Saxon succession lapsed; the last Anglo-Saxon abbot to die was Wulfstan of Worcester in 1095.[210] At the same time the episcopal bench had undergone Normanisation. Reform was in the hands of foreigners. Significantly enough, Lanfranc's *Constitutiones* are based on continental sources;[211] they betray no debt to the *Regularis concordia*, though they were intended for Christ Church, Canterbury, which possessed at least two copies of it. Lanfranc and other newcomers, both ecclesiastical and lay, had no knowledge of, nor sympathy for, the saints whom the Anglo-Saxons venerated.[212] Moreover, monastic prestige suffered from Norman apologists. The latter contended that William won at Hastings because he had God's support and apparently considered that one of the most praiseworthy results of the Conquest (and by implication one of its justifications) was the reform of

---

[209]  *Chron. Ab.*, 459–61. See above p. 59.

[210]  See Knowles, *Monastic Order*, 103–6, 111 ff.

[211]  Lanfranc's principal sources were the customs of Cluny; see Rose Graham, 'The relation of Cluny to some other movements of monastic reform', *JTS* xv (1914), 179–95 at pp. 184–5. The article is reprinted in idem, *English Ecclesiastical Studies*, London 1929, 1–29. Cf. *The Monastic Constitutions of Lanfranc*, ed. David Knowles, London 1951, pp. xii–xiii.

[212]  For Lanfranc's attitude see *The Life of St. Anselm Archbishop of Canterbury by Eadmer*, ed. and trans. R. W. Southern, London 1962, 50–4. For aspersions cast by Norman lords on St Edmund and his cult see Hermann's *De miraculis S. Eadmundi*, i. 97, 86. Cf. most recently James Campbell, 'Some twelfth-century views of the Anglo-Saxon past', in idem, *Essays in Anglo-Saxon History*, London 1986, 209 ff.

the Church carried out by Lanfranc with William's backing.[213] To highlight the reform movement Anglo-Norman writers denigrated the condition of the Anglo-Saxon Church on the eve of the Norman invasion.[214] Wholesale denigration injured the reputation of all the monasteries, but some houses suffered even worse because they were subjected to particular criticism.

However, the complete Normanisation of any monastery took time, since the pre-Conquest monks remained for the term of their lives. The amount of dislocation depended on how soon it acquired a foreign abbot and on what kind of man he was. But, without exception, the monasteries had to defend their privileges, landed property and prestige. The monks were successful partly because they had built up the strength of their houses earlier in the eleventh century. They defended privileges and landholdings by appealing to pre-Conquest charters, often revised and rewritten to meet new needs, by forging more charters if necessary and by obtaining royal confirmations. They defended their houses' prestige by proliferating hagiographies of patron saints.[215] Thus, they used the past to protect them in the present. Indeed, they met the challenge of the Norman settlement by infusing fresh vitality into their own tradition.

The Anglo-Saxon practice of writing a Life of a recently dead head of a house is known to have survived in two monasteries. At Worcester two monks, Hemming and Coleman, each wrote a *Life of Wulfstan*, bishop of Worcester (d. 1095);[216] and at Evesham a monk wrote the *Life of Abbot Æthelwig* (d. 1077).[217] Hemming's *Life of Wulfstan* and the *Life of Æthelwig* record in detail, in typically Anglo-Saxon fashion, their subjects' acquisition of property for their monasteries. Coleman's *Life of Wulfstan* has another feature characteristic of a number of pre-Conquest biographies: it is divided into sections according to subject matter. There are three sections concerning: first, Wulfstan's early life and education;

[213] It seems fair to assume that Eadmer's attitude reflects Norman propaganda; for his account of Lanfranc's reforms etc. see *Eadmeri Historia novorum in Anglia*, ed. Martin Rule (Rolls Series, 1884), 12–17. For the Norman view of Lanfranc see *Guillaume de Poitiers: Histoire de Guillaume le Conquérant*, ed., with French trans., Raymonde Foreville, Paris 1952, 126–9.

[214] Eadmer asserted that the monasteries were almost totally destroyed in Edward the Confessor's reign, *Hist. nov.*, 5. William of Malmesbury denigrated the pre-Conquest Church in general, including the monasteries. Eadmer particularly attacked the monks of Christ Church, Canterbury.

[215] For Osbern's and Eadmer's hagiographies, with references, see Southern, *Saint Anselm*, 248–51, 277–85. For those of the professional hagiographer, Goscelin, see *Life of King Edward*, 91–111.

[216] *Hemingi Chartularium ecclesiae Wigorniensis*, 2 vols, ed. Thomas Hearne, Oxford 1723, 403–8. Coleman's work, which was in OE, only survives in William of Malmesbury's Latin translation, *The Vita Wulfstani of William of Malmesbury*, ed. R. R. Darlington (Camden Society, 3rd ser. xl, 1928).

[217] *Chron. Eve.*, 87–96. Cf. Darlington, 'Æthelwig', 1–22, 177–98. For this biographical form, of which the earliest example in England is Asser's *Life of King Alfred*, see Gransden, op. cit. 51–2, 56, 88.

secondly, his episcopate; and, thirdly, his character, personal habits and miracles. These divisions closely resemble those of Ælfric's *Life of St Ethelwold*. But most remarkable is the fact that Coleman's *Life of Wulfstan* was in Old English (it survives only in William of Malmesbury's Latin translation) – surely a piece of conscious revivalism. At the same time the Anglo-Saxon tradition of historical writing was continued. It has recently been shown that Christ Church, Canterbury, was a hive of historiographical activity, all within the bounds of the Anglo-Saxon tradition; new annals were written and the Anglo-Saxon Chronicle was continued.[218] A copy of the Chronicle went from Christ Church to Peterborough, where it was continued until the accession of Henry II.[219] Worcester probably had more than one version of the Chronicle, one of which may have continued until 1130.[220] Some version (or versions) formed the basis of the Latin chronicle by the Anglo-Norman monk of Worcester, known as 'Florence', and of his continuator, John of Worcester.[221]

A measure of the monks' success was the quick recognition by the new regime of their immediate value and of the value of their past tradition. William the Conqueror soon realised that they were potentially useful allies because of their knowledge of, and power in, the localities. He used both Wulfstan of Worcester and Æthelwig of Evesham as advisers and administrators to help maintain his authority in the difficult regions bordering on Wales.[222] The lavishness of his grants of privilege to Bury St Edmunds suggests that he intended to increase the power of this loyal outpost in the rebellious Fens and against the threat of invasion from Scandinavia.[223] The abbot, Baldwin, a Frenchman appointed by Edward the Confessor, having been Edward's physician, became William's. At the same time the new ecclesiastical establishment came to accept some parts of the Anglo-Saxon tradition. It realised. that, on a national level, the

[218] See Dumville, 'Aspects of annalistic writing', 23–57 passim. For the Christ Church versions of the Anglo-Saxon Chronicle in particular see ibid. 40 ff.; Whitelock, *Anglo-Saxon Chronicle*, pp. xi–xii.

[219] *The Peterborough Chronicle, 1070–1154*, ed. Cecily Clark, 2nd edn, Oxford 1970. Moreover, the Anglo-Saxon tradition of line-drawing continued to flourish at Christ Church in the generation after the Conquest. See Francis Wormald, 'The survival of Anglo-Saxon illumination after the Norman Conquest', *Proceedings of the British Academy* xxx (1944), 127–45. Professor Wormald later slightly revised the views which he had expressed there, *English Drawings*, 53 and n. 1, 54–8.

[220] Whitelock, *Anglo-Saxon Chronicle*, pp. xiv–xvi, xx.

[221] *Chron. ex Chronicis*; and *The Chronicle of John of Worcester, 1118–1140*, ed. J. R. Weaver, Oxford 1908. For the use of the Anglo-Saxon Chronicle by the Worcester chronicler/ chroniclers see *English Historical Documents*, 120; Martin Brett, 'John of Worcester and his contemporaries', in *The Writing of History in the Middle Ages. Essays presented to Richard William Southern*, ed. R. H. C. Davis and J. M. Wallace-Hadrill, Oxford 1981, 111 and n. 3, 123–4 and n. 1. For the attribution of the chronicle to 1118 to Florence see Brett, op. cit. 104 and n. 3; below, pp. 116-17.'

[222] *Vita Wulfstani*, pp. xxvii–xxviii; *Chron. Eve.*, 89.

[223] Gransden, 'Baldwin', 67.

Church in England and, locally, each individual church, could only profit from having an ancient and often glorious history.

Anglo-Saxon saints regained respect, and the Anglo-Saxon biographical and historiographical traditions were turned to Anglo-Norman uses. Thus, Eadmer, monk of Christ Church, Canterbury, continued and developed the Anglo-Saxon biographical tradition. The subject of his biography, St Anselm, Lanfranc's successor as archbishop of Canterbury and previously prior of Bec, was one of the newcomers. Like earlier Anglo-Saxon biographers Eadmer knew his subject well; he was a member of Archbishop Anselm's household and keeper of his chapel and relics. He divided his biography, in typically Anglo-Saxon fashion, according to subject matter; it is in two parts: the *Life of St Anselm* concerns St Anselm's spiritual life and the *History of Recent Events* his 'public' career.[224] Although the two parts jointly constitute the biography, Eadmer has developed the Anglo-Saxon structural mode to such an extent that they form two separate, though complementary, books. Similarly, the Anglo-Saxon historiographical tradition was useful to the new generation. But it had to be made accessible and attractive to the new, French-speaking monks. One purpose of the spate of annalistic writing in Latin at Christ Church was to enable them to learn about Anglo-Saxon history[225] in general and about the history of Christ Church in particular. This must also have been one reason why a parallel Old English and Latin version of the Anglo-Saxon Chronicle was made there.[226] At the same time 'Florence', writing at Worcester, while using the Anglo-Saxon Chronicle as the principal source of information about English history for his (Latin) chronicle, included appropriate material about Norman and French history derived from continental sources (mainly from Marianus Scotus) to suit new interests.[227]

There is no better illustration of Norman co-operation with the Anglo-Saxons in preserving tradition and continuity than the mission to the north of England in 1077.[228] An Anglo-Saxon, Aldwin, prior of Winchcombe, was inspired to missionary activity by reading Bede and decided to refound the monasteries of Wearmouth and Jarrow. He was joined by two Anglo-Saxon monks from Evesham. The Norman bishop of Durham, Walcher, gave them the sites of Wearmouth and Jarrow, where

---

[224] Printed respectively: *Life of St Anselm*; *Hist. nov.*

[225] See Dumville, 'Aspects of annalistic writing', 54–5.

[226] F. P. Magoun (ed.) in 'Annales Domitiani Latini: an edition', *Mediaeval Studies* ix (1947), 235–95. It should, however, be remembered that the translation of the Anglo-Saxon Chronicle into Latin had begun well before the Conquest. Both Asser and Æthelweard translated substantial portions for their works. See *Asser's Life of King Alfred*, pp. lxxxii–lxxxix; Keynes and Lapidge, *Alfred the Great*, 55–6; *The Chronicle of Æthelweard*, ed. and trans. Alistair Campbell, London 1962, pp. xxiii, xxxvii.

[227] Brett, 'John of Worcester', 110–11 and n. 1.

[228] *Symeonis monachi Opera Omnia*, i. 9–11, 108 ff. Cf. Knowles, *Monastic Order*, 166 ff. For Bede's influence on the revival see above pp. 7 and n. 30, 8 and Davis, *op. cit.* (above p. 29).

they built huts for themselves and those who joined them under the ancient ruins. Walcher was himself a student of Bede and planned to refound a monastery in St Cuthbert's see at Durham, but it was his successor, another Norman and also a student of Bede, William of St Carilef, who finally, in 1083, did so. Thus, Anglo-Saxons and Normans together attempted to restore Northumbrian monasticism, and also to continue the work of the tenth-century reformers, by promoting the reflorescence of monasticism in the north.

Anglo-Norman historiography reflects both the initial hostility of the two peoples' mentalities and their partial reconciliation. The Normans' implied claim that they invaded in order to reform a corrupt Church was in actuality contradicted by those monks who were intent on recording, even glorifying, the achievements of their abbots. In the next generation Anglo-Norman historians adopted a view of the past which, to some extent, reconciled Norman propaganda with Anglo-Saxon pride. Its chief architects were Eadmer and William of Malmesbury. Both were of mixed parentage; they were at once Normans and fervent believers in the reforms of their own times and Englishmen acutely conscious that their heritage was in peril. Their divided loyalties must have made them the more anxious to produce some kind of historiographical reconciliation. Eadmer saw a pattern, which William of Malmesbury elaborated, in the history of Anglo-Saxon monasticism. The foundations of the tradition were laid during the Northumbrian renaissance, when monasticism reached a height of excellence never to be surpassed in England. Then followed a period of decline, leading to the extinction of monastic life. The latter was revived in the last half of the tenth century, a period of outstanding achievements. But again decline followed, the result in the first instance of the Viking incursions. This decline reached its nadir on the eve of the Norman Conquest and was followed by another great period of reform, that initiated by Lanfranc and carried through with William the Conqueror's help.[229] This historiographical pattern had the advantage that it allowed the Anglo-Saxon Church a glorious tradition but did not detract from the importance of the Anglo-Norman reformation. The glory of the Anglo-Saxon tradition depended on the two peak periods, of which even the most recent was well in the past, and the Anglo-Norman reformation put an end to years of decadence. Moreover, the reformation was in line with the two great periods of the Anglo-Saxon era; it was their worthy successor.

Eadmer's scheme had much truth in it and was, as a whole, perfectly plausible. The towering figure of Bede stood witness to the Northumbrian renaissance, and there was no doubt about the subsequent decline of strict monastic observance. Available evidence about the tenth-century revival

---

[229] See *Hist. nov.*, 3–5. Cf. Southern, *Saint Anselm*, 309–12; *Willelmi Malmesbiriensis monachi De gestis regum Anglorum libri quinque*, 2 vols, ed. William Stubbs (Rolls Series, 1887–9), i. 304–6.

was quite sufficient to substantiate the claims in its favour, while that for the period which followed was too scanty to disprove the theory of decline. When William of Malmesbury did research for his *Gesta pontificum*, a virtual gazetteer of monastic England, he could discover hardly anything about the eleventh century. He saw the very lack of contemporary sources, representing the monks' silence, as damning, an indication of intellectual stagnation.[230]

There is ample evidence for Anglo-Norman interest in the Northumbrian renaissance and in the tenth-century revival. Bedan studies underwent a dramatic resurgence[231] and were accompanied by the proliferation of copies of the *Ecclesiastical History*. Bede himself was eulogised, notably by Symeon of Durham and William of Malmesbury, and the *Ecclesiastical History*, the principal source for early Anglo-Saxon history, was the means of informing the Norman settlers of their new country's origins. Historians saw themselves as Bede's continuators, even as his humble imitators. Bede's influence on the actual progress of the Anglo-Norman reformation is well illustrated by the above-mentioned renewed monastic impetus in the north. Anglo-Norman interest in the tenth-century revival is shown, for example, by the fact that a number of important works written then were recopied in the late eleventh and early twelfth centuries. Indeed, to this period belongs the apparently sole surviving manuscripts of Ælfric's *Life of St Ethelwold*[232] and of St Ethelwold's treatise on King Edgar's Establishment of the Monasteries,[233] one of the only two extant manuscripts of the *Regularis concordia* and an important manuscript of St Ethelwold's translation of the Rule of Benedict.[234] The three earliest manuscripts of Abbo's *Passio Sancti Eadmundi* are late eleventh-century,[235] and the five earliest manuscripts of Wulfstan's *Life of St Ethelwold* are all twelfth-century.[236] The Anglo-Norman historian, Orderic Vitalis, produced a reworked version of the latter.[237]

---

[230] Ibid. i. 1–2; *Gesta pontificum*, 328, 331.

[231] For more details about Bede's influence in the Anglo-Norman period, with references, see above pp.7-16.    [232] *Three Lives*, 6.

[233] Printed most recently in *Councils and Synods*, 142–54. Armitage Robinson, *Times of St Dunstan*, 160–7, argues that the treatise is post-Conquest. Dorothy Whitelock, however, contends that it is by St Ethelwold, Whitelock, 'The authorship of the account of King Edgar's establishment of the monasteries', *Philological Essays, Studies in Old and Middle English Language and Literature in Honour of Herbert Dean Meritt*, ed. J. L. Rosier, The Hague–Paris 1970, 127–36. Whitelock makes a good case for dating the composition of the work to the revival. Nevertheless, she ignores the passage in the narrative which, as Robinson points out, is reminiscent of one in William of Jumièges; this parallel suggests that the narrative was at least revised after the Conquest.

[234] Cotton MS Faustina A X; N. R. Ker, *Catalogue of Manuscripts Containing Anglo-Saxon*, Oxford 1957, 194–5, 196 no. 154 B, art. 1. Printed in Schröer, *Die Angelsächsischen Prosabearbeitungen*.    [235] See Gransden, 'Baldwin', 72, 75 and nn. 146–8.

[236] *Three Lives*, 7.

[237] Printed in Jean Mabillon, *Acta sanctorum Ordinis S. Benedicti*, 9 vols, Paris 1668–1701, vii. 608–24; PL cxxxvii. 81–104. Michael Winterbottom. 'Three Lives of St. Ethelwold', *Medium Ævum* xli (1972), 196–9.

The Anglo-Norman historians were undoubtedly influenced by the tenth-century revival. Eadmer, in fact, linked his own times with the tenth-century revival by means of a theory of history. This theory underlies his historiographical pattern described above in so far as the latter relates to late Anglo-Saxon monasticism. It is based on an interpretation of an alleged prophecy of St Dunstan to King Ethelred.[238] St Dunstan said that, because Ethelred had seized the throne by shedding the blood of his brother, Edward the Martyr, his reign would be one of bloodshed; he would suffer constant invasion from abroad and his kingdom would be continually wracked by the cruellest oppression and devastation. The Viking invasions had followed (the initial cause of monastic decline) and then the Norman Conquest, and so St Dunstan's prophecy had been fulfilled. Eadmer also alleged that St Dunstan appeared in a vision to Lanfranc to encourage him during his struggle to defend the privileges of the church of Canterbury.[239] He saw St Dunstan's co-operation with King Edgar as foreshadowing that of Lanfranc and Anselm with William the Conqueror.[240]

Similarly, the Anglo-Norman historians were influenced in their writing of local history by what information they had about the tenth-century revival. They continued the Anglo-Saxon practice of seeking *topoi* from the past in order to fill gaps in their knowledge. Eadmer, William of Malmesbury and others, who were determined to prove the antiquity and unbroken history of particular monasteries, could often discover nothing about a house's foundation, unless it were early enough to have been recorded by Bede. Ignorance about monastic history from the late eighth century until the tenth-century revival was general and profound. Therefore, local historians turned to the revival itself for plausible hypotheses about what had happened. The entry under 964 in the Anglo-Saxon Chronicle saying that King Edgar expelled the clerks from the Old and New Minsters at Winchester and from Milton and Chertsey was a favourite *topos*. Another seems to have been Ælfric's and Wulfstan's statement that, on Edgar's authority, St Ethelwold gave the clerks of the Old Minster the choice of becoming monks or leaving and that the clerks left, although three of them later returned to join the new community.[241] Thus 'Florence of Worcester' (*c.* 1100) asserts (s.a. 963) that Edgar ordered the reformers to expel clerks living in communities throughout Mercia and to replace them by monks or nuns. He also states that, as a result, St Oswald expelled those clerks from Worcester Cathedral who refused to become monks and gave the habit to those who agreed,

---

[238] *Hist. nov.*, 3–5.    [239] Ibid. 18.

[240] Ibid. 3, 5. See Sally Vaughn, 'Eadmer's *Historia novorum*', *Proceedings* x (1987), 269, 276, 286. Professor Vaughn also argues that Eadmer found a number of archetypes for Lanfranc and Anselm in Bede's *HE*, ibid. 263–85. The evidence for Eadmer's use of such archetypes is implicit, not openly expressed. Nevertheless, Professor Vaughn's argument conforms with my idea of the Anglo-Saxons' backward-looking mentality and certainly, in the case of St Dunstan, is convincing.

[241] *Three Lives*, 23, 45.

appointing a monk of Ramsey, Wynsige, to be their prior.[242] Writing later, the Ramsey chronicler gives much the same account as Florence of Worcester, but in one respect he seems to follow Ælfric more closely; he asserts that Wynsige was a clerk of the old community whom St Oswald sent for training to Ramsey, before restoring him to Worcester to rule the new monastery.[243] William of Malmesbury claims that St Dunstan expelled the clerks from Malmesbury Abbey and introduced monks; similarly he alleges that Wulfsige, bishop of Sherborne (? 993–1001/2), expelled the clerks from, and established monks in, his cathedral.[244] Again, the historian of Ely (*temp.* Henry II) asserts that St Ethelwold expelled the clerks from Ely in order to introduce monks.[245]

The case of Bury St Edmunds presented a special problem since two weighty authorities, Abbo and Ælfric, made it clear that in their time, the late tenth century, St Edmund's shrine was still served by a clerical community.[246] The monastic foundation was, therefore, post-Edgarian. Nevertheless, the abbey's first historian, Hermann (writing *c.* 1100), and his successors seem to have used *topoi* drawn from the tenth-century revival for their accounts of the foundation. In fact they may well have had virtually no information about it. Hermann claims that the clerical community was replaced by a monastic one in Cnut's reign, with the king's consent and on the advice of Bishop Æflwine.[247] The Bury monk, who interpolated a copy of the chronicle of 'Florence of Worcester' in Henry I's reign, elaborated on this. He alleged that Cnut, on Ælfwine's advice, moved the clerks 'to other places' and established monks.[248] Here he was probably using the *topos* supplied by 'Florence' himself, who presumably had derived it from his principal source for pre-Conquest history, the Anglo-Saxon Chronicle.[249] The Bury interpolator also claims that Cnut gave the clerks the choice of becoming monks and staying or of leaving with adequate provision.[250] Once more his immediate model may have been 'Florence'; the ultimate source was probably Ælfric or Wulfstan. According to Hermann's narrative, one of the clerks, the

---

[242] Edgar ordered SS Dunstan, Oswald and Ethelwold 'ut, expulsis clericis, in majoribus monasteriis per Merciam constructis monachos collocarent. Unde S. Oswaldus, sui voti compos effectus, clericos Wigorniensis ecclesiae monachilem habitum suscipere renuentes de monasterio expulit; consentientes vero hoc anno, ipso teste, monachizavit, eisque Ramesiensem coenobitam Wynsinum, magnae religionis virum, loco decani praefecit': *Chron. ex Chronicis*, i. 141.       [243] *Chron. Ram.*, 40–1.

[244] For the 'refoundation' of Malmesbury Abbey see William of Malmesbury's *Vita S. Dunstani*, 301. William says nothing about the expulsion of clerks from Malmesbury in the *Gesta pontificum*, an earlier work; see ibid. 407. For Sherborne see ibid. 178.

[245] *Lib. Eli.*, 74. The passage stating that he expelled the clerks was an interpolation, presumably *temp.* Henry II, into the late tenth-century *Libellus*.

[246] *Three Lives*, 82 ff.; *Ælfric's Lives of Saints*, ii. 327 ff.

[247] Hermann, *De miraculis S. Eadmundi*, 47. See Gransden, 'Legends and traditions', 10 ff.

[248] *Memorials of St Edmund's Abbey*, i. 341–2.

[249] *Chron. ex Chronicis*, i. 141.

[250] 'aut in eodem loco ad religionis culmen erexit, aut datis aliis rebus de quibus abundantius solito victum et vestitum haberent': *Memorials of St Edmund's Abbey*, i. 342. Cf. above p. 172.

sacristan Æthelwine, did in fact stay.[251] Here again the model was probably Ælfric, who states that Eadsige, sacristan of the previous clerical community in the Old Minster, Winchester, became a monk there.[252]

The attribution by Eadmer and other Anglo-Norman historians of the decline of monasticism, which followed the tenth-century revival, in the first instance to the Viking incursions may be another example of literary borrowing. But the model was not provided by the tenth-century revival; at that time the preceding decline was ascribed, possibly partly under Bede's influence, to excessive aristocratic power, which resulted in the secularisation of monasteries and the loss of their property. Perhaps attribution to such a cause would have been distasteful to the Anglo-Norman historian, since it would have seemed suspiciously like an innuendo against the rapacity of the feudal lords of their own day. The model for the idea of the Vikings as the primary cause was probably St Dunstan's prophecy as described in Osbern's *Life of St Dunstan*.[253] Osbern was an Anglo-Saxon monk of Christ Church, who was already of mature age at the time of the Norman Conquest. After a difficult period of readjustment to the new era, he became the first monk to write Lives of the Canterbury saints.[254] Eadmer's well-known description of the pre-Conquest monks of Christ Church, Canterbury, should be seen in the light of this tendentious historiography, a historiography which often relied on literary models rather than on first hand observation or other sound evidence. Eadmer asserts that the monks lived

in omni gloria mundi, auro videlicet, argento, variis vestibus ac decoris cum pretiosis lectisterniis, ut diversa musici generis instrumenta, quibus saepe oblectabantur, et equos, canes et accipitres, cum quibus nonnunquam spatiatum ibant, taceam, more comitum potius quam monachorum vitam agebant.[255]

William of Malmesbury embroidered this description and claimed that it was applicable to most Anglo-Saxon monks before the Conquest.[256] Knowles took Eadmer's account seriously,[257] but Professor Darlington and Sir Richard Southern have pointed out that it does not accord with what other information we have about the Christ Church monks.[258] In general, historians have regarded the passage as reflecting Norman propaganda on the corruption of the late Anglo-Saxon Church. In fact, it could be at least partly a result of Eadmer's tendency to treat the Anglo-Norman monastic reformation as a reproduction of the tenth-century

[251] Ibid. i. 34–7, 53–4. Even Æthelwine's name is suspect, see Gransden, 'Baldwin', 73, 74. Cf. idem, below p. 94.    [252] *Ælfric's Lives of Saints*, i. 422–7.

[253] *Memorials of St Dunstan*, 127. Cf. ibid. 115; and Southern, *Saint Anselm*, 311. Asser, and Fulco, archbishop of Rheims, in his letter to King Alfred, had previously suggested that the Viking onslaughts were a cause of the monastic decline. Alfred, in his preface to Gregory's *Pastoral Care*, considers the invasions to have been God's punishment for the decline. See above p. 41 and n. 41.    [254] Southern, op. cit. 248–52.

[255] *Vita S. Dunstani*, 237–8.    [256] *Gesta pontificum*, 70–1.

[257] Knowles, *Monastic Order*, 79.

[258] Darlington, 'Ecclesiastical reform', 402 n. 2; Southern, *Saint Anselm*, 247 and n. 1.

revival. Possibly Eadmer based his criticisms on those levelled by late tenth-century writers against the clerks of the old communities whom the reformers ousted. Admittedly, Ælfric and the author of the first *Life of St Oswald* include among their strictures one on the clerk's non-celibate state, a criticism which Eadmer does not level at the Canterbury monks. However, he (and his audience) knew that the Anglo-Saxon monks were not married and believed them to have been celibate, but perhaps the mention of sumptuous bed-hangings (a detail omitted by William of Malmesbury) is an oblique reference to concupiscence.

## Conclusion

Historians have seen the tenth-century monastic revival and the Anglo-Norman reformation as two peaks of monastic excellence, each rising steeply from a plain of decadence. They have tended to attribute these peak periods to continental influence and to concentrate their research on the nature of that influence. At both periods the reformers themselves helped promote such a view. No doubt they saw their achievements in this light – and certainly wanted others to do so. This was because, in each case, they needed to justify, and gain support for, their takeover from the pre-existing religious 'establishment'. The Anglo-Norman reformers made this picture of the tenth-century revival even more spectacular; they regarded the reformers as their own prototypes and stressed the contrast between their high level of achievement and the low level of the previous era.

At neither period could the reformers afford to jettison the Anglo-Saxon tradition. To do so would have done irreparable damage to the prestige of the Church of England. Fortunately, there was no obstacle to prevent the tenth-century reformers from regarding the seventh century as a Golden Age; it served to emphasise the subsequent decline, which King Alfred had only partly, but they themselves had successfully, reversed. The Anglo-Norman reformers treated the seventh century in similar fashion, besides praising the tenth-century revival itself. In this way the reformers during both periods were able to shed reflected glory on their own movements and, by keeping within the Anglo-Saxon tradition, to make them more acceptable.

However, this historiographical scheme distorted historical reality. It resulted in a neglect of the achievements by religious communities in the two 'low level' periods and, worse still, led to their propagandist denigration. After the Norman Conquest a few local historians, urged on by the necessity at that hazardous time of defending the rights and prestige of their own monasteries, altered the picture in their particular regard. They showed much that was creditable to late Anglo-Saxon monasticism. This and other evidence suggest the conclusion that we should see English monastic history, at least before *c.* 1100, not in terms of plain and mountains, but of hills separated by gently undulating country.

# 3

## Legends and Traditions concerning the Origins of the Abbey of Bury St Edmunds

DAVID KNOWLES AND R. NEVILLE HADCOCK were aware of the difficulties which beset any scholar who tries to establish the precise date of the foundation of a pre-Conquest monastery. Indeed the origins of such houses were various and usually obscure.[1] The Scandinavian invasions caused a hiatus in English monastic history, and it is generally agreed that there was virtually no continuity between the period of Northumbrian monasticism and tenth-century revival. The post-Conquest houses were to all intents and purposes founded during and after that revival. The term, however, 'to found', is misleading. It denotes a multiple procedure: the formation of a monastic community, its endowment by charter, the construction of a church and monastic buildings, and the dedication of the church. The word is certainly applicable to Ramsey abbey, founded by St Oswald (bishop of Worcester 961–92, archbishop of York 972–92), in conjunction with Æthelwine the ealdorman. But is is only partially applicable to most of the other houses. Here, therefore, we use it to mean only the constitution of a regular community observing the Rule of St Benedict. The tenth-century revival marked the restoration of some ancient monasteries, notably Abingdon, Ely and Peterborough. It also saw the establishing of Benedictines in houses where there were already congregations of priests or 'canons' living semi-monastic lives. This, it seems, was the situation at Christ Church, Canterbury, Evesham, Glastonbury, Malmesbury, Winchester and Worcester. Little is known about these early congregations; pre-Conquest evidence is rare and, as will be argued below with reference to Bury St Edmunds, post-Conquest evidence should not be relied on. The priests served a cathedral or church, under the aegis of a patron saint whose relics they possessed. Three congregations, indeed, claimed to have the perfect, uncorrupt body of their patron saint; there was St Ætheldreda at Ely, St Cuthbert successively at Lindisfarne, Chester-le-Street and Durham, and St Edmund at Beodricesworth. Only in a few cases is it known with any degree of

---

1. David Knowles and R. Neville Hadcock, *Medieval Religious Houses, England and Wales* (2nd edn, London, 1971), p. 1.

certainty whether members of the pre-existing congregation stayed on, adapting themselves to the new regime, or whether they were replaced wholesale by Benedictines from elsewhere.[1]

The historian undertaking research into the origins of a pre-Conquest monastery is faced with the problem both of the paucity of contemporary evidence, and of the often biased nature of that and later evidence. The monks themselves distorted the historiography of their houses. In view of the importance attached to tradition in the Middle Ages, it is not surprising that they were eager to know their houses' history. They were interested in normal circumstance, but interest deepened in times of especial religious fervour, and of trouble. Then the monastic historian aimed to increase his monastery's fame, power and wealth by glorifying its patron saint, and when necessary by proving its rights to privileges and possessions. He would, therefore, embellish what facts he could discover with unwarranted detail, and if evidence was scanty or absent, he might use forged documents and resort to literary fabrication. Crowland, Glastonbury, Westminster and St Swithun's, Winchester, are all notorious for their tainted, tendentious histories. At first sight the origins of St Edmund's abbey present less problems than those of most houses. Scholars accept that it was founded nearly fifty years after the tenth-century monastic revival, by which time light had surely dawned. Indeed there are today a number of unquestioned beliefs about the abbey's foundation, and also about the pre-existing secular congregation, and its *raison d'être*, the cult of St Edmund – and even about the martyrdom itself. It is the purpose of this paper to examine the evidence for these beliefs, treating the subject chronologically, in order to discover how securely they are based.

The Anglo-Saxon Chronicle records s.a.870: 'that winter King Edmund fought against [the Danes], and [they] had the victory, and killed the king and conquered all the land'. The phrase 'þone cining of slogan' does not exclude the possibility that St Edmund was killed in battle and not martyred at all.[2] Numismatics prove that within twenty years of St Edmund's death, King Alfred promoted his cult and that it flourished in the Danelaw.[3] But after a while enthusiasm for the cult seems to have declined; no more St Edmund coins were minted

---

1.  Above pp. 42–4, below p. 94.

2.  *The Anglo-Saxon Chronicle*, a revised translation ed. Dorothy Whitelock with D. C. Douglas and S. I. Tucker (London, 1961), p. 46. Professor C. E. Fell has called my attention to the fact that St Olaf, king of Norway, was killed in battle (1030), but the tradition grew that he was martyred (Bollandists, *Acta Sanctorum*, July, vol. vii, p. 107). For a fourteenth-century picture of St Olaf's 'martyrdom', see *Islandske håndskrifter og dansk kultur. Udstilling på statens Museum for Kunst* (Copenhagen, 1965), p. 83. For another similarity between the St Edmund legend and that of St Olaf, see *infra* 87 and n. 6.

3.  C. E. Blunt, 'The St Edmund memorial coinage', *Proceedings of the Suffolk Institute of Archaeology*, xxxi (1970), pp. 234–55.

after about 910 or perhaps a little later, and St Edmund does not appear in the surviving liturgical calendars of the ninth, tenth and early eleventh centuries. However, at the time of the tenth-century monastic revival at least the potential of St Edmund's cult was sufficiently recognized for the monks of Ramsey to commission a Life of the saint, Abbo of Fleury's *Passio Sancti Eadmundi*.[1] The information in the *Passio* that the cult centred on a shrine of St Edmund at Beodricesworth is corroborated by the chronicle of Æthelweard the ealdorman and by *Resting Places*.[2] By this time the cult was popular enough for Ælfric to include an English rendering of the *Passio* in his *Lives of Saints*.[3] So far the evidence for the death of King Edmund and for the development of the cult to *c*.1000 is trustworthy. But Abbo puts flesh on this skeleton. He claims the highest authority. The prologue dedicates the work to St Dunstan and reveals that Abbo wrote it during his visit to Ramsey (985–7), at the request of the monks.[4] It also claims that Abbo's authority for St Edmund's martyrdom was St Dunstan himself: the latter when a boy had heard St Edmund's armour bearer telling King Athelstan, and Abbo had heard St Dunstan telling the bishop of Rochester and the abbot of Malmesbury.

It was normal in the middle ages for a religious community to commission a Life of its patron saint, and the question arises why the monks of Ramsey should have commissioned one of a saint buried elsewhere. The prologue suggests that St Dunstan himself may have originated the idea, or a request might have come from the congregation at Beodricesworth. However, although the *Passio* shows strong local attachment, it is not only to Beodricesworth – and to Ramsey – but also to the Fenland, on which it has a paean.[5] It is not improbable that Ramsey's founder, St Oswald, suggested that Abbo should write the *Passio*. His interest in the cult of saints is well known. As archbishop of York he searched for and found the relics of a number of Northumbrian saints. One Northumbrian saint, his namesake, St Oswald king and martyr, was of course an obvious parallel with St Edmund.[6] He might well have promoted St Edmund's cult

1. The most recent edition is in *Three Lives of English Saints*, ed. Michael Winterbottom (Toronto Medieval Latin Tests, 1972), pp. 67–87, the edition cited here. Another edition is in *Memorials of St. Edmund's Abbey*, ed. Thomas Arnold (Rolls Series, 1890–96, 3 vols.), i. 3–25.

2. *Passio*, p. 82; *The Chronicle of Æthelweard*, ed., with an English translation, A. Campbell (Nelson's Medieval Texts, 1962), p. 36; *Die Heiligen Englands*, ed. F. Liebermann (Hanover, 1889), pp. 13, 14; D. W. Rollason, 'Lists or saints' resting-places in Anglo-Saxon England', *Anglo-Saxon England*, vii (1978), pp. 61–93.

3. Printed in *Ælfric's Lives of Saints*, ed., with translation into modern English, W. W. Skeat (Early English Text Society, original series, lxxvi, lxxxii, xciv, cxiv, 1881–1900, 2 vols. in 4 pts), ii. 314–35, the editon used here. Another edition is in *Ælfric, Lives of Three English Saints*, ed. G. I. Needham (London, 1966), pp. 43–59.

4. *Passio*, p. 67.

5. *Passio*, pp. 69–70.

6. *The Historians of the Church of York*, ed. James Raine, jr (Rolls Series, 1879–94, 3 vols.), i. 462.

in order to add another illustrious name to the catalogue of East Anglian saints, an intention which would have appealed to the Ramsey monks. He may even have wanted to put East Anglia on a par with Northumbria. Abbo himself emphasizes the parallel between St Edmund and St Cuthbert, saying that if anyone doubts the uncorruption of St Edmund's body, he should remember the case of St Cuthbert.[1] Abbo relates that the Danish leader Ivarr captured St Edmund at 'Haeglesdun' (or, as here, 'Haegilisdun'),[2] had him tied to a tree, scourged, shot at with arrows, and finally beheaded. To prevent a decent burial, the Danes, as they returned to their boats, threw the saint's head into a thicket in 'Haeglesdun' wood.[3] Christians in the neighbourhood buried the body and when peace was restored searched for the head. At length the head attracted their attention by calling 'here, here, here', and they found it between the paws of an immense wolf, which was guarding it from other wild animals. The country folk, followed by the wolf, took the head back to their village. On arrival the wolf returned to the wood, and the villagers fitted the head back on to the body; the two miraculously reunited. The villagers buried the perfect uncorrupt body, which began to work miracles, and built a simple church over it. When the times were favourable (*ubi tempus oportunum invenit*) the body was moved to the royal vill (*villa regia*, presumably a vill owned by the king of East Anglia),[4] a suitable church built to house it, and lavishly endowed.[5] Abbo shows that the shrine was served by some kind of semi-monastic congregation. He also asserts that shortly before the time of writing (*Paulo ante nostra moderna tempora*) the body was cared for by a holy woman called Oswen, who cut its hair and nails every year.[6]

Historians have of course dismissed the miraculous elements in this story. However, they have in general treated the rest of it uncritically. The account of the martyrdom itself has been used as evidence for the way Danes executed their prisoners,[7] even for ritual sacrifice by

---

1. *Passio*, p. 68. None of the extant texts of the *Passio* was written before the Norman Conquest and the emphasis on the similarity between St Edmund and St Cuthbert could be the result of post-Conquest revision; see A. Gransden, 'Baldwin, abbot of Bury St Edmunds, 1065–1097', *Proceedings of the Battle Conference on Anglo-Norman Studies, iv, 1981* (Woodbridge, 1982), pp. 72, 73, 192, 193 nn. 99–108, 120–21, and *cf. infra* n. 4, and p. 93.

2. *Passio*, p. 73.

3. *Ibid*. p. 79.

4. *villa regia*: possibly a post-Conquest addition; see *infra*, p. 93 and n. 2. *Cf. supra*, n. 1.

5. *Passio*, p. 82.

6. *Ibid*. pp. 82–3.

7. Dorothy Whitelock, 'Fact and fiction in the legend of St. Edmund', *Proceedings of the Suffolk Institute of Archaeology*, xxxi (1970), pp. 221–2. Professor Whitelock states that 'the main facts of the martyrdom are likely to be true'. She cites as a parallel the martyrdom of St Ælfheah in 1012 by the Danes, who used him for target practice. But the parallel is not close since Ælfheah apparently was killed by being pelted with bones, stones and pieces of wood; *Anglo-Saxon Chronicle*, ed. Whitelock, pp. 91–2, and *Thietmar von Merseburg Chronik*, ed. Werner Trillmich (Ausgewählte Quellen zur Deutschen Geschichte des Mittelalters, ix, Berlin, 1962), p. 400. Whitelock ('The legend of St Edmund', p. 222 and n. 18) also states that 'the removal of the head is a well-evidenced practice among primitive peoples'; she cites three examples, none of which, however, resembles the case of St Edmund at all closely.

blood eagle.[1] This disregards the fact that there is no evidence in the literary sources that the body in the shrine had been riddled with arrows and beheaded. Abbo, in his account of St Edmund's translation to Beodricesworth, emphasizes that the body was perfect (*integer et uiuenti simillimus*), but had, as a sign of martyrdom, a thin red line like a thread of silk around its neck (*Tantum in eius collo ob signum martyrii rubet una tenuissima riga in modum fili coccinei*).[2] Allegedly the coffin was next opened and the body examined by Abbot Leofstan (?1045-1065), but more probably when St Edmund was translated to Abbot Baldwin's new church in 1095.[3] The occasion is described by Hermann who wrote c.1100 and was apparently a monk of Bury at that time. His *De Miraculis Sancti Eadmundi*[4] stresses the perfection of the body (*Jacet integer ut dormiens*).[5] He makes no mention of any mark around the neck, although he relates an improbable tale of how Abbot Leofstan conducted an experiment to see if the head had truly grown back on the body.[6] However, he does describe the body's clothing as blood stained and perforated with arrow holes (*Exuitur itaque sanctus sancti martyrii vestibus partim rubeis rubore sanguinis, partim perforatis ictibus telorum crebris*). The clothing was removed 'for restoration' for the salvation of the faithful (*sed tamen reponendis, saluti credentium profuturis*), and placed in the treasury.[7] Jocelin, of Brakelond, in his account of the examination of the body by Abbot Samson, similarly stresses the body's perfection and makes no allusion to any wounds.[8]

The signs of the martyrdom, the thin red line, the blood-stained, perforated clothing, mentioned in the sources, could obviously all have been fabricated by St Edmund's guardians. The absence of early evidence that the body in the shrine had suffered in the way Abbo

---

1. A. P. Smyth, *Scandinavian Kings in the British Isles 850-880* (Oxford, 1977), pp. 211-12, and J. M. Wallace-Hadrill, *The Vikings in Francia* (Reading, 1975), p. 10. Since I completed the present article, an article has appeared which throws grave doubt on the trustworthiness of accounts of the rite of the 'blood-eagle' in skaldic verse, and which discards the martyrdom of St Edmund as an example of the alleged rite for substantially the same reasons as I do (*infra* |87 and nn. 1, 2; see Roberta Frank, 'Viking atrocity and skaldic verse: the rite of the Blood-Eagle', *ante*, xcix (1984), 332-43).

2. *Passio*, c. 14, ll. 3-10 (p. 82).

3. A parallel would be the opening of St Cuthbert's tomb during his translation in 1104; *Symeonis Monachi Opera Omnia*, ed. T. Arnold (Rolls Series, 1882-5, 2 vols.), i. 247-61. *Cf. ibid.* i. 229 n.a., and *Symeonis Dunelmensis Opera Omnia*, ed. H. Hinde (Surtees Society, li, 1868), i. 188-97. For my reasons for doubting the story of the opening of St Edmund's tomb by Abbot Leofstan see 'Baldwin', p. 73. The story is accepted by N. Scarfe, 'The body of St. Edmund', *Proceedings of the Suffolk Institute of Archaeology*, xxxi (1970), 308-9.

4. Printed *Memorials of St Edmund's Abbey*, ed. Arnold, i. 26-92 (henceforth referred to as 'Hermann'). For Hermann see *infra* 89 and n. 7.

5. Hermann, p. 53.

6. *Ibid*, p. 54. I inadvertently overlooked this passage when I stated (citing *ibid*. p. 56) in 'Baldwin', p. 193, n. 116, that Hermann does not connect Leofstan's gout of the hands with this irreverent act.

7. *Ibid*. pp. 53-4.

8. *Chronicle of Jocelin of Brakelond*, ed., with an English translation, H. E. Butler (Nelson's Medieval Classics, 1949), p. 114.

describes has led to the suggestion that it was not St Edmund's.[1] On the other hand if it was St Edmund's, this fact undermines the credibility of the martyrdom account in the *Passio*. The latter interpretation is the most likely, since the narrative is little more than a hotchpotch of hagiographical commonplaces, a fact neglected by recent historians. Abbo himself remarks on the resemblance of St Edmund's martyrdom to that of St Sebastian who was also made a target for arrows.[2] St Sebastian was eventually cudgelled to death, while St Edmund was beheaded. Usuard provides many examples of martyrs who, having survived a series of torments, were at last decapitated.[3] Abbo's specific models may have been the *Passio SS. Dionysii, Rustici et Eleutherii* by Fortunatus (fl. 700) and the *Vita S. Dionisii* by Hilduin (d.840). It is not unlikely that Abbo of Fleury would have turned for a model to the legend of St Denis, the patron saint of the abbey of St Denis, Paris, and of the kings of France, the most venerated saint in the Île-de-France, especially since St Edmund was a king and one whose cult was, as will be seen, associated with royalty. (Hilduin's *Vita* at least was known in England by the late tenth century; it is in the 'Cotton-Corpus' Legendary, of which Ælfric's *Lives of Saints* is in effect a translation.)[4] Hilduin relates that St Denis was stretched on a rack, scourged, flung into a fire, and thrown to lions – but God saved him, as He had Daniel, by making the lions lie down peaceably before him. The reference to Daniel supports the suggestion that Hilduin was one of Abbo's models, since it could explain the presence in the *Passio* of an inapposite reference to the Daniel story: the passage relates that the country folk, on finding St Edmund's head guarded from other wild creatures by a wolf, decided that his merits must resemble Daniel's.[5]

Hilduin has the *topos* of the saint's body living after the severance of the head (St Denis walks for over two miles carrying his head until he reaches the place where he wishes to be buried). And Fortunatus has the *topos* of the head speaking.[6] The claim that St Edmund was a victim of the 'blood eagle' rests mainly on one passage in the *Passio*; Abbo states that when St Edmund was taken almost dead from the stake for execution, his ribs had been laid bare by numerous arrow wounds, as if 'he had been stretched on a rack or pierced by iron hooks' (*retectis costarum latebris praepunctionibus credis ac si raptum equuleo*

1. *Cf.* Scarfe, *op. cit.* p. 309.

2. *Passio*, pp. 78–9.

3. For examples see Migne, *PL*, cxxiii, cols. 623–4, 673–4, 681–2, 959–60; *ibid.* cxxiv, cols. 17–18, 169–70.

4. See P. H. Zettel, 'Saints' Lives in Old English: Latin manuscripts and vernacular accounts: Ælfric', *Peritia*, i (1982), 17–37. I am indebted to Dr Michael Lapidge for this reference. For Ælfric's rendering of Hilduin see *Ælfric's Lives of Saints*, ed. Skeat, ii. 168–91.

5. *Passio*, c. 12, ll. 47–8 (p. 81). *Cf.* Migne, *PL*, cvi, cols. 44–5.

6. MGH, *Auctores Antiquissimi*, iv, pt 2, p. 104, l. 13. *Cf.* Edmund Colledge and J. C. Marler, 'Céphalologie, a recurring theme in classical and medieval lore', *Traditio*, xxxvii (1981), 411f (pp. 418–19 for especial reference to the St Denis legend).

*aut seuis tortum ungulis*).[1] But racks and hooks are hagiographical commonplaces. For example St Denis, as observed above, suffered on a rack, and according to Usuard four of the martyrs who shared the same anniversary as St Sebastian (20 January) were tortured with hooks as well as the rack.[2] An exact parallel for the wolf story has proved elusive. However, the Life of St Mary of Egypt (in the *Vitae Patrum*) has a rather similar tale, although in this instance the animal in question is a lion. When Zosimus, a devout monk, went in search of St Mary in the desert, he found her dead body guarded by a huge lion, which, having helped him dig a grave, returned 'as quietly as a lamb' to its desert solitude. Since Abbo no doubt knew that there were no lions in England, he might well have considered a wolf, a savage beast well-known in western Europe, a more suitable guardian for St Edmund's head.[3]

Abbo's story of  Oswen,  the holy woman who tended St Edmund's body, is not apparently paralleled in all its details elsewhere. The *topos* itself, of a pious woman caring for a saint's body, was well-known and seems to have originated in the legend of St Sebastian, whose body was looked after by St Lucina (30 June).[4] It occurs in the St Denis legend; after his martyrdom St Denis's body was rescued and buried and his shrine built and served by a matron called Catulla.[5] The detail that Oswynn cut St Edmund's hair and nails is paralleled in the twelfth century legend of St Cuthbert and in the legend of St Olaf of Norway (d.1030).[6] Rather earlier (in 1000), when Charlemagne's tomb was opened, it was recorded that the emperor's nails had grown and needed cutting.[7] It can, therefore, be argued that Abbo's *Passio* is a patchwork of borrowings from well-known hagiographies, which Abbo adapted as he thought fit. Almost certainly he knew virtually nothing about St Edmund's death and

1. *Passio*, c. 10, ll. 27–8 (p. 79). 'seuis tortum ungulis' should be 'tortured with cruel hooks', not 'torn by savage claws', as in Dr Smyth's translation of the passage: Smyth, *op. cit.* pp. 211–12.

2. Migne, *PL*, cxxiii, cols. 673–4. *Cf.* also St Alexander, *ibid.* cxxiv, cols. 15–16.

3. I am indebted to Sister Benedicta Ward for drawing my attention to the parallel between the legend of St Mary of Egypt (Migne, *PL*, lxxiii. cols. 688–9) and that of St Edmund. Isidore (*Etymologia*, XII, cap. 2) makes a comparison between the wolf and the lion. Dr Michael Lapidge has pointed out to me that the legend of St Mary of Egypt in the *Lives of Saints* was not by Ælfric but occurs in early versions of the *Lives*, notably in BL Cotton Ms. Otho B X, an eleventh century text from Worcester, and in BL Cotton MS. Julius E VII, a twelfth century text from Bury St Edmunds: *Ælfric's Lives of Saints*, ed. Skeat, ii. 446–7; *cf. ibid.* ii. ix, xiv, xv, and N. R. Ker, *Medieval Libraries of Great Britain* (second edition, London, 1964), pp. 20, 207.

4. Bollandists, *Acta Sanctorum*, January, vol. ii, p. 257.

5. MGH, *Auctores Antiquissimi*, iv, pt 2, p. 104, l. 20; Migne, *PL*, cvi. cols. 48–9).

6. See, respectively, *Reginaldi Monachi Dunelmensis Libellus de admirandis Beati Cuthberti Virtutibus*, ed. James Raine, sr (Surtees Society, i, 1835), p. 57, and Bollandists, *Acta Sanctorum*, July, vol. vii, p. 110. For another similarity between the St Edmund legend and that of St Olaf, see *supra*, p. 2, n. 2. *Cf. The Relics of St Cuthbert*, ed. C. F. Battiscombe (Oxford, 1956), pp. 45–6. For the relationship between the legends of St Edmund and St Cuthbert see *infra*, p. 21, n. 2.

7. Robert Folz, *Le Souvenir et la Légende de Charlemagne dans l'Empire germanique médiéval* (Paris, 1950), p. 92. I owe this reference to Professor R. A. Markus.

early cult; nor could succeeding hagiographers add any new credible information. The depths of their ignorance is betrayed by their failure to agree on an important point, the exact location of the supposed martyrdom. Abbo places it at 'Haeglesdun' while later tradition (to be discussed below) places it at Hoxne.    All that is certain is that by *c.* 1000 a    shrine containng a body, supposedly that of St Edmund, was the centre of a   cult at Beodriceworth.

So far we have discussed the development of the hagiology of St Edmund in the late tenth century. The next important period of growth was the late eleventh century, to which time also belongs the genesis of the legends and traditions concerning the abbey's origins. It is essential to consider their evolution against the background of post-Conquest politics and society. It should also be remembered that the abbot, Baldwin (1065–97), was an ex-monk of St Denis and had been an intimate of Edward the Confessor (he was his physician). After the Conquest the monks of Bury had to defend themselves against Normans who tried to seize their estates[2] and even cast doubt on the actual presence of St Edmund's body in the abbey.[3] But their worst enemy was the bishop of East Anglia, first Arfast (1070–*c.*1085) and then Herbert Losinga (1090/1–1119).[4] Arfast tried to move his see from Thetford to Bury. The dispute came to a head in 1081, when, after more than a decade of contention involving appeals to Rome, and the intervention of William the Conqueror and Lanfranc,[5] the case was heard in the royal court.[6] Although judgement was given in the abbey's favour, Arfast and Losinga continued the struggle until the latter moved the see to Norwich in 1094/5. Nevertheless he and at least one of his successors towards the end of the twelfth century tried to assert authority over the abbey.[7] In the course of the dispute both parties appealed for support to historical precedents. Since very little was known about the history in Anglo-Saxon times of the East Anglian see or of the cult of St Edmund, the way was open for the disputants to interpret what little information there was as served them best, and to invent corroborative 'evidence'. Our knowledge of the controversy – its course and the protagonists' arguments – is fragmentary. Nevertheless, it undoubtedly had a profound influence on the development of St Edmund's hagiology and on that of the

---

1. *Passio*, pp. 73, 79.

2. *Feudal Documents from the Abbey of Bury St Edmunds*, ed. D. C. Douglas (London, 1932), nos. 9, 10; Hermann, pp. 58–9, 75–6, 79. *Cf.* Gransden, 'Baldwin', pp. 67, 68, and nn.

3. Hermann, p. 86. *Cf.* Gransden, 'Baldwin' , p. 73.

4. For the dispute see David Knowles, 'Essays in monastic history, IV – the growth of exemption', *Downside Review*, l (1932), 208–12, and Gransden, 'Baldwin', pp. 69–72.

5. Hermann, p. 65. *Cf. infra*, p. 91.

6. Hermann, pp. 65–7. An account of the trial is in the forged charter of privilege, allegedly of William I, to St Edmund's; see Douglas, *op. cit.* p. xxxiv, and Gransden, 'Baldwin', p. 71.

7. See *The Customary of the Benedictine Abbey of Bury St Edmunds in Suffolk*, ed. Antonia Gransden (Henry Bradshaw Society, xcix, 1973, henceforth referred to as *Bury Customary*), pp. xl, xli.

abbey's historiography, an influence which recent historians have ignored or underestimated.[1]

The popularly held belief that St Edmund was martyred and first buried at Hoxne, which by the late fourteenth century was current even at Bury[2] (despite the contrary statement in Abbo's *Passio*), seems to have originated as part of the bishop of East Anglia's case; the charter which Herbert Losinga granted to his new cathedral priory at Norwich in *c*.1100 includes among the endowments the church of Hoxne 'with the chapel of St Edmund, where the martyr was killed'.[3] The tradition was accepted at St Albans in the thirteenth century; it appears in the chronicles of both Roger of Wendover and Matthew Paris.[4] It could have reached St Albans from the latter's cell at Wymondham, within ten miles of Norwich, and then reached Bury from St Albans. Possibly it owed its origin to a simple substitution of the name of St Edmund for that of another 'martyred' king of East Anglia, St Ethelbert (who was beheaded in 794 by order of King Offa of Mercia); Ethelbert was, at latest by the mid-tenth century, the patron saint of the church at Hoxne, which had presumably acquired relics of him and was served by some kind of community.[5] The original purpose of such a substitution might well have been to provide the bishop of East Anglia's party with a precedent; Hoxne had been the bishop of East Anglia's see in the ninth century and again under Edward the Confessor;[6] therefore St Edmund's present burial place (Bury) should be the present bishop's see. Meanwhile at Bury itself Hermann, who claimed to have been in Bishop Arfast's service before becoming, as it would appear, a monk of St Edmund's,[7] wrote the *De Miraculis* as a piece of propaganda for his new home. His object was to increase St Edmund's and the abbey's prestige in order to fortify it against its enemies, especially the bishop of East Anglia. He also wrote to provide a *pièce justificative* for the monks in their dispute with Losinga. Hermann, indeed, is the

---

1. See *e.g.* p.90,n. 1 *infra*.

2. Bodley 240 (for which see *infra*, pp. 15–16 *passim*), pp. 631, 632.

3. W. Dugdale, *Monasticon Anglicanum*, ed. J. Caley, H. Ellis and B. Bandinel (London, 1817–30, 6 vols. in 8), iv. 16. *Cf*. Whitelock, 'The legend of St. Edmund', p. 223.

4. Roger of Wendover alleges that St Edmund was buried at 'Hoxe' while Matthew Paris gives 'Hore'; Matthew Paris, *Chronica Majora*, ed. H. R. Luard (Rolls Series, 1872–83, 7 vols.), i. 400 and n. 4. For the Hoxne legend see V. H. Galbraith, 'The East Anglian see and the abbey of Bury St Edmunds', *ante*, xl (1925), 223 and n. 3, and Gransden, 'Baldwin', pp. 70, 190, nn. 75–9. In modern times the legend was believed by, for example, Thomas Arnold (*Memorials*, i. xxi, 10, 16), and A. J. Robertson, *Anglo-Saxon Charters* (Cambridge, 1956), p. 425.

5. See *Anglo-Saxon Wills*, ed. and translated Dorothy Whitelock (Cambridge, 1930), no. 1. *Cf*. C. R. Hart, 'The East Anglian chronicle', *Journal of Medieval History*, vii (1981), p. 264. St Ethelbert was buried at Hereford; see Rollason, 'Resting places', pp. 64, 89.

6. Whitelock, *Wills*, pp. 4, 99, 102, and *Domesday Book* ..., ed. A. Farley (Record Commission, 1783, 2 vols.), ii. 379.

7. Hermann, pp. 62, 63, 67. *Cf. The Letters of Lanfranc Archbishop of Canterbury*, ed., with an English translation, Helen Clover and Margaret Gibson (Oxford Medieval Texts, 1979), p. 152 and n. 6. For Hermann as a propagandist for Bury, see Gransden, 'Baldwin', pp. 72–3.

earliest authority for the universally held belief[1] that St Edmund's abbey was founded in 1020 by King Canute. However, in view of the tendentious nature of his narrative this statement deserves more attention than it has hitherto received. The relevant passage reads:

> Quo [*i.e.* Canute] tetrarchizante, sanctique martyris [Eadmundi] veneratione pullulante, clericalis ordo famulatus sancto in ordinem monachicum mutatur in eodem loco, indagine veritatis talia commutando felici commercio, ut rex et martyr venerandus frequentiori famulatu necnon digniori veneraretur. Nec hoc absque regis concessu et optimatum ejus fuit assensu, sed et monitu sani consilii Ælfwini praesulis diocesiani, Eliensis quidem monachi, amatoris autem ordinis sancti, tunc tempore concessis et datis martyri sancto multis donariis, anno millesimo xx^mo Domini generationis, comitatu vero Thurcilli comitis, ad honorem sancti suppeditantis.[2]

There is nothing improbable in the story that Canute 'founded' St Edmund's abbey. His retribution for the murder by the Danes of another famous Englishman, Archbishop Ælfheah, is well known.[3] Moreover, he was the friend and benefactor of both Ely and Ramsey[4] – and in the vicinity of the latter he planned to found another religious house, a nunnery.[5] And he endowed the community at Beodricesworth, whether the pre-monastic or monastic one is not clear. Hermann states, in the paragraph preceding the foundation account quoted above, that Canute

> protectorem suum post Deum invisens sanctum [Eadmundum], actu regali xeniauit locum donis ac redditibus propriis munificauit, liberumque omni consuetudine chyrographizauit.[6]

Since the surviving diploma in Canute's name to St Edmund's contains a grant of exemption from episcopal control, it is generally believed that the monks of Bury had it forged for the 1081 trial in

---

1. The story is accepted, with varying degrees of detail and precision, by: David Knowles, *The Monastic Order in England* (2nd edn, Cambridge, 1963), p. 70; Knowles and Neville Hadcock, *Medieval Religious Houses, England and Wales*, p. 75; F. Hervey, *The History of King Eadmund the martyr and the early years of his abbey* (London, 1929), p. 32; A. Goodwin, *The Abbey of St Edmundsbury* (Oxford, 1931), p. 5; F. E. Harmer, *Anglo-Saxon Writs* (Manchester, 1952), p. 138, n. 1; Robertson, *Anglo-Saxon Charters*, p. 425; R. H. C. Davis, 'The monks of St Edmund, 1021–1148', *History*, xl (1955), 232–3; Scarfe, 'The body of St Edmund', pp. 307–8; Hart, 'East Anglian chronicle', p. 274, and the same author's *The Early Charters of Eastern England* (Leicester, 1966), p. 64.

2. Hermann, p. 47.

3. *Anglo-Saxon Chronicle*, s.a. 1023.

4. *Liber Eliensis*, ed. E. O. Blake (Camden third series, xcii, 1962), pp. 149–57 *passim*, and *Chronicon Abbatiae Rameseiensis*, ed. W. D. Macray (Rolls Series, 1886, henceforth referred to as *Ramsey Chron.*), pp. 125–6, 133–4, 139, 267. (However, many of the charters in Canute's name to monasteries are spurious; see P. H. Sawyer, *Anglo-Saxon Charters* (London, 1968), pp. 285–96 *passim*.) Another East Anglian chronicler, Henry of Huntingdon, writing in the mid-twelfth century, eulogized Canute; *Historia Anglorum*, ed. Thomas Arnold (Rolls Series, 1879, repr. Kraus 1965), pp. 188–9.

5. *Ramsey Chron.* p. 126.

6. Hermann, p. 46.

the royal court.[1] However, Miss Harmer suggests that part of it was copied from a genuine charter.[2] This section is the grant of fish due annually to Canute, a fishery, and all rights from pleas in the vills owned by St Edmund's, and the confirmation of Queen Emma's gift of 4,000 eels a year. Emma herself had bequeathed Kirby Cane in Norfolk to St Edmund's.[3] A cause and/or the result of Canute's foundation could have been the boom in the cult of St Edmund which, the liturgical calendars show, occurred in the 1020s.[4] However, too much weight should not be attached to this evidence since at this period the cult of a number of other Anglo-Saxon saints underwent spectacular development.[5]

Canute's claim in fact rests on Hermann's unsupported evidence – tendentious evidence written over eighty years after the supposed act of foundation. There is no mention of it in the forged diploma in Canute's name, nor in that in William the Conqueror's name which was probably also fabricated for the 1081 trial and includes an apparently reliable account of the proceedings.[6] When, as Hermann records, Lanfranc (sometime in the 1070s) held an inquiry to try to settle the dispute between the Bury monks and the bishop, he appealed for evidence to the aged abbot of Ramsey, Ælfwine (1043–79/80), whose memory stretched back to the time of Canute; he testified, without any allusion to the foundation story, that already in those days St Edmund's had enjoyed its privileges.[7] And neither of the contemporary authorities, the *Encomium Emmae Reginae* and the Anglo-Saxon Chronicle, mention any such matter – nor does the later but often authoritative Florence of Worcester (*c.*1118).

It seems possible that the Bury monks adopted Canute as their

---

1. Sawyer, *Anglo-Saxon Charters*, no. 980. Printed B. Thorpe, *Diplomatarium Anglicum Ævi Saxonici* (London, 1865), pp. 305–8.

2. Harmer, *Writs*, pp. 140–1, 433–5, nn. *passim.*

3. *Ibid.* pp. 148, 159–60 (no. 17), 440.

4. St Edmund is in the calendars of Christ Church, Canterbury (1012–23), and in both of those of New Minster, Winchester (1023–35, 1035 respectively); *English Kalendars before A.D. 1100, i, Texts*, ed. Francis Wormald (Henry Bradshaw Society, lxxii, 1934), pp. 124, 138, 180. St Edmund also has a special mass in the sacramentary of *c.*1020–25 which was almost certainly composed at Ely; *The Missal of Robert of Jumièges*, ed. H. A. Wilson (Henry Bradshaw Society, xi, 1896), pp. xxviii, 225–6. For the provenance of the sacramentary see J. B. L. Tolhurst, 'An examination of two Anglo-Saxon manuscripts of the Winchester School: the Missal of Robert of Jumièges, and the Benedictional of St. Æthelwold,' *Archaeolgia*, lxxxiii (1933), 27–41. St Edmund's omission from the calendar is almost certainly accidental; Tolhurst, *loc. cit.* p. 30 and n. 1.

5. See C. E. Fell, 'Edward king and martyr and the Anglo-Saxon hagiographic tradition', *Ethelred the Unready: Papers from the Millenary Conference*, ed. David Hill (British Archaeological Report, British Series, lix, 1978), p. 7.

6. Although Douglas's argument in favour of the authenticity of the diploma is unconvincing, his contention that its account of the trial is sound seems indisputable; *Feudal Documents from the Abbey of Bury St Edmunds*, p. xxxiv.

7. regis jussu Lanfrancus Cantuariae praesul, hac pro re terminato ibidem novem comitatuum cœtu, Ælfwino Ramesiensi abbate tunc pleno dierum, ac sene, cujus testimonium ex tempore regis Cnuti prolatum, voceque novem comitatuum obfirmatum; abbatia viguit praenominata tunc temporis libertate testificata; Hermann, p. 65.

putative founder in the late eleventh century. Since he was the
benefactor of their own and other monasteries he could be seen as
a latter-day King Edgar, the patron of English Benedictinism. The
monks' objective would have been to increase the abbey's reputation
and in particular to assert its independence of the bishop of East
Anglia. To have a royal founder, as well as a royal patron saint, was
particularly prestigious. In addition, to be under royal protection
and at the king's disposal, to be in effect a royal *eigenkloster*, ensured
immunity from any other authority, notably the diocesan's. Since
Abbot Baldwin's former home, St Denis, was such a royal foundation
and one throughout its history closely associated with the French
monarchy, he must have appreciated the advantages of the royal
connection. Nor would this idea have represented any break with the
abbey's tradition since it already had an established link with royalty.
Possibly the earliest royal benefactor of the community at Beodricesworth was King Edmund (opinions are divided about the authenticity of his charter).[1] As has been seen, Canute himself was probably
a benefactor of St Edmund's, and his wife Emma certainly was. But
perhaps at no time throughout its history were St Edmund's ties with
royalty closer than under Edward the Confessor. The latter regarded
St Edmund as his ancestor (two of his surviving writs refer to St
Edmund as 'my kinsman'),[2] and was a substantial benefactor. He
granted the abbey regalian rights, including the right to have a
mint;[3] most important was the grant to the second abbot, Leofstan,
of the liberty of eight and a half hundreds where abbatial authority
virtually replaced the king's;[4] this liberty, the charter states, had
previously been held by Edward's mother, Emma.[5] And in 1065
he appointed the St Denis' monk, his own physician, Baldwin, to
succeed Abbot Leofstan. David Knowles has already suggested that
Edward brought with him from Normandy the idea that a ruler might
exercise proprietary rights over an abbey under his patronage, and
that he regarded Westminster as his *eigenkloster*.[6] It seems that he saw
St Edmund's in a similar way. The question arises why Abbot
Baldwin would have preferred Canute to Edward the Confessor as
the putative founder of St Edmund's. One answer would obviously
be that Canute offered the abbey a more ancient tradition. The notion
could have been suggested by Canute's well-known generosity to the
East Anglian monasteries, which included his grant to St Edmund's,
and because of Canute's wife, Emma; she was not only a benefactor

---

1. See Sawyer, *Anglo-Saxon Charters*, no. 507, for further references.
2. Harmer, *Writs*, pp. 160–1 (no. 18), 164–5 (no. 24).
3. *Ibid*. pp. 150–1, 165–6 (no. 25).
4. For the grant see *ibid*. pp. 145–7, 154–5 (no. 9), 435–9.
5. For Queen Emma's 'miniature shire' of the eight and half hundreds, see H. W. C. Davis,
'The liberties of Bury St Edmunds', *ante*, xxiv (1909), 418–19.
6. Knowles, *Monastic Order*, pp. 579–80. For the protection and freedom enjoyed by a royal
*eigenkloster*, see *ibid*. pp. 569, 584.

of St Edmund's but also it was her estate, the liberty of the eight and a half hundreds, which became the nucleus of the abbey's property.

It remains to discuss the part played by Ælfwine, bishop of Elmham 1022–1023 x 1038. Hermann asserts that he, 'a monk of Ely and lover of the monastic life', advised Canute to introduce monks at Beodricesworth. V. H. Galbraith and Florence Harmer have already indicated their surprise that the bishop should have advised Canute to establish a highly privileged monastery within his own diocese.[1] Even supposing that the whole story is true and Hermann merely mistook the date, it is odd that he should admit Ælfwine's part. As apologist for the Bury monks against the East Anglian bishop, it was risky to ascribe a crucial role in their abbey's foundation to the diocesan. Such an admission would be particularly surprising if, as I have suggested elsewhere, the monks actually revised the *Passio* during the dispute to reduce the bishop's part in St Edmund's origins.[2] Possibly the solution of these problems is to be found in the propaganda purveyed in support of the bishop's case. In the course of the dispute Losinga's party produced a tendentious history of the East Anglian see and of the church of Beodricesworth.[3] Having alleged that Felix, a colleague of St Augustine, founded a cathedral there dedicated to the Virgin Mary (it has no reference to St Edmund), it states that Bishop Ælfwine (called Ælfric presumably in error) replaced the secular clerks by monks and that after Canute's death King Harold transformed the cathedral priory into an abbey. The passage concerning Ælfric's foundation reads:

> Is [*i.e.* Canute ] Alfricum [*sic*] monachum et priorem Elyensis monasterii ascitum in ecclesia apud Beodrichesworth pontificem elegit, obsecratus ut clericos qui ibidem irreligiose vivebant expelleret et monachos constitueret.[4]

Losinga's tract, therefore, makes Ælfwine the virtual founder. In this it is supported by the *Liber Eliensis*, which states that Ælfwine

> ipsius [Canuti] regis precepto in Betricheswrde primum monachorum adduxit catervam ... eisque affluenter subsidia detulit,ausilium impendente Thurchillo comite, insuper rebus et ornamentis ipsi loco de sua parte collatis quamplurimis, eterne libertati donavit ...[5]

However, in this instance little weight can be put on the evidence of the *Liber Eliensis*: it is a late authority (it was compiled in Henry II's reign); the passage cited appears to be based on Hermann, only

1. Galbraith, 'East Anglian see', p. 225 and n. 1; Harmer, *Writs*, p. 140 (Galbraith refers to the bishop of East Anglia as 'Ælfric' instead of 'Ælfwine', presumably having been misled by his source, the 'Losinga' tract, for which see *infra*).

2. 'Baldwin', p. 72.

3. Printed Galbraith, 'East Anglian see', pp. 226–8. For the manuscript see *infra*, p. 22 and n. 5.

4. *Ibid.* p. 226.

5. *Liber Eliensis*, p. 155.

Ælfwine is substituted for Canute as the prime mover; and, as will be seen, the compiler's information was contaminated by Norwich propaganda. The idea of attributing such a role to Ælfwine could well have originated among Arfast's apologists; by demonstrating St Edmund's abbey's initial debt to the diocesan, it strengthened the bishop's case against the Bury monks in their struggle for exemption. Hermann might have heard the story when in Arfast's service, brought it with him to Bury, and there incorporated it, suitably modified, in the *De Miraculis*.

What happened to the clerks who formed the pre-monastic congregation at Beodricesworth is problematic. Hermann indicates that one member of the previous congregation, Æthelwine, the sacristan, remained and joined the new community. His evidence accords with that of the Bury interpolator of Florence of Worcester who asserts that Canute expelled only those clerks who did not take the habit:

> presbyteros vero qui inibi inordinate vivebant aut in eodem loco ad religionis culmen erexit, aut datis aliis rebus de quibus abundantius solito victum et vestitum haberent, in alia loca mutavit.[1]

However the evidence of neither Hermann nor the interpolator is trustworthy on this point. Hermann claims that it was Æthelwine who carried St Edmund's bier to safety in 1010, and who later, when Abbot Leofstan opened the coffin, identified the body as that of St Edmund. He was, therefore, a vital witness that in Hermann's day the body in the shrine was indeed the martyr's.[2] Thus Æthelwine's role suggests the possibility that Hermann 'invented' him to serve his propagandist purpose.[3] The statement of the Bury interpolator of Florence of Worcester is equally suspect. It could be based on Hermann's evidence, or more probably on that of Florence of Worcester himself. The latter describes how St Oswald constituted the cathedral priory at Worcester. (His account derives ultimately from one in either Ælfric's or Wulfstan's *Vita S. Æthelwoldi* – their respective texts are at this point, as in so many other places, almost identical – which tells how St Ethelwold expelled the clerks from the Old Minster, Winchester.) Florence asserts that St Oswald.

> clericos Wigorniensis ecclesiae monachilem habitum suscipere renuentes de monasterio expulit; consentientes vero hoc anno, ipso teste, monachizavit.[4]

It became the accepted tradition at Bury, probably by Henry II's

---

1. *Memorials*, i. 341–2.
2. Hermann, pp. 52–3. *Cf.* pp. 40–6 *passim*.
3. Æthelwine's name itself is suspect; see Gransden, 'Baldwin', pp. 73, 74, and *infra*, p. 21, n. 2.
4. *Chronicon ex Chronicis*, ed. Benjamin Thorpe (English Historical Society, 1848–9, 2 vols.), i. 141. *Cf.* Ælfric's *Vita S. Æthelwoldi* in *Chronicon Monasterii de Abingdon*, ed. Joseph Stevenson (Rolls Series, 1858, 2 vols.), i. 260–1, and Wulfstan's *Vita S. Æthelwoldi* in *Acta Sanctorum*, 1 August, p. 92.

reign, that Canute, as a preliminary to introducing Benedictine monks at Beodricesworth, expelled all the clerks.[1] (Apparently the tradition, which does not concern us here, that Canute formed the clerks, twelve in number, into a gild, the *douzegild,* which later Abbot Baldwin provided with a parish church, originated at about the same time.)[2] However, as in the case of the story of partial expulsion, that of wholesale expulsion cannot be substantiated. It first appears in the Losinga tract, which states that Canute appointed Ælfric (*sic* for Ælfwine) to the see of Beodricesworth *ut clericos ... expelleret.*[3] Losinga's apologist may well have borrowed the idea from Florence of Worcester who, in his turn here using the Anglo-Saxon Chronicle, states (s.a.969) that King Edgar

> S. Dunstano Dorubernensis, et B. Oswaldo Wigorniensis, et S. Æthel-woldo Wintoniensis ecclesiae episcopis praecepit, ut, expulsis clericis, in majoribus monasteriis per Merciam constructis monachos collo-carent.[4]

Thus, there is no reliable evidence either that only some of the clerks were expelled, or that all were. A corollary of the accepted tradition of total expulsion was that the monastery was settled by a colony of monks from elsewhere. The full story of such colonization of Beodricesworth does not appear at Bury until the late fourteenth century, when the Life and Miracles of St Edmund (now Bodley Ms. 240) was compiled. This vast compilation includes a narrative describing the abbey's foundation. The relevant passage states that in 1020 Bishop Ælfwine 'quosdam de Hulmo sancti Benedicti, et quosdam de ecclesia Eliensi monachos ibi collocauit', citing (in the margin) as its authority 'the chronicles of Ely'. It proceeds, here citing 'the chronicles of Holme':

> Placuit enim [Canuto] regi, ut de ecclesia beati Benedicti de Hulmo antiquitus constituta pars dimidia fratrum ad ecclesiam Beodricensem dirigeretur. Ea vero tempestate xxvj. monachi, viri religiosi et bonae famae, in ecclesia de Hulmo Deo et sancto Benedicto famulabantur. De illa namque parte dimidia fratrum ad Beodricesworthe directa vir prudens et honestus Uvius erat, qui in ecclesia beati Benedicti officium prioratus agebat, et in ecclesia S. Edmundi apud Beodricesworthe abbas extitit primus ...[5]

A passage almost identical to, and possibly the source of, the citation 'from the chronicles of Ely' is in the *Liber Eliensis* (temp. Henry II).[6] The substance of the citation 'from the chronicles of

1. *Bury Customary,* p. 123 (*cf.* pp. xl, xli).
2. *Ibid.* p. 59, n. 6 for further references. See also Douglas, *Feudal Documents,* pp. 161–2.
3. *Supra,* p. 13.
4. *Chronicon ex Chronicis,* i. 141.
5. *Memorials,* i. 359.
6. *Liber Eliensis,* p. 155.

Holme' is in the two chronicles composed at Holme in the late thirteenth and early fourteenth centuries respectively, that is 'John de Oxenedes' and the so-called *Cronica Buriensis*,[1] and also in the register of Holme, of *c.* 1300.[2] The story at this stage has a detail not in the Life and Miracles of St Edmund; it states that Holme supplied St Edmund's with half of its own books, vestments, sacred vessels and the like. But there is no trace at Bury of any tradition that monks from Ely and Holme colonized St Edmund's abbey until the late thirteenth century. Neither Hermann nor the interpolator of Florence of Worcester have any such story. Nevertheless, the interpolator does mention Ufi: he asserts that Canute 'praefecitque eis patrem et abbatem nomine Uvium, virum scilicet humilem, modestum, mansuetum et pium.'[3] This passage, however, is suspiciously like the one in Florence of Worcester about the appointment by St Oswald of the first prior of Worcester: 'eisque Ramesiensem coenobitam Wynsinum, magnae religionis virum, loco decani praefecit.'[4] The earliest mention that Ely helped colonize St Edmund's is the passage in the *Liber Eliensis*,[5] but thereafter there is silence until the compilation of the Life and Miracles of St Edmund. As in the case of the Ely tradition, the one connecting Holme with the colonization of St Edmund's first appears elsewhere than at Bury itself, in fact in a Norwich source – the Losinga tract; this states that Bishop Ælfwine appointed a monk of Holme to be prior of his new cathedral priory at Beodricesworth ('Holmensis monasterii monachum priorem constituit').[6] The story appears at last at Bury late in Henry III's reign, in a register, the *Liber Albus*.[7] There a short historical narrative has the same story as was to occur shortly afterwards in the Holme sources.

The statement by a recent scholar that the special position afforded by the Customary of St Edmund's (*c.*1234) to the abbot of Holme in the chapter at Bury testifies to Holme's part in the foundation of St Edmund's abbey, is not sound.[8] The relevant passage states: 'Our prior shall yield place to no bishop or abbot in chapter, save to our

1. *Chronica Johannis de Oxenedes*, ed. H. Ellis (Rolls Series, 1859), p. 19, and *Memorials*, iii. 1. For the provenance of the *Cronica Buriensis* see *infra*, pp. 240–4.

2. BL MS. Cotton Galba E II, fo. 36ᵛ; printed in *St Benet of Holme 1020–1210. The Eleventh and Twelfth Century Sections of Cotton MS. Galba E ii. The Register of the Abbey of St Benet of Holme,* ed. J. R. West (Norfolk Record Society, ii, iii, 1932, 2 vols), i. 35–6, and in Dugdale, *Monasticon*, iii. 135. This together with the confraternity between Bury and Holme (see *infra*, p. 97), is the source of the account of the foundation of Bury in Davis, 'The monks of St. Edmund', pp. 232–3.

3. *Memorials*, i. 341.

4. *Chronicon ex Chronicis*, i. 141.

5. *Supra*, p. 95.

6. Galbraith, 'East Anglian see,' p. 226.

7. BL MS. Harley 1005, fos. 35, 35ᵛ. Cf. Gransden, 'The "Cronica Buriensis" and the abbey of St Benet of Hulme', p. 78 and n. 6.

8. Davis, 'The monks of St. Edmund', p. 233.

own abbot or to the abbot of Holme and the like, who by right ought to hear the secrets of the chapter, and to have competence to correct any abuses, according to our customs.'[1] It will be noticed that the reference to the abbot of Holme is followed by words 'and the like', presumably indicating other heads of houses to whom similar respect was due. In fact the passage probably concerns the heads of those houses with which Bury had entered into confraternity. The surviving text of the confraternity between St Edmund's and St Augustine's, Canterbury, stipulates that if the abbot of one house visited the other, he should enjoy the same rights in that house as he did in his own.[2] By the mid-thirteenth century Bury had confraternities with Peterborough, St Albans and Westminster as well as with St Augustine's.[3] There is no positive evidence that it had one with Holme before *c.*1234, the date of the Customary, although it certainly did late in Henry III's reign.[4] The passage cited from the Customary suggests that there was an earlier confraternity. Indeed the text of the extant Bury/Holme confraternity could well be based on an earlier one. It includes the provision that any monk who committed a crime (barring treachery to his house or abbot) and, therefore, fled or was expelled, might take refuge in the other house where he would live on equal terms with the monks there. This kind of provision was characteristic of early thirteenth century confraternities, or 'confederacies', as Knowles calls such agreements; Knowles describes them as 'mutual insurance policies' and tentatively attributes their proliferation in the last half of the twelfth and early thirteenth century to the 'democratic' movements which then took place in a number of houses – including Bury.[5] These could result in the flight or exile of dissidents for whom a confederate house would provide asylum.[6]

There is, therefore, no evidence of any tradition at Bury that St Edmund's abbey was colonized from Holme until late in Henry III's reign. This, combined with the even later appearance at Bury of the tradition that Ely also supplied monks, indicates that the credibility of the colonization story needs investigation. The monks of Ely

1. Prior noster nulli episcopo, nulli abbati cedat in capitulo nisi abbati proprio vel abbati de Hulmo seu tali, qui secreta capituli de iure debeat audire et excessus regulariter sciat secundum consuetudinem nostram corrigere; *Bury Customary*, p. 18, lines 7–10.

2. *Historiae Anglicanae Scriptores X*, ed. Roger Twysden (London, 1652), p. 1843.

3. A mid-thirteenth century list of the confraternities enjoyed by St Edmund's is in Harley 1005, f.250. R. M. Thomson, *The Archives of the Abbey of Bury St Edmunds* (Suffolk Records Society, xxi, 1980), p. 18, dates the index of charters, in which this list occurs, to after 1254.

4. Harley 1005, fos. 35, 35ᵛ. A text is also in the 'Cronica Buriensis' (*Memorials*, iii. 2) and in the Holme register (West, *St Benet of Holme 1020–1210*, i. 3).

5. Knowles, *Monastic Order*, pp. 474–5 and nn. For Bury see A. Gransden, 'A democratic movement in the abbey of Bury St. Edmunds in the late twelfth and early thirteenth centuries', *Journal of Ecclesiastical History*, xxvi (1975), 25–39.

6. St Albans had cells to which the abbot could exile dissidents; Abbot John (1195–1214) did so (*Gesta Abbatum Monasterii Sancti Albani*, ed. H. T. Riley (Rolls Series, 1867–9, 3 vols.), i. 251). Bury had no cells. Cf. *infra* pp. 103, 243–4.

might have claimed that their abbey helped colonize St Edmund's in order to gain reflected glory for their house; in the course of the twelfth century St Edmund's became one of the most renowned monasteries in England. However, it is certainly possible that Ely, an ancient and famous house little over twenty five miles from Beodricesworth, did provide monks for the new community, especially if Bishop Ælfwine, a monk of Ely, was instrumental in the foundation. Nevertheless, the lack of early evidence testifying to Ely's part is disturbing. In the case of Holme's participation the weight of probability is against the tradition. St Benet's was neither famous nor particularly near to St Edmund's, being nearly fifty miles away. Situated in the marshes on the Norfolk coast about eight miles north of Norwich, it emerged in the course of the eleventh century and enjoyed in Anglo-Saxon and post-Conquest times a merely local reputation. The only reliable evidence for its pre-Conquest history are a few wills containing bequests to the abbey.[1] (The charter of King Canute may well be a forgery, and that of Edward the Confessor certainly is.)[2] Scholars have accepted that Canute founded the abbey in 1019, although the earliest authority for this belief is a brief notice in 'Oxenedes'.[3] The latter, indeed, reads like a contrivance designed to make plausible the claim, which immediately follows, that Holme monks were sent in 1020 to form part of the new community established by Canute at Beodricesworth.

The tradition that monks from Holme formed part of the first monastic community at Beodricesworth could have been the result of misidentification. Ramsey abbey, as well as Holme, was dedicated to St Benedict. (Although its full dedication was to St Benedict and St Mary, charters of the Anglo-Saxon period usually call it St Benedict of Ramsey.)[4] It is certainly possible that Ramsey, one of the most influential centres of the tenth century monastic revival, helped colonize St Edmund's monastery at Beodricesworth. It had played a

---

1. Whitelock, *Wills*, nos. 25, 28, 31, 33, 34 (p. 90).

2. Sawyer, *Anglo-Saxon Charters*, nos. 984, 1055. See West, *St Benet of Holme 1020–1210*, i. 1–2 and n. 5, 3–5. For the post-Conquest charters of Holme, which are of interest for tenurial history, see F. M. Stenton, 'St Benet of Holme and the Norman Conquest', *EHR* 37 (1922), 225–35.

3. *VCH, Norfolk*, ii. 330; Knowles and Hadcock, *Medieval Religious Houses, England and Wales*, p. 75; West, *op. cit.* ii. 191. The principal sources cited by the *VCH* for the early history of Holme and the succession of its abbots are: the history of Holme to 1275 in BL MS. Cotton Nero D II (printed in *Oxenedes*, pp. 267–76); 'Oxenedes'; the Bury/Holme confraternity (see *supra*). All these sources are, at least in their present form, late thirteenth century and should not be relied on. They are also cited for the abbatial succession in David Knowles, C. N. L. Brooke and Vera London, *The Heads of Religious Houses, England and Wales, 940–1216* (Cambridge, 1972), p. 67. The latter cites in addition the more detailed information given by William Worcester, writing in 1479. Worcester had a particular interest in Holme; in the fifteenth century it was popular with the East Anglian nobility, and one of its patrons was his own patron, Sir John Fastolf. See *William Worcestre, Itineraries*, ed., with an English translation, J. H. Harvey (Oxford Medieval Texts, 1969), pp. 2, 92, 220–2, 232–4.

4. See Harmer, *Writs*, nos. 58–60, and Whitelock, *Wills*, nos. 31, 39.

crucial role in St Oswald's constitution of Benedictine communities at Worcester and Winchcombe. St Oswald's precise method of procedure with regard to Worcester is debatable. According to the Ramsey chronicler, Wynsige, the first prior of Worcester, had previously been a member of the clerical congregation there whom Oswald had sent to Ramsey for instruction before returning him to Worcester.[1] But Florence of Worcester asserts that he was a monk of Ramsey.[2] Florence is probably right, since Winchcombe would provide a parallel; St Oswald sent Germanus, prior of Ramsey, to reform the clerical congregation at Winchcombe, appointing him abbot.[3] Ramsey's reforming activity did not end with St Oswald's death. It was continued by his successor at Ramsey, Abbot Eadnoth (993– 1006) who established Benedictine communities at Slepe (afterwards St Ives, Hunts.)[4] and at Chatteris.[5] And later still, a monk of Ramsey, Ælfweard, was abbot of Evesham (*c.*1014–1035).[6] Besides its contribution to the actual establishing of Benedictine monasteries, Ramsey took an active part in fostering the cult of saints, a preoccupation no doubt encouraged by the example of Fleury, allegedly the resting place of St Benedict himself. Ramsey's lay patron, Æthelwine the ealdorman, acquired for it the relics of two Kentish martyrs, SS. Ethelbert and Ethelred,[7] and Abbot Eadnoth shared St Oswald's interest in relics; this is shown by his 'invention' of the body of St Ivo, preliminary to the foundation of the monastery of Slepe.[8] And Abbot Ælfweard of Evesham almost certainly translated the relics of St Wigstan to Evesham and bought the relics of St Odulf for the abbey.[9] To promote the growth of cult centres, Ramsey's greatest scholar, Abbo's pupil Byrhtferth, apparently wrote saints' Lives. He was probably the author of the Life of Ramsey's patron saint, St Oswald,[10] and of St Ecgwin, patron saint of Evesham.[11] Just possibly he also wrote a *Passio* of the Kentish martyrs, SS. Ethelbert and Ethelred.[12] (There were also Lives of St

1. *Ramsey Chron.* pp. 41–2.

2. *Chronicon ex Chronicis*, i. 141.

3. *Ramsey Chron.* p. 42.

4. Goscelin, *Vita S. Ivonis*, Migne, *PL*, clv. cols. 85 et seqq.; *Liber Eliensis*, p. 141 and n. 1; *Ramsey Chron.* pp. 114–15. For the endowment of St Ives and Chatteris see C. R. Hart, 'Eadnoth, first abbot of Ramsey, and the foundation of Chatteris and St Ives', *Proceedings of the Cambridge Antiquarian Society*, lvi–lvii (1964), 61–7.

5. *Liber Eliensis*, 141 and n. 5.

6. *Chronicon Abbatiae de Evesham*, ed. W. D. Macray (Rolls Series, 1863), p. 81.

7. *Ramsey Chron.* p. 55.

8. *Supra*, n. 4.

9. *Chron. Evesham*, pp. 36–8, 81–5, 314.

10. See Michael Lapidge, 'The hermeneutic style in tenth-century Anglo-Latin literature', *Anglo-Saxon England*, iv (1975), pp. 91–3.

11. Michael Lapidge, 'Byrhtferth and the *Vita S. Ecgwini*', *Mediaeval Studies*, xli (1979), 331–53.

12. Michael Lapidge, 'Byrhtferth of Ramsey and the early sections of the *Historia Regum* attributed to Symeon of Durham', *Anglo-Saxon England*, x (1981), 119–20.

Neot, patron saint of St Neot's,[1] and St Ethelbert, patron saint of Hereford and Hoxne.)[2] An important part in the expansion of Ramsey's influence was played by its lay patron, the ealdorman Æthelwine. He and his family not only endowed Ramsey but also Crowland and St Neots.[3] He died in 992 but his work was continued by Abbot Eadnoth who, with the help of his own family, endowed Slepe    and Chatteris.[4] Thus Ramsey's influence spread in the Fenlands and farther afield, to Worcester and the Severn basin. In East Anglia, however, its expansion was not without setbacks. King Edgar's death (in 975) was followed by a reaction against the monasteries, and when Æthelwine the ealdorman died (991), the ties between Ramsey and its satellites were weakened. But most serious were the renewed Viking attacks of the early eleventh century culminating in the battle of *Assandun* in 1016, in which the abbot of Ramsey was killed.[5]

It is against this background that the origins of Bury must be seen. Clearly the links between Ramsey and Beodricesworth were close. Not only was Ramsey less than forty miles away, but also some of its estates adjoined those of St Edmund's.[6] In the late 980s the Ramsey monks were already sufficiently interested in Beodricesworth as a cult centre to ask Abbo to write the *Passio* of its patron saint, a work which can be seen as a prototype of Byrhtferth's hagiographies. St Edmund figures in the late tenth century metrical calendar of Ramsey, which indicates that he must also have been in Ramsey's (now lost) liturgical calendar.[7] His martyrdom is also recorded in the late tenth century annals probably compiled at Ramsey.[8] And after the Norman conquest the monks of Bury must have believed that some knowledge of their abbey's early history was preserved at Ramsey, for they appealed to Abbot Ælfwine to give evidence at Lanfranc's inquest. There is indeed no direct evidence from Ramsey that it helped colonize St Edmund's. There is no reference to such an event in the Ramsey chronicle. However, the chronicle is a comparatively late authority, belonging to the reign of Henry II, and does

1. It has been suggested that this Life of St Neot was composed shortly after the saint's translation to Huntingdonshire towards the end of the tenth century; Hart, 'East Anglian chronicle', pp. 265–7, 278–9.

2. *Ibid.* pp. 264–5.

3. *Ibid.* p. 279.

4. *Supra*, p. 99 n. 4.

5. *Ramsey Chron.* p. 118.

6. Hart, 'East Anglian chronicle', p. 177.

7. See the forthcoming article by Michael Lapidge, 'A metrical calendar from Ramsey', *Revue Bénédictine*, xcv (1985).

8. C. R. Hart, 'The Ramsey Computus',*EHR* lxxxv (1970), 42. The 'Ramsey annals' were probably copied from the 'York annals', a copy of which possibly reached Ramsey through the agency of St Oswald, founder of Ramsey and archbishop of York; see Lapidge, 'Byrhtferth of Ramsey and the early sections of the *Historia Regum*', pp. 115–16. The version of the 'York annals' preserved by the Durham chronicler does not include the notice of St Edmund's martyrdom; Hart, *loc. cit.* p. 37.

not mention Ramsey's foundation of the albeit very minor houses at Slepe and Chatteris. And there is one piece of evidence which does suggest the possibility that some such tradition did linger at Ramsey into the Anglo-Norman period. As observed above,[1] the first hint of the Holme story, the statement that Bishop Ælfwine appointed a monk of Holme to be prior of his new monastery at Beodricesworth, is in the Losinga tract. Herbert Losinga before he became bishop of Thetford had been abbot of Ramsey for four years. Perhaps he knew a tradition that St Benedict of Ramsey helped colonize St Edmund's, but substituted St Benedict of Holme as the mother house for propagandist reasons. (My suggestion that the Norwich party substituted St Edmund for St Ethelbert as the patron saint of the church of Hoxne, would provide a parallel to the substitution of St Benedict of Ramsey for St Benedict of Holme.) It would have been inexpedient for Losinga in his struggle with the Bury monks to associate the origins of their abbey with so powerful a house as Ramsey and one, moreover, outside his diocese. St Benedict of Holme, having little prestige and being within his own diocese, was open to no such objections.

Meanwhile it seems that the monks of Bury were either ignorant or indifferent, or both, concerning the provenance of the original occupants of their abbey. Ignorance is a perfectly plausible hypothesis. The story of Æthelwine, the sacristan of the clerical congregation at Beodricesworth, bearing St Edmund's bier to London for safety in 1010 is, as I have argued elsewhere,[2] unlikely to be true at least in its present form. Nevertheless, it surely preserves some tradition that sometime during the Viking incursions the martyr's body had been moved to a safer place. In fact the incursions must have disrupted the life of the community at Beodricesworth, and by doing so disrupted its corporate memory.[3] Therefore, if the monastery was already in existence, knowledge of its origins could have been destroyed. The haziness of the monks' recollections in Anglo-Norman times, and the absence of pre-Conquest written evidence

1. *Supra*, pp. 95-6.

2. 'Baldwin, p. 74. However, I do not sufficiently emphasise there the complexity of the relationship between the legend of St Edmund and that of St Cuthbert. The earliest source for the latter's cult, the *Historia de Sancto Cuthberto* (in Symeon of Durham, *Opera Omnia*, ed. Arnold, i. 196–214) is mid-tenth century, but the earliest surviving text is mid-eleventh century. The legend was elaborated by Symeon in his *Libellus, c.* 1100 (*ibid.* i. 3–135) and again by Reginald of Coldingham in the mid-twelfth century (*supra*, p. 87 n. 6). Thus the St Cuthbert legend evolved at the same time as the St Edmund one, and mutual cross-fertilization must be expected, especially as the bishop of Durham presided over the translation of St Edmund in 1095 (*cf.* Battiscombe, *op. cit.* p. 46). Nevertheless, it seems fair to assume that the story of Æthelwine the sacristan carrying St Edmund's bier was influenced by the St Cuthbert legend, and not *vice versa*, since there is no convincing evidence that Æthelwine the sacristan was a real person, while Æthelwine, bishop of Durham, certainly was.

3. For the decline of monastic fervour and the monks' sufferings, which were real though passing, in the late tenth and early eleventh centuries, owing to the Viking raids, see Knowles, *Monastic Order*, p. 69.

about the abbey's earlier history, are demonstrated by the appeal in the trial in the royal court in 1081 to the memory of the aged Abbot Ælfwine of Ramsey. Moreover, since their main preoccupation was to establish the royal origin and connections of the abbey, the provenance of its first inmates was not their concern.

The questions arise how the Bury monks learnt the Holme story and why they adopted it late in Henry III's reign. The information could well have reached them from Norwich at that period, since there was a close historiographical connection between Norwich and Bury; from 1258 to 1263 the Norwich chronicler extracted from the chronicle composed at St Edmund's in the last half of the thirteenth century.[1] Probably Bury lent a copy to Norwich for transcription and might well have received historical material in exchange.[2] There is also evidence that the sacrist of Bury, William of Hoo (1280–94), with whose office the composition of the last section of the Bury chronicle is to be associated, had previously been precentor of Norwich.[3] His migration to Bury, perhaps a result of the Norwich riots of 1272, would have created another historiographical link.[4] The vehicle for the transmission of the Holme story could have been the Losinga tract. A possible indication that this was the source is the fact that the only known copy of the tract is in the Bury register, the *Liber Albus*, in a hand dateable to the 1260s and 1270s.[5] Although the tract only states that Bishop Ælfwine made a monk of Holme prior of the new monastery, this could be the seed of the story. The Bury monks, who of course believed that the new monastery was an abbey and not a cathedral priory, would have substituted 'abbot' for 'prior', supplied the name Ufi, since they believed he was their first abbot, and presumably invented the other details.

The Bury monks probably adopted and elaborated the story of colonization from Holme in order to provide historical justification for the exceptionally binding terms of the confederacy which they made with Holme in the last decade of Henry III's reign.[6] The

1. See Bartholomew Cotton, *Historia Anglicana*, ed. H. R. Luard (Rolls Series, 1859), pp. lii–lviii and *The Chronicle of Bury St Edmunds 1212–1301*, ed., with an English translation, A. Gransden (Nelson's Medieval Texts, 1964, henceforth referred to as *Bury Chron.*), p. xxvii.

2. For an example of an early manuscript of the Bury chronicle being 'edited' for use by the chronicler of another house, in this case Peterborough, see *Bury Chron.* p. xliv.

3. Cotton, *Hist. Angl.* p. 149; cf. A. Gransden, *Historical Writing in England, i, c.550–1307* (London, 1974), pp. 399–400.

4. Both Bartholomew Cotton and the Bury Chronicle have graphic (but not identical) accounts of the attack on Norwich cathedral. Cotton, *Hist. Angl.* pp. 146–9, *Bury Chron.* pp. 50–1.

5. BL MS Harley 1005, fos. 197, 197ᵛ. Printed Galbraith, 'East Anglian see', pp. 226–8. This text is by a scribe active at Bury in the 1260s and 1270s, who wrote a number of items in Harley 1005, for example, the best surviving text of the Bury Customary, besides additional customs compiled after 1267/8 (*Bury Customary*, p. xxxviii, Appendix II). The text of the Losinga tract has a late fourteenth century gloss by Henry Kirkstead (Galbraith, *op. cit.* pp. 226, 228), for whom see R. H. Rouse, 'Bostonus Buriensis and the author of the *Catalogus Scriptorum Ecclesiae*', *Speculum*, xli (1966), pp. 471–99 (esp. p. 484).

6. *Supra*, p. 97 and n. 4.

confederacy has an apparently unique provision: in case of disaster from fire, war or other grave misfortune, half the monks of the stricken house might reside in the other house, as full members of the community until their own house was restored to prosperity. The earliest text of the confederacy is in the hand of the above-mentioned scribe of the Losinga tract, which dates it to the 1260s and 1270s. Indeed, it is very likely that the extant confederacy was drawn up in or after 1264, as a result of the troubles with the town which beset the abbey then and thereafter. At the time of the Barons' War and again during the widespread disorders which accompanied the deposition of Edward II in 1326/7, the townsmen of Bury consti-tuted a serious threat to the abbey's security, opposing the monks with actual violence.[1] The Bury monks must also have suffered vicarious alarm in the summer of 1272, when the citizens of Norwich attacked the priory and set fire to the cathedral. In such circumstances the remote site of Holme could provide a welcome asylum to frightened monks from Bury.[2] It is in fact known that the sacrist and other monks fled there in 1327 and stayed until it was safe to return.

This inquiry into the legends and traditions concerning the origins of St Edmund's abbey does not prove that they are false, but it does suggest that they are open to grave doubt. The hagiographical character of the *Passio*, the subsequent absence of Anglo-Saxon sources apart from the charters and wills of Edward the Confessor's reign, and the propagandist bias of Anglo-Norman and later sources combine to warn us against rash acceptance of these legends and traditions. They also developed elsewhere than at Bury, and wherever they grew they too were susceptible to extraneous pressures. Such legends and traditions, far from remaining isolated, contributed to the formation of those evolving at Bury itself. The legend that St Edmund was martyred and first buried at Hoxne seems to have originated as part of the propaganda used by the bishop of East Anglia in the struggle with Bury. Once that conflict was resolved, the legend could gain acceptance at Bury with impunity; by the late fourteenth century it had become an undisputed element in St Edmund's hagiology. The tradition of Bishop Ælfwine's role in the abbey's 'foundation' may also derive from the bishop's propaganda; perhaps Hermann adopted it, suitably modified, because he thought, in view of its plausibility, that it would be rash to jettison it outright. Similarly, the seed of the tradition that St Edmund's was colonized from St Benet of Holme is to be found in the bishop's propaganda. It was only adopted at Bury in the late thirteenth century when the

1. See M. D. Lobel, *Borough of Bury St Edmunds* (Oxford, 1935), pp. 126–8, 142–4.

2. Gransden, 'The "Cronica Buriensis" and the abbey of St Benet of Hulme', pp. 81–2. In similar circumstances the monks of St Albans used their cell at Tynemouth – some of them took refuge there during the Peasants' Revolt; Thomas Walsingham, *Historia Anglicana*, ed. H. T. Riley (Rolls Series, 1863–4, 2 vols.), i. 469. See *infra*, pp. 240 and n. 6, 243–4.

monks' conflict with the town gave them a motive for fostering it.

In the absence of evidence corroborating the accepted account of the origins of St Edmund's abbey, we are justified in suggesting an alternative which fits the facts at least as well. I suggest that Ramsey was responsible for the reform of the clerical congregation at Beodricesworth. (The dedication of Holme to St Benedict suggests that it too owed its origin as a Benedictine monastery to Ramsey.) This reform could have happened during St Oswald's rule at Ramsey, in connection with Abbo's composition of the *Passio*. But, since the spectacular growth in the cult of St Edmund did not take place until the 1020s, it seems more likely that the reform was the work of St Oswald's successor, Abbot Eadnoth. Perhaps Eadnoth, imitating St Oswald's practice as exemplified at Worcester and Winchcombe, sent a monk of Ramsey to reform the clerical congregation at Beodricesworth, appointing him abbot. Life in St Edmund's new monastery would have been disrupted by the Viking incursions, but have recovered under Canute. At this point we are, so to speak, on dry land. Florence records that the church was dedicated in 1032,[1] and charters show that both Canute and Emma made grants to St Edmund's. More lavish endowment followed in the reign of Edward the Confessor, who seems, indeed, to have given the monastery his especial patronage. But although Abbot Baldwin exploited this royal connection after the Norman Conquest in the struggle against the bishop of East Anglia, its importance soon began to decline; ultimately it was the pope who was to become the abbey's principal protector.[2] These hypotheses are, like the generally accepted legends and traditions concerning the origins of St Edmund's abbey, unprovable on the present evidence. However, their plausibility at least demonstrates that the abbey's origins are obscure and problematical – the alleged certainty about them is chimera; as is the case with a number of other pre-Conquest foundations, they deserve further scholarly attention.

---

1. *Chronicon ex Chronicis*, i. 189.

2. Knowles, 'Essays in monastic history, IV – the growth of exemption', pp. 210–13 *passim*.

I am indebted to Mr Christopher Hohler and Dr Michael Lapidge for reading the typescript of this article and for making valuable comments and suggestions, especially about my discussion of the St Edmund legend. I alone, however, am responsible for any errors and for the opinions expressed.

1  David harping, from St Wulfstan's portiforium.
   *(Cambridge, Corpus Christi College, MS 391, fo. 24v)*

# 4

# Cultural Transition at Worcester in the Anglo-Norman Period

The Norman Conquest posed the monasteries of England with a problem, how to preserve the continuity of their religious traditions. Abbacies falling vacant were filled with Normans, and neither they nor the ecclesiastical authorities readily recognised the claim of the Anglo-Saxon saints to sanctity.[1] As Archbishop Lanfranc said: 'These Englishmen among whom we are living have set up for themselves certain saints whom

### SHORTENED TITLES USED

| | |
|---|---|
| *Gesta Pontificum:* | *Willelmi Malmesbiriensis Monachi de Gestis Pontificum Anglorum* ed. N.E.S.A. Hamilton (Rolls Series, LII, 1870) |
| *Gesta Regum:* | *Willelmi Malmesbiriensis Monachi de Gestis Regum*, ed. W. Stubbs (Rolls Series, XC, 1887, 1889) |
| GRANSDEN: | A. Gransden, *Historical Writing in England c. 550-c. 1307* (London 1974) |
| *Hemingi Chartularium:* | *Hemingi Chartularium Ecclesiae Wigorniensis*, ed. T. Hearne (Oxford 1723) |
| MACRAY, *Chron. Evesham:* | *Chronicon Abbatiae de Evesham*, ed. W.D. Macray (Rolls Series, XXIX, 1863) |
| *Memorials of St Dunstan:* | *Memorials of St Dunstan*, ed. W. Stubbs *(Rolls Series, LXIII, 1874).* |
| SOUTHERN (1963): | R.W. Southern, *St Anselm and his Biographer* (Cambridge 1963) |
| SOUTHERN (1970): | R.W. Southern, 'The Place of England in the Twelfth Century Renaissance', *Medieval Humanism and Other Studies* (Oxford 1970) |
| *Vita Wulfstani:* | *The Vita Wulfstani of William of Malmesbury*, ed. R.R. Darlington (Camden Society, XL, 1928) |
| WEAVER, *Chron. Worcester:* | *The Chronicle of John of Worcester* 1118-1140, ed. J.R.H. Weaver (Anecdota Oxoniensa, Oxford 1908) |

---

[1] Cf. S.J. Ridyard, '*Condigna veneratio*: Post-Conquest Attitudes to the Saints of the Anglo-Saxons', *Anglo-Norman Studies*, ix, *Proceedings of the Battle Conference, 1986* (Woodbridge, 1987), 179-206.

they revere. But sometimes when I turn over in my mind their own accounts of who they were, I cannot help having doubts about the quality of their sanctity'.[2] The Anglo-Saxon saints were on trial. Walter, the Norman abbot of Evesham (1077-1104) put the saints' relics preserved in his abbey to the test of fire: only those spared by the flames were to be accounted genuine – luckily they proved non-inflammable.[3]

By the second generation after the Conquest, Anglo-Norman writers had come to the rescue of the Anglo-Saxon saints. The loss of their reputations would have been damaging to the monasteries. The cult of saints was lucrative business. Relics attracted pilgrims and they gave offerings to the monks, an important source of income.[4] At Christ Church, Canterbury two monks, first Osbern and then Eadmer, wrotes Lives of a number of the saints connected with the cathedral. They included material relating to the history of Christ Church itself.[5] Here they were following the practice of earlier Anglo-Saxon hagiographers who, because they treated the patron saint of a monastery as the *persona*, as it were, of the place, had used hagiographies to some extent a vehicles for local history.

The scholar who did most to salvage the reputations of the Anglo-Saxon saints and to write the histories of the houses associated with them was William of Malmesbury. In 1125 he published his *Gesta Pontificum Anglorum*, which was virtually a survey of ecclesiastical England. It is divided into sections, one for every bishopric, and each section ends with an account of the religious houses, including Lives of their saints – thus nearly half of his account of Worcester is devoted to the life and miracles of St Wulfstan (bishop 1062-1095).[6] Indeed William's declared purpose was to remedy the deficiencies of the Anglo-Saxon historians and hagiographers; since Bede, he asserts, they had neglected to record their country's past and the achievements of its great men.[7]

Malmesbury Abbey, together with the great abbeys of the Severn valley, including Worcester, was in the early 12th century the centre of a remarkable cultural revival.[8] Other writers besides William were engaged

---

[2] *The Life of St Anselm Archbishop of Canterbury by Eadmer*, ed., with an English translation, R.W. Southern (Nelson's Medieval Texts, 1962), 50-2. Cf. Gransden, 105.

[3] Macray, *Chron. Evesham*, 323-4.

[4] See C.R. Cheney, 'Church-Building in the Middle Ages', *Bulletin of the John Rylands Library*, XXXIV (1951-52), 29, 32.

[5] Gransden, 127-31.

[6] *Gesta Pontificum*, 279-89, 301-3.

[7] *Ibid.*, 4, and *Gesta Regum*, I, 2.

[8] For scriptural studies in the Severn Valley see Hugh Farmer, 'William of Malmesbury's Commentary on Lamentations', *Studia Monastica*, IV (1962), 284-5; for the contributions to the study of science by Abelard of Bath see C.H. Haskins, *Studies in the History of Mediaeval Science* (Cambridge 1924), 20-42, and by Walcher of Malvern see below p. 111 and nn. 25, 27. For the historians see below.

in establishing links with the past. At Evesham the prior Dominic wrote the *Life* of the patron saint, Ecgwin, and of two other pre-Conquest saints, St Odulf and St Wistan, whose relics were preserved in the abbey.[9] Moreover, he or another monk of Evesham wrote a history of the abbey from its foundation in the 8th century until the rule of Abbot Walter.[10] This history resembles in form Bede's *Lives of the Abbots of Wearmouth and Jarrow*. The author had no doubt read the work; certainly Bede's *Ecclesiastical History* was studied at Evesham. Already in 1073 or 1074, it had inspired two of the monks to go with the prior of Winchcombe (which was at that time ruled jointly with Evesham) to visit the holy places of ancient Northumbria and emulate the asceticism of the Bedan saints. At the persuasion of Walcher bishop of Durham they refounded Jarrow, and two years later a group from the south refounded Wearmouth.[11]

Bede was also studied at Worcester. Wulfstan dedicated a church to Bede. His *Life*, which will be discussed later, notes that after the dedication, Wulfstan preached a sermon 'which sparkled with the same eloquence as had formerly moved the tongue of Bede, . . . that prince of letters among the English people'.[12] And later when Nicholas, who was prior of Worcester from *c.* 1113 to *c.* 1124, wrote to Eadmer (of Christ Church, Canterbury) on the rights of the see of York in Scotland, he cited the *Ecclesiastical History* as evidence.[13]

A recent scholar has written: 'Of all the Old English monasteries, Worcester was the most successful in preserving its links with the past'.[14] The cathedral priory flourished during the Anglo-Norman period. This may have been partly because its fame and prosperity were well established in early Anglo-Saxon times. It was already a cultural centre in the time of King Alfred who had summoned Wærferth bishop of Worcester and three of his fellow Mercians, Plegmund (later archbishop of

---

[9] Macray, *Chron. Evesham*, 1-17, 313-37. See J.C. Jennings, 'The Writings of Prior Dominic of Evesham', *E.H.R.* LXXVII (1962), 298-304.

[10] Macray, *Chron. Evesham*, 1-98. For the suggestion that Dominic wrote the History, including the *Life of Abbot Æthelwig* which it incorporates (for which see R.R. Darlington, 'Æthelwig, abbot of Evesham', *E.H.R.* xlviii (1933), 1-22, 177-98) see Jennings, op. cit., 302-3. His case, however, rests on cross-references between Dominic's Life of St Ecgwin and the History, which could have been inserted by Thomas of Marlborough who revised and continued the History in the early 13th century. Therefore, his arguments do not vitiate those I put forward against Dominic's authorship in Gransden, 113 (cf. *ibid.*, 89, 111-13, and M.D. Knowles, *Monastic Order in England* (Cambridge 1963), Appendix VIII, 704-5.

[11] For the post-Conquest monastic settlement of the north see above/below pp. 7-8, with further references.

[12] *Vita Wulfstani*, 20.

[13] *Councils and Ecclesiastical Documents*, ed. A.W. Haddan and W. Stubbs (Oxford 1869-71), II, 203, 204.

[14] Southern (1970), 168.

Canterbury), Æthelstan and Werwulf, to help him in his educational reforms: at his order Werfrith translated the *Dialogues* of Pope Gregory from Latin into Anglo-Saxon.[15] The standard of literacy at Worcester was probably maintained at least for some years after Alfred's death.[16] And during the 10th-century monastic revival it again achieved pre-eminence during the episcopate of St Oswald who became bishop of Worcester in 961 and held the see together with that of York from 972 until his death in 992. The priory had the benefit both of St Oswald's religious reputation and of his administrative ability which created the immunity of the Oswaldslow.

However, during the Danish domination in the early 11th century Worcester suffered badly. The area was ravaged by Swein, and the cathedral was despoiled and finally sacked.[17] It owed its recovery to Wulfstan, one of the greatest Anglo-Saxon bishops and one whose rule at Worcester bridged the Norman Conquest. Having been loyal to the old order, he transferred his support to William I shortly after the Conquest. He was high in the favour of both William I and William II and was often at the royal court. Locally he helped enforce order: he assisted in suppressing the baronial revolts of 1075 and 1088 and played an important part in the government of the shire, acting as a judge at least once.[18] His power in the area was only rivalled by that of Æthelwig abbot of Evesham from 1059 to 1077. Wulfstan contributed much to the welfare of the cathedral priory. He regained estates lost during the disruptions caused by the Danes and by the Norman Conquest,[19] and, in order to record the priory's rights and property, he commissioned the subprior Hemming to write a cartulary.[20] This included a short biography of Wulfstan himself which is devoted mainly to his work for the priory.[21]

According to legend, soon after the Norman Conquest Wulfstan had nearly been deposed by Archbishop Lanfranc in the presence of William I in an ecclesiastical council at Westminster. He was charged with 'simplicity and ignorance' but a miracle saved him; he refused to surrender his staff to Lanfranc, but placed it on the tomb of Edward the Confessor, from whom he had received it. The stones opened and held the end fast, so that

---

[15] *Asser's Life of King Alfred*, ed. W.H. Stevenson (Oxford 1904, reprinted 1959 with a contribution by Dorothy Whitelock), 62-3 (ch. 77), 303-5.

[16] The evidence for this is the excellent series of legal records in English bearing the names of the ealdorman Æthelred and of his wife Æthelflaed, King Alfred's daughter; F.M. Stenton, *The Latin Charters of the Anglo-Saxon Period* (Oxford 1955), 45.

[17] For a summary of the history of Worcester in the 10th and 11th centuries see V.C.H., *Worcestershire*, II, 95-7.

[18] *Vita Wulfstani*, xxvii-xxviii.

[19] See *Hemingi Chartularium*, II, 406-8, 418-19. Cf. *Vita Wulfstani*, xxvi.

[20] See *Hemingi Chartularium*, I, 1. Cf. *Vita Wulfstani*, xlii.

[21] *Hemingi Chartularium*, II, 403-8. Cf. Gransden, 87 and n. 158.

no one but Wulfstan himself could take it up: this was interpreted as indicating that God wanted him to retain the bishopric.[22]

In view of known facts about Wulfstan it seems unlikely that the charge of ignorance was justified. He started his monastic career as school-master,[23] and indeed later contributed both directly and indirectly to Worcester's cultural achievements. It was he who was responsible for the introduction at Worcester of the new movement in science which resulted from the acquisition by north-western Europe of the learning of the Arabic world and the Iberian peninsular.[24] This knowledge reached Worcester from Malvern where Walcher, a Lotharingian, was prior from 1091 to his death in 1125. He was noted as a mathematician and astronomer and used the works of the converted Spanish Jew, Peter Alphonso.[25] Already by 1092 Walcher was using the astrolabe and writing on scientific matters. His treatises show his transition from the cumbersome Roman fractions to the more precise measurements of degrees, minutes and seconds. He describes his observation of a lunar eclipse he saw in Italy in 1091 and, in more detail, one he saw in England in 1092.[26] A manuscript (now Bodleian, Auct. F.1.9) containing his lunar observations, the most up-to-date researches of the Spanish astronomers and some excellent diagrammatic illustrations, was made at Worcester *c*. 1130.[27]

Possibly Wulfstan was also interested in chronology, an interest which could well have originated with the study of Bede, the first English chronologist,[28] and been fostered by his friendship with the learned Robert bishop of Hereford (who like Walcher of Malvern was a Lotharingian). Their friendship is attested by a story given in rather different versions by a number of authorities. William of Malmesbury relates that when Wulfstan was on his death-bed, he appeared in a vision to Robert telling him to hasten to Worcester if he wanted to see him alive

[22] The story first appears in Osbert of Clare's *Vita beati Edwardi Regis*, ch. XXIX, ed. Marc Bloch in *Analecta Bollandiana*, XLI (1923), 64-6. Cf. *Vita Wulfstani*, xxxi-xxxii. On Wulfstan's alleged simplicity see Emma Mason, 'Change and Continuity in Eleventh-Century Mercia: the Experience of St Wulfstan at Worcester', *Anglo-Norman Studies*, VIII, *Proceedings of the Battle Conference, 1985* (Woodbridge 1986), 169-70, 173-4, and idem, 'St Wulfstan's staff: a legend and its uses', *Medium Ævum*, LIII (1984), 166-7.

[23] *Vita Wulfstani*, 9.

[24] Southern (1970), 168.

[25] For Walcher see C.H. Haskins, 'The Reception of Arabic Science in England', *E.H.R.* xxx (1915), 56-9.

[26] See the next note.

[27] Extracts from Bodleian MS Auct. F.1.9, including Walcher's descriptions of the lunar eclipses, are printed in Haskins, *loc. cit.*, 57-9. One of the illustrations (f. 88) is reproduced by Southern (1970), plate VIII. (For another scientific illustration from Worcester see page 8 and n. 75.) For the Worcester provenance of the manuscript see N.R. Ker, *Medieval Libraries of Great Britain* (London 1964), 208 and nn. 5, 6.

[28] For the influence of Bede on Wulfstan see above p. 109.

again. On the way Robert had another vision of Wulfstan, who announced his own death and said that Robert too would die shortly. Robert arrived at Worcester, buried Wulfstan and was presented by Prior Nicholas with the lambswool cope 'in which [Wulfstan] was wont to ride', as a token of their long friendship. But before Robert could leave he was taken ill with cold shivers and died 'with tears and sighs'.[29]

Bishop Robert had imported from Germany a copy of the universal chronicle of Marianus Scotus, an Irish monk, who lived as a recluse first at Fulda and then at Mainz.[30] His chronicle was written in annalistic form and covered the period from the Creation until A.D. 1082 (in which year Marianus probably died). It has one peculiarity: Marianus believed that the accepted date of the Incarnation was twenty two years too late – and demonstrated the chronological justification for his view at some length. Therefore he dated events doubly; according to Dionysius and according to his own computation.[31]

The introduction of Marianus's chronicle into England was important because it was the most comprehensive and up-to-date universal history yet known here. Its information on European affairs was particularly valuable because they had been neglected by the Anglo-Saxon chroniclers. It received the immediate attention of scholars. Bishop Robert himself wrote an abbreviated version,[32] and William of Malmesbury described it both in the *Gesta Pontificum* and in the *Gesta Regum*, commenting that there was much to be said for its chronological system although the latter had not been widely accepted.[33] No doubt on account of Bishop Robert's friendship with Wulfstan, a copy soon reached Worcester, and there at the command of Wulfstan, one of the monks began interpolating it with material relating to England, bringing it up to date.[34]

Wulfstan himself was interested in history. He was regarded as an authority on the pre-Conquest period. Eadmer, enumerating his virtues, concludes: 'He was above all imbued with knowledge of the ancient

---

[29] *Gesta Pontificum*, 302-3. Cf. *Vita Wulfstani*, xv, n. 2, 60-3, and *Florentii Wigorniensis Monachi Chronicon ex Chronicis*, ed. Benjamin Thorpe (English Historical Society, 1848, 1849), II, 36-7.

[30] William of Malmesbury records that Robert first brought Marianus's chronicle to England: *Gesta Pontificum*, 301.

[31] See W.H. Stevenson, 'A Contemporary Description of the Domesday Survey', *E.H.R.* XXL (1907), 73 and n. 3.

[32] See *ibid.*, 72 and n. 2, 73.

[33] *Gesta Pontificum*, 301; *Gesta Regum*, II, 345.

[34] This is the chronicle from the Creation of the World to A.D. 1140, which to 1118 is attributed to Florence of Worcester (see n. 29 above and pp. 6 *et sqq.*) and thereafter to John of Worcester (Weaver, *Chron. Worcester*). For the statement that Wulfstan commissioned the chronicle see below p. 117 and n. 62.

customs of the English'.[35] And Lanfranc's successor Anselm wrote to him to discover what the customs were relating to the archbishop of Canterbury's rights to dedicate churches on his estates outside his diocese.[36] Moreover, Wulfstan was interested in his cathedral priory's pre-Conquest history, particularly in the saints associated with it. During the trial of the dispute between him and Thomas archbishop of York, concerning the latter's claim to supremacy over the bishopric of Worcester and to some of its property, Wulfstan had with him the *Lives* of St Dunstan (bishop of Worcester from 960 until 962 when he succeeded to Canterbury) and of St Oswald.[37] He translated the relics of St Oswald when he rebuilt the cathedral between 1084 and 1088 or 1089,[38] and refounded the priory originally established by Oswald at Westbury on Trym.[39] After his death the cult of St Oswald continued to flourish at Worcester, and in the early 12th century the monks commissioned Eadmer to write a new *Life* of St Oswald.

However, the researches of hagiographers were not the most characteristic feature of cultural continuity at Worcester (Oswald's career was too recent and well known to need much study). On the other hand two literary forms typical of the Anglo-Saxon period were revived in the cathedral. Wulfstan himself contributed indirectly to the revival of one, and directly to the revival of the other. The first which will be considered is the biography arranged according to subject matter; Wulfstan's own posthumous biography was arranged in this way. The second literary form in question is the vernacular annals (that is the Anglo-Saxon Chronicle); Wulfstan himself commissioned one of his monks to write Latin annals which were partly a translation of these.

First, the bipartite biography. The earliest secular biography written in Anglo-Saxon England, Asser's *Life of King Alfred*, was divided into two parts. The first relates mainly to Alfred's public life, his career as king, and the second part to his private life – his character, family and the like. This division of the biography into two parts according to subject matter originated with Suetonius's *Lives of the Caesars* and was transmitted to Asser by Einhard's *Life of Charlemagne*.[41] It was also used in two

---

[35] *Eadmeri Historia Novorum in Anglia*, ed. Martin Rule (Rolls Series, LXXXI, 1884), 45-6.

[36] Eadmer preserves a copy of the letter; *ibid.*, 46-7.

[37] *Vita Wulfstani*, 25.

[38] *Ibid.*, xxxix, 52.

[39] *Ibid.*, xxxix, 52.

[40] Eadmer's *Vita S. Oswaldi* is printed in *Historians of the Church of York*, II, ed. James Raine (Rolls Series, LXXI, 1886), 1-59. Cf. p.      below.

[41] For Asser's arrangment of his work and use of Einhard see *Asser's Life of King Alfred*, ed. Stevenson, lxxix-lxxx, 54 (ch. 72), 294, and Marie Schütt, 'The Literary Form of Asser's *Vita Alfredi*', *E.H.R.* LXXII (1957), 209-20 *passim*.

subsequent royal biographies written in Anglo-Saxon times: the biography of King Canute (the *Encomium Emmae Reginae*)[42] and the *Life of King Edward* (the Confessor).[43] On the other hand most of the sacred biographies, that is *Lives* of saints and ecclesiastics (often the same people), written in this period were unitary – they were arranged chronologically and not divided according to subject matter. However, one saint's *Life*, Ælfric's *Life of St Ethelwold* is divided according to subject matter:[44] first it deals with St Ethelwold's parentage, infancy and career; then with his character, death and miracles. This approximates to the Suetonian division.

It was the practice among the Anglo-Saxons for the biography of a famous bishop to be written by someone who knew him well, within a few years of his death. This practice survived the Conquest – such biographies were written of Leofric of Exeter (1050-1072),[45] Gundulf of Rochester (1077-1108),[46] Anselm of Canterbury (1093-1109)[47] – and of Wulfstan of Worcester. The latter concerns us here. The author was Coleman, precentor of Worcester Cathedral, who had been Wulfstan's chaplain for fifteen years and the bishop's chancellor.[48] For the *Life* which he wrote sometime between 1095 and 1113, he adopted an arrangement very similar to Ælfric's *Life of St Ethelwold*. Book I deals with Wulfstan's birth, parentage, education and rule as bishop up to the Norman Conquest. Book II concerns his episcopate after the Conquest, and Book III relates to his private life, his death and miracles.

Coleman painted a picture of a saintly bishop of the Anglo-Saxon type, not dissimilar to St Cuthbert. Wulfstan was personally holy and assiduous in his religious life and episcopal duties. Like St Cuthbert he was constantly riding from place to place, fulfilling his pastoral duties. The *Life* says that 'he always carried in his bosom a psalter and book of prayers', and he recited the hours, psalms and prayers with his attendants.[49] Just as St Cuthbert's portable altar has survived, so also has the very portiforium, or breviary, of St Wulfstan. It is a small book, less

[42]  The *Encomium* is in three books; the first two are a biography of King Canute (the last relates to Emma and her son Harthacanute). The biography, having recounted Canute's conquests and secular activities, ends with his spiritual life and relations with the church; *Encomium Emmae Reginae*, ed. Alistair Campbell (Camden Society, LXXII, 1949), 35-9.

[43]  See *The Life of King Edward*, ed. Frank Barlow (Nelson's Medieval Texts, 1962), xx.

[44]  See Gransden, 79.

[45]  Printed in *The Exeter Book of Old English Poetry*, ed. R.W. Chambers, M. Förster and R. Flower (London 1933), 8-9.

[46]  Printed in Henry Wharton, *Anglia Sacra* (London 1691), II, 273 *et sqq.*

[47]  See p. 108 and n. 2 above.

[48]  For Coleman's career and the composition of the *Life of Wulfstan* see *Vita Wulfstani*, viii.

[49]  *Ibid.*, 95 and n. 2. Cf. *ibid.*, 49, and Dame Laurentia McLachlan, 'St Wulstan's Prayer Book', *Journal of Theological Studies*, xxx (1929), 176.

than nine inches by six, and is now in Corpus Christi College, Cambridge (MS 391)[50] (Pl. 1).

Coleman also stressed that Wulfstan (like earlier Anglo-Saxon bishops) was of consequence in national affairs.[51] And in the Anglo-Saxon manner, Coleman worked the local history of the priory into his biography. He mentions Wulfstan's reforms as prior before he became bishop, and his building activities.[52] More especially he gives a detailed account of Wulfstan's dispute with Thomas archbishop of York; thus the *Life* served as a record of Wulfstan's success and of the independence of the bishops of Worcester from the authority of the archbishops of York.[53] But Coleman's debt to the Anglo-Saxon tradition went further than the arrangement of his work and the treatment of the subject matter. He wrote the *Life* in the Anglo-Saxon vernacular. This may well have been a piece of conscious revivalism because within a generation the monks could no longer understand it. Therefore they asked William of Malmesbury to translate it into Latin – which he did, dedicating his translation to Warin, who was prior from *c.* 1124 to *c.* 1143.[54] The fact that Coleman wrote in Anglo-Saxon may also have contributed to the loss of his work – for his text we have to rely on William of Malmesbury's translation.[55] It has been suggested that the only copy of Coleman's *Life* was sent to the pope in the early 13th century as evidence in the proceedings to secure Wulfstan's canonisation and was never returned.[56]

Next to be considered is the survival of annalistic historiography at Worcester. The Anglo-Saxon Chronicle itself was firmly rooted there. It is very likely that at least two copies were continued by the monks until after the Conquest. There is good evidence that the so-called D version which went down to 1079 was written at Worcester.[57] Moreover, another version

---

[50] See Pl. 1. For the importance of this picture as evidence for the survival at Worcester of the Anglo-Saxon technique of line drawing see C.M. Kauffmann, *Romanesque Manuscripts 1066-1190* (London-Boston 1975), p. 45. The volume is described by McLachlan, *loc. cit.*, 174-7.

[51] *Vita Wulfstani*, 22-4.

[52] *Ibid.*, 11, 15, 21, 52.

[53] *Ibid.*, 16-20, 24.

[54] *Ibid.*, 1.

[55] William of Malmesbury claims (*ibid.*, 2) to have adhered closely to Coleman's text, and Professor Darlington argues that he made few alterations or additions (*ibid.* ix). I have accepted this view although Mr Farmer contends that William allowed himself considerable latitude; see Hugh Farmer, 'Two Biographies by William of Malmesbury' in *Latin Biography*, ed. T.A. Dorey (London 1967), 165-74.

[56] *Vita Wulfstani*, viii n. 4, xlvii.

[57] The Worcester provenance of the D version of the Anglo-Saxon Chronicle is supported by G.N. Garmonsway; *The Anglo-Saxon Chronicle* (London 1955), ed. G.N. Garmonsway, xxxvii-xxxix. However Dorothy Whitelock and F.M. Stenton suggest York (*The Anglo-Saxon Chronicle*, ed. D. Whitelock, D.C. Douglas and S.I. Tucker (London 1961), xv; F.M. Stenton, *Anglo-Saxon England* (Oxford 1947), 681). Charles Plummer

now lost, reaching to 1130, appears to have been used by the Anglo-Norman chroniclers at Worcester who are discussed below.[58] Nevertheless at Worcester as elsewhere the Norman Conquest ultimately killed the Anglo-Saxon Chronicle. English was no longer a language used by the literate; it was replaced by Norman French for the less formal kinds of literature, Latin of course remaining the learned language.

The survival of annalistic historiography at Worcester was partly the result of the introduction of Marianus Scotus's chronicle, and Wulfstan's command that it should be supplemented and continued, as already mentioned.[59] Thus was begun the Worcester chronicle, the so-called *Chronicon ex Chronicis* (the *Chronicle of Chronicles*), which was subsequently continued there to 1140. Nevertheless, although Marianus was responsible for the inception of the Worcester chronicle, the Anglo-Saxon Chronicle played a crucial role in its actual composition. It provided the entries on English history which the chronicler interpolated into Marianus's work, and also much of the material after Marianus ended, probably down to 1130.[60] Perhaps even more significant, it encouraged the writing of contemporary annals. Marianus, though he brought his chronicle up to date, relied mainly on earlier works; his gift was as a compiler, not a contemporary annalist. The Anglo-Saxon chroniclers, on the other hand, were distinguished as contemporary annalists; from the reign of King Alfred they had added entries to the Chronicle year by year, when news reached them. Such a chronicle was not a formal literary work, but an ever growing record of recent events. This aspect of the Anglo-Saxon Chronicle was adopted at Worcester; although until the early 12th century the Worcester chronicle is mainly a compilation, from 1121 it is a contemporary record, and from 1130 (when the lost version of the Anglo-Saxon Chronicle apparently ended), it is wholly independent of all known chronicles.

The name of the monk whom Wulfstan commissioned to write it is open to dispute. The chronicle itself has an entry under 1118 reading:

> On the nones of July died Dom. Florence monk of Worcester. This chronicle of chronicles excels all others because of his profound erudition and studious application.[61]

suggests Evesham (*Two of the Saxon Chronicles Parallel*, ed. C. Plummer (Oxford 1892, 1899), II, lxxvi-lxxvii).

[58]  Pp. 116-20.

[59]  P. 112 and n. 34. For the Worcester chronicle cf. below pp. 203-4 and nn. 21-4.

[60]  See Whitelock, Douglas and Tucker, *op. cit.* xx. Cf. R.R. Darlington and P. McGurk, 'The "Chronicon ex Chronicis" of "Florence" of Worcester and its Use of Sources for English History before 1066; *Anglo-Norman Studies*, V, *Proceedings of the Battle Conference, 1982* (Woodbridge, 1983), 185-96 *passim*.

[61]  Weaver, *Chron. Worcester*, 13.

The Worcester chronicle to 1118 has consequently gone under the name of Florence of Worcester. However when sometime early in the 12th century (the exact year is unknown), the chronicler Orderic Vitalis visited Worcester from Normandy, he found a monk called John writing the chronicle. Orderic writes:

> John was an Englishman by birth, entered the monastery of Worcester as a boy and won great repute for his learning and piety. He continued the chronicle of Marianus Scotus and carefully recorded the events of William's reign and of his sons William Rufus and Henry up to the present . . . at the command of the venerable Wulfstan bishop and monk.[62]

If Orderic had merely stated that John was writing the chronicle at the time of his visit, there would be no problem, because the chronicle itself has evidence that the latter part of it at least was by a monk called John: in the annal for 1139 it has some verses apostrophising the reader and asking for corrections to be made 'if John has offended in any way'.[63] However, it is hard to reconcile Orderic's explicit assertion that John started the chronicle, writing at Wulfstan's command, with the entry in the annal for 1118 that Florence was responsible for it up to that date. It could be assumed that Florence wrote to 1118 and John added the continuation to 1140, and that the passage in Orderic was simply the result of confusing the name of John, the writer at the time of Orderic's visit, with that of Florence, the earlier one. However, there is no stylistic indication of a break in the chronicle at 1118 – the whole reads like the work of one man.[64] A possible solution is that the chronicle was written by John using material collected by the assiduous Florence.

In its present form the chronicle was composed between 1124 and 1140. It contains some information about John himself. It records in the annal for 1132 that he was standing next to Uhtred, precentor of Worcester, at Mass when Uhtred was seized by his final illness; the author was deeply grieved because Uhtred had 'loved me like a foster-father'.[65] Probably soon after this the author must have temporarily fallen into disgrace, for he was exiled to Winchcombe Priory; while there he met Henry I's physician Grimbald who told him of the three visions experienced by the king while in Normandy in 1130.[66] He must have been back at Worcester

---

[62] *The Ecclesiastical History of Orderic Vitalis*, ed., with an English translation, Marjorie Chibnall, II (Oxford Medieval Texts, 1969), xxi, 187-8.

[63] Weaver, *Chron. Worcester*, 49.

[64] See Gransden, 144 and n. 55, and Martin Brett, 'John or Worcester and his Contemporaries', *The Writing of History in the Middle Ages. Essays presented to Richard William Southern*, ed. R.H.C. Davis and J.M. Wallace-Hadrill (Oxford, 1981), 104 and n. 3, 110.

[65] Weaver, *Chron. Worcester*, 36.

[66] *Ibid.*, 10, 33. For the visions see p. 119 and Pls. 2, 3.

by 1139 at latest, for on 7 November of that year he was at Lauds in the cathedral when the Empress Matilda's forces entered and sacked the city.[67]

The Worcester chronicle is significant in the history of historical writing for a number of reasons. It transmitted the Anglo-Saxon Chronicle to the post-Conquest period. Its extensive borrowings from the Chronicle were of course in Latin translation. The translation of the Chronicle into Latin had begun almost at the time of its inception in Alfred's reign – Asser translated the portions relating to Alfred for his *Life of King Alfred*. Later, in about 1000, Æthelweard the ealdorman had translated much of it into Latin for his chronicle.[68] and soon after the Norman Conquest a bilingual version, in Anglo-Saxon and Latin, was written at St Augustine's, Canterbury.[69] Nevertheless, despite these earlier translations, it was the Worcester chronicle which contributed most to making the text available in Latin to the Anglo-Normans.

Besides transmitting much of the contents of the Anglo-Saxon Chronicle, the Worcester chronicle also encouraged the keeping of contemporary annals in other monasteries. It was comparatively popular among the monks of the day. A copy reached Durham probably soon after 1118, where it formed the basis of the *Historia Regum*, which is commonly attributed to Symeon of Durham, for the years from 848 to 1118.[70] Soon after 1130 copies up to that date were made for the abbeys of Abingdon, Bury St Edmunds, Gloucester and Peterborough.[71]

The Worcester chronicle had features making it particularly attractive to the monks of other communities. Its literary form was different from the two other important histories written in the Anglo-Norman period, Eadmer's *History of Recent Events*, and William of Malmesbury's *Gesta Regum*. Both these works have literary shape, and deal with topics discursively even if this involved disregarding the chronological sequence. They could not, therefore, be interpolated without disturbing the structure. The Worcester chronicle on the other hand has no literary pretensions; it is a purely chronological record of events. Thus it could be interpolated at any point or continued without altering its nature, and so

[67]  *Ibid.*, 57.

[68]  See *The Chronicle of Æthelweard*, ed., with an English translation, Alistair Campbell (Nelson's Medieval Texts, 1962), xxii-xxxvii.

[69]  The old English text of F (BL MS Cotton Domitian A VIII) is printed in *The Anglo Saxon Chronicle*, ed. Benjamin Thorpe (Rolls Series, XXIII, 1861), I, 3-329 *passim*; the Latin text is printed and described F.P. Magoun, jn., 'Annales Domitiani Latini: an Edition', *Mediaeval Studies*, IX (1947), 235-95. For Thorpe's text see *ibid.*, 235 n. 3. Cf. Garmonsway, *op. cit.*, xli and n. 2.

[70]  See P. Hunter Blair, 'Some Observations on the *Historia Regum* attributed to Symeon of Durham', *Celt and Saxon*, ed. N. K. Chadwick (Cambridge 1963), 107-11.

[71]  See Weaver, *Chron. Worcester*, 5-9 *passim*.

monasteries which acquired copies could interpolate material relating to affairs of local interest and omit entries which exclusively concerned Worcester. For example the Gloucester copy inserts a notice of the death of Roger de Berkeley, a benefactor of St Peter's abbey, in 1137, and an account of King Stephen's visit to Gloucester in 1138 but omits the details of the death of the precentor Uhtred at Worcester.[72] Similarly some of the copies were continued – the Peterborough copy goes down to 1295.[73]

In addition to its usefulness in providing a framework and starting point for the chronicles of other monasteries, the Worcester chronicle has merits as a history. It includes European history and is more than a series of dry annals. To some extent it reflects the cultural achievements of Worcester at that time. It shows an interest in astronomy, having an enthusiastic outburst in favour of the Arab astronomer, Al-Kharismi.[74] It has a number of astronomical details; it records, for example, the sun spots seen on 8 December 1128, and has a good diagrammatic picture of them.[75] It is also concerned with chronology; it discusses at some length under A.D. 703 and 725 Bede's views on chronology expressed in *De Temporibus*, and gives chronological details relating to a number of dates.[76]

Moreover, the Worcester chronicle has in places the merit of readability. It includes some amusing stories. For example, there are three tales of German origin which must have been intended to entertain.[77] (It is noteworthy that William of Malmesbury included similar stories, in order, his editor suggests, to float the heavier portions of his narrative.)[78] And there is the graphic account of the visions experienced by Henry I in Normandy which were interpreted as divine admonitions to him to rule more justly. First, as he lay asleep he was threatened by a band of rustics who vanished when he leapt up to punish them. Second, a group of armed knights threatened the sleeping king; when the king attacked them with his sword, he did not wound any. And third, his bed was surrounded by prelates expostulating and waving their staffs, on account of Henry's ill-treatment of the Church. On his return to England he was nearly drowned in a storm in the channel, but was spared on vowing to stop exacting Danegeld for seven years and to go on pilgrimage to Bury St Edmunds.[79] The visions and voyage are illustrated

---

[72] *Ibid.*, 6-7, 25 n. 3, 36 n. 4, 48 n. 4.

[73] Printed in *Florentii Wigorniensis Monachi Chronicon ex Chronicis*, ed. Thorpe (English Hist. Soc., London 1848-9), II, 136-279.

[74] Weaver, *Chron. Worcester*, 53.

[75] *Ibid.*, 28. See Southern (1970), 168 and pl. VII.

[76] See Thorpe, *op. cit.*, I, 45; II, 36, and Weaver, *Chron. Worcester*, 34, 53.

[77] Weaver, *Chron. Worcester*, 34-6, 45-8.

[78] *Gesta Regum*, I, xc-xci. Stubbs suggests (*ibid.*, I, lxxxix) that some of William of Malmesbury's stories of German derivation reached him from Walcher of Malvern; John of Worcester could have obtained his from the same source.

[79] Weaver, *Chron. Worcester*, 32-4.

2 The visions of Henry I, from the chronicle of John of Worcester: Henry is beset by peasants and by knights.
*(Oxford, Corpus Christi College, MS 157, p. 382)*

3  The visions of Henry I, from the chronicle of John of Worcester: Henry
   is beset by bishops; his stormy crossing from Normandy.
   *(Oxford, Corpus Christi College, MS 157, p. 383)*

by four pictures, together covering nearly two full pages, of high quality, testifying to the abbey's artistic achievements (Pls 2, 3). The Worcester chronicle is apparently the earliest surviving illustrated chronicle produced in western Europe.[80]

The dissemination of the Worcester chronicle must also have been partly the result of Worcester's reputation as a cultural centre. It was in the Anglo-Norman period the venue of scholars. The visit of Orderic Vitalis, who was no doubt attracted by its fame, and the contact of both Eadmer and William of Malmesbury with Worcester, have already been mentioned.[81] A key person in Worcester's cultural connections was Prior Nicholas, who was interested in history.

Nicholas supplied Coleman with details concerning Wulfstan's piety which Coleman included in his *Life*.[82] He himself figures in one anecdote: it relates how Nicholas disregarded Wulfstan's prohibition of drinking in the priory (because of the brawls to which it gave rise), and was divinely punished by a nightmare which prevented him sleeping until he had confessed to Wulfstan.[83]

William of Malmesbury himself visited Worcester and became a personal friend of Nicholas. Evidence of his visit is provided, for example, by his eyewitness description of Wulfstan's tomb.[84] Besides at the monks request translating Coleman's *Life of Wulfstan* into Latin, he also used it as his main source for the account of the see of Worcester in the *Gesta Pontificum*.[85] He gives an anecdote about Nicholas as a young man, which he must surely have heard from the prior himself:

Nicholas, afterwards prior of Worcester, was a favoured pupil of Wulfstan. [One day when] he was sitting at his feet, the bishop, overflowing with joy, stroked the youth's head with a gentle hand, where the flowing hair deceptively covered a bald patch. 'I think', he said, 'you will go bald'. But the youth, who already in adolescence grieved that he was aging in that respect, lamented the ill fortune of falling hair. 'Why', he said, 'don't you hold it on for me?' The bishop replied laughing, 'Believe me, never as long as I live will the remainder fall out'. It was as he said, but in the very week when he departed this life, it all vanished – I don't know where – leaving the scalp bare.[86]

Eadmer too visited Worcester, perhaps when Nicholas was elected

---

[80] The four pictures are reproduced in Weaver, *Chron. Worcester*, frontispiece, as well as below pls. B, C. For the importance of the Worcester chronicle as perhaps the earliest example of an illustrated chronicle see C.M. Kauffmann *op. cit.*, pp. 43-50.

[81] Pp. 109, 115.

[82] See *Vita Wulfstani*, 51, 52, 54.

[83] *Ibid.*, 56.

[84] *Gesta Pontificum*, 288.

[85] *Ibid.*, 278-88. Cf. *Vita Wulfstani*, ix.

[86] *Gesta Pontificuam*, 287.

prior. It may have been on this occasion that the monks commissioned him to write the *Life of St Oswald*.[87] In it he mentions that he had seen and handled St Oswald's chasuble, which had been found intact when the saint was translated twelve years after his death, and was still in use at the time of Eadmer's visit.[88]

Relations between Worcester and Christ Church, Canterbury, were obviously close. Ties had no doubt been strengthened by Wulfstan's victory, with Lanfranc's help, over Thomas archbishop of York, which had put the diocese beyond dispute under the control of the archbishop of Canterbury.[89] Eadmer corresponded with the Worcester monks – in 1123 or 1124 he wrote exhorting them to elect a monk to the bishopric; he pointed out that in those evil times wicked men were seeking to exclude monks from the episcopal bench[90] (nevertheless, the king appointed a secular, Simon). The Worcester monks also benefited from Eadmer's work as an historian. Not only did he write the *Life of St Oswald* for them, but also soon after 1121 a copy of his *History of Recent Events* was at Worcester where it was extracted for the Worcester chronicle.[91]

But perhaps Eadmer's debt to the Worcester monks was even greater than their debt to him. There is certain evidence that they supplied him with information for his *Life of St Dunstan*, which he wrote partly to correct the errors in the *Life* by Osbern, Eadmer's predecessor as hagiographer at Christ Church.[92] He acknowledges at some length in the prologue his obligation to Ethelred, monk of Worcester, who had formerly been subprior and precentor of Christ Church.[93] There is also independent evidence that Prior Nicholas helped him. A long letter from Nicholas to Eadmer survives.[94] It was written in reply to a query concerning the mother of Edward the Martyr, and explains that Edward's mother, Æthelflaed, though never crowned queen, was legitimately married to King Edgar: on the other hand his second wife Ælfthryth was both crowned and legitimately married. Nicholas based his conclusions 'on the ancient authority both of chronicles and of songs which are known to have been composed in the vernacular at that time by learned men, and on the

[87] See above p. 113 and n. 40, and Southern (1963), 283 n. 2.
[88] *Vita S. Oswaldi*, 50.
[89] See p. 115 and n. 53.
[90] Printed in Wharton, *Anglia Sacra*, II, 238. Cf. Southern (1963), 286, and D.L. Bethell, 'English Black Monks and Episcopal Elections in the 1120s', *E.H.R.* LXXXIV (1969), 681 (Bethell reprints Wharton's copy of the letter, *ibid.*, 697-8).
[91] For John of Worcester's use of Eadmer's *Historia Novorum* see Weaver, *Chron. Worcester*, 13-16 *passim*. For the date of the *Historia* see Southern (1963), 298-309 *passim*.
[92] See Eadmer's *Vita S. Dunstani* in *Memorials of St Dunstan*, 162-3. Cf. Southern (1963), 281 n. 2.
[93] *Memorials of St Dunstan*, 163-4.
[94] Printed in *ibid.*, 422-4.

testimony of other writings'. This information enabled Eadmer to correct one of Osbern's errors[95] – he had stated that Edward's mother was a nun and not Edgar's wife.[96]

Eadmer also corrected another of Osbern's mistakes, the assertion that in Dunstan's time Worcester cathedral bore the same dedication as it did subsequently, that is to St Mary.[97] Eadmer denied this, claiming that it was dedicated then to St Peter and explaining how (in his opinion) the later dedication to St Mary arose. He writes:

> The holy and religious Oswald, who succeeded to the rule of this church when Dunstan became archbishop of Canterbury, because he could not convert the clerks living there from their depravity, nor drive them hence (since they were of noble birth and powerful), built a church nearby dedicated to Mary mother of God, where he himself would serve with the monks whom he planned to unite with Christ.[98]

Besides help with his work, Eadmer received advice on his career from Prior Nicholas. In 1120 he was invited by Alexander I, king of Scotland, to become bishop of St Andrews. However, because he demanded to pay obedience to Canterbury, not York, disputes ensued, and he resigned six months later without having been consecrated.[99] In the course of the quarrel he wrote to Nicholas for evidence that the archbishop of York had no right to consecrate the bishops of the Scottish sees. Nicholas's reply, which still survives,[100] illustrates both his historical interests and ability, and his friendship for Eadmer. He demonstrates, with appeals to precedent, that the archbishops of York had never consecrated the bishops of Scotland. He advises Eadmer to obtain consecration in Rome – and asks him to bring back as many 'white pearls' as possible, and at least four large ones.

It can, therefore, be seen that cultural life at Worcester was active during the Anglo-Norman period. The monks played an important part in

---

[95]  *Ibid*, 214.

[96]  See Osbern's *Vita S. Dunstani* in *ibid.*, 112.

[97]  *Ibid.*, 103, 106.

[98]  *Ibid.*, 197. A similar passage is in Eadmer's *Vita S. Oswaldi* in *Historians of the Church of York*, ed. Raine, II, 25. J. Armitage Robinson, 'St Oswald and the Church of Worcester', *British Academy Supplemental Papers*, V (1919), 3-4 cites the similar explanation for the change of the dedication of Worcester cathedral given by William of Malmesbury in his *Vita S. Dunstani* (*Memorials of St Dunstan*, 303-4); he overlooks the testimony of Eadmer which was almost certainly used by William of Malmesbury (see Gransden, 130 n. 170). Dr Eric John cites charter evidence which is apparently incompatible with Eadmer's explanation; see Eric John, 'St Oswald and the Church of Worcester', *Orbs Britanniae and Other Studies* (Leicester 1966), 234-48.

[99]  Southern (1963), 236.

[100]  Haddan and Stubbs, *op. cit.*, II, 202-4. Cf. p. 109 and n. 13.

saving the heritage of the Anglo-Saxons from obliteration after the Conquest. Without the work of such men much more would have been swept away by the Normans, for, in the words of St Wulfstan. 'Wretches that we are, we destroy the work of saints because we think in our pride that we can do better'.[101]

### Note

On pages 116 and 117 above I state that John of Worcester's chronicle ends in 1140. Dr Martin Brett has pointed out to me that there is no evidence that it did end in 1140 since the earliest manuscript, Corpus Christi College, Oxford, MS 157, ends incomplete. However, it must have been completed before 24 September 1143 since it mentions Henry of Blois, bishop of Winchester, as papal legate 'non tunc sed nunc'. Weaver, *Chron. Worcester*, 38 and n. 7. (Henry was a papal legate from 1 March 1139 to 24 September 1143.)

[101] *Vita Wulfstani*, 52. Cf. *Gesta Pontificum*, 283.

# 5

## Prologues in the Historiography of Twelfth-Century England

The medieval tradition of the literary prologue had its roots in Greek and Roman times.[1] The classical prologue was adapted in the early Christian era to conform to the new religious ideals.[2] In a prologue the author introduces himself to the reader, and tries to put him in a receptive frame of mind; he informs him about the purpose and scope of the work; and demonstrates his own rhetorical skill. To achieve these ends he uses a variety of literary commonplaces, *topoi*. One species of prologue was the prologue to an historical work. However, although an historical prologue might well have distinctive features, it had much in common with prologues to other classes of work: therefore, generalisations about it may also be appropriate to them.

It is the purpose of this paper to examine historical prologues as a genre. The subject will be discussed in two parts. First, the characteristics of historical prologues will be treated generally. Secondly, those written in twelfth-century England will be examined in more detail, to see how they conform to the norm.

Usually a prologue dedicates a work to some important person, and often it claims that that person, or some other named individual, ordered or persuaded the author to write.[3] Next the author may well try to disarm the reader by a declaration of modesty.[4] He is unequal to the task, unable to write good enough prose to do justice to his subject. (He may even use a

1 For the classical prologue tradition see Tore Janson, *Latin Prose Prefaces, Studies in Literary Conventions* (Acta Universitatis Stockholmiensis. Studia Latina Stockholmiensia XIII, Stockholm *et al.*, 1964).
2 For the medieval tradition to c.1200 see Gertrud Simon, 'Untersuchungen zur Topik der Widmungsbriefe mittel-alterlicher Geschichsschreiber bis zum Ende des 12. Jahrhunderts', *Archiv für Diplomatik*, iv (1958), 52–119, v–vi (1959–60), 73–153.
3 Simon, *op. cit.*, iv, 54–63; E. R. Curtius, *European Literature and the Latin Middle Ages*, translated by W. R. Trask (London, 1953), p. 85, D. W. T. C. Vessey, 'William of Tyre and the art of historiography', *Mediaeval Studies*, xxxv (1973), 436–8 (cf. below, pp. 56–7). For the classical origins of this *topos* see Janson, pp. 116–20. Cf. below, pp. 129, 131–3.
4 Simon, iv, 98–119 *passim*, Curtius, *op. cit.*, pp. 83–4, Vessey, *op. cit.*, p. 439.

diminutive of himself or his book.) He promises to write briefly,[5] and in a simple, even rustic, style, but will compensate for his lack of literary skill by his industry – perhaps claiming to have studied by night as well as by day.[6] And sometimes he will mention the work of previous historians, thus parading his learning, and discuss his sources.[7] He may admit the especial difficulty of writing contemporary history: if he criticises someone he will be accused of malice, but if he praises, he will be accused of flattery, which must be abhorrent to any historian.[8] To tell the truth, prologues commonly insist, is the historian's primary duty.[9] His narrative should be accurate, its concrete facts right and, moreover, it should be free from bias. Often an historian declares that his purpose was to preserve the memory of past deeds for posterity.[10] This done, history provides examples of good and bad conduct for the reader to emulate or eschew.[11] Above all, it shows God's dominion over man, especially how He punishes wrongdoers.[12]

Such are the principal *topoi* which tend to occur in historical prologues, treated with varying degrees of elaboration. Some authors, indeed, add little of their own. Therefore, it is debatable whether historical prologues in general are of much value as evidence to the present day historian. If the writer was merely repeating a set form, his prologue, it can be argued, tells us little about his mentality, except that he was well acquainted with the rules of rhetoric, and that he thought it appropriate to write a prologue in rhetorical style. It would tell us nothing reliable about his real thoughts about history and the historian's task, nor about the immediate occasion for his writing. This is the view taken by D.W.T. Vessey in his discussion of

Bernard Guenée, 'Les premiers pas de l'histoire de l'historiographie en occident au XIIᵉ siècle', *Comptes Rendus de l'Académie des Inscriptions et Belles-Lettres* (1983), pp. 146. For classical examples see Janson, pp. 124–49 *passim*, 159. Cf. below, pp. 137-8.

5  For promises of brevity see Simon, *op. cit.*, v–vi, 82-8, Curtius, *op. cit.*, pp. 85, 487-94. For classical examples see Janson, pp. 96-7, 154-5. Cf. below, 138.

6  See especially Bernard Guenée, 'L'histoire entre l'éloquence et la science. Quelques remarques sur le prologue de Guillaume de Malmesbury à ses *Gesta Regum Anglorum*', *Comptes Rendus de l'Académie des Inscriptions et Belles-Lettres* (1982), pp. 359, 367-9. See also Vessey, *op. cit.*, p. 441. The *topos* of historians' industriousness in pursuit of learning had well-established classical origins; see Janson, pp. 97-8, 147-8. Cf. below, pp. 139-40.

7  See Guenée, 'L'histoire entre l'éloquence et la science', p. 368, *idem*, 'Les premiers pas', pp. 136-44. For the classical origins see Janson, pp. 97, 152-3, 155-6. Cf. below, pp. 138-9, 141.

8  Simon, *op. cit.*, iv, 88-9, Vessey, *op. cit.*, p. 442-3. Cf. below, p. 143 & nn. 127, 128.

9  Simon. *op. cit.*, v–vi, 89-94, Vessey, *op. cit.*, p. 441. For the classical origins of the 'truth' *topos* see Janson, p. 67. Cf. below, pp. 128-9, 141-6.

10  Simon, *op. cit.*, iv, 78-81, v–vi, 94-111 *passim*. Cf. below, p. 134.

11  Simon, *op. cit.*, v–vi, 94-111 *passim*. Cf. below, pp. 135-6.

12  See below, pp. 135-6, 147-8.

William of Tyre's *Gesta Amalrici* (written in the 1170s). Thus, he writes: 'A prologue was, above all, a place where rhetoric and commonplace were inevitable and expected'; and again, 'It would be wrong to interpret [William's] prologue as a highly significant statement of his motives and intentions or as a declaration of deeply-felt principle.'[13] Dr Vessey questions William's claim that he wrote at King Amalric's command, and also shows that, contrary to William's assertion that he speaks the 'truth', the *Gesta* is a very sententious work.[14] (Similarly, Jeanette Beer has shown that, despite the recurrent claims in their works to veracity, William of Poitiers, the anonymous author of the *Gesta Francorum et aliorum Hierosolimitanorum*, and Villehardouin were much more concerned to persuade readers and listeners of their overall argument than to record events with factual accuracy.[15])

However, Gertrud Simon, in her detailed study of historical prologues before 1200, is more cautious. It is a problem, she admits, whether a prologue is merely a collection of *topoi*, or whether the author's own feelings predominate.[16] Other recent scholars have decided more positively in favour of the value of historical prologues. J.O. Ward writes:

> The obvious starting point for an analysis of what twelfth century historians thought they were doing is recognised to be the *exordium* prefaced to most histories. Recent research suggests that these *exordia* were meant as quite precise guides to contemporary historical ideas.[17]

The scholar who has worked most extensively on medieval historical prologues, Bernard Gienée, has no doubt of their value:

> Il est bien vrai que ces morceaux de bravoure que sont souvent les préfaces ont parfois des développements conventionnels qui justifient le peu d'intérêt qu'y prennent les lecteurs. Mais souvent aussi un auteur a mis beaucoup de lui-même dans sa préface, et il y attache une grande importance. ... En fait, dans sa préface, l'auteur prend souvent soin de dire l'historien qu'il croit être et l'histoire qu'il veut faire. Et comme je voulais approfondir et préciser mes recherches sur ce qu'avaient été l'histoire et l'historiens au Moyen Âge, l'idée s'est imposée à moi qu'il fallait systématiquement étudier ces miroirs plus

---

13  Vessey, *op. cit.*, pp. 440, 444–5.

14  *Ibid.*, pp. 436–55 *passim*.

15  J. M. A. Beer, *Narrative Conventions of Truth in the Middle Ages* (Études de philologie et d'histoire, xxxviii, Geneva, 1981), chapters 1–3.

16  See Simon, *op. cit.*, iv, 52–4.

17  J. O. Ward, 'Some principles of rhetorical historiography in the twelfth century' in *Classical Rhetoric and Medieval Historiography*, ed. Ernst Breisach (Studies in Medieval Culture, xix, Medieval Instituate Publications, Western Michigan University, Kalamazoo, 1985), p. 106 and n. 23 for further references.

au moins fidèles que sont les préfaces des oeuvres historiques d'occident mediéval.[18]

There are, therefore, divergent views about the value of prologues as historical evidence. In fact, it seems best to treat them with caution, but notwithstanding to take them seriously. Indisputably, they contain many *topoi*. Guenée points out [19] that Sallust's historical prologues, the earliest ones in Latin, and especially that to *Bellum Catalinae*, were models of primary importance throughout the Middle Ages. How meaningful particular *topoi* are is often hard to decide. Especially difficult are those concerning an author's state of mind. For instance, we cannot be sure how modest a specific author was, despite any protestations to that effect. Probably he thought he ought to be modest, but if, as well he may, he also shows pride in his calling,[20] that would be hard to reconcile with actual humility. And if humility made an historian declare that he would write briefly, for fear of boring, it did not necessarily make him do so.

Author's claims that they have written the truth are problematical in cases where their works are biased, and perhaps contain falsehoods. However, the medieval historians' concept of 'truth' differed from ours.[21] They considered that the overall truth of a work was more important than the factual accuracy of every detail. The author had to prove that what he believed to be true was correct, for example that God was on the side of the crusaders, or that a ruler was justified in conquering another country if he intended to reform the church. In the interests of such truths an author was justified in omitting discordant facts and filling gaps in knowledge with convenient probabilities.

Moreover, the historian in the Middle Ages had different standards of evidence from those of an historian today. He trusted most what he himself had seen, but this of course left much unknown. He, therefore, turned to what people of repute had written or said,[22] and accepted the truth of what was probable. Probability, that is 'verisimilitude', was not established by

---

18  Guenée, 'L'histoire entre l'éloquence et la science', p. 357.

19  *Ibid.*, p. 357, *idem*, 'Histoire, mémoire, écriture. Contribution à une étude des lieux communs', *Comptes Rendus de l'Académie des Inscriptions et Belles-Lettres* (1983), pp. 442–3.

20  See below, pp. 138–9.

21  It must, however, be admitted that exactly what authors meant by 'truth' is often far from clear. The question is discussed by, for example: Beer, *Narrative Conventions of Truth in the Middle Ages*, esp. pp. 10–11; Roger Ray, 'Rhetorical scepticism and verisimilar narrative in John of Salisbury's *Historia Pontificalis*' in Breisach, *op. cit.*, pp. 77–83 *passim*; D. J. Wilcox, *The Measure of Times Past* (Chicago UP, 1987), chapter 8 *passim*.

22  For the medieval historians' attitude to 'authority' in assessing data see especially Bernard Guenée, *Histoire et Culture historique dans l'Occident médiéval* (Paris, 1980), pp. 129–33.

invention, but by careful research and deductions drawn from concrete evidence. It was allowable to insert such probabilities as true facts without warning the reader of type of evidence used. These ideas about truth, and the evidence necessary to establish it, gave an historian considerable latitude. In the service of an overall argument, he could distort the evidence by suppression and unfair emphasis. His authorities themselves might give him false information, and the process of discovering 'verisimilitude' was inevitably partly subjective: it was a matter of opinion whether the evidence was sufficient to support any conclusion at all; the line between a reasonable deduction and one derived from inadequate evidence was a fine one.[23] An author might decide that, for instance, a certain turn of events was probable, and could, therefore justifiably be presented as concrete fact, simply because he would have liked it, or thought that it ought, to have happened. It is not, therefore, surprising that some narratives are so slanted that it is hard to reconcile them with the prohibition of bias, which was part of the 'truth' *topos*, even if we consider them in the light of medieval ideas about truth and evidence.[24] Nevertheless, despite this reservation, bearing those ideas in mind, we should read with sympathy the claims in prologues to write truth. This is especially so because they are often supported by plenty of evidence, both in prologues and in the works themselves, of great assiduity in the pursuit of information and in the assessment of its accuracy.

Indeed, there is much that can be said in defence of the value of historical prologues. They certainly should not be dismissed as mere verbiage. There is no reason to assume that an author did not believe at least most of what he wrote. It is safest to accept the truth of a statement, unless there is strong evidence to the contrary. Thus, an author's claim that he wrote at the request of a named individual should normally be believed (remembering, however, that he may have had more than one motive for writing). And, even if such a statement is false, the identity of the alleged patron would be of interest.

Prologues can tell us much about what historians in the Middle Ages thought about themselves and their calling. The very currency of the *topoi* which the historian had at hand would have helped shape his ideas. His choice of them is itself significant. Changes in the popularity of one or other *topos* suggest changes in historians' attitudes.[25] Thus, Guenée argues that as the twelfth century progressed authors laid less stress on the importance of an eloquent, persuasive style, and more on their industry and pursuit of learning: their tastes were moving from rhetoric to

23  For William of Malmesbury's methods of arguing see below, pp. 144-6.
24  For examples see above, pp. 126-7.
25  On the value of *topoi* as historiographical evidence see especially Guenée, 'Histoire, mémoire, écriture', pp. 441 *et seqq*.

scholarship.[26] An author's acknowledgement of debt to previous writers was conventional,[27] but the selection of sources cited was his own. And an author could, and often did, include his own observations in the prologue. He might, for instance, explain any distinctive structure he had adopted for his work.[28] A prologue, indeed, provided a place for miscellanea and creative writing.

Guenée has shown that the historical prologues of the twelfth century are of especial interest. He emphasises the primary importance of Hugh of St Victor's universal history, published in 1130.[29] Its influence, Guenée believes, was largely responsible for a shift from eloquent to erudite historiography. Guenée surveys prologues written throughout the medieval West, including England. Our intention here is to look at the principal English examples in greater detail.

The twelfth century was, indeed, a golden age of historiography in England, as elsewhere in Europe. Particularly famous historians are Eadmer, William of Malmesbury, Geoffrey of Monmouth, Henry of Huntingdon, Ralph Diceto, Roger of Howden, William of Newburgh, and, at the turn of the century, Gervase of Canterbury. Among the Anglo-Norman historians Orderic Vitalis, writing in Normandy,, should also be numbered. All except Roger Howden[30] start with prologues of comparable interest, although of varying lengths and sophistication. Moreover, one of the lesser twelfth-century historians, Alfred of Beverley, begins his *Annales* (which Gross considered a worthless compilation)[31] with an illuminating prologue.[32] Clearly authors recognised prologues' usefulness. William of Malmesbury wrote (c.1125) substantial prologues to each of the five books which together comprise his *Gesta Regum*,[33] and did the same for his *Gesta Pontificum*.[34] Later, towards the end of the century, Diceto included in the prologue to his *Abbreviationes Chronicorum* long passages from the

26 Guenée, 'L'histoire entre l'éloquence et la science', pp. 357-70 *passim*. Cf. above, p. 126 & n. 6 and below, pp. 150-1.
27 See above, p. 126 & n. 7 and below, p. 141.
28 See below, pp. 146-50.
29 Guenée, 'Les premiers pas', pp. 137 *et seqq*.
30 See below, p. 151.
31 Charles Gross, *A Bibliography of English History to 1485*, ed. E. B. Graves (Oxford, 1975), p. 405 (no. 2795).
32 *Aluredi Beverlacensis Annales sive Historia de Gestis Regum Britanniae*, ed. Thomas Hearne (Oxford, 1716), pp. 1-10.
33 *Willelmi Malmesbiriensis Monachi de Gestis Regum Anglorum Libri Quinque...*, ed. William Stubbs (Rolls Series, 1887-9, 2 vols), i, 1-2, 103-4; ii, 283-4, 357-8, 465-6.
34 *Willelmi Malmesbiriensis Monachi de Gestis Pontificum Anglorum Libri Quinque*, ed. N.E.S.A. Hamilton (Rolls Series, 1870), pp. 3-5, 139, 208-10, 277, 330-1.

prologues of a number of previous writers, from Justin to Ivo of Chartres.[35] And William of Newburgh made use of the prologue of his *Historia Regum Anglicarum*[36] to accommodate extraneous matter – to discuss a subject about which he apparently felt very strongly: he inserted a full-scale attack on Geoffrey of Monmouth's *Historia Regum Britanniae*; this, since Geoffrey's work concerned the ancient Britons, had no relevance to William's history, which did not deal with them at all, but began at the Norman Conquest.[37]

In our examination of the twelfth-century English historical prologues, notice will be taken of *topoi* used, and where possible their immediate source suggested. At the same time what the prologues say will be treated as evidence. Consideration will be given to the light they throw on various historiographical matters: the motives, both immediate and long term, for the writing of history; the status of historiography, and its accepted spiritual value and worldly uses: historians' view of themselves and their task; their attitude to, and treatment of, their sources; and the methods they adopted to structure their works. Finally, we will consider whether two of Guenée's general conclusions about the twelfth-century historical prologues of the medieval West apply equally to the English examples: first was the influence of Hugh of St Victor as important in England as on the continent? Secondly, was there a move from rhetoric to scholarship?

There are plenty of English examples of prologues which state that an individual work was written in response to a commission or request. Sometimes an author wrote for his monastic superior (or superiors) or fellow monks. Symeon of Durham was ordered (c.1100) to write by his monastic superiors,[38] and Orderic Vitalis started work at the command of

---

35 *The Historical Works of Master Ralph de Diceto, Dean of London*, ed. William Stubbs (Rolls Series, 1876, 2 vols), i, 20–4.

36 *Chronicles of the Reigns of Stephen, Henry II, and Richard I*, ed. Richard Howlett (Rolls Series, 1884–9, 4 vols), i, 11–19.

37 I suggest elsewhere the possibility that William originally wrote the section of the prologue which attacks Geoffrey's *Historia* (*ibid.* from p. 11, line 2, 'Qui nimirum', to p. 18, line 18, 'ab omnibus respuatur') as a propaganda tract in the royal interest to discredit the Arthurian legend; the Bretons (like the Welsh) believed that King Arthur would return and lead the British people to victory against their Angevin rulers. They seem to have identified the legendary Arthur with Henry II's grandson, the son of Geoffrey and a daughter of the duke of Brittany. He was born in 1186, baptised Arthur and reared, according to William of Newburgh (*ibid.*, i, 235) 'under the mighty omen of his name'. Near the end of his chronicle William records the Breton rebellion of 1196. See A. Gransden, 'Bede's reputation as an historian in Medieval England', *Journal of Ecclesiastical History*, xxxii (1981), above, pp. 20–2.

38 The so-called *Historia Dunelmensis Ecclesiae* in *Symeonis Monachi Opera Omnia*, ed. Thomas Arnold (Rolls Series, 1882–5, 2 vols), i, 3. The evidence for Symeon's authorship of the *Historia* is not beyond dispute; A. Gransden,

Roger, abbot of St Évroult (1091-1123), and completed it for his successor, Guérin des Essarts.[39] Eadmer was urged by friends to write the *Historia Novorum* and its companion volume, the *Vita Sancti Anselmi*,[40] and similarly friends persuaded William of Malmesbury to write Book IV of the *Gesta Regum* (despite his reluctance because of the difficulties presented by near contemporary historiography).[41] And Gervase of Canterbury wrote for 'Brother Thomas and our humble little family'.[42] Some authors wrote for distant friends. John of Salisbury wrote the *Historia Pontificalis* (? 1164) at the request of his 'dearest friend and master', Peter de Celle, abbot of St Remigius, Rheims.[43] And Richard of Devizes, a monk of St Swithun's, Winchester, wrote his *Cronicon de Tempore Regis Richardi Primi* (1192-8) at the request of his friend ('his venerable father, always his master') Robert, formerly prior of St Swithun's, but then a Carthusian monk of Witham.[44]

It seems likely that occasionally a request amounted to a commission in return for some benefit to the author, or, presumably, if the latter was a monk or regular canon, to his community. The benefit may have been money or patronage. William of Newburgh, himself an Augustinian canon of Newburgh, explains that Ernald, abbot of the Cistercian abbey of Rievaulx, asked him to write.[45] William of Malmesbury dedicated the second edition of his *Gesta Regum*[46] and his *Historia Novella* to Robert earl of Gloucester (whose patronage Malmesbury abbey badly needed during the anarchy of Stephen's reign),[47] while Geoffrey of Monmouth

*Historical Writing in England*, [i], *c.550-c.1307* (London, 1974), pp. 115-16 and nn. 66-70 for further references.

39 *The Ecclesiastical History of Orderic Vitalis*, ed. Marjorie Chibnall (Oxford, 1969-80, 6 vols), i, 130-2.

40 *Eadmeri Historia Novorum in Anglia*, ed. Martin Rule (Rolls Series, 1884), p. 1; *The Life of St Anselm Archbishop of Canterbury by Eadmer*, ed. with an English translation R. W. Southern (Nelson's Medieval Texts, 1962), p. 1.

41 *Gesta Regum*, ii, 357.

42 *Chronica* in *The Historical Works of Gervase of Canterbury*, ed. William Stubbs (Rolls Series, 1879-80, 2 vols), i, 89: 'tibi, mi frater Thoma, et nostrae familiolae pauperculae scribo'.

43 *Ioannis Saresberiensis Historia Pontificalis*, ed. with an English translation Marjorie Chibnall (Nelson's Medieval Texts, 1956), p. 3: 'Vnde voluntati tue, dominorum amicorumque karissime, libentius acquiescens . . .'.

44 *The Chronicle of Richard of Devizes of the Time of King Richard the First*, ed. with an English translation J. T. Appleby (Nelson's Medieval Texts, 1963), p. 1: 'Venerabili patri et semper domino Roberto . . .'. Richard says he writes partly to remind Robert of his friend; *ibid.*, p. 2.

45 *Chrons. Stephen, Henry II, and Richard I*, i, 3. The dedication to Abbot Ernald in fact is in a dedicatory letter, preceding the prologue.

46 See *Gesta Regum*, i, lvi-lviii; ii, 518-21.

47 *The Historia Novella of William of Malmesbury*, ed. with an English translation K. R. Potter (Nelson's Medieval Texts, 1955), p. 1. Cf. below, p. 146 and n. 141.

dedicated various copies of the *Historia Regum Britanniae* to a number of great men, including King Stephen, Robert earl of Gloucester, Waleran count of Meulan, and Alexander bishop of Lincoln.[48]

One reason why some people liked writing history was because it gave them a worthwile and enjoyable occupation. Prologues express this sentiment in various commonplace ways. William of Newburgh was grateful to Abbot Ernald for saving him from the dangers of idleness.[49] Sallust had claimed that the study of history was a more fruitful occupation for one's leisure than to spend it 'in idleness and sloth, or, by turning to farming or the chase, to lead a life devoted to servile [i.e. physical, not intellectual,] employment'.[50] William of Malmesbury seems to echo Sallust on this matter (although possibly he also had in mind the Biblical prohibition of 'servile works' on Sunday): in the prologue to Book IV of the *Gesta Regum*, he writes that, after a period of leisure and silence, his love of learning has returned; he cannot be idle and spend his time on outdoor pursuits and on those unworthy of an educated man.[51] Idleness was in any case unacceptable to any good Benedictine monk, since the Rule taught that it 'is the enemy of the soul'.[52] Gervase of Canterbury actually quotes the Rule: 'because I know that idleness is the enemy of the soul, I have occupied myself with this work' (i.e. the writing of his chronicle).[53] Alfred of Beverley, a secular clerk, wrote his *Annales* to prevent himself from wasting time. He explains in the prologue that, owing to an interdict (i.e. in 1143), the celebration of the divine office in his church had temporarily stopped. This and other sufferings of the clergy nearly drove him to despair. 'But merciful God saved me from the chasm of desperation, and led me back

---

48 *The Historia Regum Britanniae of Geoffrey of Monmouth*, ed. Acton Griscom (London, 1929, repr. Slatkine, 1977), pp. 219-20. Cf. J. S. P. Tatlock, *The Legendary History of Britain* (University of California Press, 1950), pp. 436-7, 444.

49 *Chrons. Stephen, Henry II, and Richard I*, i, 4.

50 Sallust, *Bellum Catilinae*, iv, ed. T. E. Page, E. Capps and W. H. D. Rouse, with an English translation by J. C. Rolfe (Loeb Classical Library, 1931), p. 8: '... non fuit consilium socordia atque desidia bonum toium conterere, neque vero agrum colundo aut venando servilibus officiis intentam aetatem agere ...' Cf. Leviticus 23.7: 'Dies primus erit vobis celeberrimus, sanctusque; omne opus servile non facietis in eo'. I am indebted to Professor Lewis Kelly for calling my attention to this Biblical archetype.

51 *Gesta Regum*, ii, 357: 'sed dum aliquamdiu solutus inertia vacassem, rursus solitus amor studiorum aurem vellit et manum injecit, propterea quod nec nil agere possem, et istis forensibus et homine litterato indignis curis me tradere non nossem'.

52 Rule of St Benedict, Cap. XLVIII. 1, from the Rule of the Master. *La Règle de Saint Benoit*, ed. A. de Vogüé (Sources Chrétiennes, Páris, 1971-7, 7 vols), ii, 598 and note.

53 *Gerv. Cant.*, ed. Stubbs, i, 89-90: 'Et quia novi quod otiositas inimica est animae, otium meum hoc negotio curavi occupare.'

to reason.' He decided to spend his time on the not ignoble occupation of reading;[54] and he goes on to say that what he read in particular was history – Geoffrey of Monmouth's *Historia Regum Britanniae*.

Historiography, however, did more than remove its practitioners from the temptations of idleness. It had other virtues and values. Most importantly, it was a rational study, as Gervase of Canterbury explains.[55] Sallust wrote that 'it behoves men not to go through life in silence like beasts', but to strive to excel intellectually.[56] Henry of Huntingdon applied this maxim directly to the study of history: knowledge of the past distinguishes men from brutes, whether men or beasts; the former do not know, and do not want to know, their people's origins, nor the history of their country; the latter, of course, are incapable of such knowledge, or of wishing for it.[57] History, Henry asserts, makes the past present (the lives and deaths of brutish men are assigned to everlasting oblivion).[58] It was commonplace that historiography preserves the past for posterity.[59]

But why should we remember the past? Above all history demonstrates the workings of Providence on earth. This idea, of Biblical origin and prescribed for the Middle Ages by St Augustine's *De Civitate Dei* and Orosius' *Historia contra Paganos*, underlay all medieval Christian

---

54 *Annales*, p. 2.
55 *Gerv. Cant.*, ed. Stubbs, i, 87: 'nichilque aliud comprehendere nisi quod historiae de ratione videtur competere'.
56 *Bell. Cat.*, i (Loeb edition), p. 2: 'Omnis homines qui sese student praestare ceteris animalibus summa ope niti decet ne vitam silentio transeant veluti pecora, quae natura prona atque ventri oboedientia finxit. Sed nostra omnis vis in animo et in corpore sita est; animi imperio, corporis servitio magis utimur; alterum nobis cum dis, alterum cum beluis commune est. Quo mihi rectius videtur ingeni quam virium opibus gloriam quaerere, et, quoniam vita ipsa qua fruimur brevis est, memoriam nostri quam maxume longam efficere; nam divitiarum et formae gloria fluxa atque fragilis est, virtus clara aeternaque habetur.' This paragraph is quoted here in full because it almost certainly influenced Henry of Huntingdon; see below and next note and p. 65 and n. 63.
57 Dedicatory epistle to Bishop Alexander; *Henrici Archidiaconi Huntendunensis Historia Anglorum*, ed. Thomas Arnold (Rolls Series, 1879), pp. 2–3: 'Habet quidem et praeter haec illustres transactorum notitia dotes, quod ipsa maxime distinguat a brutis rationabiles; bruti namque homines et animalia unde sint nesciunt, genus suum nesciunt, patriae suae casus et gesta nesciunt, immo nec scire volunt. Quorum, homines quidem illos infeliciores judico; quia quod bestiis ex creatione, hoc illis ex propria contingit inanitione; et quod bestiae si vellent non possent, hoc illi nolunt cum possint.'
58 *Ibid.*, p. 2: 'Historia igitur praeterita quasi praesentia visui repraesentat; ...' *Ibid.*, p. 3: 'Sed de his [hominibus brutis] jam transeundum est, quorum mors et vita sempiterno dotanda est silentio.'
59 Eadmer, *Hist. Novorum*, p. 1; William of Malmesbury, *Gesta Regum*, i, 3 (see below p. 69 and n. 101); *idem, Hist. Novella*, p. 1; Orderic Vitalis, i, 132; John of Salisbury, *Hist. Pont.*, 3; William of Newburgh, dedicatory epistle to Abbot Ernald, *Chrons. Stephen, Henry II, and Richard I*, i, 3.

historiography.[60] John of Salisbury gives it explicit expression: chroniclers have always had but one intention, to relate noteworthy matters, 'so that what was done may show the invisible God'.[61] One way in which historiography could show God's power was by recording instances of the transitory nature of all earthly glory. This was one of Henry of Huntingdon's favourite themes.[62] Sallust had remarked that 'the renown which riches or beauty give is frail and fleeting'. He adds that 'only mental excellence is a splendid and lasting possession'.[63] Henry of Huntingdon, on the other hand, saw only spiritual glory, which leads to salvation, as eternal.[64] Richard of Devizes also wrote partly to show the fickleness of fortune.[65]

Moreover, the study of history should do more than increase faith; it should also improve behaviour. One facet of the belief in providential history was the idea that God rewards the good and punishes wrongdoers. This idea was familiar from the Bible (for example from Psalms 7, 36 and 90, and the Book of Amos), and was central in Orosuis' *Historia*. Moreover, it figures large in Bede's prologue to the *Historia Ecclesiastica*: he hoped that readers would be morally, as well as spiritually, improved by the examples of this aspect of divine power to be found in his history.[66] The twelfth-century historians probably had these models in mind in their treatment of the same idea. 'What', asks William of Malmesbury, 'is more to the advantage of virtue, and more conducive to justice, than to learn about God's beneficence to the good, and vengeance on traitors?'[67] Similarly, John of Salisbury asserts that he, like other chroniclers, wrote 'so that examples of [divine] rewards and punishments may make men more zealous in fear of God and the pursuit of justice'.[68] He adds that 'whoever is ignorant of the past rushes blindly to the future. Nothing (except the grace and law of God) teaches the living more correctly and forcefully than knowledge of the deeds of the dead.'[69] And John supports his argument

---

60 See Benoit Lecroix, *Orose et ses Idées* (Montreal/Paris, 1965), esp. pt 2, chapters I and II.
61 John of Salisbury, *Hist. Pont.*, p. 3.
62 See the verses at the end of the epistle to Bishop Alexander and the prologue to Book II, pp. 3–4, 37. Cf. Gransden, *Historical Writing*, i, 197 and nn. 107–12.
63 See the last two lines of the passage in *Bell. Cat.* cited above, p. 134 n. 56.
64 *Hen. Hunt.*, p. 37.
65 *Richard of Devizes*, p. 2.
66 *Venerabilis Baedae Historia Ecclesiastica Gentis Anglorum...*, ed. Charles Plummer (Oxford, 1896, 2 vols, repr. in one vol. 1961), i, 5.
67 *Historia Novella*, p. 1.
68 *Hist. Pont.*, p. 3. For John of Salisbury's extensive and intelligent use of *exempla* see Peter Von Moos, 'The use of *exempla* in the *Policraticus* of John of Salisbury' in *The World of John of Salisbury*, ed. Michael Wilks (Studies in Church History, Subsidia 3, Oxford, 1984), pp. 207–61.
69 *Hist. Pont.*, pp. 3–4.

with a quotation from Cato's supposititious work, the *Disticha de Moribus*: 'The lives of others are our teachers.'[70] Gervase of Canterbury pursues the same theme, expounding at length the edificatory value of historiography. In his introduction (*ingressus*) to his prologue, addressed to his dear brother (presumably his fellow monk Thomas), he says that three things deliver men from evil – prohibition, precept and example, and example is generally the most effective. Knowledge of the punishments which God inflicts on wrongdoers scares men into trying to avoid similar fates, while the examples of the lives of saints and the good deeds of many others inspire emulation and love of God. Gervase's prologue takes up the theme. Historical writings are repositories of such examples; Gervase writes, therefore, for his audience's edification.[71]

Historical writings had worldly uses as well as spiritual and moral value. In very practical terms, they could, Eadmer points out, in certain circumstances provide helpful precedents. As John of Salisbury says: 'chronicles are useful for establishing or abolishing custom, for strengthening or weakening privileges'.[72] But historiography also had more general secular uses. William of Malmesbury claims that the examples in his narrative of the energy, enterprise, bravery and other merits of great men will encourage others to similar behaviour.[73] Moreover, historical writings could boost a nation's self-awareness and pride in itself. 'It is idle and ignoble', writes William of Malmesbury, 'to know about distant lands and not about one's own great men.'[74] As already mentioned (p. 64), to Henry of Huntingdon a man's ignorance of his own country's history was a piece of brutish stupidity, which doomed him to eternal oblivion.

Finally, a few of the prologues testify to the perennial value of history as a source of pleasure. William of Newburgh was grateful to Ernald for

70 *Ibid.*, p. 3. *Disticha de Moribus*, iii, 13: 'uita est nobis aliena magistra'.
71 *Gerv. Cant.*, i, 84–7.
72 Eadmer, *Hist. Nov.*, p. 1: he wrote partly 'ut posterorum industriae, si forte quid inter eos emerserit quod horum exemplo aliquo modo juvari queat, parum quid muneris impendam'. John of Salisbury, *Hist. Pont.*, p. 3: 'Valet etiam noticia cronicorum ad statuendas uel euacuandas prescriptiones et priuilegia roboranda uel infirmanda.'
73 *Gesta Regum*, ii, 283: 'de [Willelmo] talia narrabo libenter et morose quae sint inertibus incitamento, promptis exemplo, usui praesentibus, jocunditati sequentibus'. *Ibid.*, ii, 358: William says he will write about the Crusade 'quia tam famosam his diebus expeditionem audire sit operae pretium et virtutis incitamentum'. *Gesta Pontificum*, p. 4: 'Quid enim dulcius quam majorum recensere gratiam, ut eorum acta cognoscas a quibus acceperis et rudimenta fidei et incitamenta bene vivendi.' *Hist. Novella*, p. 1: 'Quid porro iocundius quam fortium facta uirorum monimentis tradere litterarum, quorum exemplo ceteri exuant ignauiam, et ad defendendam armentur patriam?'
74 *Gesta Pontificum*, p. 4.

imposing on him an easy, pleasant task (one unfitting for the monks of Ernald's own house, bound by the strict Cistercian rule). He had asked him 'to wander in the avenues of history, as if for the recreation of the spirit'.[75] Eadmer starts his prologue to the *Historia Novorum* by describing history as a solace; in his day men investigate the past in order to find 'comfort and strength'.[76] Henry of Huntingdon, at the beginning of his prologue, expresses (with echoes of Boethius) a similar sentiment: while all kinds of learning are 'a mitigation of trouble and consolation in grief', history deserves pride of place as the noblest and most delightful of studies.[77]

Despite all that historians wrote in favour of historiography, ostensibly they regarded it as a comparatively lowly pursuit. They were not, in the words of William of Newburgh, concerned with 'lofty matters and divine mysteries'.[78] Moreover, many historians made a show of their own humility in the conventional way. Rhetoric set a standard of eloquence hard to attain. Sallust had said that the writing of history was one of the most difficult tasks, partly because 'the style and diction must be worthy of the deeds recorded'.[79] William of Malmesbury was very conscious of the need for eloquence. He praises previous historians who wrote simple, persuasive Latin (especially Bede, but also Eadmer),[80] and condemns those who were verbose and obscure (notably Eddius Stephanus and Æthelweard).[81] And he felt that he himself was insufficiently eloquent to do justice to the momentous affairs of Henry I's reign. ('Hardly Cicero, whose eloquence was venerated throughout the Latin world, would attempt it, or even the Mantuan bard.')[82] Orderic Vitalis similarly protests his lack of 'literary skill and eloquence',[83] and William of Newburgh asserts that many monks in Ernald's own monastery could have written a history 'with greater ease and elegance than he'.[84] Gervase of Canterbury's humility was truly abject. He divided historical writing into two categories, histories and chronicles, which were different in narrative mode and structure. Histories were written in diffuse and elegant style. Chronicles, on the other hand, were simple and concerned with dates, and the record of the acts of kings

---

75 *Chrons. Stephen, Henry II, and Richard I*, i, 4.
76 *Hist. Nov.*, p. 1.
77 *Hen. Hunt.*, p. 1. 'Cum in omni fere literarum studio dulce laboris lenimen et summum doloris solamen, dum vivitur, insitum considerem, tum delectabilius et majoris praerogativa claritatis historiarum splendorem amplectendum crediderim'.
78 *Chrons. Stephen, Henry II, and Richard I*, i, 4.
79 *Bell. Cat.*, iii (Loeb edition) p. 6: '... in primis arduum videtur res gestas scribere; primum quod facta dictis exaequanda sunt, ...'
80 *Gesta Regum*, i, 1.
81 *Gesta Pontificum*, p. 210; *Gesta Regum*, i, 1, 3.
82 *Ibid.*, ii, 465. For the sequel to this passage see below, p. 141 and n. 109.
83 *Orderic*, i, 130.
84 *Chrons. Stephen, Henry II, and Richard I*, i, 3.

and princes, and other events.[85] Gervase berated chroniclers who exceeded the limits of the genre by writing eloquent prose – who 'make broad their phylacteries and enlarge the borders of their garments' (Matthew, xxiii.5.88). He did not claim for his 'little self' even the title of chronicler. He was a mere compiler, and his work of the utmost insignificance.[86]

In keeping with such protestations of humility were authors' assertions that they were afraid of boring.This alleged fear was in turn one reason for their expressed intention of writing briefly. Since in fact they did not write briefly, such statements must be regarded as rhetorical flourishes. Sallust had promised to be brief about the Catilinarian conspiracy.[87] William of Malmesbury made a similar promise and explained his motives: 'I shall write as briefly as I can, bearing in mind the tastes of the studious, and the scorn of the disdainful.'[88] Henry of Huntingdon claims that he wrote briefly about the Roman Emperors, because 'greater prolixity would have been boring'.[89] But brevity should not be carried to excess. Ralph Diceto writes that he will indulge neither in 'profusion and tedious chatter, nor in obscure brevity'.[90]

Historians may have been, or at least thought they ought to be modest, but a number by implication betray self-esteem and pride in their calling.[91] They tend to see themselves as heirs to a noble tradition. (Indeed, on the continent Robert of Torigni justified writing his chronicle by appealing to great predecessors, from Cyprian to Sigebert of Gembloux, whose names he recites.)[92] Both William of Malmesbury and Henry of Huntingdon declare themselves to be successors of Bede; they would continue where Bede left off.[93] Orderic Vitalis begins his prologue with a list of those 'who had previously studied and recorded all ages, the good and evil fortunes of men, for the benefit of posterity'.[94] He then lists seven great historians (including Bede), from Moses to Paul of Monte Cassino, and says that 'following the

85  *Gerv. Cant.*, i, 87.
86  *Ibid.*, i, 89: '. . . aliqua gestorum praeteriti temporis et futuri compilare potius quam scribere cupio, . . . .'; 'Me autem inter cronicae scriptores computandum non esse censeo, quia non bibliotecae publicae sed tibi, mi frater Thoma [continues as above p. 62 n. 42].' *Ibid.*, 91: 'Cronicam parvulam pusillus ego conscripturus, . . .'
87  *Bell. Cat.*, iv (Loeb edition), p. 8: '. . . de Catilinae coniuratione quam verissume potero paucis absolvam'.
88  *Gesta Pontificum*, p. 139: 'breviterque omnia digerens, quantum potero consulam studiosorum notitiae et fastidiosorum nausiae'.
89  *Hen. Hunt.*, p. 37.
90  *Diceto*, i, 34.
91  See Guenée, 'Les premiers pas', 142–8 *passim*. Professor Guenée argues that historians' pride grew in the course of the twelfth century.
92  *Chrons. Stephen, Henry II, and Richard I*, iv, 61–2.
93  *Gesta Regum*, i, 2; *Hen. Hunt.*, p. 3.
94  *Orderic*, i, 130.

early Fathers, I shall write about ecclesiastical affairs'.[95] Like Bede he called his work *Historia Ecclesiastica*. John of Salisbury starts with an even more elaborate list of historians and includes a few biographical details and brief comments on their works. Of Cassiodorus he remarks that he was a Gentile turned Christian, a senator turned monk, and he had 'many successors distinguished in this learning (*studium*)'. In his own age, John asserts, 'many wise men have laboured in this way for the benefit of contemporaries'.[96] He ends with Sigebert of Gembloux, sketching the scope of his works. The longest and most elaborate such list of historians compiled in England was by Ralph Diceto. His prologue includes a list of forty-two famous historians with notes of when and what they wrote.[97] He starts with Trogus Pompeius and ends with himself ('the most modern of the modern') 'Ralph, dean of the church of London, began the book called *Ymagines Historiarum* at A.D.1147 and continued to 1190.'[98] As Guenée points out, John of Salisbury and Diceto compiled their historiographical surveys under the influence of Hugh of St Victor[99] (whom both include in their lists). The prologue to Hugh's universal chronicle has a list of thirty-four historians.[100] Although disordered and inaccurate, it was the first list of its kind, and exerted a seminal influence on many later historians. In fact, it was an important step forward in the history of historiography.

Historians in the twelfth century, like their classical prototypes, might protest their lack of literary skill, but were happy to mention their industriousness. 'I hope', writes William of Malmesbury, 'to have credit with posterity for industry if not talent.'[101] Historiography was, indeed, regaining its

95  *Ibid.*, i, 130. Orderic himself made copy of Bede's *Historia Ecclesiastica*; see Bede's *Ecclesiastical History of the English People*, ed. with an English translation B. Colgrave and R. A. B. Mynors (Oxford Medieval Texts, 1969), p. lxi. Possibly Orderic borrowed the idea of appending an autobiography to his own work from Bede; see *Orderic*, vi, 550-6 and n.1.
96  *Hist. Pont.*, p. 2.
97  *Diceto*, i, 20-4.
98  *Ibid.*, i, 23-4.
99  Guenée, 'Les premiers pas', 139-40. See also G. A. .Zinn, 'The influence of Hugh of St Victor's *Chronicon* on the *Abbreviationes Chronicorum* by Ralph Diceto', *Speculum*, lii (1977), 38-61.
100  Hugh of St Victor's universal history is unpublished: see W. M. Green, 'Hugh of St Victor *De tribus maximis circumstantiis gestorum*', *Speculum*, xviii (1943), 484-93. The list of historians (noticed *ibid.*, 493) is printed in G. Waitz, *Archiv der Gesellschaft für ältere deutsche Geschichtskunde*, xi (1858), 307-8. Cf. Guenée, 'Les premiers pas', 137.
101  *Gesta Regum*, i, 3: habiturus, ut spero, apud posteros, post decessum amoris et livoris, si non eloquentiae titulum, saltem industriae testimonium'. *Gesta Pontificum*, 4: 'Quod cum fecero, videbor mihi rem nulli attemptatam consumasse, non meo fretus ingenio sed dignae cognitionis allectus studio.' Cf. Guenée, 'L'Histoire entre l'éloquence et la science', 359, 367-8, and above p. 56 and n. 6.

status in England of a learned subject, a status lost after the death of Bede. Importance was now attached to the accumulation and evaluation of data. Bede had set an example of assiduity in the search for material, as he reveals in his prologue. Of the twelfth-century historians perhaps William of Malmesbury took the greatest pains in this respect. He attached much importance to chronicle evidence: chronicles, he writes, 'shine like a beacon to light my path'.[102] His prologue to Book II of the *Gesta Regum* states that he 'sought chronicles far and wide' and even 'procured some histories of foreign peoples'. He was acutely aware of gaps in his knowledge. 'I confess', he sadly admits, 'I profited little from all this industry.'[103] And if he was short of material for the *Gesta Regum*, he was even shorter of it for the *Gesta Pontificum*. For that he found virtually no chronicles to help him: 'almost totally destitute of such solace, I feel my way through the shadows of gross ignorance, with no light of history to guide me'.[104] He especially laments his lack of information about saints, the result of the absence of saints' Lives, or of their domicile in distant lands.[105] He even asks readers to help him make the *Gesta Regum* more comprehensive by sending additional information; he will insert it in the margin if unable to fit it into the appropriate place in the text.[106] William's claims that he took such trouble collecting data have been amply justified by recent research. He was extraordinarily widely read, and did not claim to have used works which he did not use, at least indirectly.[107] The very fact that most of his account of the Anglo-Saxon church after Bede's time is so brief indicates that in general he accepted the limitation imposed by lack of

102 *Gesta Pontificum*, p. 4: with reference to the *Gesta Regum*. William writes 'Siquidem ibi aliquid de cronicis quae prae me habebam mutuatus, velut e sullimi specula fulgente facula, qua gressum sine errore tenderem, ammonebar.' (For the sequel to this passage see below, n. 104). For William as a learned man see below, n. 107.

103 *Gesta Regum*, i, 104: 'Chronica longe lateque corrogavi, sed nihil propemodum hac, fateor, profeci industria.' *Ibid.*, i, 103: 'Itaque, cum domesticis sumptibus nonnullos exterarum gentium historicos conflassem, familiari otio quaerere perrexi si quid de nostra gente memorabile posteris posset reperiri.'

104 *Gesta Pontificum*, p. 4 (continuing the passage cited above, n. 102): 'Hic autem, pene omni destitutus solatio, crassas ignorantiae tenebras palpo, nec ulla lucerna historiae praevia semitam dirigo.' (For the sequel to this passage see below, p. 73 n. 124.)

105 *Ibid.*, p. 277 (prologue to Book IV). For the lack of written evidence about his abbey's patron, St Aldhelm, see *ibid.*, p. 330 (prologue to Book V).

106 *Gesta Regum*. i, 104: 'ut meo stylo apponantur saltem in margine quae non occurrerunt in ordine'.

107 See R. M. Thomson, *William of Malmesbury* (Woodbridge, 1987), esp. chapters 2, 3, 6-10 and appendix I.

evidence. Moreover, the autograph manuscript of the *Gesta Pontificum* shows his use of the margins for late additions.[108]

Literary sources were, of course, of no help for contemporary history; reliance had to be placed on oral and documentary evidence. William of Malmesbury expresses regret in the prologue to Book V of the *Gesta Regum* that he will not be able to deal with Henry I's reign fully, because he is 'far from the secrets of courts', and so does not know all the king's doings and great deeds.[109] (Orderic Vitalis appeals explicitly to his monastic status as a reason for areas of ignorance: he cannot explore 'Macedonian, Greek or Roman history, or other noteworthy matters, because, being, of my own free choice, a cloister monk, I am bound irrevocably to the monastic observance'.[110]) It is well known that many twelfth-century historians made extensive use of documents. John of Salisbury's prologue mentions the searches he undertook in order to write the history of the popes after 1148 (when Sigebert of Gembloux's continuator ended): 'I could discover no chronicle, although I have found in church archives some notes of memorable events, which could be of help to any future writer.'[111]

Symptomatic of historians' concern with their sources of information was the development of the practice of discussing them in the prologue. Bede provided a model. However, since Bede had had hardly any literary sources to serve his purpose, his prologue mainly details oral ones (although it also describes his acquisition of documents). William of Malmesbury was the first historian in the twelfth century to adopt this practice. In the prologue to Book I of the *Gesta Regum* he briefly surveys the literary sources for English history to which he was indebted; he starts with Bede, 'the most learned and least proud' ('vir maximus doctus et minimus superbus'), and ends with Eadmer.[112] Such an account of sources can, of course, be indistinguishable from a list of eminent historians, of the kind mentioned above.[113] Hugh of St Victor's list combines both roles, and so to a limited extent does Ralph Diceto's. However, such coincidences are exceptional. For example, John of Salisbury's *Historia Pontificalis* begins in 1148, the year when, John states, Sigebert of Gembloux (in fact his continuator), the last author in his eminent historians' list, ended.

The English historians' attitude to truth was that typical of the Middle Ages. Sallust had declared that he hoped to write truthfully.[114] Perhaps he was William of Malmesbury's model for his claim that he means to write

108 *Gesta Pontificum*, pp. xii, 16 n. 7.
109 *Gesta Regum*, ii, 465 (prologue to Book V, here continuing the passage cited above, p. 137 and n. 82.
110 *Orderic*, i, 130.
111 *Hist. Pont.*, p. 2.
112 *Gesta Regum*, i, 1-2.
113 Above, p. 138.
114 See above, p. 138 n. 87.

the truth in *Gesta Regum* and *Historia Novella*.[115] Chronology is of course inextricably linked to historical truth: to have historical validity an event must be correctly dated. Ralph Diceto and Gervase of Canterbury make their consciousness of this clear. Diceto cites a dictum of Hugh of Fleury in his prologue: 'an event not attributable to a specific time cannot be accepted as history, but must be dismissed as an old wives' tale'.[116] Gervase, declaring that he wishes above all to keep the path of truth, confesses that the study of chronology is full of pitfalls. He laments that many errors arise because of the variety of ways used to calculate the years.

To underpin their statements historians appealed to authority. Their immediate model may have been Bede, who in his prologue disclaims responsibility for the truth of statements in the *Historia Ecclesiastica*, because he had trusted reliable witnesses.[117] William of Malmesbury refuses to vouch for his information about the distant past; veracity, he says, rests with his written authorities. For recent times he relied on what he himself had seen, or heard from trustworthy persons.[118] And Geoffrey of Monmouth tried to give credibility to his specious narrative by appealing to a (supposed) authority, 'an old book in the British language'.[119]

Occasionally   an authority was questioned. William of Malmesbury observes that Bede's account of St Wilfred has many omissions, and warns that Abbot Faritius' Life of St Aldhelm is untrustworthy, because Faritius was a foreigner (a Tuscan) and ignorant of the Anglo-Saxon language.[120] A few historians compared authorities in order to establish the truth. Alfred of Beverley clearly had doubts about the veracity of Geoffrey of Monmouth's *Historia Regum Britanniae*. He claims to have treated it with judicious caution. He asserts that he compared its text with other histories, noting agreements and disagreements; he had, he alleges, only copied into

---

115 See *Gesta Regum*, i, 284: 'Mihi haec placet provincia, ut mala, quantum queo, sine veritatis dispendio extenuem.' *Historia Novella*, 1: 'Itaque primo uocata, ut decet, in auxilium Diuinitate, rerum ueritatem scripturus, nichilque offense daturus aut gratie, ita incipiam.'

116 Diceto, i, 15: 'Res gestae quae nulla regum ac temporum certitudine commendantur non pro hystoria recipiuntur; sed inter aniles fabulas deputantur.' Diceto attributes this passage to Aimoin of Fleury, but Stubbs notes (*ibid.*, 15 n. 3) that it is by Hugh of Fleury.

117 See *Eccl. Hist.*, prologue (ed. Plummer), i, 6: 'Ut autem in his, quae scripsi, uel tibi, uel ceteris auditoribus siue lectoribus huius historiae occasionem dubitandi subtraham, quibus haec maxime auctoribus didicerim, breuiter intimare curabo.' (Bede's account of his authorities follows.) And *ibid.*, i, 8: 'Lectoremque suppliciter obsecro, ut, siqua in his, quae scripsimus, aliter quam veritas habet, posita reppererit, non hoc nobis imputet, qui, quod uera lex historiae est, simpliciter ea, quae fama uulgante collegimus,...'

118 *Gesta Regum*, i, 3.

119 *Hist. Brit.*, i, 1 (ed. Acton Griscom), p. 219.

120 *Gesta Pontificum*, pp. 210, 331 respectively.

his *Annales* passages corroborated in this way.[121] William of Newburgh knew no such moderation. He pilloried Geoffrey as an unbridled liar and totally demolished his credibility. He did so mainly be using the same comparative method as Alfred. Bede was his principle yardstick. ('Trust must be put in Bede, whose wisdom and sincerity are beyond doubt.'[122]) Gervase of Canterbury turned to authority to solve the problem of the multiplicity of chronological systems. He decides to follow earlier chronicles (notably the Worcester ones), and adopt the Dionysian era; anyone who prefers to date by the Evangelists need only subtract twenty-two years from any date. Moreover, to avoid the confusion caused by the fact that different historians might begin the year on different days (for example, the Annunciation, Nativity or Passion), he himself will start at Christmas, as most of his predecessors had done.[123] In addition, historians used probability in their search for truth. William of Malmesbury says that he will do his best to write the truth in the *Gesta Pontificum* by 'following the light of reason, since there are no chronicles to light the way'.[124] And William of Newburgh attacked Geoffrey of Monmouth's *Historia* partly on grounds of improbability.[125]

Historians were anxious to show that they recognised the need for accuracy and had taken great trouble to avoid error. Exceptionally, one might even ask the reader for help. Bede explained that he sent King Ceolwulf the *Historia Ecclesiastica* for criticism.[126] Ralph Diceto declares that he does not mind having any chronological or other errors, or stylistic infelicities, corrected.[127] William of Malmesbury's prologues show his awareness of the danger of bias entering an historical narrative. He was afraid that his account of the Norman Conquest might suffer from the bias in his authorities: Norman writers extol William the Conqueror to the skies, without discrimination, while the Anglo-Saxon ones denigrate him, because he subjugated their land.[128] But the danger of bias was worst when writing contemporary history. The problem was that an author might make enemies if he wrote the truth, and was, therefore, tempted to slant his narrative, in order to avoid the risk. Sallust asserted that, since returning

121 *Annales*, pp. 2–3. See above, pp. 19-20.
122 *Chron. Stephen, Henry II, and Richard I*, i. 18. Cf. above, pp. 20-2, 61.
123 *Gerv. Cant.*, i. 88–90 *passim*.
124 *Gesta Pontificum*, p. 4 (continuing the passage cited above, p. 70 n. 104): 'Aderit tamen, ut spero, lux mentium, ut et integra non vacillet veritas et instituta conservetur brevitas.' The substance here is very like that of the passage in Sallust, *Bell. Cat.*, iv, cited above, p. 68 n. 87.
125 See especially *Chrons. Stephen, Henry II, and Richard I*, i, 15–18.
126 *Hist. Eccl.*, prologue (ed. Plummer), i, 5.
127 Diceto, i, 19.
128 *Gesta Regum*, i, 283.

from public life, his determination to write history was strengthened, because at last his mind was at liberty, free from hope, fear or partisanship.[129] Perhaps William had this statement in mind when he wrote that friends had warned him of the peculiar danger of writing about the present: 'truth is often ship-wrecked and falsehood praised, because to speak ill of contemporaries is perilous, and good laudable'.[130] The fact that William revised the *Gesta Regum* and *Gesta Pontificum* in order to modify his criticisms of the Anglo-Norman kings and other great men of his day, indicates that his fears were real, and he acted on them.[131]

There is plenty of evidence in the prologues that historians subscribed to the ideal of historical veracity. But was this a matter of mere words? In fact, as long as they had no motives for distortion, most of them clearly took trouble to be accurate. However, historians used the latitude allowed them by the medieval concept of 'truth' and ideas of evidence outlined above (pp. 128-9), and a few wrote very biased narratives. William of Malmesbury is a good example of an historian who made a little information go a long way. His objective was to produce a coherent, meaningful narrative, rather than a string of disconnected facts, and to make it more convincing by filling gaps in his knowledge with plausible (but unverifiable) statements. A further objective was to write an account which supported, as will be seen, a certain point of view.

To achieve his ends William sometimes resorted to fallacious arguments.

---

129  *Bell. Cat.* iv (Loeb edition), p. 8: '.... eodem regressus statui res gestas populi Romani carptim, ut quaeque memoria digna videbantur, perscribere; eo magis, quod mihi a spe, metu, partibus rei publicae animus liber erat'. For the *topos* see above, p. 56 and n. 8.

130  *Gesta Regum*, ii, 357 (prologue to Book IV): 'Scio plerisque ineptum videri quod gestis nostri temporis regum scribendis stylum applicuerim; dicentibus quod in ejusmodi scriptis saepe naufragatur veritas et suffragatur falsitas, quippe praesentium mala periculose, bona plausibiliter dicuntur. Eo fit, inquiunt, ut, quia modo omnia magis ad pejus quam ad melius sint proclivia, scriptor obvia mala propter metum praetereat, et, bona si non sunt, propter plausum confingat.' However, at the urging of his friends, William decided to write about recent times. He continues, *ibid.*, ii, 358: 'Quocirca illorum, qui mihi timent ut aut odiar aut mentiar, benevolentiae gratus, ita sub ope Christi satisfaciam, ut nec falsarius nec odiosus inveniar.' See also the end of the prologue to Book I of the *Gesta Regum* (cited above, p. 69 n. 101), and *Gesta Regum*, ii, 283 (prologue to Book III): William says he will treat William the Conqueror impartially 'bene gesta, quantum cognoscere potui, sine fuco palam efferam; perperam acta, quantum sufficiat scientiae, leviter et quasi transeunter attingam; ut nec mendax culpetur historia, nec illum nota inuram censoria cujus cuncta pene, etsi non laudari, excusari certe possunt opera'.

131  *Gesta Regum.* i, xxxiii *et seqq.*, xlvii; *Gesta Pontificum*, pp. xv–xvii; Hugh Farmer, William of Malmebsury's life and work', *Journal of Ecclesiastical History*, xiii (1962), 45–6; Gransden, *Historical Writing*, i, 181–2 and nn. 130-41.

Examples of the practice may be given. The first suggests that he used the *post hoc, ergo propter hoc* method. Thus, he states that God punished Leofstan, abbot of Bury St Edmunds (1045–1065), for tampering with St Edmund's body, by inflicting him with gout of the hands, and that Baldwin, a well known physician, who later succeeded Leofstan in the abbacy, first visited Bury in order to cure Leofstan's gout.[132] It seems that William apparently constructed this narrative by giving casual connections to disparate facts, all recorded by a respected early authority: Abbot Leofstan tampered with St Edmund's body;[133] he contracted gout in his hands;[134] Baldwin was a well known physician;[135] he succeeded Leofstan.[136]

William also almost certainly used analogical arguments. For instance, there was no early authority for the pre-Conquest origins of the abbeys of Malmesbury or Sherborne. But William knew from the Anglo-Saxon chronicle that in 964 King Edgar expelled the clerks from the Old and New Minsters at Winchester, and from Milton and Chertsey, and introduced monks. He also knew that St Ethelwold's biographers, Ælfric and Wulfstan, represented Ethelwold as the moving force in the transformation of the clerical communities at Winchester into monastic ones.[137] It seems that William used these cases as analogues of what happened at Malmesbury and Sherborne ; he states that St Aldhelm drove the clerks from Malmesbury, and St Wulfsige drove them from Sherborne. (Other twelfth-century historians seem to have used the same *topoi* for the account of the pre-Conquest origins of their houses).[138]

A final example of William's apparent use of a fallacious argument is of him drawing a general conclusion from, so far as we know, an isolated case. It appears that he used Eadmer's strictures on the pre-Conquest monks of Christ Church, Canterbury,[139] as evidence for the decadence of all monasteries in the late Anglo-Saxon period.[140] If so, his deduction could reflect unwarranted bias; the Anglo-Norman historians denigrated the Anglo-Saxon church in the interest of the new régime, which justified its

132 *Gesta Pontificum*, pp. 155–6.
133 Hermann, 'De Miraculis Sancti Eadmundi' in *Memorials of St Edmund's Abbey*, ed. Thomas Arnold (Rolls Series, 1890–6, 3 vols), i, 52–4.
134 *Ibid.*, i, 56.
135 *Ibid.*, i, 56, 63.
136 *Ibid.*, i, 56.
137 *Three Lives of English Saints*, ed. Michael Winterbottom (Toronto Medieval Latin Texts, 1972), pp. 23, 45 respectively.
138 I.e. the historians of Worcester, Ely and Bury St Edmunds. See A. Gransden, 'Traditionalism and continuity during the last century of Anglo-Saxon monasticism,' Part II, *Journal of Ecclesiastical History*, above, pp. 76–8.
139 Eadmer's 'Life of St Dunstan' in *Memorials of St Dunstan*, ed. W. Stubbs (Rolls Series, 1874), pp. 237–8.
140 *Gesta Pontificum*, pp. 70–1. Cf. R. W. Southern, *St Anselm and his Biographer* (Cambridge, 1963), p. 247 and n. 1.

existence partly on grounds of its programme of ecclesiastical reform. It is very likely that William intended to support this point of view. He was certainly not free of partisan bias. He did not write contemporary history until late in life, when he wrote the *Historia Novella* for Robert earl of Gloucester.[141] Earl Robert was a patron sufficiently powerful to protect William and his abbey, and the *Historia* is strongly slanted in favour of him and his niece, the empress Matilda.

There remains to discuss the light prologues throw on the methods which an historian might adopt to structure his work. A work's structure is sometimes explained in the prologue. The twelfth century was remarkable for the elaborate ways used to construct histories. Traditionally historiography in England was annalistic, but particularly in the twelfth century a few writers broke away from the strictly chronological arrangement. Instead they gave their works unity by other kinds of structure and by overriding themes. The most ambitious authors in this respect explained their methods in their prologues.

Thus Eadmer explains how his two books on St Anselm, the *Historia Novorum* and the *Vita Sancti Anselmi* complement each other. In the prologue to the *Vita* he points out that the *Historia* dealt with the relations of the kings of England with St Anselm, but neglected his private life, character and miracles. This omission, at the insistence of his friends, he now tends to remedy. 'I have tried to adopt a plan to form a complete narrative in each case, so that neither work needs each other.' Nevertheless, in order to understand St Anselm properly, the reader should read both books.[142] Eadmer inherited the idea of dealing separately with different aspects of a man's life from the Anglo-Saxon tradition of secular and sacred biography (a tradition derived from Einhard's *Life of Charlemagne*, and thus indirectly from Suetonius' *Lives of the Caesars*). However, Eadmer developed that tradition. The pre-Conquest examples are of single biographies divided into sections, each dealing with a particular aspect: typically, a man's public life; his private life; and, if he were a saint, his miracles. Eadmer, by producing two distinct volumes, made the physical division absolute.[143]

William of Malmesbury, like Eadmer (who may well have influenced him in this matter, as he did in others),[144] saw his two principal works, the *Gesta Regum* and the *Gesta Pontificum* as complementary. In the prologue to the latter he writes: 'having formerly dealt [in the *Gesta Regum*] with the kings of England, it is not unreasonable that I should

141 *Historia Novella*, ed. Potter, p. xiii.
142 *Vita Sancti Anselmi*, ed. Southern, p. 2.
143 For the Anglo-Saxon tradition of the divided biography see Gransden, *Historical Writing*, i, 51–2 and nn. 60, 132, 136.
144 See *ibid.*, i, 169, 170.

now turn to its pontiffs.[145] Under Bede's influence, he arranged the *Gesta Regum* in five books, according to the old kingdoms of Anglo-Saxon England. He adopted the same order for the *Gesta Pontificum*, substituting 'episcopal provinces' for kingdoms.[146] But he deliberately alters the order. Both start with Kent, but whereas the *Gesta Regum* has Wessex second and East Anglia and Essex last, the latter two being, William says, 'of little interest',[147] the *Gesta Pontificum* has East Anglia and Essex after Kent because of their distinguished and still continuing series of bishops.[148] Moreover, Book V of the *Gesta Pontificum* is devoted to the patron saint of Malmesbury abbey, St Aldhelm. 'The reader like a pilgrim at last returns home.'[149] And William arranges his material about St Aldhelm's life, as he explains,[150] in four parts, according to subject matter, in the traditional Anglo-Saxon manner.

Similarly, Henry of Huntingdon explains in the prologues to Books I and V of the *Historia Anglorum* why he divided his work into five parts. His motive was thematic rather than purely structural. He made the structure reinforce his work's overall edificatory theme. Divine vengeance, he argues, had inflicted five scourges on Britain from the beginning of its history until Henry's own time. First, the Romans conquered Britain; secondly, the Picts and Scots sorely harassed it; thirdly, the Anglo-Saxons came and conquered; fourthly, the Danes wreaked havoc; fifthly, the Normans subdued the land and still rule it.[151] Henry describes the fourth scourge, England's sufferings from the Danes, particularly graphically. The Danes had descended 'like a swarm of wasps', 'sparing neither age nor sex', and decimated the country for 230 years, from the accession of King Ethelwulf (in 837) until the Norman Conquest,[152] which, by imposing law and order, gave the people 'life and liberty'.[153] They were instruments of divine vengeance elicited by religious decadence and the corruption of the Anglo-Saxon church, which had shone with such lustre in its early days.[154]

Henry's periodisation was in the mainline of the ancient tradition of Christian historiography, which saw history as the expression of God's will on earth. St Augustine had familiarised the Middle Ages with the

145 *Gesta Pontificum*, p. 4.
146 *Ibid.*, p. 4.
147 *Gesta Regum*, i, 2: 'Quod profecto fiet expeditius, si regna Orientalium Anglorum et Orientalium Saxonum post aliorum tergum posuero, quae et nostra cura et posterorum memoria putamus indigna.'
148 This is fully explained in *Gesta Pontificum*, p. 139.
149 *Ibid.*, p. 330.
150 *Ibid.*, p. 331.
151 *Hen. Hunt.*, pp. 137–8 (prologue to Book V).
152 *Ibid.*, p. 139.
153 *Ibid.*, p. 138.
154 *Ibid.*, p. 139.

concept of the Seven Ages, symbolising the seven days of the Creation.[155] Henry's version of providential periodisation was different. It was based on the Old Testament view that history illustrates God's power to punish the sinful; in his scheme God appears not as Creator, but as Judge. The immediate source of Henry's thematic structure was probably Bede, to whom he owed his nostalgic vision of the Golden Age of Northumbria.[156] Bede, following Gildas, attributed a plague and the Anglo-Saxon invasion, which successively afflicted the ancient Britons, to God's anger with the latter for their 'drunkenness, hatred, quarrelling, strife, envy, and other similar crimes'.[157] Moreover, others before Henry had seen the Viking incursions and Norman Conquest as divine vengeance on the Anglo-Saxons. King Alfred, in the preface to the *Pastoral Care*, ascribed the ninth-century Viking incursions to God's wrath at their neglect of learning.[158] Eadmer, whose *Historia Novorum* or some common source was used by Henry, regarded the Viking attacks of the eleventh century as divine punishment for King Ethelred's murder of his brother.[159] The *Anglo-Saxon Chronicle*, which Henry certainly used, states that God did not help the Anglo-Saxons against the Normans at Hastings 'because of [their] sins'.[160] Yet again, Eadmer attributes God's anger to Harold's perjury.[161] Henry, therefore, had plenty of models encouraging him to see English history as a series of divine punishments, though the causes given for them varied.

Possibly Henry derived the idea of the Danish scourge lasting 230 years from William of Malmesbury. William asserted 223 years' historiographical 'sleep' followed Bede's death.[162] This 'sleep' was the result of intellectual torpor and, since 'idleness is the enemy of the soul', it was part of the Anglo-Saxons' moral decadence. It was finally ended by a dramatic revival of religious life after the Norman Conquest. Emphasis is laid by both Norman and Anglo-Norman historians on this reformation, with the implication that it was one justification for the Conquest.[163] To highlight

---

155 The Six Ages of the World, corresponding to the six days of the Creation, and representing epochs in history, gained currency through St Augustine's *De Civitate Dei*, xxii, 30. See Auguste Luneau, *L'Histoire du Salut chez les Pères de l'Église* (Paris, 1964), pp. 285 *et seqq.*, 352 *et seqq.*
156 *Hen. Hunt.*, p. 139.
157 *Hist. Eccl.*, i, 14 (ed. Plummer, i. 30). Cf. Gildas, *De Excidio Britanniae*, cc. 22, 24.
158 Simon Keynes and Michael Lapidge, *Alfred the Great, Asser's Life of King Alfred and other contemporary sources* (Harmondsworth, 1983), p. 125.
159 *Historia Novorum*, p. 3.
160 *The Anglo-Saxon Chronicle*, ed. D. Whitelock with D. C. Douglas and S. I. Tucker (London, 1961), p. 143 (D, s.a. 1066).
161 *Historia Novorum*, p. 9.
162 *Gesta Regum*, i, 2.
163 See e.g.: *Guillaume de Poitiers, Histoire de Guillaume le Conquérant*, ed. with

the reformation it was necessary to paint a black picture of the preceding period. Indeed, the idea of the 'sleep' could have originated as part of Norman propaganda. This suggestion is perhaps supported by the fact that there is no hint of it in either Alfred of Beverley's or William of Newburgh's survey of English historiography: both say that Bede had many successors, of praiseworthy assiduity though none of comparable talent.[164] Possibly William of Newburgh was here following Alfred of Beverley, who wrote in a fairly remote place and may be supposed, therefore, to have been little, if at all, influenced by Norman propaganda. Moreover, the idea of a historiographical 'sleep' after Bede's death occurs in the work of at least one eleventh-century French historian.[165] Henry might well have thought that the period of decadence would have more or less coincided with the Danish scourge.

Ralph Diceto likewise explains the structure of his work in the prologue. He too adopted a religious periodisation. He divided his narrative into three parts, before the Law, under the Law, and of Grace, denoting the very ancient, the ancient and the modern. And he explains the problems each period presents to the would-be historian.[166] Diceto's prologue also contains much other material. Although put together in haphazard fashion, one fact clearly emerges: he had the convenience of readers much in mind. He adopted two expedients to help them. First, he lists twelve different subjects (persecutions of the church, schisms, ecclesiastical councils, royal coronations, and so on), and draws a sign after each. Any reference in the narrative to one of these subjects is indicated, as he explains, by the appropriate sign in the margin.[167] (This system of *signa* was to be

a French translation Raymonde Foreville (Les Classiques de l'Histoire de France au Moyen Age, xxiii, Paris, 1952), p. 127; Eadmer, *Historia Novorum*, pp. 12–15 *passim*; William of Malmesbury, *Gesta Regum*, ii, 326; Orderic, ii, 208 *et seqq.*

164 Alfred of Beverley, *Annales*, p. 3: 'Similiter et post Bedam plures per Anglorum ecclesias regum tempora diligencius perscrutantes, ipsorum gesta sollerti indagine annotare curaverunt, de quibus non nulla studiosius investigata huic opusculo sunt inserta.' William of Newburgh in *Chrons. Stephen, Henry II, and Richard I*, i, 18: 'Sane post Bedam non defuere, qui ab ipso seriem temporum atque eventuum nostrae insulae ad nostram usque memoriam ducerent; illi quidem minime comparandi; pro religiosa tamen opera et fideli, quanquam minus diserta narratione, laudandi.'

165 In 1044 the French historian Raoul Glaber had remarked that no one wrote history for 200 years after Bede and Paul the Deacon; Raoul Glaber, *Les cinq livres des ses histoire (900–1044)*, ed. M. Prou (Collection de textes pour servir à l'étude... de l'histoire, Paris, 1886), p. 1 (cited Guenée, 'Les premiers pas', p. 136).

166 *Diceto*, i, 18–20.

167 *Ibid.*, i, 3–4.

adopted and elaborated by Matthew Paris.[168]) Diceto's second aid to readers was to make compendia and extracts. For example, he compiled his list of historians and supplied extracts from their prologues, so that readers who had no access to their books could learn about their works.[169]

To conclude, we have to consider whether the two generalisations of Bernard Guenée mentioned above, about the twelfth-century historical prologues of western Europe, are exactly applicable to the English examples. First, was Hugh of St Victor an influence of primary importance? Certainly he had some influence on John of Salisbury, and a very strong one on Ralph Diceto. But Guenée naturally writes from a European point of view. In discussing English twelfth-century historiography, while not forgetting the native tradition,[170] he puts the emphasis on continental influence.[171] This tends to obscure the profound influence of Bede, which the English prologues make very evident. Bede was by far the most highly regarded English historian, and his *Historia Ecclesiastica* was – as it still is – an unrivalled source for England's early history. Therefore, it is not surprising that this influence was powerful and pervasive. As has been seen, William of Malmesbury and Henry of Huntingdon were Bede's self-declared continuators, and the structure of William's *Gesta Regum* and *Gesta Pontificum* was partly modelled on that of the *Historia Ecclesiastica*. The growing precision with which the prologues describe the authors' sources no doubt owed much, as Guenée points out, to Hugh of St Victor. But English historians already had the precedent of Bede's prologue to the *Historia Ecclesiastica*. Although it seems that Bede's influence waned in southern England in the last half of the twelfth century, in the north it remained as strong as ever; this is most vividly illustrated by William of Newburgh's prologue, which sets Bede's authority against that of Geoffrey of Monmouth.

The second question concerns one of Guenée's central themes. He argues that in the course of the twelfth century the dominance of rhetoric over historiography declined; instead scholarship gained supremacy.[172] Historians became less concerned with literary style and structure and more with learning – with the search for, and evaluation and even criticism of, the works of their predecessors. Rather than write history in literary mode, they began to produce compilations of extracts from standard authorities,

---

168 See Gransden, *Historical Writing*, i, 364 and n. 56.
169 *Diceto*, i, 19–20. Cf. Gransden, *op. cit.*, i, 231 and n. 102, 234, 235 and n. 130.
170 See Guenée, 'L'Histoire entre l'éloquence et la science', pp. 361–2, 363.
171 *Ibid.*, 357–70 *passim*, Guenée, 'Les premiers pas', pp. 136–52 *passim*.
172 *Idem*, 'L'Histoire entre l'éloquence et la science', pp. 357–70 *passim*, idem, 'L'Historien et la compilation au xiiie siècle', *Journal de Savants* (1985), pp. 119–35.

assembled and sorted in scholarly fashion, and presented in strictly chronological sequence. Thus twelfth-century historiography paved the way for that of the thirteenth century; then the 'monastic chronicle', which begins as a compilation and is throughout composed of annals, had a monopoly. Can this trend be detected in the English prologues?

In general the English evidence concurs with Guenée's conclusion. For example, the prologues of Eadmer and William of Malmesbury make clear their preoccupation with literary style and structure. Diceto's prologue, on the other hand, shows less concern with these matters, but is remarkable for the number of extracts it contains. Symptomatic of this trend is the prologue to Roger of Howden's chronicle. Roger did not compose it himself at all, but simply copied from Symeon of Durham.[173] Nevertheless, like all generalisations, this one of Guenée's can only be accepted with reservations. The prologues highlight static factors in twelfth-century English historiography. The influence of rhetoric by no means died; Henry of Huntingdon and Richard of Devizes amply prove this. Nor was learning a prerogative of the last half of the century. (Respect for 'authority' was perennial in the Middle Ages; this in itself always encouraged historians to study standard history books.) William of Malmesbury, indeed, was one of the most learned historians England has ever produced. And he was perfectly capable, when he wished, of effectively criticising his sources. William of Newburgh's critical acumen would have been exceptional in any age. An historiographical generalisation, like any other, can only be roughly right. Deviations inevitably occur because of the peculiar character and talents, background and immediate circumstances of individual authors.

173 *Hoveden*, i, 3–4.

# 6

## The Growth of the Glastonbury Traditions and Legends in the Twelfth Century[1]

A recent scholar has written of 'the widespread belief, by no means the monopoly of high Anglicans only, that it was to Glastonbury, first of all places in these islands of ours, that the Christian faith first came, and that Glastonbury is therefore the fountain and head-spring of Christianity in England, and indeed in the whole of the British Isles'.[2]

Glastonbury claimed in the Middle Ages to be one of the most hallowed spots in Britain not only because of its ancient tradition, but also because of the numerous relics it housed, of saints and of king Arthur and queen Guinevere. This reputation originated in the Anglo-Saxon period and grew in the four centuries following the Norman Conquest. It was mainly the result of work by the abbey's chroniclers and by others whom the monks commissioned to write. In its development the twelfth century was crucial: during this period the monks 'proved' Glastonbury's antiquity and holy associations, sowing the seeds of the more baroque manifestations of its later medieval legends.

The reasons are obvious why the monks wanted to increase the abbey's reputation by the use of literature to prove its long and holy tradition. The earlier the date of an abbey's foundation the higher its status. In particular this would give an abbot precedence at an ecclesiastical council,[3] but in a more general way antiquity gave prestige. Relics, too, contributed to prestige, and an abbey with the relics of a famous founder was especially fortunate.[4] Prestige armed a religious community against its

---

[1] This paper is based on one delivered to the Glastonbury Antiquarian Society in St. John's church, under the chairmanship of my father, Mr. Stephen C. Morland, F.S.A. I am indebted to him and to my colleague Dr. B. F. Hamilton for help on specific points.

[2] R. F. Treharne, *The Glastonbury Legends,* London 1967; reprinted, without the index, Abacus Books 1975, 4.

[3] See J. Armitage Robinson, *Two Glastonbury Legends: King Arthur and St. Joseph of Arimathea,* Cambridge 1926, 40–1 and n.1.

[4] See Jonathan Sumption, *Pilgrimage, an Image of Medieval Religion,* London 1975, 165–7.

enemies, which enabled it to defend its privileges and property more effectively. It also increased its wealth by attracting pilgrims. The crowds who came to worship, perhaps to be cured, perhaps only to look at the shrines of the saints, brought offerings which could be an important source of monastic income.[1]

At the time of the Norman Conquest Glastonbury abbey, although recognised as an ancient Christian site of outstanding holiness, needed to substantiate its traditions and legends. The circumstances of its foundation were veiled in the mists of time and lacked the picturesque details which did so much to convince the pious multitude. Moreover, although it had relics of a number of saints, many were Northumbrian or Celtic, most of whom were of limited reputation in the south. Nor did it have a famous patron saint of its own. Here it was at a disadvantage compared with other great Benedictine houses, some of which had had such patrons from their foundations: Durham had St. Cuthbert, St. Albans claimed St. Alban, Bury St. Edmunds had St. Edmund, king and martyr, and Worcester St. Oswald, to whom was added St. Wulfstan after the Norman Conquest. Westminster, too, acquired a famous saint, Edward the Confessor, in the post-Conquest period. Canterbury itself had a host of early archbishops, starting with St. Augustine, and then in 1170 gained the biggest pilgrim attraction of all, Thomas Becket. Glastonbury had no equivalent. It is true that it had some claim to St. Dunstan because he had been abbot of Glastonbury before becoming archbishop of Canterbury. But Canterbury's claim was stronger since, as was generally recognised, he was buried in the cathedral. Moreover, the monks asserted that St. Patrick the apostle of Ireland was buried in the abbey, but this claim too presented problems.[2]

The period of transition following the Norman Conquest was especially difficult at Glastonbury. The Norman abbot, Thurstan, who was appointed in about 1077, had no respect for the abbey's customs and his intransigence culminated in bloodshed in the church—at least two monks were killed and many more wounded.[3] In addition Glastonbury had difficulties similar to those faced by other pre-Conquest houses. Its estates, already impoverished by Danish raids and the dilapidations of the last two Anglo-Saxon abbots, had suffered from the Norman settlement,[4] and its prosperity was further threatened by the attrition of spiritual prestige. The new ecclesiastical hierarchy tended to regard the Anglo-Saxon saints

---

[1] For the lucrativeness of the pilgrim trade see C. R. Cheney 'Church-building in the Middle Ages', *Bulletin of the John Rylands Library,* xxxiv (1951–2), 29–32 (reprinted in Cheney, *Medieval Texts and Studies,* Oxford 1973, 346–63), and Sumption, op. cit., 158–65.

[2] For Glastonbury's claim to the relics of St. Patrick and St. Dunstan see below, 159, 162, 163-5 passim.

[3] See the Anglo-Saxon Chronicle, s.a. 1083; *The Anglo-Saxon Chronicle,* a revised translation ed. Dorothy Whitelock with D. C. Douglas and S. I. Tucker, London 1961, 160, and *Adami de Domerham Historia de Rebus gestis Glastoniensibus,* ed. Thomas Hearne, Oxford 1727, i. 113–16.

[4] *Adam de Domerham,* i. 110–13.

with scepticism. As archbishop Lanfranc said: 'When I turn over in my mind the accounts of these saints, I cannot help doubting the quality of their sanctity';[1] and he struck some from the liturgical calendar of Christ Church, Canterbury.[2]

Nor was Glastonbury's need of prestige and money particularly acute only in the Anglo-Norman period. In 1184 a catastrophic disaster struck the abbey; the church and monastic building were burnt to the ground. The place, lamented its chronicler, 'was reduced to a pile of ashes, its relics to confusion'.[3] The cost of rebuilding was immense and could only be met with the help of those impressed by its fame. The abbey's troubles lasted well into the thirteenth century. It needed all its prestige to defeat the attempt by Savaric bishop of Bath (1192–1205) and his successors first to move the see of Bath to Glastonbury and then to assert the right to overlordship of the abbey.[4] The monks' financial resources were severely strained by litigation in the royal courts and papal curia.

Monks habitually responded to such challenges by propaganda, in order to augment their houses' reputations. They wrote local histories and saints' 'Lives'. Both were probably read mainly by the monks themselves, but through them the propaganda was transmitted to neighbours and pilgrims; it was hoped that the well-informed public would give more generously. The Norman Conquest provided a strong incentive to this kind of writing: the monks of Durham and Evesham, for example, produced local histories to prove that their foundations had long and glorious traditions, unbroken by the Conquest;[5] and many houses wrote Lives of their patron saints—at Canterbury Osbern[6] and Eadmer[7] wrote in defence of the Canterbury saints, which was doubtless one reason why some were restored to the liturgical calendar.[8]

Glastonbury conformed to this general trend, but besides lacking a detailed foundation story and famous relics, the monks were apparently short of literary talent to make the best of what they had. In the twelfth

---

[1] *The Life of St. Anselm Archbishop of Canterbury by Eadmer*, ed., with an English translation, R. W. Southern (Nelson's Medieval Texts, 1962), 50. Cf. A. Gransden, *Historical Writing in England c. 550 to c. 1307*, London 1974, 105.

[2] See F. A. Gasquet and E. Bishop, *The Bosworth Psalter*, London 1908, 27–39.

[3] *Adam de Domerham*, ii. 334.

[4] For this dispute, a full account of which is given by Adam of Domerham (*Adam de Domerham*, ii. 352f. and see below, 340), see M. D. Knowles, 'Essays in Monastic History: V. The Cathedral Monasteries', *Downside Review*, li (1933), 94–6, and J. Armitage Robinson, 'The First Deans of Wells', *Somerset Historical Essays*, London 1921, 68–70. The monks appealed to the antiquity of Glastonbury in the dispute; they ask in one of their articles against Jocelin bishop of Bath (1206–42) 'An omnibus ecclesiis Angliae Glastoniensis ecclesia sit antiquior et vetustior, saltem per famam?': *Adam de Domerham*, ii. 453.

[5] Printed in *Symeonis Monachi Opera Omnia*, ed. Thomas Arnold (Rolls Series, 1882, 1885, 2 vols.), i. 3–135, and *Chronicon Abbatiae de Evesham*, ed. W. D. Macray (Rolls Series, 1863). Cf. Gransden, op. cit., 111–21.

[6] For Osbern and his hagiographies see R. W. Southern, *Saint Anselm and his Biographer*, Cambridge 1963, 248–52.

[7] For Eadmer's hagiographies, see ibid., 277–87.

[8] See Gasquet and Bishop, op. cit., 33–4.

century the abbey produced no one capable of writing in its defence. Later it was to be more fortunate. In the thirteenth century Adam of Domerham wrote its history to 1291, with the general intention of showing how the abbey's property and privileges, formerly so great but now sadly diminished, could be preserved and increased, but in particular to record its victory over the claims of the bishop of Bath.[1] And early in the fifteenth century a monk of Glastonbury called John abbreviated Adam's work, adding various embellishments, and continued it until about 1400. (A further brief continuation was added which goes down to the late fifteenth century.)[2]

Because of the paucity of literary talent at Glastonbury itself in the twelfth century, the monks turned to outsiders to record and amplify the abbey's history. They commissioned at least one well-known historian, William of Malmesbury, and, as will be suggested below, probably employed two other writers, Caradoc of Llancarfan and Gerald of Wales. It is certain that William and Gerald visited Glastonbury before writing, and Caradoc may have done so too.

The use of outsiders as propagandists was by no means unusual, and in most instances they seem to have visited the place for which they were to write. Hagiography, indeed, became such an industry in the Anglo-Norman period that a class of professional hagiographers began to develop. Many of these were foreigners. There was, for example, Goscelin from the abbey of St. Bertin's at St. Omer in Flanders, who came to England and travelled from monastery to monastery writing Lives of the patron saints.[3] Such professionals from abroad were sufficiently numerous to arouse Eadmer's anger; he wrote in disgust that they would tell any lie if paid enough.[4] (However, Eadmer was being too severe because many of the 'Lives' by foreigners, like those by the Anglo-Normans themselves, are of considerable value for local history.) The practice of commissioning outsiders to write propaganda remained common throughout the twelfth century. Thus Ailred of Rievaulx, having attended the translation of relics at Hexham in 1155 at the invitation of the canons, subsequently wrote for them an account of the Hexham saints.[5] Similarly, in 1163, the abbot of Westminster invited him to the translation of Edward the Confessor and commissioned him to write on the saint's life and miracles.[6]

---

[1] For the printed edition of Adam's chronicle see above, 154 n. 3.
[2] John's chronicle and the continuation are printed in *Johannis Glastoniensis Chronica sive Historia de Rebus Glastoniensibus*, ed. Thomas Hearne, Oxford 1726, 2 vols.
[3] For Goscelin and other foreign hagiographers see Gransden, op. cit., 107–11.
[4] Eadmer says this in his letter to the monks of Glastonbury countering their claim to have the relics of St. Dunstan (cf. below 163 & n. 4); *Memorials of St. Dunstan*, ed. William Stubbs (Rolls Series, 1874), 415.
[5] His work, *De Sanctis Ecclesiae Haugustaldensis, et eorum Miraculis Libellus*, is printed in *The Priory of Hexham, its Chroniclers, Endowments and Annals*, ed. James Raine (Surtees Society, xliv, xlvi, 1864, 1865, 2 vols.), i. 172–203.
[6] Printed in Migne, *Patrologia Latina*, cxcv, coll. 737–90, from Roger Twysden, *Historiae Anglicanae Scriptores X*, London 1652, i, 369. Cf. *The Life of Ailred of Rievaulx by Walter Daniel*, ed., with an English translation, F. M. Powicke (Nelson's Medieval Texts, 1950). xlvii–xlviii.

In order to build up the prestige of Glastonbury abbey, the twelfth century propagandists made use of two well-established literary traditions, hagiography and romance literature.

Hagiography, although centred on the lives of saints, involved an interest in local history because nearly every saint was the patron of a place, usually where he was buried.[1] The place attracted the hagiographer's attention from the time of the saint's first association with it, which in the writer's view might mark its origin; thus hagiographers tended to be interested in origins.

The romance tradition, which was influenced by classical literature, belonged, in contrast to hagiography, to the secular world. Although typified by the *chansons de geste*, features of it invaded other types of writing, for example the Latin chronicle. Its values were popularised in England by Geoffrey of Monmouth's *Historia Regum Britanniae* which was finished in 1136.[2] The hero of romance, at all times obedient to the chivalric code of behaviour, might be an historic figure, but his alleged deeds were largely imaginary. To give verisimilitude to the tale, his career was often linked to recorded events. (Brutus, for example, Geoffrey of Monmouth's eponymous hero of Britain, was an exile from the Fall of Troy.) This led to a taste for historical parallels, to place the hero in the sequence of world history; and if he were a founder, this resulted in an interest in origins.

Hagiography and romance were not, of course, totally distinct literary forms; each influenced the other. Both tended to be interested in origins, and the heroes of each were not always dissimilar. On the one hand, a saint might have the attributes of a warrior—he might even have been one earlier in life. (Alternatively a hero of romance might impinge on his career.)[3] On the other hand, a warrior hero might be represented as a Christian fighting for God, and his tomb might become the centre of a cult. Generally speaking hagiography was the principal influence on Glastonbury's literary productions up to 1184, the year of the fire; thereafter romance was the most important factor.

The influence of hagiography will be considered first. In this context the principal figure is William of Malmesbury whom the Glastonbury monks commissioned in about 1129 to write the abbey's history[4] and the life of St. Dunstan.[5] Besides his proximity, there were good reasons for

[1] For the value of hagiography for local history see Gransden, op. cit., 69, 71–3, 85–6, 89–91, 106–114 passim.

[2] Printed in *The Historia Regum Britanniae of Geoffrey of Monmouth*, ed. Acton Griscom, London 1929.

[3] For an example, see below, 169.

[4] The text of the *De Antiquitate Glastoniensis Ecclesiae* as it survives today (see below, 158 and n. 5) is dedicated to Henry of Blois, bishop of Winchester (1129–1171), who also ruled Glastonbury as abbot. But originally William addressed the work to the monks of Glastonbury; see *Adam de Domerham*, i. 121–2. Cf. Armitage Robinson, 'William of Malmesbury "On the Antiquity of Glastonbury"', *Somerset Historical Essays*, 4.

[5] For William's two *Lives of St. Dunstan* see below, 159. The surviving *Life* is printed in *Memorials of St. Dunstan*, ed. Stubbs, 250–324. For the dedication to the monks of Glastonbury, see ibid., 250.

employing him. He was a writer of ability and a recognised authority on history: he was, as it were, a specialist on the subject of continuity as well as a hagiographer. In 1125 he published his major work, the *Gesta Pontificum*,[1] which stressed that the church of his time was a continuation of the Anglo-Saxon one. His declared intention was to fill the gap between Bede and his own day, paying particular attention to the lives of the pre-Conquest saints, which, he said, the Anglo-Saxons had neglected to record.[2] Already early in the twelfth century the monks of Worcester had commissioned him to translate from English into Latin the *Life of Wulfstan*, written by one of their number, Coleman, soon after the saint's death in 1095.[3]

The Glastonbury monks wanted William both to glorify the abbey in general, and also to counter a particular attack which had recently been made on its antiquity. Osbern in his *Life of St. Dunstan* had asserted that Dunstan was the first abbot of Glastonbury.[4] The monks, of course, knew better: the abbey had a far longer history and they wanted this proved beyond dispute.

William of Malmesbury's *De Antiquitate Glastoniensis Ecclesiae* sought finally to establish that the abbey had a very long and very venerable history. Unfortunately we do not have William's original text. All that survives is the copy made by Adam of Domerham to form the early part of his own chronicle. The version of the *De Antiquitate* which Adam copied was not the text as William left it. It had numerous additions, mainly of legendary material, interpolated by the Glastonbury monks to enhance the abbey's reputation. Some idea of what William actually wrote can be gained by comparing the extant text of the *De Antiquitate* with the extracts William inserted in the third edition of his *Gesta Regum*: whatever is not in the *Gesta Regum* is suspect. Nevertheless, it is impossible to be certain of William's original text, or of the date of all the interpolations, although many were clearly added shortly after the fire of 1184.[5] Besides the *De Antiquitate* William wrote saints' 'Lives' for the

[1] Printed *Willelmi Malmesbiriensis Monachi de Gestis Pontificum Anglorum*, ed. N.E.S.A. Hamilton (Rolls Series, 1870).

[2] See ibid., 4, and *Willelmi Malmesbiriensis Monachi de Gestis Regum*, ed. William Stubbs (Rolls Series, 1887, 1889, 2 vols.), i. 2.

[3] Coleman's work does not survive but William of Malmesbury's Latin translation is extant and is printed in *The Vita Wulfstani of William of Malmesbury*, ed. R. R. Darlington (Camden Society, third series, xl, 1928).

[4] *Memorials of St. Dunstan*, ed. Stubbs, 92. See William of Malmesbury's comment in his *De Antiquitate Glastoniensis Ecclesiae; Adam de Domerham*, i. 71. William makes the same criticism of Osbern in his own *Life of St. Dunstan* (for which see below, 159); Stubbs, op. cit., 251.

[5] The interpolation of the *De Antiquitate* is fully discussed by W. W. Newell, 'William of Malmesbury on the Antiquity of Glastonbury', *Publications of the Modern Language Association of America*, xviii (1903), 459–512, and, independently, by Armitage Robinson, 'William of Malmesbury "On the Antiquity of Glastonbury"', *Somerset Historical Essays*, 1–25. For specific references to the fire in two of the interpolations see *Adam de Domerham*, i. 23, 37. Adam of Domerham's version of the *De Antiquitate* and his own chronicle (*Adam de Domerham*, i. 1–122, ii. 303–596, respectively) are in Trinity College, Cambridge,

Glastonbury monks: he wrote two 'Lives' of St. Dunstan, one of which survives and is of some value for the history of the abbey,[1] and 'Lives', now lost, of St. Patrick, St. Indract and St. Benignus.[2]

It is clear from William's *Life of St. Dunstan* that he fully appreciated the value of the earliest *Life of St. Dunstan*.[3] This was by an unknown writer, probably a foreigner, whose name began with 'B' and who wrote the 'Life' shortly after Dunstan's death partly on the information of members of the archbishop's intimate circle.[4] Although he was not a monk of Glastonbury, 'B' may have visited the abbey. William's *De Antiquitate* may be regarded as a gloss, so to speak, on two passages by 'B'. One passage, following the statement that Dunstan's father took him as a boy to visit Glastonbury, describes the place itself: 'There was within the realm of king Athelstan a certain royal island known locally from ancient times as Glastonbury. It spread wide with numerous inlets, surrounded by lakes full of fish and by rivers, suitable for human use and, what is more important, endowed by God with sacred gifts. In that place at God's command the first neophites of the catholic law discovered an ancient church, built by no human skill though prepared by heaven for the salvation of mankind. This church was consecrated to Christ and the holy Mary his mother, as God himself, the architect of heaven, demonstrated by many miracles and wonderful mysteries. To this church they added another, an oratory built of stone, which they dedicated to Christ and to St. Peter. Henceforth crowds of the faithful came from all around to worship and humbly dwelt in that precious place on the island'.[5]

The other relevant passage in 'B' says that 'Irish pilgrims, as well as other crowds of the faithful, had a great veneration for Glastonbury, particularly on account of the blessed Patrick the younger, who was said most happily to rest in the Lord there'.[6]

From these passages it could reasonably be assumed that Glastonbury was extremely ancient as a Christian site, and the burial place of St. Patrick the apostle of Ireland. But the narrative was too bald and brief to stir enthusiasm. It needed amplification, and this is what William of

---

[1] For the printed edition see above, 157 n. 5.

[2] William mentions that he wrote lives of SS. Patrick, Benignus and Indract, besides the two lives of St. Dunstan, in his prologue to the *De Antiquitate; Adam de Domerham*, i. 3; cf. ibid., 24, 113. For St. Indract and his connexion with Glastonbury see below, 349 n. 1.

[3] See *Memorials of St. Dunstan*, ed. Stubbs, 252 and n. 4, 258 and n. 1, 263 and n. 1, 265 and n. 1.

[4] For 'B' and suggestions as to his identity see Stubbs, op. cit., xi–xxvi.

[5] Ibid., 6–7.

[6] Ibid., 10–11.

---

MS.R.5.33, fols. 1–18ᵛ, 21–73ᵛ, respectively. The *De Antiquitate* and Adam's chronicle are in the same good thirteenth century charter hand to fol. 51ᵛ; thereafter the handwriting of Adam's chronicle becomes progressively rougher. Both *De Ant.* and Adam's chronicle have long marginal additions in at least three hands of the thirteenth, fourteenth and fifteenth centuries. The MS. is described in M. R. James *Catalogue of Manuscripts in the Library of Trinity College, Cambridge*. Cambridge 1900–4, ii. 199. For two other references to the MS. see below, 166 nn. 4, 6.

Malmesbury undertook. To amplify he used written evidence and the observations of his own eyes, and no doubt hearsay.

William knew from the first passage cited that in the remote past missionaries came to Glastonbury. To discover who these were he turned to Bede's *Ecclesiastical History*. There he read that at the request of king Lucius, pope Eleutherus sent missionaries to Britain in A.D. 166.[1] These were the first missionaries known to have come to Britain and so corresponded with 'B''s 'first neophites of the catholic law'. However, 'B''s statement that the missionaries found a pre-existing church 'built by no human skill' gave William more trouble. In itself it contradicted 'B''s description of the missionaries as the 'first neophites'. Here William apparently abandoned 'B' and used another now unidentified source. This authority stated that the old church was built by disciples of Christ.[2] William comments that this was not impossible, for, as Freculfus said, St. Philip preached to the Gauls, and he could have sent missionaries over the channel. 'But', William writes, 'I will leave such disputable matters and stick to solid facts'.[3]

To fill out the early history William made remarkable use of visual evidence. He gave an account of the churches at Glastonbury from his own observation and much of what he says has been confirmed by archaeology. He gives the exact location of the earliest church, which he says was of wattle but had been covered with wooden planks and roofed with lead by Paulinus archbishop of York (625–633).[4] This church was destroyed by the 1184 fire and no trace of it remains. However archaeology has revealed within the precincts a chapel of wattle,[5] a type of construction favoured by the Celts in Britain. William also records that king Ine's church, which was next to the wattle one, was enlarged by St. Dunstan by the addition of side aisles, thus changing its shape from a rectangle to a square.[6] Recent excavations have confirmed this.[7]

Most remarkable are William's observations on the two 'pyramids' or standard crosses in the cemetery.[8] He records that one was twenty-six feet

[1] *Historia Ecclesiastica*, Bk. I, cap. iv; Bk. IV, cap. xxiv; *Venerabilis Baedae Historia Ecclesiastica*, ed. Charles Plummer, Oxford 1896, i. 16, 352. The mission is also noticed in the Anglo-Saxon chronicle, s.a. 167; ed. Whitelock, Douglas and Tucker, 8.

[2] See Armitage Robinson, *Somerset Historical Essays*, 10–11.

[3] *Gesta Regum*, ed. Stubbs, i. 23–4.

[4] *Adam de Domerham*, i. 17–18, 28, 53–4. A parallel to this method of renovating a wattle church is in Bede who states that bishop Finan (651–661) built the church at Lindisfarne of hewn oak and thatched it with reeds. Bishop Eadbert (688–698) removed the reeds and covered the whole with plates of lead: *Historia Ecclesiastica*, Bk. III, cap. xxv; ed. Plummer, i. 181 (cf. Joan and Harold Taylor, 'Pre-Norman Churches of the Border', *Celt and Saxon: Studies in the Early British Border*, ed. N. K. Chadwick, Cambridge 1963, 254 and n. 1.). Similarly Wilfrid re-roofed the church at York with lead: *The Life of Bishop Wilfrid by Eddius Stephanus*, ed., with an English translation, Bertram Colgrave, Cambridge 1927, 34 (cap. xvi; cf. Plummer, op. cit., ii. 188).

[5] See Taylor and Taylor, op. cit., 256.

[6] *Adam de Domerham*, i. 54, and *Memorials of St. Dunstan*, 271.

[7] Taylor and Taylor, op. cit., 256, and the same authors' *Anglo-Saxon Architecture*, Cambridge 1965, i. 251.

[8] *Adam de Domerham*, i. 44–5.

high and had five panels on which were carvings of people with their names transcribed beneath. The other cross was eighteen feet tall and had four similar panels. Although the names were, as William says, almost illegible with age, he managed to transcribe most of them. He identified them as abbots of Glastonbury, thus disproving Osbern's assertion that Dunstan was the first of the line. Modern scholarship does not suggest that these were in fact the names of abbots,[1] but clearly William was right to describe the 'pyramids' as 'extremely ancient'; they must have belonged to the same period, the seventh century, as the Northumbrian crosses at Ruthwell and Bewcastle.

In order to give what account he could of the Anglo-Saxon abbots from the seventh century onwards, William used the evidence of early charters which enabled him to record the abbots' acquisition of lands.[2] He also testified to the burial at Glastonbury of the relics of a number of Irish, Welsh and Northumbrian saints. Here he must have derived his information from the shrines he saw in the abbey and perhaps also from the liturgical calendar used by the monks. There is, in fact, tenth century evidence supporting his claim with regard to some of the saints.[3]

[1] See Aelred Watkin, 'The Glastonbury "Pyramids" and St. Patrick's "Companions" ', *Downside Review*, lxiii (1945), 30–41. However, Dom Aelred Watkin's identifications are, perhaps, more definite than the evidence warrants.

[2] William of Malmesbury's information, brief though it is, on the Anglo-Saxon charters of Glastonbury, which date back to the seventh century, is of great value because many of the texts are lost. See H. P. R. Finberg, *The Early Charters of Wessex*, Leicester 1964, 15 (Professor Finberg includes William's particulars in his hand-list; op. cit., 109 f.).

[3] For William on Glastonbury's relics see *Adam de Domerham*, i. 18–30 passim (cf. Armitage Robinson, *Somerset Historical Essays*, 17–21, and the same author's *The Times of St. Dunstan*, Oxford 1923, 98–103). William includes SS. Ceolfrid, Aidan, Benedict Biscop, Gildas (see below, 163 and n. 1), and Patrick (see below and the next note). Evidence on the association with Glastonbury of a number of Northumbrian and Celtic saints in the tenth century is provided by the calendar of the Bosworth Psalter from Christ Church, Canterbury, which is based on a Glastonbury calendar almost certainly taken to Canterbury by Dunstan when he became archbishop, in the late tenth century Glastonbury calendar in the Leofric Missal, and in a late tenth or early eleventh century tract on the resting places of saints: printed respectively in *Bosworth Psalter*, ed. Gasquet and Bishop, 76–118, cf. P. M. Korhammer, 'The Origins of the Bosworth Psalter', *Anglo-Saxon England*, ed. Peter Clemoes, Cambridge 1972–5, ii. 175–80; *Leofric Missal*, ed. F. E. Warren, Oxford 1883, 23–34 (for the association of the calendar in the Leofric Missal with Glastonbury, see ibid., liv); *Die Heiligen Englands*, ed. F. Liebermann, Hannover 1889. The Bosworth Psalter and Leofric Missal both state that abbot Ceolfrid was buried at Glastonbury: Gasquet and Bishop, op. cit., 21, 106; Warren, op. cit., 31. The Leofric Missal and the tract on the resting places of saints state that Aidan was buried there: Warren, op. cit., 30; Liebermann, op. cit., 17. Moreover, the calendars show that besides the feasts of Ceolfrid and Aidan, those of Benedict Biscop (12 January), Gildas (29 January) and Bridget (1 February) were kept at Glastonbury. Relics of the Northumbrian saints may have reached Glastonbury between c. 900 and c. 970: see Christopher Hohler, 'Some service books', *Tenth Century Studies: essays in commemoration of the millenium of the Council of Winchester and the Regularis Concordia*, ed. David Parsons, London and Chichester 1975, 69–71 (cf. *Adam de Domerham*, i. 29). It should also be noted that the calendars in the Bosworth Psalter and Leofric Missal show that the feast of Paulinus (10 October) was observed at Glastonbury, which confirms that he had traditionally some connection with

It was particularly necessary to emphasise that St. Patrick was buried in the abbey.[1] The second passage quoted above from 'B' states explicitly that it was St. Patrick the younger, that is the bishop, and the apostle of Ireland. This positive assertion indicates that Glastonbury's claim had already been questioned, as well it might, because it was far more likely that he was buried in Ireland, as the Irish contended. Probably the suggestion had been made that it was 'the elder', not his famous namesake, who rested at Glastonbury.

Generally speaking William of Malmesbury's treatment of the antiquity and relics of Glastonbury was restrained and scholarly. The same cannot be said of those who succeeded him as the abbey's historians. As the twelfth century proceeded the monks' interest by no means declined but study became more disreputable; they stopped at neither fantasy nor forgery.

Soon after William of Malmesbury wrote the *De Antiquitate*, a Welshman, Caradoc of Llancarfan, composed a *Life of St. Gildas* for the Glastonbury monks.[2] Little is known for certain about Caradoc—only a colophon in one MS. of the *Life* attributing the work to him,[3] and a brief notice by Geoffrey of Monmouth: Geoffrey speaks of him as a contemporary who wrote a history of the later Welsh kings, from the point where his own history ended.[4] This work has not survived, but Geoffrey's statement suggests that Caradoc was a writer of some reputation. It has been argued on the grounds of the pro-Glastonbury bias in the *Life of St. Gildas* that Caradoc, having been a canon of Llancarfan, became a monk of Glastonbury.[5] However, it seems equally likely that the Glastonbury monks commissioned him to write. His *Life* amplifies a brief statement by William of Malmesbury that Gildas spent many years at Glastonbury,

---

[1] William of Malmesbury had stated that St. Patrick the apostle of Ireland came to Glastonbury; ibid., 18–19 (cf. Armitage Robinson, *Somerset Historical Essays*, 12–17). Besides the passage cited from 'B', the two calendars cited in the previous note show that the feast of Patrick 'the bishop', i.e. the apostle of Ireland (17 March), was kept at Glastonbury. The tenth-eleventh century list of saints' resting places states simply that 'St. Patrick' was buried there (Liebermann, op. cit., 17). The two calendars also show that the feast of Patrick 'the elder' (24 August) was kept at Glastonbury, and the Bosworth calendar adds that he rested there; see Gasquet and Bishop, op. cit., 21. For the problem as to which St. Patrick was buried in the abbey see *Memorials of St. Dunstan*, ed. Stubbs, lxxviii n. 3, 10 and n. 8; C. H. Slover, 'William of Malmesbury and the Irish', *Speculum*, ii (1927), 271–3; H. P. R. Finberg, 'St. Patrick at Glastonbury', *Irish Ecclesiastical Record*, cvii (1967), 345–54 passim; the latter article is reprinted in the same author's *West-Country Historical Studies*, Newton Abbot 1969, 70–88. Cf. below, 165.

[2] Printed in T. Mommsen, *Monumenta Germaniae Historica, Auctorum Antiquissimorum, xiii, Chronica Minora*, Berlin 1898, iii. 107–10.

[3] Ibid., 3, 110. Cf. J. S. P. Tatlock, 'Caradoc of Llancarfan', *Speculum*, xiii (1938), 140.

[4] *Historia Regum Britanniae*, Bk. xii, cap. xx; ed. Acton Griscom, 124 and n. 2, 125, 536.

[5] Tatlock, op. cit., 141.

---

the abbey (see above, 344 and n. 3). I am indebted to Mr. Christopher Hohler and Mr. C. P. Wormald for help with the subject matter of this note.

died there and was buried in front of the altar in the wattle church.[1] To this outline Caradoc added graphic details of Gildas's flight from his hermitage near the Bristol channel and his stay at Glastonbury, ending with his urgent request on his deathbed to be buried in the abbey, and his honourable burial 'in medio pavimento ecclesiae sanctae Mariae'.[2]

The fire of 1184 was a stimulus to further invention; undoubtedly most of the interpolations in the *De Antiquitate* were made soon afterwards. One of them, the so-called charter of St. Patrick, clearly shows concern for the pilgrim trade. This document is dated A.D. 430 but is in fact a forgery probably made in the post-fire period. It reinforces Patrick's connexion with Glastonbury by giving full details of his arrival and career as the first abbot. It describes how he climbed the Tor, fighting his way through the undergrowth, and discovered St. Michael's oratory built by the two first missionaries. And here the Charter makes specific concessions to pilgrims—all who visit the oratory will have thirty days indulgence, and those clearing the approaches 'with axes and hatchets, to make access easier for pious Christians' are to have a hundred days indulgence.[3]

The monks not only tried to strengthen their claim to St. Patrick's relics, they also staked a claim to St. Dunstan's. Already in William of Malmesbury's time a rumour was current that St. Dunstan was buried at Glastonbury, and not in Canterbury cathedral. His body, it was asserted, had been stolen and brought to Glastonbury a hundred years earlier. Eadmer wrote a long, angry letter (the only known evidence for the rumour) abusing the monks for their mendacity: had he not as a boy seen the elevation of St. Dunstan's body in the cathedral before a great multitude? Did they not remember the annual pilgrimage from Canterbury to Glastonbury in honour of the saint?[4] The story with full elaboration and with its *denouement* after the 1184 fire is narrated in one of the interpolations to the *De Antiquitate*.[5] It tells of the removal of Dunstan's body to Glastonbury in the early eleventh century and its 'rediscovery' in the abbey church after the fire. This far-fetched tale culminates in an account of the actual 'rediscovery'; which may well describe an event actually staged by the monks. The whole is worth closer examination because it foreshadows the 'discovery' of the bodies of king Arthur and queen Guinevere a few years later.

The story has numerous circumstantial details to make it sound convincing. It alleges that shortly after Canterbury was burnt to the ground

---

[1] *Adam de Domerham*, i. 18. For a tenth-century tradition connecting Gildas with Glastonbury see above, 161, n. 3.

[2] For references to king Arthur in Caradoc's *Life* see below, 353.

[3] *Adam de Domerham*, i. 19–22. The charter is printed in translation and discussed in Armitage Robinson, *Somerset Historical Essays*, 12–16. Cf. Finberg, 'St. Patrick at Glastonbury', 345–6.

[4] Eadmer's letter, which provides the evidence for Glastonbury's claim, is printed in *Memorials of St. Dunstan*, 412–22. Cf. ibid., cxv–cxvi, and Southern, *St. Anselm and his Biographer*, 282, 285.

[5] *Adam de Domerham*, i. 35–8; cf. ibid., ii. 335–6.

by the Danes in 1012, king Edmund happened to visit Glastonbury. He told the abbot about events at Canterbury. The abbot was grief-stricken, and, telling the king of St. Dunstan's virtues, asked for help in bringing his relics to Glastonbury where he had 'first imbibed the milk of religion'. The king agreed to a plan and four monks were sent to Canterbury. Their names are given and the author alleges that they had been chaplains to St. Dunstan at Canterbury and had attended his funeral. (This should reassure readers that they knew the exact location of his tomb.) Subsequently they had served his successor St. Elphege until his martyrdom. When they arrived at Canterbury they found Dunstan's tomb, his bones and ring lying on gold and topaz exactly as they remembered. On their return to Glastonbury with the relics there was much discussion about how to hide them safely in case, when peace returned, the archbishop wanted them back. Eventually it was decided that their burial place should be known only to two wise old monks, who each on his deathbed should each pass on the information to another wise old monk. The box in which the relics were placed is then carefully described. (To leave the reader in no doubt that it was the same which was later 'rediscovered'.)

The story proceeds to tell how the secret of Dunstan's burial place was at last revealed after the 1184 fire. Previously a gifted young monk called John de Watelege acquired influence over his master, John Canan, at that time the possessor of the secret. Eventually after much asking, Canan gave Watelege a cryptic indication of the relics' whereabouts. But his words, though they were common knowledge after his death, baffled the monks. It was only after the fire that light dawned on two particularly assiduous brethren, Richard of Taunton and Ralph Toc. They went to the place, removed a stone and there found the box. They called the prior and convent. (The reader needed to know that there were witnesses to what followed.) The box was unmistakably the same as that previously buried. Nor could there be any doubt whose relics it contained because one end was inscribed 'S' and the other 'D'. The box was opened and inside lay Dunstan's bones and ring. The relics were carefully removed and placed with due reverence in a reliquary already containing an arm and leg of St. Oswald.

It is hardly necessary to point out that this story is full of inconsistencies. Why did the abbot hear of the sack of Canterbury from king Edmund when apparently the four monks of Glastonbury who had been serving archbishop Elphege returned at that time? Why did only one monk, John Canan, know of the hiding place, when according to the original arrangement two wise old monks should have known it? Why was it only after the 1184 fire that his cryptic words were understood? Clearly the story was concocted to add the relics of an important saint to Glastonbury's store, and incidentally to deprive Canterbury of them.

At the same time the monks were at pains to stress that the fire had not destroyed the abbey's other relics. Adam of Domerham's chronicle specifically mentions the salvaging of the relics of St. Patrick, St. Indract and St. Gildas.[1] Glastonbury was, indeed, rich with relics; it would, an interpolator of the *De Antiquitate* writes, take an immense volume to enumerate them all. He continues: 'In addition to the relics of the blessed Patrick and of those saints we have mentioned, the church of Glastonbury houses many more. No place you can walk lacks relics of the blessed—the paving stones, the areas beside and above the high altar, the very altar itself, are full of relics. No wonder the resting place of so many saints is called a celestial sanctuary on earth! How happy are those, dear Lord, whose lives are changed for the better by this holy place! None can fail of salvation who has the favour and intercession of such saints! I do no injustice to religion if I believe that wherever a stone triangle or square is deliberately placed in the paving, carefully set and bonded with lead, there lies some hidden, holy relic. The place's antiquity and the abundance of saints command reverence; by night no one presumes to loiter in the church, and during the day no one would dare spit—one shudders all over at such a disgusting thought!'[2]

Nevertheless, despite the labours of William of Malmesbury and his successors, the abbey still towards the end of the twelfth century lacked one famous saint exclusively its own. Its claim to St. Dunstan was more than dubious. Nor was its claim to St. Patrick generally accepted. One reason why John of Glastonbury wrote his chronicle was to disprove a statement of Ranulf Higden in his very popular work written early in the fourteenth century, the *Polychronicon*.[3] Higden asserted that the St. Patrick buried at Glastonbury could not be the apostle of the Irish because he was buried, as was well known, in Ireland. It was in fact St. Patrick the abbot who lived in about 850. John angrily denied this, using various specious arguments.[4]

What the Glastonbury monks needed above all after the 1184 fire was an outstanding patron saint. At this point, their study of hagiography having failed, they turned to another  great literary tradition, that of romance. Surely this would yield more spectacular results. And indeed it did, for in 1191 they exhumed the bodies of king Arthur and queen Guinevere.

The story of the exhumation is so well known that it is not necessary to dwell on it. Briefly, in 1191 the abbot Henry de Soilli ordered the monks

---

[1] Ibid. ii. 335. St. Indract was according to tradition the son of an Irish king who followed St. Patrick to Glastonbury and was murdered in the vicinity with his companions by robbers. William of Malmesbury wrote his Life, now lost (see above, 159 and n. 2), and asserts that king Ine translated his relics to Glastonbury and placed them in a pyramid on the left of the high altar (*Adam de Domerham*, i. 35–6), which may be true; see G. H. Doble, 'Saint Indract and St. Dominic', Somerset Record Society, lvii (1942) *Collectanea*, iii, 3, 21. There is evidence suggesting that he was venerated at Glastonbury at least by the early eleventh century; ibid., 1.

[2] Ibid., i. 27.

[3] *Polychronicon Ranulphi Higden Monachi Cestrensis*, ed. Churchill Babington and J. R. Lumby (Rolls Series, 1865–86), v. 304, 306.

[4] *Johannes Glastoniensis*, i. 7–8.

to dig between the two pyramids in the cemetary. They, surrounded by a crowd but screened from direct view by curtains, dug down over sixteen feet. Eventually they found an oak coffin containing the gigantic bones of a man, with a huge skull bearing the marks of ten wounds, and the skeleton of a woman with a lock of beautiful golden hair: one monk, jumped impetuously into the hole to seize the hair which turned to dust at his touch. In the grave was a lead cross, inverted under a stone, and on it was a Latin inscription: 'Here lies buried the renowned king Arthur on the Isle of Avalon'. The monks then reburied the bones in a mausoleum in their church.[1] (The presence of witnesses and the inscription identifying the bones recalled the 'rediscovery' of St. Dunstan's bones.)

The narrative of the exhumation has to be reconstructed from a number of sources, all of which have some information not in the others. Only one, the latest in date, is by a monk of Glastonbury, Adam of Domerham.The earliest known accounts are by Gerald of Wales. He wrote two: one is in his *De Principis Instructione* which he began before 1192;[2] the other is in his *Speculum Ecclesiae*, written in about 1217.[3]

Adam of Domerham's chronicle also has two accounts, both shorter than Gerald's and one a marginal addition.[4] The latter is derived almost word for word from the *Speculum Ecclesiae* or from a common source.[5] The other, although expressed in different words,[6] is substantially the same as Gerald's account with the exception of one or two additional statements (notably the mention of the curtains). It seems most likely that

---

[1] What is meant by the monks' church baffled Dr. Nitze, who argues that the Lady Chapel is intended. This, however, leads to problems with the texts which are unnecessary if it is assumed that the new tomb was put in the abbey church even though rebuilding was in progress. See W. A. Nitze, 'The Exhumation of King Arthur at Glastonbury', *Speculum*, ix (1934), 360–1.

[2] *Giraldi Cambrensis Opera*, ed. J. S. Brewer and others (Rolls Series, 1861–91, 8 vols.), viii. 126–9. For the date of *De Principis Instructione* see ibid., xiv–xviii.

[3] Ibid., iv. 47–51. For the late date of the *Speculum Ecclesiae* see *The Autobiography of Giraldus Cambrensis*, ed. and translated H. E. Butler, with an introductory chapter by C. H. Williams, London 1937, 351.

[4] Both accounts are on fol. 26ᵛ in Trinity College, Cambridge, MS.R.5.33: printed partly in two columns in *Adam de Domerham*, ii. 341–3 (the added account is in the right hand column on page 341 and in the left on page 342, and continues on page 343 which has no columns).

[5] For an addition to the account in the *Speculum* see below, 170 n. 4.

[6] One short passage (*Adam de Domerham*, ii. 342) resembles the *Speculum Ecclesiae*. It reads 'Dehinc tumbam reginae, Arturo consepultae, aperientes, tricam muliebrem flavam et formosam, miroque artificio consertam, inveniunt'. The *Speculum* (*Giraldus Cambrensis*, iv. 47) reads 'inventa fuit in eodem sepulchro trica muliebris, flava et formosa, miroque artificio conserta et contricata, uxoris scilicet Arthuri, viro ibidem consepultae'. However, this does not prove that the author of the account in Adam was here copying the actual words of the *Speculum* because the passage is apparently the work of a reviser, being mainly on an erasure and with one word in the margin. Another passage in Adam (*Adam de Domerham*, ii. 342) resembles one in Gerald's *De Principis Instructione*. It reads 'os unius tibiae a terra usque ad medium cruris et amplius in magno viro attingeret'. The passage in *De Princ. Instr.* (*Giraldus Cambrensis*, viii. 129) reads 'Os enim tibiae ipsius appositum [tibiae] longissimi/viri loci, quem nobis abbas ostendit et juxta pedem illius terrae affixum, large tribus digitis trans genu ipsius se porrexit'.

Gerald's and Adam's narratives descend from some exemplar which contained all the details now divided between the two authors.[1]

None of the above accounts give the date of the exhumation. This appears in two Cistercian chronicles, that of Ralph de Coggeshall (written c. 1223)[2] and that of Margam abbey in Glamorgan (of c. 1234).[3] Comparison of the entries makes it clear that Coggeshall's is a shortened version of that in the Margam chronicle.[4] Since direct borrowing is most unlikely, it must be supposed that there was a common exemplar. This narrative, despite one important variant,[5] in general follows Gerald of Wales.[6]

The postulated exemplar from which the extant accounts by Gerald of Wales and Adam of Domerham descend was almost certainly by Gerald himself. This is suggested by the fact that he seems to have attended the exhumation and written from his own observation.[7] The graphic details must surely have been written by an eyewitness: there are the mention of

---

[1] The evidence does not warrant the firm opinion expressed by Dr. Nitze (op. cit., 360) that Adam's account is independent of Gerald's. Professor Treharne and Professor Alcock also treat Gerald and Adam as independent sources: Treharne, *The Glastonbury Legends*, 102–3, and Leslie Alcock, *Arthur's Britain*, London 1971, 74, respectively.

[2] *Radulphi de Coggeshall Chronicon Anglicanum*, ed. Joseph Stevenson (Rolls Series, 1875). 36.

[3] The chronicle of Margam in *Annales Monastici*, ed. H. R. Luard (Rolls Series, 1864–9), i. 21–2.

[4] Nitze's contention (op. cit., 359) that the entry in the Margam chronicle is dependent on Coggeshall cannot be sustained. Coggeshall follows almost *verbatim* the Margam text for three quarters of the account and then ends abruptly.

[5] In addition to the important variant discussed below (172) the version of the inscription on the lead cross differs in both Margam and Coggeshall from that given by Gerald of Wales, and agrees with that given by Adam of Domerham: Gerald alone adds 'cum Wenneuereia vxore sua secunda'. As this reference to Guinevere does not appear in the copy of the inscription given by Camden (see below, 352 n. 7), it seems likely that it was Gerald's invention. Professor Alcock argues that Coggeshall's account differs from Gerald's in another particular, i.e. in the description of the coffin: Coggeshall states that the bones lay 'in quodam vetustissimo sarcophago', while Gerald places them 'in terra quercu concava': *Coggeshall*, 36; *Giraldus Cambrensis*, viii. 127; Alcock, *Arthur's Britain*, 74. However, there is no conflict here because in the medieval period the word *sarcophagus* does not necessarily mean, as it did in Roman times, a stone coffin; it merely signifies a coffin: see R. E. Latham, *Revised Medieval Latin Word-List*, London 1965, 419, under *sarcographia*. Indeed, Adam of Domerham describes the coffin in question as *sarcophagum ligneum mirae magnitudinis*: *Adam de Domerham*, ii. 341.

[6] Although there is general similarity in content, verbal echoes are hard to find because the Margam account is so much shorter than Gerald's narratives. Professor Treharne and Professor Alcock both treat Coggeshall as an independent authority for the exhumation: Treharne, op. cit., 93, and Alcock, op. cit., 74. As they overlook the Margam chronicle they fail to recognise that it and Coggeshall's account derive from an exemplar which may well have been of Glastonbury provenance (see below, 172 and n. 2).

[7] Treharne (*Glastonbury Legends*, 97) expresses the opinion that Gerald wrote his account after visiting Glastonbury in 1192 or 1193. The evidence for this date is the fact that Gerald saw the new tomb already prepared, but while Henry de Soilli was still abbot (he was consecrated bishop of Worcester in December 1193). However, it seems almost certain that he was an eyewitness; he could have seen the tomb on a later occasion, or heard about it.

the curtains[1] and the description of the monk jumping into the hole to seize the lock of hair.[2] Gerald's extant accounts refer to the author's presence. Abbot Henry 'showed us' the tibia of one of Arthur's legs, demonstrating its size by holding it against the leg of the tallest man present—it reached three inches above the knee.[3] Similarly, having described the exact position of the lead cross, Gerald writes that 'it was removed from under the stone and handed round by abbot Henry so that we could examine it and read the inscription'.[4]

There can be no reasonable doubt that the exhumation of king Arthur and queen Guinevere was bogus, a spectacle put on for the credulous public.[5] The very existence of king Arthur is not established beyond dispute[6] and certainly Guinevere was a figment of the imagination. The conclusion cannot be avoided that the Glastonbury monks deliberately buried two skeletons, complete with inscribed cross, and then staged the 'discovery'. The circumstances are hard to explain in any other way. The 'discovery' was so very opportune in view of the abbey's financial plight (the inscribed cross itself presents serious problems).[7] And why the curtains if not to conceal the details of what was going on?

The reasons why the monks decided to adopt king Arthur as their patron, which made it necessary to find his body so that his tomb could become the centre of a cult, are not immediately obvious. Probably a number of factors attracted the monks to the idea. The fame of king Arthur was widespread, particularly among the nearby Welsh. The oral

---

[1] *Adam de Domerham*, ii, 341.

[2] *Giraldus Cambrensis*, iv. 47–8; viii. 127.

[3] Ibid., viii. 129; cf. above, 166 n. 6.

[4] Ibid., iv. 50.

[5] Professor Alcock argues in favour of the authenticity of the exhumation. He asserts that though the forgery of documents was well known in the Middle Ages, 'the Glastonbury exhumation, if it was a fake, was of a quite different character from the general run of monkish forgeries' (op. cit., 76). His argument neglects the probability that the monks themselves had recently faked the 'discovery' of St. Dunstan's relics. Professor Alcock also states that he would find it easier to accept that the exhumation was bogus if 'we believed that Glastonbury already had a traditional Arthurian connection' (op. cit., 80; cf. 75–6). Here he overlooks the fact that Glastonbury had already been associated with king Arthur in Caradoc of Llancarfan's *Life of St. Gildas* (a work not referred to by Professor Alcock); see below, 169.

[6] For a summary of the evidence on king Arthur's historicity see J. S. P. Tatlock, *The Legendary History of Britain* (University of California Press 1950), 178–229. See also Thomas Jones, 'The Early Evolution of the Legend of Arthur', *Nottingham Mediaeval Studies*, viii (1964), 3–21, (this article was first published in Welsh in *Bulletin of the Board of Celtic Studies*, xvii (1958), 237–52, and was translated by Gerald Morgan), and K. H. Jackson, 'The Arthur of History', *Arthurian Literature in the Middle Ages*, ed. R. S. Loomis, Oxford 1959, 1–11. Professor Alcock argues in favour of the authenticity of the Arthurian entries in the *Annales Cambriae*; the extant text is mid-tenth century although it used earlier material; Alcock, op. cit., 45–55.

[7] William Camden gave the inscription but did not reproduce the cross itself in his *Britannia*, London 1586, 104. In the sixth edition (London 1607), 166, he gives a picture of the cross with the inscription on it. All discussion of the cross and inscription depends on accepting that Camden's picture of the cross and his epigraphy of the inscription is correct (it could of course be the result of his antiquarianism). Professor Alcock's opinions (op.

legends had received definition and elaboration in Geoffrey of Monmouth's *Historia*, a best seller,[1] which had popularised Arthur's reputation as never before. In one respect Arthur was a very suitable patron for Glastonbury. Geoffrey, following Nennius,[2] said that Arthur fought with the image of the Virgin Mary on his shield 'which forced him to think perpetually of her':[3] the abbey church, then in process of rebuilding, was dedicated to St. Mary.

However, Geoffrey of Monmouth did not associate king Arthur with Glastonbury. This connexion was apparently first made in writing by Caradoc of Llancarfan in his *Life of St. Gildas*. Caradoc wrote under the influence of romance literature as well as hagiography, and brought king Arthur to Glastonbury at the time when Gildas was living there. Arthur 'the tyrant' came with an army to snatch Guinevere back from her abductor, the wicked king Melvas. A reconciliation between the kings was achieved by the abbot and Gildas, and in return both kings granted lands to the abbey, promising reverence and obedience, and never to injure it.[4]

Caradoc says nothing of Arthur's burial at Glastonbury. For this the monks had to rely on the passage in Geoffrey's *Historia* which stated that Arthur when mortally wounded at the battle of Camlan    was carried to the Isle of Avalon.[5] All that was necessary was to identify Avalon with

---

[1] For the popularity of the *Historia* see Gransden, *Historical Writing in England c.* 550–c. *1307*, 201–2 and nn.

[2] See *Historia Brittonum*, cap. lvi; ed. T. Mommsen, *M.G.H., Auctorum Antiquissimorum*, xiii, *Chronica Minora, iii.* 199.

[3] *Historia Regum Britanniae*, Bk. IX, cap. iv; ed. Acton Griscom, 438.

[4] Mommsen, op. cit., 109–10.

[5] *Historia Regum Britanniae*, Bk. XI, cap. ii; ed. Acton Griscom, 501.

---

cit., 78–80), which coincide with those of C. A. Ralegh Radford (see *The Quest for Arthur's Britain*, ed. Geoffrey Ashe, London 1968, 126–38 passim), deserve attention. Accepting Camden's reproduction as accurate, he dates the epigraphy to the tenth or eleventh century. He suggests that the monks of St. Dunstan's time copied a sixth century inscription, perhaps reading 'Hic sepultus iacit Arturius,' which marked the burial place of king Arthur which was, it is postulated, next to a mausoleum in the old cemetery. They copied it to mark Arthur's grave when the mausoleum was demolished, prefixing 'Rex inclitus' and appending 'in insula Avalonia'. It should be noted that Professor K. H. Jackson dates the epigraphy of the inscription to the sixth century (see his review of Professor Alcock's book in *Antiquity*, xlvii (1973), 81); this suggests the possibility that the cross was the actual one used to mark Arthur's original burial. However, it seems much more likely that the monks faked the cross in 1191 and deliberately used archaic letter forms. It is most improbable that the monks of St. Dunstan's day (and even less of the sixth century) would have added 'in Avalonia', because the identification of Glastonbury with Avalon was first made, at least in writing, by Gerald of Wales (below, 170 & n. 1) . And they might well have imitated the lettering of an old inscription, perhaps one in the cemetery; the ancient letters on the two pyramids had certainly attracted attention (see above, 345, and *Giraldus Cambrensis*, viii. 127). In this context an example of visual antiquarianism at Wells may be noted. Early in the thirteenth century the canons commissioned a series of effigies of the pre-Conquest bishops of Wells, to increase their prestige in their struggle with the monks of Bath over the right to elect the bishops. Two of these wear the low, rounded mitres and simple dress of the Anglo-Saxon period ('clear signs of genuine antiquarianism'): Lawrence Stone, *Sculpture in Britain in the Middle Ages,* Penguin Books 1955, 106–7. I am indebted in writing this foot-note to a discussion with Mr. P. W. Dixon.

Glastonbury. This identification first appears in Gerald of Wales.[1] It may well have been thought that people could easily be persuaded to accept it because Glastonbury was surrounded by lakes and marshes, and the Tor has a mysterious appearance. There is, however, no proof that the actual suggestion originally came from the monks. Possibly it came from the royal court, from Henry II himself. Gerald of Wales asserts rather vaguely that the king 'told the monks everything', having 'heard about it from an ancient Welsh bard knowledgeable on history', that is, exactly where and how deep to dig and what they would find.[2] He also advised them to lay the bones in a marble tomb.[3] The addition to Adam of Domerham asserts that abbot Henry de Soilli, who was elected in September 1189, was a relative and former friend of king Henry.[4]

Gerald may well have been right in attributing the suggestion to Henry II. Romance literature and the cult of king Arthur flourished at court. King Henry had been brought up partly by his uncle, Robert of Gloucester, to whom Geoffrey of Monmouth dedicated the first issue of his *Historia*,[5] and Henry himself commissioned a romance history, the *Roman de Rou*.[6] In addition Henry was very concerned over the abbey's financial troubles. The abbacy was vacant from 1180, when abbot Robert died, until Henry de Soilli's succession, and after the fire Henry II allowed what revenues remained after the monks had been provided with their necessities, to contribute to the rebuilding rather than go to the royal exchequer.[7] He may have realised that a flourishing Arthurian cult would help matters. It would also be useful to him politically because it would publicise that king Arthur was actually dead: in current folklore it was believed that he merely slept on the Isle of Avalon and would one day awaken and again lead the Britons to victory. Such a view was damaging to a king trying to subdue the Welsh.[8]

---

[1] *Giraldus Cambrensis*, iv. 49; viii. 128.

[2] 'Rex Angliae Henricus secundus, sicut ab historico cantore Britone audierat antiquo, totum monachis indicavit, quod profunde, scilicet in terra per xvi. pedes ad minus, corpus invenirent, et non in lapideo tumulo sed in quercu cavato': ibid., viii. 128. 'Dixerat enim ei [i.e. to Abbot Henry] pluries, sicut ex gestis Britonum et eorum cantoribus historiis rex audierat, quod inter pyramides duas, quae postmodum erectae fuerant in sacro coemeterio, sepultus fuit Arthurus ...': ibid., iv. 49.

[3] 'Dictus autem abbas corpore reperto, monitis quoque dicti regis Henrici, marmoreum ei sepulchrum fieri fecit egregium ...': ibid., iv. 51.

[4] 'Conditus fuit Rex Arthurus (sicut per regem Henricum abbas Henricus didicerat, cujus consanguineus et dudum familiaris extiterat: qui eciam Rex hoc ex gestis Britonum, et eorum cantoribus historicis, frequenter audierat ...': *Adam de Domerham*, ii. 341.

[5] See J. S. P. Tatlock, 'Geoffrey and King Arthur in *Normannicus Draco*', *Modern Philology*, xxxi (1933), 124–5.

[6] *Maistre Wace's Roman de Rou et des Ducs de Normandie*, ed. H. Andresen, Heilbronn 1877, 1879, and *Chronique des Ducs de Normandie par Benoit*, ed. Carlin Fahlin, Lund 1951–67. See Tatlock, *Legendary History of Britain*, 465, 467, and M. D. Legge, 'The influence of Patronage on Form in Medieval French Literature', *Stil- und Formprobleme in der Literatur*, ed. Paul Böckmann, Heidelberg 1959; Vorträge des VII Kongresses der Internationalen Vereinigung für moderne Sprachen und Literaturen in Heidelberg, 139.

[7] *Adam de Domerham*, ii. 334–5.

[8] Tatlock, 'Geoffrey and King Arthur in *Normannicus Draco*', 122–3.

Court interest in the Arthurian cult at Glastonbury did not end with Henry II. In 1278 Edward I, his queen Eleanor, and their retinues, visited Glastonbury. The tomb of king Arthur and queen Guinevere was solemnly opened in their presence. Adam of Domerham describes the occasion in detail.[1] The next day the king placed Arthur's bones in one casket and the queen placed Guinevere's in another; each sealed the respective casket with the royal seal, and the caskets were put back in the tomb, which had been moved, at Edward's command, to a place in front of the high altar. Edward's motives for the disinterment were similar to those of Henry II: he was a devotee of the cult of king Arthur;[2] he wanted to help the monks raise money (in this instance partly to finance abbot John of Taunton's building activities);[3] and, because of his attempts to impose English rule on the Welsh following the treaty of Conway (November 1277), he needed it to be known that king Arthur was dead.[4]

An objection to attributing the monks' decision to 'discover' king Arthur to the influence of Henry II is the time factor: Henry died in July 1189 and the monks did not dig until 1191. But this does not present an insuperable difficulty. Henry's advice would not necessarily have been taken at once, and after his death the need for money became even more acute: in the words of Adam of Domerham, king Richard 'turned his mind to matters of war and took no interest in our new church, and so work on the building came to a standstill because there was no one to pay the labourers'.[5]

Once the monks had made the decision, maximum publicity was desirable. It seems likely, therefore, that lacking a writer of their own, they invited Gerald of Wales to attend the exhumation and commissioned him to write it up afterwards (in the same way as the canons of Hexham and the abbot of Westminster had commissioned Ailred of Rievaulx).[6] They would have considered Gerald a suitable person: it is even possible that Henry II himself suggested him, because in about 1184 Gerald had entered royal service.[7] Gerald was accustomed to recording his experiences and observations: he wrote on the Irish campaign of 1187 on which he accompanied John at king Henry's command;[8] and he wrote on

---

[1] *Adam de Domerham*, ii. 588–9.

[2] For Edward I's interest in king Arthur (with a reference to his visit to Glastonbury) see R. S. Loomis, 'Edward I, Arthurian Enthusiast', *Speculum*, xxviii (1953), 114–27.

[3] See *VCH, Somerset*, ii, 91. For a list of buildings put up by John of Taunton see *Adam de Domerham*, ii. 573.

[4] See F. M. Powicke, *King Henry III and the Lord Edward*, Oxford 1947, ii. 724.

[5] *Adam de Domerham*, ii. 341. Treharne (*Glastonbury Legends*, 106) does not accept that Henry II could have originated the idea of the search for king Arthur's bones.

[6] Above, 156.

[7] *The Autobiography of Giraldus Cambrensis*, ed. Butler, 81 and n. 1.

[8] Ibid., 86 ff. After the campaign Gerald wrote the *Expugnatio Hibernica* and the *Topographia Hibernica* (printed in *Giraldus Cambrensis*, v); he dedicated the *Topographia* to Henry II (ibid., 20) and the *Expugnatio*, first to king Richard and then to king John (ibid., 222, 405).

archbishop Baldwin's tour of Wales in 1188, when he helped to preach the crusade.[1]

The attempts of the monks of Glastonbury to publicise king Arthur's exhumation probably extended further than the commissioning of Gerald. It is likely that they distributed propaganda pamphlets to other religious houses,[2] which probably had at least one important variant from the original narrative. As has been mentioned[3] both Coggeshall and the Margam chronicler, who surely derived their accounts from some such broadsheet, differ in one particular from Gerald and Adam. Instead of attributing the discovery to deliberate excavation undertaken on Henry II's advice, they ascribe it to chance: a monk had expressed a strong desire to be buried between the pyramids and the gravediggers unexpectedly came upon the bones of Arthur and Guinevere.[4] Presumably the monks of Glastonbury suppressed the part played by Henry II because they considered that the story sounded less contrived without it. They may also have feared that mention of king Henry's involvement would alienate readers because he was not popular with the Church.

Although Gerald of Wales gave a full record of king Arthur's exhumation, his work as a piece of propaganda had one weak link: unless the public were sure that Glastonbury had once been Avalon, it was impossible to be certain that the bones discovered were really those of Arthur and Guinevere, or that the inscription on the lead cross was not a fake. Gerald had simply stated that Glastonbury was the former Avalon, giving independent etymologies of both names.[5] Glastonbury meant the glassy borough in the English language, and Avalon was the island of apples in Celtic. But there was nothing to connect the one with the other. In order to secure the identification the monks adopted and elaborated a pre-Conquest eponymous foundation story. Their version of the eponym is one of the interpolations in the *De Antiquitate*.[6] It alleges that Glastonbury took its name from a swineherd called Glasteing. He lost his sow, a remarkable creature with eight legs, and pursued her for a long distance. Eventually, taking the track known as 'Sugewege' (in Celtic 'the marshy way') from Wells, he reached Glastonbury. There he found his sow suckling her piglets under an apple tree. Delighted with the fertility of the place, he made it his home with his family.

Thus Glastonbury took its name from Glasteing. By adopting this

---

[1] Ibid., 99 ff. After the tour Gerald wrote the *Itinerarium Kambriae* and the *Descriptio Kambriae* (printed in ibid., vi.).

[2] A copy may have reached Christ Church, Canterbury, in the early thirteenth century: this is suggested by the fact that Gervase of Canterbury knew of the identification of Avalon, as Arthur's burial place, with Glastonbury. See *The Historical Works of Gervase of Canterbury*, ed. William Stubbs (Rolls Series, 1879, 1880), ii. 19.

[3] Above, 167. The Margam chronicle also alleges that Mordred was buried with Arthur and Guinevere.

[4] *Radulfus de Coggeshall*, 36; *Annales Monastici*, i. 21.

[5] *Giraldus Cambrensis*, iv. 49; viii. 128.

[6] *Adam de Domerham*, i. 16–17.

etymology the monks were abandoning Gerald of Wales's. But they kept his explanation of Avalon, as the island of apples, adding, however, that it was probably so called because Glasteing found his sow under one of the apple trees. And so the story proved that Glastonbury and Avalon were one and the same place.[1] The Celtic affiliations of the eponym are well known.[2] There was an early tale that St. Patrick had resurrected and baptised a swineherd called Cass mac Glaiss. In the course of the ninth century the name became Glass mac Caiss and the story was localised at Glastonbury. Here were the seeds of the later eponym—but nothing to identify Glastonbury with Avalon.

Concentration on the Celtic aspects of the story has tended to overshadow the influence of romance literature on its final form. Eponyms were a feature of romance and had their roots in classical antiquity. Virgil had, for instance, asserted that Rome took its name from Romulus. Moreover, an animal often played an essential part in ancient foundation myths. There was the wolf in the Romulus and Remus story, and even more relevant to our purpose the sow in the story of the foundations of Rome's ancestor cities, Lavinium and Alba Longa. Virgil mentions the white sow and her thirty piglets in this context,[3] while the Greek historian Dionysius relates that the sow was pursued by the Trojans over a distance of twenty-four stades and was found giving birth to her litter on the site of the future city.[4]

However, the direct influence on the Glastonbury monks was Geoffrey of Monmouth. The writer's account of the source of his story is itself reminiscent of Geoffrey: he states that it was taken 'from ancient books of the Welsh';[5] Geoffrey had claimed that the source of the *Historia* was 'an ancient book in the Welsh tongue'.[6] Moreover, the form of the story may well have been borrowed from Geoffrey. He was particularly fond of eponyms, alleging, for example, that Britain took its name from the first settler Brutus, London from king Lud, and Colchester from king Cole. It should be noted that the Glastonbury eponym incorporates a mini-eponym, as it were: the sow is the eponymous heroine of 'Sugewege' which the monks by a false etymology now called Sows' Way.[7] (To this day a farm off the Wells Road is called Southway.)

The monks of Glastonbury had, therefore, by the end of the twelfth

[1] Previous scholars do not seem to have appreciated the use of the Glasteing eponym in linking Glastonbury with Avalon.
[2] See Slover, 'William of Malmesbury and the Irish', 276–80 and nn. for further references, and Finberg, 'St. Patrick at Glastonbury', 354–5 and n. 36.
[3] *Aeneid*, Bk. III, lines 389–93; Bk. VIII lines 42–5.
[4] See Virgil, *Aeneid Book VIII*, ed. K. W. Gransden, Cambridge 1976, 188.
[5] 'Haec de antiquis Britonum libris sunt': ibid., 17.
[6] Geoffrey states that his source was a book lent him by Walter, archdeacon of Oxford— 'quendam britannici sermonis librum vetustissimum': *Historia Regum Britanniae*, Bk. I, cap. i; ed. Acton Griscom, 219.
[7] The false etymology resulted from the confusion of *sugga*, a marsh, with *sugu*, a sow; see Finberg, op. cit., 354.

century at last acquired in king Arthur a much needed patron, exclusively theirs. But a famous patron constituted only half, so to speak, of an abbey's prestige; the other half was its antiquity.[1] The story of Glasteing only gave an explanation of Glastonbury's origin as an inhabited place, not as a Christian centre. And for propaganda purposes the monks needed to trace their community's Christian origins. To do this they resorted after the 1184 fire to both the hagiographical and to the romance literary traditions. The results of their researches are to be found in the so-called Charter of St. Patrick. By reference to Geoffrey of Monmouth they were able to enlarge on William of Malmesbury's statement that, as far as could be known with any certainty, the founders of the abbey were two missionaries sent by pope Eleutherus in A.D. 166.[2] Geoffrey supplied the missionaries' names (although he made no mention of them coming to Glastonbury); they were called Fagan    and Deruvian.[3]

William of Malmesbury had hinted at even earlier origins, tentatively suggesting that the church ('built by no human skill') which the two missionaries found was the work of disciples of St. Philip.[4] Now the monks were more specific: the charter of St. Patrick states categorically that both St. Philip and St. James had sent twelve disciples who, as instructed by the archangel Gabriel, had built the church at Glastonbury.[5] The date of the conversion of Britain was, therefore, almost contemporary with that of France and Spain, an idea sure to appeal to the incipient patriotism of the late twelfth century. The Glastonbury monks had only to find a leader for the twelve founding disciples and supply an exact date. This they did in the mid-thirteenth century. They set St. Joseph of Arimathea, whose cult was growing in popularity, at the head of the band, and dated the arrival at Glastonbury to A.D. 63.[6]

Thus Glastonbury abbey acquired the earliest foundation date of any in England, and a patron whose fame survives even to this day. The monks dove-tailed the legend of St. Joseph into that of king Arthur by asserting that St. Joseph was an ancestor of king Arthur—Adam of Domerham gives the genealogy in true romance style.[7] Henceforth the legends of both developed side by side; but their later evolution, which can be read in the pages of John of Glastonbury, belongs to literature rather than historiography.

[1] See above, 153.
[2] Above, 160.
[3] *Historia Regum Britanniae*, Bk. IV, cap. xix, ed. Acton Griscom, 328-9; *Adam de Domerham*, i. 19-21.
[4] Above, 160.
[5] *Adam de Domerham*, i. 20.
[6] See Armitage Robinson, *Two Glastonbury Legends*, 28.
[7] *Johannes Glastoniensis*, i. 56-7.

Note: For revisory notes to this chapter see below pp. 329-30.

# Realistic Observation in Twelfth-Century England

T. D. KENDRICK has already commented on "nascent medieval topography" (which he describes as "rather casual") in England, and cites examples of topographical descriptions from chronicles.[1] It is proposed here to examine in more detail the ability of medieval writers in twelfth-century England to see and describe the world around them. Besides topographical observation, I shall include observation of small objects (such as goldsmiths' work and books), of mankind itself (people's physical appearance, character and behaviour both individually and corporately as social beings), and of animals and birds.

Writers had various motives for descriptive writing. Admiration of the beautiful and wonder at the extraordinary were constant motives throughout history. Moreover, a writer often had a commemorative intention: he might, for example, want to preserve for posterity the appearance of a great man, or of a work of art in order to commemorate the artist.[2] But to some extent visual sense is an individual gift. Therefore some writers (such as William of Malmesbury), with a developed visual sense, will always turn more readily than others to descriptive writing.

Two intellectual trends could also encourage realistic description. The first was Christian piety. A writer's spiritual love, centred on God and his saints, stirred his interest in any person or object with a holy association. His earthly loyalty and affection were centred on his own home — usually a monastery. Therefore he was likely to observe carefully anything contributing to its reputation — for example, any building of outstanding beauty, or one which proved the place's great antiquity, or a relic of the patron saint, which demonstrated its holiness. Visual perception became particularly acute if the house's business interests were at stake. Monks began to study palaeography and diplomatic because they needed to defend their houses' property and privileges against enemies armed with forged charters.

The second intellectual trend encouraging descriptive writing was the study of the classics. The influence of classical antiquity took various forms. Admiration for classical civilization sometimes led to an interest in archaeological remains of Roman Britain. Moreover, study of some classical authors provided models for descriptive writing. Thus Suetonius' *Lives of the Caesars* had descriptions of the Caesars' physical appearance. (William of Malmesbury adopted the Suetonian mode for his descriptions of the Anglo-Norman kings). Probably more important for our purpose was the attitude of mind engendered by classical studies. The

---

[1] T. D. Kendrick, *British Antiquity* (London, 1950), p. 134. For a large collection of extracts from printed editions of early documents and literary sources relating to art and architecture, including some of the passages cited below, see O. Lehmann-Brockhaus, *Lateinische Schriftquellen zur Kunst in England, Wales und Schottland vom Jahre 901 bis zum Jahre 1307* (München, 1955–1960, 5 vols.; *Veröffentlichungen des Zentralinstituts für Kunstgeschichte in München*, no. 1 etc.).

[2] This motive is explicitly stated by Matthew Paris; see below p. 178 & n. 15.

idea of Rome as a city of art treasures and monumental buildings provoked the competitive spirit: England too had treasures and fine cities. Furthermore, such classical authors as Sallust fostered an interest in the trivialities of everyday life.

It must, of course, be remembered that the hagiographical tradition and classical studies could both discourage realistic descriptive writing. For example, the hagiographer and the author influenced by classical works usually aimed at giving the general rather than the particular truth about their hero, to show how such a saint or king would have behaved and what he would have looked like, not his actual behaviour and appearance. Similarly descriptions of inanimate objects and of the outside world were sometimes based on classical models. Therefore the reader must be on his guard against idealization and literary imitation.[3] However, the examples given below which are surely authentic, suggest that it is easy to overestimate the extent to which mediaeval writers were bound by these literary conventions.

The twelfth century was, until the literary developments of the fourteenth and fifteenth centuries, pre-eminent for descriptive writing. A number of writers described what they saw in detail and a few drew rational deductions from their observations. The use of observations as evidence amounted to rudimentary historical research. (Perhaps, therefore, Professor V. H. Galbraith's statement that "It would be a brave man who sought to widen the list of medieval achievements by the inclusion of historical research"[4] needs slight modification). Both the religious motive and the incentive provided by classical studies gained momentum in the twelfth century. Generally speaking, the former was strongest early in the twelfth century and the latter towards the end.

The Norman Conquest and settlement presented the Anglo-Saxon church with a challenge and put its saints on trial. (Archbishop Lanfranc questioned the right of some Anglo-Saxon saints to liturgical commemoration).[5] The reputation of the Anglo-Saxon church as a whole, and the prestige and prosperity of each monastery in particular, depended on having an unbroken and glorious history. Therefore hagiographers and historians turned with enthusiasm to the study of ecclesiastical history, determined to prove that the Anglo-Saxon church had a creditable past. The influence of classical authors is already apparent early in the century (notably in the works of William of Malmesbury), but it is particularly marked in the works of such late twelfth-century "humanists" as Gerald of Wales and Walter Map, and resulted occasionally in objective curiosity.

[3] For the influence of classical literature on mediaeval representations of heroes and rulers, and of landscape, see E. R. Curtius, *Europäische Literatur und lateinisches Mittelalter* (Bern, 1948), chapters ix, x.

[4] V. H. Galbraith, *Historical Research in Medieval England* (London, 1951), p. 7.

[5] For Lanfranc's attitude to Anglo-Saxon saints see *The Life of St. Anselm Archbishop of Canterbury by Eadmer*, ed., with an English translation, R. W. Southern (Nelson's Medieval Texts, 1962), pp. 50–54. For the changes made by Lanfranc in the liturgical calendar of Christ Church, Canterbury, see F. A. Gasquet and E. Bishop, *The Bosworth Psalter* (London, 1908), pp. 37–39. For the test of fire to which Walter, the Anglo-Norman abbot of Evesham (1077–1086) submitted the relics at Evesham see *Chronicon Abbatiae de Evesham*. ed. W. D. Macray (Rolls Series, 1863), p. 323.

Although the twelfth century was most remarkable for descriptive writing, the preceding period and the thirteenth century also produced examples. Gildas, Bede and Nennius were all capable of using archaeology as historical evidence.[6] But here they were exceptional. Realistic descriptions by other writers were the result of admiration, wonder and piety towards saints. The description of Romano-British buildings in the Old English poem the *Ruin* was obviously written because of admiration and wonder.[7] Eddius Stephanus must have intended to praise Wilfrid by describing his churches and the treasurers at Hexham and Ripon.[8] (Presumably the biographer of Edward the Confessor had the same motive for describing the abbey church at Westminster).[9] And the reference to ancient remains in Bede's *Life of St. Cuthbert*[10] and in Felix's *Life of St. Guthlac*[11] are incidental to the hagiographical theme. Such examples of realistic descriptions are "casual" and isolated; clearly as yet authors had no compelling motive to write them.

Again in the thirteenth century examples of realistic observations are sporadic,

[6] For Gildas on the Roman wall see *De Excidio Britanniae et Conquestu*, cc. 15–18, ed. T. Mommsen in *Monumenta Germaniae Historica, Auctorum Antiquissimorum*, xiii, *Chronica Minora Saeculi iv–vii*, iii (Berlin, 1898), 33–35; Gildas' interpretation of the evidence is discussed by C. E. Stevens, "Gildas Sapiens" in *EHR*, lvi (1941), 356–360. For Bede's derivation of the name Horsa apparently from a Roman tombstone see *HE*, i. 15; *Venerabilis Baedae Historia Ecclesiastica Gentis Anglorum*, ed. C. Plummer (Oxford, 1896, 2 vols.), i. 31 (*cf.* H. M. Chadwick, *The Origin of the English Nation* [Cambridge, 1924], pp. 42–43). For Nennius' interpretation of archaeological evidence at Cair Segeint (Segontium) see *Historia Brittonum*, c. 25, ed. Mommsen, *op. cit.* iii, 166. *Cf.* F. Lot, *Nennius et l'Historia Brittonum* (Paris, 1934), pp. 59–60. For hoards of coins found at Segontium see R. E. M. Wheeler, "Segontium and the Roman Occupation of Wales" in *Y Cymmrodor*, xxxiii (1923), 111 *sq.* Alcuin mentions the Roman walls at York; see *De Pontificibus et Sanctis Ecclesiae Eboracensis Carmen*, lines 19–37, printed in *Monumenta Alcuiniana praeparata a Philipp Jaffé*, ed. W. Wattenbach and E. Dümmler (Aalen, 1964), p. 82. For a description of Bugga's church by Aldhelm see *Carmen in Ecclesia Mariae a Bugge exstructa*, printed in *Aldhelmi Opera*, ed. R. Ehwald in *Mon. Germ. Hist. Auctorum Antiquissimorum*, xv (Berlin, 1919), 14–18. Brief descriptions of the topography of Lindisfarne and of the author's own monastery are in Æthelwulf's *De Abbatibus*, ed., with an English translation, A. Campbell (Oxford, 1967), pp. 10, 12.

[7] For internal evidence suggesting that *The Ruin* refers to Bath, see *Three Old English Elegies, The Wife's Lament, The Husband's Message, The Ruin*, ed. R. F. Leslie (Manchester, 1961), pp. 23–26. For the poet's talent for vivid description see *ibid.* pp. 28–29.

[8] For Eddius' description of York, Ripon and Hexham see *The Life of Bishop Wilfrid by Eddius Stephanus*, ed., with an English translation, Bertram Colgrave (Cambridge, 1927), pp. 35, 37, 47; *cf.* H. M. Taylor and J. Taylor, *Anglo-Saxon Architecture* (Cambridge, 1965, 2 vols.), i, 301; ii, 516–518, 700–709. For Eddius' description of the Gospels in gold letters on purple parchment which Wilfrid gave to Ripon see Colgrave, *op. cit.* p. 37; for such gospel-books, executed from the sixth to the twelfth centuries, see E. Maunde Thompson, *An Introduction to Greek and Latin Palaeography* (Oxford, 1912), pp. 32–33.

[9] *The Life of King Edward*, ed., with an English translation, Frank Barlow (Nelson's Medieval Texts, 1962), pp. 45–46.

[10] St Cuthbert was looking at the Roman walls of Carlisle, and a Roman well, when he had his vision of King Ecgfrith's defeat; *Two Lives of St. Cuthbert*, ed., with an English translation, Bertram Colgrave (Cambridge, 1940), p. 122.

[11] For a description of the prehistoric or Roman barrow inhabited by Guthlac see *Felix's Life of St. Guthlac*, ed., with an English translation, Bertram Colgrave (Cambridge, 1956), pp. 92–95, 182–184.

the result of individual interest rather than a general trend. Matthew Paris, himself an artist, had a developed visual sense. He wrote the well-known description of Henry III's elephant,[12] and also described the buffalo, specimens of which were owned by Richard of Cornwall.[13] Especially notable are his descriptions of works of art (for example of the wash-bowl presented by Queen Margaret of France to Henry III).[14] His aesthetic sense was augmented by a desire to commemorate the artists who had worked at St. Albans.[15] (The *Gesta Abbatum* is partly a history of the abbey's art and architecture). The monks of Bury St. Edmunds had a considerable antiquarian interest in their house[16] and also left a graphic description of the abbey's twelfth-century illuminated Bible (now Corpus Christi College, Cambridge, MS 2).[17] But only at the beginning of the century and at the very end (perhaps in the early fourteenth century) do we find lifelike descriptions of people's appearances and characters comparable to those written in the late twelfth century. Jocelin of Brakelond's description of Samson abbot of Bury St. Edmunds (1182/3–1211)[18] can be regarded as an extension of the twelfth-century mode, while Nicholas Trevet's descriptions of Henry III and Edward I were the product of another humanist revival.[19]

Realistic observation in the twelfth century will be discussed in two parts.

---

[12] See Brit. Mus. MS. Cotton Nero D i, f. 168ᵛ and attached slip, and the flyleaves of Matthew's autograph of the *Chronica Majora* in Corpus Christi College, Cambridge, MS. 16. See also *Chronica Majora*, ed. H. R. Luard (Rolls Series, 1872–1884, 7 vols.), v. 489; F. Madden, "On the Knowledge possessed by Europeans of the elephant in the thirteenth Century" in *The Graphic and Historical Illustrator*, ed. E. W. Brayley (London, 1834), pp. 335–336, 352; and R. Vaughan, *Matthew Paris* (Cambridge, 1958), pp. 256–257.

[13] *Chronica Majora*, v. 275.

[14] *Ibid.* v. 489. Another product of Matthew's visual sense was his work on heraldry; for the coats of arms he inserted in his historical works see *Rolls of Arms: Henry III*, ed. T. D. Tremlett (Harleian Society cxiii–iv, 1961–1962).

[15] Recording the artistic achievement of St. Albans, Matthew writes: "Haec idcirco scripturae immortali, ac memoriae, duximus commendanda, ut penes nos, haud ingratos, eorum vigeat cum benedictionibus recordatio, qui studioso labore suo opera ecclesiae nostrae adornativa post se reliquerunt"; *Gesta Abbatum Monasterii Sancti Albani*, ed. H. T. Riley (Rolls Series, 1867–1869, 3 vols.), i. 233.

[16] This appears, for example in: the thirteenth-century tract on the dedication of the altars, chapels and churches at Bury St Edmunds, in Brit. Mus. MS. Harley 1005, ff. 217ᵛ–218ᵛ (extracts are printed in M. R. James, *On the Abbey of St. Edmund at Bury* (Cambridge Antiquarian Society, octavo series, xxviii, [1895], pp. 161–162); the account of the uncovering of the walls of an ancient round church at Bury in 1275; *The Chronicle of Bury St. Edmunds 1212–1301*, ed., with an English translation, Antonia Gransden (Nelson's Medieval Texts, 1964), p. 58; and in the thirteenth century *Gesta Sacristarum*, printed in *Memorials of St. Edmund's Abbey*, ed. T. Arnold (Rolls Series, 1890–1896, 3 vols.), ii. 289–296.

[17] *Ibid.* ii. 290. For this passage concerning the Bury Bible in the *Gesta Sacristarum* see E. G. Millar, *English Illuminated Manuscripts from the tenth to the thirteenth Century* (Paris-Brussels, 1926), pp. 30–32.

[18] *The Chronicle of Jocelin of Brakelond*, ed., with an English translation, H. E. Butler (Nelson's Medieval Classics, 1949), pp. 39–40.

[19] *Nicholai Triveti Annales*, ed. T. Hog (English Historical Society, 1845), pp. 279–283. *Cf.* F. M. Powicke, *King Henry III and the Lord Edward* (Oxford, 1947, 2 vols.), ii. 686–687. Trevet also gives a good topographical description of Winchelsea; *Annales*, p. 167.

First, it will be considered as exemplifying the Christian motive for writing. Second, it will be considered as a response to classical studies.

The desire to establish continuity with the Anglo-Saxon past is a marked feature of the history of Durham written in the early twelfth century, probably by the monk Symeon of Durham.[20] The author's obsession with continuity permeates the work, and caused him to describe some material objects. It also accounts for some statements which are of dubious credibility. The author wanted to give venerable associations even to flaws in Durham's treasures. Thus he asserts that the crack in the stone cross (which, he alleges, was the cross of Ethelwold, the bishop of Lindisfarne who died in 740), standing in St Cuthbert's cemetery, was acquired when the Danes raided Lindisfarne.[21] Similarly he tells a story apparently to provide a creditable explanation for a flaw, a slight water stain at the top of some pages, in the precious Gospel-book then owned by Durham cathedral (now the Lindisfarne Gospels in the British Museum). Having briefly described the book which, he states, was written by Eadfrith, and bound with wonderful decoration in gold and gems, by the hermit Billfrith at the order of Bishop Ethelwold,[22] he relates how, when the book was borne from Lindisfarne with St Cuthbert's body and carried to the mouth of the Derwent for embarkation (which was divinely prevented) to Ireland, it accidentally fell in the sea, to be miraculously recovered three days later from the beach at Whithorn.[23] This story can hardly be true, because Whithorn is thirty miles from the mouth of the Derwent. However, the legend that the Gospels accompanied St Cuthbert's body is itself quite plausible.[24]

In the south of England the man to contribute most to vindicate the reputation of the early Anglo-Saxon church and to establish continuity between past and present was William of Malmesbury. He accused the Anglo-Saxons of neglecting

[20] Printed *Symeonis Monachi Opera Omnia*, ed. T. Arnold (Rolls Series, 1882–5, 2 vols.), i. For post-Conquest interest in Bedan Northumbria see *ibid.* i. 108 *sq.*, and M. D. Knowles, *The Monastic Order in England* (Cambridge, 1949), pp. 165–171. Already in the tenth century St. Oswald had searched for relics of the Northumbrian saints and tried to refound Ripon (*Historians of the Church of York*, ed. James Raine, [jn.] Rolls Series, 1879–1894, 3 vols., i. 462), and in the early eleventh century Alured, sacrist of Durham (great-grandfather of Ailred of Rievaulx) went relic-hunting in Northumbria; see *Symeon*, i. 88–89, and *The Priory of Hexham, its Chroniclers, Endowments and Annals*, ed. James Raine (Surtees Society XLIV, 1864, 2 vols.), i. liii.

[21] *Symeon*, i. 39. For a reference to two marvellously carved stone crosses at the head and foot of Acca's tomb (one of which is probably to be identified with the cross now in Durham cathedral) see *ibid.* ii. 33, and Taylor and Taylor, *op. cit.* i. 305.

[22] *Symeon*, i. 67–68. This passage is fully discussed by T. J. Brown in *Codex Lindisfarnensis*, ed. T. D. Kendrick and others (Oltun and Lausanne, 1960, 2 vols.), i. 5–11.

[23] *Symeon*, i. 64–68. This story is fully discussed by T. J. Brown, *loc. cit.* i. 21–23.

[24] See *ibid.* i. 23–24. The Stonyhurst Gospel, which had a close connection with St Cuthbert, were found in St Cuthbert's tomb when it was opened in 1827; see R. A. B. Mynors, "The Stoneyhurst Gospel" in *The Relics of Saint Cuthbert*, ed. C. F. Battiscombe (Oxford, 1956), pp. 357–358.

their past.[25] No one since Bede had tried to record English history and few had troubled to write the lives of saints. To remedy the deficiency William wrote the *Gesta Regum* and the *Gesta Pontificum* in 1125, and also hagiographies and his book on the antiquity of Glastonbury, the *De Antiquitate Glastoniensis Ecclesiae*. His corpus of works concerns both Anglo-Saxon history in general, and also the history of his own abbey, Malmesbury, and of Glastonbury abbey.

Besides recording in the *Gesta Pontificum* all he could discover about the lives of the Anglo-Saxon archbishops, bishops and saints, William included what is virtually a gazetteer of ecclesiastical England. He divided the work into bishoprics. He begins each section with a description of the episcopal see, its site and buildings (the careers of the successive bishops follow), and ends with an account of the religious houses in the diocese, complete with topographical descriptions. It is likely that most (perhaps all) of William's descriptions were based on personal observation, not hearsay. He was, therefore, the first Englishman to travel to get his evidence — to write history from information collected on the spot. His notices of the generous hospitality of some monasteries (such as Reading and Tewkesbury)[26] may represent formal thanks for a visit. The surviving autograph copy of the *Gesta Pontificum* is a small volume which could have fitted into his pocket.[27]

*The Gesta Pontificum* has descriptions of numerous churches and their treasures. Thus William describes St Wulfstan's tomb at Worcester,[28] and mentions the splendid glass in Rochester cathedral,[29] both of which have long since vanished. Of particular value to the architectural historian today is his account of the round church built at Athelney by King Alfred (of which no trace now remains), still served in William's day by a community of ascetic monks. It was built, William records, in a novel style: "Four posts fixed in the earth support the whole structure, and it has four aisles with round ends arranged around the spherical building."[30]

---

[25] William of Malmesbury, *Gesta Regum*, ed. William Stubbs (Rolls Series, 1887–1889, 2 vols.), I. 2; *Gesta Pontificum*, ed. N. E. S. A. Hamilton (Rolls Series, 1870), p. 4.

[26] *Gesta Pontificum*, ed. Hamilton, pp. 193, 295.

[27] Magdalen College, Oxford, MS. 172. Five pages of this MS are reproduced in facsimile by Hamilton, *op. cit.* who gives in the footnotes William's revisions of his text.

[28] *Gesta Pontificum*, p. 288.

[29] *Ibid.* p. 138.

[30] "[Rex Elfredus] fecitque ecclesiam, situ quidem pro angustia spatii modicam, sed novo edificendi modo compactam. Quattuor enim postes solo infixi totam suspendunt machinam, quattuor cancellis opere sperico in circuitu ductis"; *ibid.* p. 199. For the value of William's description see G. Baldwin Brown, *The Arts in Early England* (London 1903–1937, 6 vols.; new edition of vol. 2, "Anglo-Saxon Architecture", London 1925), II. 196. For King Alfred's foundation of the monastery see *Asser's Life of King Alfred* c. 92, ed. W. H. Stevenson (Oxford, 1904), pp. 79–80. William of Malmesbury also mentions the Anglo-Saxon church at Bradford-upon-Avon: *Gesta Pontificum*, p. 346; *cf.* Baldwin Brown, *op. cit.* II. pp. 17, 160, 297, 302–303. William mentions an Anglo-Saxon church, now lost, at St. Albans: *Gesta Pontificum*, p. 316; *cf.* Baldwin Brown, *op. cit.* II. 187. William's description of Hexham (*Gesta Pontificum*, p. 255) is mainly based on that by Eddius Stephanus (see above p. 31 and n.8 and Baldwin Brown, *op. cit.* II. 175–176), and is of less interest than the detailed description written by Richard of Hexham soon after 1138, which is printed in *The Priory of Hexham*, ed. Raine, I. 10–14,

The fifth book of the *Gesta Pontificum* is devoted to the life of St Aldhelm, patron and co-founder of Malmesbury abbey.[31] William included in it information about local history. Like Symeon of Durham, he shows a penchant for giving local antiquities religious associations, in order to enhance the reputation of his house. He connected material objects with St Aldhelm. There was preserved at Malmesbury a beautiful old cope. It was, William records, of fine scarlet silk and had peacocks enclosed in black roundels embroidered on it. William asserts that this cope had belonged to St Aldhelm.[32] He also states that the series of free standing stones near Malmesbury were erected to mark the places where the bearer of St Aldhelm's body rested on the way from Doulting, where St Aldhelm died, to Malmesbury, where he was buried.[33] And William claims that a crack in the altar at Bruton, a gift, according to William, from Pope Sergius to St Aldhelm, was caused by the fall of the animal (perhaps a camel) which carried it over the Alps.[34]

William of Malmesbury's most ambitious and intelligent excursion into local history was in the *De Antiquitate Glastoniensis Ecclesiae*, written sometime between 1129 and 1139.[35] The reasons, perhaps biographical,[36] for William's close interest in Glastonbury, are obscure. But he certainly wrote to please Henry of Blois, bishop of Winchester, who ruled Glastonbury abbey during his episcopate (1129–1171),[37] and to counter the assertion by Osbern, the Canterbury hagiographer, in his *Life of St Dunstan*, that Dunstan was the first abbot of Glastonbury, which impugned Glastonbury's claim to a long and venerable Christian past.[38] William sought to prove Glastonbury's antiquity as an abbey and its even greater antiquity as a holy place. He used, besides documentary evidence, extant antiquities to prove his thesis. He particularly called attention to two "pyramids," or burial crosses, in the cemetery.[39] One, he states, was

---

and fully discussed in Baldwin Brown, *op. cit.* II. 149–184 *passim. Cf.* Taylor and Taylor, *op. cit.* I. 297–312 *passim* and A. W. Clapham, *English Romanesque Architecture* (Oxford, 1930–1934, 2 vols.), I. 44–45, 72–73.

[31] The *Gesta Pontificum* is divided into five books; the last is a Life of St. Aldhelm, and includes much historical material concerning Malmesbury abbey.

[32] *Gesta Pontificum*, p. 365. The peacock motif was popular from the seventh century, or earlier, until the thirteenth century: I owe this information to Mr. Donald King, Deputy Keeper of Textiles in the Victoria and Albert Museum.

[33] *Gesta Pontificum*, pp. 383–384.

[34] *Ibid.* p. 373. However Hugh Farmer, "William of Malmesbury's Life and Work" in *Journal of Ecclesiastical History*, XIII (1962), p. 40, accepts William's statements concerning the cope and the Bruton altar.

[35] Printed in *Adami de Domerham Historia de Rebus Gestis Glastoniensibus*, ed. Thomas Hearne (Oxford, 1727, 2 vols.), I. 1–122.

[36] For criticism of William's work see *Gesta Regum*, II. 357. For the possibility that he was passed over for the abbacy in 1120 see *ibid.* I. xxxviii–ix.

[37] See J. Armitage Robinson, "William of Malmesbury 'On the Antiquity of Glastonbury' " in his *Somerset Historical Essays* (Oxford, 1921), pp. 3, 4.

[38] See *Domerham*, p. 71, and Armitage Robinson, *loc. cit.* pp. 3, 23.

[39] *Domerham*, pp. 44–45. This passage is printed in translation by Aelred Watkin, "The Glastonbury 'Pyramids' and St. Patrick's 'Companions' " in *Downside Review*, LXIII (1945), pp. 30–31. The

twenty-six feet high and had five storeys, on four of which ancient names could be deciphered, though the stone was weathered. William copies the names. He also copies the names from the other "pyramid" which had four storeys and was eighteen feet high. William states that these were the names of the abbots before Dunstan, thus proving, on his own evidence, the abbey's great antiquity: William may well have been partly right, because some of the names probably did commemorate the earliest abbots of Glastonbury, of the late seventh and eighth centuries.[40] He was certainly right in his general view that Glastonbury had been a holy place from the early Christian period in Britain.[41] And his obviously eye-witness description of the "pyramids" is particularly valuable to the historian today because no trace of them now remains.[42]

Besides William of Malmesbury, Osbern and Eadmer, both monks of Christ Church, Canterbury, made intelligent use of antiquities. Their hagiographies contributed much to re-establishing the reputations of the Anglo-Saxon saints connected with Canterbury after the Conquest. Osbern, an Englishman who found it difficult to adapt to Norman rule (Lanfranc sent him for two years to Normandy to help him readjust), visited Glastonbury when writing his *Life of St Dunstan*. He saw Dunstan's cell which he described precisely, using it to demonstrate the saint's austerity. This den, "more like a tomb for the dead than a habitation for the living," was so small ("not more than five feet long and two and a half feet wide") that Dunstan could never have lain down to sleep, and the door, with a small window in it, constituted one wall.[43]

Eadmer, best known as biographer of Anselm, archbishop of Canterbury (1093–1109), resembled Osbern in his concern for preserving the memory of the Anglo-Saxon saints. Besides the threat to continuity offered by the Norman Conquest, he responded to an additional challenge. Canterbury cathedral was burnt to the ground in 1067. The cathedral's reputation could have suffered serious damage if contemporaries had believed that the relics it housed had been lost in the conflagration. Therefore Eadmer wrote a work, *De Reliquiis Sancti Audoeni et quorundam aliorum sanctorum quae Cantuariae in aecclesiae domini Salvatoris habentur*, to prove that the relics from the old choir had been safely placed in the new one.[44] He described the exact location of the relics in the old

---

rendering in Robinson, *loc. cit.* p. 21, is less precise than that by Watkin (see Watkin, *loc. cit.* p. 30 n. 5).

[40] See the suggested identifications of the names given by Watkin, *loc. cit.* pp. 35–40.

[41] For what is known today of the Anglo-Saxon churches at Glastonbury, with references to William of Malmesbury's information, see Taylor and Taylor, *Anglo-Saxon Architecture*, i. 250–257. See also the same authors' "Pre-Norman Churches of the Border" in *Celt and Saxon, Studies in the Early British Border*, ed. N. K. Chadwick (Cambridge, 1963), pp. 256–257.

[42] The "pyramids" remained standing until the eighteenth century, when they were dragged away. They were remarked on by other writers from the late twelfth century onwards, but by then their inscriptions were indecipherable; see Watkin, *loc. cit.* pp. 31–35.

[43] *Memorials of St. Dunstan*, ed. William Stubbs (Rolls Series, 1874), pp. 183–184.

[44] Printed A. Wilmart, "Edmeri Cantuariensis cantoris nova opuscula de sanctorum veneratione et obsecratione" in *Revue des Sciences religieuses*, xv (1935), 362–370. The architectural description in this work is also printed with an English translation (together with other references in the works of

choir, and this caused him to describe its architecture. Therefore he wrote what was in fact the first architectural history to be composed in England — a precedent which, as will be seen below, was not neglected at Christ Church. A characteristic passage reads: "Beyond the middle of the length of the nave there were two towers which projected above the aisles of the church. The south tower had an altar in the middle of it which was dedicated in honour of the blessed pope Gregory, and at the side was the principal door, which formerly was called by the English — and still is — the Suthdure."[45]

The Norman Conquest resulted in the most serious, but not the only, threat to the continuity of the monastic tradition in mediaeval England. The anarchy of King Stephen's reign (1135–1154) and Henry II's judicial reforms also made monks fear for their ancient rights and privileges. Again monks showed a heightened interest in their houses' past. In the first half of Henry II's reign chronicles were written in numerous monasteries, for example at Ely, Peterborough, Ramsey and Battle, which were principally intended to record the houses' history, authenticated with copies of documents, as far back as possible. The Ely chronicler begins with a Life of the patron saint, St Etheldreda, and uses visual evidence to connect the abbey's treasures with the Anglo-Saxon past. He describes a precious altar cloth; it was of blood-coloured satin on top, and had green sides decorated with gold thread and gems and edged with gold fringe — it was, he said, the work of, and a gift from Queen Emma.[46]

The Ramsey chronicler was particularly interested in remains from the Anglo-Saxon period. He gives a valuable description of the earliest stone church at Ramsey, the tower of which fell in St Oswald's time, because of faulty foundations. Nothing now remains of this church which was in the Carolingian style:

Two towers overshadowed the roofs; the smaller one, at the west end, at the front of the church, presented a beautiful spectacle from a long way off to those entering the island; the larger one, in the centre of the quadrifid structure, was supported by four columns, one attached to the next by spreading arches to prevent them falling apart. According to the architecture of that distant age, this was a fine enough building.[47]

The Ramsey chronicler also mentions the ruins of an old crypt in the cemetery, which, he stated, were "witness and evidence" of a nunnery which King Canute and Bishop Æthelric had intended to found there. But God in His mercy had prevented them![48]

---

Eadmer and other early writers throwing light on the architectural history of Christ Church) in R. Willis, *The Architectural History of Canterbury Cathedral* (London, 1845), pp. 9–13. See also R. W. Southern, *Saint Anselm and his Biographer* (Cambridge, 1963), pp. 262 n. 2, 370–371.

[45] "Dein sub medio longitudinis aulae ipsius duae turres erant, prominentes ultra aecclesiae alas. Quarum una, quae in austro erat, sub honore beati Gregorii papae altare in medio sui dedicatum habebat, et in latere principale octium aecclesiae, quod antiquitus ab Anglis et nunc usque Suthdure dicitur;" Wilmart, *loc. cit.* p. 365.

[46] *Liber Eliensis*, ed. E. O. Blake (Camden Soc. third series, XCII, 1962), p. 149. For a description of the altar at Ramsey see *Chronicon Abbatiae Rameseiensis*, ed. W. Dunn Macray (Rolls Series, 1886), p. 90.

[47] *Ibid.* p. 41. See Baldwin Brown, *op. cit.* II. 268–269; Clapham, *op. cit.* I. 90. See *Historians of the Church of York*, ed. Raine, I. 434 for an earlier reference to this church.

[48] *Chron. Abb. Ram.* p. 126.

But the Ramsey chronicler had more than a nostalgic, antiquarian interest in the Anglo-Saxon past. Of all the twelfth-century chroniclers, he took the most methodical interest in charters. He explicitly states that the anarchy of Stephen's reign provided the incentive: he wanted to provide written evidence of the abbey's titles to land and privilege in case these were again challenged in a period of chaos.[49] Therefore the Ramsey chronicler copied numerous charters into his chronicle. He concentrated particularly on pre-Conquest charters, thus becoming one of the earliest Anglo-Saxon scholars. He examined "very ancient schedules of charters and cyrographs," which, as they were "nearly all in English", he translated into Latin. He comments on the poor condition of some of the documents, "disintegrating with age."[50]

The Ramsey chronicler was also interested in seals. He appreciated the additional authority given to a charter by the royal seal, and remarks on the fact that in early times only the king and great men, not people of lesser importance had seals.[51] The same point is made in the contemporary chronicle of Battle abbey which records that Richard de Lucy, the justiciar, when defending in court the authenticity of an unsealed charter of Battle abbey, pointed out that in the old days "not every little knight had his own seal, but only kings and really important people."[52] Interest in the physical appearance of devices for the authentication of documents is vividly demonstrated in "Benedict of Peterborough": it has a drawing of the rota of King William II of Sicily, at the end of a copy of William's charter granting dower to his betrothed, Henry II's daughter Joan    [53] (Pl. 4).

Forgery, a weapon against attacks on rights to property and privilege, provided a powerful incentive to palaeographical and diplomatic study, because suspect charter were examined attentively.[54] Thus Gervase of Canterbury, writing between about 1188 and 1199, records how a forgery was detected in 1181. In order to strengthen their claim to exemption from obedience to the archbishop of Canterbury, the monks of St Augustine's produced what purported to be a papal diploma granted to St Augustine of Canterbury. But, Gervase records, though the parchment (actually a reused piece) was old, the handwriting, style and leaden bull were not.[55]

---

[49] *Ibid.* p. 4.

[50] *Ibid.* pp. 65, 176–177.

[51] *Ibid.* p. 65.

[52] *Chronicon Monasterii de Bello*, ed. J. S. Brewer (Anglia Christiana, London, 1846), p. 108.

[53] See also *Gesta Regis Henrici Secundi Benedicti Abbatis*, ed. William Stubbs (Rolls Series, 1867, 2 vols.), I. 172 n. 4. A picture of the same rota is also in Roger of Howden's chronicle; see *Chronica Magistri Rogeri de Houedene*, ed. William Stubbs (Rolls Series, 1868–1871, 4 vols.), II. 98. (For evidence suggesting that Roger of Howden wrote "Benedict" see D. M. Stenton, "Roger of Howden and 'Benedict'" in *EHR*, LXVIII (1953), 574–582 *passim*). For a reference to this rota, on a diploma dated at Palermo in 1182, see Arthur Engel, *Recherches sur la Numismatique et la Sigillographie des Normands de Sicile et d'Italie* (Paris, 1882), p. 87.

[54] For examples of the criticism of documents at the papal curia in the twelfth century see R. L. Poole, *Lectures on the History of the Papal Chancery* (Cambridge, 1915), pp. 143–162.

[55] *The Historical Works of Gervase of Canterbury*, ed. William Stubbs (Rolls Series, 1879, 1880, 2 vols.), I. 296–297. For this case see M. D. Knowles, "The Growth of Exemption" in *Downside Re-*

4 'Benedict of Peterborough' (*rota* of William II of Sicily).
*(London, British Library, MS Cotton Vitellius E xvii, fo. 28)*

5 A cripple from Gerald of Wales, *Topographia Hibernica*, dist. iii, cap. xxxv.
*(London, British Library, MS Royal 13 B viii, fo. 30v)*

6 Irish hornblowers from Gerald of Wales, *Topographia Hibernica*, dist. iii, cap. xxxiv.
*(London, British Library, MS Royal 13 B viii, fo. 30)*

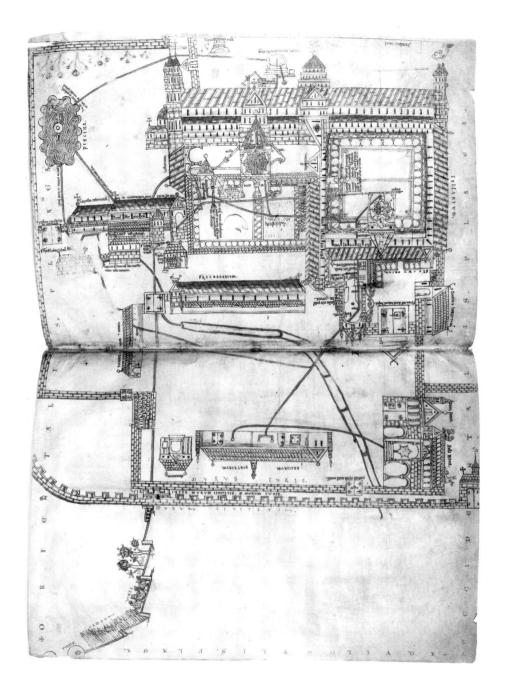

7  Plan of waterworks of Christ Church, Canterbury, *c.* 1165.
*(Cambridge, Trinity College, MS R.17.1, fos. 284v-285)*

Gervase of Canterbury was the last representative in the twelfth century of the monastic antiquarian tradition exemplified by William of Malmesbury. Like William he was interested in the monastic geography of England. His *Mappa Mundi*,[56] compiled to preserve the memory of the England of his own day, is a nearly complete list of the monasteries of England (he gives four hundred and thirty eight houses), grouped in counties, arranged in three columns: in the first column is written, as relevant, "archbishopric," "bishopric," "abbey" or "priory"; in the second is the name of the place and the patron saint; and in the third column is the order to which the house belonged.

But Gervase's antiquarian interest was mainly centred on Christ Church. Like Eadmer, he faced a challenge to the continuity of the cathedral's spiritual tradition. In 1174 the choir of the cathedral was again burnt to the ground, to be rebuilt in the next decade by William of Sens and his successor. Once again it was necessary to prove that no relics had been lost, and that the tombs of the archbishops, especially that of Thomas Becket, had been safely disposed in the new choir. Gervase begins his Chronicle with an account of the fire and of the rebuilding, including an architectural history of the cathedral from Anglo-Saxon times and a vivid description of the new choir.[57] His purpose was, he states, to prevent the two previous churches, both destroyed by fire, from ever being forgotten. He probably had a personal reason for strong interest in and detailed knowledge of the new cathedral's architecture. It is likely that he was the monk appointed by William of Sens to oversee the workmen after William had been incapacitated by a fall from the scaffold.[58]

Gervase's interest in architectural history was stimulated, like Eadmer's, by preoccupation with relics. "It is impossible," he writes, "to show clearly the resting-places of the saints, which are in various parts of the church, without first describing the building itself where they are housed."[59] He copies Eadmer's account of the location of the relics in the pre-Conquest church, and describes exactly where they and the archbishops' tombs were placed in the new choir — the climax is the account of the translation of Thomas Becket.[60]

Gervase traced the cathedral's architectural history in great detail. He relied on Eadmer for his account of the pre-Conquest church, but described the

---

*view*, L (1932), 411–415. For a similar case, of 1221, involving Dunstable priory see *Annales Monastici*, ed. H. R. Luard (Rolls Series, 1864–1869, 5 vols.), III. 66, and V. H. Galbraith, *Studies in the Public Records* (London, 1948), pp. 48–52.

[56] Printed in *Gervase of Canterbury*, II. 414–449. It is fully discussed by M. D. Knowles, "The Mappa Mundi of Gervase of Canterbury" in *Downside Review*, XLVIII (1930), 237–247.

[57] *Gervase*, I. 7–29, *passim*. For an English translation see R. Willis, *The Architectural History of Canterbury Cathedral*, pp. 32–62 *passim*.

[58] *Gervase*, I. 20, records that William of Sens after his accident, "veruntamen quia hiems instabat, et fornicem superiorem consummari oportebat, cuidam monacho industrio et ingenioso qui cementariis praefuit opus consummandum commendavit, unde multa invidia et exercitatio malitiae habita est, eo quod ipse, cum esset juvenis, potentioribus et ditioribus prudentior videretur". The omission of the young monk's name would be surprising if he were not Gervase himself.

[59] *Ibid.* I. 12.

[60] *Ibid.* I. 22–3.

nave of Lanfranc's church, which had survived the 1174 fire, from his own observation. (He admits that he cannot describe Lanfranc's choir because it was pulled down by Prior Conrad in Archbishop Anselm's time in order to build the new one). He describes Conrad's choir from memory, and compares it with the new choir in order to highlight the latter's architectural novelties. He points out that the new columns were nearly twelve feet higher than the old ones, and unlike the latter had carved capitals. He states that the new rib-vaults replaced plain stone vaults and painted wooden roofs, and notices that the new choir had two triforiums instead of one, was higher and lighter, and was richer in marble and carving. He ends by explaining why the new choir narrowed at the end. Gervase concludes with an appreciation of the value of visual evidence: "All these things can be more clearly and pleasurably seen with the eye than learnt about from the written or spoken word."[61]

Gervase' strong interest in the architecture of Christ Church was undoubtedly aroused by the fire of 1174. However it should be noted that about ten years earlier another event had stimulated the monks' interest in the architecture of their monastery. Sometime between 1153 and 1167 they had installed a new system of water distribution and drainage within the precincts. This gave rise to the two earliest known surveys made in England, in order to show where the pipes lay. One survey is a plan of the monastery, showing the cathedral and principal buildings, which though not correct in all details is in general accurate   (Pl. 7). The other is a plan of the extra-mural waterworks.[61a]

I turn now to descriptive writing encouraged by study of the classics. William of Malmesbury himself was much influenced by the classics. His admiration for classical antiquity is well demonstrated by his inclusion in the *Gesta Pontificum*, a work devoted to Christian history, of a description of the ruins of an impressive Roman hall in Carlisle, and a transcription of the inscription on it.[62] But the most important result of William's study of the classics, especially of Suetonius' *Lives of the Caesars*, was on his perception of people. Suetonius provided William of Malmesbury with models for the physical description of people and taught him a technique for illustrating facets of character. William, the first writer in England to write more than one pen-portrait,[63] used the Suetonian method of short,

---

[61] *Ibid.* I. 28.

[61a] Both surveys are discussed and reproduced in *The Canterbury Psalter* ed. M. R. James (London, 1935) pp. 53–56, and end of volume.

[62] *Gesta Pontificum.* p. 208. This inscription is in R. G. Collingwood and R. P. Wright, *The Roman Inscriptions of Britain* (vol. 1 only published, Inscriptions on Stone, Oxford, 1965), I. 316–317 (no. 950).

[63] A few pre-Conquest writers described men's physical appearance. Bede briefly but graphically described the appearance of Bishop Paulinus (*HE*, ii. 16). Alcuin, writing abroad, described Willibrord, in the Suetonian style (quoted *HE*, ed. Plummer, II. 293). There is a description of Edward the Confessor in the anonymous Life, apparently based on a description of St. Omer in a contemporary hagiography; *The Life of King Edward*, ed. F. Barlow, p. 12 and n. 1. The earliest description of an

snappy descriptions.[64] How far his descriptions are realistic is hard to say. As they have verbal echoes of Suetonius and it is unlikely that William had met the men he describes, they could be literary rhetoric, without historical basis. This is probably true of his portrait of St Wulfstan, bishop of Worcester (1062–1095) which has no distinctive features — Wulfstan was "of medium height, overtopped by the very tall, but exceeding the very short, and all his limbs were well-porportioned."[65]

On the other hand, William's pen-portraits of the Anglo-Norman kings are sufficiently concrete to justify credence. He could have obtained his information from people who had seen the kings. For example, he writes that William Rufus "was squarely built, had a florid complexion and yellow hair, an open countenance and multi-coloured eyes, varied with glittering specks; he was of astonishing strength, though not very tall, and had a protruding stomach."[66] William also adopted the Suetonian technique of illustrating character, both good and bad traits, by recounting anecdotes and trivial details. A good example of William's use of anecdote is a story he tells to show William Rufus' extravagance. Rufus reprimanded his chamberlain for buying him a cheap pair of boots, exclaiming angrily, "Only three shillings!? you son of a whore, since when has a king worn such cheap boots? Go and bring me a pair worth a silver mark!"[67] Moreover William probably borrowed from Suetonius his method of writing passages exclusively devoted to sketching characters in some detail. (He treats the Anglo-Norman Kings in this way).[68]

The classics and romance literature (itself indebted to classical studies) fostered interest in secular life. William of Malmesbury was the first writer to divide secular from ecclesiastical history explicitly, dealing with the former in the *Gesta Regum* and the latter in the *Gesta Pontificum*. And the first pen-portrait of a layman other than a king was written in the mid-twelfth century: Ailred of Rievaulx gives a vivid description in the Suetonian style of Walter Espec, lay patron of Rievaulx abbey — a very tall man, with black hair, a bold, lined

---

Englishman is that of Pelagius by Jerome, who knew him well ("a huge, fat highland dog" who "walked like a tortoise"); see J. N. L. Myres, "Pelagius and the End of Roman Rule in Britain" in *Journal of Roman Studies*, L (1960), 24.

[64] See *e.g.* Suetonius, *Duodecim Caesares*, ed. Maurice Rat, with a French translation (Paris, 1931, 2 vols.), I. 51; II. 65, 127 (Caesar, c. XLV; Caligula, c. 1; Claudius, c. XXX). For the influence of Suetonius on William of Malmesbury treated generally see M. Schütt, "The Literary Form of William of Malmesbury's 'Gesta Regum' " in *EHR*, XLVI (1931), 255–260.

[65] *The Vita Wulfstani of William of Malmesbury*, ed. R. R. Darlington (Camden Society, third series, XL, 1928), p. 46. For a similar description of Thomas archbishop of York (1070–1100) see *Gesta Pontificum*, p. 257.

[66] *Gesta Regum*, II. 374. For descriptions of William I and Henry I see *ibid.* II. 335, 488. For a short reference to King Athelstan's appearance, based on observations made when his tomb at Malmesbury was opened, see *ibid.* I. 148.

[67] *Ibid.* II. 368.

[68] See *ibid.* II. 335–336, 366–371, 488. A character-sketch of William the Conqueror occurs in the Anglo-Saxon chronicle, *s.a.* 1087; *The Anglo-Saxon Chronicle*, a revised translation ed. D. Whitelock with D. C. Douglas and S. I. Tucker (London, 1961), pp. 163–164.

face, with a voice like a trumpet, "uniting eloquence with a certain majesty of sound."[69]

The twelfth century is notable for numerous topographical descriptions of castles. These reflect contemporary interest in warfare, encouraged both by romance literature, popularized by Geoffrey of Monmouth's *Historia Regum Britanniae* (published *ca.* 1136), and by conditions during the anarchy of Stephen's reign. They also reflect men's response to the impressive castles which played a crucial role during the anarchy. Geoffrey of Monmouth himself briefly describes the Tower of London.[70] And so many topographies of castles (of Exeter, Bristol, Bath, Oxford, Cricklade and Faringdon)[71] occur in the *Gesta Stephani* as to suggest that the author had some particular reason for interest in their defensive potential. For example, he writes of Oxford:

The city is very securely protected, inaccessible because of the very deep water that washes it all round, most carefully encircled by the palisade of an outwork on one side, and on another finely and very strongly fortified by an impregnable castle and a tower of great height.

A similar topography of Scarborough castle is in the late twelfth-century chronicle of William of Newburgh, an Augustinian canon:

A huge rock, almost inaccessible on account of precipices on all sides, drives back the sea which surrounds it, except for a narrow ascent on the west. On its summit is a beautiful grassy plain, more than sixty acres in area, with a spring of fresh water issuing from a rock. At the entrance, which is difficult of access, there is a royal castle, and below the incline begins the town which spreads to the south and north but faces west, defended on this side by its own wall, on the east by the castle rock, while both sides are washed by the sea.[72]

Most remarkable for realistic descriptive writing were a group of writers working in the last decade of Henry II's reign and in the reign of Richard I. Their common features were, in varying degrees, an interest in man as an individual and an objective curiosity about man's environment. All were influenced, to a greater or lesser extent, by classical studies, but none imitated exactly any particular classical author. Foremost were Gerald of Wales, Walter Map, and William Fitz Stephen. Other writers sharing some of their characteristics were Adam of Eynsham, chaplain and biographer of St Hugh of Lincoln, Ralph Diceto, dean of St Paul's (1180/1–1202), Richard of Devizes, a monk of St Swithuns, Winchester, and Lucian, a monk of St Werburgh's, Chester. All these men, except apparently Richard of Devizes and Lucian, had contact, with one or more of the famous schools of the day. Gerald of Wales, Walter Map and

[69] Ailred, *Relatio de Standardo*, in *Chronicles of the Reigns of Stephen, Henry II, and Richard I*, ed. Richard Howlett (Rolls Series, 1884–1889, 4 vols.), iii. 183.

[70] Geoffrey of Monmouth, *Historia Regum Britanniae*, c. iii. 10; ed. Acton Griscom (London, 1929), p. 291. Cf. *ibid.* c. i. 17; c. iii. 20 (pp. 252, 301, respectively).

[71] *Gesta Stephani*, ed., with an English translation, K. R. Potter (Nelson's Medieval Texts, 1955), pp. 22, 37–38, 38–39, 92, 113, 120, respectively. For a detailed account of the Isle of Ely's natural defences and a brief comment on Bedford see *ibid.* pp. 66, 155.

[72] William of Newburgh, *Historia Rerum Anglicarum*, in *Chrons. Stephen, Henry II, and Richard I*, ed. Howlett, i. 104.

Adam of Eynsham had connections with Oxford[73] and Lincoln cathedral[74]— Gerald mentions the schools at Lincoln.[75] Fitz Stephen, who describes the schools in London,[76] and Diceto were Londoners, and both Gerald and Walter Map (who held a prebend at St Paul's)[77] often lived in the capital. Gerald[78] and Walter Map,[79] and probably Diceto had studied at Paris university,[80] and all three had close connections with the Angevin court, a notable cultural center.

Gerald of Wales and Walter Map both give pen-portraits of Henry II, whom they knew personally. (Walter Map entered royal service soon after 1160[81] and Gerald of Wales in about 1184).[82] Gerald's description, as the most graphic of the two, may be quoted. Henry was:

a man of reddish, freckled complexion with a large round head, grey eyes which glowed fiercely and grew bloodshot in anger, a fiery countenance and a harsh, cracked voice. His neck was poked forward slightly from his shoulders, his chest was broad and square, his arms strong and powerful. His frame was stocky, with a pronounced tendency to corpulance, due to nature rather than indulgence, which he tempered by exercise.[83]

---

[73] Gerald read one of his works to the students of Oxford in about 1185, and spent two years in Oxford from 1193 to 1194; see *Giraldi Cambrensis Opera*, ed. J. S. Brewer and others (Rolls Series, 1861–1891, 8 vols.), I. 72, 294. *Cf. The Autobiography of Giraldus Cambrensis*, ed. H. E. Butler (London, 1937), pp. 97, 139 and n. 5. Walter Map became archdeacon of Oxford in 1196; J. Le Neve, *Fasti Ecclesiae Anglicanae* (Oxford, 1854, 3 vols.), II. 64. Adam, a monk of Eynsham (about five miles from Oxford), was of an Oxford burgher family; see *The Life of St. Hugh of Lincoln*, ed. D. L. Douie and H. Farmer (Nelson's Medieval Texts, 1961–1962, 2 vols.), I. viii–ix.

[74] Gerald of Wales retired to Lincoln to write and study in 1196; *Giraldus*, I. 93, and Butler, *op. cit.* p. 127 and n. 2. Map was precentor of Lincoln; J. Le Neve, *op. cit.* II. 82. Adam lived partly at Lincoln as St. Hugh's chaplain from 1197 to Hugh's death in 1200; *Life of St. Hugh*, I. x–xi.

[75] See *Giraldus*, I. 93.

[76] See Fitz Stephen's description of London in his *Life of Saint Thomas* in *Materials for the History of Thomas Becket*, ed. J. C. Robertson and J. B. Sheppard (Rolls Series, 1875–1885, 7 vols.), III. 4–5.

[77] J. Le Neve, *Fasti Ecclesiae Anglicanae 1066–1300*, I, compiled by D. E. Greenway (London, 1968), p. 60.

[78] *Giraldus*, I. 23, 45 *sq.*; VIII. 292.

[79] For Map's stay in Paris see Walter Map, *De Nugis Curialium*, ii. 7; *cf.* v. 5: ed. M. R. James (Anecdota Oxoniensia, 1914), pp. 69, 225. *sq.*

[80] Diceto studied in Paris, probably at the university and had other close contacts with France and the Angevin empire; see *The Historical Works of Master Ralph de Diceto*, ed. William Stubbs (Rolls Series, 1876, 2 vols.), I. xvii *sq.*, xxxi *sq.*

[81] See *De Nugis*, ii. 3; v. 6: ed. James, pp. 65–66, 246, *Cf.* T. Wright's introduction to his edition of *De Nugis* (Camden Society L, 1850), p. vi.

[82] See Butler, *op. cit.* p. 81 and n.l.

[83] *Expugnatio Hibernica*, in *Giraldus*, v. 302; the pen-portrait and character-sketch (discussed below) is printed, in an English translation, in *English Historical Documents 1046–1089*, ed. D. C. Douglas and G. W. Greenaway (London, 1953), pp. 386–388. Walter Map's pen-portrait of Henry II is in his character-sketch of the king; see Walter Map, *De Nugis Curialium*, v. 6, ed. James, p. 237 and the next note. For another contemporary pen-portrait and character-sketch of Henry II see Peter of Blois' *Epistola* 66 (written in 1177), printed in *Materials for the History of Thomas Becket*, ed. Robertson and Sheppard, VII. 571–575 (and in *Petri Blesensis Bathoniensis archidiaconi Opera omnia*, ed. J. A. Giles, Oxford 1846–1847, 4 vols.). Peter was a prolific writer whose career resembled that of Gerald of Wales though much of it was on the continent. He was born at Blois, took orders, studied at Bologna and taught at Paris. He was successively tutor of William II of Sicily, and secretary to Rotrou archbishop of Rouen, to Baldwin archbishop of Canterbury, and to Queen Eleanor,

Moreover, Gerald of Wales and Walter Map give detailed character-sketches of Henry II. They treat the subject *en bloc*, besides telling numerous illustrative anecdotes in Suetonian fashion. Map's description of Henry mainly concerns his abilities as a ruler (he had "discretion in the making of laws and the ordering of all government, and was a clever deviser of decisions in difficult and dark cases"). But Map also gives some more personal touches. He ascribes Henry's restless energy, which made him a tireless traveller "tolerant of the discomforts of dust and mud," and exhausted his household, to his fear of growing too fat. And he describes his good temper and good manners, but criticises him for a tendency to withdraw from company when away from home.[84] Equally vivid is Gerald of Wales' description of Henry's character.[85] Like Map, he comments on his extraordinary energy; after a day of strenuous physical activity he would sit neither before, or after supper, so that "by such great and wearisome exertion he would wear out the whole court by continually standing."

Adam of Eynsham in the *Life of St Hugh* illustrates character with anecdotes and trivial details, even mentioning facets of St Hugh's character which were not entirely creditable — he relates that Hugh was sometimes irritable when he presided over the chapter at Lincoln.[86] He recounts anecdotes about the kings which show Henry II's quick temper and sense of humour,[87] Richard I's forgiving nature,[88] and King John's lack of religious feeling, meanness, and worldly ambition. (He illustrates John's unpleasant character partly with a story of how St Hugh showed him a carving of the Last Judgment on the tympanum at Fontevrault, hoping that the sight of the torments of the damned would frighten him into repentance: but John turned away to look at some carvings of proud kings, saying it was them whom he would emulate.)[89] Adam also had an eye for everyday life. He describes a baby's response to the saint's presence:

The tiny mouth and face relaxed in continuous chuckles. . . . It then bent and stretched out its little arms, as if trying to fly, and moved its head to and fro. . . . Next it took St. Hugh's hand in both of its small ones, and using all its strength raised it to his face, immediately licking rather than kissing it.[90]

A feature of a number of late twelfth-century writers was an interest in towns,

---

and became archdeacon of Bath in about 1175 and of London in about 1192. He knew Henry II well. Short pen-portraits and character-sketches of Thomas Becket occur in the Life by William Fitz Stephen (*Materials*, III. 17) and in the Icelandic Life (*Thómas Saga Erkibyskups*, ed. E. Magnùsson, Rolls Series, 1875, 1883, 2 vols., I. 29).

[84] *De Nugis*, v. 6; ed. James, pp. 237–242 *passim*. Map records that he once crossed the channel with Henry II (*ibid*. p. 242). His character-sketch of Henry is printed, in an English translation, in Douglas and Greenaway, *op. cit.* pp. 389–390. Map also gives character-sketches of King Canute and Henry I; *De Nugis*, v. 4; v. 5: ed. James, pp. 211, 218–220.

[85] *Giraldus*, v. 301–306. Gerald also gives character-sketches of Henry II's sons and of William Longchamp; *Giraldus*, v. 193–201; IV. 399 *sq.*, respectively.

[86] See *The Life of St. Hugh of Lincoln*, ed. Douie and Farmer I. 124.

[87] *Ibid*. I. 115–119.

[88] *Ibid*. II. 101. Cf. *ibid*. I. xlii–iv.

[89] *Ibid*. II. 140–141.

[90] *Ibid*. I. 129–130.

both in their topography and in the customs of their citizens. This interest developed throughout the twelfth century (writers in earlier periods rarely refer to towns)[91] as a result of a number of factors. Towns were playing an increasingly important part in the economic and social life of England. Moreover, the idea of the city was fostered by trends in European history. The reform of the papacy attracted attention to Rome. William of Malmesbury copied a poem in praise of Rome, and gives a topography of the Eternal City.[92] Interest in cities was further encouraged by the crusades — cities of Byzantium and in the crusading states were famous and prosperous. William of Malmesbury gives topographical accounts of Constantinople, Antioch and Jerusalem,[93] and the author of the Itinerary of Richard I describes Jerusalem and its holy places.[94] And early in the thirteenth century the Cistercian chronicler Ralph of Coggeshall gave a detailed, though rather inaccurate account of the topography of Constantinople.[95]

Study of the classics also fostered an interest in cities, the centres of ancient civilization. Geoffrey of Monmouth derived his interest in the derivation of the names of towns from the classics. Virgil explained the derivation of the name Rome with an eponym (the story of Romulus and Remus): Geoffrey used eponyms to explain the names of London,[96] Gloucester,[97] and Leicester.[98] And by calling London "New Troy," Geoffrey shows that he regarded London as a reincarnation, so to speak, of that ancient city. Although the descriptions of cities written in England in the late twelfth century are not modelled exactly on any classical work, they, like those by classical authors, divide into two categories, the laudatory[99] and the satirical.[100] William Fitz Stephen's description of London, Lucian's description of Chester, and Ralph Diceto's description of

---

[91] Gildas realized the importance of cities in Britain; *De Excidio*, c. 3; ed. Mommsen, p. 28. Alcuin praised York as a center of commerce; *De Pontificibus . . . Carmen*, lines 19–37; ed. Wattenbach and Dümmler, p. 83. The 11 th-century hagiographer Goscelin mentioned London's commercial prosperity; C. H. Talbot, "The Liber Confortatorius of Goscelin of Saint Bertin" in *Analecta Monastica* III, xxxviii; Rome, 1955), p. 49. For a similar passage see *The Life of King Edward*, ed. Barlow, p. 44.

[92] *Gesta Regum*, ii. 402–408. For the poem and the topography (which dates from the late seventh or early eighth century) see *ibid*. ii. cxxi–ii, and J. K. Hyde, "Medieval Descriptions of Cities" in *Bulletin of the John Rylands Library*, xlviii (1966), 321.

[93] *Gesta Regum*, ii. 411–412, 415–416, 422, respectively. For William's sources for these descriptions see *ibid*. ii. cxxii–cxxiii.

[94] *Itinerarium Peregrinorum et Gesta Regis Ricardi* in *Chronicles and Memorials of the Reign of Richard I*, ed. William Stubbs (Rolls Series, 1864–1865, 2 vols.), i. 435.

[95] *Radulphi de Coggeshall Chronicon Anglicanum*, ed. Joseph Stevenson (Rolls Series, 1875), pp. 149–150.

[96] *Historia Regum Britanniae*, iii. 20; ed. Acton Griscom, p. 301. See also Geoffrey's derivations of Billingsgate and Ludgate, *ibid*. iii. 10, 20; ed. Acton Griscom, pp. 291, 302.

[97] *Ibid*. iv. 15; ed. Acton Griscom, p. 324.

[98] *Ibid*. ii. 11; ed. Acton Griscom, p. 262.

[99] The laudatory attitude to cities in classical literature is well represented by Aelius Aristides' Roman Oration; printed in translation by J. H. Oliver, *The Ruling Power* (Transactions of the American Philosophical Society, *new series*, xliii, pt. 4, 1953), pp. 895–907. Virgil praises Rome throughout the *Æneid*.

[100] An obvious classical prototype is Juvenal's *Satire* III, on Rome.

Angers, are laudatory, while Richard of Devizes' accounts of English towns are satirical.

Richard of Devizes, who wrote his chronicle between 1192 and 1198, frequently cites from such authors as Virgil, Horace, Juvenal, Lucan and Ovid.[101] He includes satirical references to a number of English towns, dissociating himself from his remarks by a literary conceit: he puts them into the mouth of a French Jew advising a Gentile youth where to settle in England.[102] The young man should avoid London, a sink of iniquity, crowded with pimps, gamblers and parasites ("actors, smooth-skinned boys, belly dancers" and the like). The youth should also avoid Canterbury, Rochester, Chichester, Oxford, Exeter, Worcester, Chester, Hereford, York, Durham, Norwich, Lincoln and Bristol — Richard gives a brief reason for the undesirability of each. For example, York "is full of Scotsmen, filthy and treacherous creatures scarcely men," Bath "is placed or rather dumped down in the midst of valleys in an exceedingly heavy air and in sulphurous vapour, at the gates of Hell,"[102a] and at Bristol "there is no-one who is not or has not been a soap maker, and every Frenchman loves soapmakers as he does a dung-heap." The Jew concludes by advising the youth to settle in Winchester, "the city of cities, the mother of all and better than all others," the only city tolerant of Jews, where men can study and the citizens are generous and courteous. But Richard adds a satirical remark even here — Winchester is full of gossip and rumours.

The account of London written sometime between 1173 and 1175 by William Fitz Stephen, a clerk who had been in the service of Thomas Becket, is the most detailed and realistic description of a city written in mediaeval England.[103] It has many allusions to and citations from classical authors — for example Virgil, Horace, Persius and Ovid. Fitz Stephen wrote primarily because of the circumstances of his times. His love of and loyalty to London were roused by the attention paid to Canterbury as a result of the martyrdom of Thomas Becket in the cathedral. Fitz Stephen prefixed the description of London to his *Life of Saint Thomas*, the pretext being that Becket, like Fitz Stephen, was a Londoner — and just as Sallust had described Africa in his history of the Carthaginian war, so Fitz Stephen would describe London. London, he writes, was once a metropolitan see (a reference to Gregory the Great's arrangements for the ecclesiastical organisation of England), and would, "it is thought," be so again, unless the martyr Thomas' fame perpetuates the honour for Canterbury where his body lies. But London could justly dispute Canterbury's claim to close association with Becket because, though he died in Canterbury, he was born in London.[104]

[101] See, for example, *The Chronicle of Richard of Devizes*, ed., with an English translation, J. T. Appleby (Nelson's Medieval Texts, 1963), pp. 63–64 and n. 3.

[102] *Ibid.* pp. 65–67.

[102a] A more favourable description of Bath, which mentions the popularity of its health-giving hot springs, is in the *Gesta Stephani*, ed. K. R. Potter, pp. 38–39.

[103] The text is in *Materials*, III. 2–13 (see above note 76). For an English translation, by H. E. Butler, see F. M. Stenton, *Norman London* (Historical Association Leaflets nos. 93, 94, 1934). See also Hyde, *loc. cit.* pp. 324–325.

[104] *Materials*, III. 2–3.

Fitz Stephen describes the topography of London, the Tower, the walls with their towers and gates, the Thames ("teeming with fish"), the suburban houses with wells and spacious gardens, the meadows and forests beyond. Even more remarkable is his long account of the social customs and pastimes of the Londoners. He describes the horse fair at Smithfield, and the cook-shops on the banks of the Thames, which catered for rich and poor and were especially handy if guests arrived unexpectedly. He mentions the disputations of students studying in London, thus providing evidence for the existence of schools in the capital. Then he describes the games of young Londoners, the ball-games, horse-races and dangerous ice sports played on the frozen Thames. Like Rome in ancient and in Christian times, London was notable both for the usefulness and hard work of its citizens, and also for its pleasures and entertainments.[105] Following Geoffrey of Monmouth, Fitz Stephen asserts that London ("New Troy") produced "not a few men who subdued many nations and the Roman empire to their sway" in the pre-Christian era. He ends his account of famous men with Thomas Becket " 'than whom she bore no whiter soul nor one more dear' (Horace, *Sat.* l. v. 41–2) to all good men in the Latin world."

The two other laudatory descriptions of cities written at this period have less detail than Fitz Stephen's. Lucian, in his work in praise of Chester, *De Laude Cestrie*,[106] written in about 1195, gives numerous references to classical authors, especially to Horace, Virgil, Ovid and Seneca, besides citing the Bible and the Fathers[107] — and Geoffrey of Monmouth.[108] The influence of Rome appears in the comparison of the church of St Peter at Chester with St Peter's, Rome.[109] Apparently the work originated as a series of sermons intended to please and edify the citizens of Chester,[110] for it has long, homiletic passages, and many allegories (for example, the two Roman streets meeting in the city center symbolize the cross, the four gates angelic guardians).[111] Nevertheless, Lucian describes the plan of the city and its geographical position.[112] He also describes the city walls, the river Dee with its daily tide, wide sands and busy harbour, frequented by merchants from Spain, Ireland, Aquitaine and Germany, and by fishermen.[113]

The other laudatory description of a city, the account of Angers in Ralph Diceto's *Ymagines Historiarum*,[114] is more straightforward. It is uncertain whether Diceto was himself the author or whether he copied it from some now lost Angevin source.[115] The description of the bridge at Angers is particularly

---

[105] *Ibid.* III. 8–9.

[106] Printed *Liber Luciani de Laude Cestrie*, ed. M. V. Taylor (Lancashire and Cheshire Record Society, LXIV, 1912). For the date of the *De Laude* see *ibid.* pp. 8–10.

[107] See *ibid.* p. 15.

[108] *Ibid.* p. 64.

[109] *Ibid.* p. 52.

[110] See *Ibid.* pp. 19–20.

[111] *Ibid.* pp. 46–47.

[112] *Ibid.* pp. 44, 45, 58.

[113] *Ibid.* p. 46.

[114] Diceto, *Works*, ed. Stubbs, II. 291–292.

[115] The description of Angers also occurs in the *Historia Comitum Andegavensium*; see *Chroniques*

8 A crane, *grus*, from Gerald of Wales, *Topographia Hibernica*, dist. i, cap. xiv.
*(London, British Library, MS Royal 13 B viii, fo. 9)*

9 A swan from a bestiary of *c.* 1200.
*(Oxford, Bodleian Library, MS Ashmole 1511, fo. 71)*

10 Pigeons from a bestiary of *c.* 1120-30.
*(Oxford, Bodleian Library, MS Laud Misc. 247, fo. 161v)*

alpa dicta quod sit dampnata cecitate
perpetua tenebris. Est enim absq; oclis
semp terram fodit; 7 humum egerit. 7 radices
subter frugib; comedit op gri aphala vocant.

11   Hedgehogs from a bestiary of *c.* 1200.
     *(Cambridge, University Library, MS Ii.4.26, fo. 28v)*

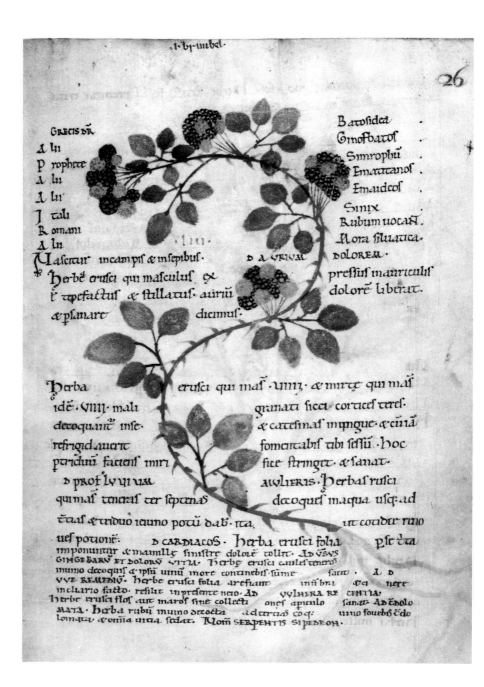

12 A bramble from an early twelfth-century herbal.
  *(Oxford, Bodleian Library, MS Bodley 130, fo. 26)*

erbe simphomace radix alligata infomore. / DINCVINV DOLOREM
mimu dolore tollit.        D PEDVM DOLOREM.
imphomaca alligata pedu dolore tollit. & sup pedes imposita
mire tumore & dolore tollit.        D PECLIHEL I ET
MVLIERVM    DOLOR    E    M . ——
    imphomace sucus mixtus cu croco dab potione.
    mirabile effectu habet.    D OCIHERV DOLORE ET ADPVL
MOHVM VEXATIONEM. Simphomace sucu da bibere. suma ad
miratione sanabit.

Sowethastel

·lxiii·

ascitur secus
mollib; guttis
Herba uipina trita
mirifice;
ac.

flumina aut insertis folus
uspo. Advipe noov.
cu uino & potu data
mox uipu sanat & uentuu disti
LEGES EAM MENSE APR'L·

13   A milk thistle from an early-twelfth century herbal.
   (Oxford, Bodleian Library, MS Bodley 130, fo. 37)

vivid: it had "workshops in little houses (of earth, wood and stones) . . . placed opposite each other and arranged under one almost uniform roof so making the bridge (which is mainly wood in the middle) like a real street, always open to passers-bye but sheltered from the sun."[116]

Diceto also has a passage (probably copied from a lost continental source), on the social customs of the people of Aquitaine, including a description of their cullinary methods. It states, for example, that "the men of Poitou love beef for daily fare. When the pepper and garlic have been mixed together in a mortar, the fresh meat needs as a condiment either the juice of wild apples or that of young vine shoots, or grapes."[117] This interest in social customs, reminiscent of Fitz Stephen's account of the Londoners, is particularly characteristic of Gerald of Wales. But while Diceto and Fitz Stephen concentrated on civilized man, Gerald turned his attention to primitive peoples, describing the customs of the Irish and Welsh in his *Topographia Hibernica*[118] and in the *Descriptio Kambriae*.[119] Ostensibly he wrote about the Irish and the Welsh because he thought writers had neglected them. But he seems also to have wanted to point out the short-comings of civilized life by implicitly contrasting it with the primitive condition.[120] His view of both peoples as barbarians (with consequent vices and virtues) probably owed something to classical literature.

Gerald of Wales collected his information for the *Topographia Hibernica* when he visited Ireland with Prince John in 1185, and for the *Descriptio Kambriae* when he toured Wales with Archbishop Baldwin, who was preaching the crusade, in 1188. Much of what he says about the Irish is based on folk-lore, not fact, but he records some vivid details which are surely authentic. Most of his information about the Welsh seems to be based on objective observation. He says that both

---

*des Comtes d'Anjou*, ed. P. Marchegay and A. Salmon, with an introduction by E. Mabille (Société de l'Histoire de France, 1856, 1871), pp. 336–338. Stubbs suggested that Diceto was the author of the *Historia*; Diceto, *Works*, II. xxiv–xxix. If so, it is likely that Diceto wrote the description. Stubbs also suggested that the description of the customs of the people of Aquitaine (see below), which is not in the *Historia*, was by the same author, whether Diceto or not, as the description of Angers. See *ibid.* II. 293 n.l.

[116] For the bridge see C. Port, *Dictionnaire Historique Géographique et Bibliographique de Maine-et-Loire* (Angers, 1874–1878, 3 vols.), I. 105–106.

[117] *Diceto*. I. 293–294. Unlike the descriptions of food cited by Curtius, *op. cit.* pp. 189–190, this passage appears to be realistic.

[118] Printed *Giraldus*, v. 3–204.

[119] Printed *ibid.* VI. 155–227. Gerald's *Itinerarium Kambriae*, which also has a few first-hand observations, is printed in *ibid.* VI, 3–152.

[120] Such a contrast seems to be implied, for example, in the account of the natural growth of the Irish from their infancy: ". . . fere cuncta naturae relinquuntur. Non in cunabulis aptantur; non fasciis alligantur; non frequentibus in balneis tenera membra vel foventur, vel artis juvamine componuntur. Non enim obstetrices aquae calentis beneficio vel nares erigunt, vel faciem deprimunt, vel tibias extendunt. Sola natura quos edidit artus, praeter artis cujuslibet adminicula, pro sui arbitrio et componit et disponit." And the Irish grow up fine, handsome men. *Ibid.* v. 150. The same criticism of civilized man seems implicit for example in the account of the hospitality of the Welsh. The Welsh feed guests lavishly, but "non ferculis multis, non saporibus et gularum irritamentis coquina gravatur; non mensis, non mappis, non manutergiis, domus ornatur. Naturae magis student quam nitori." *Ibid.* VI. 183.

peoples neglected agriculture, trade, and all productive labour.[121] He describes the primitive clothes of the Irish in realistic terms: they wore close fitting hoods hanging over the shoulders, "of parti-coloured strips sewn together," under which they had rugs instead of cloaks, and breeches often with socks attached to them.[122] The Welsh slept all together, in their day-clothes, a thin cloak or tunic, on a coarse blanket spread on the floor along the side of the room, keeping each other warm, and before they turned over warming themselves by the fire.[123] Gerald describes how the Irish rode, bareback, without boots or spurs, but with a sort of riding crop, and reins which served both as bridle and bit.[124] He appreciated the virtues of these hardy peoples (especially those of the Welsh). The Irish had by nature fine physiques — they needed no human skills to help their growth.[125] They loved leisure and liberty above all else, and were gifted musicians.[126] The Welsh too were very musical,[127] and they were also brave soldiers[128] and most generous to guests (Gerald describes their customs at table in detail) — and they kept their teeth the cleanest in the world (they made them "gleam like ivory by constant rubbing with green hazel and by wiping them with a woollen cloth").[129] Moreover, the *Topographia Hibernica* has lively illustrations in the margins, in pen and colour, of scenes from Irish life and other subjects (Pls. 5, 6, 8).    As these pictures are in the earliest known manuscript of the work (from St Augustine's, Canterbury) it seems likely that the originals were executed by Gerald himself, or at least under his supervision.

Gerald of Wales was a remarkably acute observer of other aspects of the outside world besides people and social anthropology. He also noticed and vividly described antiquities and natural history. His principal motives were objective curiosity and aesthetic appreciation. The former motive probably elicited his description of Stonehenge. Having accepted Geoffrey of Monmouth's statement that Stonehenge had been magically transported from Kildare in Ireland, he proceeds with an eye-witness description. "It is wonderful" he writes "how stones of such huge size were ever collected together and erected in one place, and how equally large stones were so skilfully placed on top of such immensely tall stones; thus they seem to hang suspended, as if in mid-air, appearing to be supported more by the artifice of craftsmen than by the tops of the upright stones."[130]

---

[121] *Ibid.* v. 151–152; vi. 180.

[122] *Ibid.* v. 150.

[123] *Ibid.* vi. 184.

[124] *Ibid.* v. 150.

[125] See above p. 48 n. 120.

[126] *Ibid.* v. 152 *sq.*

[127] *Ibid.* vi. 186 *sq.*

[128] *Ibid.* vi. 180–181.

[129] *Ibid.* vi. 185.

[130] *Ibid.* v. 100–101. Gerald says that the stones were transported from Kildare, where they were known as the Giants' Ring, and that originally they came from Africa. Here Gerald was following Geoffrey of Monmouth, who had also apparently seen Stonehenge; see *Historia Regum Britanniae*, viii. 10–12; ed. Acton Griscom, pp. 409–414. *Cf.* J. S. P. Tatlock, *The Legendary History of Britain, Geoffrey of Monmouth's Historia Regum Britanniae and its early vernacular versions* (California, 1959), pp. 40–43. Geoffrey's view that the stones had been brought to Stonehenge from afar is of course

Moreover Gerald was interested in Roman remains. He comments on the charred walls of the ancient fort at Carmarthan ("the magnificent walls, still partly standing, situated on the noble river Towy"),[131] and describes Roman Caerleon, "where you can still see many remains of its former grandeur; . . . the spacious palaces (which formerly had guilded roofs in the Roman fashion. . .), an enormous tower, remarkable baths, the ruins of temples, and a theatre all enclosed with a fine wall, parts of which still stand." Gerald also remarks on the subterranean structures and the acquaducts, and particularly on the hypocaust system "constructed with wonderful art."[132] His aesthetic motive is well illustrated by his graphic description of an illuminated manuscript he saw in Ireland, probably the Book of Kells.[133]

Moreover, to this period belong the earliest realistic descriptions of animals and birds,[134] for which the ever-curious Gerald of Wales was mainly responsible. He describes, for example, the Irish hare and the habits of the bear,[135] but most remarkable is his descriptions of St Hugh of Lincoln's pet swan:

It was about as much larger than a swan as a swan is than a goose, but in everything else, especially in its colour and whiteness, it closely resembled a swan, except that in addition to its size it did not have the usual swelling and black streak on its beak. Instead that part of its beak was flat and bright yellow in colour, as were also its head and the upper part of its neck.[136]

It is possible to identify Hugh's swan from this description as a whooper swan. Gerald accompanies this description with details about its habits, how "it would fly over the surface of the river, beating the water with its wings, and giving vent to loud cries." Adam of Eynsham, who copied Gerald's account, added some details, notably concerning the swan's affection for St Hugh.[137]

Finally, it should be noted that the occurrence of realistic descriptive writing in twelfth-century England has a counterpart in art. Despite the dominance of Romanesque, a heavily stylized and conventionalized art form, there are examples of realistic pictures. Gerald of Wales, in the *Topographia Hibernica*, was probably responsible not only for the vivid scenes from Irish life, but also for

---

correct (they probably came from the Prescelley mountains in Pembrokeshire); see Stuart Piggott, "The Stonehenge Story" in *Antiquity*, xv (1941), 305–319.

[131] *Giraldus*, vi. 80.

[132] *Ibid*. vi. 55–56.

[133] *Ibid*. v. 123–124. For the identification of the book described by Gerald with the Book of Kells see *The Book of Kells*, ed. E. H. Alton and P. Meyer (Bern, 1950–1951, 3 vols.), iii. 14–16.

[134] William Fitz Stephen's description of the action of horses is probably an example of classical influence and not of realistic observation. He describes the 'rocking-horse' action and the 'lateral trot' action, both of which occur frequently in classical sculpture and numismatics; *Materials for the History of Thomas Becket*, ed. Robertson and Sheppard, iii. 6.

[135] *Giraldus*, v. 57 (cf. *ibid*. v. lxxii–lxxiii); vi. 114–117, respectively. Gerald's knowledge of natural history is fully discussed by U. T. Holmes, "Gerald the Naturalist" in SPECULUM xi (1936), 110–121.

[136] *Giraldus*, vii. 74.

[137] *Life of St Hugh*, ed. Douie and Farmer. i. 105–109.

illustrations of animals, birds and fishes in Ireland. Particularly remarkable is the fairly accurate coloured drawing of a crane (Fig. 5).[138]

Even the Bestiaries and Herbals of the period have a few realistic pictures. Usually an artist faithfully copied the traditional, often fanciful, picture in his exemplar, especially if it was of a creature or plant (such as an elephant or a delphinium[139]) which he had never seen. However, if he knew from personal observation what his subject looked like, he might draw it realistically. Thus there are, for example, realistic pictures of a swan, pigeons, hedgehogs, a bramble and a thistle (Pls. 9–13).[140] These pictures (with the exception of the two plants which could have been drawn from life) were probably drawn from memory and are not accurate in every detail: they are slightly stylized and show a tendency to conflate one species with another. Nevertheless, they demonstrate that some artists, like some writers, had closely observed the world around them.[141]

[138] Illustrating Gerald of Wales' *Topographic Hibernica*, dist.i, cap. xiv. The pronounced tail resembles that of a crane, although the general shape is most like a heron (whose favourite food is the eel), and the colouring (black with white breast and belly, red bill and legs) is that of a black stork. Holmes, *loc. cit.* p. 117, unequivocally identifies the drawing as a black stork. I owe the comments on the birds in this (pl. 8) and the next two plates (9 and 10) to my colleague in the University of Nottingham, Dr. A. K. Kent.

[139] See *The Herbal of Apuleius Barbarus from the early twelfth century Manuscript formerly in the Abbey of Bury St Edmunds*, ed. R. T. Gunther (Roxburghe Club, 1925), pp. xxiv–xxv.

[140] Plate 9, a swan, from a Bestiary of ca. 1200 (Oxford, Bodleian Library, MS. Ashmole 1511, f.71) is a reasonably life-like representation of a mute-swan. However, the beak is not the correct shape or colour and is closer to that of a goose than a swan.

Plate 10, pigeons, from a Bestiary of ca. 1120–1130 (Oxford, Bodleian Library, MS, Laud Misc. 247, f.161[v]); the beak and legs are not correct, but the preening-action of the second from the left, and the landing-action of the second from the right, are very lifelike.

Plate 11, hedgehogs, from a Bestiary of ca. 1200 (Cambridge, University Library, MS. Ii.3.26,f.28[v]); reproduced *The Bestiary, being a Reproduction of the Manuscript Ii.4.26 in the University Library, Cambridge*, ed. M. R. James (Roxburghe Club, 1928).

Plate 12, a bramble, from the early twelfth-century Herbal reproduced by Gunther, *op. cit.* (Oxford, Bodleian Library, MS. Bodley 130, f.26).

Plate 13, a milk thistle, from the same Herbal (f.37). This milk thistle, *Carduus Mariannus*, does not illustrate the text which describes snakeweed: see Gunther, *op. cit.* p. 113.

[141] Brunsdon Yapp, having studied pictures of birds in medieval manuscripts, came to this conclusion: 'Not until the mid-13th century, in Gothic manuscripts, does there appear any attempt at the kind of accurate drawing that might satisfy a modern illustrator . . . There is then a sudden flowering of birds in decoration, which reaches its climax in England in the early years of the 14th century, and soon afterwards ceases even more abruptly than it began.' W. Brunsdon Yapp, *Birds in Medieval Manuscripts* (British Library, 1981), p. 71. This indicates that the twelfth-century examples which I mention are rare. Brunsdon Yapp also points out that the vast majority of the realistic pictures of birds in 13th–early 14th century manuscripts are not found in bestiaries at all, but in other kinds of book, such as bibles and psalters. The artists of pictures in bestiaries were almost always dominated by the traditional bestiary illustrations, much as the authors of the texts relied generally on the authority of the *Physiologus* (probably of the second century A.D.), Pliny, Isidore, the bible, Fathers of the church and the like, and not on personal observation. See *ibid.* 114 and most recently: Xenia Muratova, 'Workshop Methods in English Late Twelfth-Century Illumination and the Production of Luxury Bestiaries' in *Beasts and Birds of the Middle Ages*, ed. W. B. Clark and M. T. McMunn (University of Pennsylvania Press, Philadelphia, 1989), pp. 56–7, and J. B. Friedman, 'Peacocks and Preachers: Analytic Technique in Marcus of Orvieto's *Liber de Moralitatibus*, Vatican lat. MS 5935' in *ibid.* 185–6.

# 8

# The Chronicles of Medieval England
# and Scotland

## *Introduction*

The aim of the following study is to classify and characterise the chronicles of medieval England and, to a lesser extent, of Scotland. Attention is especially paid to their later sections, those dealing with the authors' own times. The subject will be dealt with in seven parts:

1. Definition of the term 'chronicle', and the usage adopted here
2. A brief survey of chronicle writing
3. The provenance of chronicles
4. Motives for writing chronicles
5. The government's use of, and influence on, chronicles
6. Suggested reasons for the decline of the chronicle as an historiographical genre
7. The composition of the 'contemporaneous' sections of chronicles.

## *1. Definition of the term 'chronicle'*

The first step in any attempt to characterise the chronicles of medieval England and Scotland must be to classify them, that is to distinguish them from other kinds of historical writing. This is necessary because the term 'chronicle' has been used so loosely in medieval and modern times that it has lost any precise meaning. Here it will be used only of general, serious historical writings. Therefore, local histories and biographies, such as the 'chronicle of Battle Abbey' and the 'chronicle of Jocelin of Brakelond', will be excluded. Also to be excluded are histories in the romance style, most of which are in French, for example the *Chronique* of Jordan Fantosme. Because their primary purpose was to entertain, they do not share a number of the features typical of chronicles as characterised below.

Chronicles, then, by our definition fall into the category of general, serious history. However, further classification is necessary, because the category itself is composite. It includes both 'histories' and 'chronicles'. The distinction between these two genres was already recognised in classical times,[1] and was well expressed in the late twelfth century by Gervase of Canterbury:

> It is characteristic of history to tell the truth, to persuade those who read or hear it with soft words and elegant phrases and to inform them about the deeds, ways and lives of anyone it truthfully describes; it is an essentially rational study. A chronicle, on the other hand, reckons the years, months and Kalends from the Incarnation of our Lord, briefly tells of the deeds of kings and princes which happened at those times, besides recording any portents, miracles or other events.[2]

Thus histories were in literary form, and, although their contents were expected to be 'true', they were selected in order to suit a theme. They observed chronology, but were not structured by it. Chronicles, on the other hand, were dominated by their chronological structure; a chronicler entered the events of each year under the appropriate year-date. Examples of histories are Eusebius' *Ecclesiastical History*[3] and Bede's *Ecclesiastical History of the English People*.[4] Examples of chronicles are Eusebius' *Chronicle*,[5] and the two chronicles which Bede appended to his two books on time.[6]

However, the two genres of histories and chronicles tended to overlap. A chronicler might write eloquently and at length, revealing his own opinions, so that his work acquired features of a history. Gervase of Canterbury deplored this tendency. Quoting Matthew 23.5, he said: 'They make broad their phylacteries, and enlarge the borders of their garments.'[7] Examples of chroniclers who thus exceeded the limitations of

---

[1] Cicero had distinguished between the early annalists and the later rhetorical historians: *De Oratore*, II, 51-64; cf. *Latin Historians*, ed. T.A. Dorey (London, 1966), pp. xii-xiii.

[2] *The Historical Works of Gervase of Canterbury*, ed. William Stubbs (Rolls Series, 1879-80, 2 vols), i. 87; cited V.H. Galbraith, *Historical Research in Medieval England* (London, 1951), repr. in *idem*, *Kings and Chroniclers* (Hambledon Press, London, 1982), p. 2.

[3] *The Ecclesiastical History*, ed., with an English translation, K. Lake and J.E.L. Oulton (Loeb Classical Library, London, 1949-57, 2 vols).

[4] The standard edition is *Venerabilis Baedae Historia Ecclesiastica gentis Anglorum . . .*, ed. Charles Plummer (Oxford, 1896, 2 vols). A more recent edition, with an English translation, is by Bertram Colgrave and R.A.B. Mynors (Oxford Medieval Texts, 1969).

[5] For St Jerome's Latin translation of Eusebius' *Chronicle* see *Die Chronik des Hieronymus: Hieronymi chronicon*, ed. Rudolph Helm (*Eusebius Werke*, vii, *Die Griechischen Christlichen Schriftsteller des Ersten Jahrhunderts*, xlvii, 24 and 34, Berlin, 1956).

[6] Bede's chronicles, one from the Creation to 703 and the other from the Creation to 725, form the last part of his *De Temporibus* and *De Temporum Ratione* respectively; printed parallel *Monumenta Germaniae Historica, Auctores Antiquissimi*, xiii, *Chronica Minora Saeculi iv-vii*, vol. 3, ed. T. Mommsen (Berlin, 1898), 247-317, 247-327.

[7] *Gervase of Canterbury*, ed. Stubbs, i. 87-8.

their genre are Henry of Huntingdon[8] and Matthew Paris.[9]

Chronicles, therefore, must be differentiated from histories. A further distinction has to be made, between chronicles and annals. The term 'annals' itself is confusing, since a chronicle consists of individual 'annals', an 'annal' being the entry for each year. Used generically, the term 'annals' is usually understood to mean a chronicle with very short yearly entries. The earliest annals written in the Christian West were notes of a line or two made in the margins of Easter Tables, opposite the appropriate years. By process of evolution annals came to be written independently of Easter Tables.[10] The entries might be copied from an earlier work or works, or composed by the author himself fairly soon after the events they record happened. However, the distinction between chronicles and annals defined in this way is blurred. A work might, and often does, start with brief annals and then become prolix, or, which is rarer, *vice versa*. Bernard Guenée adopts another distinction between them.[11] In his view a chronicle is a compilation from various written sources, mainly standard works, while annals are a more or less contemporaneous account of events. But this definition, like the other, has a drawback, because very often a work begins as a compilation, and continues as a contemporary account. It is with the last kind of work, combined chronicle and annals according to Guenée's definition, that this article is concerned, and for convenience they will all be called chronicles.[12]

## 2. Survey of Chronicle Writing in England

The chronicle tradition in England goes back at least to the eighth century, when somewhere in Northumbria Latin annals were added to the

---

[8] *Henrici Archidiaconi Huntendunensis Historia Anglorum*, ed. Thomas Arnold (Rolls Series, 1879).

[9] *Matthaei Parisiensis, Monachi S. Albani, Chronica Majora*, ed. H.R. Luard (Rolls Series, 1872-83, 7 vols).

[10] See R.L. Poole, *Chronicles and Annals* (Oxford, 1926), pp. 5 *et seqq.*; P. Grosjean, 'La date du Colloque de Whitby', Appendix 'Sur les annales anglaises du VIIᵉ siècle jointes à des tables pascales', *Analecta Bollandiana*, lxxviii (1960), 255-60; *The Anglo-Saxon Chronicle*, ed. G.N. Garmonsway (Everyman's Libary, London, 1953, revised ed. 1954), pp. xx-xxii and n. 2 and plate.

[11] Bernard Guenée, *Histoire et Culture Historique dans l'Occident Médiéval* (Paris, 1980), pp. 203-4.

[12] This usage is narrower than that adopted by John Taylor, *The Use of Medieval Chronicles* (Helps for Students of History, no. 70, Historical Association, 1965). For example, he includes in his survey the St Albans' *Gesta Abbatum* (p. 12), a local history, Higden's *Polychronicon (p. 4)*, largely an encyclopaedia, and the works of Langtoft (p. 9) and Froissart (p. 17), both in the romance style. None of these fall within our category.

chronological summary of Bede's *Ecclesiastical History*.[13] But it owed its extraordinary vitality to the Anglo-Saxon Chronicle which, although based up to the early ninth century on now lost Latin annals, was first composed (to 890) in Wessex in the reign of King Alfred.[14] Copies were sent to important churches where they were continued. At this period its history is obscure, but, by the late tenth century, copies were at the Old Minster Winchester, Abingdon, Ripon and either at Evesham, Worcester or York.[15] In the eleventh century Christ Church and St Augustine's, Canterbury, and Peterborough all had copies. Other copies are lost.[16] A few bridged the Norman Conquest; the Peterborough one continued until the accession of Henry II.[17]

Although the Norman Conquest doomed the Anglo-Saxon Chronicle, since English was no longer the language of educated people, its influence survived. Once translated into Latin it could continue in serviceable use in the many monasteries where it had taken root. The task of translation had begun almost at the time of its inception. Asser translated a substantial portion for his *Life of King Alfred*,[18] and Aethelweard the ealdorman did the same for the chronicle which he composed in about 1000.[19] However, the first translation of the whole was apparently made shortly after the Norman Conquest, in the late eleventh century, at Christ

[13] See: *Historia Ecclesiastica*, ed. Plummer, i. 361-3, ii. 345 note; *Chronica Magistri Rogeri de Houedene*, ed. William Stubbs (Rolls Series, 1868-71, 4 vols), i. xxviii-xxx; P.H. Blair, 'Some observations on the "Historia Regum" attributed to Symeon of Durham', *Celt and Saxon*, ed. N.K. Chadwick (Cambridge, 1963), pp. 86-99. See also D.N. Dumville, 'A new chronicle fragment of early British history', *English Historical Review*, lxxxviii (1973), 312-14.

[14] See: *The Anglo-Saxon Chronicle*, ed. D.N. Dumville and Simon Keynes, iv, *MS. B*, ed. Simon Taylor (D.S. Brewer, Cambridge, 1986), p. xi; J. B. Bately, 'Manuscript layout and the Anglo-Saxon Chronicle', *Bulletin of the John Rylands Library*, lxx (1988), 23 and nn.

[15] For the claims of Evesham, Worcester and York see respectively: *Two of the Saxon Chronicles Parallel*, ed. Charles Plummer, on the basis of an edition by J. Earle (Oxford, 1892-9, 2 vols, repr. 1952 with two notes by D. Whitelock), ii. lxxv-lxxvii; *Anglo-Saxon Chronicle*, ed. Garmonsway, p. xxxvii; F.M. Stenton, *Anglo-Saxon England* (3rd edn, Oxford, 1971), p. 681, supported by *The Peterborough Chronicle*, ed. D. Whitelock (Early English Manuscripts in facsimile, iv, Copenhagen, 1954), pp. 29-30. For the continuations in general see Plummer and Earle, *op. cit.*, ii. xxxvii *et seqq.*

[16] Plummer and Earle, *op. cit.*, ii. cxxv-cxxvii and *Anglo-Saxon Chronicle*, ed. Whitelock, pp. xvii-xxi.

[17] *The Peterborough Chronicle, 1070-1154*, ed. Cecily Clark (2nd edn, Oxford, 1970).

[18] *Asser's Life of King Alfred . . .*, ed. W.H. Stevenson (Oxford, 1904; new impression with a contribution by D. Whitelock, 1959), pp. lxxxii-lxxviii, xcix-c, and Simon Keynes and Michael Lapidge, *Alfred the Great: Asser's Life of King Alfred . . .* (London, 1982), pp. 55-6 (for further references see *ibid.*, index under 'Asser: learning of').

[19] *The Chronicle of Æthelweard*, ed., with an English translation, Alistair Campbell (Nelson's Medieval Texts, 1962), pp. xvii-xviii, xxi-xliv *passim*.

Church, Canterbury (BL Cotton MS Domitian A VIII).[20]

The Anglo-Saxon Chronicle bequeathed two things to the post-Conquest period: a fund of information about Anglo-Saxon times, and a historiographical model. The first chronicler to make extensive use of it was apparently the monk of Worcester commonly referred to as Florence,[21] who started the *Chronicon ex Chronicis* in the late eleventh or early twelfth century. For Anglo-Saxon history up to the eighth century Bede was, of course, the Worcester monk's principal authority, but thereafter he relied mainly on the Chronicle; in fact much of his material is little more than a Latin translation. Subsequent chroniclers followed suit in recognising that the Chronicle was a source of basic importance. Moreover, it provided an historiographical model for the writing of annals shortly after the events to be recorded took place, and also provided a starting point for continuation. No doubt its existence encouraged the Worcester monk to compile his chronicle in the first place. (There was also another model, one brought from the continent by Robert Losinga, bishop of Hereford (1079-95), that is the Universal Chronicle by the German, Marianus Scotus.)

At Worcester, therefore, the annalistic tradition was adapted to the needs of the post-Conquest period. Worcester itself became a centre of historiography. Copies of the *Chronicon ex Chronicis*, which was continued at Worcester ultimately to 1140 by a monk called John, soon reached other monasteries. A copy was at Durham probably shortly after 1119,[22] and almost immediately John had completed the annal for 1130 other monasteries received copies. By the end of the twelfth century copies were at, for example, Abingdon, Coventry, Gloucester, Bury St Edmunds and Peterborough.[23] The influence of the Worcester chronicle continued to

---

[20] See N.R. Ker, *Catalogue of Manuscripts containing Anglo-Saxon* (Oxford, 1957), no. 148. The Latin text is edited by F.P. Magoun, jr, 'Annales Domitiani Latini: an Edition', *Mediaeval Studies*, ix (1947), pp. 235-95. For a detailed account of Canterbury as an historiographical centre in the late Anglo-Saxon period and under the Anglo-Normans see D.N. Dumville, 'Some aspects of annalistic writing at Canterbury in the eleventh and early twelfth centuries', *Peritia*, ii (1983), 23-57.

[21] Florence's part in the composition of the Worcester chronicle is problematical. See: *Vita Wulfstani*, ed. R.R. Darlington (Camden Society, third series, xl, 1928), pp. xi-xviii; *idem, Anglo-Norman Historians* (London, 1947), p. 14; Martin Brett, 'John of Worcester and his contemporaries', in *The Writing of History in the Middle Ages, Essays Presented to R.W. Southern*, ed. R.H.C. Davis and J.M. Wallace-Hadrill (Oxford, 1981), p. 104 (and n. 3 for further references); above pp. 116-20, 123. 'Florence' is printed *Florentii Wigorniensis Monachi Chronicon ex Chronicis*, ed. Benjamin Thorpe (English Historical Society, 1848-9, 2 vols, repr. Krau, Vaduz, 1964). Cf. above p. 123 Note.

[22] Hunter Blair, 'Some observations on the *Historia Regum* attributed to Symeon of Durham', pp. 107-10.

[23] See: *The Chronicle of John of Worcester 1118-1140*, ed. J.R.H. Weaver (Anecdota Oxoniensia, 1908), pp. 4-9; Brett, *loc. cit.*, pp. 106-10.

spread in the thirteenth century.[24]

By that time the most important centre of historical writing was St Albans. There, in about 1259, Matthew Paris wrote an abbreviated version of his *Chronica Majora*, the *Flores Historiarum* which was a chronicle from the Creation to 1258. It was continued by another monk of St Albans to 1265. A copy with the continuation went to Westminster abbey where it was further continued to 1307 and then to 1326.[25] From Westminster copies with all or part of the continuation to 1307 soon reached, for example, St Augustine's Canterbury, St Swithun's (as the Old Minster was now called) Winchester, Rochester, Norwich and St Benet of Hulme.[26] Nor was its popularity confined to the Benedictines; the Augustinians of Merton (in Surrey),[27] the Cistercians of Tintern, and the secular canons of St Paul's and also those of St Mary's Southwark, all had copies, which their chroniclers plundered and continued.[28] Moreover, the citizen of London who wrote the *Annales Londonienses* (1194-1316) extracted from the *Flores* to 1306 and continued his chronicle to 1330;[29] the *Flores* thus contributed to the evolution of a new species of chronicle, the London chronicle.

Another historiographical centre in the thirteenth century was Bury St Edmunds. The first recension of its chronicle, by the monk John Taxter, covered the period from the Creation to 1265; it was later continued to 1296 and then to 1301.[30] The recension to 1296 was influential especially

[24] A copy of the Worcester chronicle (or extracts from it) was available at St David's in Wales, in the thirteenth century; see Kathleen Hughes, 'The Welsh Latin chronicles: *Annales Cambriae* and related texts', *Proceedings of the British Academy*, lix (1973), 246.

[25] Matthew Paris's *Flores* and its St Albans and Westminster continuations are printed *Flores Historiarum*, ed. H.R. Luard (Rolls Series, 1890), 3 vols).

[26] Bodleian Library Laud MS 572. See *Flores*, ed. Luard, i. xxxi-xxxiii, xvii-xviii (cf. N.R. Ker, *Medieval Libraries of Great Britain* (2nd ed., London, 1964), p. 201), xxvi-xxvii, xxix, xxii-xxiv, respectively. Variants from the standard Westminster text of the *Flores* in the Rochester version are printed in *Flores*, ed. Luard, iii. 327-8.

[27] For the Merton copy, which apparently preserved an otherwise lost Westminster version of the *Flores*, see below pp. 247-8.

[28] *Ibid.*, i. xxii-xxiv, xxvii-xviii, xxix, respectively. The variants from the standard Westminster text of the *Flores* in the Tintern version are printed in *ibid.*, iii. 328-48.

[29] *Chronicles in the Reigns of Edward I and Edward II*, ed. W. Stubbs (Rolls Series, 1882-3, 2 vols), i. xvii-xviii, and J. Catto, 'Andrew Horn: law and history in fourteenth-century England' *The Writing of History in the Middle Ages*, ed. Davis and Wallace-Hadrill, pp. 367, 375.

[30] The Bury chronicle is printed from 1212, *The Chronicle of Bury St Edmunds*, ed., with an English translation, A. Gransden (Nelson's Medieval Texts, 1964). For discussion of how the contemporary annals were composed see below pp. 226-38 *passim*.

in East Anglia;[31] it was plundered by the chroniclers of Norwich,[32] St Benet of Hulme,[33] Peterborough[34] and Spalding.[35] In the early fourteenth century much of it was copied by the chronicler of St John's, Colchester,[36] and by the middle of that century an abstract was with the Grey Friars of Babwell, near Bury St Edmunds, which later passed to the Grey Friars of Lynn.[37] Although only exceptionally did the influence of the Bury chronicle spread outside eastern England, it was known to a chronicler in Wales, probably a monk of the Cistercian abbey of Whitland, in the late thirteenth century,[38] and in the late fourteenth century a copy of 'Taxter' was in the Augustinian friary in York.[39]

The thirteenth century was the heyday of the monastic chronicle, when, as will be seen, chronicles fulfilled an important record function. Most monasteries, besides those already mentioned, kept chronicles; for example, the Benedictine houses of Burton,[40] Tewkesbury,[41] Battle,[42] St Swithun's and Hyde abbey in Winchester,[43] and Worcester,[44] and the

---

[31] For the dissemination of the Bury chronicle see below pp. 226-35 *passim*, 241-3. A similar centre of chronicle writing was St Swithun's Winchester. See N. Denholm-Young, 'The Winchester-Hyde chronicle', *English Historical Review*, xlix (1934, repr. in *idem*, Collected Papers on Medieval Subjects* (Oxford, 1946)), 85-93, and see below n. 43, pp. 211 and n. 64, 225 and n. 122, 235 and n. 184.

[32] See *Bartholomaei de Cotton Monachi Norwicensis Historia Anglicana 449-1298*, ed. H.R. Luard (Rolls Series, 1859), pp. lii-lviii.

[33] *Chronica Johannis de Oxenedes*, ed. Henry Ellis (Rolls Series, 1859).

[34] The Peterborough version (Corpus Christi College, Cambridge, MS 92) of the Bury chronicle, which covers the years from 1152-1294 and is a continuation of the chronicle of 'Florence' and John of Worcester, is printed in *Chronicon ex Chronicis*, ed. Thorpe ii. Cf. below pp. 228, 237, 238.

[35] Printed in Joseph Sparke, *Historiae Anglicanae Scriptores Varii* (London, 1723, 2 vols), pp. 1-137, and reprinted as *Chronicon Angliae Petriburgense*, ed. J.A. Giles (Caxton Society, 1845). Cf. Felix Liebermann, 'Ueber Ostenglische Geschichtsquellen', *Neues Archiv*, xviii (1892), 235-45.

[36] The Colchester annals are described and printed in Felix Liebermann, *Ungedruckte Anglo-Normannische Geschichtsquellen* (Strasburg, 1879), pp. 158-65.

[37] See below p. 279-80.

[38] Hughes, *loc. cit.*, pp. 247-9.

[39] *Bury Chronicle*, ed. Gransden, pp. xxxvii-xxxviii.

[40] A.D. 1004-1262, printed in *Annales Monastici*, ed. H.R. Luard (Rolls Series, 1864-9, 5 vols), i. 183-500.

[41] A.D. 1066-1262, printed in *ibid.*, i. 43-170. For another chronicle, 1258-1263, copied at Tewkesbury but not necessarily composed there, see below p. 216 n. 83.

[42] Brutus to 1264 (continued to 1286), mainly unpublished. Described and annals 1258-65 printed in Charles Bémont, *Simon de Montfort Comte de Leicester* (Paris, 1884, repr. Geneva, 1976), pp. xiv-xv, 373-80.

[43] The chronicles of these two houses are closely related. A version, A.D. 519-1277, is printed in *Ann. Mon.*, ii. 3-125. Cf. Denholm-Young, 'Winchester-Hyde chronicle', pp. 86-93.

[44] Incarnation-1308; printed in *Ann. Mon.*, iv. 355-560. Cf. Denholm-Young, *loc. cit.*, p. 88, and below p. 208 and n. 55.

Cistercian abbeys of Margam and Waverley, and Melrose in southern Scotland.[45] Similarly, chronicles were kept by the Dominican priory of Dunstable and the Augustinian abbey of Osney.[46] These chronicles, with few exceptions, end late in Henry III's reign or early in Edward I's. In the fourteenth century the monks' near monopoly of chronicle writing was increasingly challenged by secular clerks and then by laymen. Nearly all the chroniclers belonging to these classes were Londoners; men such as Adam of Murimuth, a prebendary of St Paul's,[47] and Robert of Avesbury, registrar at the court of the archbishop of Canterbury at Lambeth,[48] besides, of course, the authors of the London chronicles proper.[49] The most popular of all fourteenth-century chronicles were the *Brut* chronicles, which apparently originated in the reign of Edward I; probably they too were by secular clerks, and written in London.[50]

The monastic tradition of chronicle writing enjoyed its last period of vitality in Richard II's reign. Indeed, at St Albans the revival lasted well into the fifteenth century. There Thomas Walsingham, the last great St Albans' chronicler, brought Matthew Paris' *Chronica Majora* up to date.[51] However, in the fifteenth century the writing of chronicles became primarily an activity of secular clerks and laymen. They managed to keep the chronicle tradition alive because they accommodated it to the rise of

[45]  The Margam chronicle (1066-1232) and the Waverley chronicle (Incarnation-1291) are printed in *Ann. Mon.*, i, 3-40, ii. 129-411. The Melrose chronicle, A.D. 731-1275, is edited in facsimile by A.O. and M.O. Anderson (limited edn, London, 1936); see below Plate V.

[46]  The Dunstable chronicle (Incarnation-1297) and Osney chronicle (A.D. 601-1297) are printed in *Ann. Mon.*, iii. 3-408, iv. 3-352. For the Dunstable chronicle see below pp. 226, 237.

[47]  Printed in *Adae Murimuth Continuatio Chronicarum. Robertus de Avesbury De Gestis Mirabilibus Regis Edwardi Tertii*, ed. E. Maunde Thompson (Rolls Series, 1889), pp. 3-219.

[48]  Printed in *ibid.*, pp. 279-471. For what is known about Avesbury's life see: *ibid.*, pp. xxii-xxiii; C.L. Lethbridge, 'Robert de Avesbury', *English Historical Review*, xxii (1907), 292.

[49]  The earliest London chronicle in print is the *Cronica Maiorum et Vicecomitum Londoniarum*, probably by Arnold Fitz Thedmar, an alderman; printed in *De Antiquis Legibus Liber*, ed. Thomas Stapleton (Camden Society, original series, xxxiv 1846), pp. 1-77. The author of the *Annales Londonienses* may well have been Andrew Horn, fishmonger, alderman and chamberlain of London (see above, p. 204 and n. 29). See also, with further references, A. Gransden, *Historical Writing in England*, [i], *c. 500-c. 1307* (London, 1974), pp. 509-17 and nn., and, for the fifteenth-century versions, below p. 207 n. 52.

[50]  Printed *The Brut or the Chronicles of England*, ed. F.W.D. Brie (Early English Text Society, cxxxi, cxxxvi, 1906, 1908, 2 vols, repr. 1960); cf. *idem, Geschichte und Quellen der mittelenglischen Prosachronik the Brute of England oder the Chronicles of England* (Marburg, 1905), and John Taylor, *English Historical Literature in the Fourteenth Century* (Oxford, 1987), Chapter 6.

[51]  For Thomas Walsingham and the St Albans' tradition of historiography see: *The St Albans Chronicle 1406-1420*, ed. V.H. Galbraith (Oxford, 1937), pp. xxvii-lxxi; Gransden, *Historical Writing*, [i], Chapter 16; *idem, Historical Writing in England, ii, c. 1307 to the Early Sixteenth Century* (London, 1982), ii, Chapter 5; Taylor, *English Historical Literature*, pp. 59-78.

the vernacular. In the same way as the tradition survived the Norman Conquest because the Anglo-Saxon Chronicle was translated into Latin, so now it survived because chroniclers wrote in English. The earliest versions of the *Brut* chronicle are in French, but by the late fourteenth century they were being composed in English. So too were the closely related London chronicles, which proliferated in the fifteenth century and were particularly favoured by the merchant class.[52]

The longest of the *Brut* chronicles ends in 1475, and the longest London ones in the early sixteenth century. Nevertheless, the influence of the London chronicles survived in the Tudor period. Some of them supplied Robert Fabyan with information for his *New Chronicles of England and France* (completed in 1504), which preserved many of their characteristics, notably, besides the chronological structure, the interest in, and knowledge of, the City of London.[53] Furthermore, the chronicle of the Grey Friars of Newgate, and its continuation from the friary's dissolution in 1538 to the accession of Queen Mary, are virtually a London chronicle.[54] The influence of the London chronicles is very evident in the works of the Tudor historians Edward Hall, John Stow and Raphael Holinshed. They used the London chronicles as sources, and retained the chronological structure. John Stow's *Chronicles of England* (1580) was in fact a re-edition of the old London chronicles; Stow borrowed from them, and when they came to an end he added new annals up to his own day. The subsequent fate of the chronicle tradition will be discussed in Part 6 below.

## 3. The Provenance of Chronicles

Monasteries, especially Benedictine ones, were the homes *par excellence* of chronicle writing. Their chronicles are more numerous, and on average of better quality, than those of other institutions or of individual non-monastic authors. They offered chroniclers from generation to generation a combination of facilities. Their libraries contained standard histories and chronicles, which could serve as historiographical models. Such books also provided information necessary for the compilation of early history. Although monastic archives consisted principally of the house's charters and other business documents, a few 'public records' were

---

[52] For the fifteenth-century London chronicles see: C.L. Kingsford, *Chronicles of London* (Oxford, 1905); *The Great Chronicle of London*, ed. A.H. Thomas and I.D. Thornley (London, privately printed, 1938); with further references, Gransden, *Historical Writing in England*, ii 227-48 and nn.

[53] *The New Chronicles of England and France by Robert Fabyan . . .*, ed. Henry Ellis (London, 1811).

[54] A.D. 1189-1556, printed in *Monumenta Franciscana*, ed. J.S. Brewer and Richard Howlett (Rolls Series, 1858, 1882, 2 vols), ii. 143-260.

usually stored with them. The archives themselves impressed on monks the virtue of record-keeping, besides supplying material for the history of the not-so-distant past, and for recent and contemporary history. Moreover, the monastic chronicler was well placed to hear news by word of mouth. For local affairs he had the benefit of his house's position as a landowner, since this entailed close contact with tenants and neighbours. For national affairs he could question visitors to the guest house.

Once a tradition of chronicle writing was established in a monastery it tended to be self-perpetuating; one chronicle provided a model, and also the foundation stone, or at least a quarry, for another. The tradition at Worcester, for example, may well have begun as early as the late tenth century, and lasted until towards the end of the thirteenth,[55] while that at St Albans lasted from the early thirteenth century until the early fifteenth.

Other institutions, notably secular cathedrals and the City of London, could supply chroniclers with facilities similar to those enjoyed by monastic chroniclers, but to a lesser extent. In fact, no secular cathedral except St Paul's in London established a flourishing chronicle tradition.[56] Although London chronicles proliferated in the late Middle Ages, nearly all were apparently individual compositions – few can be proved to have been officially sponsored by the Guildhall.[57] They lacked, therefore, stable corporate backing, and, indeed, their quality does not compare with that of the best monastic chronicles.

## 4. Motives for Writing Chronicles

In a few cases there is evidence suggesting that a chronicle was written as a result of a direct commission, but usually the reasons are more obscure and less simple. One or other of a variety of reasons, or several, might

[55] For Worcester's claim to have been the home of one version (D) of the Anglo-Saxon Chronicle see above, p. 202. and n. 15. For versions of the Anglo-Saxon Chronicle which were at Worcester after the Norman Conquest but are now lost see *Anglo-Saxon Chronicle*, ed. Whitelock, p. xx. For post-Conquest chronicles written at Worcester see above pp. 203 and nn. 21, 23, 24, 205 and n. 44.

[56] Two chronicles survive from St Paul's, written in the last half of the thirteenth century and in the first half of the fourteenth (other St Pauls' chronicles may well be lost): *Annales Sancti Pauli* (1064-1274), described and extracts printed by F. Liebermann, *Monumenta Germaniae Historica, Scriptores*, xxviii (Hannover, 1888), pp. 548-51; *Annales Paulini* (to 1341, printed in *Chronicles of the Reigns of Edward I and Edward II*, ed. William Stubbs (Rolls Series, 1882-3, 2 vols). Murimuth (d.? 1347) was a prebendary of St Paul's (above p. 206). Earlier, the prolific chronicler, Ralph Diceto, was dean of St Paul's (1180/1-1201); see *Radulphi de Diceto Lundoniensis Opera Historica*, ed. W. Stubbs (Rolls Series, 1876, 2 vols).

[57] Some of the London chronicles were quasi-official productions, that is, they were by authors who held office in the City and used City records. But there is no evidence that any was actually commissioned by the mayor and corporation; see: D.C. Cox, 'The French chronicle of London', *Medium Aevum*, xlv (1976), 207; Gransden, *Historical Writing*, [i], 511-14; *ibid.*, ii, 71, 230-3, 242.

encourage or cause someone to write a chronicle. Therefore, for the sake of clarity, the subject will be discussed from a number of angles in two main sections, each with sub-sections, first, 'internal' incentives, and, secondly, 'external' ones.

### i. 'Internal' incentives

These comprise the chronicler's spontaneous motives, not those he might adopt on account of external circumstances and pressures. However, these motives were not peculiar to the chronicler as an individual, but as a member of the community to which he belonged, whether a monastery, the City of London, or whatever.

#### (a) RELIGIOUS PURPOSE

It is commonly held that chronicles were intended to be edifying and serve a religious purpose, to strengthen Christian faith and improve behaviour.[58] It is true that any account of past events could be seen as demonstrating the workings of God's providence on earth. However, the edificatory element in chronicles has been exaggerated, perhaps as a result of applying to 'chronicles' a characteristic feature of 'histories' and even more of hagiographies. In general only those chroniclers who 'broaden their phylacteries', writers such as Henry of Huntingdon and Matthew Paris, point out and dwell upon examples of divine retribution and the like. Bede had adopted for his two World Chronicles the periodisation of the Seven Ages, symbolising the seven days of the Creation and the seven stages of a man's life.[59] Matthew Paris adopted these divisions for his *Chronica Majora*, but he was exceptional in this respect (as in many others). Most chroniclers were satisfied with the simple annalistic arrangement. Although Robert Fabyan divided his chronicle into seven books, these symbolised the Seven Joys of the Virgin Mary, not the days of the Creation.[60] And although Ranulph Higden used the divisions of the Seven Ages for his *Polychronicon*,[61] the latter is not a 'chronicle' by our definition.

#### (b) INFORMATORY PURPOSE

There can be no doubt that one of a chronicler's main motives was to satisfy man's natural curiosity about the past and his desire for contemporary news; a chronicle was both a history book and a newspaper.

---

[58] See e.g. R.G. Collingwood, *The Idea of History* (Oxford, 1946), pp. 52-6 *passim*, and J.R. Hale, *The Evolution of British Historiography* (London, 1967), pp. 9-10.

[59] The concept of the Seven Ages derived from St Augustine, *De Civ. Dei*, xxii, 30. See: Auguste Luneau, *L'Histoire du salut chez les Pères de l'Énglise* (Paris, 1964), pp. 285 *et seqq.*, 352 *et seqq.*; C.A. Patrides, *The Grand Design of God* (London, 1972), pp. 18-22 and nn.

[60] See Gransden, *Historical Writing in England*, ii. 246 and n. 175.

[61] See John Taylor, *The Universal Chronicle of Ranulf Higden* (Oxford, 1966), p. 39.

It is noticeable that newsworthy events, such as the Viking invasions during the Anglo-Saxon period, the Barons' War in Henry III's reign, the Peasants' Revolt of 1381 and the deposition of Richard II, were all accompanied by a spate of chronicle writing, and may in some instances have provided the initial incentive to composition.[62] The chronicler's immediate audience, his own community, might well have encouraged him to write simply because he presented information in an attractive form; his chronological, episodic narrative suited medieval taste.

Whatever sentiments and opinions a chronicler expressed were bound to please his fellow monks, since in normal circumstances they would have been their own. Although undoubtedly monks of a community might be bitterly divided concerning internal matters, it is unlikely that they often were about national politics and other external affairs. Their strong sense of corporate identity and their communal self-interest must have militated against divergence in attitude, and (as should become apparent in the next section) a chronicler was his community's mouthpiece. The fact that nearly all the thirteenth-century chronicles share a common outlook, makes it fair to conclude that the predominant element in the total monastic population also did so; one result of this would have been that the information purveyed in the chronicle of one house would have been congenial to monks of another.

### (c) CHRONICLES AS RECORDS

Besides serving a general, informatory purpose, chronicles had particular, local interest and utility. A chronicler's concern for his own monastery, or its equivalent, tended to override all other considerations. He fitted the history of his own institution into the framework of general history, which gave the chronicle additional interest to his audience. Moreover, it was useful to have local history in such a context. For example, a monastery's comparative antiquity might be demonstrated in this way, which would enhance its prestige. More specifically, a chronicle with notices of a community's acquisition of property and privileges and of its important lawsuits, perhaps including the citation *in extenso* of relevant documents, could serve as a business record.

There is no doubt that often an important motive for composition was to provide a useful record. The record element is clear in many monastic chronicles and also in the fifteenth century London ones. It is especially characteristic of the monastic chronicles of the thirteenth century. As records, chronicles had an advantage over cartularies or registers; information and documents in them were in strictly chronological order. This was no small advantage especially in the thirteenth century when the

---

[62] For the suggestion that the baronial opposition to Henry III, the Peasants' Revolt and Richard II's deposition prompted the writing of chronicles see: Gransden, *Historical Writing*, [i]. 407; *ibid.*, ii. 142, 162-3.

monasteries were proliferating and accumulating innumerable documents, but when the organisation of archives was in its infancy.[63] It was becoming increasingly difficult to find a specific document; but if its date were known, there was at least a chance of finding it in a chronicle.

Although the thirteenth-century monastic chronicle, like other chronicles, was a literary production and usually seems to have been kept in the monastic library, it is best regarded as a product of the record-keeping mentality. It was apparently an 'official' production in the same way as cartularies and registers were. This is implied by the passage in the prologue of the Winchester/Worcester chronicle which describes how contemporaneous annals should be written.[64] Having specified that current news should be noted in plummet on a schedule of loose leaves attached to the end of the chronicle, the author proceeds:

> At the end of each year let he who is ordered, not just anyone who likes, record for posterity what he thinks best, entering it briefly at the end of the book.

This shows that in this instance at least a monastic superior commissioned the chronicler. It also shows that a chronicle might be by more than one monk (the same passage later mentions that a chronicle 'was composed by various people'). Thus chronicles were corporate productions. Most are anonymous; only the more sophisticated ones have names attached. Their anonymity, however, is of little importance since the resources which a chronicler used and, in normal circumstances, the views he expressed (as I have argued above) must surely have been those of his community, at least so far as they related to national affairs.

*ii. 'External' incentives*

Influences from outside might impinge on any chronicler, whether monk, secular clerk or layman, and cause or encourage him to write. He might receive a commission from the government or from an individual, or simply intend to please a patron, or he might be inspired by patriotism. These possibilities will be considered in turn.

---

[63] See M.T. Clanchy, *From Memory to Written Record* (London, 1979), pp. 122-47 (esp. pp. 123, 139, 143, 147).

[64] The passage is printed from the Worcester chronicle, which copied it from a lost Winchester chronicle (Denholm-Young, *op. cit.*, p. 88), in *Annales Monastici*, ed. Luard, iv. 355. It is cited by V.H. Galbraith (who ascribes it to the Worcester chronicler), 'The St. Edmundsbury chronicle, 1296-1301', *English Historical Review*, lviii (1943), 53; cf. C.R. Cheney, 'The making of the Dunstable Annals, A.D. 1233 to 1242', in *idem, Medieval Texts and Studies* (Oxford, 1973, first publ. in *Essays in Medieval History presented to Bertie Wilkinson*, ed. T.A. Sandquist and M.R. Powicke (Toronto, 1969)), p. 228. For the light which the passage throws on the compilation of the contemporary annals of a chronicle see below p. 235 and n. 184 (for the text itself).

## (a) ROYAL AND GOVERNMENT SPONSORSHIP

There was no tradition of official, in the sense of government sponsored, historiography in medieval England. Not one chronicle explicitly acknowledges commission by the king. However, the content and tone of some chronicles provide evidence, convincing in some cases, that they were official.

A case can be made for regarding the Anglo-Saxon Chronicle to 890 as an official history. If it was, it would be the earliest surviving English example.[65] It may well have owed its inception to someone at the court of King Alfred, if not to the king himself. Since it is in Old English, it could well have been a product of Alfred's policy of promoting the vernacular as a written language. His intention was to raise the standard of education, primarily of the clergy, but also of thegns. The Chronicle demonstrates the rise of the West Saxon dynasty and of Alfred's achievements, and at the same time relates the history of the English people as a whole. Copies of the Chronicle were sent to important churches for preservation and continuation, but the various local versions seem to have retained some connections with the royal court. Apparently, indeed, the Chronicle was continued at Edward the Elder's court; a version survives which is strongly biased in Edward's favour.[66] Even those chroniclers composing continuations locally received common instalments from some centre, probably one connected with court of the kings of Wessex at least for the earlier periods, for the years 892-924, 925-975 and 983 1018.[67]

After the Norman Conquest very few historical works were written which can be regarded as official. Nor do any of the most obvious examples, all of them fifteenth-century, fall within our definition of

[65] Plummer and Earle, *Two of the Saxon Chronicles Parallel*, ii.civ, take the view that King Alfred himsef wrote or commissioned the Chronicle, R.H.C. Davis, 'Alfred the Great: propaganda and truth', *History*, lvi (1971), 173-7, considered that its purpose was to rally support for Alfred in his struggle against the Vikings, even by distorting facts in Alfred's favour. Dorothy Whitelock, however, argues strongly against this opinion; D. Whitelock, *The Importance of the Battle of Edington, A.D. 878* (lecture to the Annual meeting of the Friends of Edington Priory Church, 1977, Westbury, Wilts.), pp. 1-4. Janet Bately supports her view; J.B. Bately, 'The compilation of the Anglo-Saxon chronicle, 60 BC to AD 890', pp. 127 and n. 3, 128. For a balanced judgement see Keynes and Lapidge, *Alfred the Great*, pp. 39-41.

[66] For the Edwardian version of the Anglo-Saxon Chronicle see *The Chronicle of Æthelweard*, ed., with an English translation, Alistair Campbell (Nelson's Medieval Texts, 1962), pp. xxviii-xxix.

[67] See Plummer and Earle, *op. cit.*, ii. cxiv-cxxii, and *The Battle of Brunanburh*, ed. Alistair Campbell, (London, 1938), pp. 1-7, 34-6. For the idiosyncratic character of the annals for Ethelred II's reign (979-1016) in the Chronicle, which were compiled *en bloc* after his death, see Simon Keynes, 'The declining reputation of King Aethelred the Unready', in *Ethelred the Unready: Papers from the Millenary Conference*, ed. David Hill (British Archaeological Report, British Series, lix, 1978), pp. 229-36.

'chronicle'.[68] They are the *Gesta Henrici Quinti*,[69] John Capgrave's *Liber de Illustribus Henricis*,[70] and the two propaganda tracts of Edward IV's reign, the *Chronicle of the Rebellion in Lincolnshire* and the *Historie of the Arrivall of Edward IV in England and the Finall Recoverye of his Kingdomes from Henry VI, 1471*.[71]

Four other works approach nearer to our 'chronicle' classification. They are all arranged in chronological order, in annals, but on the other hand their last annals were not apparently composed contemporaneously with the events recorded; rather they seem to have been written *en bloc* retrospectively, though soon after the date of the concluding annal. The two earliest, the so-called 'Merton' *Flores Historiarum* (to 1306) and its continuation (to 1326) by Robert of Reading, were written in Westminster abbey.[72] It appears, indeed, that in the early fourteenth century the monks of Westminster were writing official history for the kings of England. If so, for this brief period they can be compared with the monks of St Denis, in so far as the latter throughout the Middle Ages composed the official history of the kings of France. Westminster stood in similar relation to the kings of England as St Denis to the kings of France; the king was the abbey's patron, and the abbey was the scene of coronations, a royal mausoleum and situated close to the seat of government.

The fulsome terms used by the 'Merton' *Flores* to praise Edward I are best explained by assuming that it was written to please king and court. Perhaps it was intended for Edward I himself. However, the fact that the account of each reign, from King John's to Edward I's, is prefaced by a picture of the respective king in full regalia sitting on the coronation throne, and that the series ends with a similar but rather larger picture of

---

[68] Earlier, in Richard I's reign, a history in monograph form was written in favour of the king's opponents, the Appellants; *Historia sive Narracio de Modo et Forma Mirabilis Parliamenti apud Westmonasterium Anno Domini Millesimo CCCLXXXCI ... Thomas Favent Clericum indictata*, ed. May McKisack (Camden Miscellany, xiv, 1926), pp vi-viii, 1-27.

[69] Printed *Gesta Henrici Quinti*, ed. F. Taylor and J.S. Roskell (Oxford, 1975). For the *Gesta*'s purpose of promoting the French war see *ibid.*, pp. xxiii-xxviii.

[70] Printed *Johannis Capgrave Liber de Illustribus Henricis*, ed. F.C. Hingeston (Rolls Series, 1858).

[71] Printed *Chronicle of the Rebellion in Lincolnshire, 1470*, ed. J.G. Nichols (Camden Miscellany, i, 1847), and *Historie of the Arrivall of Edward IV in England and the Finall Recoverye of his Kingdomes from Henry VI, A.D. M.CCCC.LXXI*, ed. John Bruce (Camden Society, original series, i, 1838). For these works as official histories see Gransden, *Historical Writing*, ii. 261-5, and *idem*, 'Politics and historiography during the Wars of the Roses', *Medieval Historical Writing in the Christian and Islamic Worlds*, ed. D.O. Morgan (School of Oriental and African Studies, University of London, 1982), pp. 128-31.

[72] These continuations of the *Flores* are discussed below pp. 245-65. The version of the *Flores* eulogizing Edward I is preserved in a copy made for Merton priory; the manuscript is described and the variants from the standard version are printed in *Flores Historiarum*, ed. H.R. Luard (Rolls Series, 1890, 3 vols), i. xv-xvii, iii. 239-327. Robert of Reading's chronicle is printed in *ibid.*, iii. 137-235.

Edward II,[73] suggests the possibility that the 'Merton' *Flores* was written for presentation to Edward II, perhaps on the occasion of his coronation. Robert of Reading, writing about Edward II's reign, also produced a strongly biased narrative in highly coloured prose. In his case the bias was not in favour of the king, but against him. His consistent and eloquent vilification of Edward II indicates that he wrote for Queen Isabella and Roger Mortimer, to justify their seizure of power and Edward's deposition.

The two other historical works which may be official are Robert of Avesbury's *De Gestis Mirabilibus Edwardi Tertii* and Thomas Walsingham's *Ypodigma Neustriae*. Avesbury eulogises Edward III, especially as a hero of chivalry,[74] and is at pains to justify the French war and Edward's claim to overlordship of Scotland.[75] His subject-matter, therefore, suggests the possibility that he wrote for the king. It is not inconceivable that the king commissioned him to write, since Avesbury was a well-educated Londoner (the fact that he gives details about the riot in Oxford in 1355 suggests that he had studied there).[76] Walsingham explicitly dedicates the *Ypodigma* to Henry V in the prologue, and states that his intention is to provide the king with a history of Normandy, to justify the Norman campaigns.[77] Again, it is not impossible that Henry V commissioned the work. Walsingham lived within fifteen miles of London and was a chronicler of wide reputation. Moreover, after Henry Bolingbroke's coup of 1399 he wrote in the Lancastrian interest, including in his narrative propagandist material issued by the new regime.[78] Nevertheless, too much weight should not be attached to the dedication as evidence that Henry V commissioned the *Ypodigma* or even that it was intended for his eyes. Such a dedication was a literary commonplace. The practice of dedicating a work to a famous person began in ancient times, and flourished throughout the Middle Ages.[79] The suggestion that the

[73] The picture of the coronation of Henry III and that of Edward I are reproduced Pls 28, 29.

[74] See e.g. *Avesbury*, ed. Thompson (above p. 206 n. 48), pp. 285, 390-1, 409-10, 413, 451, 455.

[75] *Ibid.*, pp. 286-97, 302-3, 339.

[76] *Avesbury*, pp. 421-3, noticed H. Rashdall, *The Universities of Europe in the Middle Ages*, ed. F.M. Powicke and A.B. Emden (Oxford, 1936, 3 vols), iii. 98 n. 2. For the riot see *The History of the University of Oxford*, ed. J.I. Catto (Oxford, 1984), p. 167.

[77] *Ypodigma Neustriae a Thoma Walsingham*, ed. H.T. Riley (Rolls Series, 1876), pp. x, 3-5.

[78] See: Gransden, *Historical Writing*, ii. 139, 140 and nn. 159, 161, 141; G.B. Stow, jr, 'Richard II in Thomas Walsingham's chronicles', *Speculum*, lix (1984), 91-8.

[79] See: Tore Janson, *Latin Prose Prefaces* (Acta Universitatis Stockholmiensis. Studia Latina Stockholmiensia XIII, Stockholm etc., 1964), pp. 95, 116-45 *passim*; Gertrud Simon, 'Untersuchungen zur Topik der Widmungsbriefe Mittelalterlicher Geschichtsschreiber bis zum Ende des 12. Jahrhunderts', *Archiv für Diplomatik*, iv (1958), 54-63 *passim*; *ibid.*, v-vi (1959-60), 136-46; D.W.T.C. Vessey, 'William of Tyre and the art of historiography', *Mediaeval Studies*, xxxv (1973), 436-8. See above pp. 125, 127, 129.

dedication may be no more than a conventional flourish, receives some support from the fact that the *Ypodigma* soon abandons the history of Normandy, and concentrates on that of England.

*(b) PATRONAGE*

A few chronicles were written to please a patron, perhaps even in response to a commission. Some monasteries had individual patrons, and all had benefactors. The monks were grateful to them for past benefits and hoped for future ones. They also needed their protection, and that of any powerful figure, especially in troubled times. Patronage was even more important for secular clerks and laymen than for monks. The same considerations weighed with them, and in addition they needed the help of patrons for advancement in their careers. Historiography provided a means of expressing gratitude and currying favour. Any historical work which touched on the activities of the patron was biased towards him and tended to reflect his viewpoint; the same applied to its treatment of his relatives. (Often, of course, authors writing for patrons did not adopt the chronicle mode; they preferred to write history in verse, in the romance style.)[80]

As in the case of official chronicles, explicit evidence of commission by individual patrons is lacking. Again we have to rely on the content and tone of the work. It is impossible to be certain whether the bias in a chronicle implies that it was actually commissioned by a patron, or merely reflects the chronicler's respect for him, accompanied perhaps by the desire to cultivate his good graces. A few examples may be cited of chronicles which were at least strongly influenced by patronage. During the anarchy of Stephen's reign Malmesbury abbey fell within Robert of Gloucester's orbit. William of Malmesbury dedicated the *Historia Novella* to Earl Robert;[81] it is slanted in his favour and includes much eulogy of him.[82] None of the thirteenth-century chronicles shows convincing signs

---

[80] Examples of verse histories for patrons are: *L'Histoire de Guillaume le Maréchal*, ed., with an abridged translation into modern French, Paul Meyer (Société de l'Histoire de France, 1891-1901, 3 vols), commissioned by the Marshal's son, William, fifth earl of Pembroke (1219-31); *The Metrical Chronicle of Robert of Gloucester*, ed. W.A. Wright (Rolls Series, 1887, 2 vols) (part of the text 1262-4 is also in *Early Middle English Verse and Prose*, ed. J.A.W. Bennett and G.V. Smithers (2nd edn, Oxford, 1968), pp. 158-64, 394-53 and see below), perhaps written for Sir Warin of Bassingbourn (see, with citations from Wright, rendered in modern English, of passages relating to Sir Warin, *Warin of Bassingbourn fortified his Manor*, no author or date, ?1982, Cam. d. 982.5 in Cambridge University Library, and Gransden, *Historical Writing*, [i], 436); *The Chronicle of John Hardyng*, ed. Henry Ellis (London, 1812, repr. 1974), written to please various patrons (see C.L. Kingsford, 'The first version of Hardyng's chronicle', *English Historical Review*, xxvii (1912), 465 *et seqq.*, and Gransden, *op. cit.*, ii. 274-82 *passim*.
[81] See *The Historia Novella by William of Malmesbury*, ed., with an English translation, K.R. Potter (Nelson's Medieval Texts, 1955).
[82] *Ibid., passim* (esp. pp. 64-7).

that it was written as a result of patronage.[83] However, examples survive from the fourteenth century.

It is likely that the secular clerk who wrote the French *Brut* to 1333 had some connection with the house of Lancaster; this would account for his Lancastrian bias, which appears especially in the fulsome praise of Thomas of Lancaster.[84] The principal patron of Geoffrey le Baker (*fl.* 1350) was Sir Thomas de la More, but Baker's sympathetic interest in, and knowledge of, Humphrey, earl of Hereford, and other evidence indicate that he also had a Bohun patron.[85] In Richard II's reign, Henry Knighton's hostility to king and government was no doubt partly because the earls and dukes of Lancaster were patrons of his abbey, St Mary's in the Meadows, Leicester.[86] Adam of Usk (*fl.* 1352-*c.* 1421) was another Lancastrian partisan, partly no doubt because he wrote under the patronage of the earl of March and Archbishop Thomas Arundel.[87] Conversely, it may well be that the Westminster chronicler gives a relatively favourable portrait of Richard II during the last decade of his rule because the king, the abbey's patron, was on good terms with the monks at that time.[88]

*(c) PATRIOTISM*

A number of chronicles have passages with a patriotic ring. National

---

[83] The chronicle from 1258 to 1263 preserved in a manuscript copied in Tewkesbury abbey (printed *Ann. Mon.*, ed. Luard, i. 174-80). It is so pro-baronial in viewpont that it might well have been composed for a member of the house of Clare. The fact that a copy of the chronicle was made at Tewkesbury may be explained by the fact that the Clare earls of Gloucester were the abbey's patrons. (For the burial of the earls in Tewkesbury abbey see Michael Altschul, *A Baronial Family in Medieval England: the Clares, 1217-1314* (Baltimore, 1965), pp. 34, 60, 92, 155, 164.) However, these two facts are insufficient to prove that the chronicle was actually composed there. Indeed, it seems unlikely that it was, since it makes no mention of Tewkesbury.

[84] The version of the *Brut* to 1333, printed *The Brut or the Chronicles of England*, ed. Brie, i. For its Lancastrian bias see Gransden, *op. cit.*, ii. 74-5. John Taylor, however, regards the *Brut*'s judgment on Thomas of Lancaster as an expression of popular opinion; Taylor, *English Historical Literature*, p. 113.

[85] For Baker's patrons see: *Chronicon Galfridi le Baker de Swynebroke*, ed. E. Maunde Thompson (Oxford, 1889), pp. x-xvi; Taylor, *op. cit.*, p. 13.

[86] *Chronicon Henrici Knighton vel Cnitthon Monachi Leycestrensis*, ed. J.R. Lumby (Rolls Series, 1889-95, 2 vols). See: V.H. Galbraith, 'The chronicle of Henry Knighton', *Fritz Saxl 1890-1948. A volume of Memorial Essays from his friends in England.*, ed. D.J. Gordon (London, 1957), p. 136; Gransden, *op. cit.*, ii. 178-81; Taylor, *op. cit.*, pp. 13, 18.

[87] For Adam of Usk's career and patrons see: *Chronicon Adae de Usk de A.D. 1377-1421*, ed., with an English translation, E. Maude Thompson (2nd edn., London, 1904), pp. xi-xxix; Taylor *op. cit.*, pp. 11-12. For the bias in his chronicle see Gransden, *op. cit.*, ii. 183 *et seqq.*

[88] See *The Westminster Chronicle 1381-1394*, ed., with an English translation, L.C. Hector and B.F. Harvey (Oxford Medieval Texts, 1982), pp. lxxiv-lxxv, for a different interpretation. But cf. *Nottingham Medieval Studies*, xxviii (1984), pp. 102-3.

triumphs are duly celebrated and national disasters bewailed. Such patriotic manifestations were not necessarily the result of a chronicler's spontaneous feelings. If he was an 'official' chronicler (as probably the author of the Alfredian Anglo-Saxon Chronicle and Robert of Avesbury were), or was influenced by government propaganda (a subject to be discussed in the next section), his patriotic tone might reflect the government's point of view rather than his own. On the other hand, the opinions and sentiments of chronicler and government might coincide. In any case, only rarely can patriotism have been strong enough to provide the initial motive for composition. Nevertheless, in some circumstances it must have encouraged chroniclers to write.

A marked characteristic of the chronicle tradition in England is the propensity for criticising king and government. To suppose that such criticism necessarily reveals a chronicler's independence of mind would be an over-simplification. As has been seen, some chroniclers were influenced by patrons, and a patron might be a magnate in opposition to the king. As will be shown (in the next section) some of the chroniclers writing about Richard II's reign succumbed to Lancastrian propaganda which was spread under Henry IV to discredit Richard. These reservations aside, critical passages in general suggest that on occasion a chronicler's patriotism could override both his obsession with his own locality and his loyalty to the king. Then his criticisms were the result of genuine concern for the English people, a concern which made him take a detached view. Good examples of this phenomenon occurred in the late Anglo-Saxon period and in the thirteenth century.

A sense of national identity distinct from the monarchy appears in the eleventh-century annals of the Anglo-Saxon Chronicle. Having noted, *s.a.* 1009, that King Ethelred allowed the large fleet, which he had built and assembled at Sandwich, to disperse, the chronicler comments: '[thus] the toil of all the nation [came] lightly to naught; and no better than this was the victory which all the English people had expected.'[89] The threat of civil war under Edward the Confessor again aroused the chronicler's patriotism.[90] When the host of Earl Godwin and his sons faced the king's forces in 1051, he writes: 'some thought it would be a great piece of folly if they joined battle, for in the two hosts there was most of what was noblest in England.' Similarly, he states uner 1052, on recording Godwin's return from Flanders with a strong force, that 'it was hateful to almost all [of his soldiers] to fight against men of their own race, for there was little else that was worth anything apart from Englishmen on either side.'

This incipient nationalism was accompanied by xenophobia. King Edgar, the chronicler alleges under 959, 'indulged excessively in one bad

---

[89] *Anglo-Saxon Chronicle*, ed. Whitelock, p. 89.
[90] *Ibid.*, pp. 118, 123-4.

practice: he loved evil foreign customs and was too persistent in bringing heathen manners into this land; and he attracted hither foreigners and enticed harmful people to this country.'[91] On the death of Hardacnut, the chronicler welcomes the restoration of the English dynasty: 'all the people then received Edward the Confessor as was his natural right'.[92] But later it deplores the favour Edward showed to 'Frenchmen', who 'promoted injustices and passed unjust judgment and [gave] bad counsel in this country', and caused discord between the king and Earl Godwin.[93] Patriotism is, therefore, a characteristic of the Anglo-Saxon Chronicle. It may have been one reason why a version survived the Conquest by almost a century; it survived at Peterborough, in a pocket of English resistance.

The thirteenth-century chroniclers almost without exception supported the barons against King John and Henry III. They expended some of their most eloquent prose on the Barons' War; the barons, in their eyes, were acting for the benefit of the realm, upholding the ancient laws and customs of England and the liberty of the Church, in face of encroachment and abuse by the central authority.[94] The St Albans' *Flores Historiarum* (*s.a.* 1259/60) claims that the baronial reforms revived 'the spirit of justice'.[95] Many chroniclers appealed to the right of the community of the realm to act against bad government, and to the barons' privilege of advising the king as his 'natural counsellors'.[96] As in the tenth and eleventh centuries, the chroniclers hated foreigners. They attacked the queen's Savoyard relatives because, in their opinion, they usurped the barons' rightful influence over the king and became excessively rich; the Oseney chronicler feared they would 'overthrow the native inhabitants'.[97]

---

[91]  *Ibid*, p. 75.

[92]  *Ibid.*, p. 106.

[93]  *Ibid.*, pp. 124, 125-6.

[94]  See Gransden, *Historical Writing*, [i], Chapter 18 *passim* (esp. pp. 407, 414-17, 421-3 and nn. for further references). For the extreme pro-baronial attitude of a chronicle from Tewkesbury abbey see above p. 216 and note 83. For Matthew Paris's partisanship see: Richard Vaughan, *Matthew Paris* (Cambridge, 1958), p. 137-43; V.H. Galbraith, *Roger Wendover and Matthew Paris* (Glasgow, 1944, repr. 1970 and in *idem, Kings and Chroniclers*), p. 20; Gransden, *op. cit.*, [i]. 368 *et seqq.*

[95]  *Flores Historiarum*, ed. Luard, ii. 439.

[96]  For references, variously expressed, to the community of the realm etc., see: Matthew Paris, *Chronica Majora*, ed. H.R. Luard (Rolls Series, 1872-83, 7 vols), iii. 495, v. 21; *Flores Historiarium*, ed. Luard, ii. 426-7; *Ann. Mon.*, ed. Luard, i. 471. For reference to the king's reliance on bad counsellors, neglect of the barons' advice, etc., see: Matthew Paris, *Chron. Maj.*, iii, 395; *Flores Historiarum*, ed. Luard, ii. 464, 466, 470; *Ann. Mon.*, ed. Luard, ii. 351.

[97]  *Ann. Mon.*, ed. Luard, iv. 150-1. For other anti-alien passages see: Matthew Paris, *Chron. Maj.*, ed. Luard, v. 229, 316-17; *Flores Historiarum*, ed. Luard, ii. 463, 479; *Ann. Mon.*, ed. Luard, ii, 349, 355.

## 5. *The Government's Use of, and Influence on, Chronicles*

The scarcity of official chronicles in medieval England could be understood to mean that in general the kings did not consider chronicles very useful. This would be a false conclusion. Although the kings commissioned few themselves, they recognised the value of other people's chronicles, as sources of information, records and potential vehicles of propaganda.

It was pointed out above that in the thirteenth century the growth of monastic archives had outstripped the ability to organise them.[98] The consequent problem of retrieving information from archives in a monastery was but a microcosm of those suffered by the central government. Edward I gave spectacular recognition to the value of chronicles, which stored information in chronological order, in 1291. When he claimed the right to try the case of the disputed succession to the Scottish throne, he turned for evidence of his overlordship not only to the public records but also to the monks, with a request that they consult their chronicles for precedents.[99] Their findings helped furnish the historical proofs of the English king's overlordship which were cited during the trial.[100]

Further examples of royal appeals to chronicle evidence survive from the fourteenth century. Such an appeal was made some time early in the 1340s, though no details are known about it: a letter survives from the abbot of Nutley to the Chancellor saying that he cannot provide a transcript of a chronicle because it is on loan to the dean of Wells.[101] Another instance is known to have occurred in 1352, but again there are no details: Edward III summoned Ranulph Higden to come 'with all your chronicles and those in your charge to speak and treat with the council concerning matters to be explained to you on our behalf'.[102] In 1399 Henry Bolingbroke used chronicles to justify Richard II's deposition, and in 1400, as Henry IV, to substantiate his claim to overlordship of Scotland.[103]

---

[98] Above p. 210-11.

[99] See J. Bain, *Calendar of Documents relating to Scotland* (Edinburgh, 1881-8, 4 vols), ii. 122, nos 503, 504; F. Palgrave, *Documents and Records illustrating the History of Scotland* (Record Commision, 1837), pp. xcvi-xcvii and n. Cf. E.L.G. Stones, 'The appeal to history in Anglo-Scottish relations between 1291 and 1401', *Archives*, ix (1969), 11-21 *passim*. Cf. below p. 232, 237.

[100] E.L.G. Stones and G.G. Simpson, *Edward I and the Throne of Scotland 1290-1296: An Edition of the Record Sources for the Great Cause* (Oxford, 1978, 2 vols), i. 137-62, ii. 296-309.

[101] PRO, Ancient Correspondence (S.C.1), vol. xxxix, no. 161 (c. 1341-3). I owe this reference to Professor M.C.E. Jones.

[102] J.G. Edwards, 'Ranulf, monk of Chester', *English Historical Review*, xlvii (1932), 94.

[103] See *Chronicon Adae de Usk*, ed. Thompson, pp. 29-31, and Stones, 'The appeal to history in Anglo-Scottish relations', pp. 80-3.

Kings appreciated that chronicles, besides providing useful information, were suitable places to preserve copies of documents of propagandist value. In 1291 Edward I sent copies of the letters of submission to his authority of the competitors for the Scottish throne,[104] and in 1399 the new Lancastrian government distributed copies of the official 'record and process' of Richard II's deposition to important monasteries for inclusion in their chronicles.[105]

Since on occasion chronicles attracted the attention of the central government, the question arises to what extent their authors enjoyed freedom of expression. The fact that many severely criticised king and government suggest that they wrote what they liked. Presumably they might feel particularly confident if they lived in a remote place, beyond the reach of retribution. An even stronger safeguard would have been a sympathetic, protective audience. This most monastic chroniclers had, since they wrote primarily for their own communities and also perhaps for those of neighbouring religious houses. However, the monks themselves were apparently not the only possible readers of monastic chronicles. It is likely that visitors to a religious house might read, or at least learn about the contents of, its chronicle. This is indicated by the fact that occasionally the author of some fairly ordinary chronicle admits that he considers it risky to express himself freely. Thus the Osney chronicle has an early note in the margin after the notice of the battle of Lewes (1264) which reads:

> because of the malice of the times it is not safe to tell the whole truth, so at present we will be silent concerning the names of the magnates who fled, and who were captured in the battle; and we have omitted from this history much else that was done in these days, for the sake of readers' peace, because what

---

[104] See: the Canterbury chronicle in *The Historical Works of Gervase of Canterbury*, ed. Stubbs, ii. 297-9; *Bury Chronicle*, ed. Gransden, pp. 100-3; *Bartholomaei de Cotton . . . Historia Anglicana*, ed. Luard, pp. 180-2; the Peterborough chronicle in *Florentii Wigorniensis . . . Chronicon ex Chronicis*, ed. Thorpe, ii. 247-50 (however, the copy of the letter in the Peterborough chronicle may be a doctored version of the copy in the Bury chronicle; see below p. 237); the chronicles of Merton and Rochester in *Flores Historiarum*, ed. Luard, i. xvi, iii. 72 n.1; and the chronicles of Dunstable, Waverley and Worcester in *Ann. Mon.*, ed. Luard, ii. 411, iii. 368-9, iv. 507-9. For the letters of submission in the chronicles of St Benet of Hulme see below p. 236.

[105] See *Johannis de Trokelowe . . . Chronica et Annales*, ed. H.T. Riley (Rolls Series, 1866), pp. 252-86; *Eulogium Historiarum*, ed. F.S. Haydon (Rolls Series, 1858-63, 3 vols), iii. 382-4; *Historia Vitae et Regni Ricardi Secundi*, ed. G.B. Stow, jr (Pennsylvania, 1977), pp. 157-61; *Chronicles of London*, ed. Kingsford, pp. 16-47. Cf. M.V. Clarke, and V.H. Galbraith, 'The deposition of Richard II', *Bulletin of the John Rylands Library*, xiv (1930, repr. in *Fourteenth Century Studies by M.V. Clarke*, ed. L.S. Sutherland and May McKisack (Oxford, 1937)), 144-6 *passim*; H.G. Richardson, 'Richard II's last Parliament', *English Historical Review*, lii (1937), 41.

might please the king's men would displease those who favoured the barons.[106]

The chronicler of Furness in Lancashire also reveals unease. He notes that after the battle of Evesham (1265) people dared not speak of the miracles worked by Simon de Montfort's body for fear of the king.[107] The Dictum of Kenilworth (1266), Chapter 8, prohibited such tales. Perhaps it was in response to this decree that mention of such miracles was erased from the chronicle of Bury St Edmunds.[108]

It is well known that two chroniclers, Matthew Paris and Thomas Walsingham, carried out drastic revision of their chronicles to reduce the anti-government element. Matthew Paris revised his chronicles to suppress or modify his abuse of the king, the queen's French relatives and other members of the 'establishment',[109] and Thomas Walsingham did the same to his scurrilous attacks on John of Gaunt.[110] Although William of Malmesbury's *Gesta Regum* and *Gesta Pontificum* are not strictly speaking 'chronicles', they deserve mention in this context because they provide an early example of similar revision. Late in life William modified his censure of William the Conqueror, William Rufus, and their ministers and officials.[111]

Fame had deprived Matthew Paris and Thomas Walsingham (as it had also William of Malmesbury) of the relative immunity which protected more obscure monastic chroniclers; it had brought them and their chronicles to the notice of important people. Such attention, facilitated by St Albans' proximity to London, must have made them circumspect, since it was necessary to keep on good terms with the great. At the same time it exposed them to the full brunt of government propaganda. Caution and the influence of propaganda were probably Walsingham's principal

---

[106] 'Et quia propter temporum maliciam non est tutum omnia vera loqui, ideo ad praesens tacemus nomina magnatum, [qui] fugerant et qui capti fuerant in bello predicto. Multa etiam alia quae sunt facta hiis diebus omittimus huic historiae interserere propter pacem legentium, quia forte quod placeret regalibus displiceret baronum fautoribus'; *Ann. Mon.*, ed. Luard, iv. 148-9. Exactly who read, or listened to, monastic chronicles remains problematical.

[107] The chronicle of Furness in *Chronicles of the Reigns of Stephen, Henry II, and Richard I*, ed. Richard Howlett (Rolls Series, 1884-9, 4 vols), ii. 548.

[108] *Chronicle of Bury St Edmunds*, ed. Gransden, p. 33 and n. *a*. Cf. below p. 229 and Plate 15.

[109] See: Vaughan, *Matthew Paris*, pp. 64-5, 117-24.

[110] V.H. Galbraith, 'Thomas Walsingham and the Saint Albans chronicle, 1272-1422', *English Historical Review*, xlvii (1932), 21-5; *The St Albans Chronicle 1406-1420*, ed. *idem* (Oxford, 1937), p. li.

[111] *Willelmi Malmesbiriensis Monachi de Gestis Regum Anglorum Libri Quinque*, ed. William Stubbs (Rolls Series, 1887-9, 2 vols), i. xxxiii *et seqq.*, xlvii; *Willelmi Malmesbiriensis Monachi de Gestis Pontificum Anglorum Libri Quinque*, ed. N.E.S.A. Hamilton (Rolls Series, 1870), pp. xv-xvii; Hugh Farmer, 'William of Malmesbury's life and work', *Journal of Ecclesiastical History*, xiii (1962), 45-6.

reasons for revision. He revised his chronicles after the 1399 revolution to make them conform with the Lancastrian viewpoint. Besides rehabilitating John of Gaunt, Henry IV's father, he underlined criticism of Richard II and his government (partly by extracting material from the 'record and process', which included a damning account of Richard's reign). His revision, therefore, not only improved the image of the Lancastrian dynasty, but in addition helped justify Henry's usurpation.

Caution and the influence of propaganda may not have been Thomas Walsingham's only reasons for revision. Improved knowledge of public affairs and public figures could well have resulted in a more sympathetic attitude. This may have been so in Thomas Walsingham's case; it was almost certainly true in Matthew Paris's. Matthew came to know Henry III personally (he records that in 1247 and 1257 Henry gave him information for inclusion in his chronicle),[112] and he composed and illustrated Saints' Lives in French verse for Queen Eleanor and for at least two noble ladies.[113] It seems very likely that such acquaintance caused a genuine change of mind on Matthew's part.

## 6. Suggested Reasons for the Decline of the Chronicle

Why the chronicle tradition was moribund by the end of the fifteenth century is uncertain. A few possible reasons may be suggested. As has been seen, the strength of the tradition had lain in the monasteries. Most monasteries seem to have stopped producing chronicles in a routine way as part of their archives early in the fourteenth century. The Indian Summer of the monastic chronicle in Richard II's reign and in the early fifteenth century was transient. Apparently monks no longer felt the urge to record national events. Perhaps they found other means of learning news, for example by newsletters, more satisfactory,[114] or perhaps they had become more 'parochial' in their outlook. This last suggestion receives support from the number and generally high quality of the domestic histories of religious houses composed in the first half of the fifteenth

---

[112] *Chron. Maj.*, ed. Luard, iv. 644-5, v. 233-4, 617-18. Cf. Vaughan, *Matthew Paris*, p. 3.

[113] See Vaughan, *op. cit.*, pp. 170, 173, 178; Gransden, *Historical Writing*, [i]. 358-9 and nn.

[114] Newsletters were a source of information from the twelfth century onwards, and their value was fully recognised by chroniclers, who used them for information. See, with further references, E.L.G. Stones, 'The surrender of King John of Scotland to Edward I in 1296: some new evidence', *Bulletin of the Institute of Historical Research*, xlviii (1975), 103 and nn. 3, 4; A.E. Prince, 'A letter of Edward the Black Prince describing the Battle of Najera', *English Historical Review*, xli (1926), 417; C.A.J. Armstrong, 'Some examples of the distribution and speed of news in England at the time of the Wars of the Roses', *Studies in Medieval History presented to F.M. Powicke*, ed. R.W. Hunt, W.A. Pantin and R.W. Southern (Oxford, 1948, repr. 1969), p. 432; Gransden, *Historical Writing*, ii (see index under 'newsletters'); Taylor, *English Historical Literature*, pp. 140, 229, 270, 320.

century.[115] One object of a 'house' history was to satisfy the monks' curiosity about their monasteries' origins and history. Another purpose was to improve *esprit de corps* by dwelling on (and often exaggerating) an individual monastery's antiquity and glorious past. This aspect of a 'house' history was also useful to the monastery in its external relations. It increased its prestige and recorded its rights and privileges, which strengthened its defences in an increasingly less sympathetic environment. These histories were both a manifestation of, and an incentive to, the growth of monastic localism.

Another external circumstance may have discouraged the writing of chronicles. As the fifteenth century progressed writers' desire to keep or court the king's favour, or at least not to risk his displeasure, grew. It is known that such feelings influenced authors of histories which do not fall within our definition of 'chronicles'. This is proved by the fact that a number were turncoats: John Hardyng, John Capgrave and William Worcester switched sides from the Yorkist to the Lancastrian 'party', and John Rous, having supported the Yorkists, became an ardent partisan of Henry Tudor.[116] Clearly these writers (like Sir John Fortescue)[117] considered it expedient to support whichever party was in power. Monastic chroniclers had shown themselves vulnerable to government pressure from Edward I's reign onwards; perhaps during the Wars of the Roses and thereafter, in those increasingly difficult and insecure times, the religious preferred not to risk recording national events.

The London chronicles flourished until towards the end of the fifteenth century. Their authors were in a different position from the monks. Since they wrote under the patronage of a strong, close-knit community, the London oligarchy, they had a comparatively safe environment. They consistently present the merchants' political (pro-Yorkist) viewpoint. Although the last of the actual London chronicles came to an end in the early sixteenth century, their influence continued. As has been seen, the chronicle of the Grey Friars of Newgate, which continued to Queen Mary's accession, is more or less indistinguishable from a London chronicle, and John Stow's *Chronicles of England* not only used the London chronicles as sources, but also, when they ended, continued to his own day with additional annals.

Nevertheless, the tradition of adding annals year by year to a chronicle was dying even in London. Its demise was probably mainly owing to the introduction of printing, a decline in demand for news in the form of annals, and a change in historiographical taste. William Caxton printed the *Brut* in 1480 and the *Polychronicon* in 1482, and by the end of the

[115] See Gransden, *Historical Writing*, ii, Chapters 12 and 13 *passim*.

[116] See Gransden, 'Politics and historiography during the Wars of the Roses', pp. 133-6.

[117] See P. E. Gill, 'Politics and propaganda in fifteenth century England: the polemical writings of Sir John Fortescue', *Speculum*, xlvi (1971), 333-47.

sixteenth century several of the most important chronicles were in print.[118] The multiplication of copies meant that a chronicle once in print was easier to borrow and cheaper to buy. At the same time the text lost its 'organic' quality: it was now fixed, not fluid. In addition, the demand for news in annalistic form probably declined. Such a 'news-medium' was slow and tended to be sketchy. Londoners can have had little difficulty in learning about current events; the City was the centre of national life, and a hub of news, from royal proclamations, public ceremonies and celebrations, verbal exchange and the like. Meanwhile the chronicle mode had become old-fashioned. Under the Tudors the factual record of events characteristic of the medieval chronicle lost favour; taste turned to histories, which, though still in chronological order, had a strong theme (usually in support of the Tudor dynasty).[119]

## 7. The Composition of the 'Contemporaneous' Sections of Chronicles

> The author wrote his book and then, like William of Malmesbury, invited his readers to send him, or like Matthew Paris or Thomas Walsingham, himself loaded the margins with, notes suggested by further reading and reflection. This process occupied many years and at any stage a copy might be bespoken by another religious house or a lay patron. In this way endless recensions arose, and not until the work became a classic, like Bede's *Ecclesiastical History*, was the text in any way fixed.[120]

V.H. Galbraith wrote this passage in 1959 to introduce his exposition of the evolution of Higden's *Polychronicon*. Although the latter is an encyclopaedia rather than a chronicle by strict definition, Galbraith's generalisation is certainly appropriate to the composition of a typical monastic chronicle except that nearly all, far from being potential 'classics', were second- or third-rate pieces of work. In these cases it was not 'classical' status which fixed their texts, but printing. As long as a chronicle remained in manuscript it had an 'organic' existence; only if and when printed did its text become static – but even then only barring new editions.

The early part of a chronicle, which begins well before the author's own time, for example at the Creation, Incarnation or Norman Conquest, was, of course, a compilation from usually well-known authorities. Later, when the author wrote of the period within living memory, he used in addition oral information. Editors and other scholars have in general taken pains to

---

[118] For the first appearance of chronicles in print see F.J. Levy, *Tudor Historical Thought* (Huntington Library, San Marino, California, 1967), pp. 120, 133-4.

[119] For historical writing in the Tudor period see Levy, *op. cit.*, and May McKisack, *Medieval History in the Tudor Age* (Oxford, 1971).

[120] V.H. Galbraith, 'An Autograph MS of Ranulph Higden's *Polychronicon*', *The Huntington Library Quarterly*, xxiii (1959-60), p. 3.

identify chroniclers' sources. Most recently L.C. Hector and Barbara Harvey in their edition of the Westminster chronicle have given a thorough analysis of that chronicle's sources, and D.E.R. Watt has done the same in his edition for the last two Books of the *Scotichronicon*.[121] Such analyses include the specific problem of the relationship of one monastic chronicle with others composed at about the same time. This inter-relationship of chronicles has been the subject of a few specialist studies: for example, N. Denholm-Young tried to unravel the intricate relationship of the Winchester, Hyde, Waverley and Worcester chronicles.[122]

A chronicler's greatest problem was how to compose the contemporary part of his work. Perhaps he was in touch with the chronicler of a nearby religious house. If so, he might be sent intalments about recent events by that chronicler, as the latter added them to his own work. He was, therefore, borrowing from a chronicle which itself was no more than a draft, still in a very unfixed state. Apart from such a possible chronicle source, a chronicler had little or no control over what or when news reached him, and had to impose chronological order and narrative coherence on a miscellaneous collection of items arriving sporadically, sometimes after he had composed the relevant annal. Galbraith did much to illuminate the composition of the contemporaneous section (1392-1422) of the St Albans chronicle, when Thomas Walsingham was writing within two or three years of the events which he recorded. Galbraith described the process of composition: it was 'one of ceaseless experiment and change'; 'Closely connected with this fluid character of the text, inevitable in an age when there was nothing equivalent to the publication of a book, is the annalistic nature of Walsingham's . . . chronicle'; 'Such piecemeal composition inevitably involved a good deal of recasting from time to time on grounds of style, or because fresh information came to hand, or because the writer's feelings changed.'[123]

Apart from Galbraith, scholars do not seem to have appreciated the problem of how the contemporary sections of chronicles were compiled. But the St Albans chronicle was a monastic chronicle *par excellence*. Matthew Paris and Thomas Walsingham wrote with a degree of detail and eloquence unmatched by other monastic chroniclers, and the number of surviving copies of their works is exceptionally great. It is the intention in what follows to examine the methods apparent in more typical

[121] *The Westminster Chronicle, 1381-1394*, ed. Hector Harvey, pp. xliii-liv. For Professor Watt's edition of the *Scotichronicon* see below, p. 226 n. 133.

[122] The chronicle of St Swithun's, Winchester, was used by the chroniclers of Hyde, Waverley and Worcester; see N. Denholm-Young, 'The Winchester-Hyde Chronicle', *EHR*, xliv (1934), 85-93 (repr. *idem, Collected Papers on Medieval Subjects* (Oxford, 1946, new edn. Cardiff, 1969), pp. 86-95.

[123] *The St. Albans Chronicle, 1406-1420*, ed. Galbraith, p. lxiii.

monastic chronicles, of how their authors wrote contemporaneously. The related problem of the dissemination of a chronicle, from its place of origin to other religious houses, will also be considered. The argument will be centred on the chronicle of Bury St Edmunds,[124] a normal monastic chronicle and a product of the thirteenth century when the chronicle genre had its heyday (as explained above, pp. 205-6, 210-11).

In its final form the Bury chronicle covered the period from the Creation to 1301. Its first recension, to 1265, was by John de Taxter, a monk of Bury. Another (anonymous) Bury monk wrote a second recension. He revised Taxter's chronicle and continued to 1296. A second continuator (also anonymous) then added annals to 1301. The Bury chronicle's strictly annalistic structure and the nature of its contents resemble those of many other monastic chronicles. For purposes of comparison a selection of these will be referred to below: the chronicle of John of Worcester (Creation to c. 1140);[125] the Winchcombe 'Annals' (1182-1232);[126] the chronicle of Melrose (Roxburghshire, 731-1275);[127] the chronicle of St Swithun's, Winchester (519-1277);[128] the Norwich chronicle (Incarnation to 1291);[129] the chronicle of St Benet of Hulme (Norfolk), which goes under the name of 'John of Oxenedes' (Creation to 1292);[130] The Dunstable 'Annals' (Incarnation to 1297);[131] and the Westminster chronicle (1381-94);[132] Walter Bower's *Scotichronicon* (Noah to 1437)[133] will also be mentioned, although it is not a typical monastic chronicle. (It has many features of a history in literary form, but nevertheless has a fair number of annalistic entries which are of use in the

[124]  *The Chronicle of Bury St Edmunds 1212-1301*, ed. Gransden.
[125]  *The Chronicle of John of Worcester, 1118-1140*, ed. Weaver.
[126]  'The Winchcombe annals 1049-1181', ed. R.R. Darlington, in *A Medieval Miscellany for Doris Mary Stenton*, ed. P.M. Barnes and F.C. Slade (Publication of the Pipe Roll Society, new series, xxxvi, 1960). See also Eric John, 'A critical study of the sources of the annals of Winchcombe, Faustina B I, ff.21-29^b (1182-1232)', M.A. thesis, University of Manchester (1949).
[127]  *The Chronicle of Melrose, a facsimile edition from Cotton MS. Faustina B ix*, ed. A.O. Anderson and M.O. Anderson (London, 1936).
[128]  Printed in *Annales Monastici*, ed. Luard, ii. 3-125.
[129]  This Norwich chronicle was incorporated by Bartholomew Cotton in his chronicle; *Bartholomaei de Cotton, Historia Anglicana*, ed. Luard, pp. 47-182. Cf. *ibid.*, pp. xxiii-xxiv.
[130]  *Chronica Johannis de Oxenedes*, ed. Ellis.
[131]  Printed in *Annales Monastici*, ed. Luard, iii. 3-408.
[132]  For the standard edition see above p. 216 n. 88.
[133]  To 1383 Bower incorporated most of John Fordun's *Chronicon Gentis Scotorum*. His own chronicle is virtually a continuation of Fordun's. The whole is ed. Walter Goodall (Edinburgh, 1759, 2 vols). For an up-to-date edition of four of the books see *Scotichronicon by Walter Bower in Latin and English*, general editor D.E.R. Watt, ii, *Books III and IV*, ed. John and Winifred MacQueen (Aberdeen, 1989), viii, *Books XV and XVI*, ed. D.E.R. Watt (Aberdeen, 1987). The remaining books in this edition are planned to appear within the next decade.

study of how chronicles were composed.)

In general, the length of individual annals in a chronicle increases as the chronicler nears his own day. Starting with brief, piecemeal entries, the prose tends to become fluent when it concerns events more or less contemporary with the author. The Bury chronicle conforms to this model. From 1264 Taxter was writing fairly soon after the events he recorded, and gives a detailed account of the Barons' War. His first continuator wrote more or less contemporaneously at least from the mid-1280s, and probably did so throughout. The near contemporaneity of a substantial part of the Bury chronicle make it a suitable focus of attention for our study.

The Bury chronicle has in addition other advantages which few other chronicles possess in combination. Of those listed above, excluding Bower because he is untypical, only John of Worcester has them all, and he does not belong to the thirteenth century, from which most of our examples are drawn. Part of the Bury chronicle survives in an early draft. It is true that the later annals of quite a few of the chronicles listed (John of Worcester, and the Winchcombe, Melrose, Dunstable and Westminster chronicles) survive in early drafts,[134] but, with the exception of John of Worcester and the Dunstable chronicle, there is only one manuscript of each. The Bury chronicle, on the other hand, survives in a number of manuscripts and, moreover, was plundered by the chroniclers of quite a few other religious houses. None of the chronicles listed enjoyed comparable popularity – except the Winchester chronicle and, again, John of Worcester.[135]

The best text of Taxter's chronicle is British Library Cotton MS Julius A 1, ff. 3-43ᵛ.[136] It is a fair, but early, copy in one hand throughout. There is one other copy of Taxter, of the last half of the fourteenth century, College of Arms Arundel MS 6, ff. 109-24. Although not copied directly from Julius A 1, it is a descendant of it.[137] The best text of the second recension of the Bury chronicle, and the only one of the second continuation, is College of Arms Arundel MS 30, ff. 97-205. To 1285 it is a fair copy, with only one change of hand, in the middle of the annal for 1268. From 1270 there are signs of early revision (see e.g. below Plate 14). Most significantly, from 1286 to 1296 there are many changes of ink and apparently of hand. Clearly this part of the manuscript is a draft, not a fair

---

[134] For descriptions of the manuscripts of these chronicles respectively see: Weaver, *op. cit.*, pp. 4-10; Darlington, *loc. cit.*, pp. 111-12, and John, *loc. cit.*, pp. 1-2; *Melrose, ut. cit.*, pp. x *et seqq*; Cheney, 'The making of the Dunstable Annals, A.D. 1233 to 1242', pp. 210-13, 219; *Westminster Chronicle*, ed. Hector and Harvey, pp. xiv-xxi.

[135] See above p. 203 and n. 23.

[136] For descriptions of the manuscripts of the Bury chronicle see *Bury Chronicle*, ed. Gransden, pp. xxxv-xliv, and for more detail *idem, A Critical Edition of the Bury St Edmund's Chronicle in Arundel MS 30 (College of Arms)*, Ph.D. thesis, University of London (1956), pp. 21-68.

[137] But see below p. 229.

14   The Chronicle of Bury St Edmunds; the first continuation (London, College of Arms, MS Arundel 30, fo. 167v). The end of the annal for 1279 and the beginning of that for 1280. An early reviser made corrections to the text in plummet in the margin, and these were incorporated in the text in ink. A passage (a notice of an eclipse, and a notice of William de Hoo's succession to the office of sacrist of Bury St Edmunds) is marked *vacat* in the margin in plummet.

15   The Chronicle of Bury St Edmunds; the first recension by John Taxter (London, British Library, MS Cotton, Julius A 1, fo. 43v). The end of the last annal, for 1265, with the passage alleging that Simon de Montfort's corpse worked miracles erased.

16  The Chronicle of Bury St Edmunds (London, College of Arms, MS Arundel 30, fo. 150). Annals from 1260 to 1263, with spaces between the annals for 1260 and 1262. A note of the birth of John de Hastings to Joanna, wife of Henry de Hastings, has been added at the end of the annal for 1262 (the Hastings were hereditary stewards of St Edmund's Liberty).

17 The Chronicle of Bury St Edmunds (Bury St Edmunds, Moyses Hall, MS, fo. 103v). The end of the annal for 1282. A space has been left after the notice of the birth of a daughter to Queen Eleanor for her name. The text in the College of Arms calls her Elizabeth, but Bartholomew Cotton has 'Walkiniana'. 'Oxenedes' has 'Elysabeth' written on an erasure.

18   The Chronicle of Melrose Abbey (London, British Library, MS Cotton, Faustina B IX, fo. 28v). Annals from 1208 to 1210, with spaces between the annals. A note recording the death of Richard abbot of Coupar-Angus and the succession of Abbot Alexander has been added at the end of the annal for 1209.

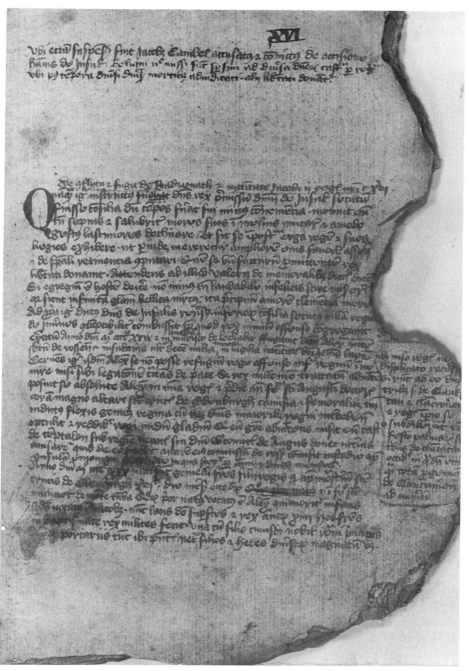

19 *Scotichronicon* by Walter Bower (Cambridge, Corpus Christi College, MS 171, fo. 343).
Book 16, the end of Chapter 15 and the beginning of Chapter 16, 1428–30. A space of
about nine lines has been left after Chapter 15. The last sentence, 'Reliqui...donantur',
was added in a similar, but smaller hand and in darker ink. The original scribe made a
marginal addition.

20    The Chronicle of Bury St Edmunds, the first continuation (London, College of Arms, MS Arundel 30, fo. 179). Part of the annal for 1291. By the copy of Edward I's letter to the abbot and convent of Bury St Edmunds ordering them to copy into their chronicle the letters of submission to his judgement of the competitors for the Scottish throne, a scribe has written *Sancti Petri de Burg'* in plummet; clearly this was in preparation for a copy being made for Peterborough. Edward I's and the competitors' letters must have been copied into the chronicle before the historical matter introducing them; since the scribe did not leave enough space for the latter, the final words were relegated to the margin.

21 The Chronicle of Bury St Edmunds, the first continuation (London, College of Arms, MS Arundel 30, fo. 190). Part of the (penultimate) annal for 1295. The scribe left a space after the notice of the dismissal of William March from the office of Treasurer. An early reviser recorded the succession of Walter Langton in plummet in the margin, and inserted it in ink in the space. Three passages are marked *vacat*. The first concerns the treason of Thomas de Turbeville; the second records March's disgrace and Langton's succession as Treasurer; and the third names the tax collectors in Suffolk.

22  The Westminster Chronicle (Cambridge, Corpus Christi College, MS 197A, p. 197). Annal for 1390, including a notice of the consecration of Brother Alexander [Bache] as bishop of St Asaph. The scribe left a blank space for the surname which was later inserted.

23 The Chronicle of Bury St Edmunds; the first recension by John Taxter (London, British Library, MS Cotton, Julius A 1, fo. 23v). A marginal addition (extracted from Ralph de Diceto's *Abbreviationes Chronicorum*, s.a. 773) to the annal for 772.

24 The Chronicle of Winchcombe Priory (London, British Library, MS Cotton, Faustina B I, fo. 13). The annals from 1074 to 1088. The chronicler wrote an annal, abridged from a Tewkesbury chronicle, after the year date, and then added material in blocks around it.

25   The Chronicle of Bury St Edmunds (London, College of Arms, MS Arundel 30, fo. 188v). Part of the annal for 1294. The succession of William de Hothum to the archbishopric of Dublin has been added in the margin.

26 The Chronicle of St Benet of Hulme commonly known as 'John de Oxenedes' (London, British Library, MS Cotton, Nero D.II, fo. 235v (new foliation)). Part of the annal for 1282. The name of Queen Eleanor's new born baby, 'Elysabeth', is written by a different scribe on an erasure.

27   The St Albans copy of Ralph Diceto's *Ymagines Historiarum* (London, British Library, MS Royal 13 E VI, fo. 134v). The annal for 1198, 'edited' for the scribe making an abbreviated version for Dunstable priory; the passages to be copied are marked with a diagonal stroke in the left-hand margin in reddish brown pencil. Compare the Dunstable chronicle, s.a. 1198 (Luard 1864–9:3.27).

copy. Another manuscript of the second recension, also written at Bury, is now in the Moyses Hall Museum at Bury St Edmunds. It is in one neat book hand, apparently the same as that which wrote the annals from 1268 to 1285 in Arundel 30, but only goes down to 1283. From 1269 its variants from the text in Arundel 30 become important.[138] It is a very early copy, made shortly after the date of its last annal.[139]

To these manuscripts must be added the chronicles of the principal borrowers from the Bury chronicle. In fact it was used by a number of chroniclers in various religious houses, mostly in East Anglia and adjoining regions, in the thirteenth and fourteenth centuries.[140] However, only those chronicles which reproduce substantial parts of the text, that is the chronicles of Norwich, St Benet of Hulme and Peterborough, are helpful for the present inquiry. The Norwich chronicle copies Taxter for the annals from 1258 to 1263, and the second recension from 1279 to 1284.[141] The Hulme chronicle uses the second recension for the annals from 1020 to 1169, and 1258 to 1292.[142] The Peterborough chronicle also copies the second recension (probably Arundel 30 itself), from 1152 to 1295.[143]

Light is thrown on the Bury chronicle's evolution and dissemination by various kinds of evidence: study of the contents of the chronicle, and of the early manuscripts; collation of the various manuscripts of it,[144] and of the relevant sections in the partly derivative chronicles; and study of the derivatives themselves. As stated above, Taxter wrote fairly contemporaneously from 1264. This conclusion is based partly on the immediacy of the narrative. Moreover, it conforms with evidence provided by Taxter himself. He states at the end of the annal for 1244: 'hoc anno scriptor presentis voluminis habitum suscepit monachicum dictus I. de Taxter'.[145] Therefore, if he wrote in the 1260s, he would have been a monk for upwards of twenty years, which is perfectly feasible. This

---

[138]  Gransden, *A Critical Edition*, p. 38.

[139]  The annals for 1267 and 1268 are also preserved in the early fourteenth-century Bury customary, BL Harley MS 3977, ff. 55ᵛ-9. This text has small variants from both Arundel 30 and the Moyses Hall MS, but will not be considered here.

[140]  See above pp. 204-5.

[141]  See *Cotton*, ed. Luard, pp. lii-liv, lv-lviii.

[142]  Another chronicle mostly compiled at Hulme, the so-called 'Cronica Buriensis', also contains citations from the Bury chronicle, probably from the version used by 'Oxendes'. The 'Cronica Buriensis' is a history of St Edmund's abbey from 1020 to 1346. It is mainly a compilation and there are changes of authorship at least in 1327 and 1335. Certainly to 1327 and probably to 1335 it was compiled at Hulme, but thereafter was continued at Bury. See below pp. 239-44.

[143]  Printed in *Florentii Wigorniensis Monachi Chronicon ex Chronicis*, ed. Thorpe, ii. 136-279. Cf. *Bury Chron.*, pp. xvii, xliv.

[144]  A full collation of the texts is in the footnotes in Gransden, *A Critical Edition*. Selected variant readings of the texts, from 1212 onwards, are in the footnotes in *Bury Chron.*, ed. Gransden.

[145]  *Bury Chron.*, p. 13 n. *b*.

evidence from the chronicle's subject matter is corroborated by the earliest manuscript, Julius A 1. The handwriting could well belong to the 1260s. In addition, an erasure suggests the possibility that it was written before the Dictum of Kenilworth, 30 October 1266. The statement under 1265 that Simon de Montfort's body worked miracles has been carefully scraped out[146] (see Plate 15). An erasure can, of course, be made at any time, but possibly this one was a result of the Dictum: Chapter 8 forbade men to speak of Simon's alleged miracles.[147] If this were so, the copy of Taxter from which Arundel 6 descends and the earliest draft of the second recension of the chronicle must already have been made, since both have the original reading.

Taxter's continuator started by revising his exemplar. His main alterations were to insert a number of passages about classical history to the early part, and to omit the entry under 1244 that Taxter took the habit.[148] He also made one small revision to the contemporaneous section: to the notice under 1265 about de Montfort's miracles he added 'as many say' ('ut plurimis dicitur').[149] Perhaps this was in response to the changed political climate after Henry III's resumption of power. His continuation, as mentioned above, was probably composed fairly close to events at least from the early 1280s. Explicit evidence of the near contemporaneity of one annal, that for 1287, occurs in the annal itself. It describes how in that year St Edmunds abbey lost its manors of Semer and Groton in a judicial duel. Lamenting this misfortune, the chronicler observes that there was no hope of recovering them.[150] But we know from other records that negotiations for their recovery were crowned with success in 1290.[151]

The manuscripts indicate that from the 1260s the author of the second recension took into account the need to allow for the inclusion of late news. The scribe of Arundel 30 left three lines blank after the annal for 1260 and two after that for 1262 (Plate 16). From 1265 he regularly left such spaces after each annal. Similar, but longer, spaces, comprising up to nine blank lines, occur after each annal in the Moyses Hall MS from 1265 onwards (Plate 17). In one instance both Arundel 30 and the Moyses Hall MS have a space near the beginning of an annal, after the first two brief entries of the annal for 1279.[152]

---

[146] *Ibid.*, p. 33. Cf. above p. 221.
[147] R.E. Treharne, *Documents of the Baronial Movement of Reform and Rebellion 1258-1267* (Oxford Medeival Texts, 1973), p. 322.
[148] See *Bury Chron.*, p. xix.
[149] *Ibid.*, p. 33 and n.*a*.
[150] *Ibid.*, p. 89.
[151] *CCR, 1288-96*, p. 126. See V.H. Galbraith, 'The death of a champion', in *Studies in Medieval History presented to F.M. Powicke*, ed. Hunt, Pantin and Southern (repr. in Galbraith, *Kings and Chroniclers*), p. 292.
[152] *Bury Chron.*, p. 67 n.*c*.

These spaces were intended for additions. In fact, an addition has been inserted in Arundel 30, in another hand than that of the scribe of the rest of the text, at the end of the annal for 1262: it records the birth to Joanna, wife of Henry de Hastings, of a son, John, at Allesley (in Warwickshire) on 6 May[153] (Plate 16). This was a matter of particular interest to a Bury chronicler, because the Hastings were hereditary stewards of St Edmunds's Liberty. John succeeded his father on the latter's death in 1268/9. It is tempting to conclude that the addition was made at about that time, when information about John would have been especially topical. In any case, it may well have been made before the Moyses Hall MS was copied, since the entry is in the text in the hand of the original scribe in that manuscript (and in the Peterborough version of the second recension. It is not in Taxters's chronicle).[154]

A number of other chronicles have blank lines between annals for additions. A good example is the thirteenth-century chronicle of Melrose.[155] Only one manuscript survives of the Melrose chronicle, which was probably the only one of it ever written. Therefore, the many changes of hand, blank spaces, and insertions in them and in the margins reflect the actual process of composition (see Plate 18). Another example of the practice of leaving spaces is provided by the very different *Scotichronicon* composed by Walter Bower, prior of Inchcolm (1417-49). Bower borrowed from John Fordun's chronicle until that ends in 1483. Thereafter his chronicle derives from no other chronicle, and from the early fifteenth century until 1438, when it ends, it was increasingly based on Bower's own experiences and observations.[156] It is a much more sophisticated work than the Melrose chronicle, and survives in a number of copies. It is not in all respects a typical monastic chronicle. One untypical feature is that the chronology of the annals tends to be confused, and its main divisions are into books (for the reigns of the kings of Scotland), and chapters each approximating to an annal. The earliest manuscript (Corpus Christi College, Cambridge, MS 171) was copied under Bower's supervision, and substantial spaces were left between chapters for additions. Entries were inserted into two of these at an early date[157] (Plate 19).

There is evidence indicating that the Moyses Hall MS of the Bury

---

[153]   That this was the birthday of John de Hastings, 1st baron Hastings 1290-1312/13, is confirmed by an inquisition 'post mortem'; *Cal. Inq. Post Mortem, Henry III*, v. 229, no. 719. For the Hastings' hereditary stewardship of St Edmund's Liberty see L.J. Redstone, 'The Liberty of St. Edmund', in *Proceedings of the Suffolk Institute of Archaeology and Natural History*, xv (1915), pp. 207-9.

[154]   *Bury Chron.*, p. 89 n. *d*.

[155]   See above p. 226 and n. 127.

[156]   See Professor Watt's introduction to *Scotichronicon*, viii, ed. Watt, pp. xvi-xx.

[157]   *Ibid.*, pp. xiv, 238 n. *b*, 260 n. *w*.

chronicle and the Corpus MS of the *Scotichronicon* were each copied from exemplars which also had spaces between their respective annals or chapters, and that additions had been inserted into some of them. Collation shows that the Moyses Hall MS has three sentences, two under 1274 and one under 1277, which are not in Arundel 30.[158] They record respectively that: Edward I forfeited the Limousin and Provence in the court of the king of France, and the countess of Provence was awarded them instead; the king of Spain opposed the election of the king of Germany as emperor of the Romans, with the agreement of the Genoese and the marquess of Montferrat; King Edward forfeited the castle of Fronsac (Gironde) in the king of France's court. The first of these additions occurs one sentence before the end of the annal for 1274, the second at the end, and the third is fairly near the beginning of the annal for 1277. It seems likely that at least the first two entered the chronicle as additions in a space at the end of the annal for 1274 in some now lost draft. The same may also be true of the third addition; as noted above, the annal for 1279 in Arundel 30 and the Moyses Hall MS has a space near the beginning. It is noteworthy that all three additions concern foreign affairs, about which one would expect news to arrive late. In the case of the *Scotichronicon* the significant feature is that a number of chapters end with short, inconsequential entries; these could well have originated as additions made in blank spaces left in the copyist's exemplar.[159]

Thus, it can be seen that spaces between annals were intended, and sometimes used, for additions. They were particularly useful for information which came to hand after the annal for the relevant year had been composed. Spaces left elsewhere in a manuscript were similarly used. When the scribe of the Corpus MS of Bower's chronicle listed the chapter heads at the beginning of each book of the *Scotichronicon*, he left the verso blank. Two of these blank pages provided room for the insertion of four important letters: a letter of Pope Gregory XI and one of David II were inserted at the beginning of Book XV; and two of Henry IV of England are on the blank page at the beginning of Book XVI, with a heading indicating that they should be inserted in Chapter 30 ('Hec sequentes littere deberent situari infra sequentem librum XVI[tum] ad

---

[158]  *Bury Chron.*, pp. 57 nn. *d,f*, 63 n. *a*. However, these additions could have originated as marginalia. For the use of margins for additions see below pp. 233-4. It is hard to interpret the fact that an early annotator of Arundel 30, whose notes in faint plummet appear frequently in the margins, has written the incipits of each of these three additions at the appropriate places. It seems most likely that he collated the text in Arundel 30 with the Moyses Hall MS or its exemplar, and noted these additions in this way.

[159]  See e.g. *Scotichronicon*, viii, ed. Watt, pp. 80-2, 86, 124, 254, 264, 266, 276, 292, 296-8. The spaces in Corpus MS 171 were little used (see n. 157 above); it is only to be expected that more use would have been made of those in an earlier draft. However, Professor Watt tells me that these short entries almost certainly came from some pre-existing St Andrews' chronicle. For spaces left between annals for additions see below p. 249.

XXX capitulum') – where they duly occur in the later manuscripts of the *Scotichronicon*.[160] Whether or not these pages had been left blank on purpose for late additions is not clear.

Sometimes it seems that a document might be copied in first and the explanatory narrative introducing it inserted afterwards. The Bury chronicle in Arundel 30 has the letters of submission to Edward I's judgement of the competitors for the Scottish throne, 5 June 1291, copied in a different hand from the preceding account of the dispute; the last nine words of the latter are written in the margin, obviously for want of space[161] (Plate 20). Edward I himself had ordered (9 July 1291) specific religious houses, including Bury, to have these letters copied into their chronicles.[162] Presumably the royal mandate was the immediate cause of their inclusion here. It would seem that the chronicler obeyed Edward's command promptly, before composing the introductory matter; he, therefore, left a space, but it proved too short.

To leave a small gap in a line of text for some snippet of information not yet to hand was a common practice. The scribe of the Bury chronicle in Arundel 30 left such a gap in the annal for 1295 after an entry about the dismissal of William March from the office of Treasurer. Another early hand has filled it in with: 'cui successit Walterus de Langeton'[163] (Plate 21). In fact March was dismissed on 16 August 1295, and Langton appointed on the following 28 September. The Moyses Hall MS of the Bury chronicle (copied in, or shortly after, 1283) leaves a gap under 1282 for the name of the daughter who, it records, was born to Queen Eleanor at Rhuddlan (actually August, 1282)[164] (Plate 17). The Westminster chronicle, which was written more or less contemporaneously probably from the late 1380s, and survives in an early copy, Corpus Christi College, Cambridge, MS 197A, has a similar gap. Under 1390 it notes the consecration by the archbishop of Canterbury on 8 May of Brother Alexander as bishop of St Asaph; a blank is left for his surname (Bache)[165] (Plate 22). In the same way Bower leaves small gaps for names he does not know under 1277 and 1433.[166] In one place the Westminster chronicle leaves a gap for another kind of information: it records that in 1390 Richard II created William count of Ostrevantz, a knight off the Garter and conferred 500 marks on him – but the '500' is in darker ink than the

[160] Corpus Christi College, Cambridge, MS 171, 336ᵛ. Cf. *Scotichronicon*, viii, ed. Watt, pp. xiv, 310-13.
[161] *Bury Chron.*, p. 100 n. *a*.
[162] See Stones and Simpson, *Edward I and the Throne of Scotland*, i. 65, 160, 178; ii. 120 (no. D. 46).
[163] *Bury Chron.*, p. 129 n. *b*.
[164] *Ibid.*, p. 77 n. *a*. Cf. below p. 234.
[165] *Westminster Chronicle*, ed. Hector and Harvey, p. 434.
[166] *Scotichronicon*, viii, ed. Watt, pp. 98 and n. *j*, 286 and n. *a*.

rest of the text, which indicates that it was inserted later.[167]

Margins were, of course, useful places for additions. The scribe of Taxter's chronicle in Julius A 1 made marginal additions, especially to the early part (see Plate 23). The new material was derived from standard literary sources. These marginalia are incorporated in the text of the Arundel copy of Taxter, and in the second recension of the Bury chronicle.[168] Bower used the margins of the *Scotichronicon* in the same way for additions, but even more extensively (see Plate 19); these too were incorporated in the texts of the later copies. But perhaps the most striking example of such marginal additions is provided by the Winchcombe chronicle. The holograph manuscript, British Library Cotton MS Faustina B I, ff. 21-29[b], shows that the chronicle was little more than a skeleton fleshed with copious marginalia (see Plate 24). C.R. Cheney describes the chronicler's method: 'He set the entry for each year as an island in a little sea of parchment. Then he added new islets of text, spread all round the original entry: sometimes there are as many as six for one year.'[169]

The sources of the Winchcombe chronicler's additions were other monastic chronicles, but margins were especially useful for the insertion of late news, both oral and documentary. Various examples of this usage could be cited, but three from the Bury chronicle in Arundel 30 illustrate it well. The above mentioned addition (p. 232) in a gap in the text, recording the succession as Treasurer of Walter de Langton in 1295, was probably made in response to a note in plummet in the margin: 'cui successit Walterus de Langeton' Angl' thes'.' The other two examples both occur under 1294. They are by one annotator writing soon after the scribe of the text, in the margin in ink. The first note is next to the chronicler's entry recording that Edward I took over the religious houses and their revenues, putting his officials in charge of them and ordering a fixed allowance for each monk still resident. The annotator added: 'that is, 18d. a week per monk' ('videlicet cuilibet monacho per ebdomados xviij. d' ').[170] The other marginal addition occurs by the notice that John de Sanford, archbishop of Dublin, who had been on an embassy to the king of Germany, returned to Yarmouth and died a few days later. The annotator wrote: 'Brother William de Hothum of the Order of Preachers succeeded him' ('Cui successit frater Willelmus de Hodone de ordine

---

[167] *Westminster Chronicle*, p. 452. For a similar example see *Scotichronicon*, viii. 262 and n. *e*, and below Plate 19. The scribe left a marginal note incomplete at the end, not adding the number comprising 'the whole membership of Clan Cameron'. The note remained incomplete, and when subsequent scribes incorporated it into the texts of their copies of the *Scotichronicon* they left a small gap for the still unknown number.

[168] *Bury Chron.*, pp. xxxvii-xxxviii.

[169] Cheney, 'The making of the Dunstable Annals', p. 227.

[170] *Bury Chron.*, p. 123 and n. *c*.

predicatorum')[171] (Plate 25). Since Sanford died on 2 October 1294, and Hotham was provided to Dublin on 24 April 1296, this addition (and presumably the other one) was made after the latter date.

Study of manuscripts, therefore, can throw light on a chronicle's development. Moreover, if there are more than one manuscript of a chronicle, the collation of the texts may well be revealing. Again, the Bury chronicle provides good examples. Comparison of the texts of the chronicle itself and also of it with its derivatives, the chronicles of Norwich, St Benet of Hulme and Peterborough, produces significant results. Collation of Arundel 30 with the Moyses Hall MS shows the presence in the latter of the three extra sentences under 1274 and 1277, discussed above.[172] It also shows that one of them (that recording Edward I's forfeiture of the Limousin and Provence) was copied into the Hulme chronicle.[173] These variants indicate that both Arundel 30 and the Moyses Hall MS descend from an earlier draft which was in process of revision.

It is noticeable that from the early 1280s the Norwich, Hulme and Peterborough chronicles differ increasingly from their Bury exemplar, again indicating the latter's progressive revision. It was observed above that the Moyses Hall MS leaves a gap for the name of Queen Eleanor's daughter born in 1282.[174] But Arundel 30 has 'Elizabeth'.[175] The Hulme chronicle similarly has 'Elysabeth', but on an erasure, in a darker ink, and apparently not in the hand of the original scribe, though in a nearly contemporary one[176] (Plate 26). This suggests that new information occasioned revision. The Norwich chronicle calls the baby 'Walkiniana'.[177] It would seem from these scraps of evidence that there was some delay before a name reached the chronicler at all, and then some confusion over what it was.

From 1286 onwards the Hulme chronicle diverges more and more from the surviving text of the Bury chronicle. In some instances it seems that the latter was corrected after the Hulme chronicle was written. For example, the Hulme chronicle asserts wrongly that Edward I crossed to France in about the middle of Lent, 1286;[178] the Bury chronicle states that he did so after Easter (14 April), in May, which is correct.[179] Again, under 1290, the Hulme chronicle wrongly names the duke of Brabant Walter;[180]

---

[171]  *Ibid.*, p. 124 and n. *b*. Cf. above p.232 and n. 163 and Plate 21.
[172]  Above p. 231.
[173]  *Oxenedes*, p. 246. Cf. *Bury Chron.*, p. 57 n. *d*.
[174]  Above p. 232 and n. 164.
[175]  *Bury Chron.*, p. 77.
[176]  BL Cotton MS Nero D II, f. 235ᵛ (new foliation); *Oxenedes*, p. 260.
[177]  BL Cotton MS Nero V, f. 206 (new foliation); *Cotton*, ed. Luard, p. 162.
[178]  *Oxenedes*, p. 267.
[179]  *Bury Chron.*, p. 86.
[180]  *Oxenedes*, p. 276.

the Bury chronicle rightly calls him John.[181] In another instance both chronicles are wrong, but disagree nonetheless: under 1286 the Hulme chronicle states that Hugh Balsham, bishop of Ely, died on 5 Ides July (11 July);[182] the Bury chronicle gives 5 Ides June (9 June);[183] in fact 5 Kal.July (16 July) was the date of his death.

So far we have been concerned with methods of expanding annals already composed for specific years, in order to include extra information, and with their revision. The next problem is how a chronicle was continued from year to year, in such a way that incoming material was digested and a coherent annal composed. The Winchester chronicler recommends a method in his prologue:

> Let it be your responsibility that a sheaf of loose leaves be added to the end of the book, on which should be noted in plummet the deaths of illustrious men and anything memorable you hear concerning the state of the kingdom. At the end of each year let he who is ordered, not just anyone who likes, record for posterity what he thinks best, entering it briefly at the end of the book.[184]

The Winchester chronicler explains why he insisted that 'not just anyone who likes' should write an annal: it was because he deplored any annal in 'rough, unpolished Latin'. One such might easily occur because, 'since the book is added to every year and is, therefore, composed by various people, it may fall into the hands of someone who writes barbariously.'[185] In fact, most monastic chronicles seem to have been the work of one monk and of one or more continuators, each covering several years. Nor by any means were they all kept up from year to year; two, three or even more yearly intervals were apparently not uncommon. Moreover, there is no positive evidence as to how widespread the practice was of appending a schedule of blank leaves to a chronicle. No manuscript of a chronicle petrified, as it were, in process of production, with a sheaf still attached, seems to survive. However, the argument of probability, and evidence provided by collation of texts, suggest that some such

---

[181] *Bury Chron.*, p. 95.
[182] *Oxenedes*, p. 267.
[183] *Bury Chron.* p. 86.
[184] *Annales Monastici*, iv. 355. See above p. 211 and n. 64. The whole passage reads: Considerantes pro multis causis in religione chronicas esse necessarias, istas vobis de vetustis rotulis neglectisque scedulis excerpsimus; et quasi de sub mensa Domini fragmenta collegimus, ne perirent. Non enim debet vestras urbanas aures offendere rudis et inculta Latinitas, qui soletis in scripturis magis sensui quam verbis incumbere, fructui potius quam foliis inhærere. Nec mirandum, si liber annuatim augmentatur, ac per hoc a diversis compositus, in alicujus forte manus inciderit, qui proloquens fecerit barbarismum. Vestri itaque studii erit; ut in libro jugiter scedula dependeat, in qua cum plumbo notentur obitus illustrium virorum et aliquod de regni statu memoriale, cum audiri contigerit. In fine vero anni non quicunque voluerit, sed cui injunctum fuerit, quod verius et melius censuerit ad posteritatis notitiam transmittendum, in corpore libri succincta brevitate describat; et tunc veteri scedula subtracta, nova imponatur.
[185] See previous note.

method was used to compile the more ambitious kind of chronicle. Obviously a chronicler had to assemble his material, documentary and other, before writing an annal; to attach it to the end of the chronicle would have been a sensible way of keeping it safe and readily accessible.

The practice of appending a collection of relevant documents to an historical work was not unknown. The best surviving example is, of course, Matthew Paris's *Liber Additamentorum*.[186] But a collection of this sort was supplementary to an historical work; it was not meant to provide material for composing the narrative. However, it is likely that the copies of documents which form the last part of Thomas Elmham's *Speculum Augustinianum* represent a collectanea made preparatory to composition.[187] Elmham planned to write accounts of the sixty-one abbots of St Augustine's, up to his own time, the early fifteenth century. But he only completed sections on the first fourteen abbots, to 806. He then gives brief particulars to 1087 and finally a collection of documents to 1191.

In this context the Bury chronicle and its derivatives are again suggestive. The divergencies in their texts, which have already been mentioned, become even more marked as the years pass. It would appear that the borrowers were not using the Bury chronicle itself, nor even a proper draft, but merely notes and documents acquired from Bury. This is most vividly illustrated by an example from the Hulme chronicle: it has a Latin version of the letters of submission of the competitors for the Scottish throne to Edward I's judgement, while the Bury chronicle has a French one; in both chronicles Edward's covering letter is addressed to the abbot and convent of St Edmunds.[188]

Study of individual manuscripts and collation of texts illuminates some aspects of the dissemination of a chronicle from the monastery where it was composed to other religious houses. Some 'parent' manuscripts show traces of preparation for use as an exemplar by the scribe of a derivative

---

[186] Printed in *Chronica Majora*, ed. Luard, vi. The Bridlington chronicler (temp. Edward II, early Edward III) often refers readers to his *Incidentia Chronicorum*, which must have been a register of documents relevant to his narrative, similar to Paris's *Liber Additamentorum*. See *Chronicles of the Reigns of Edward I and Edward II*, ed. Stubbs, ii. xxiv and n. 3, 40, 53, 78 etc., and V.H. Galbraith, *Historical Research in Medieval England* (London, 1951, repr. in *idem, Kings and Chroniclers*), p. 32 n. 1. Documents were thought to add authority to a text. It was for this reason that Eadmer crowded the last part of his *Historia Novorum*, mainly concerning the Canterbury/York controversy, with documents. See *Eadmeri Historia Novorum in Anglia*, ed. Martin Rule (Rolls Series, 1884), esp. pp. 198 *et seqq.* Alan of Tewkesbury regarded his collection of Becket letters as of primary importance, and his Life of St Thomas as introductory to it. See *Materials for the History of Thomas Becket*, ed. J.C. Robertson and J.B. Sheppard (Rolls Series, 1875-85, 7 vols), ii. 300, 351, and Anne Duggan, *Thomas Becket: A Textual History of his Letters* (Oxford, 1980), esp. Chapter 3.

[187] *Historia Monasterii S. Augustini Cantuariensis*, ed. Charles Hardwick (Rolls Series, 1858), pp. 347-479.

[188] *Oxenedes*, p. 136; *Bury Chron.*, p. 100. Cf above p. 232.

chronicle. Thus Arundel 30 of the Bury chronicle has a note in plummet in the margin by Edward I's letter ordering the abbot and convent of St Edmunds to insert the submissions of the Scottish competitors into their chronicles: it reads 'Sancti Petri de Burg'[189] (Plate 20). This must have been an instruction to a scribe making a copy of the chronicle intended for Peterborough abbey: he was to substitute an address to the abbot and convent of Peterborough for the existing one to the abbot and convent of Bury. The Peterborough version of the chronicle has the revised address.[190]

The annals from 1268 to 1295, the end of the first continuation, in Arundel 30, have numerous passages marked 'vacat' in the margins, in plummet.[191] A number of the passages relate to Bury; others concern foreign affairs, particularly Sicily and the papacy, and Edward I's relations with Wales. A few are notices about the weather and other natural phenomena, while some seem purely miscellaneous. The 'vacat' passages were presumably to be omitted by some copyist. In view of the fact that a sizeable proportion concern Bury, it seems safe to conclude that the copy was intended for some other house. The fact that the 'vacat' hand could well be the same as the 'Sancti Petri de Burg" one suggests the possibility that the house in question was Peterborough. If so, the resultant chronicle cannot be the Peterborough chronicle preserved in the Corpus MS, since very few of the 'vacat' passages correspond with those it omits.

The copy of Ralph Diceto's *Ymagines Historiarum* belonging to St Albans is a convincing example of a chronicle marked for a scribe making a copy for another religious house.[192] It has passages marked by small diagonal strokes in plummet in the margins (see Plate 27). These were directions for a copyist, and in this case it is known for which house the copy was intended. It was Dunstable priory. The passages marked generally correspond with those extracted for the Dunstable 'Annals'.[193]

Adaptation of a parent chronicle can also be detected by collation. For example, the Hulme chronicler kept the passage in the Bury chronicle recording that in 1275 the monks of Bury pulled down the ancient round of St Edmund, but added 'apud Sanctum Ædmundum', and substituted 'creditur' for 'credimus' in the sentence 'credimus illam [capellam] fuisse

---

[189] *Bury Chron.*, p. 100 n. *b*.

[190] *Ibid.*, p. 100 n. *b*. and *Florentii Wigorniensis Monachi Chronicon ex Chronicis*, ed. Thorpe, ii. 247.

[191] The passages marked 'vacat' in Arundel 30 are noted in *Bury Chron.*, pp. 39-129 nn. *passim*. Some of the marks are almost, and a few completely, illegible. For Matthew Paris's use of 'vacat' marks when revising his own chronicles, to alter their political tone etc., see Vaughan, *Matthew Paris*, pp. 64-5, 117-24.

[192] BL Royal MS 13 E VI (C in *Radulphi de Diceto Lundoniensis Opera Historica*, ed. William Stubbs (Rolls Series, 1876, 2 vols)).

[193] See Cheney, 'The making of the Dunstable annals', pp. 216-17.

que ad opus sancti Eadmundi primo fuit constructa'.[194] Similarly, collation shows that the chronicler of St Peter's, Gloucester, when in the mid-twelfth century he copied the chronicle of John of Worcester, added a notice of the death of Roger de Berkeley, patron of St Peter's, but omitted the account of the sudden (and soon fatal) illness during mass of Uhtred, precentor of Worcester.[195]

The question arises whether a chronicle was lent to another house for copying or whether the copy was made in the house of its origin. Maybe more research, for example on the palaeography of the manuscripts concerned, would provide answers. No doubt practice varied. In the case of the Bury chronicle in Arundel 30 there is evidence suggesting that at least the Peterborough copy was made at Bury itself: the hand which wrote 'Sancti Petri de Burg'' in plummet in the margin almost certainly wrote 'Nota' in the same way by a number of entries about Bury. Particularly convincing evidence that the hands are identical is provided by two longer 'nota' marginalia; that is, 'Nota de Capella Marie' and 'Nota de Mort' abb[a]t[is] Simon' by the relevant entries in the annals for 1275 and 1279 respectively.[196] The references are to the notice in the text to Abbot Simon de Luton's construction of the Lady Chapel in St Edmund's conventual church, and to his death.[197]

The Bury chronicle, therefore, considered together with its derivatives, throws light on how the contemporary part of a chronicle might be written, and how its text might spread to other religious houses. It is a fairly safe basis for generalisation since it is typical of its genre, and, as has been seen, parallels for the methods of composition which its authors employed can be found in other chronicles.

[194] *Bury Chron.*, p. 58; *Oxenedes*, p. 246.
[195] *Chronicle of John of Worcester*, pp. 25 n. 3, 36 and n. 4.
[196] Arundel 30, ff. 162ᵛ, 166ᵛ. *Bury Chron.*, p. 58 n. c; Gransden, *A Critical Edition*, p. 413 n. 1282.
[197] A copy of Matthew Paris's *Flores Historiarum* was executed at St Albans *c.* 1250 probably especially for the monks of Westminster, to whom it was later transferred. See below p. 245.

# 9

## The *Cronica Buriensis* and the Abbey of St Benet of Hulme

THE *Cronica Buriensis*, so called by its editor, Thomas Arnold,[1] is a history of the Benedictine abbey of Bury St. Edmund's from its refoundation by King Canute in 1020 to 1346. The only known text is a fair copy of about 1400 in a volume from the library at St. Edmund's abbey, now Cambridge University Library Additional MS. 850, fos. 25v–48v: it is incomplete at the end, a gathering of eight leaves having been lost.[2]

The *Cronica* is not a methodical record of events with entries for each year. It has the succession of the abbots of Bury and notices of important events in the abbey's history, omitting many years altogether. Arnold treated the *Cronica* as the work of one man. It is, however, almost certainly a composite work, compiled by more than one author and at more than one time. Exactly how many contributed is unknown but there is evidence suggesting changes of authorship in 1327 and 1335. The work must have been completed before about 1400, the approximate date of the manuscript. The annal of 1327 reads like a contemporary account of the events it records.

---

[1] *Memorials of St. Edmund's Abbey* (3 vols., Rolls Ser., 1890–6), iii, pp. vii–xv, 1–73 (hereafter referred to as Arnold).

[2] The medieval foliation jumps from fo. ccxxi (fo. 48 of the modern foliation) to fo. ccxxx (now fo. 49). The *Cronica* today ends with a complete sentence as the first word or two of the next sentence, at the end of the last line on fo. 48v, have been totally erased by scraping. Arnold does not note that the text is incomplete.

The choice of events to be recorded may have been determined partly by the availability of material. To 1292 the text is mainly composed of extracts from other chronicles; and from 1301 (there are no entries for the years 1293 to 1300) of documents. There are a few passages which are neither citations from known literary works nor from documents. Two of them have information not to be found in other literary sources. One relates to the collection of an aid in 1212 from the town of Bury by a monk, instead of as was customary by the burgesses.[1] The second is the account of the revolt of the town against the abbey in 1327; this is independent of the account written at Bury, the *Depraedatio Abbatiae*.[2]

Arnold's identification of citations from, and passages reminiscent of, other chronicles in the *Cronica* is incomplete and somewhat misleading. He printed citations in small type with the name of the work in which they occur in the margin. He also printed letters and other documents in small type. He does not, however, mention that the *Cronica* is also related to a number of other works. The account at the beginning of the *Cronica* of the refoundation of Bury by monks of St. Benet of Hulme and of Ely appears to be mainly a conflation of the account inserted in the mid-twelfth-century copy of Florence of Worcester from St. Edmund's abbey (MS. Bodley 297, p. 350)[3], that in the registers of Hulme and Bury (Brit. Mus., Cotton MS. Galba E. ii, fo. 36v[4], and Brit. Mus, Harley MS. 1005, fos. 35, 35v respectively), both of about 1300, and that in the volume of St. Edmund's life and miracles, written in the last half of the fourteenth century (MS. Bodley 240, fo. 638; the passage has the rubric 'ex cronicis de Hulmo').[5] The details of the confraternity between Hulme and Bury which follow in the *Cronica* are almost verbatim in Cotton MS. Galba E. ii, fo. 36v and Harley MS. 1005, fos. 35, 35v.[6] The succession, with short lives, of the Bury abbots recorded in the course of the *Cronica* is probably derived from a list like that in the fifteenth-century Lakynhethe register of Bury (Brit. Mus., Harley MS. 743, fos. 52–3)[7] and the notice of Abbot Baldwin's building activities resembles that in Hermann's *De*

---

[1]Arnold, iii. 9–10. Noticed by M. D. Lobel, *The Borough of Bury St. Edmunds* (Oxford, 1935), p. 124.

[2]Printed Arnold, ii. 327–54. For the account in the *Cronica* see below 243-4. For the revolt see M. D. Lobel, 'A detailed account of the 1327 rising at Bury St. Edmund's and the subsequent trial', *Proc. Suffolk Inst. Archaeol.*, xxi (1933), 215–31.

[3]Printed Arnold, i. 341–2.

[4]Printed W. Dugdale, *Monasticon Anglicanum*, ed. J. Caley, H. Ellis and B. Bandinel (6 vols. in 8, 1817–30), iii. 135 (hereafter referred to as *Mon. Angl.*).

[5]Printed Arnold, i. 359.

[6]The version in the *Cronica* ('Crescente autem ibidem religione . . . unus fratrum loci illius collocetur:' Arnold, iii. 2) differs from that in Cotton MS. Galba E. ii (printed *Mon. Angl.*, iii. 135) and Harley MS. 1005 in omitting a sentence reading 'quod usque in eternum gratia Dei firmiter observabitur' after 'omnibus aliis bonis Deo placitis' and adding two sentences at the end reading 'Abbates vero utriusque ecclesie . . . frequentius exhibetur'. Cf. above p. 97.

[7]Printed *Mon. Angl.*, iii. 155–6.

*Miraculis Sancti Eadmundi.*[1] There are citations which appear to be from the chronicle of John of Wallingford.[2]

Arnold recognized citations from, and passages reminiscent of, Jocelin's life of Abbot Samson,[3] the *Annales Sancti Edmundi* (a chronicle of the world from the Incarnation to 1212 compiled at Bury),[4] the *Electio Hugonis* (an account, with documentation, of the disputed election as abbot of Bury of Hugh de Northwold 1213–14),[5] and the *Chronica Maiora* of Matthew Paris.[6]

He noticed that the *Cronica* contains citations from the chronicle, compiled at Bury in the last half of the thirteenth century, covering the period from the Creation to 1301, which has been attributed to John de Everisden. But, though he identified some citations from 'Everisden', he overlooked many more. He used the only printed text of 'Everisden', appended by Benjamin Thorpe to his edition of Florence of Worcester (English Historical Society, 1848/9). Thorpe printed from the version of 'Everisden' in Corpus Christi College, Cambridge, MS. 92, which was written for Peterborough abbey. It only covers the years from 1152 to 1295 and omits many passages relating to Bury which occur in the best text of the chronicle written at Bury.[7] The *Cronica* cites many of these

[1] Printed Arnold, i. 26–92. Cf. *ibid.*, iii. 4 and i. 85.

[2] Brit. Mus., Cotton MS. Julius D. vii, fos. 61–110, for which chronicle see R. Vaughan, 'The chronicle of John of Wallingford', *Eng. Hist. Rev.*, lxxiii (1958), 66–77, and the same, 'The chronicle attributed to John of Wallingford', *Camden Miscellany*, xxi (1958). Citations from it in the *Cronica* are: *s.a.* 1210 (Arnold, iii. 9) 'cum filio suo capta . . . ibidem fame interiit'; *s.a.* 1214 (*ibid.*, pp. 10–11) 'Hic legationis suae officium. . . His ita gestis ad propria remearunt'.

[3] The account of St. Edmund's translation in 1198 in the *Cronica* (Arnold, pp. 7–9) is related to that in Jocelin (*The Chronicle of Jocelin of Brakelond*, ed. H. E. Butler (1949), with an English translation, pp. 112 *sqq.*).

[4] The work is incomplete at the end owing to the loss of leaves. Extracts printed Arnold, ii. 3–25, and F. Liebermann, *Ungedruckte Anglo-Normannische Geschichtsquellen* (Strassburg, 1879), pp. 97–115. The account of Abbot Samson's death in the *Cronica* (Arnold, iii. 9) is a citation from it.

[5] Printed Arnold, ii. 29–130. The account in the *Cronica* (*ibid.*, iii, pp. vii, 11–26) has briefer narrative passages than the *Electio* but has transcripts of three letters not in the *Electio*, viz: the letter ratifying Hugh's election (*ibid.*, p. 14), letter from the archbishop of Canterbury, Stephen Langton, to Pope Innocent III (*ibid.*, pp. 15, 16), letter from Eustace, bishop of Ely, to Pope Innocent III (*ibid.*, p. 16).

[6] The notice of the death of Hugh de Northwold, bishop of Ely, formerly abbot of Bury, in 1248 (*ibid.*, p. 29), 'quandoque abbas sancti Edmundi . . . ita et episcopus episcoporum coruscauit', is in *Matthaei Parisiensis Chronica Majora*, ed. H. R. Luard (7 vols., Rolls Ser., 1872–83), v. 454–5.

[7] College of Arms, MS. Arundel 30. For the 'Everisden' chronicle and the manuscript texts see V. H. Galbraith, 'The St. Edmundsbury chronicle, 1296–1301', *Eng. Hist. Rev.*, lviii (1943), 51 *sqq.* Since Professor Galbraith wrote his article another manuscript (to 1283) of 'Everisden' has come to light, which is now in the Moyses Hall Museum at Bury St. Edmunds. An edition of MS. Arundel 30 has been prepared by the present writer for future publication in *Nelson's Medieval Texts*.

passages omitted in the Peterborough text: Arnold did not recognize them.

Arnold indicated that the *Cronica* has citations from the chronicle of English history to 1292 composed at St. Benet of Hulme and attributed to John de Oxenedes.[1] Yet the passages which he ascribed to 'Oxenedes' are citations in 'Oxenedes' from 'Everisden'.[2] Collation of the *Cronica*, 'Everisden' and 'Oxenedes' suggests that these passages in the *Cronica* are citations from 'Everisden' and not'Oxenedes'[3]: only two passages (not identified by Arnold) in the *Cronica* are in 'Oxenedes' and not in 'Everisden'.[4] Collation also indicates that the *Cronica* and 'Oxenedes' cite the same version of 'Everisden', but that this version differed from those surviving today. Thus *s.a.* 1071 both the *Cronica* and 'Oxenedes' omit the first line of the verse inscribed on the altar which Pope Alexander II gave to Baldwin abbot of Bury; the line is in all the known texts of 'Everisden'.[5] Another variant suggests that the lost version was not written at Bury: *s.a.* 1275 the *Cronica* and 'Oxenedes' add the phrase 'apud sanctum Edmundum' to the statement in 'Everisden' that the chapel

---

[1] *Chronica Johannis de Oxenedes*, ed. H. Ellis (Rolls Ser., 1859) (hereafter referred to as Ellis).

[2] 'Oxenedes' has citations from 'Everisden' for the years 1020 to 1169 and 1258 to 1292 (the St. Albans chronicles are the main sources for the intervening period). Ellis apparently only knew the text of 'Everisden' from Thorpe's edition of Florence of Worcester and so did not identify many of the citations from it in 'Oxenedes'. The connexion between 'Oxenedes' and 'Everisden' is noticed in *Bartholomaei de Cotton, monachi Norwicensis, Historia Anglicana*, ed. H. R. Luard (Rolls Ser., 1859), p. lvii.

[3] 'Oxenedes' has passages from 'Everisden' not in the *Cronica*, and the *Cronica* has some not in 'Oxenedes'. It is possible that the *Cronica* cites 'Oxenedes' for passages common to 'Oxenedes' and 'Everisden', and only cites 'Everisden' directly for passages not in 'Oxenedes'. However it is more likely that the *Cronica* throughout cites 'Everisden' directly, as 'Everisden' is a better authority for Bury history than 'Oxenedes'. Collation supports this view: some of the 'Everisden' citations in the *Cronica* are fuller than in 'Oxenedes' which omits short sentences (e.g. 'Oxenedes' omits from 'Everisden' citations *s.a.* 1279 'Dominica videlicet in albis, .. manerium suum,' *s.a.* 1282 'Fraternitas etiam Duodene ... xii marcas fuit taxata'; both sentences are in the *Cronica*: see Ellis, pp. 253, 259; College of Arms, MS. Arundel 30, fos. 166v, 169; Arnold, iii. 33, 35). Also 'Oxenedes' has some readings in 'Everisden' citations different from those in both 'Everisden' and the *Cronica* (e.g. *s.a.* 1275 'fuerunt' before 'apud sanctum Edmundum'; 'Everisden' and the *Cronica* read 'venerunt': Ellis, p. 246; College of Arms, MS. Arundel 30, fo. 162; Arnold, iii. 31). Similarly 'Oxenedes' does not derive 'Everisden' citations from the *Cronica* as it has phrases from 'Everisden' not in the *Cronica* (e.g. *s.a.* 1282 like 'Everisden' it has 'modo predicto' before 'cepit contributionem'; the *Cronica* omits these words: Ellis, p. 258; College of Arms, MS. Arundel 30, fo. 169; Arnold, iii. 34).

[4] Details of the expulsion of the Jews, *s.a.* 1290, and of the king's visit to Bury in 1292 (Arnold, iii. 35–6) are in 'Oxenedes' (Ellis, pp. 277, 285) but not in 'Everisden'. Cf. the briefer entries in College of Arms, MS. Arundel 30, fos. 177v, 184v.

[5] Cf. Arnold, iii. 3; Ellis, p. 34; College of Arms, MS. Arundel 30, fo. 133v.

of St. Edmund was pulled down; in the same entry they read 'creditur' for 'credimus' at the beginning of the sentence 'illam [capellam] fuisse que ad opus sancti Edmundi primo fuit constructa'.[1]

Collation of 'Oxenedes' with the extant texts of 'Everisden' suggests that the lost version ended in 1290. Though the annals for 1291 and 1292 in 'Oxenedes' appear to be related to 'Everisden', they contain such striking variants as to suggest that the author was using a draft of 'Everisden' and some of the same documents as the Bury chronicler used, together with his own knowledge. For example, the copy of Edward I's letter of 1291 relating to the Scottish succession case is addressed to the abbot and convent at Bury, but the letters recited in it of submission of the competitors to Edward's judgment are in Latin, though in 'Everisden' they are in French.

The probability, although unknown to Arnold, that the *Cronica* cites the same version of 'Everisden' as the Hulme chronicle attributed to Oxenedes, supports his view that the *Cronica* was compiled at Hulme. Arnold writes (p. vii) of the *Cronica*: 'this chronicle, as many indications go to show, was written by a monk of St. Benet Hulme'. Undoubtedly three indications led Arnold to his conclusion. The first was the opening paragraph concerning the part played by St. Benet of Hulme in the foundation of Bury and the close relationship between the houses. The second was the presence of twelve letters to the abbot of Hulme, mostly from the abbot, prior and others at Bury, and of two from him (all relating to Bury), dated or dateable 1301 to 1335 (the last letter cannot be dated exactly but was probably written after 1335 and certainly before 1346).[2]

Arnold's third probable reason for ascribing the *Cronica* to Hulme was the inclusion in the vivid and surely contemporary account of the revolt of the town of Bury, which broke out on 14 January 1326/7, of a description of the flight of the sacrist, William de Stowe, to Hulme.[3] It relates that Stowe hardly escaped, climbing the town wall with a ladder, helped by a carpenter, in the middle of the night, and reached Hulme only after evading an ambush at Newmarket. The *Cronica* does not record the length of his stay: it reads 'venit ad sanctum Benedictum die Dominica proxima sequente, ibique moratus est usque ad . . .', leaving a blank for the date of his departure. Presumably Stowe was still at Hulme at the time of writing. One of the letters, dated 1 February [1326/7], is from the abbot of Bury thanking the abbot of Hulme for his hospitality to the unfortunate Stowe and asking for its extension.[4] The *Cronica* records that other Bury monks, who were on holiday in the country, took refuge at Hulme but returned to Bury where they were imprisoned. It is not

---

[1] Cf. Arnold, iii. 32; Ellis, pp. 246–7; College of Arms, MS. Arundel 30, fo. 162v.

[2] Arnold, iii. 48. It is a letter from William de Stowe as prior of Bury to John abbot of Hulme (1325–46) asking him to send three or four monks to the feast of St. Edmund. It follows a letter dateable to 1335.

[3] *Ibid.*, p. 39.                    [4] *Ibid.*, p. 41.

unlikely that the chronicler obtained his information from the refugees themselves.

This evidence only suggests that the *Cronica* as far as the end of the fourteen 'Hulme' letters was composed at Hulme. It is likely that the rest of it was written at Bury, for its contents have nothing to do with Hulme. They are documents relating to the dispute between William de Bernham, abbot of Bury 1335 to 1361, and John, abbot of the Premonstratensian house of Langley, over the reception at Bury of a fugitive canon of Langley, and to the dispute, 1345 to 1346, between Abbot William and William Bateman, bishop of Norwich, over the abbot's spiritual jurisdiction.

The reason why a history of Bury should have been written at Hulme is obscure. Possibly it was one result of the close relationship between Bury and Hulme. The *Cronica* shows that it was customary for the abbots to attend each other's election, installation and funeral.[1] The deed of confraternity which must underlie part of the opening paragraph stipulated that the houses were to help each other in times of poverty or trouble (such as fire or war), if necessary harbouring half the inmates of the stricken house. This deed of confraternity seems to have belonged to the type which Professor Knowles suggests was 'a kind of insurance on the part of the communities'.[2]

The interest of the Hulme monks in Bury must have been stimulated by the town's attack on its privileges and the flight of monks to Hulme. Seven of the fourteen 'Hulme' letters and one other document[3] in the *Cronica* relate to the revolt. One is a papal bull appointing the abbot of Hulme legate to announce the excommunication of the rioters. If the revolt was the cause of the writing of the *Cronica* to 1327, the possibility cannot be disregarded that one of the Bury refugees at Hulme had a hand in it.

## ADDITIONAL NOTE

*Page 241 n.5.* There is a new edition of the *Electio Hugonis: The Chronicle of the Election of Hugh Abbot of Bury St. Edmunds and Later Bishop of Ely*, ed., with an English translation, R. M. Thomson (Oxford Medieval Texts, 1974).

— *n.7.* My edition of the Bury Chronicle in Arundel MS 30 in the College of Arms is published: *The Chronicle of Bury St. Edmunds 1212–1301*, ed., with an English translation, A. Gransden (Nelson's Medieval Texts, 1964).

# 10

## The Continuations of the *Flores Historiarum* from 1265 to 1327

MATTHEW Paris started the *Flores Historiarum*, a general history based on his own works, at the Creation of the world, and ended in 1249.[1] A copy of this chronicle (now MS. 6712 in Chetham's Library, Manchester) was made at St. Albans under Matthew Paris's supervision; he himself wrote the text from 1241 to 1249[2] and helped his pupils draw the series of pictures of the coronations of English kings (Arthur, Edward the Confessor, and the kings from William the Conqueror to John).[3] This manuscript was probably executed specially for the monks of Westminster in about 1250.[4] However, it was not transferred to Westminster until 1265, after a continuation from 1250 to 1265 had been added at St. Albans.[5]

The *Flores Historiarum* was continued in Westminster Abbey from 1265 to 1327. The first continuation ends abruptly in February 1307, and the second continuation begins with a notice of Edward I's death, on 7 July, 1307, and ends with Edward III's accession, on 25 January, 1327. The problems raised by both continuations have been studied with especial reference to the manuscript evidence by a number of scholars, F. Mad-

1 Matthew Paris' *Flores Historiarum* and its continuations are printed in *Flores Historiarum*, ed. H. R. Luard, 1 (Rolls Series, 1890, 3 vols.).

2 See R. Vaughan "The Handwriting of Matthew Paris," *Transactions of the Cambridge Bibliographical Society*, (1953), 384, 390, and N. R. Ker, "From 'Above Top Line' to 'Below Top Line'," *Celtica*, 5 (1960), 15-16. I am grateful to Miss Hilda Lofthouse, librarian of Chetham's Library, for allowing me facilities for examining the manuscript.

3 The pictures are described and reproduced by A. Hollaender, "The pictorial work in the *Flores Historiarum* of the so-called Matthew of Westminster," *BJRL*, 28 (1944), 361-381. The picture of Henry III's coronation is missing because of the loss of a leaf. The picture of Edward's coronation was executed at Westminster.

4 See *Matthaei Parisiensis Monachi Sancti Albani, Historia Anglorum*, ed. F. Madden (Rolls Series, 1866-1869, 2 vols.), I. 24 n. 1, and V. H. Galbraith, *Roger Wendover and Matthew Paris* (Glasgow, 1944, reprinted 1970), p. 25 and n. 2. To this evidence may be added the fact that the picture of the coronation of Edward the Confessor in the Chetham MS. (f. 115v of the library's foliation) is twice as big as the other coronation pictures, covering half a page.

5 See Madden, *op. cit.* i. xxiii-xxiv.

den,[6] H. R. Luard,[7] W. Stubbs[8] and T. F. Tout.[9] Nevertheless, problems concerning the composition and authorship, and even the provenance of one version, remain. By reviewing the manuscript evidence again in close conjunction with the style and content of the continuations, it is possible to make new suggestions which could contribute to the solution of some of these problems.

The first continuation, from 1265 to 1307, survives in a number of manuscripts and in two versions. Luard describes the Chetham MS. and fourteen other manuscripts containing the same version of the text, none of which is the author's/ authors' autograph.[10] The Chetham MS., which also contains the text of the second continuation, to be discussed below, is itself a copy made by a number of scribes, mostly of the late thirteenth and *f*arly fourteenth centuries. The annals from 1298 to 1302 are in a later fourteenth-century hand, which may also have written the last part of the annal for 1326 and that for 1327 in the second continuation:[11] certainly this section was copied well after the events it records. Other manuscripts of this version, which for convenience may be called the 'Westminster' *Flores*, are known to have belonged in the middle ages to the monasteries of Norwich, Rochester and Tintern, and one was owned by St. Paul's cathedral.

The other version of the 1265-1307 continuation of the *Flores* is based on the 'Westminster' *Flores* but has considerable variants, omissions and additions. The earliest known manuscript of this version was copied at or more probably for the Augustinian priory of Merton in Surrey, and is now MS. 123 in Eton College Library.[12] All the six copies of this version, which we will call the 'Merton' *Flores*, described by Luard apparently descend from the Merton manuscript.[13] The evidence that the

---

6 Madden, *op. cit.* i. xxiv-xxvii and nn.

7 *Flores*, ed. Luard, i. xii-xvii, xl-xliii.

8 *Chronicles of the Reigns of Edward I and Edward II*, ed. William Stubbs (Rolls Series, 1882-1883, 2 vols.), ii. xii-xiii.

9 T. F. Tout, "The Westminster Chronicle attributed to Robert of Reading," *EHR*, 31 (1916), 450-464 (reprinted in *The Collected Papers of T. F. Tout* (Manchester, 1932-1934, 3 vols.), ii. 289-304).

10 *Flores*, i. xii-xxxiii.

11 See *Flores*, i. xiv, and Tout, *op. cit.* pp. 459-460.

12 I am indebted to Mr. Patrick Strong, librarian of Eton College, and to the College authorities, for depositing Eton College MS. 123 in the British Museum for me to study. The text is a fair copy in a book-hand, although from the end of 1284 there are occasional changes of ink and perhaps of handwriting. The manuscript ends incomplete in 1306 because of the loss of a leaf, but there is no reason to suppose that it did not once extend to the beginning of 1307 where the 'Westminster' *Flores* ends, as do the descendants of the Eton MS.

13 Luard, *op. cit.* i. xv-xvii, xxix-xxxiii. The so-called Tenison MS., formerly Phillipps MS. 15732, is now MS. 426 in the Beinecke Rare Book and Manuscript Library in Yale University Library. (See the catalogue of H. P. Kraus, New York, no. 117, 1967, item 29). A microfilm is in Nottingham University Library. The text is a conflation of the 'Merton' *Flores* and the 'Westminster' one, which

Eton College MS. was made for the canons of Merton is irrefutable: the manuscript has early notices concerning Merton priory in the margins,[14] and the letter of Edward I containing the submissions of the competitors for the throne of Scotland to his judgement as overlord, of 1291, in the text is addressed to the prior and convent at Merton.[15] Therefore, it has generally been accepted that the 'Merton' *Flores* was actually composed at Merton.[16] Nevertheless the evidence for this is inconclusive. The 'Merton' *Flores* only copies two of the four entries in the 'Westminster' *Flores* relating to Merton priory,[17] and shows no especial interest in the Augustinian order in general. (On the other hand, one of its long additions to the 'Westminster' *Flores* concerns the fate of a Benedictine abbey, Dunfermline, which was sacked by the Scots in 1303).[18]

It seems more likely that the exemplar of the Eton College MS. was written at Westminster. The Eton College MS. itself provides some evidence supporting this view. It has a series of pictures of the coronations of the kings of England from William the Conqueror to Edward I, of better quality than the rather mediocre handwriting seems to justify, which were presumably copied from its exemplar. As has been seen Matthew Paris provided a similar series of pictures for the copy of the *Flores* which he apparently intended for the Westminster monks, who had of course a close interest in the coronation ceremony. Not only was the coronation performed in their church, but they also had custody of the regalia and of the books relating to the service.[19] The artist of the exemplar of the Eton College MS. has one detail which shows

---

accounts for the fact that its copy of Edward I's letter on the Scottish succession case (see below) is addressed to the abbot and convent of Westminster, not to the prior and convent of Merton. The annal for 1306 and the first part of that for 1307 derive from Nicholas Trevet's *Annales*. It ends with the appreciation of Edward I (for a small addition see below n. 82) and an account of events up to the deposition of Edward II, from Murimuth. It ends with two lines of verse:

> Carneruam natus, princeps Edwardus amatus;
> Ingratis gratus, est morte graui cruciatus.

For references to other conflated texts see *Flores*, i. xx.

14 See *Flores*, iii. 250 n. 1, 292, 302 n. 4 (Eton College MS. ff. 227, 251ᵛ, 254ᵛ). For an insertion in the text concerning Merton priory see *ibid*. iii. 84.

15 See *Flores*, i. xvi.

16 However, Richard Vaughan doubts the Merton provenance of the exemplar of the Eton College MS.; see his *Matthew Paris* (Cambridge, 1958), p. 101.

17 *Flores*, ii. 46, 51. For the entries in the 'Westminster' *Flores* concerning Merton priory omitted in the 'Merton' *Flores* see *ibid*. ii. 81 and n. 3, 88 and n. 1.

18 *Flores*, iii. 311-312.

19 See P. E. Schramm, *A History of the English Coronation*, translated from the German by L. G. Wickham Legg (Oxford, 1937), pp. 40, 75, 80.

28  The 'Merton' *Flores Historiarum*: the coronation of Henry III.
*(Windsor, Eton College, MS 123, fo. 194)*

29 The 'Merton' *Flores Historiarum*: the coronation of Edward I (who
holds the rod with the dove).
*(Windsor, Eton College, MS 123, fo. 237)*

his knowledge of the regalia. He depicts Edward I holding the rod with the dove, carefully delineated, in his right hand.[20] The rod with the dove also appears in the picture of King John's coronation, only less well drawn. This emblem is not generally represented in fourteenth and fifteenth century art, although it was in use in the coronation service at least from the time of Richard I. Usually the king is shown holding a rod with a floriated finial in his right hand (he held the sceptre with fleur-de-lis and orb in his left hand), as in the other coronation pictures in the Eton College MS. It is surely likely that the rod with the dove had attracted the especial attention of the artist of the exemplar of the Eton College MS. If he was working at Westminster his interest in the emblem could have been aroused at the time of Edward I's funeral, because the king was buried in full regalia, holding the rod with the dove. The actual rod, which was described in detail after Edward's tomb was opened in 1774, bore a close resemblance to the artist's representation.[21] The artistic evidence could, therefore, be interpreted as indicating that the 'Merton' *Flores* was composed and illustrated at Westminster soon after Edward I's funeral. More evidence supporting this hypothesis will be adduced when discussing the author's outlook and argument.[22]

Neither version of the continuation of the *Flores Historiarum* from 1265 to 1307 has an ascription of authorship. On the other hand the continuation from 1307 to 1327 was according to its own evidence composed by a monk at Westminster called Robert of Reading up to the beginning of the annal for 1326. The relevant passage reads:

> Sicque frater Robertus de Redinge, quondam monachus ecclesiae beati Petri Apostoli Westmonasterii, cronicarum, vitae quoque suae, finem conclusit. Et in praemissis magister Adam Murimoth, olim canonicus ecclesiae sancti Pauli Apostoli Londoniarum, qui texuit ab anno regni regis Edwardi secundi post conquestum sexto usque ad annum regni regis Edwardi tertii filii ejusdem vicesimum, luculentius procedit.[23]

Tout has already discussed the problems inherent in this passage.[24] It

20 Eton College MS. 123, f. 237. (The picture of King John's coronation is on f. 184). For the rod with the dove see L. G. Wickham Legg, *English Coronation Records* (Westminster, 1901), pp. lii-liii.

21 See Joseph Ayloffe, "An Account of the Body of King Edward the First, as it appeared on opening his Tomb in the Year 1774," *Archaeologia*, 3 (1775), 384.

22 Below pp.252ff.

23 *Flores*, iii, 232.

24 Tout, *op. cit.* pp. 450-455. For a payment by the prior of Westminster to "brother Robert de Rading," dated 5 Ocotober 1305, see *Documents Illustrating the Rule of Walter de Wenlok, Abbot of Westminster, 1283-1307*, ed. B. F. Harvey (Camden fourth series, ii, 1965), pp. 91-92.

is not impossible that Robert of Reading was the author, but if so, there must have been more than one monk of that name at Westminster during Edward II's reign, because a Robert of Reading died in 1317, too early for the chronicler. The ascription-passage itself does not have the authority of contemporaneity. The reference to Adam Murimuth 'formerly' canon of St. Paul's dates it to after 1347, the year of Murimuth's death.[25] Moreover, as Tout has pointed out, the author of the remainder of the chronicle after the ascription-passage used not only Murimuth's chronicle but also that of Robert of Avesbury which was composed at the earliest after September 1356.[26] Therefore, the passage was written well after the middle of the fourteenth century. The manuscript evidence agrees with this conclusion. The earliest text of the 1307-1327 continuation, as of the 'Westminster' *Flores*, is in the Chetham MS. (The only other medieval copy, in Cottonian MS. Cleopatra A xvi in the British Museum, is of the fifteenth century.)[27] The change of hand at the beginning of the annal for 1326 noted above,[28] occurs at the ascription-passage. The handwriting up to this point, though clearly not the author's autograph, is of the first half of the fourteenth century. (Its near contemporaneity with the events it records is demonstrated by the fact that substantial blank spaces, some of more than half a column, are left at the end of each annal for the addition of late news). We are mainly concerned with this part of the text preceding the ascription-passage, which will be called the 1307-1326 continuation.

To turn now to the question of literary style. Tout argued on stylistic grounds, irrespective of Robert of Reading's authorship, that one author must have written not only the 1307-1326 continuation but also the annals of the 'Westminster' *Flores* from about 1298.[29] The whole, as Tout pointed out, is in a distinctive style: the prose is florid and bombastic with rhetorical invocations and numerous biblical allusions and citations, and is punctuated with couplets of verse. In fact these stylistic features occur in the 'Westminster' *Flores* almost from the beginning in 1265,[30] although they become much more noticeable after 1298: this

---

25 See *Adae Murimuth Continuatio Chronicarum. Robertus de Avesbury De Gestis Mirabilibus Regis Eduardi Tertii*, ed. E. M. Thompson (Rolls Series, 1889), p. ix.

26 *Ibid.*, p. xxii; Tout, *op. cit.*, p. 454.

27 Cleopatra A xvi, ff. 67-193, contains the 'Westminster' *Flores* from 1298 to 1307 and then the 1307-1326 continuation. This is followed by the chronicles of Adam Murimuth and of John of Reading, consecutively, thus producing a continuous history from 1298 to 1367.

28 Above p. 246.

29 Tout, *loc. cit.* pp. 456-457.

30 See for examples of biblical citations (from 1266), *Flores*, iii. 8, 9, 13, 111, 115-120 *passim*, and of verse couplets (from 1272), *ibid.*, iii. 29, 75.

suggests that the original series of annals to about 1298, which were probably written fairly close to the events recorded, were refurbished and continued to 1307 in the florid style in the early fourteenth century. This style is particularly characteristic of the 'Merton' *Flores* (which apparently Tout did not distinguish from the 'Westminster' one).

Two passages may be quoted, one from the 'Merton' *Flores* and one from the 1307-1326 continuation, to show the marked stylistic similarity between these works. The passage in the 'Merton' *Flores* describes the plight to which England was reduced by the Provisions of Oxford. It reads:

> Reliqua autem hujus provisionis, videlicet causam, exordium, et processum, regni vero divisionem et desolationem, contentiones et discordias, depraedationes et incendia, intrusiones ecclesiarum, persecutiones clericorum, obsidiones castrorum, tribulationes civitatum, exhaeredationes procerum, gemitus pauperum, extorsiones plebium, redemptiones captivorum, defectus senum, miserias orphanorum, deflorationes et suspiria virginum, fletus et lamenta viduarum, praelia et seditiones, et caetera dampna et gravamina, quae ab initio praedictae provisionis usque post bellum Eveshamiae illius occasione in regno Angliae acciderant et fiebant, quae vox, quae poterit lingua retexere?[31]

The 1307-1326 continuation has a similar lament on the state of England after the battle of Boroughbridge, reading:

> Planxerunt mulieres generosae maritorum privationem et natorum, luxerunt ingenui parentum amissionem, doluerunt cives urbium desolationem, deflevit Ecclesia propriam et regni subitam confusionem, quibus communitas undique vallata, liber et servus, dives et pauper, quisque recenter sumpsit lamentum, et qui videbantur laetitiam in vultu praeferre, genas suas occultis lacrimis lugentes regabant.[32]

Two examples may be given to illustrate the use in both works of biblical allusions and citations. The passage from the 'Merton' *Flores* is part of the account of Edward I's siege of Stirling castle in 1304. It has extracts from 2 Reg. xi. 20, 21 (here printed in italics), Joab's advice to David, woven into its text:

> Res stupenda nimis, ex turbine molae violentissimo, quasi ad ictum tonitrui, dextrarius regis resupinatis pedibus corruit, *quasi asina Balaam dans locum exterminatori.* Et accurrentes commilitones traxerunt regem per declivum montis, increpantesque dixerunt, "*Domine, quare proprius*

---

31 *Flores*, iii. 248.
32 *Flores*, iii. 213.

caeteris inermis ad murum acceditis, ut praeliamini? *An ignoras quod multa desuper ex muro tela mittantur ? Quis percussit Abimelech filium Jerobaal ? Nonne mulier misit super eum fragmentum molae de muro, et interfecit eum in Thebes ?* Manete amodo in papilionibus. *Sive enim fugerimus, non magnopere de nobis ad eos pertinebit, sive media pars de nobis ceciderit, non satis curabunt, quia* sola persona vestra *pro decem milibus computatur. Melius est igitur ut sitis nobis* alior-sum *in praesidio."*[33]

The comparable passage in the 1307-1326 continuation describes the escape of Roger Mortimer, the younger, from the Tower of London in 1323. It uses the account of St. Peter's escape from prison, in Act. xii. 4, 6-11, and reads:

misit rex crudelis ministros detestabiles ad Turrim Londoniarum, ubi Rogerus et Rogerus de Mortuo Mari compedibus habebantur constricti, ut denuo majori artarentur supplicio dolentes, *volens* post paucos dies juniorem Rogerum *producere populo* et acerba morte dampnare. *Cumque producturus eum esset* rex, ecce *in nocte* sancti Petri ad Vincula Spiritus Domini astitit et gratia ejus affuit in habitaculo carceris, tactoque corde Rogeri *excitavit eum dicens, 'Surge velociter et sequere me.* Et egressus *sequebatur eum, quia verum est quod fiebat* per Christum; non ergo *aestimabat se visum videre. Transiens autem primam et secundam custodiam* pervenit ultra Thamense flumen ...[34]

Comparison of these four passages surely helps dissipate any remaining doubts as to the Westminster provenance of the 'Merton' *Flores*. Moreover, the isolation of this literary style links both versions of the *Flores* from 1265 to 1307, and the 1307-1326 continuation to two other works. The account in the 'Westminster' *Flores* of the burglary of the royal treasury at Westminster in 1303[35] refers in its concluding words to its source:

"Subsequitur passio monachorum Westmonasteriensium secundum Johannem, cujus copiam non habentas quaerant et invenient et postulantes accipient."

This tract on the burglary, the "passion according to John," is now apparently lost. On the evidence of the extract in the 'Westminster' *Flores*, which has a bombastic tirade, replete with biblical citations, against the imprisonment by the king of ten Westminster monks accused of complicity, the original tract must have been in the same style as the 'Mer-

---

33 *Flores*, iii. 318.

34 *Flores*, iii. 217.

35 *Flores*, iii. 115-117. For reference to this account of the burglary see T. F. Tout. "A Mediæval Burglary," *BJRL*, 2 (1914-1915), 364. For the burglary in general see *ibid.* pp. 348-369, E. H. Pearce, *Walter de Wenlok, Abbot of Westminster* (London, 1920), pp. 146-166, and H. F. Westlake, *Westminster Abbey* (London, 1923, limited edition, 2 vols.), ii. 430-446.

ton' *Flores* and the 1307-1326 continuation. The fourth work in this group is the *Commendatio Lamentabilis in Transitu Magni Regis Edwardi*, a lamentation on the death of Edward I addressed to his queen, Margaret, by 'John of London'.[36]

The *Commendatio Lamentabilis* starts with a eulogistic description of Edward's appearance and character (modelled on Peter of Blois' description of Henry II) and proceeds with panegyrics on him, spoken, as it were, by Margaret and various social groups (the bishops, the earls and barons, the knights, and the like). It has obvious stylistic affinities with the 'Westminster' and 'Merton' *Flores*, with the 1307-1326 continuation and, judging from the surviving extract, with the tract on the burglary. The 'Merton' *Flores* and the 1307-1326 continuation both have passages in the threnetic mode (for example the laments on the condition of England quoted above),[37] while the extant passage from the tract on the burglary is virtually a lament on the fate of the suspect monks. Furthermore, the *Commendatio Lamentabilis* is in the characteristic florid prose, with biblical allusions and rhetorical invocations. To illustrate the similarity a passage in the *Commendatio Lamentabilis* may be compared with one in the 'Merton' *Flores*. Addressing Edward I's knights the *Commendatio Lamentabilis* recalls the peace imposed by the king; it reads, with an allusion to Isai. ii. 4 ('Et conflabunt gladios suos in vomeres'): "Gladii nostri conflabuntur in vomeres et in falces bellastices lanceae redigentur." It then invokes England: "O felix Anglia et vere beata terra cujus rex est nobilis .... Quo proficiscente in regione viventium et ejus regnante vocabulo pax vigescit, aemulus obmutescit, et tranquillitate ecclesia reflorescit."[38] The comparable passage in the 'Merton' *Flores* is in an invocation of England, with reference to her sufferings during the Barons' War. The author recalls her previous peace and prosperity: "In te, gladiis conversis in vomeres, pax et religio viguerunt, ut caeteris omnibus regnis catholicis speculum sisteres et exemplum."[39]

There is some, though inconclusive, evidence concerning the authorship of these works. The 'John' who wrote the burglary-account could of course be 'John of London,' the author of the *Commendatio Lamentabilis*. However, such an identification is only valid if this John of London was a monk of Westminster, which cannot, because the name was a

---

36 The *Commendatio Lamentabilis* is printed *Chrons. Edward I and Edward II*, ed. Stubbs, ii. 3-21. Its view of history is discussed in B. Smalley, *English Friars and Antiquity in the early fourteenth Century* (Oxford, 1960), pp. 9-12.

37 Above  p. 250.

38 *Chrons. Edward I and Edward II*, ii. 16.

39 *Flores*, iii. 267.

common one, be proved. Nevertheless, there was a monk at Westminster called John of London in the early fourteenth century.[39a] He is
apparently to be identified with John Bever, a monk at Westminster.[40]
This identification provides corroborative evidence for his authorship
of the 'Merton' *Flores*, because one fourteenth-century copy (an abbreviated text from St. Augustine's Canterbury), has a note contemporary with the manuscript attributing the work to John Bever.[41]
There is, therefore, the possibility that John of London *alias* John Bever,
monk of Westminster, wrote the 'Merton' *Flores,* the burglary-account
and the *Commendatio Lamentabilis.* He may also have been responsible for
the 'Westminster' *Flores* in its present form: he may have revised a
preexisting continuation of the St. Albans' *Flores Historiarum* to about
1298 and then continued it to 1307. (The reference to John's *passio
monachorum* could be to the author's own work). On stylistic evidence he
could also have written the 1307-1326 continuation. However, this conclusion would be rash because it would involve discarding the medieval
attribution to Robert of Reading, who, as a product of the same literary
school, might well have written a similar florid prose.

It is now necessary to examine the light thrown on the continuations
of the *Flores Historiarum* from 1265 to 1327 by their outlook and
argument. Just as the continuations have a distinctive prose style, so

39ª "A 'John of London' appears among the monks of Westminster indicted by Edward I for
complicity in the burglary of the royal treasury in 1303; *CPR, 1301-1307,* p. 195: For an identification of John of London, the monk of Westminster, with a former rector of Newland in the
Forest of Dean (1264-1302), of the same name, see C. Fortescue-Brickdale, 'A Gloucestershire Rector's Lament for Edward I', *Transactions of the Bristol and Gloucestershire Archaeological Society,* 61 (1939),
p. 195. The evidence there adduced is quite inconclusive. I owe this reference to Miss E. Danbury.

40 The identification of the author John of London with John Bever is suggested by T. D. Hardy,
*Descriptive Catalogue of Materials relating to the History of Great Britain and Ireland* (Rolls Series, 1862-1871,
3 vols.), iii. 282. The evidence that the monk John of London was also called John Bever is a mandate preserved in Westminster Abbey from the commissary general of the archdeacon of London to
the archdeacon of Westminster to publish the excommunication of "brother John de London, dictum Le Bevere," for contumacy in respect of a summons for a crime committed within the arch-
deaconry of London, dated 28 March 1310. This identification does not, however, prove that this
John of London was the author of the *Commendatio Lamentabilis.* Nevertheless, Madden, *Historia
Anglorum,* i. xxiv-xxv and n. 1, tentatively accepts that he was the same man, and the possibility is
discussed by Stubbs, *Chrons. Edward I and Edward II,* ii. xi-xiii. On the other hand, Miss Smalley
maintains the work's anonymity; Smalley, *op. cit.* p. 9 n. 1.

41 BM MS. Harley 641. At the foot of f. 1 is written in a fifteenth-century hand: "Cronica de
edicione domini Johannis dicti Bever" monachi Westmonasterii. De libraria monasterii Sancti
Augustini Cantuariensis Distinct' T. Abbatis.' (A similar inscription is at the end of the chronicle, f.
115ᵛ). The reference is to Thomas de Fyndone, abbot of St. Augustine's 1283-1310. The earlier part
of the text is based on Geoffrey of Monmouth. Then at the Norman conquest it begins to follow
the 'Merton' *Flores* which it slightly abbreviates, and also interpolates a few paragraphs; see *Flores,* i.
xxxi-xxxiii. It is noteworthy that the five texts of the *Commendatio Lamentabilis* used by Stubbs all
follow copies of the *Flores;* see Hardy, *op. cit.* iii. 309, and *Chrons. Edward I and Edward II,* ii. vii-xi.

also do they have distinctive attitudes to politics. When the *Flores* left St. Albans for Westminster in 1265, it acquired a new political bias. Matthew Paris and his continuators at St. Albans (like the great majority of contemporary chroniclers) were harsh critics of the central government and ardent supporters of the baronial cause. At Westminster the *Flores* was continued in a royalist tone. Thus the 'Westminster' *Flores* calls Henry III an innocent, God-fearing man whose dearest wish was to end civil discord.[42] Recording Henry's death, it writes: "God and those who faithfully supported Henry knew what an innocent, patient man he was, and with what devotion he worshipped the Saviour. And, above all, the miracles which followed his death, show how God valued his life.[43] The 'Westminster' *Flores* estimate of Edward I, despite occasional criticism, tends to be eulogistic. (In general the other chroniclers also favour Edward). It enthusiastically supports his Scottish policy. Edward was Scotland's rightful lord, the glorious victor,[44] the most fortunate king, who "trampled on the horns of the proud and silenced the roar of rebels."[45] The very walls of Stirling castle, captured in 1303, bore witness to his glory: the damage done to them by the besiegers' missiles were "indelible tokens of the lasting victory and great triumph of this magnificent king."[46]

This royalist bias is even more marked in the 'Merton' *Flores*. The author modified the few passages in the 'Westminster' *Flores* which were critical of the king. For example he rewrote the passage on Edward I's oppressive treatment of the clergy when they refused an aid in 1296, thus omitting a particularly biting piece of invective. ("The king turned to cruelty, and the clergy were so constantly afflicted that it was as if the madness of Nero was revived in England").[47] Under 1303 he shortened the tirade against Edward for the imprisonment of the monks suspected of complicity in the robbery of the royal treasury, and rewote it in such a bombastic style that it is almost incomprehensible.[48] Besides copying the passages in the 'Westminster' *Flores* which favour the king, the author of the 'Merton' *Flores* added more of his own. He inserted a

42 *Flores*, iii. 15.

43 *Flores*, iii. 28.

44 *Flores*, iii. 112.

45 *Flores*, iii. 118.

46 *Flores*, iii. 119-120.

47 *Flores*, iii. 99. The author of the 'Merton' *Flores* diverted some of the blame on to the *falsi clerici*, *aulici curiales; ibid.* iii. 291.

48 *Flores*, iii. 313.

resumé of events culminating in the battles of Lewes and Evesham which justifies the monarchy and discredits the barons.[49] He accuses the baronial leaders whom he calls 'princes of faction', of being moved by hate, ambition and greed rather than by patriotism,[50] and of causing untold suffering by the civil war, which they engendered.[51] He insists on the ultimate legitimacy of monarchy,[52] defending the king's right to endow his foreign relatives[53] and arguing that Henry could have annulled the Provisions of Oxford, which he refers to as the *proditiones Oxoniae*, by 'common consent' because they had been agreed by 'common consent' — only his scrupulousness made him seek papal absolution from his oath to observe them.[54] Henry was a man of peace, and monarchical government was the custodian of peace. Henry's restoration to power in his "perfect and spacious vineyard" represented the restoration of peace.[55] The author gives a paean on peace, contrasted with horrors of civil war, in his most eloquent prose.[56]

The 'Merton' *Flores* praises Edward I. The author emphasises, in the account of events immediately preceding the battle of Evesham, the part played by the then Lord Edward in securing his father's victory over Simon de Montfort.[57] Later, when Edward was king, he treats him as the architect of peace. He was especially interested in Edward's Scottish campaigns which tried to impose peace on the north. His most eulogistic passages are in his elaboration of the account in the 'Westminster' *Flores* of the siege of Stirling castle.[58] Edward was brave and wise, his interference in Scotland was justified by historical precedents, and during the siege he was protected by the angel of the Lord from the blows of the devil. The biblical citations and allusions, discussed above,[59] serve to embellish Edward's *persona* as the Lord's annointed.

The strength of the political bias in the 1307-1326 continuation of the *Flores* rivals that in the 'Merton' *Flores*. However, the bias is in the opposite direction. No other chronicler attacks Edward II with such unremitting virulence. He is eloquent on Edward II's malefactions and

49 *Flores*, iii. 251-266.
50 *Flores*, iii. 252-254.
51 *Flores*, iii. 248. (See above p. 250).
52 *Flores*, iii. 254.
53 *Flores*, iii. 252.
54 *Flores*, iii. 255.
55 *Flores*, iii. 266.
56 *Flores*, iii. 266-268.
57 *Flores*, iii. 264-265.
58 *Flores*, iii. 315-321.
59 Above pp. 250-1.

accuses him of tyranny. The king, "paralysed by sloth, won disgrace not fame."[60] The author dwells on the failure of his Scottish campaigns[61] and his virtual loss of Gascony.[62] Edward was a coward in battle, fleeing in terror from the Scots in 1322, "spurring on his horse, trembling and defenceless," and allowing the English to suffer all the miseries of defeat.[63] And so he lost the glory and power won by his famous ancestors whose fame was extolled throughout the world.[64] He broke his oath to observe the Ordinances[65] and habitually "forgot in the morning what he had promised in the evening."[66] His avarice was insatiable, with the result that the exactions of the royal justices reduced many counties to irremediable poverty,[67] and he "stretched forth his hand to vex" not "certain of the church" (Acts xii.i) but every single prelate by his wicked ferocity![68] He followed evil counsel[69] and made decisions "in secret in his chambers with his intimates"[70] and tried to circumvent opposition in parliament by delay, so that the lords, their patience and money exhausted, agreed to his demands.[71] He preferred the company of the lowborn to that of the nobles[72] whose counsel he neglected and whom he grievously oppressed, planning to humble and even to exterminate them. Under 1321 he writes: "In his insane fury he hated all the magnates with such wicked hatred that he plotted to overthrow completely the great men of the realm together with the whole English nobility."[73]

Conversely, the author of the 1307-1326 continuation praises the barons for their wisdom and magnanimity, their strength and courage in protecting England by war.[74] They were steadfast in their support of their leader, Thomas of Lancaster, preferring in 1321 to die in the faith

---

60 *Flores*, iii. 192.
61 *Flores*, iii. 159, 176, 190 and *passim*.
62 *Flores*, iii. 221-223.
63 *Flores*, iii. 210.
64 *Flores*, iii. 192-193.
65 *Flores*, iii. 201.
66 *Flores*, iii. 222. (Cf. *ibid*. iii. 228).
67 *Flores*, iii. 218.
68 *Flores*, iii. 218.
69 See e.g. *Flores*, iii. 143-144, 148, 192-193, 209, 230.
70 *Flores*, iii. 219.
71 *Flores*, iii. 220.
72 The chronicler describes how Edward amused himself "relicto nobilium consortio ... orientalia stagnorum aequora in comitatu Cantebrugge cum simplicium personarum magna comitiva ...;" *Flores*, iii. 173.
73 *Flores*, iii. 200.
74 *Flores*, iii. 149, 188.

of Christ for the liberty of the church and realm, rather than to violate their oath to uphold the Ordinances.[75] Thomas himself died a martyr to the cause, and "the manifold goodness of this famous man, the generous alms he gave, his pious acts when alive and the merits of his posthumous miracles, worked by divine clemency, require a book on their own.[76] Moreover, the author consistently supports Isabella and Mortimer (unlike Adam Murimuth and Geoffrey le Baker who are bitterly hostile to them). In the passage quoted above on Mortimer's escape from the Tower, he implies, by the use of biblical citations, a comparison of Mortimer with St. Peter.[77] He is outspoken about Edward II's treatment of Isabella, who, he asserts, pleaded with the king in 1311 to turn from his intimates (*confabulatores*) "to the excellence of the magnates, the wisdom of the clergy and the protection of the community," for the sake of peace.[78] Later, in 1324, he accuses the king of cruelty to the queen, by depriving her of her household, and exclaims: "On the insane stupidity of the king of England, which must be condemned by God and man! He should not love his own infamy and illicit bed, full of sin, and should never have removed from his side his noble consort and her tender wifely embraces, in contempt of her noble birth!"[79] The author's Francophilia appears in the assertion that Isabella's brother, Charles IV and the nobility of France, grieved at her ill-treatment (and impressed by the good looks and good manners of her son Edward, the heir-presumptive), will help her to invade England.[80]

We have, therefore, two chronicles, the 'Merton' *Flores* and the 1307-1326 continuation, of exceptionally strong political bias. Both stop short just before the end of the reign to which they relate, one in February 1307 and the other in February 1326. However, there is evidence suggesting the possibility that the text of the 'Merton' *Flores*, or at least drafts for it, did originally extend until the death of Edward I on 7 July, 1307, and that part of this continuation may be recovered from the chronicle of Adam Murimuth, who, as he himself states, used Westminster material.[81] Murimuth's appreciation of Edward I's achieve-

---

75 *Flores*, iii. 204.
76 *Flores*, iii. 214.
77 Above, p. 478.
78 *Flores*, iii. 148.
79 *Flores*, iii. 229.
80 *Flores*, iii. 231.
81 Murimuth states that he found chronicles in Westminster Abbey up to 1305 and that from that year he wrote from his own knowledge; *Murimuth*, pp. 3-4. However, it is likely that Murimuth used historical material at Westminster to a later date (see the next note).

ments following the notice of his death coincides in tone with the account of the king in the 'Merton' *Flores*. It specifically attributes the defeat of Simon de Montfort and the barons to Edward's heroism, and recites his victories over England's enemies, especially the Scots, both of which subjects figure large in the 'Merton' *Flores*.[82]

Similarly, there is a possiblity that the 1307-1326 continuation originally went as far as the accession of Edward III. The ascription-passage, at the beginning of the annal for 1326 which states that Robert of Reading ended both his chronicle and his life, does not preclude such a conclusion. It could merely signify the point at which Robert stopped writing, not the date of his death. Perhaps he even left drafts for his continuator. If so, it is likely that this continuation is partly preserved by Murimuth. The account of Edward II's deposition in his chronicle sustains the theme of the 1307-1326 continuation of the *Flores*. It represents Edward as abdicating voluntarily, admitting his own unworthiness to rule, saying: "I greatly lament that I have so utterly failed my people, but I could not be other than I am; I am pleased that my son who has been thus accepted by all the people should succeed me on the throne." And so "the whole community of the realm immediately received the young Edward as king."[83]

It remains to examine possible causes for the extreme bias in favour of Henry III and Edward I in the 'Merton' *Flores*, and against Edward II in the 1307-1326 continuation. The problem is whether the affection of the Westminster monks for Henry III and Edward I, and their hatred of Edward II are sufficient explanation. Certainly it is not surprising that the 'Westminster' *Flores* adopted a pro-royalist attitude to Henry III. It supported the king partly no doubt from reasons of circumspection, because the governement was next door to the abbey (the royal treasury was in the abbey itself). But their support was surely sincere because Henry, as the abbey's patron, was a generous benefactor and

---

82 *Murimuth*, p. 10. Murimuth follows the notice of the funeral with two lines of verse celebrating the peace which Edward I imposed. The presence of the same lines in the *Flores* (iii. 128) suggests that Murimuth was still using Westminster material for his annal for 1307. The lines read:

> Dum viguit, rex, et valuit tua magna potestas,
> Fraus latuit, pax magna fuit, regnavit honestas.

The so-called Tenison MS. (see above p. 246 n. 13) adds two more lines of verse:

> Scotos Edwardus, dum vixit, suppeditavit,
> Terruit, afflixit, depressit, dilaniavit.

83 *Flores*, iii. 235. See below p. 262.

the builder of their new church. The 'Westminster' *Flores* describes how when Henry was ill in 1271 "the monks of Westminster, fearing to lose their patron, processed with bare feet, in the rain to the New Temple and there celebrated mass for him to the Blessed Virgin Mary."[84] However, such good relations with Henry III expressed in the 'Westminster' *Flores* do not explain the rewriting for the 'Merton' *Flores* of the account of the Barons' War in an even more royalist tone, in the early fourteenth century. Moreover, the abbey's relations with Edward I, despite his gift of the regalia of the Scottish kings and the Stone of Scone to the abbey in 1297,[85] were not always sufficiently good to explain the revision of the 'Westminster' *Flores* to produce in the 'Merton' version an even more eulogistic account of him. Conversely, relations between Edward II and the abbey were hardly bad enough to justify the invective against him in the 1307-1326 continuation, although they were sometimes strained.[86] (The chronicler expressed the anger of the Westminster monks at the removal in 1319 of the royal Exchequer and court of King's Bench from Westminster palace to York,[87] and under 1320 he records that Edward occupied, "not without sacrilege," a cottage within the abbey precincts "called Borgoyne, for (Edward) preferred to have the title 'of Borgoyne' rather than the titles used by his glorious predecessors."[88]

Another explanation may be tentatively suggested for the political bias of the 'Merton' *Flores* and the 1307-1326 continuation. Perhaps they were official histories, written in response to royal command. Such an hypothesis would explain some of the problems raised by these works. With regard to the 'Merton' *Flores,* the following suggestions may be made. It was written by John of London, *alias* John Bever, a monk of Westminster, after the death of Edward I (7 July, 1307), at the command of Edward II, perhaps for presentation on the occasion of his coronation (24 February, 1308). John based the work on the 'Westminster' *Flores,* for the composition of which he himself was partly responsible. (The eulogy of Edward I in the account of the siege of Stirling castle in the 'Westminster' *Flores* suggests the possibility that

---

84 *Flores*, iii. 22-23.

85 *Flores*, iii. 101.

86 The monks of Westminster clearly objected to Edward I's oppressive taxation of the clergy, and came into conflict with him over the indictment of some of their number for complicity in the burglary of the royal treasury; see above    p. 251 & n. 35.

87 *Flores*, iii. 191.

88 *Flores*, iii. 193. For minor causes of conflict between Edward's II's household and Westminster Abbey see Tout, *op. cit.* p. 457 n. 2.

John wrote this passage at the command of Edward I to celebrate his victory).

There is evidence corroborating the hypothesis that the 'Merton' *Flores* was written for Edward II's coronation. The coronation pictures in the earliest text, the Eton College MS., show a preoccupation with the coronation ceremony, and the careful delineation of the rod with the dove could be interpreted as indicating that the pictures were executed soon after Edward's funeral when the emblem, may have attracted especial attention.[89] The theme of the 'Merton' *Flores* also supports our hypothesis. It commemorates the acts of Edward I, the new king's father, emphasising his military victories — his contribution, as the Lord Edward, to the defeat of Simon de Montfort, and his victories, as king, over the Scots. It is noteworthy that the new *ordo* compiled for Edward II's coronation included a prayer that the king should succeed against enemies and rebels.[90] Its interest in the Barons' War, apparent in the long resumé of events leading up to the battle of Evesham, and the eloquent paean on peace[91] are explicable if the work was written at Edward II's accession, because the king was again under baronial pressure.[92] The author must surely have been thinking of his own times when he wrote that even if Henry III did have shortcomings, they did not vitiate his heirs' monarchical rights, because "both divine and human law provide that once the fault or defect ceases, the punishment is never transmitted to the heirs, lest the iniquity of the father should attend the son and the punishment exceed the crime."[93] (That the author wrote 'heirs' not 'heir' shows that he was thinking further ahead than Edward I). Moreover, the only shortcoming of Henry III which the author specifically mentions is his 'intolerable prodigality' which made the baronial take-over necessary:[94] this can be regarded as a veiled admonition to Edward II lest the same fault on his part should lead to a similar result.

Additional support for the suggestion that the 'Merton' *Flores* was started immediately after Edward I's funeral is provided by the *Com-*

---

89 See above pp. 247-8.

90 "Tribue ei, optimus Deus, ... ut sit fortissimus regum, triumphator hostium, ad opprimendas rebelles et paganas nationes; sitque suis inimicis satis terribilis, praemaxima fortitudine regalis potentiae. *Foedera* (Record Commission edition), ii. pt. i, 34.

91 See above pp. 254-5.

92 See Schramm, *op. cit.* pp. 76, 207-208, and M. McKisack, *The Fourteenth Century* (Oxford, 1959), pp. 4 sq.

93 *Flores*, iii. 254. The coronation *ordo* of 1308 laid especial emphasis on Edward II's succession by hereditary right.

94 *Flores*, iii. 254.

*mendatio Lamentabilis.* This lament, described by Stubbs as a "sort of mortuary Éloge or funeral sermon,' must have been written soon after the king's death. The close similarity between its point of view and that of the 'Merton' *Flores* suggests that the latter was written at about the same time. The *Commendatio Lamentabilis,* like the 'Merton' *Flores,* emphasises that the Lord Edward helped Henry III defeat the barons: the knights say that they, with the great Edward, "snatched England, from the lion's jaw when they freed Henry III, like Daniel, from that wild beast, Simon de Montfort."[95] And it too praises Edward when king for his wisdom, bravery and success in war which won for England the benefits of peace.[96]

With regard to the 1307-1326 continuation, it seems likely that it was written after the deposition of Edward II and before the fall of Isabella and Mortimer in October 1330. It may have been intended for presentation to Edward III on the occasion of his coronation, and is best understood as a *pièce justificative* for Isabella's and Mortimer's coup. It reads as if it were intended to substantiate the accusations levelled against Edward II in the assembly held on 13 January, 1327, which deposed him. The chronicle of the Cistercian abbey of Pipewell gives the fullest account of the proceedings. It records :

> There, by common assent of all, the archbishop of Canterbury declared how the good King Edward when he died had left to his son the lands of England, Ireland, Wales, Gascony and Scotland in good peace; how Gascony and Scotland had been as good as lost by evil counsel and evil ward; how, further, by evil counsel the son had destroyed the greater part of the noble blood of the realm, to the dishonour and loss of himself, his realm and all the people; and how he had done many other marvels.[97]

It will be noticed that the charges made against Edward are precisely those enlarged on in the 1307-1326 continuation.[98] Moreover, assuming that Murimuth preserves the lost ending of the chronicle, its account of

95 *Chrons. Edward I and Edward II,* ii. 14. The *Commendatio Lamentabilis* compares Edward I with David and Solomon. It is noteworthy that prayers in the coronation *ordo* of Edward II ask God to endow the king with the qualities of various Old Testament figures such as Abraham, Moses, David and Solomon; see *Foedera,* ii, pt. i, 33-34.

96 *Chrons. Edward I and Edward II,* ii. 16 and *passim.* See above p. 254.

97 The translation is that in M. V. Clarke, "Committees of Estates and the Deposition of Edward II," *Historical Essays in Honour of James Tait,* ed. J. G. Edwards, V. H. Galbraith and E. F. Jacob (Manchester, 1933), p. 35. (The Anglo-Norman text is printed in *ibid.* p. 44 and in M. V. Clarke, *Medieval Representation and Consent* (London-New York-Toronto, 1935), pp. 194-195). The accusations against Edward II appear in an expanded form in Adam de Orlton's *Apologia* of 1334; Twysden, *Decem Scriptores,* c. 2765, and *Foedera,* ii. pt. i, 650.

98 See above p. 257.

Edward II's abdication and Edward III's accession had a propagandist element, for clearly the chronicler was trying to make what was illegal seem legal. Its assertion that the abdication was 'voluntary' reflects Isabella's and Mortimer's insistance on a formal resignation,[99] and Edward's alleged confession of his unworthiness to rule may well be a fiction suggested by the proceedings of the deposition assembly. Finally, the author calls the assembly itself a parliament: but it hardly deserved the appellation.[100]

If our hypothesis that the 'Merton' *Flores* and the 1307-1326 continuation are official histories is correct, it provides a possible explanation of the fact that each stops just before the end of the reign which it describes. Perhaps only one complete copy of the original draft of each chronicle was made in Westminster Abbey. These complete copies were presented to the kings. Edward II's book could well have been lost during the upheaval of the deposition, and meanwhile at Westminster no other complete copy had been made; perhaps the monks, satisfied with the 'Westminster' *Flores*, were not sufficiently interested. Therefore, in order to meet outside demand, it was necessary for scribes to use as exemplar the incomplete copy made for Merton priory. With regard to the 1307-1327 continuation, political considerations may explain the survival of only one early copy, itself incomplete. Edward III's copy might have been deliberately destroyed after the fall of Isabella, because its favourable attitude to them was no longer acceptable. The same factor could have resulted in the destruction at Westminster of other early copies and it is likely that it would have discouraged the making of more.

Official histories were rare in medieval England and those which seem to deserve the title were by secular clerks.[101] Thus, in the twelfth

99 See W. Stubbs, *The Constitutional History of England* (fifth edition, Oxford, 1891-1906, 3 vols.), ii. 379-380.

100 See B. Wilkinson, "The Deposition of Richard II and the Accession of Henry IV," *EHR*, 54 (1939), 223-230.

101 Before the Norman Conquest, the Alfredian Anglo-Saxon chronicle and the version written under Edward the Elder were almost certainly written to please Alfred and Edward and are biased accordingly: Plummer argues that the former was written under Alfred's 'direction and supervision'; see *Two of the Saxon Chronicles Parallel*, ed. C. Plummer, on the basis of an edition by J. Earle (Oxford, 1892, 1899, 2 vols., reprinted with two notes by D. Whitelock, 1952), ii. civ. For the 'official' element in the Edwardian chronicle see *The Chronicle of Aethelweard*, ed., with an English translation, Alistair Campbell (Nelson's Medieval Texts, 1962), pp. xxvii-xxxii. It should also be noted that the Norman accounts of William the Conqueror, especially that by William of Poitiers (*Histoire de Gillaume le Conquerant*, ed., with a French translation, R. Foreville, Les classiques de l'histoire de France au moyen age, xxiii, Paris, 1952), are official histories in the sense that they praise the king and justify the Conquest. Moreover, the Norman work which formed the basis of *L'estoire de la*

century the chronicle of Roger of Howden, a clerk in the king's service, has features of an official history.[102] In the fourteenth century the *De Gestis Mirabilibus Regis Edwardi Tertii* by Robert of Avesbury, recorder of the archbishop of Canterbury, could, judging from its eulogistic tone, have been written to please Edward III, even at his command. And in the fifteenth century a chaplain of the royal household wrote the *Gesta Henrici Quinti*, "an outstanding piece of propaganda, designed to justify the king's character and policy."[103] Nevertheless, it is not unlikely that the monks of Westminster should have produced two official histories in the first third of the fourteenth century.

Initially it is possible that Matthew Paris undertook to write the *Flores Historiarum* for Westminster Abbey as a result of royal encouragement. In October, 1247, when he attended the translation of Edward the Confessor at Westminster, Henry III told him to record the proceedings;[104] the translation is duly noticed in the *Flores* which he completed soon afterwards.[105] 'Such an undertaking in response to the king would accord with evidence supplied by his *Chronica Majora* and *Historia Anglorum* which shows that at about this time Matthew adopted a more favourable attitude to Henry. Both works in their original form are notable·for their strong anti-royalist bias. But in 1250 Matthew decided to modify his invective. He marked some passages in the *Chronica Majora* as offensive: many of these were omitted by the scribe making a new copy for St. Albans in 1250 or soon after. Matthew also erased some passages, substituting milder ones, and he revised the *Historia Anglorum*

---

*guerre sainte* (ed. Gaston Paris (Paris, 1897)) and of the *Itinerarium Peregrinorum et Gesta Regis Ricardi* (printed in *Chronicles and Memorials of the Reign of Richard I*, ed. W. Stubbs (Rolls Series, 1864, 1865, 2 vols.), i), eulogizes Richard I, in chivalric terms, and justified his behaviour during the crusade. Cf. J. G. Edwards, *"The Itinerarium Regis Ricardi* and the *Estoire de la Guerre Sainte"* in *Historical Essays in Honour of James Tait*, ed. Edwards, Galbraith and Jacob, pp. 59-77, and *Das Itinerarium Peregrinorum*, ed. H. E. Mayer (*MGH, Schriften*, xvii, Stuttgart, 1962), pp. 80-102. The *Gesta Stephani* (ed., with an English translation, K. R. Potter (Nelson's Medieval Texts, 1955)), which may also be of foreign authorship (see *ibid.* pp. xxx-xxxii) praises King Stephen as a chivalric hero.

102 Printed *Chronica Magistri Rogeri de Hoedene*, ed. W. Stubbs (Rolls Series, 1868-1871, 4 vols.). See also F. Barlow, 'Roger of Howden', *EHR*, 65 (1950), 352-360, and D. M. Stenton, 'Roger of Howden and *Benedict*', *EHR*, 68 (1953), 574-582.

103 J. S. Roskell and F. Taylor, "The Authorship and Purpose of the *Gesta Henrici Quinti*: i," *BJRL*, 53 (1970-1971), 428. The *Gesta* is printed *Henrici Quinti, Angliae Regis, Gesta*, ed. B. Williams (English Historical Society, 1850).

104 Matthew Paris, *Chronica Majora*, ed. H. R. Luard (Rolls Series, 1872-1883, 7 vols.), iv. 644-645. For a translation of the passage see Vaughan, *Matthew Paris*, p. 3. Henry's interest in Matthew Paris' historical work also appeared when he visited St. Albans in 1257, on which occasion he gave Matthew a list of the canonized kings of England and the names of two hundred and fifty English baronies.

105 See Vaughan, *op. cit.* pp. 108-109.

even more drastically.[105a] Perhaps the dedication of his *Life of Edward the Confessor*, in Anglo-Norman verse, which he wrote at about the same time, to Henry's queen, Eleanor of Provence, is also indicative of a rapprochment with the royal family.[106]

There is more evidence for Edward I's interest in history than there is for Henry III's. His appreciation of the value of chronicles as records of precedents, and of the uses of historiography for propaganda is well-known. His clerks searched the chronicles for evidence relating to the case of the competitors for the Scottish throne in 1291, and he wrote to the monasteries ordering the monks to search their chronicles for similar material.[107] The evidence collected was synthesized by the royal clerk, John of Caen, into the official account of the proceedings, the *Processus Scotiae,* which gave an account of Anglo-Scottish relations from 901 to 1252 strongly biased in favour of Edward's claims.[108] Edward also ordered chroniclers throughout England to insert in their works copies of the competitors' letters of submission to Edward as overlord.[109] Furthermore, there was a literary interest in history at court, fostered by the cult of King Arthur. The Dominican, Nicholas Trevet, wrote a chronicle in Anglo-Norman dedicated to Edward I's daughter Mary.[110] And a number of books and works of art (including a coronation throne) were executed at Westminster for the king and members of the royal family.[111]

Moreover, the possibility of French influence cannot be discounted. In the late thirteenth and early fourteenth centuries cultural connections between England and France were close, reinforced by the marriage of Edward I with Margaret, daughter of Philip II of France (in September 1299), and by Edward II's marriage with Isabella, daughter of Philip the Fair (in January 1308). The official chronicle of the kings

105a *Ibid.* pp. 64-5, 117-124.

106 See *La estoire de seint Aedward le rei,* ed., in facsimile, M. R. James (Roxburghe Club, 1920), pp. 12, 17. For date of work see Vaughan *op. cit.* p. 168.

107 Edward I's appeal to historical precedent in the Scottish succession case is fully discussed by E. L. G. Stones, "The Appeal to History in Anglo-Scottish Relations between 1291 and 1401: i," *Archives,* 9 (1969), 11-21 *passim.* For Edward I's letters to the religious houses see *ibid.* p. 12 and n. 8, J. Bain, *Calendar of Documents relating to Scotland* (Edinburgh, 1881-1888, 4 vols.), ii. 110, no. 470, and F. Palgrave, *Documents and Records illustrating the History of Scotland* (Record Commission, 1837), pp. 60-67.

108 *Foedera,* i. pt. ii, 762-784. See V. H. Galbraith,*Historical Research in Medieval England* (London, 1951), p. 36, and Stones, *op. cit.* pp. 17-19. Edward I again appealed to history to defend his claim to overlordship of Scotland against Boniface VIII; see *ibid.* pp. 19-21.

109 See Bain, *op. cit.* ii. 122, nos. 503-504, and Palgrave *op. cit.* pp. xcvi-xcvii and n. *.

110 This chronicle is unpublished; see M. D. Legge, *Anglo-Norman Literature and its Background* (Oxford, 1963), pp. 299-302.

111 See Peter Brieger, *English Art 1216-1307* (Oxford, 1957), chapter xii *passim.*

of France, the *Grandes chroniques*, described by its modern editor as "a monument raised to the glory of the French monarchy,"[112] provides a continuous history from the origins of the monarchy in the sixth century, until, ultimately, the end of the fifteenth century. It was begun in the mid-thirteenth century and later continued by the monks of the royal foundation of St. Denis, near Paris. If we are correct in our hypothesis that the 'Merton' *Flores* and the 1307-1327 continuation are an official history by the monks of Westminster, the English monarchy had for a short period a comparable work produced by a comparable royal foundation.

112 *Les Grandes chroniques de France*, ed. J. Viard (Soc. de l'histoire de France, 1920-1953, 10 vols.), i. viii. See also A. Molinier, *Les sources de l'histoire de France* (Paris, 1901-1904, 5 vols.), iii, no. 2530, and the unpublished Ph. D thesis for Edinburgh University (1969) by Sarah Murphy Farley, *French Historiography in the Later Middle Ages with special Reference to the 'Grandes chroniques de France.'*

Note

For an additional note to pp. 259–61 see below pp. 332–33.

# 11

## The Alleged Rape by Edward III of the Countess of Salisbury[1]

THE story of the rape by Edward III of the countess of Salisbury in 1342 has five component episodes:

(1) Edward III falls in love with the countess when he visits the castle of William Montagu, first earl of Salisbury (1337–44), during a campaign against the Scots;

(2) in order to see the countess again Edward holds a grand tournament in London to which the earl of Salisbury is commanded to come with his wife;

(3) Edward returns to the earl's castle and rapes the countess;

(4) the countess confesses to her husband;

(5) the earl takes consequent action.

The full story of this *villain cas* is told by the Hainault chronicler, Jean le Bel, who wrote more than fifteen years after the alleged incident.[2] The last three episodes are briefly noticed in the *Chronographia Regum Francorum*, a chronicle compiled in the early fifteenth century in the abbey of St. Denis in Paris, based on earlier historical collections made at St. Denis.[3] The same three episodes are similarly noticed in other continental chronicles: these will not be cited in evidence here because they are closely related to the *Chronographia*.[4]

1. I am indebted to my colleague Dr. M. C. E. Jones, and to my husband K. W. Gransden, for kindly reading this article in typescript and making useful comments and suggestions. I am also grateful to Professor E. L. G. Stones for help on specific points. However, I am responsible for any errors or omissions.

2. *Chronique de Jean le Bel*, ed. J. Viard and E. Déprez (Soc. de l'histoire de France, 1904, 1905, 2 vols.), i. 290–4; ii. 1–4, 30–33. For the date when these parts of the chronicle were written see *ibid*. i. pp. xiv–xvi.

3. For the composition of the *Chronographia* see the printed edition, *Chronographia Regum Francorum*, ed. H. Moranvillé (Soc. de l'histoire de France, 1891–7, 3 vols.), i. pp. xliii–xlvii.

4. These episodes are in: *Chronique normande du xiv<sup>e</sup> Siècle*, ed. A. and É. Molinier (Soc. de l'histoire de France, 1882), pp. 54, 59–60; *Istore et cronique de Flandres*, ed. K. de Lettenhove (Brussels, 1879-80, 2 vols.), ii. 6, 9; the *Chronique de Flandre* in L. Delisle, *Histoire du château et des sires de Saint-Sauveur-le-Vicomte suivie de pièces justificatives* (Valognes, 1867), pp. 89–90. These chronicles are in French and the relevant passages in all three are almost identical. Scholars disagree concerning the relationship of the *Chronographia* to the *Chronique normande* and the *Istore et cronique de Flandres*. Moranvillé, *op. cit.* i. pp. v–xxvi *passim* argues that the *Chronique normande* and the *Istore* used the same St Denis source as the *Chronographia*. On the other hand H. Pirenne, 'Les sources de la chronique de Flandre jusque'en 1342', in *Études d' histoire du moyen âge dédiées à Gabriel Monod*, ed. E. Lavisse (Paris, 1896), pp. 367-370, and his 'L'Ancienne chronique de Flandre et la *Chronographia Regum Francorum*', in *Compte rendu de séances de la commission royale d'histoire ou recueil de ses bulletins*, cinquième série, tome viii, iv<sup>e</sup> bulletin (1898), pp. 199–208, and A. Molinier, in *Revue historique*, lxvii (1898), 90–92, and his

Episode (5) differs in substance in Le Bel from the account in the *Chronographia.*[1]

Froissart (the first and second redactions of whose chronicle follow Le Bel closely) explicitly condemned Le Bel's story. In the first redaction he suppressed the prediction of the rape at the end of episode (1) and the rape itself, episode (3). In the second redaction (the version in the Amiens MS.) he again suppressed the prediction of the rape, and added instead the famous description of the game of chess played by the king and the countess.[2] Moreover, besides omitting episode (3), he inserted, *s.a.* 1345, a critique of its veracity. He writes:

> You have heard me speak above of Edward's love for the countess of Salisbury. The chronicle of Jean le Bel speaks of this love less properly than I must, for, please God, it would never enter my head to incriminate the king of England and the countess of Salisbury with such a vile accusation. If respectable men ask why I mention that love, they should know that Jean le Bel relates in his chronicle that the English king raped the countess of Salisbury. Now, I declare that I know England well, where I have lived for long periods mainly at the royal court and also with the great lords of that country. And I have never heard tell of this rape although I have asked people about it who must have known if it had ever happened. Moreover, I cannot believe and it is incredible that so great and valiant a man as the king of England would have allowed himself to dishonour one of the most noble ladies of his realm and one of his knights who had served him so loyally all his life.[3]

In the third redaction of his chronicle Froissart suppressed all reference to the countess of Salisbury at the grand tournament of 1342, and also the additions relating to the rape-story in the second redaction.[4] Kervyn de Lettenhove, after research on the records and other chronicles of the period, exposed some errors in Le Bel's story

---

*Les sources de l'histoire de France* (Paris, 1901–6, 6 vols.), iv. 23–26, argue that the *Chronique normande* is the primary source of the other chronicles, However, if this is the case' it would not vitiate the probability that the author of the *Chronique normande* used some material from St. Denis in common with the author of the *Chronographia.* Certainly the latter cannot have copied his account of our episode (5) from the extant text of the *Chronique normande,* because the *Chronographia* has one passage, *et ea hereditavit filiam suam quia masculinum heredem non habebat* (see below p. 337) which has no equivalent in the *Chronique normande.* It should be noted that the passages in question are not in the *Grandes chroniques* written at St. Denis. The latter copies many passages from the same source as the *Chronographia* until well into the fourteenth century. However, from 1340 to 1350 it has an original account apparently written by a monk of St. Denis contemporaneously with the events recorded, and was one source used by the *Chronographia*; see *Grandes chroniques de France,* ed. J. Viard (Soc. de l'histoire de France, 1920–53, 10 vols.), viii. pp. xiii–iv; ix. pp. iv–vi, and below p. 339 n. 4.

    1. See below pp. 273 ff.

    2. See *Chroniques de Jean Froissart,* ed. S. Luce, G. Raynaud and L. and A. Mirot (Soc. de l'histoire de France, 1869–1966, 14 vols., in progress), ii. 135, 340–2.

    3. *Ibid.* iii. pp. xviii–xix, 293 (*cf.* i. pp. lxiv–lxv).

    4. *Ibid.* iii. pp. 198, 294 ff. (*cf.* i. p. lxxiv).

and concluded that Froissart's disbelief was justified.[1] Le Bel's editor, Jules Viard, could only point out in Le Bel's defence that part of the story is also in the *Chronographia* and two other continental chronicles: he did not mention that these chronicles have a common historiographical archetype.[2]

An examination of the story concerning the alleged rape shows that it is a mixture of fact, error and the unverifiable. The five episodes will be discussed in turn. (Le Bel and the *Chronographia* will be provisionally treated as primary authorities, postponing for now the consideration of the possibility that both relied on a common source.)

Episode (1). Edward III went to relieve 'the castle of Salisbury', where the countess was staying, after the retreat of David Bruce. It was being held for the earl of Salisbury by 'a gentle esquire, the son of the earl's sister, who bore the name William Montagu after his uncle.'[3] Le Bel places this episode in 1342. It could have happened in December 1341 or January 1342, when Edward was campaigning in the north.[4] The castle in question must have been Wark-on-Tweed which Edward had granted to the earl of Salisbury in 1329 for life (and in 1333 in fee tail).[5] There is no known evidence corroborating either that the countess of Salisbury was at Wark at this time, or that the castle was being held, in the absence of the earl (who was a prisoner in France from Easter 1340 until early in June 1342),[6] by the young William Montagu. Moreover, the passage almost certainly has one error. The young William Montagu who succeeded to the earldom of Salisbury in 1349 is generally accepted as the son of the first earl and his wife Katharine.

Episode (2). The grand tournament in London to which King Edward summoned the earl of Salisbury. Here for the first time Le Bel names the countess of Salisbury. He calls her Alice.[7] In fact the wife of William Montagu first earl of Salisbury was Katharine. Le

1. Lettenhove examines the story in *Oeuvres de Froissart, Chroniques*, ed. Kervyn de Lettenhove (Brussels, 1867–77, 25 vols.), iv. 458–62 (cf. iii. 517–24).

2. Le Bel, ii. 30 n. 2; *cf.* above p. 333 n. 4.

3. *Ibid.* i. 285–94 *passim*. Froissart follows Le Bel in stating that the young William Montagu was the first earl's nephew; Froissart, ed. Luce, ii. 129, 346.

4. The statement that Edward III visited Wark is accepted as probably true by C. J. Bates, *The Border Holds of Northumberland*, i (Newcastle, 1891), pp. 359–69, who dates the visit to sometime between 13 and 20 Dec., 1341 (*ibid.* p. 364).

5. C[alendar of] P[atent] R[olls], *1327–1330*, p. 392; CPR, *1330–1334*, p. 462. Cf. K. H. Vickers in *A History of Northumberland* (issued under the direction of the Northumberland County History Committee, Newcastle, 1893–1926, 12 vols.), xi. 52. It is not possible to substantiate Lettenhove's assumption that Wark castle was being held by Edward Montagu in 1341/2. See Lettenhove, *op. cit.* iii. 516.

6. For the agreement between William Montagu, earl of Salisbury, and Philip VI, for the earl's release in exchange for the earl of Moray, dated 2 June 1342, see J. du Tillet, *Recueil des guerres et traictez d'entre les roys de France et d'Angleterre* (Paris, 1588), fo. 62ᵛ, and Lettenhove, *op. cit.* iii. 524–6. Apparently the earl of Salisbury was actually released on 4 June; *ibid.* iv. 459.

7. *Le Bel*, ii. 2.

Bel's error could have been the result of one of two simple confusions.[1] On the one hand he may have confused Katharine with Alice, the aged widow of Thomas of Lancaster. This Alice, who died in 1348 was *suo jure* countess of Lincoln and Salisbury. If anyone had been asked the name of the countess of Salisbury whom King Edward had (allegedly) raped, Alice's name might well have come to mind, especially as her matrimonial career had won her some notoriety.[2] On the other hand Le Bel could have confused the countess Katharine with the wife of Edward Montagu, brother of the first earl of Salisbury, who was called Alice.[3] If this was the cause of the error, it would partly explain another probable mistake in Le Bel, the statement that the young William Montagu was the earl's nephew.[4] He was of course the nephew of Edward Montagu and Alice. In conclusion, the mistakes made by Le Bel (which are reproduced by Froissart) concerning the earl of Salisbury's family connections could be the result of ignorance.

Le Bel dates the grand tournament to the middle of August 1342.[5] There is no evidence to corroborate that a tournament was held at that time. Le Bel makes two statements about the tournament which suggest that he misdated a conflation of two tournaments held in the spring of 1342. He records the death in the jousts of John, the eldest son of Henry Beaumont. Adam Murimuth records John's death at the tournament at Northampton on 14 April.[6] Le Bel also mentions the presence of William, count of Hainault; Murimuth states that a tournament was held in the count's honour at Eltham on 9 May.[7] However, there is an objection to the hypothesis that Le Bel intended to refer to a grand tournament in the

1. For the suggestion that Le Bel may have confused the name deliberately see Margaret Galway, 'Joan of Kent and the Order of the Garter', *University of Birmingham Historical Journal*, i (1947), 36–40, who argues that the countess of Salisbury in question was Joan of Kent who married William Montagu, second earl of Salisbury (1344–97) probably in 1340/1 and certainly before 1343; she was divorced in or before October 1349. See G. E. C[ockayne], *Complete Peerage*, xi. 389–90 and n.a.

2. See *ibid.* vii. 687–8. In 1317 Alice, who was born in 1281, was carried off by Sir Richard de St. Martin who claimed to have known her before her marriage to Thomas of Lancaster. In 1335/6 she married as her third husband Sir Hugo de Freyne (by whom she had previously been ravished), despite a vow of chastity.

3. See *ibid.* ix. 84–85. It should also be noted that William Montagu, second earl of Salisbury, contracted a marriage with Alice, younger daughter of Thomas of Brotherton before marrying Joan of Kent; *ibid.* xi. 389 n. k.

4. Above p. 269, and below p. 273 n. 3.

5. *Le Bel*, ii. 2. Froissart borrows Le Bel's date in the first redaction of his chronicle, but alters it to Candlemas (2 Feb.) in the second redaction; *Froissart*, ed. Luce, iii. 2, 197. Tournaments on neither date are mentioned by D. Sandberger, *Studien über das Rittertum in England vornehmlich während des 14 Jahrhunderts* (Berlin, 1937).

6. *Adae Murimuth Continuatio Chronicarum. Robertus de Avesbury De Gestis Mirabilibus Regis Edwardi Tertii*, ed. E. M. Thompson (Rolls Series, 1889), p. 124. The inquisition *post mortem*, dated 26 June 1342, does not give the date of the death of John Beaumont, son of the late Henry Beaumont earl of Buchan; *Cal[endar of] In[quisitions] p[ost] m[ortem]* viii, n. 381. (*Cf. ibid.* viii. n. 271 and G. E. C[ockayne,] *op. cit.* ii. 61).

7. *Le Bel*, ii. 3; *Murimuth*, p. 124. *Cf.* Sandberger, *op. cit.* p. 54.

spring of 1342. The earl of Salisbury could not have taken his wife to a tournament at that time because he was not released by the French until early in June 1342.[1] Therefore Le Bel must presumably have been referring to a summer tournament. Possibly the fact that he records an embassy to Edward III from Brittany immediately after the tournament provides a clue to the date.[2] This embassy from John de Montfort's party was, Le Bel states, immediately followed by another one. (He incorrectly asserts that the second embassy was headed by the  duchess  de Montfort herself.)[3] He records that as a result of these embassies which asked for help against Charles of Blois, Edward sent an expedition led by Robert of Artois and the earl of Northampton. It is known that representatives of John de Montfort's cause were active negotiating with Edward III in 1341 and until the summer of 1342.[4] On 23 July 1342 Edward at Windsor confirmed an agreement, of 21 February 1342, with de Montfort's party.[5] The agreement stipulated the terms on which Edward would send military aid under Artois and Northampton. Possibly Le Bel had in mind the negotiations resulting in this indenture. If so, the grand tournament could be dated to sometime after early June (when the earl of Salisbury was released by the French), and before 23 July (the date of the indenture). It may be suggested that Le Bel's erroneous date, mid-August, for the grand tournament, arose from confusion with the date when the expeditionary force sailed for Brittany – 14 August.

Episode (3). The rape. Le Bel tells the story in highly-coloured dramatic prose. The *Chronographia* states briefly: 'The king of England violated the wife of the earl of Salisbury.' Both authorities place the alleged event in 1342, in the same chronological context; after the earl of Salisbury left with Robert of Artois on the Breton expedition, on 14 August. (Le Bel infers that Edward sent the earl purposely, so that he could pursue his intention with the  duchess ),[6] and before Edward himself sailed for Brittany, in mid-October (he landed at Brest on 19 October).[7] It is not impossible that between

---

1. See above p.26 9and n. 6.                          2. *Le Bel*, ii. 4–6.
3. *Ibid.* ii. 7–8. *Cf. Chron. norm.* ed. Molinier, p. 259 n. 1, and A. Le Moyne de la Borderie, *Histoire de Bretagne* (Rennes and Paris. 1896–1914, 6 vols.), iii. 447. The *Chronographia* also incorrectly states that the du ch ess de Montfort came on an embassy to Edward III in 1342; *Chronographia*, ii. 196.
4. See *Murimuth*, p. 121; *Foedera* (Record Commission edition), ii. pt. 2, 1189, 1205; Borderie, *op. cit.* iii. 447; J. Le Patourel, 'Edward III and the kingdom of France,' *History*, xliii (1958), 187.
5. P[ublic] R[ecord] O[ffice], Duchy of Lancaster, Cartae Miscellaneae (D.L.36), i. no. 198. I owe this reference to Dr. M. C. E. Jones, who also called my attention to a payment to Amaury de Clisson and Bernard de Guyngen, for expenses for a visit to England, dated 7 March 1342; P.R.O., E 403/323, m. 31.          6. *Le Bel*, ii. 4. 30.
7. M. C. E. Jones, *Ducal Brittany 1364–1399* (Oxford, 1970), p. 143, citing the chronicle of Richard Lescot. This date is corroborated by a warrant under the privy seal, dated at Brest, 19 Oct. 1342; P.R.O., C. 81, 287, no. 15132. However, Adam Murimuth dates Edward III's departure for Brittany 23 Oct.; *Murimuth*, p. 128. Perhaps Murimuth

these dates Edward paid a fleeting visit to Wark, but there is no known evidence of it.[1]

Episode (4). The countess's confession. This is described in graphic detail by Le Bel and noticed more briefly in the *Chronographia*.[2] Both authorities, which are uncorroborated by other evidence, date it to after the return of King Edward and the earl from Brittany: they landed at Weymouth on 2 March 1343.[3]

Episode (5). The action taken by the earl of Salisbury as a result of the confession. Here Le Bel and the *Chronographia* have, besides points of coincidence, both complementary and conflicting information. Le Bel states that the earl of Salisbury was grief-stricken at the countess's revelations, particularly because of the king's manifest ingratitude for his faithful service. He therefore undertook to give half his property to the countess and their son, who was twelve years old. He then went to London, confronted the king with his iniquity and handed back everything he held of the king, 'for the aid of his son.' He ended his harangue: 'Neither you nor anyone else in this land will ever set eyes on me again.' Thereupon he left to fight the Moors in Spain, and was killed at the siege of Algeciras.[4] The *Chronographia* similarly represents the confrontation between the king and the broken-hearted, angry earl, but asserts that the earl took his friends with him. He disseized himself of all his lands in the presence of his peers and 'ea hereditavit filiam suam quia masculinum heredem non habebat, sic quod uxor eius haberet doagium quamdiu viveret.' Next, he left the court, defied Edward and crossed to France. He went to Philip VI and handed him letters of confederation (*litteras de confederatione*) of Oliver de Clisson and

---

derived his date from knowledge that governmental business under the privy seal continued to be conducted at Portsmouth until 23 Oct.: this is demonstrated by the fact that the extant privy seal warrants, except the one mentioned above, were issued at Portsmouth from 19 to 23 Oct.; P.R.O., C. 81. 287, nos. 15129–15131, 15133–15155. (There is then a gap in the dates of the privy seal warrants until 1 Nov., when they are dated at Plouguerneau and Brest. For problems in reconstructing the royal itinerary see the next note.)

1. Kervyn de Lettenhove (*Froissart*, iv. 459) concluded, on the evidence of the documents printed from the chancery rolls in *Foedera*, that Edward III did not go north in the period between 14 Aug. and 23 Oct. 1342. However, H. C. Maxwell-Lyte, *Historical Notes on the Use of the Great Seal of England* (London, 1926), pp. 71–72, 80, 236, 247–8, 251 ff., 405–9, has demonstrated that the chancery records do not provide infallible evidence for the king's itinerary at this period. See also P. Chaplais, *English Royal Documents, King John to Henry VI*, 1199-1461 (Oxford, 1971), pp. 26, 39–45. Nevertheless, a search through the privy seal warrants (P.R.O., C. 81/285–287) and the wardrobe accounts (P.R.O., E. 101/389/14, E. 101/390/1 and E 36/204) corroborates the evidence of the chancery records in this instance. I am indebted to Miss Elizabeth Danbury for making a preliminary search of E. 36/204. The expenses of Edward III at Newcastle-on-Tyne recorded in E. 101/389/40, were almost certainly all incurred during his Scottish campaign in the winter of 1341.

2. *Le Bel*, ii. 32–33; *Chronographia*, ii. 204. See below pp. 342-3.

3. C[alendar of ]C[lose] R[olls], *1343–1346*, p. 97.       4. *Le Bel*, ii. 33–34.

Godfrey de Harcourt with Edward III. Soon afterwards he left France 'and was never again seen by anyone'.[1]

There is nothing in the public records to confirm that Edward III and the earl of Salisbury had this bitter quarrel after their return from Brittany. Nor is there any evidence confirming the earl's alleged arrangements for his property: on the contrary, on his death Katharine had dower in his possessions, and subsequently, in 1349, William Montagu, second earl of Salisbury, had livery of the inheritance, in accordance with the normal procedure.[2] The statement in the *Chronographia* that the earl had no male heir is contrary to the evidence that the second earl of Salisbury was son and heir to the first earl.[3] Similarly, its assertion that the earl defied the king cannot be substantiated. Moreover, Le Bel's statement that the earl was killed at Algeciras is demonstrably untrue; he died of a wound inflicted in the tournament at Windsor in April 1344.[4]

However, episode (5) in both Le Bel and the *Chronographia* has some true facts. Le Bel correctly associated the earl with the war in Spain. By 30 August 1343 he was with the earl of Derby in Castile, negotiating on Edward III's behalf with King Alfonso, and he probably later fought the Moors.[5] The precise date when he left England is apparently unknown, but he could have visited Paris before joining the earl of Derby (who left England before the middle of March 1343)[6] in Castile. It is, therefore, not impossible that he visited Paris on the way. If so, he could have betrayed Oliver de Clisson and Godfrey de Harcourt to King Philip.[7] Oliver de Clisson, one of the principal Breton lords who had supported Charles of Blois' claim to the duchy of Brittany,[8] and Godfrey de Harcourt, a powerful Norman lord, had both been captured by the

1. *Chronographia*, ii. 204–5. The *Chronique normande*, p. 59, omits the statement that the earl gave his inheritance to a daughter because he had no male heir. The *Istore et croniques de Flandres*, p. 9, and the Flemish chronicle in Delisle, *op. cit.* p. 90, omit the statement that the earl had no male heir.

2. See *CCR, 1343–1346*, p. 307; *CCR, 1346–1349*, p. 450; *CCR, 1349–1354*, p. 107; *Cal. Inq. p.m.* ix. nos. 64, 310.

3. See *Cal. Inq. p.m.* viii. no. 532. For a suggestion that Le Bel's statement that the young William Montagu was the nephew of William Montagu first earl of Salisbury (above p. 269 and n. 3), was intended to cast doubt on the second earl's legitimacy, see Galway, *loc. cit.* pp. 39–40 (*cf. ibid.* pp. 24–25).

4. This is recorded in a version of Murimuth's chronicle; *Murimuth*, p. 232.

5. *CCR, 1343–1346*, p. 226 (a transcript of this entry on the Close Roll is printed in *Foedera*, ii. pt. 2, 1232). *Cf.* G.E.C., *Complete Peerage*, xi. 387 and n.h.

6. See Kenneth Fowler, *The King's Lieutenant, Henry of Grosmont, First Duke of Lancaster 1310–1361* (London, 1969), pp. 45–46. *Cf.* Froissart, ed. Lettenhove, iv. 459–60.

7. This possibility is mentioned by Raymond Cazelles, *La société politique et la crise de la royauté sous Philippe de Valois* (Paris, 1958), p. 153. The alleged incident is also mentioned by Siméon Luce, *Histoire de Bertrand du Guesclin* (Paris, 1876), p. 47 n. 2, who cites P. H. Morice, *Histoire ecclésiastique et civile de Bretagne* (Paris, 1750, 1756, 2 vols.), i. 268; however Morice was here citing the chronicle of Flanders, not an independent source (see above p. 267 and n. 4).

8. For Oliver de Clisson, brother of Amaury de Clisson (for whom see above p. 271 n. 5) see Cazelles, *op. cit.* pp. 143, 147, 153–4.

English at Vannes in December 1342, and had apparently come to terms with their captors.[1] Harcourt rebelled against King Philip in 1343.[2] Philip carried out a purge of these and other traitors in May 1343; Clisson was executed in Paris, on 2 August 1343, and Harcourt was exiled. How Philip discovered Clisson's treason is unknown (the records of his and Harcourt's trial are lost),[3] but the possibility of a revelation by the earl of Salisbury cannot be discounted.

On the evidence available, allowing the chroniclers a due margin of error, it is surely impossible to decide how much truth there is in the story, with its complex of related incidents, of the rape of the countess of Salisbury. There is undoubtedly a possibility that Edward III raped the countess Katharine (or some other lady). The contrast between the ideals of chivalric society (which are reflected in Froissart's protestation concerning the rape-story), and the actual practice of those violent times is a truism. However, irrespective of how much truth the rape-story contains, it can be regarded from another angle. It can be considered as a piece of political propaganda. Propaganda was one by-product of the Hundred Years War. Probably there was a propagandist element in the anti-French bias evinced by the English chroniclers, especially by Adam Murimuth and Geoffrey le Baker. Murimuth argues at length the legal case for Edward III's claim to the crown of France, and stresses that the French were opposing the 'true heir' (John de Montfort) in Brittany.[4] He consistently refers to Philip VI as Philip de Valois, not as king of France. Baker is more virulent, calling Philip a pseudo-king and tyrant, who planned to annihilate England, and was, like his subjects, inflated with pride.[5] In France, the abbey of St. Denis, Paris, was the home of the official histories of the kings of France.[6] During the Hundred Years War its historical productions

1. *Chronographia*, ii. 202–3; *Grandes chroniques*, ed. Viard, ix. 241–2.
2. Cazelles, *op. cit.* pp. 152–3. Cf. *Grandes chroniques*, ed. Viard, ix. 243.
3. Cazelles, *op. cit.* p. 155 n. 6.                 4. *Murimuth*, pp. 100–1, 121.
5. *Chronicon Galfridi le Baker de Swynebroke*, ed. E. M. Thompson (Oxford, 1889), pp. 54, 55, 123, 143.
6. The first recension of the *Grandes chroniques*, written at St. Denis and started at the request of Louis IX, presents an account of French history strongly biased in favour of the French monarchy to 1340. Its continuation, also written at St. Denis, to 1350 has an even more marked 'official' bias, as a result of increased royal interest in the work (John II was anxious to whitewash the failures of Philip VI, notably in the Hundred Years War). The second recension was commissioned by Charles V, soon after his accession in 1364. His councillor Pierre d'Orgement (who became chancellor in 1373) produced the new recension as 'official' propaganda, with an especial bias against the English. I owe this information partly to an unpublished Ph.D. thesis for Edinburgh University (1969) by Sarah Murphy Farley, *French Historiography in the Later Middle Ages with Special Reference to the 'Grandes Chroniques de France'*, (see especially pp. 276–84, 361–8, 380–98). See also D. Hay, 'History and historians in France and England during the fifteenth Century', *Bulletin of the Institute of Historical Research*, xxxv (1962), 111–5, and, with reference to a later period, P. S. Lewis, 'War propaganda and historiography in fifteenth-century France and England', *Transactions of the Royal Historical Society*, xv (1965), 1–21.

show a marked anti-English bias. Moreover, there is at least one continental example of a sophisticated propaganda piece. *Les Voeux du Héron*,[1] a poem in French, was apparently written to denigrate the English army commanders. It laid the blame for the start of the Hundred Years War on Robert of Artois, recounting how, embittered against King Philip by exile and disgrace, he came to the court of Edward III to incite him to renew his claim to the French crown. It relates that Edward and his nobles, whom it satirizes *en passant*, swore at a feast, on a roasted heron, to fight in France. The same story appears in an even more bitterly anti-English form in the *Chronographia*, a product of the abbey of St. Denis.[2] (It contains little historical truth, though some such ceremony may have been performed at Edward's court.)

The story of the rape of the countess of Salisbury can be considered as a piece of political propaganda, a deliberate 'smear' on Edward III. It may be suggested that behind both Le Bel's account and the *Chronographia* lies some now lost tract, or even a poem, aimed at discrediting Edward III.[3] If such a work existed, the discrepancies between the episodes in Le Bel and those in the *Chronographia* need explanation. It may be postulated that Le Bel copied his source closely, but because of his fair-mindedness and wish to praise Edward III,[4] he suppressed some details. Thus he omitted the statement that the first earl of Salisbury had no male heir. This statement was particularly libellous because by inferring that the second earl was not the first earl's son, it could be regarded as an innuendo against the countess. Le Bel also suppressed the earl's betrayal of Clisson and Harcourt, which in the full story appears as the damaging result of Edward's crime. He could well himself have added that the earl of Salisbury died at Algeciras. Knowing that the earl was at the siege, and reading in his source that he was never seen again after leaving France, Le Bel may have concluded that he died in Spain. In fact, the most scurrilous version of the story without any romantic embellishments, is that in the *Chronographia*. This suggests the possibility that the hypothetical propaganda piece was composed, like the *Chronographia* itself, by a monk of St. Denis.

1. The poem is printed and translated in *Political Poems and Songs . . . . from the Accession of Edward III to that of Richard III*, ed. Thomas Wright (Rolls Series, 1859, 1861, 2 vols.), i. 1–25. It is fully discussed by B. J. Whiting, 'The Vows of the Heron', *Speculum*, xx (1945), 261–78, who suggests that *Les Voeux* was a piece of anti-war propaganda composed in Hainault. For Robert of Artois in England see H. S. Lucas, *The Low Countries and the Hundred Years' War, 1326-1347* (University of Michigan, 1929), p. 124.                                     2. *Chronographia*, ii. 36–38.

3. To accept that Le Bel used a written source for the story makes it necessary not to interpret literally the statement with which he prefaces his account of the rape, that he 'heard it': 'Or vous vueil je conter le villain cas que fist le roy Edowart, dont on le pouoit blasmer, car il ne fut pas petit, ainsy que je l'ay ouy dire'; *Le Bel*, ii. 30.

4. For passages eulogizing Edward III see *Le Bel*, ii. 65–67, *passim*, 168. (*Cf*. i. pp. xii–xiii).

One of the literary affiliations of the rape-story seems obvious; it is hard to avoid the conclusion that it is indebted to Livy's account of the rape of Lucretia.[1] The use of a classical model would not be surprising. The Scottish barons in 1320 quoted from Sallust's *Cataline* in the Declaration of Arbroath.[2] Moreover, Livy, who had been outside the tradition of the medieval schools, received increasingly close attention in the fourteenth century, in the course of which a more complete text became available.[3] He was much studied by humanists in France, Italy and England. Petrarch's annotated copy of Livy still survives,[4] and the English Dominican Nicholas Trevet wrote the earliest known commentary on the first and third decades. He wrote at the request of Pope John XXII, whose court at Avignon was the centre of a group of humanists. There were copies of the commentary not only in France but also in Italy.[5] The Benedictine Pierre Bersuire translated Livy at the order of King John II, the Good (1350–1364).[6] The Lucretia legend itself was studied both from Livy and from Ovid.[7] (The moral problems it posed had fascinated writers from the earliest Christian times.)[8] There is abundant evidence of its popularity in fourteenth-century England, which had very close cultural ties with France.[9] The Dominican scholar Robert Holcot, lecturing at Cambridge sometime between 1334 and 1342, used Lucretia as an example of a faithful (pagan) wife.[10] Ranulph Higden discussed the Lucretia legend in the *Polychronicon*.[11] Both Chaucer and John Gower wrote poems on the theme.[12] Chaucer,

1. *Livy*, i. 57–59.

2. See J. R. Philip, 'Sallust and the Declaration of Arbroath', *Scottish Historical Review*, xxvi (1947), 75–78.

3. For the study of Livy by the early fourteenth-century humanists and the availability of the text see Beryl Smalley, *English Friars and Antiquity in the Early Fourteenth Century* (Oxford, 1960), pp. 60–61, 64, 86, 92–93. (For further references see the index under Livy.)

4. See R. J. Dean, 'The Earliest Commentary on Livy is by Nicholas Trevet', *Medievalia and Humanistica*, iii (1945), 86, and Smalley, *op. cit.* pp. 289–90, 295. Petrarch read Trevet's commentary on Livy; *ibid.* p. 64.

5. For Trevet's commentary see Dean, *loc. cit.* pp. 86–98, and Smalley, *op. cit.* pp. 60–65.          6. See Smalley, *op. cit.* p. 262.

7. Ovid, *Fasti*, ii. 721–852. The account of the rape of the countess of Salisbury follows Livy rather more closely than Ovid.

8. *E.g.* Augustine, *Civ. Dei*, i. 19. For further references see R. M. Ogilvie, *A Commentary on Livy Books 1–5* (Oxford, 1965), p. 220.          9. See Hay, *loc. cit.* pp. 111–15.

10. Smalley, *op. cit.* pp. 155–6, 322.

11. *Polychronicon Ranulphi Higden*, ed. Churchill Babington and J. R. Lumby (Rolls Series, 1865–86, 9 vols.), iii. 156 ff. Higden cites Livy for the Lucretia legend (*ibid.* iii. 158), but it is not certain that he used him at first hand; see John Taylor, *The Universal Chronicle of Ranulf Higden* (Oxford, 1966), p. 76.

12. Chaucer, *The Legend of Good Women*, lines 1680–1885 (*The Works of Geoffrey Chaucer*, ed. F. N. Robinson, 2nd ed. Oxford, 1957, pp. 507–9); John Gower, *Confessio Amantis*, lines 4754–5130 (*The Complete Works of John Gower*, ed. G. C. Macaulay, Oxford, 1899–1902, 4 vols., iii, 367–77).

who regarded Lucretia as a model of virtue and steadfastness, even mentions her as a saint and says that her day was hallowed.[1]

The parallels between the Lucretia legend in Livy and the story of the rape of the countess of Salisbury are striking. In both emphasis is laid on the virtue of the victim, her faithfulness to her husband and fear of dishonour. In both the rape is preceded by a friendly visit of the would-be-lover. Lucretia's husband Collatinus brought Sextus Tarquinius, son of Tarquinius Superbus king of Rome, with other young men to his house, where they were hospitably dined, and Sextus Tarquinius fell passionately in love with Lucretia's beauty and virtue. Edward III came to the earl of Salisbury's castle with ten or twelve knights and was hospitably received by the countess. He was astounded by her beauty, noble bearing and gracious manner, and fell so deeply in love that he could hardly eat the dinner she provided. However, she rejected his declaration of love.

Both Sextus Tarquinius and Edward paid a second visit. Tarquinius rode, with one companion, from Ardea to Collatia near Rome, a distance of about twenty miles. Edward, apparently alone, undertook a longer journey, from London to Wark. Both were again kindly received, and each went to his bedroom and waited until the household was asleep (although Edward had to warn the countess's personal servants, who were still awake, not to interfere). Then each went to the lady's room. Sextus Tarquinius approached with a drawn sword, terrified Lucretia into silence and made her submit by fear and force. Edward's violence appeared in other ways; he stopped the countess's mouth before she could utter more than two or three cries, and 'having forced on her such grief and martyrdom', he left her bleeding, in a faint. Neither Livy nor Ovid mention that Lucretia fainted, but Chaucer says that she fainted 'for fer of sclaunder and drede of deth'.[2] Sextus Tarquinius left immediately, and Edward returned to London the next morning. Subsequently each victim, overcome with grief, voluntarily confessed to her husband, whose sorrow was only equalled by his anger with the culprit. Although no blame in either case was imputed to the wife, neither couple continued to live together; Lucretia killed herself, and the earl of Salisbury left for ever.

After the confession scene it is harder to find similarities between the two works. However, by pursuing the comparison it is possible tentatively to suggest the purpose of, and an approximate date for, the postulated work on the rape of the countess of Salisbury. The

1. *The Legend of Good Women*, line 1871. This 'canonization' of Lucretia was suggested by the fact that Ovid gives her story under a particular day, analogous to a saint's day; *cf*. W. G. Dodd, *Courtly Love in Chaucer and Gower* (Gloucester, Mass., 1959), pp. 227–8.

2. *The Legend of Good Women*, lines 1814–15.

Lucretia legend provided the cause of the fall of the Tarquins. Lucretia pledged Collatinus and her father Brutus to avenge her lost honour. As a result Brutus roused the people against Tarquinius Superbus, and closed the gates of Rome against him. Sextus Tarquinius himself was slain by 'revengers of old quarrels'. The author of our tract could have had this denouement in mind. Edward's vile act, like Sextus Tarquinius', had momentous political consequences. The earl of Salisbury betrayed Edward's new allies, Oliver de Clisson and Godfrey de Harcourt. Their trial and punishment, part of Philip VI's round-up of traitors in 1343, constituted a breach of the truce of Malestroit, concluded on 19 January 1343 between King Edward and King Philip to stop the Breton war, and marked the resumption of hostilities.[1]

It is noticeable that the rape-story is set throughout against a background of Anglo-Breton history: messengers from Brittany come to Edward immediately after the grand tournament of 1342; Edward rapes the countess after the earl had been sent to Brittany and before Edward's own departure there; and his crime resulted in the renewal of the Breton war. A monk of St. Denis, writing to please King Philip, would reflect the official French attitude to Edward's interference in Breton affairs. Brittany had become a battleground for Edward and Philip. On the death of Duke John III in April 1341, without direct male heir, Edward supported one claimant to the duchy, John de Montfort (consanguineous younger brother of John III), and Philip supported the other, Charles of Blois (his nephew and husband of the daughter of a younger full brother of John III). De Montfort's party, in return for military support, recognized Edward as king of France and suzerain of Brittany. It seems likely that the rape-story was written as a propaganda tract soon after the breach of the truce of Malestroit. Its object could well have been to emphasize Edward's ultimate responsibility for the renewal of fighting, and perhaps even to justify Philip's breach of the truce. Moreover, the tract could have had a prophetic purpose; to show, on the analogy of the Lucretia legend, that Edward was doomed to disaster, because of his crime.

If, as suggested, the rape-story is an example of war propaganda, it was a more subtle and insidious composition than *Les Voeux du Héron*. It was better calculated to deceive because it was set in the context of well-known events and contained nothing which was likely to appear demonstrably false to a Frenchman. In it fact and fiction were so cleverly interwoven (it is impossible to be sure of their relative proportions), that the whole was credible.

---

1. For the view that Philip's purge of traitors constituted a breach of the truce of Malestroit see *Avesbury*, ed. Thompson, p. 355, and Borderie, *op. cit.* iii. 482–3.

# 12

# A Fourteenth-Century Chronicle from the Grey Friars at Lynn

ALL that remains today of the Grey Friars' house at Lynn is the fine late fourteenth-century tower; the only manuscript from their library is a book of sermons, preached early in the fifteenth century by Friar Nicholas Philipps in East Anglia and written down by him at Lynn (and elsewhere).[1] To these may now be added two pages of a chronicle in the form of tabular annals for the years 1349, 1360–77, written apparently between those dates on folios 19–20 of a mid-fourteenth-century commonplace book, now British Museum Additional MS. 47214.

The volume has forty-eight paper leaves [2] measuring about $11\frac{1}{2}$ in. × $7\frac{1}{2}$ in., arranged in three gatherings (at least one gathering is missing after the first). The back cover of the original binding of soft white leather on sheets of stiff vellum remains. Possibly the book was still in the hands of Grey Friars at the end of the fourteenth century; a hand of about 1400 has inscribed on folio 48, ' iste quaternus est fratris Iohannis Medilton de dono fratris Nicholai Fakynham magistri '. A late sixteenth-century hand has added below ' vide Johannem Baleum de Nicholao Fackenhamo cent. 7ª fol. 530 '. The reference is to the second edition of Bale's Catalogue (1557) which describes Nicholas Fakenham of Norfolk as professor and doctor of Oxford and provincial minister of the Franciscans in England 1395–?1401. He died in 1407. The sixteenth-century annotator's identification of the inscription may be right, but Fakenham is a common East Anglian name.[3]

The whole volume, except for the Grey Friar's annals, is written by one scribe in a mid-fourteenth-century charter hand. The contents are a miscellany of legal and historical pieces. It is impossible to say who the scribe was, or where he was writing, but there is evidence to suggest that it was somewhere in East Anglia. He begins, folios 2ᵛ–17, with annals from the Incarnation to 1314. To 1295 these annals are brief extracts (usually one line long) from a chronicle compiled at Bury St. Edmunds,[4] which was popular

---

[1] Bodley MS. Lat. Th. D. 1, described by A. G. Little, *Franciscan Papers, Lists and Documents* (1943), pp. 244-5. For the house of the Grey Friars at Lynn see A. R. Martin, *Franciscan Architecture in England* (1937), pp. 101–5.

[2] The water mark of the first gathering is a T and of the second and third an eagle; *cf.* C. M. Briquet, *Les Filigranes*, no. 9089 (Palermo 1361) and no. 77 (Longwy, Udine and Pisa, mid-fourteenth century) respectively.

[3] For Nicholas Fakenham see A. G. Little, *op. cit.* p. 198, and *ibid. Grey Friars in Oxford* (1892), pp. 252-3. There was a prosperous family of Fakenhams in Lynn; H. Ingleby, *Red Register of King's Lynn* (1919 &c.), i. 155-6.

[4] For the Bury chronicle see above pp. 204 and n. 30, 205, 226–38 passim.

in East Anglia but not elsewhere. The extract has a few unimportant additions to the Bury chronicle; one, under 672, is a synopsis of the history of the abbey of Ely. On folios 20$^v$–21$^v$ are lists of the kings of the Heptarchy including notes on East Anglian kings and saints. Chief justice Thomas Weyland, a Norfolk man and great landowner in East Anglia, is mentioned in the annals under 1289, 'obsessio fratrum minorum apud Babbewelle pro Thoma Weiland', and he appears again in the last item of the volume (fos. 45–7$^v$) among the French civilians and canonists who in 1292 advised Edward I on the law of succession to the throne of Scotland.[1] The house of the Grey Friars at Babwell, Suffolk, is also mentioned under 1259, 'fratres minores post venerunt apud sanctum Edmundum et expulsi erant extra villam, propter privilegium ecclesie sancti Edmundi usque Babbewelle'.[2] The annals quoted above for 1289 and 1259 are both lifted from the Bury chronicle, but the name itself, Babwell, is an addition. There is not enough evidence, however, to conclude that the commonplace book was compiled for the Grey Friars. The contents suggest rather that it was compiled for some East Anglian lawyer who took an interest in Scottish affairs. Its principal contents, excluding the items already noticed, are: a list of the kings of Scotland 844–1285 (fo. 22$^v$), Boniface VIII's letter to Edward I, 1299, about the imprisonment of Scottish ecclesiastics,[3] and notes for Edward's answer, 1304,[4] the version of the coronation service used at Edward II's coronation [5] (fos. 24$^v$, 25), Anglo-Saxon and Norman laws, incomplete at the beginning (fos. 26–44), the reissue of King John's charter, 13 January 1215, granting freedom of election to the churches [6] and his letters patent, 1213, revoking 'ut legatio' [7] (fos.

---

[1] The lawyers' opinions are printed from a later text (mid-fifteenth century) in Johannis de Fordun, *Scotichronicon cum supplementis ac continuatione Walteri Berveni*, ed. W. Goodall (1759), ii. 139–45. Edward's consultation and the opinions have received little attention from historians. F. Michel, *Les Écossais en France, Les Français en Écosse* (1862), i. 41-2, dates Edward's consultation with the lawyers 1286. But probably it took place during the adjournment of the proceedings at Norham in 1292; *Foedera*, i. 777, records that at that time Edward 'per sollempnes nuncios de consilio suo, super facto illo, diversarum regionum consulet sapientes'. One of the lawyers who gave an opinion was master Giles Lambert, described as 'decanus' of Tours; he was dean 1290-1313; E. R. Vaucelle, 'La Collégiale de Saint-Martin de Tours, 397-1328, in *Bulletin et Mémoires de la Société Archéologique de Touraine: Mémoires*, no. 46 (1907), p. 441. See also below p. 288.

[2] A late medieval hand has written in the margin by these entries 'nota pro inhabitacione fratrum Babwell', and 'obsessio pro Weylond'.

[3] *Foedera*, i. 907-8.

[4] *Ibid*. i. 932, 933. *Cf*. Rishanger, *Chronica et Annales*, ed H. T. Riley (Rolls Series), pp. 208–10.

[5] The *ordo* printed by L. G. W. Legg, *English Coronation Records* (1901), pp. 83–112, reference O in the footnotes. The text in Add. MS. 47214 agrees closely with that in Harley MS. 2901, for which see H. G. Richardson in *Bull. Inst. Hist. Research* (1938–9), xvi. 10-11.

[6] *Statutes of the Realm*, i. 5.

[7] T. D. Hardy, *Rotuli Litterarum Patentium* (1835), i. 100.

44$^v$, 45), and the form of homage made by Edward I to Philip IV in 1294 [1] (fo. 45).

When the scribe had written the annals from the Incarnation to 1314 on folios 2$^v$–17, he tabulated the next three leaves (fos. 17$^v$–20) for the annals from 1316–77; he wrote the year date in Roman numerals and the Dominical letter in the left hand margin, leaving a space for the annal before writing the next year date. There are ten years on each page. The general appearance is like that of a modern diary. The scribe then copied in neatly annals for the years 1340, 1345–1348, 1356, 1357, and 1360. His entry for 1345, about the murder of the abbot of Combe, contains information not found elsewhere.

The remaining spaces were used by the Grey Friar of Lynn. He wrote in annals for the years 1346, 1361–70, and 1373–7. The annals themselves provide the evidence of authorship. Four entries suggest that they were written by a Grey Friar (those for 1349, 1362, 1366, and 1375) as they contain references to the Franciscans. An entry under 1364 suggests that the friar belonged to the Grey Friars' house at Lynn; it notes that 'post complein dictum in choro quasi usque ad mediam noctem erat fulmen horribile quasi continuum et grando Lenn'. Events at Lynn are also mentioned under 1363, 1374, and 1377.

It is well known that most medieval religious houses kept chronicles as part of their archives. The grand chronicles, such as those of St. Albans, have survived, partly because more than one copy was made. But many less important works have disappeared. This Grey Friar's chronicle is interesting as one of the few survivors. It represents the humble attempt of a small house to write history and may be compared with the short chronicle of Butley priory in Suffolk [2] and that of the Grey Friars of London.[3] The page format, the arrangement of spaces headed by the year date for the insertion of annals, also occurs in the mid-thirteenth-century annals of St. Augustine's Canterbury (the scribe tabulated annals from the Incarnation to 1300 and made entries to 1234),[4] and in the late thirteenth-century annals of Hickling in Norfolk (the scribe tabulated annals from the Incarnation to 1532, made entries to 1294 and other scribes added more entries later).[5] The Winchester chronicler advocated composing a chronicle year by year on a schedule attached to the end of a volume and copying the annal in neatly at the end of the year.[6] But here was another way of writing a chronicle.

[1] *Foedera*, i. 807.
[2] *Register or Chronicle of Butley Priory, Suffolk, 1510–1535*, ed. A. G. Dickens (1951).
[3] *Monumenta Franciscana*, ed. R. Howlett (Rolls Series), ii. 143–260.
[4] Cotton MS. Julius D 11, fos. 3–21. [5] Egerton MS. 3142, fos. 83$^v$–104$^v$.
[6] Cotton MS. Vespasian E iv, fo. 153, printed from a derivative text (see N. Denholm Young, *EHR*, xlix (1934), 85–93 in *Annales Monastici*, ed. H. R. Luard (Rolls Series), iv. 355. Cf. above p. 205 and n. 43.

The Grey Friar of Lynn writes bad Latin in a cramped charter hand.  His Latin shows the influence of the vernacular (for example, *complein* for *completorium* under 1364 and *princissa* for *principissa* under 1365).  Only once, under 1373, does he associate cause with effect.  But his chronicle gains value from its very unpretentiousness.  The chronicler was not tidily copying written sources.  From 1361 it is fairly certain that he was writing more or less contemporarily with the events described.  The shade of ink and width of pen strokes varies from annal to annal.  The entry for 1364 got so long that it spilt over into the space for 1365, which annal is longer still and almost crowds out that for 1366.  The author seems to have obtained much of his news as an eye-witness and listener: under 1365 he says ' hec et alia multa retulit qui interfuit ', and ends the annal for 1375 with ' ut dicebatur a multis '.  He is more than a parochial antiquary.  He mentions his own house only once and makes a bold attempt at a general history; he notes events of national importance and does not ignore the European scene.  He must have profited from being at Lynn, a busy market place and port.  He adds a number of facts to our knowledge, particularly of East Anglian history.  He is apparently the only authority for the removal and reburial of Elizabeth Ufford's body in 1362, for the fires at the Austin  friary , Orford, and in the tolbooth and Carmelite convent, Lynn, under 1363, for the celebrations on the occasion of Princess Joan's purification in 1365, for the flood and high price of water at Lynn in 1374, for the information about the Franciscans in 1375 and for the interdict on Lynn in 1377.

BRITISH MUSEUM ADDITIONAL MS. 47214.

### fo. 18ᵛ. 1340

In [1] festo nativitatis beati Iohannis Baptiste,[2] statim post horam nonam, fuit bellum navale in Swyna Flandrie inter regem Anglie [Edwardum] tercium a conquestu et navigium regis Francie, ubi Deo opitulante rex Anglie triumphavit et cepit circiter viii naves, defensoribus et gubernatoribus earundem submersis et occisis.

### 1345

Duo albi monachi de monasterio de Koumbe [3] pro morte eorum abbatis capti, et per aliquod tempus in prisona de Warwyk' detenti, demum die sancti Laurencii [4] apud Rokeby per Justiciarios domini regis E[dwardi]

---

[1] Punctuation, the use of capitals, *u, v, i, j*, are the editor's.  The years are written in Arabic instead of Roman numerals and the dominical letters omitted.

[2] 24 June.                                    [3] Combe, co. Warwick, Cistercian abbey.

[4] 10 August, at Rugby.  For this murder, which is not mentioned by the other chroniclers, see *Cal. Pat. Rolls, 1343–1345*, pp. 573, 580, and *Cal. of Inquisitions, Misc.* 11. 483.

tercii, anno regni sui xix°, de morte et prodicione eorum patris arrainiati et coram eis caucius convicti, privilegio clericali non obstante, tanquam proditores eodem die tracti fuerunt et suspensi.

## 1346

Bellum apud Cressy in Picardia inter Edwardum regem Anglie tercium a conquestu et Philippum de Valoys regem Francie, ubi ex parte dicti regis Francie ceciderunt rex Boemie, dux Lothoringie, comites de Flandrie, de Alasonn, de Bloys, de Alba Marla, de Bello Monte, de Harecourt cum duobus filiis et plures alii tam de Francia quam Alemannia; [1] et dominus rex Francie cum filio regis Boemie fugit.[2]  Et cito post rex Anglie incepit eodem anno obsidionem de Caleys.  Eodem anno David rex Scocie captus est.

## 1347

Villa de Caleys fere per unum annum per Edwardum regem Anglie tercium post conquestum obsessa, et demum fame subacta, iiii[to] die Augusti eo anno per diem sabbati eidem regi cum castro reddita fuit capitaneo, et omnibus aliis in eisdem existentibus in gratia domini Regis de vita et membris, bonis et catallis se ponentibus.

## fo. 19. 1348

Isto anno apud Melcoumbe in comitatu Dorsate parum ante festum nat' sancti Iohannis Baptiste,[3] due scaphe, quarum una erat de Bristollia, applicuerunt, in quibus naute de Vasconia venientes quadam inaudita pestilencia epidemia nominata infecti, homines illius ville de Melcoumbe primo in Anglia inficiebant, ubi incole morbo illius pestilencie trium dierum ad plus infirmati in vigilia sancti Iohannis Baptiste primo inde ibi mori ceperunt.

## 1349

Isto anno circa pascha vel modicum ante incepit pestilencia in custodia [4] Cantebrigiense et duravit per totam estatem.

## 1356

Bellum iuxta Pictaviam inter Iohannem regem Francie et Edwardum primogenitum regis Anglie principem Wallie, ubi dictus rex succubuit et captus est cum filio Philippo et multis comitibus et dominis Francie

---

[1] This list is inaccurate and incomplete.

[2] The flight of Philip with the son of the king of Bohemia, Charles IV of Luxembourg, is mentioned by the continuator of Murimuth; *Chronica Adae Murimuth et Roberti de Avesbury*, ed. E. M. Thompson (Rolls Series), p. 247. Froissart, *Chroniques*, ed. S. Luce (Soc. de l'Hist. de France), iii. 179, says of Charles, ' il s'en parti: je ne sçai pas quel chemin il prist ', and states that Philip fled with Jean de Hainault and others to Labroye and on to Paris (*ib.* iii. lvii, and 184). *Les Vrayes Chroniques de Messire Jehan le Bel*, ed. M. L. Polain, ii. 89, also mentions his flight with Jean de Hainault.

[3] The authorities give various dates.  Malvern, *Polychronicon*, ed. R. Lumby (Rolls Series), viii. 355, gives about the feast of St. John the Baptist.

[4] *Custodia ;* an administrative division of the Franciscan province; that of Cambridge covered East Anglia.  Easter was on 12 April; A. Jessop states that the plague entered East Anglia in March; ' Black Death in East Anglia ' in *The Coming of the Friars* (1890), pp. 208-9.

xix⁰ die Septembris, . . primogenito filio suo Dolphino cum acie sua a prelio fugiente.

## 1357

Edwardus princeps Wallie, regis Edwardi tercii a conquestu primogenitus, de Vasconia in Angliam rediit et xi die mensis Maii per diem iovis [1] apud Plummouth prospere applicuit, Iohannem regem Francie, Philippum filium suum et quosdam alios in bello iuxta Pictaviam captos de Burdegale secum ducens. Eodem anno circa festum nat' sancti iohannis duo cardinales in Angliam venerunt pro pace inter regna Francie et Anglie reformanda.[2] Eodem anno mense Septembris David de Brus rex Scotie a custodia regis Anglie liberatus fuit, certis obsidibus pro redemptio[n]e sua in Angliam missis.[3]

## fo. 19ᵛ. 1360

Isto anno incepit pestilencia apud London' iam circa festum sancti Michaelis [4] ubi primo infantes in magno numero delevit; et post pascham [5] proximam sequens (*sic*) homines et mulieres in maxima multitudine decesserunt.

## 1361

Isto anno fuit pestilencia in partibus australibus Anglie maxime et mors puerorum et iuvenum et divitum; hec tamen pestilencia fuit multo minor quam precedens (*sic*) anno 13ᵐᵒ.[6] Eodem anno secundum cursum ecclesie Anglicane 18 Kal. Februarii [7] et sequente nocte fuit ventus vehemens qui campanilia et ecclesias et domos destruxit et discooperuit et arbores evertit.

## 1362

Isto anno in die sanctorum Gervasii et Prothasii [8] fuit corpus domine Elizabet, uxoris domini Thome Ufford heredis [9] et filii comitis Suffolchie,[10] exhumatum apud Campese [11] et deportatum ad fratres minores Gipp' [12]

---

[1] This date is wrong; Edward arrived on 5 May; *Chronicon Angliae* (Rolls Series), ed. E. M. Thompson, p. 37. He left Bordeaux on 11 April; *Grandes Chroniques*, ed. R. Delachenal (Soc. de l'Hist. de France), i. 110.

[2] Nicholas Cappochi, cardinal-priest of St. Vitalis; Talleyrand of Perigord, cardinal-bishop of Albano.

[3] David Bruce was released on the conclusion of the treaty of Berwick, 3 October 1357; *Foedera*, iii. 372–3.

[4] This approximate date, about 29 September, is roughly six months earlier than that given by the other authorities.

[5] 5 April 1361.                    [6] Thirteen years previously, *i.e.* 1348.

[7] 15 January 1362.                [8] 19 June.

[9] The description of Thomas as ' heir ' may mean that this annal was written after 1366, as Thomas, the second son (d.? 1368), had an elder brother Robert who is supposed to have been alive in 1366; there is, however, so little evidence about the date of Robert's death that it is impossible to say when Thomas became heir: G. E. C. *Complete Peerage*, xii. 432.

[10] Robert, 1st earl of Suffolk, 1337–69.

[11] Campsey Ash, Suffolk; the Uffords were patrons of the house of Austin canonesses there; R. E. Chester Waters, *Genealogical Memoirs of the Extinct Family of Chester of Chicheley* (1878), i. 325.

[12] Ipswich. That this was Elizabeth's burial place is confirmed by J. Weever, *Funeral Monuments* (1767), p. 487; the story of her reburial does not seem to survive elsewhere.

ac sepultum coram magno altari in choro; quod iacuerat apud Campese plus quam per 24 ebdomadas in terra; discussa enim veritate quomodo corpus suum legaverat sepeliendum in loco fratrum predicto, comes, qui erat homo bone consciencie, permisit corpus levari per fratres.

## 1363

Isto anno in vigilia translationis sancti Thome Cantuariensis archiepiscopi,[1] in nocte quando fratres fuerunt in matutinis, fuit fulmen tam horribile quod combussit ecclesiam et chorum Carmelitarum Lenn' et tolbothe in eadem villa eodem tempore; et anno proximato (*sic*) precedente combussit fulmen locum fratrum Augustinensium apud Orforde et consimili tempore anni. Isto etiam anno fuit magnum gelu incipiens in medio Decembris et durans quasi usque ad medium 40^me proximato (*sic*) sequentis.

## 1364

Isto anno obiit Iohannes rex Francie London' cito post pascha, qui ante captus fuit in bello iuxta Pictaviam cum filio Philippo et multis aliis nobilibus; iste vero Iohannes predictus post captivitatem rediit ad Franciam et postea reversus ad Anglicam, London' mortuus est. Item eodem anno iv Kalendas Augusti,[2] post complein [3] dictum in choro, quasi usque ad mediam noctem, erat fulmen horribile quasi continuum et grando Lenn' et in villis quibusdam [4] vicinis mari, tam horribile quod lapides descenderunt ad quantitatem pomi, et alibi multo maiores, ita quod impetu sui decensus terram penetraverunt ad magnam profunditatem et quasi in terra se occultaverunt, et blada destruxerunt, et feras et cuniculos, aves et lepores (destru) [5] interfecerunt.

## 1365

Isto anno fecit Edwardus, primogenitus regis Anglie et princeps Aquitanie et Wallie, in quindena pasche, in Aquitania civitate Angilem,[6] maximam sole[m]pnitatem in purificatione princi[pi]sse [7] post partum filii sui primogeniti nomine Edwardi. Ubi fuerunt vii^c et vi milites et 154 domine, et duravit sole[m]pnitas per dies 10, et equi [8] in expensis principis fuerunt xviii^m per dictam sole[m]pnitatem; ubi et princi[pi]ssa habuit de camera sua 24 milites et tot dominas in [9] apparatu solempni pro hastiludiis, tripudiis et aliis solaciis transitoriis; pro qua sole[m]pnitate cera empta excessit in precio iiii^c libras argenti. Hec et alia multa retulit qui interfuit.

## 1366

Isto anno in parliamento suo celebrato apud Westmonasterium post pascham dominus rex cassavit et adnullavit [10] statutum novum editum

---

[1] Thursday, 6 July.         [2] 29 July.         [3] gplem in manuscript.
[4] quibusdam in margin with tie-mark in manuscript.         [5] Deleted in manuscript.
[6] Sunday, 27 April, at Angoulême. *Cf.* Avesbury's account of similar festivities on the queen's purification after the birth of Thomas of Woodstock in 1355; *Chronica Adae Murimuth et Roberti de Avesbury*, ed. E. M. Thompson (Rolls Series), p. 422.
[7] pi interlin. in a later hand in manuscript.
[8] eq in manuscript. An écu.
[9] A word has been erased and crossed out in manuscript.
[10] statū added and expunged in manuscript.

per universitates Oxoniensem et Cantebrigiensem contra fratres; [1] de hac materia plenius supra anno bł.[2] Item isto anno in mense Septembris frater Marcus, fratrum minorum generalis minister, factus est cardinalis et alius de ordine predicatorum.[3]

## 1367

Bellum in Hispania iuxta aquam Nazers,[4] ubi Edwardus primogenitus regis Anglie vicit bastardum Hispanie intrusorem [5] et legitimum [6] restituit in regnum, captis 2 milibus Valencium et plusquam quinque milibus occisis.   Hoc factum est 3° die Aprilis. Eodem anno statim post pascham Urbanus V$^{tus}$ recessit de Avinione cum cardinalibus transferens sedem Viterbium.

## fo. 20. 1368

Isto anno dominus archiepiscopus Cantuariensis factus est cardinalis.

## 1369

Hoc anno renovata est guerra inter Angliam et Franciam, per falsitatem quorundam de Francia, qui contra concordiam firmatam invaserunt terras regis Anglie in partibus transmarinis.   Item pestilencia magna fuit magnatum et puerorum.

## 1370

Isto anno fuit magna caristia bladi per totam Angliam et maxime in estate, ita quod quarterium frumenti valuit xx solidos et in quibusdam partibus 2 marcas.[7]

## 1373

Isto anno transfretavit magnus excercitus contra Francos, videlicet dux Lancastrie, dux Britannie, comes Sutfolch, comes Warwyc,' et alii comites et nobiles; modicum tamen profecerunt, quia fame magna pars excercitus interiit, propter defectum capitaneorum,[8] ut dicebatur a multis.[9]

---

[1] Oxford University passed a statute, 1365, forbidding the friars to receive into their orders those who had not yet completed their eighteenth year; *Statuta Antiqua Universitatis Oxoniensis*, ed. S. Gibson (1931), pp. 164-5.   Such a statute for Cambridge University has not survived.   The Parliament at Westminster, May 1366, quashed the Universities' statute; *Rot. Parl.* ii 290.   For details of the controversy see J. R. H. Moorman, *The Grey Friars in Cambridge* (1952), pp. 105 *seq.*

[2] The meaning of this passage is obscure; the manuscript reads de hc̄ m̄ pleni' s̄ an̄ bł.

[3] Mark of Viterbo, minister general of the Friars Minor, 1359-66, cardinal-priest of St. Praxidius, 1366.   William Sudre, cardinal-priest of St. John and St. Paul, 1366.

[4] *Aquam Nazers*; the battle of Najera, 3 April 1367, was fought on the banks of the river Najerilla.

[5] Henry of Trastamara.                            [6] Peter, king of Castille.

[7] Wheat was 3$^s$ a bushel (24$^s$. a quarter), as a result of the plague and floods of the preceding year, according to *Chronicon Anglia* ed. E. M. Thompson (Rolls Series), p. 65; the Annals of Bermondsey record, ' vendebatur busshellus frumenti Calisiae pro iii$^s$. iv$^d$. (26$^s$. 8$^d$. a quarter), luna currente per iii'; *Annales Monastici*, ed. H. R. Luard (Rolls Series), iii. 478.

[8] capit' in manuscript.

[9] For contemporary comments on John of Gaunt's inefficiency see *Eulogium Historiarum*, ed. F. S. Haydon (Rolls Series), iii. 336; Walsingham, *Historia Anglicana*, ed. H. T. Riley, (Rolls Series), i. 316.

## 1374

Isto anno 3º die mensis Decembris circio ¹ flante formidine fuit fluxus maris terribilis Lenn', cooperiens pro maiori parte magnum forum ibidem, terras etiam villarum adiacencium et domos intrans et submergens, naves etiam in mari ad terram per magnam distantiam elevans et proiciens, et pecora in pascuis submergens.  Et cito post sequebatur magnum gelu durans usque ad vigiliam natalis Domini.  Quo tempore fuit magna penuria aque recentis in Lenn' ita quod pipa aque recentis quandoque ² vendebatur pro 12d.

## 1375

Isto anno dominica 4ª quadragesime,³ que fuit ⁴ in octavis annunciationis Virginis gloriose, tanta ⁵ aquarum inundacia Oxonie in conventu predicatorum ⁶ quod populus venit ad locum fratrum minorum ⁷ et ibidem frater predicatorum predicavit sermonem illorum ad populum in domo fratrum minorum.   Item in eadem quadragesima fuit frater Leonardus ⁸ generalis minister fratrum minorum in Anglia et tenuit concilium suum cum magistris et custodibus Anglie Bedefordie, et fuit ibi tamen per 3 dies et statim disponit se ad recessum de Anglia; dies autem convocationis magistrorum et custodum fuit dominica in passione Domini.⁹

## 1377

Hoc anno in vigilia sancti Albani ¹⁰ obiit rex Anglie Edwardus 3ᵘˢ post conquestum, anno regni sui 51, sepultus ad quindenam post eodem die, scilicet die dominica;¹¹ et statim post (in die sanctorum Quirici et Iulitte¹² coronatus est rex Ricardus filius filii supradicti Edwardi anno etatis sue 11ᵐᵒ)¹³ 17 Kalendas Augusti¹⁴ rex Ricardus coronatus, filius filii supradicti Edwardi, etatis sue anno 11ᵐᵒ.  Item eodem anno fuit villa Lenn' supposita interdicto a 5ᵗᵒ Idibus Iunii ¹⁵ usque ad vigiliam sancti Laurencii ¹⁶ eiusdem anni, propter violenciam factam per quosdam fatuos eiusdem ville in personam domini Henrici de Dispensariis episcopi Norwyc'.

¹ *Circius* ;  a violent wind (in Roman times W.N.W.).

² ' va ' added and expunged in manuscript.

³ 1 April.

⁴ ' illo anno ' added and deleted in manuscript.

⁵ ' fuit ' added and deleted in manuscript.

⁶ The buildings (1245) of the Oxford Dominicans lay close by the Isis outside the south gate in St. Ebbes.

⁷ The Church of the Grey Friars, Oxford, stood ' from the south end of Paradise Place, where the wall juts out southwards for a few yards, to a point about the north end of King's Terrace ', A. G. Little, *Grey Friars in Oxford*, p. 23.

⁸ Leonardus Rossi de Giffono, minister general of the Friars Minor 1373-8. Gregory XI in 1374 ordered him to visit Umbria and other provinces to reform observance of the rule; *Analecta Franciscana*, vii. 349-50. His visit to England does not seem to be mentioned elsewhere.

⁹ 8 April.  A. G. Little, *Franciscan Papers, Lists and Documents*, p. 215, notes that a provincial chapter was held in England in 1375, date and place unknown.  For the problems connected with the composition, &c., of the provincial chapters and other less formal assemblies of the Friars Minor see *ibid.* pp. 156-78 passim.

¹⁰ 21 June.              ¹¹ 5 July.              ¹² 16 June.

¹³ Deleted in manuscript.      ¹⁴ 16 July.              ¹⁵ 9 June.

¹⁶ 9 August.  For a full account of Despenser's quarrel with Lynn see *Chronicon Angliae*, pp. 139-40; Walsingham does not mention the interdict.

## ADDITIONAL NOTE

*Page 280 and n. 1.* The lawyers' opinions copied into BL MS Additional 47214, ff. 45–47ᵛ, are most recently discussed and printed in E. L. G. Stones and G. G. Simpson, *Edward I and the Throne of Scotland: An Edition of the Record Sources for the Great Cause* (Oxford, 1978, 2 vols), ii. 358–64. See also G. J. Hand, 'The opinions of the Paris lawyers upon the Scottish Succession Case', *The Irish Jurist*, v (1970), 141–54.

# 13

## The Date and Authorship of John of Glastonbury's *Cronica sive Antiquitates Glastoniensis Ecclesie*[1]

John of Glastonbury's *Cronica* is a history of Glastonbury abbey from the legendary foundation of the first church by St Joseph of Arimathea until the succession to the abbacy of Walter de Monington (1342-75). Although the *Cronica* is a 'house-history', it includes occasional entries about the kings of England; these become rather more detailed in the fourteenth century. As a local history, it is based on William of Malmesbury's *De Antiquitate Glastoniensis Ecclesie*, and then to 1290 on Adam of Domerham's chronicle. The information from them is embellished with much legendary material and eloquent verbiage. From 1290 the text derives either directly or indirectly (perhaps in part from some intermediate Glastonbury annals) from documentary and also probably from oral evidence.

The final version of the *Cronica*, together with the brief continuation to 1497 composed by William Wyche at the order of Abbot Richard de Beere, was printed by Thomas Hearne (Oxford, 1726). He based his text on a later fifteenth century manuscript now in Princeton University Library (Robert Garrett MS 153, ff.2-147$^v$), and took into consideration two other manuscripts, also of the late fifteenth century. It is an excellent edition by the standards of its time, but unfortunately Hearne overlooked a manuscript of the *Cronica* which is much earlier than those he used, now Trinity College, Cambridge, MS R.5.16, pp. 27-214. Scholars therefore welcomed the modern edition (excluding Wyche's continuation) by James P. Carley, first printed in paperback in 1978 (Oxford, British Archaeological Reports, xlvii, i and ii), and reprinted in hardback, with some revision and an English translation by David Townsend, in 1985 (Boydell and Brewer, Woodbridge). Except for the translation, the 1985 edition, the one cited below, is substantially the same as the 1978 one. Carley based his text on the Trinity MS, giving variant readings from the other known manuscripts in footnotes. Because leaves at the beginning of

---

[1] The present article is based on the two reviews I wrote of Carley's 1978 and 1985 editions respectively; *English Historical Review*, xcv (1980), 358-63, and *Albion*, xix (1987), 54-8. For another review of the 1985 edition see David Corner, *EHR*, ciii (1988), 173. Cf. below and next note.

the text in the Trinity MS are missing (Carley, pp. 2-86), Carley reconstructed that part from the best readings in the other manuscripts. In addition, Carley provided subject notes at the end of the volume; of particular value are those on the sources of the *Cronica*.

Carley's Introduction contains the fruits of his researches on the chronicle itself and on its historiographical and historical background at Glastonbury. He pays particular attention to the question of the chronicle's date of composition and its authorship. His conclusions, the substance of which had already appeared in his article in *Mediaeval Studies*, xl (1978), 478-83, deserve careful attention because his dating of the chronicle differs from the previously accepted one, and he is the first scholar to claim to have identified the author, 'John'. They have been accepted without question by some scholars,[2] although the evidence presented by Carley does not warrant certainty. This is recognised by John Taylor in his definitive study of fourteenth-century English historical literature: 'a final judgement,' he says, 'cannot yet be given'.[3] Since Taylor wrote a new piece of evidence has come to light which may be relevant to the date problem. But before discussing that evidence, it is necessary to examine the evidence available to Carley and to test the soundness of his conclusion about the date of composition to which it led him. His identification of the author depends on his dating and will therefore be considered last.

Since the chronicler states in the prologue (p. 6) that he has written the history of the abbey to about 1400, Hearne and subsequent scholars concluded that *Cronica* was composed at that time. Carley, however, rejects this approximate date, postulating instead a date between 1340 and 1342 or more generally to the 1340s (pp. xxv-xxviii). This would explain the fact that the *Cronica* ends in 1342 and not c. 1400. Moreover, in Carley's opinion the Trinity MS, a composite volume, provides evidence of an earlier date than the accepted one. He bases his conclusion on the argument that the copy of the *Cronica* in the Trinity MS cannot have been made as late as c. 1400. The Trinity text is a copy and not the author's draft and was likely, Carley speculates (p. xxvi), to have been made quite a while after the original composition since 'from what we know about the Glastonbury library it seems unlikely that a text such as the *Cronica* would have been immediately duplicated'. (However, if the early draft was untidy, it seems probable that a fair copy would soon have been made).

[2] Carley's redating is accepted by J.R. Maddicott in his review of Carley's 1985 edition; *Journal of Ecclesiastical History*, xxxvii (1986), 490-1. Both the redating and the identification of the author are accepted by the editors of the Annals of St. Neots; *The Anglo-Saxon Chronicle, a collaborative edition*, ed. D.N. Dumville and Simon Keynes, xvii, *The Annals of St. Neots with Vita Prima Sancti Neoti*, ed. Dumville and Michael Lapidge (Cambridge, 1985), p. cxv.

[3] John Taylor, *English Historical Literature in the Fourteenth Century* (Oxford, 1987), p. 45.

The Trinity text is in a good bookhand and is followed without a break or a change of handwriting by a list of sixty-three monks who professed under Monington. Since this list includes John Chinnock, Monington's successor to the abbacy (1375-1420) and refers to him as *postea abbas*, it must have been copied after Chinnock's succession; Carley believes that this would not have been done much after 1375. This argument is purely speculative, since obviously a copy can be made at any time. More crucial to Carley's conclusion is the date of the handwriting of the *Cronica* in the Trinity MS. Carley cites the opinion of an eminent palaeographer, Father Leonard Boyle, that the copy was made in the last half of the fourteenth century 'and can probably be dated to the last quarter of the century' (p. xxv). Carley concludes: 'A palaeographical analysis, then, shows that the text cannot have been written as late as 1400'. However, it is surely rash to argue that the copy could have been made just before 1400, but not c. 1400. It is a truism that an old man might write a hand current in his youth, and that a whole scriptorium might be old fashioned, especially one in an out-of-the-way place – like Glastonbury.

Carley's redating of the *Cronica* to 1340-2 (or the 1340s) raises two problems. First, the *Cronica* refers to one of Chinnock's acts as abbot (p. 45). Carley warns the reader of this difficulty in a footnote (p. xxvi n. 5 and cf. p. xxviii), observing that 'By my calculations this must be an interpolation'. The second problem is the statement in the prologue that the author had continued the *Cronica* down until c. 1400. Carley argues that this was the result of a scribal error. The scribe miscopied the date because he was misled homoeoteleuton and so wrote *ad annum domini millesimum circiter quadringentesimum* instead of *ad annum domini circiter quadragesimum tercentesimum*. Thus Carley concludes that the author started writing in 1340.

There are objections to these two *ad hoc* hypotheses. The manuscript evidence does not support them. The Trinity MS, owing to the loss of leaves, throws no light on the matter, but the other manuscripts all have the passage about Chinnock *in textu* and the date 'c. 1400' in the prologue. This makes it necessary for Carley to claim (pp. xxii-xxiii) that all the surviving manuscripts descend from a common exemplar, since it is most unlikely that the interpolation would have been made and the year date miscopied in two independent manuscripts. Carley identifies this exemplar with the Trinity MS, which, he argues, in view of the relatively high quality of its text, is a copy of the original. (He does not consider the possibility that it had benefited from scribal correction.) Nevertheless, on Carley's own showing (p. xxiii), one of the other copies, the Princeton MS, does not share the few errors in the Trinity MS: this fact (which Carley attributes to scribal correction) suggests that perhaps the Trinity MS is not its exemplar.

Carley's evidence, therefore, for redating the *Cronica* is not, as he suggests (p. xxx) 'incontestable'. At most it suggests a possibility. And meanwhile a good case can be made for the traditional date. The textual evidence is on its side. Furthermore, Carley himself pointed out in his 1978 edition[4] (i.xxxvii n. 1) that it is hard to find a chronicle composed in the fourteenth century comparable with the *Cronica*. But it would fit well into the historiography of the early fifteenth century, which includes a number of similar works: Abbot William Frocester's history of St Peter's, Gloucester;[5] Thomas Elmham's history of St Augustine's, Canterbury,[6] Thomas Burton's history of Meaux;[7] and possibly the 'pseudo-Ingulf' of Crowland abbey.[8] Later in the century other monastic histories were written: Prior John Wessington's history of St Cuthbert's, Durham;[9] Thomas Rudborne's history of St Swithun's, Winchester;[10] Prior John Flete's history of Westminster abbey;[11] the history of Bermondsey abbey;[12] and the history of Hyde abbey, Winchester.[13]

When John Chinnock was abbot the situation at Glastonbury would have been particularly conducive to the composition of a monastic history. The principal purpose of a work of this kind was to increase prestige and improve the *esprit de corps* of a house by demonstrating its long and creditable past. External hostility and internal trouble both tended to result in such productions. Glastonbury abbey, having enjoyed harmony and prosperity earlier in the fourteenth century, suffered discord and economic reverse under Chinnock. Chinnock's election was disputed by another monk, Thomas Coffyn, who had a substantial following, and whose opposition was only finally defeated in 1408.[14] (It is noteworthy that Thomas Burton started writing in similar circumstances. He was elected abbot of Meaux in 1396, but there was a rival candidate, and his

---

[4] Carley (1978), i. xxxvii n. 1.

[5] *Historia et Cartularium Monasterii Sancti Petri Gloucestriae*, ed. W.H. Hart (Rolls Series, 1863-7), i. 3-58.

[6] *Historia Monasterii S. Augustini Cantuariensis*, ed. Charles Hardwick (R.S., 1858).

[7] *Chronica Monasterii de Melsa*, ed. E.A. Bond (R.S., 1866-8, 3 vols).

[8] *Rerum Anglicarum Scriptorum Veterum Tom. I*, ed. William Fulman (Oxford, 1684), pp. 1-133. H.T. Riley, 'The history and charters of Ingulfus considered', *Archaeological Journal*, xix (1862), 114-28, dates the pseudo-Ingulf to *c.* 1414, but W.G. Searle, *Ingulf and the Historia Croylandensis* (Cambridge Antiquarian Society, octavo series, xxvii, 1894), p. 207, dates it to the mid-fifteenth century, and F. Liebermann, 'Ueber Ostenglische Geschichtsquellen des 12., 13., 14. Jahrhunderts, besonders den falschen Ingulf', *Neues Archiv der Gesellschaft für ältere deutsche Geschichtskunde*, xviii (1892), 262-3, to the mid-fourteenth century.

[9] Unpublished. See H.S. Offler, *Medieval Historians of Durham* (Durham, 1958), p. 17, and R.B. Dobson, *Durham Priory 1400-1450* (Cambridge, 1973), pp. 379-81.

[10] *Anglia Sacra*, ed. Henry Wharton (London, 1691), i. 177-286.

[11] *History of Westminster Abbey*, ed. J.A. Robinson (Cambridge, 1909).

[12] *Annales Monastici*, ed. H.R. Luard (R.S., 1864-9, 5 vols), iii. 423-87.

[13] *Liber Monasterii de Hyda*, ed. E. Edwards (R.S., 1866).

[14] For an account of Chinnock's rule see Ian Keil, 'Profiles of some Abbots of Glastonbury', *Downside Review*, lxxxi (1963), 356-62.

election entailed so much discord that he resigned in 1398. He wrote his chronicle in retirement in the abbey.) The conflict at Glastonbury not only lowered morale, but also resulted in expensive litigation. The abbey's finances deteriorated further owing to a rise in prices and a decline in profits and rents. It is, therefore, likely that the monks would have turned to their legends for help, in the same way as they had done after the fire which devastated the abbey in 1184. Chinnock was the first abbot actively to promote the cult of St Joseph of Arimathea at Glastonbury, which cult had lain more or less dormant since its inception there in the thirteenth century.[15] In 1382 he dedicated a chapel which he had restored in the cemetery to St Michael and St Joseph. He may also have commissioned the *Magna Tabula* and had it put in the abbey church for the benefit of pilgrims. The *tabula*, comprising folding wooden boards with parchment pasted on them, is almost exclusively devoted to the legends of the abbey's foundation and early history, all derived from the *Cronica*.[16] Chinnock's responsibility for it is suggested by the fact that its one entry not copied from the *Cronica* records his dedication of the chapel of St Michael and St Joseph.[17]

Circumstances at Glastonbury would have provided Chinnock with ample reason for commissioning the *Cronica* at any time during his abbatiate. However, he may have had an immediate incentive, at a specific date. Perhaps this incentive took the form of encouragement by the king, Henry IV, himself. Chinnock's contact with the Lancastrians is proved by the fact that in 1399 he was one of the delegation sent to Richard II to announce his deposition.[18] From the twelfth to the fourteenth centuries there had been sporadic royal interest in the Glastonbury legends.[19] Henry II probably had some part in Abbot Henry de Soilli's decision to turn the Arthurian legends to the abbey's advantage, and both Edward I[20] and Edward III[21] visited King Arthur's tomb there. Royal fostering of the legends was not always the result only of concern for the abbey's welfare or of chivalric enthusiasm for the cult of King Arthur. At

[15] See V.M. Lagorio, 'The evolving legend of St. Joseph of Glastonbury', *Speculum*, xlvi (1971), 213-18.

[16] The *tabula*, now MS Lat. Hist. A. 2 in the Bodleian Library, is described and discussed by J.A. Bennett, 'A Glastonbury Relic', *Proc. Somersetshire Arch. and Nat. Hist. Soc.*, xxxiv (1886), 117-22.

[17] *Ibid.*, p. 120.

[18] *Rot. Parl.*, iii. 422.

[19] See *Journ. of Eccles. Hist.*, xxvii (1976), 354-5.

[20] For Edward I's visit in 1278 see R.S. Loomis, 'Edward I, Arthurian enthusiast', *Speculum*, xxviii (1953), 115-16.

[21] For Edward III's visit in 1331 see *The Great Chartulary of Glastonbury*, ed. Aelred Watkin, i (Somerset Record Soc., lix, 1947), 194-5.

least Henry II and Edward I had in addition a political motive;[22] demonstrable proof that Arthur was dead and would not return, as some believed, to lead the Britons to victory against the English, strengthened their hands against the Welsh. Henry IV may well have seen the legend of Joseph of Arimathea at Glastonbury as a weapon against the French at the Council of Pisa in 1409. The precedence of the 'nations' at the general councils was determined by the date of the country's conversion. A corollary of the legend of St Joseph at Glastonbury was the apostolic conversion of the English. This put Christianity in England on an equal footing with that in France; although the French claimed actual conversion by St Denis, they asserted that the first mission was by Mary Magdalen, Martha and Lazarus to Provence. In fact the legend of St Joseph was cited by the English party to back its claim to precedence at a series of general councils – at Pisa, Constance (1417), Siena (1424) and Basle (1434)[23] Chinnock, therefore, may have commissioned the *Cronica* preparatory to the Council of Pisa, which he himself attended.[24] Perhaps he was also at the Council of Constance,[25] and his successor Nicholas Frome was at both the Council of Siena and that of Basle.[26] If the composition of the *Cronica* was at least in part the result of the conciliar movement, it might have a historiographical parallel. It is likely that Henry V commissioned the *Gesta Henrici Quinti* as propaganda partly to fortify his position at the Council of Constance.[27] However, no doubt Chinnock would not have commissioned the *Cronica* solely to help the English party at Pisa; he would also have intended that it would provide

---

[22] For Henry II's political motive for fostering the cult of King Arthur at Glastonbury see R.F. Treharne, *The Glastonbury Legends* (London, 1967), pp. 105-6, and for Edward I's see F.M. Powicke, *King Henry III and the Lord Edward* (Oxford, 1947), ii. 724. The hope of Arthur's return may also have encouraged the Celts to resist Henry II in Normandy; see J.S.P. Tatlock, 'Geoffrey and King Arthur in *Normannicus Draco*', *Modern Philology*, xxxi (1933-4), 122-3. See also above pp. 170-1.

[23] See C.J. Hefele, *Histoire des conciles*, ed. H. Leclercq (Paris, 1907-38, 20 vols), vii, pt. i, pp. 31-2 n. 2, and J. Ussher, *Britannicarum Ecclesiarum Antiquitates* (London, 1687), pp. 13-14.

[24] G.D. Mansi, *Sacrorum conciliorum . . . collectio* (Florence etc., 1759-1962, 31 vols), xxvii, col. 349.

[25] The list of delegates to the Council of Constance (*ibid.* xxviii. coll. 626-54) does not include Chinnock, but a recent scholar presumes he was there; Logario, *loc. cit.*, p. 223 n. 64.

[26] For Frome's presence at Siena see Hefele, *op. cit.*, vii, pt. i, p. 614, n. 3, and at Basle see Thomas Rymer, *Foedera* (London, 1704-35, 20 vols), x. 577, and *Official Correspondence of Thomas Bekynton*, ed. George Williams (R.S., 1872, 2 vols), ii. 259.

[27] See J.S. Roskell and F. Taylor, 'The authorship and purpose of the *Gesta Henrici Quinti*: Part I', *Bull. John Rylands Lib.*, liv (1971-2), 227-40. It is of course possible that the *Cronica* was likewise written preparatory to the Council of Constance. However, it seems more likely that it was written preparatory to the Council of Pisa; there is no certain evidence that Chinnock was at Constance, and the date of that council is further removed from the chronicler's target of *c.* 1400 than that of Pisa.

proof, to be rehearsed with full publicity before an international audience, of his abbey's priority of foundation.

We must, I believe, accept that the weight of the evidence favours the traditional date, *c.* 1400, for the composition of the *Cronica*. Nevertheless, the problem remains how to explain the fact that the *Cronica* ends in 1342 while the author claims in the prologue to have written to *c.* 1400. He may have composed the prologue before, or in the course of, writing the *Cronica*, and then failed to complete his task. Indeed, the Trinity MS contains , besides the John of Glastonbury's *Cronica*, numerous documents relating to the abbacy of Walter de Monington , which could be collectanea made in preparation for the composition of an account of his rule.) A parallel case would be Thomas Elmham (d.? 1426) who makes plain his intention to write the history of St. Augustine's, Canterbury, up to his own day but only reached 806, leaving only brief particulars to 1089 and then a collection of documents to 1191.[28] Similarly, neither John Flete nor John Wessington ever completed their histories of Westminster abbey and the see of St. Cuthbert respectively.[29] However, other possible reasons for the discrepancy between the actual terminal date of the *Cronica* and that given in the prologue is suggested by a piece of evidence which has recently come to light. Professor Donald Watt has called my attention to a passage in Walter Bower's *Scotichronicon*. Bower, writing in the 1440s, was pro-Richard II and in his annal for 1398 explains how Henry Bolingbroke was not the nearest heir to the throne. He continues:

> Iste Henricus Lancastrie dux Herfordie et comes de Darby quando sibi regni diadema de facto assumpsit misit abbati de Glasynbiri pro actis parliamenti et cronica que posuerunt filias Rogeri de Mortuomari debere succedere, et quia excusando negavit, recognovit temporalitatem donec cronicam optinuit et incendit ac novas pro se facientes fabricare jussit.[30]

There seems no reason to disbelieve this story, especially as it accords with the Lancastrians' propagandist use of chronicles in their attempt to prove that Bolingbroke had a hereditary right to the throne.[31] According

[28] See *Historia Monasterii Sancti Augustini Cantuariensis*, ed. Hardwick, p. 344 n. 1.

[29] Wessington, prior of Durham 1416-46, completed his history only to 1362 (his history is unprinted; see A. Gransden, *Historical Writing in England, ii, c. 1307 to the Early Sixteenth Century* (London, 1982), p. 393 n. 13), and Flete, prior of Westminster 1457-65, completed his history only to 1386 (*The History of Westminster Abbey*, ed. Robinson, pp. 1, 33).

[30] *Scotichronicon by Water Bower*, ed. with an English translation, general editor D.E.R. Watt (Aberdeen, 1987-, 9 vols, in progress), viii, *Books XV and XVI*, ed. D.E.R. Watt (Aberdeen, 1987), pp. 21-2.

[31] Adam of Usk was one of the commission appointed to examine the legal justification for Bolingbroke's succession to the throne; *Chronicon Adae de Usk A.D. 1377-1421*, ed., with an English translation, E. Maunde Thompson (2nd edn., Oxford U.P., London, 1904), pp. 29-31.

to John Hardyng (writing in the 1460s), John of Gaunt had a chronicle forged and distributed to various monasteries, in support of the claim of his son, Bolingbroke, which alleged that Edmund Crouchback, the Lancastrians' ancestor, and not Edward I, from whom the Mortimers derived their claim, was Henry III's eldest son.[32] The claim to the throne of Roger Mortimer, fourth earl of March, was through his mother, Philippa, daughter of Lionel of Clarence, Edward III's third son, and wife of Edmund, third earl of March. The *Eulogium Historiarum* asserts that in the October parliament of 1385 Richard II proclaimed that Roger was next heir to the throne.[33] Although historians have tended to dismiss this statement,[34] the March claim was undoubtedly good, and Roger's successor, Edmund, fifth earl of March, became the focus of revolt and sedition early in Henry IV's reign.[35]

Bower's reference to the right of succession to the throne of Roger's daughters is puzzling. Roger himself was killed on 20 July 1498. He had four children: Anne, born 27 December 1388; Edmund, born 6 November 1391; Roger, born 23 April 1393; and Eleanor, the date of whose birth is not apparently known.[36] It is tempting to place Eleanor's birth between Anne's and Edmund's. In that case, if we accept Bower's evidence, the entry in the Glastonbury chronicle to which he refers was probably written in, or shortly before or after, 1390. Possibly the chronicle was continued after that date to the end of the century. If so, John's chronicle as it survives today may be a copy of a truncated text; perhaps originally it extended to the late fourteenth century, but Henry destroyed the section from 1342, which would have contained the offending passage or passages. An objection to this theory is that the chronicle is a local history of Glastonbury abbey, not a national history. However, it does have passages concerning political events, and these might have increased in proportion as the author reached Richard II's exciting reign, which culminated in the deposition. An alternative interpretation is that Henry destroyed the whole of some other Glastonbury chronicle of a general nature, and the extant *Cronica*, which would have positively pleased him,

[32] *The Chronicle of John Hardyng*, ed. Henry Ellis (London, 1812, repr. New York, 1974), pp. 353-4.

[33] *Eulogium Historiarum* . . ., ed. F.S. Haydon, (R.S. 1858-63, 3 vols), iii, 361.

[34] See T.F. Tout, *Chapters in the Administrative History of Medieval England* (Manchester, 1920-33, 6 vols), iii. 396 n. 1; M.V. Clarke, *Fourteenth Century Studies*, ed. L.S. Sutherland and M. McKisack (Oxford, 1937), p. 107 n. 5; Anthony Tuck, *Richard II and the English Nobility* (London, 1973), p. 205. However, Anthony Steel, *Richard II* (Cambridge, 1962), p. 214, gives the story more credence.

[35] *Usk, op. cit.*, p. 82. Cf. G.L. Harriss, *Henry V, The Practice of Kingship* (Oxford U.P., 1985), p. 32.

[36] G.E. C[okayne], *Complete Peerage of England, Scotland, Ireland, Great Britain and United Kingdom* . . ., new edn by Vicary Gibbs *et al.* (London, 1910-59, 12 vols, vol. xii in two parts), viii. 449-450 and n. a.

was composed to replace it.

Finally, there is the question of the identity of 'John', the author of the *Cronica*. He declares himself in the prologue as 'Iohannes, abiectissimus et humilimus eiusdem venerabilis loci quamuis indignus confrater et monachus' (Carley, i.5). Carley's candidate is John Seen, a monk of Glastonbury who received a D.Th. from Oxford in 1360, and who Carley thinks died before 1377 (Carley, pp. xxix-xxx). Obviously if the *Cronica* was written, as I believe, *c.* 1400, Seen cannot have been the author. Even supposing that the *Cronica* was written between 1340 and 1342, the case for his authorship is slim. He composed a now lost history of the Trojan war, and in addition, is referred to in a letter of John Grandison, bishop of Exeter, to Walter de Monington: '. . . venerabilis et religiosus vir dompnus Iohannes Sene domus vestre commonachus inter omnes huius regni peritos de gestis antiquis et cronicis magis novit . . .'. Carley suggests that the *gestae antiquae* was Seen's history of the Trojan War, and that *cronicae* denoted the *Cronica*. However, the reference is probably to Seen's historiographical learning, not to any activity as a chronicler. It should perhaps be observed that twenty-three of the sixty-three monks in the list of those who professed under Monington have the Christian name 'John'.

## Note

Pages 290-7. Most recently Professor Carley's redating of John of Glastonbury's *Cronica* has been accepted without reservation as correct by C.T. Wood, 'Fraud and its Consequences: Savaric of Bath and the Reform of Glastonbury' in *The Archaeology and History of Glastonbury Abbey*, ed. Lesley Abrams and J.P. Carley (Woodbridge, 1991), p. 282. (See also Wood's review of Carley's edition of the *Cronica* in *Speculum*, lxi (1987), 427-9.) Wood claims that the *De Gestis Mirabilibus Edwardi Tertii* by Robert of Avesbury (d. 1359) provides conclusive evidence for Carley's dating. He asserts that the *De Gestis*, which he dates *c.*1350, traces King Arthur's ancestry back to Joseph of Arimathea. Since John of Glastonbury also gives this genealogy (ed. Carley, p. 56), which was otherwise unknown in the fourteenth century, Avesbury's information, Professor Wood argues, must have come from John's *Cronica*. Wood's reasoning here is not sound because Avesbury could have derived the genealogy from some other, now lost, source, perhaps the same one as John used. But more important, Wood's premise is itself false. Avesbury's in his *De Gestis* (written in 1356 or shortly afterwards) gives no genealogy of King Arthur. The genealogy in question occurs in some notes appended to the earliest extant manuscript of the *De Gestis*, BL MS. Harley 200, a copy made in the early fifteenth century. The notes are in the same hand as, or in a hand contemporaneous with, that of the scribe of the *De Gestis*. (See *Adae Murimuth Continuatio Chronicorum. Robertus de Avesbury De Gestis Mirabilibus Regis Edwardi Tertii*, ed. E. Maunde Thompson (Rolls Series, 1889), pp. xxiii-xxiv.) Thomas Hearne printed the notes as 'Minutae' in his edition of the *De Gestis* (*Historia de Mirabilibus Gestis Edwardi III* (Oxford, 1720), pp. 256-66; Arthur's genealogy is on p. 259). Except for one note (a genealogy of Edward III) Hearne did not believe that the notes were by Avesbury (*ibid.*, pp. x-xi). Carley in the introduction to his edition of John's *Cronica* (p. xxviii) describes the notes (which he dates *c.*1350) as anonymous. He cites R.H. Fletcher, *The Arthurian Material in the Chronicles* (Harvard Studies and Notes in Philology and

Literature, x, 1906), pp. 176, 189; Fletcher, who cites Hearne p. 259, describes the notes as of uncertain authorship.

Therefore, since the *De Gestis* does not contain Arthur's genealogy and the note which does was almost certainly not by Avesbury, Wood cannot use the evidence of the genealogy to prove that John of Glastonbury's *Cronica* was Avesbury's source. For the sake of accuracy it should also be mentioned that Wood's belief that the notes occur in only one manuscript of the *De Gestis* is inexact. The other two surviving copies have some of the notes appended, though slightly differently arranged. Both these copies of the *De Gestis* were made in the first half of the fifteenth century and derived from Harley 200 (Maunde Thompson, *op. cit.*, pp. xxv-xxvi).

# 14

# Antiquarian Studies in Fifteenth-Century England

Antiquarian studies in medieval England have had a bad press. To Professor McKisack such studies begin with John Leland:[1]

> As has long been recognized, Leland's distinction as an antiquary derives, first and foremost, from the fact that he was a pioneer in the method of direct enquiry and first-hand observation, the forerunner of Camden. The originality of his approach [is] revealed in the *Itinerary* . . .

And yet over twenty years before Sir Thomas Kendrick had done ample justice to the fifteenth-century antiquaries, John Rous and William Worcester.[2] However, he treats them as heralds of a new era. While admitting that previously attempts had been made to study the past 'through the intelligent use of archives and visible monuments' (he cites a few examples from the twelfth and thirteenth centuries),[3] he characterizes the antiquarianism of medieval England as fanciful and prone to fiction.[4] The chronicler, Sir Thomas asserts, had no training in criticism, and his view of the past was dominated by the British History.[5] This corpus of legend owed its origin to Geoffrey of Monmouth, but, in the words of Sir Thomas, it was 'not a static system of antiquarian belief. . . but a thriving garden of spurious history in which any transitory nonsense about the remote past might take root and flourish'.[6] In fact Sir Thomas saw the

---

[1] May McKisack, *Medieval History in the Tudor Age* (Oxford, 1971), p. 11.

[2] T.D. Kendrick, *British Antiquity* (London, 1950), pp. 18-33.

[3] *Ibid.*, p. 18 and nn. 3-4.

[4] For example, Sir Thomas states that Leland, like many antiquaries of his day, remained 'medieval in mind'; he was 'a man two-faced, in one direction looking hopefully forward into a new era of empirical research and practical survey, and at the same time looking with affection backward to the writing-desk of the medieval scholastic chronicler-antiquary where a traditional fable might be repeated without unrestful inquiry or impertinent sixteenth century doubt'; *ibid.*, p. 63. Similarly, Sir Thomas comments that in the sixteenth century 'antiquarian thought tended to remain medieval in kind – medieval in credulity and in recklessness of conjecture'; *ibid.*, p. 65.

[5] *Ibid.*, pp. 2 *et seq.*

[6] *Ibid.*, p. 15.

history of antiquarianism from the sixteenth century onwards as a battle between the British History and the new criticism of the Renaissance. In my opinion this view is misleading: it exaggerates the impact of the Renaissance on historiography in England and underemphasizes the continuity from medieval to modern times. Indeed Sir Thomas neglected a vast area of medieval antiquarian study – local history.

Sir Richard Southern has provided a partial antidote. He has paid tribute to the monastic historians in the Anglo-Norman period.[7] Fired by the desire to prove the continuous history of their houses from Anglo-Saxon times, and so counter the threat to tradition posed by the Norman Conquest, they undertook minute research on monastic archives and antiquities. Unfortunately Sir Richard ends his account on a false note:[8]

> In historical research they had no successors. The monastic historians of the later Middle Ages abandoned historical research for contemporary journalism, and relied on their predecessors for their record of the past.

Thus he overlooks the important research done by the monks on local history in the reign of Henry II, not to mention Gervase of Canterbury's architectural history of Canterbury Cathedral and Matthew Paris's work on the antiquities of St Albans. He also passes over the fifteenth-century antiquaries, not only Rous and Worcester, but many others besides. Together these men make the fifteenth century (with which we are here concerned) remarkable for the quantity and quality of its antiquarian research.

The fifteenth-century antiquaries fall into two groups: the monks and the seculars (we include in the term 'secular' both secular clergy and laity). The monks were active in the first half of the century, and the seculars in the second half. We will consider the monks first.

A number of incentives urged monks to study the past, most emanating from their *esprit de corps*. Again, as in the Anglo-Norman period, the monks felt threatened, though this time their enemies were different. Since the twelfth century the regular and secular canons were their rivals and now, in the fifteenth, the Lollards and other 'dispossessioners' were their enemies. There were also litigious neighbours, interfering diocesans and rapacious tax collectors. And meanwhile some houses suffered from internal dissension.

The monks, therefore, did everything they could to defend themselves and improve monastic morale. One method was by propagandist writing. Towards the end of the fourteenth century a monk of Bury St Edmunds

---

[7] R.W. Southern, 'Aspects of the European tradition of historical writing: the sense of the past', *T.R.H.S.* 5th ser. xxxiii (1973), 246-56.
[8] *Ibid.*, 263.

had already produced a tract proving the antiquity of monasticism.[9] He traced its history back to its earliest origins, far beyond the date when, according to tradition, St Augustine instituted the regular canons. In the fifteenth century various versions of this tract were current in the monasteries and elsewhere.

Individually each house might try to prove that it had a long and glorious past – the longer its tradition, the greater its reputation. The monastic historian would trace his house's history back to its origins. He would include information on its treasures and notable inmates – these subjects could also be dealt with in shorts tracts. Thus he strengthened the monastery's fortifications in a general way. But he might also fight its battles on specific issues. He might record evidence of its right in a particular legal case. Such information could be put into a narrative history or into a tract. The monastic historian had other motives. He wrote to edify his fellow monks by describing the past achievements of the community, and to inform them so that they would be knowledgeable guides for visitors. He also wrote as an act of piety. But another motive is often apparent: he wrote to record the results of painstaking research undertaken to satisfy his own curiosity – simply because he was interested.

In his search for the past, the historian did not rely exclusively on verifiable fact. Vital evidence of early foundation might be lost, or the circumstances of the foundation be forgotten owing to the passage of time. So a historian might copy forged documents to substantiate what he himself believed, or he might adopt some legend to convince the reader of what he wanted him to believe. Legends, if derived from a standard authority such as Geoffrey of Monmouth, were used indiscriminately with verifiable fact. Generally speaking they only came under fire if they conflicted with an author's tendentious purpose. And then, having demolished one inconvenient legend, the author might well adopt another, equally unlikely, because it suited him. Neither forgery nor legend was totally inimical to the development of antiquarian studies. To achieve verisimilitude, the forger had to study the form and content of ancient documents and books – he might even plunder genuine material and copy archaic scripts. And a legend stimulated interest in the past, attracting immediate attention to any place or object connected with it.

It is now necessary to discuss individually some of the works produced by the monasteries. First, the histories may be considered, and, secondly, a few examples of the tracts. The principal monastic histories, arranged as far as possible in chronological order of composition, are: John of

---

[9]  For this tract, its versions and their dissemination, see W.A. Pantin, 'Some medieval English treaties on the origins of monasticism', *Medieval Studies presented to Rose Graham*, eds. Veronica Ruffer and A.J. Taylor (Oxford, 1950), pp. 189-215.

Glastonbury's history or Glastonbury Abbey (A.D. 31-1342), *c.* 1400;[10] Walter Frocester's history of St Peter's, Gloucester (A.D. 681-*c.* 1412), early fifteenth century;[11] Thomas Elmham's history of St Augustine's, Canterbury (A.D. 597-806, with notes and documents to 1191), early fifteenth century;[12] Thomas Burton's history of the abbey of Meaux (1150-1396, with a continuation to 1417), first third of the fifteenth century;[13] the annals of the (Cluniac) abbey of Bermondsey (1042-1432), *c.* 1432; [14] John Wessington's history of St Cuthbert's, Durham (A.D. 635-1195), first half of the fifteenth century;[15] Thomas Rudborne's history of St Swithun's, Winchester (A.D. 164-1141), mid-fifteenth century;[16] John Flete's history of Westminster Abbey (A.D. 184-1386), mid-fifteenth century;[17] the Crowland chronicle (eighth century-1148), ? mid-fifteenth century;[18] and the history of Hyde Abbey, Winchester (the so-called Book of Hyde, A.D. 455-1023), which, I suggest, was written in the mid-

[10] Printed *The Chronicle of Glastonbury Abbey . . . John of Glastonbury's 'Cronica sive Antiquitates Glastoniensis Ecclesie'*, ed. J.P. Carley, with an English translation by D. Townsend (Woodbridge, 1985). Professor Carley in the introduction to his edition argues against the traditionally accepted date, *c.* 1400, for the composition of the chronicle. However, I do not find his arguments convincing; see pp. 291-8 above.

[11] Printed *Historia et Cartularium Monasterii Sancti Petri Gloucestriae*, ed. W.H. Hart (Rolls Series, 1863-6, 3 vols.), i, 3-58. For the composition and value of this chronicle see C.N.L. Brooke, 'St Peter of Gloucester and St Cadoc of Llancarfan', *Celt and Saxon. Studies in the Early British Border*, ed. N.K. Chadwick (Cambridge, 1963), pp. 260-70, 277-9.

[12] Printed *Historia Monasterii S. Augustini Cantuariensis*, ed. Charles Hardwick (Rolls Series, 1858). Its medieval title was *Speculum Augustinianum*.

[13] Printed *Chronica Monasterii de Melsa*, ed. E.A. Bond (Rolls Series, 1866-8, 3 vols.).

[14] Printed in *Annales Monastici*, ed. H.R. Luard (Rolls Series, 1864-9, 5 vols.), iii, 423-87.

[15] John Wessington's *Libellus de exordio et statu ecclesie . . . Dunelmensis, ac de gestis pontificum eiusdem* [635-1195] is unpublished. For the three manuscripts of the *Libellus* see H.H.E. Craster, 'The Red Book of Durham', *E.H.R.*, xl (1925), 504-14 *passim*. See also H.S. Offler, *Medieval Historians of Durham* (Durham, 1958), p. 17, and R.B. Dobson, *Durham Priory 1400-1450* (Cambridge, 1973), pp. 379-81.

[16] The *Historia Major . . . Ecclesie Wintoniensis* of Thomas Rudborne is printed in *Anglia Sacra*, ed. Henry Wharton (London, 1691, 2 vols.), i, 177-286.

[17] Printed *History of Westminster Abbey by John Flete*, ed. J. Armitage Robinson (Cambridge, 1909).

[18] Printed in *Rerum Anglicarum Scriptorum Veterum Tom. I*, ed. William Fulman (Oxford, 1684), pp. 1-132. Various dates have been suggested for the composition of the Crowland chronicle, but the most recent scholar to study the question argues in favour of the mid-fifteenth century; W.G. Searle, *Ingulf and the Historia Croylandensis* (Cambridge Antiquarian Soc., 8vo ser. xxvii, 1894), p. 207. Cf. H.T. Riley, 'The history and charters of Ingulfus considered', *Arch. J.* xix (1862), 114-28, and F. Liebermann, 'Ueber ostenglische Geschichtsquellen des 12, 13, 14 Jahrhunderts, besonders den falschen Ingulf', *Neues Archiv der Gesellschaft für ältere deutsche Geschichtskunde*, xviii (Hanover and Leipzig, 1892), 262-3.

fifteenth century, perhaps by Thomas Rudborne himself.[19]

This list illustrates that the author's primary interest tended to be in the foundation and early history of his house. Indeed only three of the ten works, Thomas Burton's history of the abbey of Meaux, the Bermondsey annals, and Walter Frocester's history of St Peter's, Gloucester, reach the author's own time. The rest stop short of it – some, notably Thomas Elmham, well short. A number were written by eminent men, which shows the importance attached to such histories. Two were well-known writers. Thomas Rudborne, author of the history of his monastery of St Swithun's, Winchester, and possibly of the Book of Hyde, also wrote other histories,[20] and his reputation is witnessed by John Rous.[21] Thomas Elmham, after he left St Augustine's in 1414, wrote a successful verse Life of Henry V. He had studied at Oxford, and left St Augustine's to become prior of the Cluniac priory of Lenton in Nottinghamshire, and in 1415 he became vicar-general of the Cluniacs in England and Scotland.[22] Four of the authors were heads of their houses. Walter Frocester was abbot of St Peter's, Gloucester, from 1382 to 1412;[23] John Wessington was prior of Durham from 1416 to 1446; John Flete was prior of Westminster from 1457 to 1465. And Thomas Burton was briefly abbot of Meaux from 1396 until 1399 – he was forced to resign because of discord in the convent, and wrote his chronicle in retirement.[24] It is relevant to note that John Rous tells us that the Book of Hyde was in the abbot's keeping.[25] The esteem in which such works were held is underlined by the fact that all (except the

---

[19] Printed *Liber Monasterii de Hyda*, ed. Edward Edwards (Rolls Series, 1866). The possibility that Rudborne was the author of the *Liber* is suggested by the similarity of its arrangement, under kings, with that of the *Historia Major*, and also by the fact that it uses two of the unidentified sources cited in the *Historia Major* – Girardus Cornubiensis's *De Gestis Regum West-Saxonum* (see *Hist. Major*, pp. 189, 201, 204 etc., and, for Girardus, T.D. Hardy, *Descriptive Catalogue for Materials relating to the History of Great Britain and Ireland to 1327* (Rolls Series, 1862-71, 3 vols. in 4 pts., reprinted New York, 1963, iii, 50-1)), and 'Vigilantius' (for which see p. 304 and nn. 31, 32 below); see Edwards, *op. cit.*, p. xxi. The evidence of the only extant manuscript is compatible with this suggestion; see p. 305 and n. 40 below. Perhaps further research would result in a firm conclusion.

[20] For works attributed to Rudborne, see Wharton, *op. cit.*, i, pp. xxvi-xxviii. However, Wharton's list needs revision. For Rudborne's possible authorship of the Book of Hyde see above and previous note.

[21] *Joannis Rossi Antiquarii Warwicensis Historia Regum Angliae*, ed. Thomas Hearne (Oxford, 1716), p. 73. For references to the *Historia Major* see *ibid.*, pp. 78, 82, 96, 98.

[22] For Elmham's career see J.S. Roskell and Frank Taylor, 'The authorship and purpose of the *Gesta Henrici Quinti*: I', *Bulletin of the John Rylands Library*, liii (1970-1), 455-61, and C.L. Kingsford, *English Historical Literature in the Fifteenth Century* (Oxford, 1913, reprinted New York, 1962), pp. 45-6.

[23] For Frocester's authorship of the Gloucester history see Brooke, *op. cit.*, p. 260 and n. 3.

[24] See *Chron. Mon. de Melsa*, i, lxii-lxx; iii, 239-40, 258-71, 274-5.

[25] See Rous, *Historia Regum*, p. 96. Cf. p. 305 and n. 39 below.

Bermondsey annals) are on a massive scale, and some survive in handsome manuscripts. Most magnificent is the manuscript of Elmham's history, now in the library of Trinity Hall, Cambridge.[26]

We must now consider the contents of these histories. The one which contains the most forgery is the Crowland chronicle – it is spurious from beginning to end. It shows the lengths to which a forger would go to make his work appear authentic. The author foisted the section to 1089 on Ingulf, abbot of Crowland from 1085/6 to 1109, and the section from 1089 to 1148 on the twelfth-century writer, Peter of Blois.[27] 'Ingulf' starts in traditional style by declaring his intention to commemorate the abbey's founders and benefactors, and to record its history and acquisition of property.[28] Besides citing numerous (forged) charters in full, he claims to have consulted Domesday Book – which he thought was in roll form.[29] 'Peter of Blois' opens by quoting a (spurious) letter of the abbot, Henry de Longchamp; in it Abbot Henry asks him to continue the chronicle and undertakes to bring documents to London from the abbey muniments. In his reply Peter praises Ingulf's work, promises to correct it, and says he will use the documents provided.[30]

Many of the other writers copied forged charters, but Thomas Rudborne probably used a literary forgery as well. He cites Vigilantius, *De Basilica Sancti Petri*, for the pre-Conquest history of the Old Minster.[31] 'Vigilantius' is also cited in some of the other works which may be by Rudborne.[32] Professor Robert Willis used Rudborne's citations for his architectural history of the Old Minister, and concluded that 'Vigilantius' wrote shortly before the Conquest.[33] More recently the late Roger Quirk has accepted 'Vigilantius's' evidence.[34] But there are apparently no references to the work, which does not survive, prior to those just mentioned. Professor D.J. Sheerin of the University of North Carolina has

---

[26] Trinity Hall, Cambridge, MS.1. See M.R. James, *A Descriptive Catalogue of the Manuscripts in the Library of Trinity Hall, Cambridge* (Cambridge, 1907), pp. 1-3.

[27] The Crowland chronicle is discussed: Riley, *op. cit.*, pp. 32-49, 114-33; Liebermann, *op. cit.*, pp. 249-67; Searle, *op. cit.*, *passim*.

[28] Fulman, *op. cit.*, p. 1.

[29] *Ibid.*, pp. 80, 83. Cf. Searle, *op. cit.*, pp. 7-12.

[30] Fulman, *op. cit.*, 108-10.

[31] e.g. Rudborne, *Hist. Major*, pp. 181, 186, 199, 223.

[32] The chronicle from Lucius to the beginning of Henry VI's reign, Corpus Christi College, Cambridge, MS. 110, pp. 213 *et seq.* (for which see M.R. James, *A Descriptive Catalogue of Manuscripts in the Library of Corpus Christi College, Cambridge* (Cambridge, 1909-12, 2 vols.), ii, 235, and R.N. Quirk, 'Winchester Cathedral in the tenth century', *Arch. J.* cxiv (1957), 57, n. 1); the *Epitomes Historiae Majoris Ecclesiae Wintoniensis* (for which see Wharton, *Anglia Sacra*, i, xxvi); the Book of Hyde (see p. 303 and n. 19 above).

[33] R. Willis, 'Architectural history of Winchester Cathedral', *Proc. of the Royal Architectural Institute, Winchester* (1845), p. 3, n.a.

[34] Quirk, *op. cit.*, p. 29, n. 2.

pointed out to me[35] that the account of the foundation of the Old Minster attributed to Vigilantius cannot be earlier than Geoffrey of Monmouth. This is proved by the fact that it states that the minster was founded by King Lucius and consecrated by the missionaries Phagan and Deruvian[36] – all three first appear in Geoffrey's pages.[37] Probably 'Vigilantius' was written later still. When the monks of St Swithun's wrote in defence of their privileges in the late thirteenth century and claimed a British origin for their house, they made no mention of King Lucius, or of Fagan and Deruvian.[38] Indeed Rudborne's is the earliest known reference to them in this context.

Perhaps 'Vigilantius' never existed as an independent work and Rudborne's appeal to it to substantiate his history was in imitation of Geoffrey of Monmouth's appeal to an ancient book as his authority. It is worth noting that Rous describes the Book of Hyde, which the abbot showed him, as a fine copy in a recent hand made from a very old manuscript in case the latter perished.[39] A recent scholar has dated the extant text to the fourteenth or fifteenth century. It may be suggested that the manuscript is mid-fifteenth-century and that the work was composed then.[40]

Rudborne wrote partly to establish the Old Minster's priority of foundation. He may have had in mind the claims of the Glastonbury monks, who alleged that their abbey was founded by Joseph of Arimathea. Perhaps he chose Phagan and Deruvian as the consecrators of the minster because Glastonbury named them as the refounders of their abbey.[41] He

---

[35] In a letter of 7th December 1976. For a fuller discussion see A. Gransden, *Historical Writing in England*, ii, *c.1307 to the Early Sixteenth Century* (London, 1982), pp. 493-4 (Appendix D).

[36] *Hist. Major*, pp. 181-2.

[37] *The Historia Regum Britanniae of Geoffrey of Monmouth*, ed. Acton Griscom (London, 1929), pp. 328-30 (Bk IV, cap. xix).

[38] The monks were attempting to prove that the king, not the bishop of Winchester, was their patron; see *Registrum Johannis de Pontissara Episcopi Wyntoniensis*, ed. Cecil Deedes (Canterbury and York Soc., xix, xxx, 1915, 1924, 2 vols.), ii, 609-15. For the conflict between the bishop and his chapter see *ibid.*, i, xx-xxi; 676-94. The monks even earlier had falsified the history of the Old Minster; see H.P.R. Finberg, *The Early Charters of Wessex* (Leicester, 1964), pp. 226-44 *passim*.

[39] For the foundation of Cambridge University, Rous cites a chronicle of Hyde which must surely be the extant Book of Hyde (for the account in it of the foundation of Cambridge University see *Liber Monasterii de Hyda*, ed. Edwards, p. 11). He writes that he found the passage 'in dicta abbathia [de Hyde] in quadam bene indicta nobili Chronica, quae de vetusta et antiqua manu iterum, ne periret, nova manu et placida scripta est, ut egomet vidi benevola licentia domini abbatis ejusdem loci'; *Historia Regum Angliae*, p. 96.

[40] G.R.C. Davis, *Medieval Cartularies of Great Britain* (London, 1958), p. 121, no. 1051. The manuscript is owned by the earl of Macclesfield and is in the library of Shirburn Castle. A page is reproduced in facsimile as a frontispiece to Edwards, *op. cit.*

[41] *Chronicle of Glastonbury Abbey*, ed. Carley, p. 56.

states categorically that Glastonbury Abbey was founded by King Ine.[42] Moreover, he writes slightingly of King Arthur, who was supposedly buried there. For example, he proves from literary evidence that Arthur could not have defeated an emperor called Lucius, because no emperor of that name lived in his (supposed) time.[43]

Legends are a common ingredient of the monastic histories, but none contains as many as John of Glastonbury's. John wrote initially to counter Higden's assertion that the St Patrick buried at Glastonbury was not the apostle of Ireland, but a ninth-century abbot. And he wrote to show that previously the abbey was more privileged and prosperous than it was in his day, but had suffered from the neglect of 'certain prelates', the depredations of Danish and Norman invaders, and from the oppression of the bishops of Bath.[44] Using the earlier histories of Glastonbury and perhaps his own imagination, John produced a definitive history of the abbey to his own day, replete with legends of Joseph of Arimathea and King Arthur.[45]

It is not, however, for the use of forgeries and legends that most of the monastic historians are remarkable, but for the sound research they did. They cite charters and other domestic documents, and even public records – presumably from extracts in monastic registers. Dr Craster imagined John Wessington 'sitting down, with a pile of manuscripts from the conventual library at his elbow, to compile a history of his monastery'.[46] Some also used visual evidence. Even Rudborne, who leant heavily on written sources, described the tombs in Winchester Cathedral, and copied the inscriptions.[47] Flete's notices of the tombs of the abbots in Westminster Abbey are crucial evidence for the abbatial succession.[48] But most outstanding in their use of documentary and visual evidence are Thomas Elmham and Thomas Burton, who will be discussed in more detail.

Elmham's commemorative intention, his need to express his piety and satisfy his curiosity, are all evident in his work. But he wrote primarily to defend the privileges of St Augustine's. The abbey's perennial enemy was

---

[42] *Hist. Major*, p. 194.

[43] Ibid., pp. 187-8.

[44] *Chronicle of Glastonbury Abbey*, ed. Carley, p. 8.

[45] For the legends in John of Glastonbury see J. Armitage Robinson, *Two Glastonbury Legends: King Arthur and St Joseph of Arimathea* (Cambridge, 1926), *passim*.

[46] Craster, *op. cit.*, p. 514.

[47] For his record of the original burial place of St Swithun (*Hist. Major*, p. 203) see Quirk, *op. cit.*, 65 and n. 6, and Martin Biddle and R.N. Quirk, 'Excavations near Winchester Cathedral, 1961', *Arch. J.* cxix (1962), 174 and n. 6.

[48] See *Flete*, pp. 22-4. Flete also mentions the tapestries in the church, and the sumptuous mosaic pavement before the high altar; *ibid.* pp. 105 (cf. pp. 24-9), 113.

the archbishop of Canterbury:[49] the archbishops had periodically challenged its right to exemption from episcopal control.[50] By Elmham's day the matter had been settled in the monks' favour, but he mentions certain trouble-makers who scoffed at their claims.[51]

Elmham explicitly states his respect for documentary evidence. When, he writes, the guiding light of Bede failed, by good fortune he could turn to the archives of his house, to papal and royal documents, to bulls and charters, sealed and indented; few historians before him had enjoyed such a benefit.[52] He studied both the content of documents and their physical appearance – he had a developed visual sense which was supported by talent as a graphic artist. He paid close attention to the abbey's four 'earliest' documents, all in fact late eleventh-century forgeries,[53] the privilege of St Augustine and the three charters of King Ethelbert. It was no doubt to reaffirm their authenticity, which had been called in question by the archbishops of Canterbury in the twelfth and thirteenth centuries,[54] that Elham reproduced them in facsimile as well as in the handwriting of his own time. He copied the privilege of St Augustine (pl. 30) and Ethelbert's third charter in uncials, and Ethelbert's first and second charter in Anglo-Saxon script;[55] he has reproduced, he claims, referring to Ethelbert's third charter, the size and script of the original, for the benefit of posterity.

During the abbey's struggle with Archbishop Richard in Henry II's reign, one of the faults found with the privilege of St Augustine was its leaden bull. The archbishop's party objected that only popes used such bulls.[56] No doubt to demonstrate its genuineness Elmham drew its

---

[49] For a synopsis of the causes of contention between St Augustine's and the archbishops of Canterbury, see Wilhelm Levison, *England and the Continent in the Eighth Century* (Oxford, 1946), pp. 182-3.

[50] See *ibid.*, and in particular M.D. Knowles, 'Essays in monastic history, iv. The growth of exemption', *Downside Review* 1 (1932), 401-15.

[51] Elmham, *op. cit.*, pp. 87-8. Elmham also had to counter the attacks of the canons of St Gregory's, Canterbury, who claimed to have the relics of St Mildred; *ibid.*, pp. 218-19, 225-6. See M.L. Colker, 'A hagiographic polemic', *Mediaeval Studies*, xxix (1977), 61-2.

[52] *Ibid.*, pp. 309-10.

[53] Levison, *op. cit.*, pp. 205-6; Elmham, *op. cit.*, pp. xxvii-xxxiv.

[54] Knowles, *op. cit.*, p. 414 and nn.; Elham, *op. cit.*, pp. xxvii-xxxiv; *William Thorne's Chronicle of Saint Augustine's Abbey Canterbury*, translated by A.H. Davis, with a preface by A. Hamilton Thompson (Oxford, 1934), pp. liv-lvi, 116 *et seq.*

[55] Elmham, *op. cit.*,pp. 109 and n. 4, 110, 111 and n. 1, 112-13, 114 and n. 1, 115-16, 119 and n. 3, 120-1. The facsimiles are described and some reproduced in Michael Hunter, 'The facsimiles in Thomas Elmham's History of St Augustine's, Canterbury', *The Library*, 5th ser. xxviii (1973), 215-20.

[56] Elmham, *op. cit.*, pp. 122-4. Elmham erroneously dates this dispute to Henry III's reign, apparently because he identified Archbishop Richard as Richard Grant, archbishop 1229-31. However, the reference (see below) to Philip, count of Flanders (1168-91) makes it clear that the archbishop concerned was Richard of Dover (1173-84). This conclusion is

obverse and reverse, with an explanatory note and a copy of the inscription.[57] And he pointed out that St Augustine, as a Roman and a papal legate, might have used a bull. Indeed, he asserts, in later times popes had occasionally granted a bishop the right to use one. He records that, to counter Archbishop Richard's objection, Philip, count of Flanders, had sent the abbot a bull to use in evidence: Philip said that it had been given to him by a bishop, who alleged that he and his predecessors had used it.[58] The abbey's enemies had objected to the three charters of Ethelbert because they had no seals. Elmham rejoins, more or less correctly, that the practice of sealing documents was introduced after the Conquest: previously only King Canute, a foreigner, had used a seal; the Anglo-Saxon kings had authenticated documents with the sign of the cross.[59]

Since the eleventh-century forgeries are lost, we do not know if they were in facsimile, or whether the idea of producing fascimiles was Elmham's own. Examples of the imitation of archaic scripts occur from the tenth century onwards.[60] (At St Augustine's plenty of palaeographical models were at hand among its early books and charters.)[61] Nor was it unprecedented to copy authenticating devices: twelfth-century examples survive from St Augustine's itself.[62] However, reproduction of the total format of a document does seem to be a new concept.

Elmham's interest in documents extended beyond the four 'earliest' charters of St Augustine's. Although, as is to be expected, he copied the eleventh-century forgeries without question, his treatment of documents was in general well-informed and judicious. He could read Anglo-Saxon[63]

confirmed by the account of the dispute between St Augustine's and Archbishop Richard of Dover given by Gervase of Canterbury, which mentions that the leaden bulla was then called in question; *The Historical Works of Gervase of Canterbury*, ed. William Stubbs (Rolls Series, 1879-80, 2 vols.), i, 296-7.

[57] Reproduced Hunter, *op. cit.*, pl. III.

[58] Elmham, *op. cit.*, p. 123.

[59] *Ibid.*, p. 118. Rous made a rather similar statement; see p. 320 and n. 123 below.

[60] See N.R. Ker in Margaret Deanesly, 'The court of King Æthelberht of Kent', *Cambridge Historical Journal*, vii (1942), 107, n. 11.

[61] Elmham's library list (see p. 310 below) includes at least one ancient manuscript in uncials. For the school of uncial writing at Canterbury, *c.* 700, see E. Maunde Thompson, *An Introduction to Greek and Latin Palaeography* (Oxford, 1912), pp. 384-5. Professor Deanesly argues that Elmham's facsimiles of Ethelbert's charters are in Merovingian script and are based on genuine documents; Deanesly, *op. cit.*, pp. 103-10 *passim*, and the same author's 'Early English and Gallic minsters', *T.R.H.S.* 4th ser. xxiii (1941), 53-66 *passim*, and 'Canterbury and Paris in the reign of Æthelberht', *History*, xxvi (1941), 101-4. However, Levison, *op. cit.*, pp. 174 *et seq.*, has demonstrated that this view is not sound.

[62] BL MS. Cotton Vitellius A II, folios 14, 19, 19ᵛ; see Hunter, *op. cit.*, 218 and pl. VI (a)-(c). See also the picture of the *rota* of William II of Sicily in 'Benedict of Peterborough': BL MS. Cotton Vitellius E XVII, fo. 28; see p. 184 and pl. 4 above.

[63] Elmham copies a passage in Anglo-Saxon from a charter and supplies a Latin translation; Elmham, *op. cit.*, p. 332.

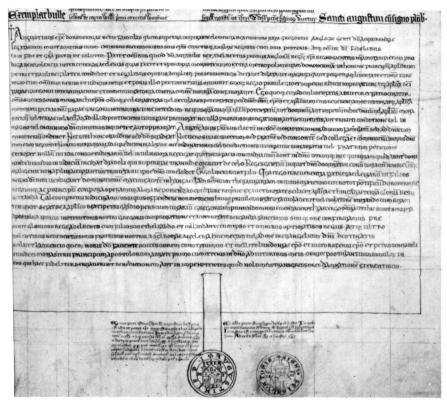

30 Thomas Elmham's facsimile of the (forged) privilege of St Augustine to St Augustine's, Canterbury.
*(Cambridge, Trinity Hall, MS I, fo. 2)*

31 Thomas Elmham's picture of the seal of an abbey dedicated to St Stephen.
*(Cambridge, Trinity Hall, MS I, fo. 24)*

32  Thomas Elmham's plan of the high altar and sanctuary at St Augustine's, Canterbury.
*(Cambridge, Trinity Hall, MS I, fo. 77)*

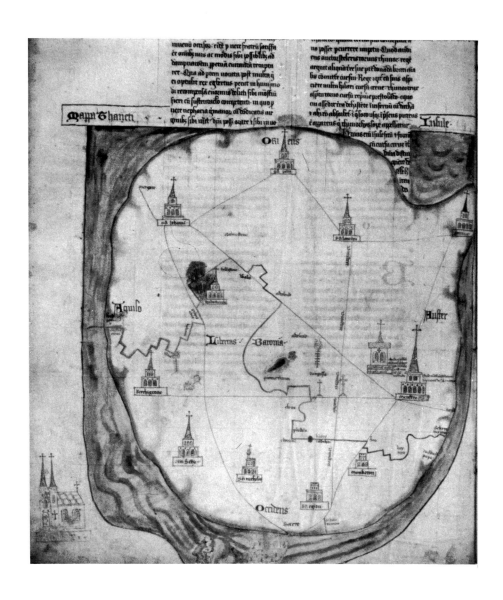

33 Thomas Elmham's map of Thanet.
*(Cambridge, Trinity Hall, MS I, fo. 42v)*

34  Arthgallus, a legendary British earl of Warwick, from John Rous's 'Yorkist' Warwick roll.
*(London, British Library, MS Add 48976)*

35   Ufa, from John Rous's 'Yorkist' Warwick roll.
*(London, British Library, MS Add 48976)*

36 The seal, 1353-54, of Thomas Beauchamp, earl of Warwick (1329-62).
*(London, British Library, seal no. xliii. 18)*

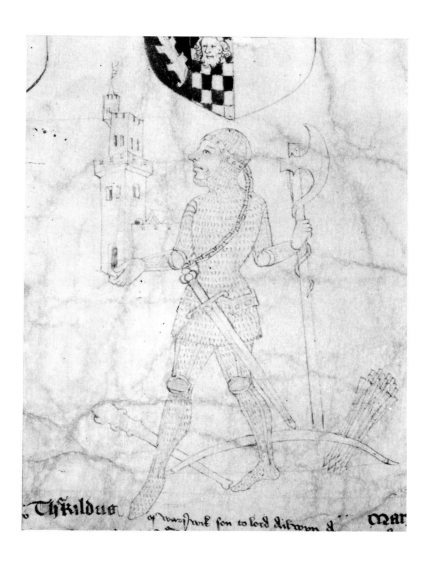

37  Thurkill, from John Rous's 'Yorkist' Warwick roll.
    *(London, British Library, MS Add 48976)*

38  William de Newburgh, earl of Warwick (d. 1184), from John Rous's 'Yorkist' Warwick roll.
*(London, British Library, MS Add 48976)*

39 Waleran de Newburgh (d. ?1203), from John Rous's 'Yorkist'
Warwick roll.
*(London, British Library, MS Add 48976)*

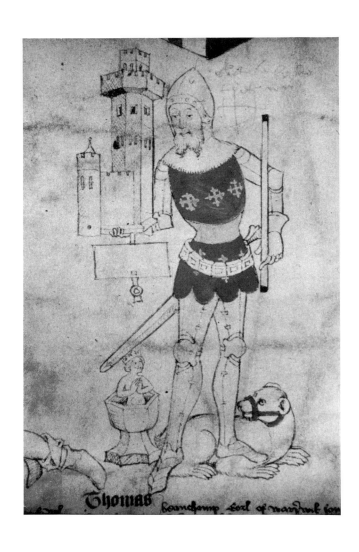

40   Thomas Beauchamp, earl of Warwick (1370-1401), from John Rous's
'Yorkist' Warwick roll.
*(London, British Library, MS Add 48976)*

41 Richard Beauchamp, earl of Warwick (1403-39), from John Rous's 'Yorkist' Warwick roll.
*(London, British Library, MS Add 48976)*

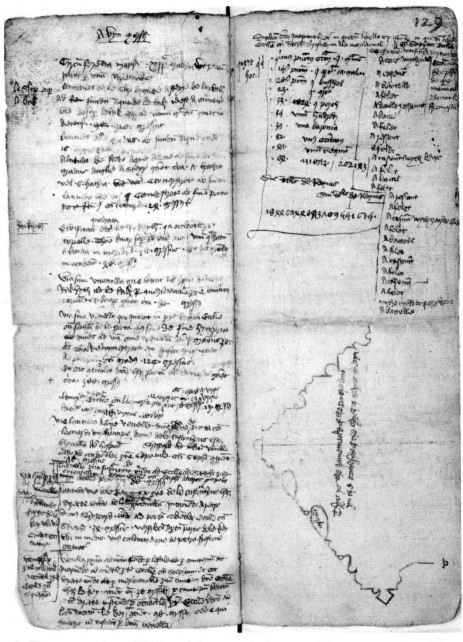

42  Two pages from William Worcester's *Itinerary*. The page on the right shows a cross section of the mouldings of the south porch of St Stephen's church, Bristol.
*(Cambridge, Corpus Christi College, MS 210, fo. 129)*

and appreciated that documents are usually more authoritative than literary sources; he twice corrects the accepted length of a reign on charter evidence.[64] He also states that an original document has more authority than a copy: he collated two originals with copies in registers, noting discrepancies, which he attributed 'either to the carelessness of the scribes or to the inability of the compiler to read Anglo-Saxon script correctly'.[65]

Nor was Elmham's interest in authenticating devices limited to the problems raised by the abbey's four 'earliest' charters. For example he drew the leaden bull attached to the privilege of Boniface IV,[66] and the *bene valete* and *rota* of Lucius II,[67] at the end of his transcriptions of their grants to St Augustine's. Sometimes his interest was objective – his observations could not have helped the abbey defend its rights. He comments that the leaden bull given by Philip, count of Flanders, was not, as the count asserted, a bishop's: the inscription and picture on the obverse showed that it had belonged to some monastery dedicated to St Stephen; he drew the obverse (pl. 31), and remarked that it was almost impossible to discern the picture on the reverse, on account of its age.[68] He also describes two curious examples of seals. One, a seal of William, first earl of Warenne, attached to a charter in the Cluniac priory of St Pancras at Lewes, contained some of the earl's hair. The other, the seal of an earl of Lincoln attached to a charter at the priory of Castle Acre, a cell of Lewes, bore the imprint of the earl's teeth; it had the subscription: 'In evidence of this I have impressed the seal with my teeth, as Muriel my wife witnesses.'[69]

---

[64]  *Ibid.*, pp. 137, 324.

[65]  *Ibid.*, pp. 233, 237-8.

[66]  Trinity Hall MS. 1, fo. 26ᵛ.

[67]  *Ibid.*, fo. 90ᵛ. See Hunter, *op. cit.*, p. 217, and his pl. I (b).

[68]  Elmham, *op. cit.*, p. 123.

[69]  *Ibid.*, pp. 118-19. The foundation charter of Lewes priory, granted by William de Warenne, first earl of Surrey, makes no reference to the presence of the earl's hair in the seal; *Early Yorkshire Charters*, ed. C.T. Clay (Yorkshire Archaeological Soc. record ser., extra ser. 1935-65, 10 vols.), vi, 54-5, no. 2. However, the confirmation by William de Warenne, third earl of Surrey (1138-48), notes that he gave seizin of a tenth penny of his rents 'by hair of his own head and that of Ralph de Warenne his brother, cut with a knife by Henry, bishop of Winchester, before the altar'; printed *ibid.*, vi, 84-5, no. 32. Cf. V.H. Galbraith, 'Monastic foundation charters of the eleventh and twelfth centuries', *Cambridge Historical Journal*, iv (1934), 211. The entry concerning the seal at Castle Acre is even more problematical. Elmham states that the earl of Lincoln in question 'pluribus possessionibus eandem ecclesiam dotavit'. But the founder of Castle Acre priory was William de Warenne, first earl of Surrey (1088) and its benefactors were his successors as earls of Surrey; see *V.C.H., Norfolk*, ii, p. 356, and G.E. C[ockayne], *The Complete Peerage*, ed. Vicary Gibbs *et al.* (London 1910-59, 13 vols.), xii, pt. i, 494-7 *passim*. None of the known names of their wives is Muriel; however, the name of the first earl's second wife is unknown (G.E. C[ockayne], *op. cit.*, xii, pt. i, 494); possibly she was called Muriel. None of the countesses of Lincoln was called Muriel, as far as is known.

Elmham was interested in other remains of the abbey's past besides its early documents. Again his attention was first attracted to antiquities associated with St Augustine himself. He intended to record the translation of his relics in 1091 by Abbot Scotland, but never reached that date. However, he included a note on St Augustine's previous burial places, and a pictorial plan of the high altar and sanctuary with their shrines (pl. 32).[70] He also gives an account of the eight books which, according to tradition, St Augustine gave to the monks. He lists their contents and describes their appearance,[71] noting, for example, that the Bible in two volumes had pages tinted purple or pink, and that the psalter on the high altar bore on its bindings silver images of Christ and the four evangelists. The accuracy of his descriptions is testified by the fact that Humphrey Wanley was able to suggest an identification for one of the books, an identification accepted by later scholars.[72] Elmham used Bede to discover the plan of the earliest church. He concluded that it was narrower than the church of his own day, that the altar of St Gregory was more or less in the middle, and that the porticus of St Martin was on the south side.[73]

On the rare occasion when Elmham cites a legend, he adds sound antiquarian observations. He tells the story of Domne Eafe's hind. (He was interested in the minster on the Isle of Thanet, of which Domne Eafe's was the founder and first abbess, because after its destruction by the Danes King Canute gave its lands to St Augustine's.) According to legend King Edgar promised to give the minster the area delineated by the course of the hind running across the island. But a wicked thegn, Thunor, tried to frustrate his generous intention by stopping the hind. Luckily the earth opened and swallowed Thunor up.[74] To illustrate this tale Elmham supplied a map of Thanet, marking the hind's course and the spot where Thunor disappeared. But he also showed, with pictures, the churches assigned to the sacristy of St Augustine's. Although the map itself is inaccurate, the pictures and relative positions of the churches seem to be correct. There was apparently a linch along the boundary of St Augustine's lands which roughly followed the hind's course as plotted on the map. There was also probably a pit on the spot marked on the map

[70] Trinity Hall MS, I, fo. 63; cf. Elmham, *op. cit.*, pp. 286, n. 1, 346, n. 1. The plan is discussed by W. Urry and reproduced in *Local Maps and Plans from Medieval England*, ed. R.A. Skelton and P.D.A. Harvey (Oxford, 1986), pp. 107-17.

[71] Elmham, *op. cit.*, pp. 96-9.

[72] See *The Vespasian Psalter* ed. D.M. Wright (Copenhagen, 1967), p. 37-43.

[73] Elmham, *op. cit.*, pp. 132-3 (cf. Bede, *H.E.*, II, 3). This passage is not cited as evidence for the church built by King Ethelbert in H.M. Taylor and Joan Taylor, *Anglo-Saxon Architecture* (Cambridge, 1965, 2 vols.), i, pp. 135-7.

[74] Elmham, *op. cit.*, pp. 207-9 *passim*. See D.W. Rollason, *The Mildrith Legend: A Study of Early Medieval Hagiography in England* (Leicester, 1982), chs 3-4.

where Thunor was engulfed (pl. 33).[75]

We turn now to the other outstanding monastic antiquary, Thomas Burton, whose history of Meaux is the most comprehensive and scholarly of the local histories written in medieval England.

Burton's purpose was partly commemorative. He wanted to commemorate the past abbots. (Perhaps he hoped that he himself would be similarly commemorated and his troubled rule vindicated: in the event, the monk who continued his chronicle did render him this service.[76]) He was grieved, he states, because he saw 'the memory of those illustrious men, the abbots of Meaux, almost lost and their light obscured owing to the sloth of the negligent'.[77] He also wanted to commemorate the achievements of outstanding monks, and the generosity of benefactors.

His desire to commemorate the abbey's benefactors helps explain the presence in his history of numerous pedigrees of local families. But there is also another explanation. Burton wanted to record the abbey's acquisition of property. The benefactors' pedigrees were inextricably connected with the descent of the properties which they had given. Burton's meticulous record of the descent of such properties, if possible from the date when the abbey acquired them until his own time, is as remarkable as that of the pedigrees themselves.[78] Two of the pedigrees were included not from the commemorative motive, but as part of Burton's record of a legal dispute. They are the two versions of the pedigree of a bondman, Richard de Aldwyne, who rebelled against Abbot Robert de Beverley (1356-67).[79] Aldwyne argued that he belonged to the king, not the abbot, and produced a pedigree to prove it. But the abbot produced a pedigree showing that Richard descended from one of his bondmen.

The desire to substantiate the abbey's case in various disputes was one reason why Burton wrote. Before becoming abbot Burton had been the bursar. This no doubt accounts for his particular interest in any dispute

[75] Trinity Hall MS, I, fo. xxviii\*. Discussed by F. Hull and reproduced in Skelton and Harvey, *op. cit.*, pp. 119-26.

[76] *Chron. de Melsa*, iii, 237-76. Cf. *ibid.*, i, xlviii-xlix.

[77] *Ibid.*, i, 71.

[78] e.g. the pedigrees of the families of Sayers (*ibid.*, i, 96), Scures (*ibid.*, i, 97-8), Fossard (*ibid*, i, 104), and Sculcottes (*ibid.*, i, 169-70). The pedigree of the Etton family of Gilling, which is combined with the history of its estates (*ibid.*, i, 316-18, and other references, for which see the index in *ibid*, iii), provided much of the information used in John Bilson, 'Gilling Castle', *Yorks. Arch. J.* xix (1907), 105-22 *passim*. Burton also gives the pedigree of the Forz family (the counts of Aumale), the founders of the abbey, and the descent of the honour and of the lordship of Holderness; *Chron. de Melsa*, i, 89-93.

[79] *Chron. de Melsa*, iii, 130, 134. For this case see R.H. Hilton, 'Peasant movements in England before 1381', *Essays in Economic History*, ed. E.M. Carus-Wilson (London, 1954-62, 2 vols.), ii, 89 (the article is reprinted in the same author's *The Decline of Serfdom in Medieval England* (London-New York, 1969)).

involving money. The abbey was in financial straits – Burton gives many details about its debts. The burden of taxation must have fostered interest in the abbey's estates. This conclusion is suggested by the fact that it was usual for most of the clergy to be taxed with the laity on property acquired under licence of mortmain after 1291, that is for spiritualities and temporalities acquired after the valuation in that year of Pope Nicholas IV.[80] Burton explains clearly about the impact on the monks of Meaux of the ninth granted by parliament in 1339. Of the clergy only the bishops and 'parliamentary' abbots (who did not, of course, include the abbot of Meaux) were liable for the tax, since they had agreed to the grant in parliament. Nevertheless, in 1341 it was specially ordered in parliament that lands acquired by the clergy after 1291 should be taxed for the ninth. Since the assessment was severe, the clergy raised objections. Burton gives details, apparently copied from the public records, of the negotiations of the abbot of Meaux with the royal officials, to obtain exemption from the ninth for certain estates, which had been assessed although the abbey had acquired them before 1291.[81] To prove the pre-1291 date of an estate involved, of course, research into its origins.

Taxation may also have encouraged interest in the topography of some of the abbey's estates. Its properties in the levels of Holderness had been diminished by erosion by the sea and by the river Hull.[82] In Burton's day the monks were trying to obtain a reduction of the tax assessment on these properties.[83] Burton himself wrote a tract putting the case to the royal officials. Research on the extent of the erosion must have involved examining it on the spot. This must help explain why Burton gave such detailed and vivid descriptions of the floods and of the damage they did, a topic which will be discussed below. Finally, the abbey's financial

[80] For the practice with regard to the taxation of clerical properties see W. Stubbs, *Constitutional History of England*, ii (3rd edn., Oxford, 1887), pp. 416 n. 1, 443, n. 4, 580; J.F. Willard, 'The taxes upon movables of the reign of Edward II', *E.H.R.* xxix (1914), 318; W.E. Lunt, *The Valuation of Norwich* (Oxford, 1926), p. 72, n. 6; J.F. Willard, *Parliamentary Taxes on Personal Property 1290 to 1334* (Cambridge, Mass., 1934), pp. 94 *et seqq.* For the ninth granted in 1339 in particular see Natalie Fryde, 'Edward III's removal of his ministers and judges, 1340-1', *Bulletin of the Institute of Historical Research*, xlviii (1975), 152. For help on the subject of clerical taxation and for the above references I am indebted to Dr Gerald Harriss and Professor E.B. Fryde.

[81] *Chron. de Melsa*, iii, 24-9. Cf. *Rot. Parl.* ii, 129, 130. Collation of the relevant entry on the Memoranda Rolls, in the *Recorda* for Trinity term, 18 Edward III (P.R.O., E 159/120 membrane 245) with the text in the chronicle shows that the latter is slightly shorter, has the king in the third person instead of the first, and uses the past instead of the present tense.

[82] *Ibid.*, iii, 123, 247 *et seqq.*

[83] The tract is among the material appended to one of the two manuscripts of the chronicle, BL MS. Egerton 1141, the revised version; see *Chron. de Melsa*, i, liii-liv. Cf. the account of the struggle between the abbey and the royal assessors in the continuation to Burton's chronicle; *ibid.*, iii, 279 *et seqq.*

difficulties drew Burton's attention to other aspects of local history. There was apparently resentment at a royal imposition on the East Riding, for which Burton is the only authority. It was a due of four measures (thraves) of corn from every carucate, dating back to the reign of Athelstan. It was called 'hestcorn' – but, Burton relates, now certain wicked people call it 'bestcorn'.[84]

The wish to commemorate the abbey's inmates and benefactors and to provide information about its disputes were certainly among Burton's motives for writing the history. But objective curiosity was a powerful incentive. The work was the occupation of his retirement, and his researches went far beyond the needs of his house.

As Meaux was of comparatively recent foundation, Burton had no need to resort to forgery or legend for its early history. He himself mentions his sources in the preface: 'No one who finds anything in what follows, which he did not know before, should think I invented it: let him rest assured that I have only included what I have found written in other works, or in a variety of documents, or have heard from reliable witnesses, or have myself seen.'[85] As bursar Burton must have been well trained in the use of documents. Besides the chronicle he has left collectanea – a register and the documentary material which he appended to his chronicle. These comprise series of documents, digests of charters, and tracts; all relate to various aspects of the abbey's history.[86] For the chronicle, Burton writes, 'I collected together many ancient documents and long forgotten parchments: I found some which had been exposed to the rain, and others put aside for the fire.'[87] Unlike most chroniclers Burton did not copy documents in full. As he explains 'I have abridged their great length and illuminated their obscurities . . . and finally I have combined the total results into this one volume with the greatest care.'[88] Like Elmham he understood that an original document has more authority than a copy. He claims to have 'read through the registers and added from the original documents whatever they omit'.[89]

Burton's history, therefore, rests on a substratum of documentary evidence, and where comparison can be made between the text of the chronicle and the underlying document, Burton's accuracy is apparent. For example, his account of the abbey's foundation is corroborated by the

---

[84] *Ibid.*, ii, 236. See *Early Yorkshire Charters*, ed. William Farrer (Edinburgh, 1914-16, 3 vols.), i, 95-6.

[85] *Ibid.*, i, 71-2.

[86] The register is now BL MS. Cotton Vitellius C VI; see *Chron. de Melsa*, i, lvi-lviii. For the collectanea appended to one of the two manuscripts of the chronicle see p. 312 n. 83 above.

[87] *Chron. de Melsa*, i, 71.

[88] *Ibid.*, i, 71.

[89] *Ibid.*, i, 71.

count of Aumale's foundation charter.[90] Most of Burton's information on the antiquities of the abbey buildings he derived from written sources, but he also used visual evidence. He has practically nothing on the abbey church itself except the usual record of burial places.[91] However, his notice of one of the epitaphs, that of Abbot Robert de Beverley, has a critical comment: the dates were wrong; the sculptor invented them because he lost the sheet given him to copy.[92] Two of Burton's observations concern other buildings in the precincts. He notes the beauty of the crucifixion in the lay brothers' church, which he attributed to the sculptor's piety (he would only carve on Fridays when fasting on bread and water), and to his use of a nude model.[93] And he records that the foundations of the chantry chapel which Abbot Adam de Skyrne (1310-39) had begun to build above the great gate, but which Abbot Hugh de Leven (1339-49) had pulled down, were still visible in his day: Abbot Hugh used the stone to improve the brewery; he made a handsome tank next to the malt kiln for the fermentation of the malt and barley.[94]

More remarkable are Burton's observations on the topography of the abbey's estates. He had obviously tried to trace the original boundary of the manor of Meaux. Using charter evidence he records that it was marked by a mound in the form of a kiln, a large stone under a bridge, a buried cow, and holes in the ground three feet wide and a stone's throw apart. 'But,' he comments, 'as the marks are now wholly unknown, we must examine the boundary as it exists today.'[95] He also has an excellent account of the topographical changes resulting from silting and erosion. He explains how the vill of Wick, which was washed on two sides by the Humber and the Old Hull, had once been in Holderness but was now part of Harthill. The New Hull to the east of Wick had grown, while the Old Hull had become a mere trickle ('hardly deserving to be called a drain'). And so the New Hull 'now divides Holderness and Harthill', leaving Wick on the Harthill side. In Burton's time the grange there, 'now called Grangewick', had been abandoned, though 'its ruins can easily be seen'.[96]

[90] *Ibid.*, i, 81. For the charter see *Early Yorkshire Charters*, ed. Farrer, iii, 89-91, 93. Compare also Burton's detailed account of the foundation of a chantry in the abbey with the inspeximus of 1238 on the Charter Rolls; *Chron. de Melsa*, ii, 59-62; *Cal. Charter Rolls*, i, 233-4.

[91] For the burial places of abbots see e.g. *Chron. de Melsa*, i, 107, 234, 380; ii, 119; iii, 167, 234. Burton states that the burial place of Abbot Robert de Skyrne (1270-80) is unknown; *ibid.*, ii, 157. For the burial places of laymen see *ibid.*, i, 260; ii, 106; cf. i, 212.

[92] *Ibid.*, iii, 152.

[93] *Ibid.*, iii, 35-6.

[94] *Ibid.*, iii, 36.

[95] *Ibid.*, i, 78-81. Cf. *ibid.*, iii, 1 and n. 2.

[96] *Ibid.*, i, 168-9. For the vill of Wick, later the site of Kingston-upon-Hull, see *ibid.*, ii, 186, 192, and *V.C.H.*, *Yorks.*, *East Riding*, i, p. 16. For Grangewick see also *Chron. de Melsa*, ii, 192.

Burton gives vivid descriptions of the flooding, twice in the mid-fourteenth century, of Ravenser Odd, a small port at the extreme end of Holderness.[97] The first flood devastated the abbey's church there, washing the bodies and bones from their graves in the cemetery – 'a horrible sight'. The second time the village was surrounded by 'a towering wall of water'. The inhabitants fled, never to return. And so Ravenser Odd disappeared into the Humber, although its ruins remained, a danger to sailors. Burton explains that it must not be confused with Old Ravenser, a manor set back from the sea and the Humber, which still existed in his day. He describes the remains of the road which once led from Old Ravenser to Ravenser Odd.[98]

It is sandy and scattered with round, yellow pebbles, and is raised very little above water-level, and is hardly a bowshot in width, but it has resisted the flooding of the sea on the east and the constant battering of the Humber on the west in a truly wonderful fashion.

Before leaving the subject of the monks as antiquaries, something must be said about their historical tracts. Each tract tends to highlight one of the principal motives which led monks to antiquarian studies – the commemorative, the instructive and the legalistic. And many betray antiquarian curiosity.

Two examples of non-legalistic tracts from St Albans, written early in the century, may be considered first.[99] One, a commemorative tract,

---

[97] *Ibid.*, iii, 79, 120-1. The latter passage is noticed by N. Denholm-Young in his account of Ravenser Odd in 'The Yorkshire estates of Isabella de Fortibus', *Yorks. Arch. J.* xxxi (1934), 404, n. 2. For Ravenser Odd and Old Ravenser, with references to Burton's chronicle, see George Poulson, *The History and Antiquities of the Seigniory of Holderness* (Hull, 1840-1, 2 vols.), ii, pp. 529-40, Barbara English, *The Lords of Holderness 1086-1260* (Oxford, 1979), pp. 211-13.

[98] The passage occurs twice in the chronicle; *ibid.*, ii, 30; iii, 121-2.

[99] A number of other examples can be cited of tracts written with a commemorative intention but which show antiquarian interests. Some of John Wessington's tracts (see p. 316 and n. 108 below) are primarily commemorative. One, for example, gives the scriptural references to the inscriptions beneath the images (or pictures) of the hundred and forty-eight monks at the altar of SS. Jerome and Benedict in Durham Cathedral, and names some of the hitherto unidentified figures: Durham Cathedral Library MS. B III 30, folios 6-25ᵛ; partly printed in *Rites of Durham*, ed. J. T. Fowler (Surtees Soc., cvii, 1903), 124-36; cf. *Historiae Dunelmensis Scriptores Tres, Gaufridus de Coldingham, Robertus de Graystanes, et Willielmus de Chambre*, ed. James Raine (Surtees Soc., ix, 1839), cclxix, Pantin, 'Some medieval treatises on the origins of monasticism', 200, Dobson, *Durham Priory 1400-1540*, p. 382. Wessington worked on the books in the cloister and cathedral library; Raine, *op. cit.*, cclxx. The desire to instruct and antiquarian interest were probably the main reasons why at Christ Church, Canterbury, William Glastonbury described the scenes in the twelve windows of the choir, partly from his own observation. His description is noticed and printed *The Chronicle of William Glastynbury, Monk of the Priory of Christ Church, Canterbury, 1418-48*, ed. C. E. Woodruff in *Arch. Cant.* xxxvii (1925), 123-5, 138, 139-51.

describes the altars, monuments and graves in the abbey church.[100] The author records the names of those buried, whom he identified by reference to 'the Book of Benefactors on the high altar',[101] documents in the keeping of the almoner, William Wintershull,[102] and Thomas Walsingham's *Gesta Abbatum*.[103] He was interested in past as well as in present arrangements. He points out, relying on written evidence and pictures, that the cult of the Virgin Mary was observed in the abbey before the chapel where her altar now stood had been built. Masses for her were celebrated in the chapel of St Blase which used to be by the abbey gate; no trace of it remained in the author's day.[104] The other tract describes the statues and pictures in the abbey church and explains their iconography.[105] It was probably written partly for the benefit of visitors,[106] but again it shows antiquarian interest. For example, it relates that formerly the statues of St Laurence and St Grimbald had been in the almonry chapel. But when the latter was pulled down, to make room for the new gatehouse and infirmary, they had been moved, 'in accordance with the tenor of the constitution then drawn up', to their present place, so that they could be venerated as before.[107]

As examples of legalistic or quasi-legalistic tracts, those by John Wessington may be cited. He produced at least forty.[108] A contemporary wrote of him:[109]

He compiled [the tracts] not without labour and study, for the perpetual preservation and defence of the rights, liberties and possessions of the church . . . against the malice and machinations of would-be molesters.

The scribe of the tract defending the prior's archidiaconal jurisdiction over his churches, remarked that it 'would be of value against the

---

[100] Printed in *Annales Monasterii S. Albani a Johanne Amundesham*, ed. H. T. Riley (Rolls Series, 1870-1, 2 vols.), i, 431-49. Described *ibid.*, ii, lix-lxii.

[101] *Ibid.*, i, 431-2. Cf. *ibid.*, i, 434-41 *passim*. Perhaps this Book of Benefactors is to be identified with that by Thomas Walsingham, now BL MS. Cotton Nero D VII, for which see *The St. Albans Chronicle 1406-1420*, ed. V. H. Galbraith (Oxford, 1937), pp. xxxvi-xxxvii.

[102] *Amundesham*, ed. Riley, i. 448.

[103] *Ibid.*, i, 433-4.

[104] *Ibid.*, i, 445-6.

[105] Printed *ibid.*, i, 418-30. Described *ibid.*, ii, lviii-lix.

[106] See *ibid.*, i, 418.

[107] *Ibid.*, i, 421.

[108] Wessington's tracts, not all of which survive, were listed by a contemporary on a roll, three copies of which are preserved in Durham Cathedral Library; Dobson, *op. cit.*, p. 379, and n. 2. One copy is printed in Raine, *op. cit.*, cclxviii-cclxxi. See also Craster, *op. cit.*, 515 and n. 2. Rather similar tracts were written at Bury St. Edmunds early in the fifteenth century, e.g. the *Visitatio Thome de Arundel*, the *Contentio cum Episcopo Eliensi*, and the *Pensio de Woolpet*; printed *Memorials of St. Edmund's Abbey*, ed. Thomas Arnold (Rolls Series, 1890-6, 3 vols.), iii, 183-8, 188-211, 78-112, respectively.

[109] Raine, *op. cit.*, cclxviii-cclxix.

archdeacon of Durham'.[110]

Not all of Wessington's tracts, however, have a litigious or even a tendentious purpose. For example, he wrote the *Jurisdictio Spiritualis* simply to try to determine whether during a vacancy the see of Durham's spiritual jurisdiction should be administered by the cathedral chapter or by the archbishop.[111] For evidence of past vacancies he examined not only Robert Graystanes's history of Durham, but also the archives of the prior and chapter. He cites a certificate of the archdeacon of Durham, which had 'many seals',[112] and an indenture 'with the seals of Archbishop John, Antony bishop of Durham, Ralph bishop of Carlisle, and the chapter of York'.[113]

I have tried to show that some generalizations about the motives and methods of the monastic antiquaries are possible. The case with the seculars, John Hardyng, William Worcester and John Rous, is different. It is hard to decide in what ways they were unlike the monks but like each other: however, their interests were not so centred on one locality; loyalty was primarily to a patron, not a place (Rous is a partial exception). And they travelled around much more. But, like the monks, they accepted legends equally with verifiable fact.

Of the three, Rous most closely resembled a monastic antiquary. Having studied at Oxford, he became a chaplain of the earl of Warwick in the chantry chapel at Guy's Cliff, near Warwick.[114] He had a strong local attachment to both his homes, Oxford and Warwick, and as a chantry priest had a powerful incentive to commemorate his patrons in the first instance, but also others. His *Historia Regum Angliae* shows a close interest in Oxford and Warwick. He has a number of passages on the antiquities of Oxford. Although his account of the foundation of the university is legend, he follows it by accurately locating some of the halls in his day.[115] (Elsewhere he has left a topographical list of all the halls, including six

[110]   *Ibid.*, cclxix.

[111]   Durham Dean and Chapter Archives, Register III, fo. 211-211$^v$. Discussed and printed by Robert Brentano, 'The *Jurisdictio Spiritualis*: an example of fifteenth-century English historiography', *Speculum*, xxxii (1957), 326-32. Professor Brentano (*op. cit.*, 327) only tentatively ascribes the work to Wessington (it is not in the contemporary list of his works), but his authorship is accepted by Professor Dobson (*op. cit.*, p. 386). Another tract written to establish the truth about the past, without litigious or even tendentious purpose, was written at St Albans: it explains exactly how the abbot of St Albans had lost his right precedence in parliament in the reign of Richard II; printed *Amundesham*, i, 414-17.

[112]   Brentano, *op. cit.*, 331.

[113]   *Ibid.*, 331 and n.g. Cf. *ibid.*, 327-8.

[114]   For Rous's career see William Courthope's introduction to *This rol was laburd and finished by Master John Rows of Warrewyk* (London 1845-59, repr. with an historical introduction by Charles Ross, Alan Sutton, 1980), and Kendrick, *op. cit.*, pp. 19-20.

[115]   *Ibid.*, pp. 77-8. For another example in the *Historia* showing Rous's antiquarian interest in Oxford, see his account of the processional cross and stone cross owned by the university; *Historia*, pp. 201-2.

pulled down 'before my time', and six more pulled down 'in my time in Cat Street for [All] Souls College'.)[116] Similarly, although he recounts the legendary origins of Warwick, he carefully describes where a monastery and a nunnery, destroyed by the Danes, had been situated.[117]

The history of Warwick is one theme of Rous's two Warwick rolls, but their principal subject was the history of the earls of Warwick. In their production Rous was strongly influenced by the heraldic tradition. Heraldry, with its dependence on genealogy, made an important contribution to antiquarian studies. Rous's Warwick rolls are not the only example of armorial genealogies,[118] but they are the best. One of them was executed in about 1477 but revised in Richard III's reign, when the other was executed.[119] The purpose of both was to commemorate the earls and countesses, and others closely connected with the family and town, who are depicted with biographical captions and their coats of arms. Rous begins with the legendary British earls, but as soon as he reaches historic times his account is sound.

The antiquarian interest of the rolls has long been recognized. Rous appreciated the value of pictures to the historian. Indeed he claims to have anticipated Bernard of Breydenbach who took an artist with him to the Holy Land in 1483, to provide him with a pictorial record: apparently Rous had earlier advised John Tiptoft, earl of Worcester, to do just that when he visited the Holy Land.[120] The pictures on the Warwick rolls not

---

[116]   The holograph of Rous's list has not survived, but there are a number of copies, the best of which is printed in '*Survey of the Antiquities of the City of Oxford' composed in 1661-6 by Anthony Wood*; i. *The City and Suburbs*, ed. Andrew Clark (Oxford Historical Soc. xv, 1889), pp. 638-41. See T. H. Aston, 'Oxford's medieval alumni', *Past and Present*, no. 74 (1977), 36-8 and nn. It should be noted that the remarkably accurate bird's eye view (executed *c.* 1463) of New College by the warden Thomas Chandler, belongs to this period; see A. H. Smith, *New College, Oxford, and its Buildings* (Oxford, 1952), p. 179 (see also pp. 43, 49, 109) and frontispiece.

[117]   *Historia*, ed. Hearne (see p. 303  n. 21 above), pp. 45-6, 58, 60, 104.

[118]   For other examples of genealogies, some with armorial and/or historical details, see the note at the end of this article (pp. 326-7 below).

[119]   The latter, the so-called Yorkist roll, the text of which is in English, now BL MS. Additional 48976, is printed with line reproductions of the pictures, by Courthope, *op. cit.* See also C. E. Wright, 'The Rous Roll: the English version', *British Museum Quarterly*, xxx (1955-6), 79. The revised roll, the so-called Lancastrian roll, preserved in the College of Arms, has not been published but its text, which is in Latin, is printed in footnotes to the descriptions of the plates in Courthope, *op. cit.*, and there is a good account of it in A. R. Wagner, *A Catalogue of English Mediaeval Rolls of Arms* (Harleian Soc., c (1948) and Oxford, 1950), 116-18. Pictures from it are reproduced in A. G. B. Russell, 'The Rous Roll', *Burlington Magazine*, xxx (1917), 31 and pl. I; J. G. Mann, 'Instances of antiquarian feeling in medieval and renaissance art', *Arch. J.* lxxxix (1932), pls. II (2), III, IV, opposite pp. 259, 260, 261, respectively, and in Kendrick, *op. cit.*, pls. II (b)-IV.

[120]   *Historia*, p. 5. For the life of Bernard de Breydenbach, dean of Mainz, and the artist, Erhard Reuwich of Utrecht, who accompanied him to the Holy Land, see H. W. Davies, *Bernhard von Breydenbach and his Journey to the Holy Land 1483-4* (London, 1911, reprinted

only record the coats of arms of the individuals depicted, but also show each earl in the armour which Rous considered appropriate to his time.

Thus Rous tried to show the evolution of medieval armour. In a general way he got it right: he traces the development from chain mail, to mail and plate, to full plate; he was also correct on some of the details.[121] He obviously had no idea what the (legendary) British earls of Warwick might have worn, and depicts them in long chain mail with coifs in one piece, a style characteristic of the late twelfth century (pl. 34). He shows the early Anglo-Saxon earls in short mail hauberks, and hemispherical ribbed helms, styles in use from the seventh to the eleventh centuries. He represents the helms, some of which the earls carry on staves or lances, as chained to the pommel of the sword (pl. 35). Here he made a mistake, no doubt led astray by the practice, which was fairly widespread in the fourteenth century, of chaining loose pieces of equipment to the hauberk. Rous shows the late eleventh-century and twelfth-century earls in mail with knee and elbow caps, a type of armour introduced in the mid-thirteenth century (pl. 37). The thirteenth- and early fourteenth-century earls are in the mixed mail and plate worn in the first half of the fourteenth century. Thereafter the chronology of the progression from mixed mail and plate to full plate in the last half of the fourteenth century and in the fifteenth century is correct (pls 39-41). Rous dates correctly the introduction of two pieces of outfit: the war hat, a protective head-piece introduced in the late twelfth century, and the armorial surcoat, introduced in the early thirteenth century; William de Newburgh (d. 1184) is the first earl depicted in a war hat, and Waleran de Newburgh (d. 1203 or 1204) the first wearing a surcoat (pls 38, 39).

It may well be that Rous obtained information about armour from suits preserved in Warwick castle. He may also have examined the effigies in St Mary's church at Warwick. The suit shown in his portrait of Thomas Beauchamp, earl of Warwick 1329-69, is identical with that represented on the earl's effigy. (Rous depicts Thomas's son and heir, Thomas Beauchamp, earl 1370-1401, in the same suit; pl. 40.) Similarly, the suit

---

Utrecht, 1968), pp. i-iii, xxi. See also J. R. Mitchell, *John Tiptoft (1427-70)* (London, 1938), p. 28.

[121] Rous's pictorial history of medieval armour is discussed by Kendrick, *op. cit.*, pp. 28-9, and by Mann, art. cit., p. 262. For full mail with coifs in one piece, resembling that worn by the British earls of Warwick in Rous's pictures, see G. F. Laking, *A Record of European Armour and Arms through Seven Centuries* (London 1920-2, 5 vols.), i, 66-70. For a ribbed helm like those worn by the early Anglo-Saxon earls in Rous's pictures, see *ibid.*, i, 8, fig. 11. For a reconstruction of an Anglo-Saxon warrior not unlike those depicted by Rous, see *ibid.*, i, 31, fig. 39. For the introduction of mixed mail and plate in the mid-thirteenth century see *ibid.*, i, 121 *et seqq.*, and for its development in the fourteenth century see *ibid.*, i, 145. For the introduction of war-hats and surcoat see respectively *ibid.* ii, 57, 66; i, 124. For the suit on Richard Beauchamp's effigy, itself an important landmark in the history of armoury, see Laking, *op. cit.*, i, 163-70. See also the next note.

in which Rous depicts Richard Beauchamp, earl 1403-39, is the same as that represented on his effigy (pl. 41). In addition, Rous may have used the evidence of seals. Possibly his mistake over the chaining of the early Saxon earls' helms was the result of misinterpreting the picture on one of the Beauchamp seals. A surviving example shows the sword chained to the shoulder of the hauberk in such a way that it could give the impression of being chained to the helm (pl. 36).[122] Rous's interest in seals appears in the *Historia Regum Angliae*. He notes more or less correctly that Henry I started the practice of sealing documents with wax seals, instead of authenticating them with a cross and sign manual, as had been the previous practice.[123] And he remarks, rather less correctly, that after the mid-fourteenth century ('the capture of King John of France' in 1356), the English nobility replaced equestrian figures on their seals with coats of arms.[124]

Rous was also interested in the history of costume; although he did not try to establish the sequence of fashions, he did depict or describe individual styles in particular periods. He shows the countesses and other ladies wearing old-fashioned clothes, but of the fourteenth century, not those appropriate to the era in which they lived. Thus King Alfred's daughter Æthelflaed wears clothes similar to those of the effigy of Catherine, wife of Thomas Beauchamp, earl of Warwick 1329-69.[125] The *Historia* has a number of (brief) descriptions of dress: in Anglo-Saxon times, under William II, Edward III and Richard II, and in his own day, besides that of the Jews and that of the canons of the Holy Sepulchre.[126] However, not all these passages are antiquarian in tone. Those

[122] For an English example of the helm chained to the hauberk see the brass (*c.* 1300) of Sir Roger de Trumpington; reproduced Daniel Lysons and Samuel Lysons, *Magna Britannia* (London, 1806-22, 6 vols.), ii, opposite p. 65. For a German example see the effigy of Heinrich von Seinsheim (d. 1360) in Wurtzburg Cathedral; reproduced Paul Martin, *Armour and Weapons*, trans. René North (London, 1968), p. 70 and pl. 63. For an example of the sword and dagger chained to the hauberk see the brass (1370) of Ralph de Knevyngton in Aveley church, Essex (reproduced Laking, *op. cit.*, iii, 5); for similar fourteenth-century examples from Germany see Martin, *op. cit.*, pp. 52, 57, 70, and pls. 51, 52, 55, 58, 62, 65. I am indebted to Mr A. R. Dufty for supplying some of the references for this note.

[123] *Historia*, p. 138. In fact Edward the Confessor was the first king to use a great seal, which is of wax; *Facsimiles of English Royal Writs to A.D. 1100 presented to Vivian Hunter Galbraith*, ed. T. A. M. Bishop and Pierre Chaplais (Oxford, 1957), pp. xix, xxii, and Pierre Chaplais, *English Royal Documents, King John to Henry VI, 1199-1461* (Oxford, 1971), p. 2. However, surviving examples of Henry I's seals are more numerous than of those of previous kings; see W. de G. Birch, *Catalogue of Seals in the Department of Manuscripts in the British Museum* (London, 1887-1900, 6 vols.), i, pp. 2-8.

[124] *Historia*, p. 204. In fact this change took place early in the thirteenth century; C. H. Hunter Blair, 'Armorials upon English seals from the twelfth to the sixteenth centuries', *Archaeologia*, lxxxix (1943), 1-26 *passim*.

[125] Kendrick, *op. cit.*, p. 28.

[126] *Historia*, pp. 106, 110, 204, 205, 131, 202, 139-40, respectively.

concerning the fashionable clothes of William II's time and of Rous's own day have a homiletic ring, and were no doubt partly inspired by the preaching tradition. (It should be noted that a number of fourteenth-century chroniclers described the extravagent fashions worn by their contemporaries, while inveighing against the worldliness they revealed.)[127] The *Historia* proves that Rous's horizon was not limited by his own loyalty to Oxford, or to the town and earls of Warwick. Indeed, he travelled quite widely. He visited London (where he worked in the libraries of St Paul's and the Guildhall) and Windsor, and the abbeys of St Albans, Osney, and of St Swithun's and Hyde, Winchester, besides going further afield, to North Wales and Anglesey.[128] He cared for England as a whole, and wrote the *Historia* partly to commemorate the great people in English history. He started the *Historia* after a visit to 'the newly built college at Windsor'. There he saw niches left for statues of the famous. John Seymour, whom Rous calls master of the works, asked him 'to write a little book on the kings, the princes of the church and the founders of cities, so that statues of them could be honourably placed in the niches for the perpetual remembrances of their names'.[129] The founders of towns and universities included by Rous are nearly all legendary and belong to the remote past,[130] but his founders and benefactors of churches, colleges and the like in the post-Conquest period are historical.[131] His interest in founders was combined with an interest in origins in general, whether of the shire system, tournaments or the side-saddle.[132]

However, some of Rous's best research was elicited neither by his commemorative intention nor by objective curiosity, but by the desire to persuade. The monks had used historical evidence to defend their houses; Rous used it to defend the common weal.[133] One reason why he wrote the

[127] *Chronica Johannis de Reading . . .*, ed. James Tait (Manchester, 1914), p. 167; *Chronicon Henrici Knighton*, ed. J. R. Lumby (Rolls Series, 1889-95, 2 vols.), ii, 229; *Eulogium Historiarum*, ed. F. S. Haydon (Rolls Series, 1858-63, 3 vols.), iii, 230-1; *Historia Vitae et Regni Ricardi Secundi*, ed. G. B. Stow (University of Pennsylvania, 1977), p. 168.

[128] *Historia*, pp. 69 and 200 (London), 120 (Windsor), 60 (St Albans), 203 (Osney), 73 (St Swithun's), 96 (Hyde), 54 (North Wales and Anglesey).

[129] *Ibid.*, p. 120. There is no evidence confirming the statement that John Seymour, a canon of St George's chapel, Windsor, was master of works at the chapel at the end of the reign of Edward IV. However, he was in charge of repairs to the college early in Henry VII's reign. See *The History of the King's Works*, ed. H. M. Colvin (London, 1963-76, vols. i-iii, v, vi, and a volume of plans published to date), iii, pt. i, 305-6.

[130] e.g. *Historia*, pp. 22-7 *passim*, 96, 119.

[131] e.g. *ibid.*, pp. 140-1, 203, 204, 210-11, 215-16.

[132] *Ibid.*, pp. 66, 194-5, 205.

[133] Rous denies that he undertook his research on enclosures for its own sake; he states that 'pro certo nunquam aliud intendebam quam honorem dei, et regis ac totius rei publicae proficuum, ut deus novit'; *ibid.*, p. 86.

*Historia* was because he and others objected to the enclosure movement. He had, he tells us, petitioned the parliament held at Covenry in 1459 to remedy the evil by legislation.[134] The petition itself has not survived but it is tempting to think that the long tirades against enclosures in the *Historia* are extracts from it.[135] His arguments are various – philosopical, theological, legal, humanitarian and expediential.

To prove that enclosures were not in the country's best interests, Rous appealed to history. He listed fifty-eight of the villages near Warwick, and, to show the extent of depopulation, studied twelve in more detail. He compared their present condition with that in Edward I's reign as recorded in the Hundred Rolls.[136] Using his own observation, he expatiates in general on the ruin of villages and the deterioration of roads,[137] and sometimes gives specific details. For example,[138]

> At Fulbrook, where there was formerly a rectory, the church is destroyed, the villeins fled, and only the manor remains. The rest was enclosed for a park by John duke of Bedford, brother of King Henry V, who built a noble square tower for the castle, but now almost nothing is there. Also Joan, Lady Bergavenny, built a splendid gate-house inside the park fence, suitable to welcome her noble lord – to please him on arrival; now this too is destroyed.

In his research on enclosures Rous was a pioneer; no one had previously tried to assess their extent and results, and the government undertook no comparable inquiry until the early sixteenth century.[139]

The desire to persuade was one reason why John Hardyng turned to antiquarian research. He had started life as an esquire in the household of

---

[134] *Ibid.*, pp. 120-1. For his petition to the Coventry parliament of 1459 see M. W. Beresford, *The Lost Villages of England* (London, 1954), pp. 102, 148, idem, 'The deserted villages of Warwickshire', *Transactions . . . of the Birmingham Archaeological Soc. for . . . 1945 and 1946*, lxvi (1950), 53-4, C. C. Dyer, 'Deserted Medieval Villages in the West Midlands', *Economic History Review*, xxxv (1982), 25.

[135] *Historia*, pp. 39-43, 87-96, 112-37.

[136] *Ibid.*, pp. 122-4. Rous was a pioneer in his use of the Hundred Rolls; Beresford, *op. cit.*, p. 282. Rous also cites Domesday Book; *Historia*, p. 107. However, recent research shows that, although Rous seems to be fairly reliable on the desertion of villages in his own locality in his own day, his information about the movement in the past should be treated with caution. See Dyer, *op. cit.*, 25-6, C. J. Bond, 'Deserted villages in Warwickshire and Worcestershire', *Field and Forest, An Historical Geography of Warwickshire and Worcestershire*, ed. T. R. Slater and J. P. Jarvis (Norwich, 1982), pp. 150-2. I am indebted to Dr Christine Carpenter for the references to recent work on Warwickshire enclosures.

[137] *Ibid.*, pp. 125-6.

[138] *Ibid.*, pp. 123-4; cf. *V.C.H., Warwick.*, iii, 91-2. For Joan, Lady Bergavenny (d. 1435), wife of William Beauchamp, Lord Bergavenny (1392-1411) see G. E. C[ockayne], *Complete Peerage*, ed. Vicary Gibbs *et al.* (London, 1910-59, 13 vols.), i, p. 26.

[139] See Beresford, *op. cit.*, pp. 81-2, 117, 148-9, and *Deserted Medieval Villages: Studies*, ed. M. W. Beresford and J. G. Hurst (London, 1971), p. 11.

Sir Henry Percy ('Hotspur').[140] Hardyng then entered the service of Sir Robert de Umfraville, and came into contact with Henry V. In 1418 the king, who was contemplating enforcing the claim of the English crown to overlordship of Scotland, sent Hardyng there 'to spy out with all kinds diligence' how best to invade the country, and to collect evidence proving his claim.[141] He stayed three years and subsequently presented documents to Henry V, Henry VI and Edward IV successively: modern research has shown that seventeen of the nineteen extant documents are forgeries. It is believed that Hardyng himself forged them,[142] and, in the opinion of Sir Francis Palgrave, they show that he was 'a diligent antiquary'.[143]

Hardyng began his *Chronicle* in about 1440.[144] One of his reasons for writing was to persuade the king (he presented copies to both Henry VI and Edward IV)[145] to enforce his right by invading Scotland. He recites every instance he knew of a Scottish king doing homage to an English one.[146] Although he attributes a legendary origin to Scotland, he makes sound antiquarian observations. He notes, for example, that until Henry V's reign the king's head on Scottish coins faced sideways, as a sign of submission 'to his sovereign lord of England', while thereafter it looked straight ahead, as a sign of equality. Numismatically Hardyng's observation is more or less correct.[147]

---

[140] For John Hardyng's career see C. L. Kingsford, 'The first version of Hardyng's chronicle', *E.H.R.*, xxvii (1912), 462-9.

[141] *Ibid.*, 463-7 *passim*, 741-3, 751.

[142] Palgrave prints the eight documents preserved in the Public Record Office; *Documents and Records illustrating the History of Scotland*, ed. Francis Palgrave (London, 1837, one vol. only printed), i, pp. 367-76. Cf. Kingsford, *op. cit.*, p. 468, and, with particular reference to the documents relating to the Great Cause, *Edward I and the Throne of Scotland, 1290-1296: an Edition of the Record Sources for the Great Cause*, ed. E. L. G. Stones and G. G. Simpson (published for the University of Glasgow, Oxford, 1978, 2 vols.), ii, pp. 385-7.

[143] Palgrave, *op. cit.*, p. ccxxiii. Palgrave was referring to the content of the forgeries, not to their handwriting which is that of Hardyng's own time.

[144] The original version is discussed and part printed in Kingsford, *op. cit.*, 469-82, 740-53. The revised version is printed *The Chronicle of John Hardyng*, ed. Henry Ellis (London, 1812, reprinted New York 1974). For the date when Hardyng started the chronicle see Kingsford, *op. cit.*, 465.

[145] See *ibid.*, 465-7.

[146] *Chronicle*, ed. Ellis, pp. 42-3, 159, 166, 210, 212, 214, 223, 228, 235-6, 240, 243, 247, 253-4, 256, 262, 269, 270, 276, 283, 294, 296, 299, 323.

[147] *Ibid.*, pp. 87-8. The bust of the king on Scottish coins was in profile probably until the reign of Robert III (1390-1406); thereafter the head was full-face: see H. A. Grueber, *Handbook of the Coins of Great Britain and Ireland in the British Museum* (revised ed., London, 1970), pp. 170 *et seqq.*, and P. F. Purvey, *Coins and Tokens of Scotland, Seaby's Standard Catalogue of British Coins*, iv (Seaby's Numismatic Publications Ltd., London, 1972), pp. 13-34. However, the full-face portrait may have been introduced at the end of the reign of Robert II (1371-90); Edward Burns, *The Coinage of Scotland* (Edinburgh, 1887, 3 vols.), i. 364. Hardyng also suggests etymologies for the name of the Scots, and gives the (legendary) history of the Stone of Scone; *Chronicle*, ed. Ellis, pp. 86, 87, respectively.

To help the royal campaign, Hardyng supplied an itinerary from Berwick via Edinburgh to Ross,[148] the route taken by Henry IV in 1400, with distances between the towns.[149] He also provided a map, the earliest known of Scotland: it marks the towns, with conventional pictures of fortifications, the principal rivers and seas.[150] Neither itinerary nor map is accurate, but they show remarkable interest in, and knowledge of, Scottish geography. As Hardyng's first editor, Richard Grafton, wrote, with more truth than elegance, in his verse preface:[151]

> Neither is there any that ever wrote,
> Which in matters of Scotland could better skill . . .,
> Or better knew water, wood, town, vale and hill.

The desire to persuade the king to foreign conquest was also one factor leading William Worcester to historical study, but in this case the foreign country was France. Worcester was born in Bristol in 1415, and spent his working life as secretary to Sir John Fastolf, a veteran of the French wars, who had served John, duke of Bedford, as major-domo when the duke was the king's lieutenant in Normandy (1422-35).[152] Worcester wrote the *Boke of Noblesse* shortly after 1451 partly to please Fastolf.[153] But his principal object was to persuade Henry VI to enforce his claim to the throne of France. He uses stock chivalric arguments in favour of war, but he supports his thesis with considerable research on the chronicles from which he drew precedents for such a conquest in ancient and medieval history. In addition, he collected relevant documents, most illustrating the duke of Bedford's success in France, which he appended as a 'codicil' to his *Boke*. Later he adapted the preface of the 'codicil', substituting Edward IV for Henry VI in the address, so that he could present a copy of both *Boke* and 'codicil' to Edward IV in 1475 on the eve of his French

[148] There are two versions of the itinerary, one in verse, in the original chronicle, and one in prose, in the revised version. Both are printed by Ellis; *Chronicle*, pp. 422-9, 414-20, n. 12, respectively.

[149] *Ibid.*, p. 414, n. 12.

[150] Three copies are known. One is in the original chronicle and is reproduced by D. G. Moir, *The Early Maps of Scotland to 1850* (Royal Scottish Geographical Soc., Edinburgh, 1973), facing p. 5. The two others are in the revised version; one is reproduced in R[ichard] G[ough], *British Topography* (London, 1780, 2 vols.), ii, p. 579, and in *Facsimiles of National Manuscripts of Scotland*, photozincographed by Colonel Sir Henry James (Record Publications, Edinburgh, 1867-72, 3 pts.), pt. ii.

[151] *Chronicle*, p. 11. For the value of Hardyng's maps see Moir, *op. cit.*, pp. 6, 163.

[152] For Worcester's life see K. B. McFarlane, 'William Worcester: a preliminary survey', *Studies presented to Sir Hilary Jenkinson*, ed. J. Conway Davies (Oxford, 1957), pp. 196-221.

[153] Printed *The Boke of Noblesse*, ed. J. G. Nichols (Roxburghe Club, London, 1860, reprinted New York, 1972). It is discussed by McFarlane, *op. cit.*, pp. 210-15.

campaign.[154]

Fastolf worked Worcester hard, and even after his death in 1459, his business affairs, which he had left in confusion, occupied Worcester for nearly twenty years more. Worcester was only able to retire in 1478, and only then, less than five years before his own death, was he free to concentrate on antiquarian studies. At once he set out on his travels: in 1478 he rode from Norfolk to London and on again to St Michael's Mount; in 1479 he travelled in Norfolk; and in 1480 he rode from London to Glastonbury.[155]

It is true that on his journeys he exercised his piety,[156] transacted business[157] and discovered what he could about Sir John Fastolf's family[158] – and his own.[159] But his overwhelming motive was curiosity. Everywhere he went he took sheets of paper[160] and jotted down what he saw and heard (pl. 42). His interests were multifarious[161] and history was one of them. He was an enthusiastic student of the British History, enquiring at Glastonbury Abbey for chronicles on King Arthur.[162] But he also copied inscriptions and any notice of historical interest in churches, and examined and extracted from numerous martyrologies, chronicles and the like.[163] However, his principal concern was topography. He described the appearance of places, and recorded (not always accurately) the distances between them and the measurements of buildings: no man previously had paced out buildings with such assiduous regularity.[164] And his survey of Bristol was the first methodical topographical survey of an English town, foreshadowing John Stow's survey of London.[165]

The fifteenth century was, therefore, a period of importance in the development of antiquarian studies. Alongside traditional belief in legends, and even the willingness to accept forgeries, sound methods of documentary research and first-hand observation were growing. Many

---

[154] The 'codicil' is printed in *Letters and Papers illustrating the Wars of the English in France*, ed. Joseph Stevenson (Rolls Series, 1861-4, 2 vols. in 3 pts.), ii, pt. ii, 521-742. It is discussed in McFarlane, *op. cit.*, pp. 210-13.

[155] For a map of Worcester's itineraries see the end of the printed edition; *William Worcestre, Itineraries*, ed., with an English translation, J.H. Harvey (Oxford Medieval Texts, 1969).

[156] *Ibid.*, pp. xiii-xiv.

[157] See e.g. *ibid.*, pp. 18, 76, 260.

[158] See e.g. *ibid.*, pp. 180, 184, 220.

[159] See *ibid.*, 306-12 *passim*.

[160] For the manuscript of the *Itinerary* see *ibid.*, pp. xviii-xxi.

[161] For his various interests see *ibid.*, pp. x-xi.

[162] *Ibid.*, pp. 260, 292, 293, n. 2.

[163] See e.g. *ibid.*, pp. 100, 101, n. 1, 112, 122, 148, 154, 164, 224, 236, 312.

[164] See *ibid.*, pp. xi-xii.

[165] Worcester's survey of Bristol is not included in Harvey's edition, but is printed by James Dallaway, *Antiquities of Bristowe* (Bristol, 1834).

scholars contributed to these studies, and ensured that the medieval antiquarian tradition survived until the eve of the sixteenth century, when it was to be taken over and extended by scholars in the Tudor period.

The monastic antiquaries, though their views were distorted and their outlook limited by local loyalty, were well educated and intelligent. The seculars were less restricted in vision and scope, but were perhaps less thorough. And both groups show that objective curiosity was often a motive for studying the past. This was history for its own sake, or, in the words of V.H. Galbraith, 'history for the sake of the historian – the indulgence of boundless curiosity, the thrill of discovery and the satisfaction of detecting error'.[166]

## Note

A now lost chronicle composed in the 1360s and 1370s in the interest of the Mortimers, earls of March, included a genealogy back to the legendary kings of Britain; see John Taylor, 'A Wigmore Chronicle, 1355-77', *Proceedings of the Leeds Philosophical and Literary Society* (Literary and Historical Section), xi (1964), pt. v, 81-94. Another Mortimer genealogy was compiled soon after 1385 (to prove the claim of Roger Mortimer to the throne) probably under the direction of John Othelake, March herald; see M. E. Giffin, 'A Wigmore manuscript at the University of Chicago', *National Library of Wales Journal*, vii (1951-2), 321-4. A genealogy and armorial roll of the earls and dukes of Gloucester was compiled *c.* 1435, almost certainly for Isabella Beauchamp, widow of Thomas Despenser, earl of Gloucester. It is now Bodleian Library MS Lat.misc.6.2 (R). An early sixteenth-century armorial genealogy of the Clares is in the benefactors' book of Tewkesbury abbey. The best surviving copy is now Bodeleian Library MS Top.Glouc.d.2. It is described by C. H. Bickerton Hudson in *Transactions of the Bristol and Gloucestershire Archaeological Society*, xxxiii (1910), 60-6. A version is printed in W. Dugdale, *Monasticon Anglicanum*, ed. John Caley, Henry Ellis and Bulkeley Bandinel (London, 1817-30, 6 vols. in 8 pts.), ii. 59-65. A page from each of these Clare armorial genealogies is reproduced in Colin Platt, *The Abbeys and Priories of Medieval England* (London, 1984), pp. 108-9. I am grateful to Dr Martin Kauffmann, Assistant Librarian at the Bodleian, for information about these manuscripts. Besides armorial genealogies made for members of the nobility a number of genealogical chronicles of the kings of England were produced in the fifteenth century. Some had a propagandist purpose similar to that of the Mortimer genealogy; they demonstrated the legitimacy of the king's claim to the English throne. In the case of Henry VI, they showed that he had a right to both the throne of England and that of France; see J. W. McKenna, 'Henry VI of England and the dual monarchy: aspects of royal political propaganda, 1422-1432', *Journal of the Warburg and Courtauld Institutes*, xxviii (1965), 145-62. For royal genealogical chronicles in the vernacular see *A Manual of the Writings in Middle English 1050-1500*, ed. A. E. Hartung, viii, E. D. Kennedy, XII *Chronicles and Other Historical Writings* (New Haven, Connecticut, 1989), pp. 2674-9, 2888-91.

   A rather similar roll to the Rous rolls was executed in the mid-fifteenth century for the Sudeleys and Botelers of Sudeley castle. The roll is now in the New York Public Library, Spenser Collection MS 193. It comprises a history of England, the royal pedigree with portraits of the kings in roundels, and the pedigree of the Sudeleys and Botelers, with heraldic shields; see Lord Sudeley, 'Medieval Sudeley. Part I. The Sudeleys and Botelers

---

[166] V.H. Galbraith, *Historical Research in Medieval* (London, 1951), pp. 42-3.

of Sudeley Castle', *Family History, the Journal of Heraldic and Genealogical Studies*, x (1977), 9-20, and D. Winkless, 'Medieval Sudeley. Part II. The fifteenth century roll chronicle of the kings of England, with Sudeley and Boteler pedigree. The Latin text and roundels', *ibid.*, 21-39. For another roll chronicle of the Sudeleys and Botelers see *Heralds' Commemorative Exhibition 1484-1934 . . . Catalogue* (London, 1936), p. 38, no. 68.

# Appendix

## Additional Notes to Chapter 6

*Page 155 and n. 2.* Edmund Bishop's attribution of the pruning of the calendar of Christ Church, Canterbury, to Lanfranc (F.A. Gasquet and E. Bishop, *The Bosworth Psalter* (London, 1908), pp. 27-39), is now known to be wrong. The revision took place in the early eleventh century. See Nicholas Brooks, *The Early History of the Church of Canterbury* (Leicester, 1984), pp. 252, 265 and refs.

*Page 156 n. 2.* Since the publication of this article (in 1976) a new edition of John's chronicle, but not of the continuation, has appeared: *The Chronicle of Glastonbury Abbey . . . John of Glastonbury's Cronica sive Antiquitates Glastoniensis Ecclesie*, ed. J.P. Carley, with an English translation by D. Townsend (Woodbridge, 1985). Cf. above, pp. 289-97.

*Page 157 n. 4.* See now the new edition: *The Early History of Glastonbury . . . William of Malmesbury's De Antiquitate Glastonie Ecclesie*, ed., with an English translation, John Scott (Woodbridge and Totowa, 1981), 41, 42.

*Page 158 n. 4.* For '*Adam de Domerham*', i. 71' read '*De Ant.*, ed. Scott, 144'.
— *n. 5 line 5.* Insert after 1-25 'and in *De Ant.*, ed. Scott, 27-33 and end notes passim'.

*Pages 159 and n. 2.* For '*Adam de Domerham*, i. 3; cf. ibid., 24, 113' read '*De Ant.*, ed. Scott, 40'.
— *penultimate line.* Insert after 'ii. 199', 'and in *De Ant.*, ed. Scott, 34-9'.

*Page 160 n. 4.* For '*Adam de Domerham* . . . 53-4' read '*De Ant.*, ed. Scott, 52-4, 66-8, 94'.
— *n. 6.* For '*Adam de Domerham*, i. 54' read '*De Ant.*, ed. Scott, 94'.
— *n. 8.* For '*Adam de Domerham*, i. 44-5' read '*De Ant.*, ed. Scott, 84'.

*Page 161 n. 3 top line.* Delete 'William on'. For '*Adam de Domerham.*, i. 18-20 passim' read '*De Ant.*, ed. Scott, 64-78 passim 193-5'.
— *n. 3 third line from end.* For '*Adam de Domerham*, i. 29' read '*De Ant.* ed. Scott, 68'.

*Page 163 n. 1.* For '*Adam de Domerham*, i. 18' read '*De Ant.*, ed. Scott, 54'.
— *n. 3.* For '*Adam de Domerham*, i. 19-22' read '*De Ant.*, ed. Scott, 54-8'.
— *n. 5.* For '*Adam de Domerham*, i. 35-8; cf. ibid.' read '*De Ant.*, ed. Scott, 72-8; cf. *Adam de Domerham*'.

*Page 165 n. 4.* For '*Johannes Glastoniensis*, i. 7-8' read '*John of Glastonbury*, ed. Carley, 6, 8'.

*Page 166 n. 3.* Add 'Cf. now also R. Barber, "Was Mordred buried at Glastonbury? Arthurian tradition at Glastonbury in the Middle Ages", in *Arthurian Literature*, iv, ed.

R. Barber (Woodbridge and Totowa, 1985), 44-50'.

*Pages 168-9 n. 7.* Add 'The words on the leaden cross probably derive from Geoffrey of Monmouth's *Historia Regum Britanniae*; see S.C. Morland, "King Arthur's Leaden Cross", *Somerset and Dorset Notes and Queries*, xxxi (1984), 215, reprinted in idem, *Glastonbury, Domesday and Related Studies* (Glastonbury Antiquarian Society, 1991)', pp. 59-60.

*Page 174 n. 5.* For '*Adam de Domerham*, i. 20' read '*De Ant.*, ed. Scott, 44, 56'.
— *n. 7.* For '*Johannes Glastoniensis*, i. 56-7' read '*John of Glastonbury*, ed. Carley, 54, 280-1 n. 83'.

## Additional Note to Chapter 8

Pages 211, 235. Professor Joan Greatrex has called my attention to, and kindly sent me transcripts of, entries in the fourteenth- and fifteenth-century precentors' accounts of Worcester cathedral, which concern the writing of a chronicle. Possibly the payments which these entries record resulted from the use of the method of up-dating a chronicle as described in the prologue of the thirteenth-century Winchester/Worcester chronicle. (A lost Winchester chronicle to 1281, which was apparently a contemporary account of events from about 1264, was the source of the thirteenth-century Worcester chronicle.)[1] The prologue specifies that a sheaf of loose leaves should be attached to the end of the chronicle, upon which important current events should be noted; at the end of the year an annal was composed, using the notes, and copied neatly on to the end of the chronicle; the sheaf of rough notes was removed and a new sheaf substituted.[2] The entries in the Worcester precentors' accounts, which may relate to this practice, number nearly twenty, range in date from 1346/7 and 1425/6, and usually occur under the heading 'Minute Expense' but occasionally under 'Forinsece Expense'. The accounts themselves are in Worcester Cathedral Muniments, reference numbers C.351 (1346/7), C.352 (1348/9), C.353 (1349/50), C.354 (1350/1), C.355 (1354/5), C.356 (1358/9), C.357 (1360/1), C.358 (1361/2), C.361 (1374/5). C.361a (1376/7), C.363 (1383/4), C.364 (1384/5), C.367 (1390/1), C.370 (1400/1), C.375 (1419/20), C.376 (1422/3) and C.377 (1425/6). The entries in question record various payments of 2d, 3d, 4d, 6d, 8d, 12d or 2s to a scribe for writing, 'altering' or 'emending' the chronicle (e.g., 'In cronic[is] scribend[is]', 'scriptori scribent[i] cronicas', 'In cronic[is] mutand[is]', 'In emendac[ione] cronic[arum]', 'pro

---

[1] See N. Denholm-Young, 'The Winchester-Hyde chronicle', *English Historical Review*, xlix (1934, repr. in idem, *Collected Papers on Medieval Subjects* (Oxford, 1946), pp. 86-9.
[2] See above pp. 211 and n. 64, 235 and n. 184.

cronic[is] emend[andis']. The exact meanings here of the verbs 'mutare' and 'emendare' are unclear but the words seem to be used synonymously with 'scribere'. The scribe worked, it seems, on leaves added to the chronicle; in two cases the cost of parchment for him is mentioned (4d in 1354/5 and 8d in 1358/9). Moreover, the work was done annually; the scribe often includes 'hoc anno' in his entry.

Thus far the precentors' accounts concur with the evidence in the prologue of the Winchester/Worcester chronicle. They have in addition two pieces of information for which the prologue provides no parallel. Two mid-fourteenth century (1346/7, 1348/9) entries state that the chronicle was 'written' in preparation for Easter ('In cronic[is] scribend[is] ad pasch[am] 6d', 'In cronic[is] scribend[is] contra Pascham 6d'). The second entry, also mid-fourteenth century (1349/50), unparallelled in the Winchester/Worcester prologue, records that 12d was paid to the scribe of the 'great chronicle hanging in the church' (solut[os] cuidam scribent[i] magnas cronicas pendent[es] in ecclesia 12d). This suggests the possibility that neither this entry nor those already mentioned concern the up-dating of a chronicle of general history akin to the twelfth and thirteenth-century Worcester chronicles. Perhaps 'the great chronicle hanging in the church' served the same purpose as, or even was, a *tabula* of the kind which hung in a number of great churches from the fourteenth to the sixteenth centuries. A *tabula* was a board, or boards hinged to form pages, as it were, of a 'book'. On it were pasted sheets of parchment bearing the history of the church to which it belonged and/or, if the church were a conventual one, of the appropriate religious order. The purpose of the *tabula* was to inform visitors either at first hand or by supplying their guides with necessary information. A good example, of c.1400, survives from Glastonbury. It comprises a folding wooden frame 3 ft 8 ins high and 3 ft 6 ins broad when open. It encloses two smaller folding boards. All six sides of the boards are faced with parchment and bear the legendary history of Glastonbury, nearly all derived from John of Glastonbury's chronicle.[3]

However, it does not seem very likely that the references in the

---

[3] For the Glastonbury *tabula* see above p. 293 and n. 16. For other examples of *tabulae* see: H.E. Savage, *The Lichfield Chronicles* (Lichfield, 1915), pp. 8-10; G.H. Gerould, ' "Tables" in medieval churches', *Speculum*, i (1926), pp. 439-40; N. Denholm-Young, 'The birth of a chronicle', *Bodleian Quarterly Record*, vii (1933), pp. 236 and n. 5, 237-8; W.A. Pantin, 'Some medieval English treatises on the origin of monasticism' in *Medieval Studies presented to Rose Graham*, ed. Veronica Ruffer and A.J. Taylor (Oxford, 1950), pp. 200-1, 207-8. J.S. Purvis, 'The Tables of the York Vicars Choral', *Yorkshire Archaeological Journal*, xli (1966), 741-8. (I owe this last reference to Professor Greatrex; the example, Additional MS 533 in York Minister Library, is described in *Medieval Manuscripts in British Libraries* iv: Paisley-York, ed. N.R. Ker and A.J. Piper (Oxford, 1992), pp. 824-5). Cf. A. Gransden, *Historical Writing in England*, ii, *c.1300 to the Early Sixteenth Century* (London, 1982), p. 495 (Appendix E).

Worcester precentors' accounts are to a *tabula*. The entries recording the purchase of parchment for the chronicle indicate a book of the normal kind. Nor does it seem probable that a chronicle of local history or an historical monograph, such as are found on *tabulae*, would have required the annual writing and revision revealed by the precentors' accounts. These procedures seem more appropriate to a chronicle of general history. The reference to a chronicle hanging in the church recalls the words of Gaimar (writing c.1140) who states that at King Alfred's command a copy of the Anglo-Saxon Chronicle was kept chained in Winchester cathedral.[4] The truth of Gaimar's assertion has been doubted[5] (it has been suggested that he confused the Chronicle with Alfred's translation of the *Pastoral Care*), and no surviving copy has marks indicating that it was ever chained.[6] However, considered in the light of the other evidence, there seems just a faint possibility that Gaimar was right. If, as is possible, the Alfredian chronicle was originally composed at Winchester,[7] this fact lends weight to Gaimar's mention of a chained copy in the cathedral. It is not unlikely that Worcester was among the first churches to receive a copy of the Chronicle, and a church which had a copy would continue it. Therefore, the instructions on the writing of a chronicle in the prologue of the thirteenth-century Winchester/Worcester chronicle, and the entries in the Worcester precentors' account showing that a chronicle in book form hung in the church and was 'written in' and 'emended' every year, suggests the merest chance that a method of chronicle writing introduced under King Alfred survived at Winchester at least until the thirteenth century, and at Worcester at least until the mid-fifteenth century.[8]

### *Additional Note to Chapter 10*

On pages 259-61 above, I suggest that the 'Merton' *Flores* was written after the death of Edward I (7 July, 1307) at the command of Edward II, perhaps for presentation at his coronation. As I explained, the subject matter supports this dating. However, Adelaide Bennett, while accepting my contention that the 'Merton' *Flores* is an 'official' history, argues, for

---

[4] Gaimar, *L'Estoire des Engleis*, ed. A. Bell (Anglo-Norman Text Society, xiv-xv, 1960), 11. 2327-36.

[5] See *The Anglo-Saxon Chronicle*, ed. Dorothy Whitelock with D.C. Douglas and S.I. Tucker (London, 1961), pp. xix-xx.

[6] I owe this information to Dr Mildred Budny.

[7] *The Anglo-Saxon Chronicle, a Collaborative Edition*, ed. David Dumville and Simon Keynes, iii, *MS A*, ed. J.M. Bately (Cambridge and Woodbridge, 1986), pp. xiv and n. 6, xxxii-xxxiii.

[8] See above p. 202 and n. 15.

'codicological, artistic and iconographic reasons', in favour of a late thirteenth-century date. (A. Bennet, 'A late thirteenth-century Psalter-Hours from London', in *England in the Thirteenth Century, Proceedings of the 1984 Harlaxton Symposium*, ed. W.M. Ormrod (Harlaxton College, 1985), 21 n. 20). I had decided that since the 'Merton' *Flores* is a revised version of the 'Westminster' *Flores* it would have been composed after the latter work was completed; the last entry in the 'Westminster' *Flores* is for early February 1307 and so presumably the chronicler stopped writing shortly after that date. The changes of hand in the Eton MS of the 'Merton' *Flores* which, as Dr Bennett points out, occur from the annal for 1295 onwards, and the other codicological irregularities, could have been the result of the manuscript being handed around the scriptorium to various scribes in the process of copying. (Cf. my *Historical Writing in England*, [i], *c.550-c.1307* (London 1974), 458 n. 157). It could also be argued that artistic evidence seldom leads to exact dating.

Nevertheless, in certain circumstances Dr Bennett's dating of the Eton MS could be right. Possibly from the late thirteenth-century the annals of the 'Westminster' *Flores* and those of the 'Merton' *Flores* were composed concurrently at Westminster, fairly close in time to the events they recorded. The text, therefore, of the 'Westminster' *Flores* would have been in a fluid state and wide differences would have been possible between it and its derivative, the 'Merton' *Flores*; the latter could easily have been adapted to suit the needs of the king. The relationship of the 'Westminster' *Flores* to the 'Merton' *Flores* would be analogous to that of the chronicle of Bury St Edmunds to the chronicle of St Benet of Hulme in the 1290s (above pp. 235-8).

If, indeed, the 'Merton' *Flores* was started in 1295 or shortly afterwards, this would lead to the interesting conclusion that the Westminster monks started producing an 'official history for Edward I during his lifetime and just when royal propaganda was busy trying to stimulate enthusiasm for the Scottish war. (See M. Prestwich, *War, Politics and Finance under Edward I* (London, 1972), 240-2, D. Burton, 'Requests for prayers and royal propaganda under Edward I', in *Thirteenth Century England*, III, ed. P.R. Coss and S.D. Lloyd (Woodbridge, 1991), 25-35, and A. Gransden, 'John de Northwold, Abbot of Bury St Edmunds (1279-1301) and his defence of its liberties', in *ibid.*, 111-12.) This conclusion would not affect my overall argument that: the 'Merton' *Flores* was an official history; a copy might have been made for presentation to Edward II on the occasion of his coronation; *Murimuth* preserves otherwise lost material from it.

# Index

Runcton, Norfolk 46 and n. 64
Ruthwell, Dumfreiss., Anglo-Saxon cross
  at 161

St Albans, Herts., Benedictine abbey 89,
  97, 103 n. 2, 154, 178, 263 n. 104, 300,
  315-16, 317 n. 111, 321 and n. 128
—, 'Book of Benefactors' 316
—, chronicles written at 242 n. 2, 254, 281
—, —, *Flores Historiarum*, continuation
  (1250-65) of Matthew Paris's 204, 218,
  245
—, —, —, copy of, at Westminster 245 and
  n. 4. See also Westminster, Benedictine
  abbey, chronicles written at
—, —, see also: Paris, Matthew;
  Walsingham, Thomas; Wendover,
  Roger of
—, abbots of, see: Gorron, Geoffrey de;
  John
—, almoner of, see Wintershull, William
St Asaph, bishop of, see Bache, Alexander
St Benet of Hulme (or St Benet of Holme),
  Norfolk, Benedictine abbey 57, 95-8
  passim, 101-4 passim, 240 and n. 6, 243-4
—, chronicles written at
—, —, 'John de Oxenedes' 96, 226, 228
  and n. 142, 234-7 passim, 240, 242
  and nn. 1-4, 243, pl. 26
—, see also under Bury St Edmunds . . .
  abbey, chronicles, *Cronica Buriensis*
—, copy of *Flores Historiarum* at 204
—, abbot of, see Aylesham, John of
St Carilef, William of, bishop of Durham
  (1081-96) 7, 8 and n. 38, 13 n. 74, 74
St Cuthbert's, see 12, 13, 28, 37, 74, 81, 317
—, clerical community attached to 7, 45,
  47, 49, 50, 81
—, see also: Chester-le-Street; Durham;
  Lindisfarne
St David's, Pembrokes., bishopric 23
—, ?Worcester chronicle at 204, n. 24
St Ives, Hunts. (formerly Slepe) 53, 54,
  99, 100, 101
St Neots, Hunts. 53, 64, 100
St Omer, Pas-de-Calais, St Bertin's,
  Benedictine abbey 156
Saint-Sauveur-le-Vicomte, Manche,
  chateaux and lords of, history of
  see *Histoire du chateau et sires de*
St Stephen's, unidentified monastery 309
St Victor, Hugh of 130, 131, 139, 141, 150
saints, cults of 45-6, 49-50, 51-4 and nn.,
  60, 81 et seqq., 108-9, 113, 154-5, 161 and

n. 3, 162-3, 165, 179 and n. 20, 185
—, see also Edmund, St
Salisbury
—, countess of, see 'Alice'. See also Lincoln
  and Salisbury, countess of
—, earls of, see: Montagu, William;
  Montagu, William
Salisbury, John of, *Historia Pontificalis* 132,
  135, 136, 139, 141, 150
Sallust 128, 176, 192
—, *Bellum Catalinae* 128, 133-43 passim
Samson, abbot of Bury St Edmunds (1182-
  1211) 85, 178, 241 n. 4
—, Life of, see Brakelond, Jocelin of
*Sanctilogium*, see Tynemouth, John of
Savaric, bishop of Bath (1192-1205) 155
Sanford, John de, archbishop of Dublin
  (1286-94) 233-4
Scarborough, Yorks., castle 188
Scollandus, see Scotland (Scollandus)
*Scotichronicon*, see Bower, Walter
Scotland 267, 323
—, relations of, with Edward I, see
  Edward I, relations of, with
—, succession question (1291-2), 219-20
  and nn., 236, 243, 264 and nn. 107-8, 280
—, map of 324
—, kings
—, —, list 280
—, —, regalia 259
—, —, see also: Alexander I; David II
Scotland (Scollandus), abbot of
  St Augustine's (1070-87) 310
scripts, see: Anglo-Saxon; uncial
seals, 184, 308, 309 and n. 69, 317, 320 and
  nn. 123, 124, pl. 36
Sebastian, St 86, 87
Seen, John, D.Th., monk of Glastonbury
  297
Seinsheim, Heinrich von 320 n. 122
Semer, Suffolk 229 and n. 151
Segontium, see Cair Segeint
Seneca 193
Sens, William of, master builder 185
Sergius II, pope (844-7) 62, 181
Seven Ages, the, periodization of 209 and
  n. 59
Sextus Tarquinius 277
Seymour, John, canon of St George's,
  Windsor 321 and n. 129
SHEERIN, D.J. 304-5 and n. 35
Sherborne, Dorset, bishops of, see:
  Hermann; Wulfsige
Sherborne, cathedral priory 57, 59, 145

# Index of Manuscripts